Yours, Al

BOOKS BY AL PURDY

POETRY

The Enchanted Echo (1944)

Pressed on Sand (1955)

Emu, Remember! (1956)

The Crafte So Long to Lerne (1959)

The Blur in Between: Poems 1960–61 (1962)

Poems for All the Annettes (1962)

The Cariboo Horses (1965)

North of Summer: Poems from Baffin Island (1967)

Wild Grape Wine (1968)

Love in a Burning Building (1970)

The Quest for Ouzo (1971)

Hiroshima Poems (1972)

Selected Poems (1972)

On the Bearpaw Sea (1973)

Sex and Death (1973)

In Search of Owen Roblin (1974)

The Poems of Al Purdy: A New Canadian Library Selection (1976)

Sundance at Dusk (1976)

A Handful of Earth (1977)

At Marsport Drugstore (1977)

Moths in the Iron Curtain (1977)

No Second Spring (1977)

Being Alive: Poems 1958–78 (1978)

The Stone Bird (1981)

Birdwatching at the Equator: The Galapagos Islands (1982)

Bursting into Song: An Al Purdy Omnibus (1982)

Piling Blood (1984)

The Collected Poems of Al Purdy (1986)

The Woman on the Shore (1990)

Naked With Summer in Your Mouth (1994)

Rooms for Rent in the Outer Planets (1996)

To Paris Never Again (1997)

Beyond Remembering: The Collected Poems of Al Purdy (2000)

OTHER

No Other Country (prose, 1977)

The Bukowski/Purdy Letters 1964–1974: A Decade of Dialogue (with Charles Bukowski, 1983)

Morning and It's Summer: A Memoir (1983)

The George Woodcock/Al Purdy Letters (edited by George Galt, 1987)

A Splinter in the Heart (novel, 1990)

Cougar Hunter (essay on Roderick Haig-Brown, 1993)

Margaret Laurence–Al Purdy: A Friendship in Letters (1993)

Reaching for the Beaufort Sea: An Autobiography (1993)

Starting from Ameliasburgh: The Collected Prose of Al Purdy (1995)

No One Else is Lawrence! (with Doug Beardsley, 1998)

The Man Who Outlived Himself (with Doug Beardsley, 1999)

EDITOR

The New Romans: Candid Canadian Opinions of the US (1968)

Fifteen Winds: A Selection of Modern Canadian Poems (1969)

Milton Acorn, *I've Tasted My Blood: Poems 1956–1968* (1969)

Storm Warning: The New Canadian Poets (1971)

Storm Warning 2: The New Canadian Poets (1976)

Andrew Suknaski, *Wood Mountain Poems* (1976)

Yours, Al

THE COLLECTED LETTERS
OF AL PURDY

Edited by Sam Solecki

HARBOUR PUBLISHING

Harbour Publishing Co. Ltd.
P.O. Box 219
Madeira Park, BC
V0N 2H0
www.harbourpublishing.com

THE CANADA COUNCIL | LE CONSEIL DES ARTS
FOR THE ARTS | DU CANADA
SINCE 1957 | DEPUIS 1957

Edited by Sam Solecki
Cover design by Roger Handling
Cover photo by D'arcy Glionna
Printed and bound in Canada

BRITISH
COLUMBIA
ARTS COUNCIL
Supported by the Province of British Columbia

Harbour Publishing acknowledges financial support from the Government of Canada through the Book Publishing Industry Development Program and the Canada Council for the Arts, and from the Province of British Columbia through the British Columbia Arts Council and the Book Publisher's Tax Credit through the Ministry of Provincial Revenue.

Library and Archives Canada Cataloguing in Publication

Purdy, Al, 1918–2000
    Yours, Al : the collected letters of Al Purdy / edited by Sam Solecki.

Includes index.
ISBN 1-55017-332-4

    1. Purdy, Al, 1918–2000—Correspondence. 2. Poets, Canadian (English)—20th century—Correspondence. I. Solecki, Sam, 1946– II. Title.

PS8531U8.Z48 2004   C811'.54   C2004-903015-9

INTRODUCTION

Think of Al Purdy's letters as an almost unexpurgated companion to his 1997 autobiography, *Reaching for the Beaufort Sea*. Like any body of interesting correspondence, they offer a perspective on the life and times of an individual from a viewpoint unavailable to anyone else. If, to quote the title of one of Purdy's last books, *No One Else Is Lawrence!*, it is also true that no one else is quite like Purdy. And we read letters, whether Lawrence's or Purdy's, to encounter those very qualities that make him unique, or in Mary Wordsworth's more figurative phrase, "to see the breathing of the inmost heart upon paper." What we discover as well are the various, sometimes contradictory aspects of a great writer's self caught in the voices and personae of letters written to various people at different times and on different occasions. We get a more complex, almost cubist self-portrait in various styles and in nearly countless typefaces than we find in an autobiography (or biography). In Purdy's case, the "picture" is the result of thousands of individual texts produced over a period of half a century and illustrates Proust's suggestion that "On ne se réalise que successivement," a notion that finds some incidental confirmation in Purdy's uncertainty for many years in his letters and his books about his name: was he Alfred Wellington Purdy, Alfred W. Purdy, A.W. Purdy, Alfred Purdy or Al?

Reaching for the Beaufort Sea, on the other hand, was the product of an extended period of difficult and reluctant writing near the end of his life, and shows a remembrance of things past from the perspective of a nearly completed story. In a manner of speaking, both he and his readers knew the book's "plot." It's worth noting that when he wrote the memoir he did not have access to most of his correspondence or papers, certainly to none before 1980, and he did not do any research in libraries. As a result, more than most writers of memoirs he depended almost completely on memory. I'm not suggesting that we need to choose between the different "truths" of the letters or the autobiography. But the former do have the immediacy, incompletion and suspense of an epistolary novel and are revealing in roughly the same way. In the letters, we read the life almost *as it happens* written by a man who before his mid-forties wasn't sure whether he would achieve success in anything, much less as a writer. Letter by letter, we can watch his development as a man, a husband and a poet; we follow his various relationships; and we learn what he thought, discussed, read and wrote at various periods in his life.

By including letters written to Purdy in this edition, I have tried to recreate some sense of the dialogue entailed by an extended correspondence of the kind he had, among many others, with Earle Birney, George Bowering, Charles Bukowski, Dennis Lee, George Woodcock, George Galt, H.R. Percy, Fraser Sutherland, myself and, especially, Margaret Laurence. Purdy was a faithful, even compulsive correspondent who wrote one or more letters each day and usually answered almost immediately. He would have agreed with Jean Renoir's comment, "Don't think that this is a letter. It is only a small eruption of a disease called friendship."

And friendship itself is a frequent topic. Because he lived most of his adult life in Trenton, Ameliasburgh (his preferred spelling) and Sidney, BC, each of which is "a little adjacent to where the world is / a little north of where the cities are" ("The Country North of Belleville"), letters kept him informed about what other writers were doing, in touch with editors and publishers, and abreast of the gossip drifting through the cultural community. Purdy was that anomaly, the gregarious man who was also shy, and letters, unlike the telephone, allowed an oblique contact with the world. They were also much cheaper, not an insignificant consideration for a man whose income rarely rose high enough to attract the attention of Revenue Canada. Purdy's letters often arrived accompanied with poems or articles cut out from magazines and newspapers that he thought his correspondent might find interesting. And the files in the archives at Saskatoon and Queen's are full of similar cuttings and magazines that his friends sent. Many of his letters contain drafts of poems; in several instances I have printed poems, especially those that Purdy didn't publish. There are also countless letters from unknown individuals asking for his opinion of their work. Mindful of the kindness of editors, including Earle Birney, Northrop Frye and Milton Wilson, who had commented on his poems of the 1940s and early 1950s, Purdy almost always replied. Before e-mail and before scanning, the letters were part of a complex information grid with Ameliasburgh often the centre.

One doesn't have to read far into the correspondence to sense that Purdy enjoyed writing letters for many reasons, not the least of which was that they made it possible for him to write during those fallow periods of ennui and boredom when the poems wouldn't come and there were no articles to be written for *Maclean's, Weekend Magazine* or *Canadian Literature*. It's as if he were keeping the engine warm for that moment when the hint of a poem might appear. Anyone familiar with the poetry will experience an occasional sense of déjà vu reading those letters in which Purdy describes in prose an experience that eventually morphs into lyric.

The letters also gave him a chance to write informally about poets and poetry. In the Birney-Purdy letters we observe how the master-pupil relationship of the late 1940s and 1950s slowly develops into a friendship and a relationship of equals as Purdy finds his confidence and his voice. There is a great deal of give and take here. In the early years, from 1947 to 1960, it's obvious that Birney is as grateful for Purdy's interest and praise as Purdy is for Birney's attention and detailed responses to his poems. In the succeeding two decades, each knows that the other will offer a sympathetic reading to his work. Along the way they conduct a seminar on poetry that includes discussions of rhyme and metre, influence, creativity, greatness, the Canadian canon, the relationship of Canadian poetry to the British and American traditions, and other poets. With George Bowering, Purdy argues about Whitman, Williams, Olson and the Black Mountain poets, always insisting, contra the very patient Bowering, that none are particularly interesting as poets and, with the exception of Bowering, neither are most of their West Coast acolytes. Though Purdy doesn't come out and say so, it's obvious he thinks that loyalty to Black Mountain is in some deep sense anti-Canadian because it looks for a Canadian poetics in what Williams called "the American grain." George Johnston's poems and translations lead him into a discussion of rhyme, metre and stanzas— what T.S. Eliot called "conservative verse"—and their place in his ostensibly free verse poems. From Bowering, one of our best poet-critics, Purdy learns more about contemporary movements in poetry than he wants to; Johnston, on the other hand, exposes him to the world of the Norse sagas which he has spent much of his life translating. For Purdy, the high-school dropout and autodidact, these exchanges are the open university in which he continues his education.

The dialogue with poets and other writers is echoed in similar exchanges with literary critics that gain momentum after *The Cariboo Horses* wins the Governor General's prize in 1965. Though there is an obvious anti-academic bias in some of Purdy's comments about university professors—it never matches Layton's in energy or venom—he read articles written about him and, on occasion, wrote to their authors. Letters to Milton Wilson, Mike Doyle, Bowering, Dennis Duffy, Stan Dragland and myself often offer the poet's comments on, and explications and evaluations of, his own work. And like most writers, Purdy paid close attention to reviews and references to him in the press. Jack McClelland, his publisher, might try to reassure him that there is no such thing as a bad review, since every review at least advertises a book's publication, but Purdy knew better: a bad review was an attack both on his most recent book—and for the first few months after completion he described each as among his best—and on his critical standing. Not far behind in his list of concerns was the effect a bad review might have on sales. Auden may be right in suggesting that "poetry makes nothing happen," but the royalties often made a significant difference in the family finances. For anyone interested in how poets without university appointments made (or did not make) a living in the second half of the twentieth century, Purdy's letters are as revealing as Layton's.

If poetic concerns were one source of letters, travel was another. Like Birney and Layton, Purdy travelled as often as he and his wife Eurithe, the family accountant and travel agent, could afford it. Together they saw most of Canada, though Al went alone to Baffin Island. They wintered often in Mexico and Florida; they travelled to the Soviet Union, Greece, Turkey, England, the Galapagos and Italy; and Al went alone to France, England, Japan and South Africa. Though he wrote many postcards and letters home and published several articles about these trips, it's obvious that he is less interested in these places *as* places than as occasions for poems. Unlike Graham Greene and D.H. Lawrence, two of his favourite writers, he's not really a travel writer by nature, perhaps because he's too self-conscious about looking for a poem, looking for what might be called a poetry-opp. He's aware of this in poems like "The Horseman of Agawa" and "The Battlefield of Batoche," which describe his wife as more attentive to the moment precisely because she is not concerned with turning it into a poem. As a result she can sense and enter the aura of another place and time, and he can't. He originally considers his stay at Hiroshima a success because it results in several poems; the 1977 tour of Russia and some of the Soviet republics is summed up both in the letters and in the autobiography as a poem-writing contest between Purdy and Ralph Gustafson: "Every day while we were in the Soviet Union, he wrote a poem. I believe he ended up with about eighteen, and I with a mere dozen. At the end of our trip I said, 'Gus, you out-poemed me nearly two to one. How about it if you trade me ten of yours for one of mine? Would that be a fair trade?' His answer was indecipherable" *(Reaching for the Beaufort Sea,* p. 259). In the end, only one of these poems—"Remembering Hiroshima"—made it into *Beyond Remembering: The Collected Poems of Al Purdy.*

Like the poems, for which they often prepare the ground, the letters—whether funny, affectionate, consolatory, nostalgic, argumentative, celebratory or angry—describe Al Purdy's multi-faceted vision of the world, his way of "being alive."

Editorial Note

Al Purdy kept copies of almost all of his letters and put a publication restriction on only a handful. The two most obvious gaps are letters to his mother, Eleanor Ross Purdy, and to his wife, Eurithe. Purdy once told me that he always felt guilty that he wrote so rarely to his mother, and I found only one letter to her among his papers. On the other hand, the paucity of letters to Eurithe Purdy is the result, as she told me, of the fact that she and Al were very rarely apart during the fifty years of their marriage. By contrast, some readers may wonder why there are so many letters to and from Earle Birney between 1946 and 1970 and to and from me during the last decade of the poet's life. In the first instance, Birney was Purdy's primary correspondent in the early years, as important then as Margaret Laurence would become during the late 1960s and throughout the 1970s. In my case, Purdy and I were often in touch while I researched and wrote *The Last Canadian Poet: An Essay on Al Purdy* and we worked on *The Woman on the Shore* (1990), *Naked with Summer in Your Mouth* (1994), *Starting from Ameliasburgh: The Collected Prose of Al Purdy* (1995), *Rooms for Rent in the Outer Planets: Selected Poems* (1996) and *Beyond Remembering: The Collected Poems of Al Purdy* (2000). As a result we got into the habit of seeing each other often, talking regularly on the phone, and writing frequently.

The majority of the letters are printed in full. Some have been edited for a variety of reasons. For instance, I knew from Purdy's response to my request for permission to use his letters in *The Last Canadian Poet* that he did not want to see in print any epistolary comments he had made that might offend anyone he was particularly fond of or loved. I have also cut passages that repeat material from an earlier letter or whose contents are unlikely to be of general interest. As a result, some of the letters to Margaret Laurence first published in *Margaret Laurence–Al Purdy: A Friendship in Letters* are shorter in this edition. (I'm grateful to John Lennox, the editor of that volume, for allowing me to use his footnotes.) All cuts have been indicated. The large majority of the letters are at Queen's University; the University of Saskatchewan has a handful of files of letters to Al Purdy from, among others, Northrop Frye, John Glassco, Earle Birney and Margaret Atwood. I am grateful to the archivists—especially Don Richan at Queen's and the late Glen Makahonuk at Saskatchewan—for their help. I am also grateful to the following for their help: Shyla Seller, Vici Johnstone, Mary White, Howard White, my copy editor Patricia Wolfe, and Eurithe Purdy. A special thanks to all of Al Purdy's friends who let me include their letters to him; to Dennis Lee for his encouragement; and to Anne Michaels for reminding me about Truffaut.

—SAM SOLECKI

1918 Born December 30 at Wooler, Ontario, to Eleanor Ross Purdy and Alfred Wellington Purdy Sr. After his father's death in 1920, his mother sells the farm and moves to Trenton: "Anyway, I'm now sitting in a room full of books overlooking the snowcovered Trent River in the dreary little town of Trenton, wishing to jesus that antho were over and done. Trenton amounts to the dingy reality of my misspent youth. The house here amounts to the shell of a huge snail that I can't seem to get rid of, marine creatures, some of them, can leave their shells but must scuttle back at signs of danger, and so do I it seems. Goddam umbilical cord to the past" (Letter to Margaret Laurence, December 31, 1967, written at 134 Front St., the house to which his mother moved after selling the farm. He also describes the house in *Reaching for the Beaufort Sea* and in the late poem, "134 Front St., Trenton.")

1925–33 Attends Dufferin Public School, Albert College and Trenton High School

1933 Publishes three poems in *Spotlight*, his high-school magazine, each under a different version of his name. One of the poems is titled "Canada."

1936–37 After dropping out of school after Grade 10, rides the boxcars to Vancouver and back

1939–45 Serves in the RCAF in Canada

1941 Marries Eurithe Mary Parkhurst from McArthur's Mills, 80 miles north of Belleville, whom he met in 1940; is posted to Vancouver, then Woodcock and Kitsilano, BC

1940–45 Continues writing poems and submitting them to Canadian and American magazines like *Driftwood*, *The Lyric West*; publishes occasionally in the weekend poetry pages of the *Vancouver Sun* and *News Herald*: "The *News Herald* also had a continuous competition in its weekend edition, one that involved completing limericks after being provided with the first couple of lines, but adding the names of the particular advertiser, dry cleaners, clothing stores and suchlike. Of course the lines you wrote were always complimentary to the advertisers. The prizes for this contest were two tickets to the Vogue Theatre on Granville Street, which meant that Eurithe and I got to see a lot of mediocre movies. As well, over a period of about two

and a half years, I appeared in the *Sun* poetry page over forty times"
(*RBS*, 102–3).

1944 Publishes at own expense *The Enchanted Echo*; heavily influenced by
the poetry of Bliss Carman, the volume falls, to quote David Hume,
"stillborn from the press." None of the poems appear in subsequent
selected or collected editions of his work.

1945 Son, Alfred Alexander (Jim) Purdy, is born

1945–48 Purdy and his father-in-law, James Parkhurst, operate Diamond
Cab in Belleville

1947 Writes to *Canadian Poetry Magazine* and makes contact with the editor, Earle Birney. They remain friends until Birney's death in 1995.
"Earle Birney and I were friends, despite the obvious differences in
temperament and character. We got along well most of the time. Of
course, there was a huge wall of reserve in him that you'd encounter if you pushed farther on some subjects than a tacitly agreed on
boundary . . .

"At times I felt awe of Birney, sometimes impatience, perhaps
even a little fear, but always respect. He was obdurate, stubborn,
combative and occasionally unfriendly; all these things to the degree that he resembles descriptions I have heard about myself when
young: and denied vociferously. He was a friend" (*RBS*, 234).

1950 Wins the Second Prize, $15, in the A. Louisa Peacock and Macnab
Awards for the poem "Bubo Virginianus"

1950–55 Family moves to Vancouver, where he works for Sigurdson's
Lumber Co. and then Vancouver Bedding; Purdy meets Curt Lang,
Doug Kaye and Steve McIntyre with whom he begins his education
in modern poetry, reading Hopkins, Pound and Thomas: "Up to
that time my own literary gods were Bliss Carman, G.K. Chesterton,
W.J. Turner, etc. . . . But suddenly I found myself reading T.S. Eliot,
Dylan Thomas, W.B. Yeats, Ezra Pound and others. I had realized
that my own writings were, if not precisely mediocre, certainly
not immortal literature either. I simply wasn't saying things that I
should have been capable of saying" (*RBS*, 135).

1952 Meets Malcolm Lowry

1955 Has a bit part as a drunken sailor in a Vancouver production of
Mister Roberts (Bruno Gerussi and Craig Stevens are the stars).
During a two-month trip to Europe he sees Paris, the south of
France, London, Scotland and New York. The family moves to
Montreal where he begins writing radio plays for CBC (*A Gathering*

of Days is the first to be accepted) and meets Irving Layton, F.R. Scott, Louis Dudek, Leonard Cohen and other writers: "Irving Layton was the Montreal magnet for me: a man with a word for everything; never in the time of my knowing him did he appear to be at a loss. Irving seemed to hypnotize himself with his own voice, feeding on echoes of his own opinion. But warm, with a feeling for other people. And the warmth made the rest bearable. I felt about him as I had not about any other Canadian writer, a kind of awe and surprise that such magical things should pour from an egotistic clown, a charismatic poseur. And I forgive myself for saying those things, which are both true and not true" (*RBS*, 155).

1956 Alfred W. Purdy publishes *Emu, Remember!*

1957 Family moves to his mother's house at 134 Front St., Trenton. They buy land at Roblin Lake where, with help from Jim Parkhurst, Milton Acorn and CPR lumber, they build an A-frame cottage. Describing these difficult years of poverty and failure in his auto-biography, Purdy refers to them as "The Bad Times": "But those awful depressions I went through, sometimes lasting for several weeks! Poverty is like that. Reading Orwell's *Down and Out in Paris and London* and Norman Levine's *Canada Made Me* is depressing and exhilarating. To endure such experiences is to be transformed into a socialist or a nihilist. I was neither, but suicide sometimes did enter my mind. As something to think about, as a trapdoor if all else failed, as an ending for the unendurable present.

"We ground it out, the time, the bad experiences, and poverty that seemed to have no ending.

"But what do you do, how do you stand it: poverty, failure, all the rest. There is no answer. You go on, or you don't" (*RBS*, 164–5).

1958 Both Eurithe and Al work at Jay Sprague's Mountainview Canning Factory. Mother dies in Trenton. "I was one of the world's losers at the time" (*RBS*, 171). During the next six years, he writes a dozen plays for CBC radio.

1959 Alfred Purdy publishes *The Crafte So Longe to Lerne*, dedicated to Irving Layton and Milton Acorn. None of the poems from the first three collections appear in *Beyond Remembering: The Collected Poems of Al Purdy*.

1960 "I received a thousand dollars from a Canada Council grant in the spring of 1960. I bought a train ticket to Vancouver ... During the tenure of my short-term grant, I planned to revisit the places where

I'd been stationed during the war, at Woodcock in the Hazelton area of northern BC.

"Driving an old 1948 Pontiac from a Vancouver used car lot, I drove north, sleeping in the car. In fact I lived in that car for nearly twenty-four hours a day. Parked on a side road in the Hazelton wilderness area, I set up literary shop. My idea was to write about Indians and whites, loggers and miners and trappers.

"I drank beer with them in the local pubs, talked to everyone, from Mounties to railways workers. And wrote poems. Once I interviewed an Indian while drinking beer with him . . . His expression while I asked my questions was most peculiar. It turned out he was the son of the Chinese Canadian hotel owner in Hazelton village" (*RBS*, 174).

1962 Publishes *Poems for All the Annettes*, his breakthrough book

1963 Has a memorable first meeting with Margaret Atwood at D.G. Jones's

1964 Begins correspondence with Charles Bukowski. The two never meet, and eventually quarrel over Purdy's inclusion of Bukowski's letters in a sale of his papers.

Travels to Mexico and Cuba. "Travelling from Canada to Cuba couldn't be done in a straight line, across the US to Miami, say, then south to Havana. American hostility to Fidel Castro and his nation precluded such a simple trip. One had to book for Mexico City, then wait for a scheduled Cubana Airlines flight instead . . .

"Two Montreal lawyers were with our contingent, both French Canadian. One spoke very little. The other was lean-faced, middle height, and balding, his manner self-possessed and confident. During one long discussion I had with him he described his formula for Quebec's relations with the rest of the country. I was impressed but forgetful, and later asked him to repeat again some key portions of his thesis. He refused, and nothing more could be said on the subject. His name was Pierre Trudeau" (*RBS*, 200).

1965 "From 1965 on, life opened up for me. At that time it became entirely feasible for me to go anywhere on earth and to write about it. I was also confident that I would 'write' well: and I hope that doesn't sound overweeningly sure of myself . . . And the last twenty-five years have not really been dominated by riding freight trains, unemployment, military servitude or the taxi business. I've been on my own, entirely responsible for what I was and am, nobody to praise or blame but my inescapable self.

"Baffin Island in 1965 was a beginning. Leaving Montreal in early June, flying over Ungava and Hudson Straits to Frobisher Bay and snowsplashed hills of Baffin like recumbent Jersey cows—that was exciting . . . No other poet I knew of had ever gone to the Arctic (except Robert Service, and he didn't count), it was virgin territory for me, untouched except for the mundane prose of explorers and scientists" (*RBS*, 190).

Publishes *The Cariboo Horses*, his first book with McClelland and Stewart; the book wins the Governor General's Award and establishes his reputation.

1966 Begins correspondence with Margaret Laurence. Is awarded the President's Medal by the University of Western Ontario for "The Country North of Belleville."

1967 *North of Summer: Poems from Baffin Island.* The Purdys travel to Newfoundland: "In the late 1960s my wife and I mounted a home-made camper on a pickup truck and drove to Newfoundland, picking wild raspberries along the road, stopping for the night in old gravel quarries, buying salmon and cod from fishermen, getting eaten ourselves by no-see-ums . . . The land seemed endless, despite the finitude of road maps. One is misled by maps into feeling that anything that can be crammed onto paper and seen there in its entirety can't be that impressive in actuality.

"But you traverse a country foot by foot in shoe leather, and mile by mile with automobile tires. The elastic landscape stretches and stretches, the mind can't take it all in . . . When I wrote poems along the road, once again there was the feeling of mapping the country, giving it an additional persona and identity. Not ego in doing so, but in the naming of things there is a knowing, a forging of bonds between . . . I mean: you can get some feedback from a dog or cat or human, a word or growl or meow—but from the land there is nothing but a great silence, unless you build a word-bridge to help you understand a thing that may be beyond understanding . . .

"One of the reasons for our Newfoundland trip was the Norse site at L'Anse aux Meadows, discovered by Norwegian explorer and writer Helge Ingstad. Along the road I was writing a review of Farley Mowat's *Westviking* for a literary magazine. When we arrived, Ingstad was amazingly still there, puttering around the Norse site with his archaeologist wife, Anne Stine. White-haired and bony looking, I thought Ingstad was. Lean with high cheekbones and ruddy complexion; both he and his wife cordial to these southern strangers" (*RBS*, 238–9).

1968 Edits *The New Romans*, a collection of Canadian essays on the American empire. *Wild Grape Wine.*

1969 The Purdys travel to Athens, Rome and Pompeii. They stay in England with Margaret Laurence when Eurithe needs surgery. The friendship with Laurence lasts until her death in 1987. Their extensive correspondence is published in 1993 as *Margaret Laurence–Al Purdy: A Friendship in Letters.*

1970 George Bowering publishes *Al Purdy*, the first monograph on Purdy's work. The Purdys return to Turkey in March. For the next several years he frequently writes articles for *Weekend* and *Maclean's*; most are collected in *No Other Country* (1977) and *Starting from Ameliasburgh: The Collected Prose of Al Purdy* (1995).

1971 Travels alone to Japan

1972 Travels alone to South Africa

1973–74 Writer in Residence at Loyola University, Montreal

1974 *In Search of Owen Roblin*

1975–76 Writer in Residence at the University of Manitoba

1977 The Purdys travel with Ralph and Betty Gustafson to the Soviet Union. Writer in Residence at the University of Western Ontario during the academic year 1977–78.

1979 To Machu Picchu and the Galapagos Islands. "When 'Birdwatching at the Equator' was published in a magazine, a Conservative Member of Parliament noticed it and read it aloud to the Liberal government in the House of Commons in Ottawa. His object was undoubtedly to embarrass the Liberals, to say, in effect: 'Is this the kind of shit you people encourage through Canada Council grants?'" (*RBS*, 264).

1980 *The Stone Bird*

1982 Order of Canada

1984–85 F.R. Scott dies (1899–1985). *Piling Blood.*

1986 Order of Ontario. Milton Acorn dies (1923–86). The Purdys buy a house in Sidney, British Columbia. From now on they spend their summers at Ameliasburgh and winters on Vancouver Island. They travel to Turkey; visit Troy.

1987 Margaret Laurence dies (1926–87). Governor General's Award for *The Collected Poems of Al Purdy*: "[Jean Sauvé, the Governor

General,] seemed unaccountably nervous when talking with me, as if my fly was open" (*RBS*, 188).

Purdy is Writer in Residence at the University of Toronto from September 1987 to April 1988. A conference on his work is held on March 25,1988.

1990 November 12 is declared Al Purdy Day in Trenton. *The Woman on the Shore.*

1991 Wins the Milton Acorn People's Poet Award

1993 *Reaching for the Beaufort Sea: An Autobiography.* Special Purdy issue of *Essays on Canadian Writing* includes essays and appreciations by Louis Mackendrick, Peter Stevens, Sam Solecki, George Woodcock, Rosemary Sullivan and W.J. Keith.

1995 *Starting from Ameliasburgh: The Collected Prose of Al Purdy*

1996 *Rooms for Rent in the Outer Planets: Selected Poems.* Harbourfront holds an evening celebrating his career on November 15; the speakers include Margaret Atwood, George Bowering and Dennis Lee.

2000 Publishes *Beyond Remembering: The Collected Poems of Al Purdy* with forewords by Margaret Atwood and Michael Ondaatje

Dies on April 21 in Sidney, and his ashes are buried beside the mill pond in Ameliasburgh. A memorial celebration takes place in Ameliasburgh in June.

October 4: a memorial service is held at Harbourfront in Toronto. October 19: an Al Purdy Night is held in Belleville.

2003 December 1–13: in Toronto CBC presents "Al Purdy at the Quinte Hotel," written by Dave Carley and featuring Gordon Pinsent as the poet. The play is broadcast on February 29, 2004.

Earle Birney (1904–95): Chaucer scholar, editor, novelist (*Turvey*, 1949), and poet. His poem "David" (1942) is a Canadian classic. One of his obituaries referred to him as "The West's Trotskyite troubadour," an allusion to his radical politics and to his meeting with Leon Trotsky in Norway in 1939. As a teacher of creative writing at the University of British Columbia, Birney influenced a generation of Canadian writers. As can be seen from his forty-year correspondence with AP, he was very influential in the latter's development as a poet. His *Collected Poems* appeared in 1977.

To Earle Birney (Vancouver), from Belleville, Ont., October 20, 1947

Dear Mr. Birney,

Just a note to let you know the verse I sent you has not been published before nor will it be except in *Canadian Poetry Magazine*.

I sometimes wonder when I read *CPM* at the change of editorial policy that seems to accompany each new editor. In my own mind I have you labelled as an extreme liberal and Watson Kirkconnell[1] as a progressive-conservative. When I write poetry, I consciously strive for beauty as well as something that makes a person think a bit. Some people say that the poetry of a nation closely resembles its conversation. I thought that point was particularly true of your long poem "David." Yet the trend of most modern poetry seems to be away from this principle and toward hyphenated words and phrases that you would think a bit odd found in prose. I notice this tendency in part of yours and all of Anne Marriott's[2] for instance. Don't think I'm acting the part of a critic but rather an observer with somewhat more than an ordinary interest. I would like very much to know whether it's a permanent trend—this swing to the ultra-modern. Well I guess I've used (if not wasted) enough of your time.

Sincerely yours,
Alfred W. Purdy

1. Watson Kirkconnell (1895–1977): poet, translator, professor of English (University of Manitoba, McMaster University and Acadia University) and literary critic. A prolific writer, Kirkconnell is probably best remembered today for his three studies of John Milton and for his championing of Canadian writing in languages other than English and French.
2. Anne Marriott (1913–97): BC poet best known for *The Wind is Our Enemy*

(1939), *Calling Adventurers!* (1941; Governor General's Award) and *The Circular Coast* (1981).

The typescript of the letter in the Birney papers at the University of Toronto has Birney's handwritten note—"ans. EB. Nov. 6"—at the bottom of the page. Nearly every letter that Birney answered has a similar annotation.

From Earle Birney (Vancouver), to Belleville, Ont., November 5, 1947

Dear Mr. Purdy,

The difference between me and Watson Kirkconnell editorially is not so much that of an "extreme liberal" as against a "progressive-conservative," as a very ordinary liberal against an incipient fascist. In Kirkconnell's regime only a limited group of very traditional writers ("traditional" in a mid-Victorian sense) were welcomed; all others were attacked, lumped together as "reds," etc. In my regime, both you and the "ultra-moderns" as you call them, have a chance, as I believe in giving any craftsman a chance if he is a good enough craftsman. As for the strangeness and stylistic differences which you ask about in my verses and others—wouldn't it be more surprising, and a good deal duller, if everybody wrote the same all the time? Every poetic generation has had to fight against the people who wanted to keep things just the way they were in grand-dad's day—that's true of all art, and all life. I'd rather be on the side of the present, the creative, the changing—but I'll still give a place in *CPM* for the good writer in the old forms, so long as he *is* good in them and has something to say. And I demand as much, if not more, from the experimentalist.

Sincerely yours,
Earle Birney

To Earle Birney (Vancouver), from Belleville, Ont., November 22, 1947

Dear Mr. Birney,
(Sounds very formal doesn't it?) You must understand that whatever I might say that I certainly mean no offence in any way and actually feel quite cordial. I don't think a discussion like this will ever come to mutual agreement but none the less I feel impelled to add an explanatory million words or so to my first letter. First of all I was quite aware that Watson Kirkconnell was definitely conservative having discussed him with Joan Buckley[1] but I didn't know that he was "hidebound" enough to exclude something really good from *CPM* in modern form because he didn't approve said form. I don't dislike modern verse because the

term "modern" is applied to it. After all the most desired quality of poetry is that it be good regardless of date, period or anything else and some present day writers write very good verse without belonging to any particular class or school. I shouldn't have used the term "modernist" at all because it can't be classified that way. Perhaps I sound a little mixed up. I hope not. Frankly I like *CPM* better now under your editorship than before. There is more variety, more of the unexpected but I do have to disagree with some things. I noticed a radio play in one issue. I didn't read all of it but I didn't think it was exactly in a proper environment. Of course I have to allow that some people probably like it but unless the magazine intends to become the medium for several forms of literature I thought it out of place. My idea of poetry is that it has no date, form or special identifying feature, it is a higher form of entertainment or enjoyment by the mind but nevertheless should be couched in the language of its own time. I believe anything that is stilted or grotesque in language is doomed to swift extinction UNLESS the message or beauty presented is so striking as to preclude this happening. Further I would say that anything stilted or grotesque militates against beauty. My whole contention is that poetry should use not everyday but natural English. I have no doubt that you can marshal your words together and shake my arguments at their foundation because I have left many loopholes. Perhaps the reason is that I don't state my case in enough detail. I'm fully aware that because I don't like a thing does not signify that my opinion is universal. I believe that the only excuse for obscurity is if it adds something to the value of a poem which it may in the hands of the proper writer but obscurity coupled with the grotesque does not make a good combination. Here's a line from a recent issue "Disentangle lush water-lily cables, Thick as a wrestler's arm . . ." In the first place I dislike the word "lush" and the comparison of water-lily stems to a wrestler's arm is grotesque to my mind or to say the least unlovely. Of course that's far from the best or worst example. I'll have to admit I like the rest of the poem. Also I like most of the verse in *CPM* so what am I arguing about? Here's something I don't like . . .

> He had passed, inconscient, full gaze,
> The wide-banded irides
> And botticellian sprays implied
> In their diastasis;

Which anaethesis, noted a year late,
And weighed, revealed his great affect,
(Orchid), a mandate
Of Eros, a retrospect.

Beautiful, isn't it? Pound![2] If I got a dictionary and looked up the words I might understand. Here's one of my favourites . . .

SPANISH JOHNNY

The old West, the old time,
The old wind singing through
The red, red grass a thousand miles—
And Spanish Johnny, you!
He'd sit beside the water ditch
When all his herd was in,
And never mind a child, but sing
To his mandolin.

The big stars, the blue night,
The moon-enchanted lane;
The olive man who never spoke,
But sang the songs of Spain.
His speech with men was wicked talk—
To hear it was a sin;
But those were golden things he said
To his mandolin.

The gold songs, the gold stars,
The world so golden then;
And the hand so tender to a child—
Had killed so many men.
He died a hard death long ago
Before the road came in—
The night before he swung, he sang
To his mandolin. (Willa Cather)[3]

You might call that symbolic of my point of view but I don't mean it that way. I simply like it. I have a definite dislike of hyphenated words generally speaking because they are nearly always ugly or grotesque coupled. Among modern Canadians (there's that word again) I would single out Anne Marriott to bear the brunt of my opprobrium. Of course I wouldn't tell her so. I'd remain non-commital. If you care to answer this I'll be glad to hear from you. I won't expect it but if you don't I'll assume that my arguments are unworthy of consideration and what kind of a spot does that put you in. You understand, of course, that I'm not presenting my own verse as a model of my viewpoint. You can and will take that or leave it as you undoubtedly will. I merely have an idea and try to live up to it. Lucidity and modern usage (not slang) are the main points. I enclose a poem finished a minute before I wrote this letter. If you do write let me know what you think of it then.

Sincerely,
Alfred W. Purdy

VERSION

If it hadn't been for Ariadne's wheedling, cheek
and bosom pressing against him when
they walked, and Pasiphae's innocent sort of look,
as if she'd like to make him happy,
but really shouldn't—
the wandering tinker, the great mechanic,
might never have watched his island-hopping son
sink like a stone. True the wings were a copy,
and chancy things at best.
But Icarus was a laconic
youth who hated his father and wouldn't
admit that Minos hated HIM,
flew at the sun and shook his fist
at the dwindling world and the anxious man below;
hesitated, and cursed himself for a yellow
coward: after that the slow
man-fall to the sea's pillow.
The old perfectionist
sighed helplessly and went on.

Everybody knows what happened,
a *cause célèbre* for a time.

Of course the courts took no action
against the father, called it an accident.
Faulty materials, it seems
to me they said. The crops ripened
much as before; Poseidon's ocean
found a place for the new chum
in a basement room; and Daedalus,
the old roué, appears
sometimes to be a little glum,
is staying with Cocalus,
working on the drafting table, one hears.

And Ariadne in the family way somewhere in the Mediter-
ranean area smiles at the sea, and continues her slow audit.

INVOCATION
(To be spoken aloud in a land without snow.)

Mourn for snow: the sun-staring, the blue-memory
Of hip-high drifts and town mirage;
The shading, the symmetry of trees beneath slow
Flakes, flowers in a lonesomeness of young age.
And morning, white morning after the windy
Yesterdays in the forest of always Sunday.

Roads in white nowhere on strange errands.
Only wire-hum, foot-heart-beat audible
And terror-telling: the steady sky-falling torrents,
As a woman should be, a woman most beautiful.

The horse-clopping, the bell-ringing time of earth,
The cloud-beaten, wind-bullied hammers of blood
Bursting in noiseless thunder—no sound heard—
Only the sky emissaries slow going to bed.

Send snow: Send it white in this land of green trees
And small brown people—comptroller of all my days.

1. "All these dollar poems in the *Vancouver Sun* caused me to be in touch with
Joan Buckley, who edited the *Sun* poetry page. I met her in late 1943. Joan was

perhaps thirty-five years old then, her legs crippled by polio years before . . . Occasionally I'd take the bus to Langley to visit Joan and the Buckleys. I'd sit with her in the sun or beside her bed, talking about everything and learning much. Joan had self-published a couple of small chapbooks of some poems, and another on how to write poetry. They sold well locally" (*RBS*, 103).

2. Ezra Pound (1885–1972): a critic and poet (*Homage to Sextus Propertius* [1919] and *Cantos*), among many other things, Pound was arguably the most influential literary figure of the twentieth century. AP recognized his importance, but admired only some of the early poems such as "The Seafarer" and "The River Merchant's Wife." In "Pound" (*Naked with Summer in Your Mouth*), AP describes him as "Old Ez: the man who knew everything," and concludes with "We humans: there is no explaining us / our cruelty and nastiness and nobility / and all you can do now is read 'The River Merchant's Wife' / and say 'Pound' / and shrug your shoulders." The two quoted stanzas are from the second section of Pound's "Mauberley."

3. Willa Cather (1876–1947): though she wrote poetry (*April Twilights*, 1903), Cather was much better known as a novelist (*My Antonia*, 1918). "Spanish Johnny" is from *April Twilights*.

Northrop Frye (1912–91): a long-time professor of English at the University of Toronto and one of the major literary critics of his generation, his internationally influential books include *Fearful Symmetry: a Study of William Blake* (1947), *Anatomy of Criticism* (1957) and *The Great Code: the Bible and Literature* (1982). On at least two occasions, he wrote letters in support of AP's grant applications. AP heavily annotated Frye's essay "Conclusion to the *Literary History of Canada*" in his copy of the book. When he reviewed it for *Books in Canada* in 1977, he paid particular attention to Frye's contribution.

From Northrop Frye (Toronto), to Belleville, Ont., May 18, 1948

Dear Mr. Purdy,

Thanks very much for the enclosed: we are taking "Reaction," "Druid," and "Defense Counsel." You say in your letter that you are anxious for criticism, which is why I write this, as your poetry interests me very much. You have a fine sinewy fluency in your writing, and everything about your rhythm, rhymes and diction has great energy and point. There are no virtues without their characteristic defects, and the dangers in your virtues are those of monotony and diffuseness. The smoother and less obscure the writing, the more sharply the ideas stand out, and any touch of commonplaceness in the thinking is more noticeable than it would be in a less honest poet. It is because the general level of writing is so high that "A thin and pious self-important sneer" seems a padded line, "This place of garish sound and revelry" a commonplace one, and the rhymes "paralleled" and "qualified" in "Adventurers" forced. You seem to have discovered the main essentials of your style very quickly, and your central line of development is in the direction of polishing and cutting out the duller bits.

Yours sincerely,
Northrop Frye
Managing Editor
[*The Canadian Forum*, Toronto][1]

1. AP refers to this letter in *Reaching for the Beaufort Sea*: "I cut out all my own [published] poems religiously, gluing them into a scrapbook. Northrop Frye was then some kind of editor on the *Canadian Forum*. I asked him for criticism on my stuff, and he sent me a full-page letter analysing it. I included his letter in the scrapbook as well; but the whole collection got lost on one of our moves from one lodging place to another" (103). In fact, the scrapbook is at the University of Saskatchewan.

To Earle Birney (Vancouver), from Vancouver, March 7, 1955. The letter was written by AP and his friend Curt Lang.[1]

Dear Dr. Birney,
This is a letter from two poets, to which there is no particular point, nor any particular reverence for your own undoubted status as a great poet. Has anybody told you that? I suppose they have not since your friends would think it too obvious a statement. But to get to this particular point in a letter without a dominating motive for being written, we think you are the greatest poet in Canada today. Better than Pratt, A.J.M. Smith, Klein[2] etc., and almost as good as Birney.

That should dispense with the flattery. Because you haven't written anything good since *Strait of Anian* [1948], which contained "Mappemounde," a large masterpiece. I meant to say in the previous paragraph that I regard you as better than any English poet such as Empson[3] et al. Nevertheless you will never be known beyond the confines of Canada, at least I don't think so, since a book has to be published outside of Canada in order to receive critical acclaim. It would seem we are still a colony therefore. I regard that as a special tragedy that such poems of yours as "David," "Slug in Woods," "Vancouver Lights," "Mappemounde," "Reverse on the Coast Range" and others should not be known and acclaimed as the very best. You will notice that in the last sentence "we" is abandoned since I am speaking for myself. But the world will lose much richness because it knows not Birney.

New paragraph. Lest the preceding flattery should go to your head, your later stuff is just ordinary. I dislike saying that, but think it true. *Trial of a City* [1952] was uninteresting to me, and you may put me down as an unperceptive pseudo-intellectual if you like. My likes and dislikes are honest, however. The tragedy is that you could still write great poetry under certain conditions and locale.

Poet number two now wrests the keyboard from resisting hands. What does the established poet think? Is he established even to himself? You are of course established, entrenched quite firmly, even, to coin, betextbooked. I speak recklessly you may see, but I am young, and a little in wine, so damn my hidden censor. But it seems to me that most poets do write their best before good taste does rear itself, for instance Donne and Eliot.[4] Certainly their later work is more responsible, more finely turned, but what can I say, you either know what I mean or you do not. Still, I wonder.

Yes, he is young, a malady not without remedy. I am fairly old. I am 36. If there was a subject and motive for this letter it was that we would like to talk to you, but I doubt that is possible. We can talk to anyone but I doubt that you can. It seems to me that a professorship or doctorate makes too much difference. I don't know if your classes are accessible to my friend and I; but in any case we are too lazy to go out to UBC. Do not mistake me. That is not indifference. You do not know if either of us can write poetry or are worth talking to. You may have seen my name, if not you very likely will. My friend may take longer.

But aside from that I'd like to see you write some good poetry again. Are we impertinent? I suppose it takes some special provocation to speak seeming truth even to oneself, in this case wine. Therefore you may ignore this missive, saying to yourself such words as may suit the situation, and letting it fade into the sea of high time. In your case perhaps I should.

Alfred W. Purdy

Curt Lang

1. Curtis Lang (1937–98): AP and Lang were close friends during AP's Vancouver years: "Curt Lang, a precocious teenager I had met at a science-fiction fan club

gathering. Curt was one of those preternaturally brilliant youngsters who antagonize their elders by being too obviously intelligent. He was also a science-fiction
buff. Curt admired my rather puerile poetry, which really doesn't speak well for
that aforementioned intelligence" (*Reaching for the Beaufort Sea,* 135). Lang and AP
went to Europe together in 1955. BC writer and publisher (Harbour Publishing)
Howard White summed up Lang as follows: "Curt was a legendary personality
on the Vancouver art scene, first showing up as a teenage prodigy attached to the
Birney–Lowry art set in the 1950s writing Rimbaudesque poetry and playing be-
bop sax. Lowry, in a much repeated and probably not very sober pronouncement,
hailed him as the most promising writer since Shakespeare. But Curt remained
promising all his life, preferring to sample a bewildering range of activities rather
than to master any. At different times he was a photographer, a boat designer and
builder, an inventor, a publisher, and a computer analyst as well as being a writer
and musician. Everybody knew him, and most people counted him as brilliant,
but he left remarkably little on the printed record. Al met him in his prodigy phase
and kept up periodic contact with him until he died. Presentation House in North
Vancouver had a tribute night for him." "For Curt Lang" is one of AP's last poems
(*Beyond Remembering: The Collected Poems of Al Purdy*).
2. E.J. Pratt (1882–1964): the pre-eminent and most popular poet of his generation, Pratt edited *Canadian Poetry Magazine* from 1936 to 1943, taught at the
University of Toronto until 1953 and was awarded three Governor General's
Awards. *E.J. Pratt: The Complete Poems* was published in 1989. The following
comment from *Reaching for the Beaufort Sea* is characteristic of AP's view of
Pratt's work: "It's the lack of a single personal human face behind E.J. Pratt's epics that leaves me indifferent to him and them." A.J.M. Smith (1902–80): a critic,
poet (*News of the Phoenix*, 1943) and anthologist (*Book of Canadian Poetry: A
Critical and Historical Anthology*, 1943; *Oxford Book of Canadian Verse: in English
and French*, 1960), Smith was one of the most influential figures in Canadian
poetry of his era. A.M. Klein (1909–72): novelist (*The Second Scroll*, 1951), Joyce
scholar and poet (*The Rocking Chair*, 1948; *Complete Poems*, 1990). Though never a popular poet, Klein was always highly regarded by critics and other poets.
3. William Empson (1906–84): though best known as a literary critic (*Seven
Types of Ambiguity*, 1930), Empson was, and continues to be, highly regarded as
a poet (*Collected Poems*, 1955); he is one of only two contemporary poets praised
in F.R. Leavis's influential *New Bearings in Modern Poetry* (1932). Among AP's
friends who were poets, only George Johnston was interested in him.
4. John Donne (1572–1631): best known for his early metaphysical love poems
("The Sun Rising," "The Canonization"). AP admired these and returned to
them in the years just before his death in *The Man Who Outlived Himself* (2000)
in which he and Doug Beardsley commented on the poems and rewrote five of
them. "For Ann More: 1584–1617)," written by AP alone, is one of the last poems
in *Beyond Remembering: The Collected Poems of Al Purdy*.
   T.S. Eliot (1888–1965): the dominant literary figure of his time, Eliot, helped
by Pound, changed the course not only of English but of European poetry (his
translators include Czeslaw Milosz and George Seferis). "The Waste Land" (1922)
is probably the single most famous poem in English of the twentieth century. His

books include *Prufrock and Other Observations* (1917), *Four Quartets* (1943) and several collections of very influential critical essays. He received the Nobel Prize in 1948.

From Earle Birney (Vancouver), to Vancouver, March 15, 1955

Dear Alfred Purdy and Curt Lang,
Glad to hear from you. By coincidence I'd just got *Pressed on Sand* out of the University library—mainly as a result of liking some of your pieces I'd seen in the *CF* and *SN*, Mr. Purdy. Confess I dont know your work, Mr. Lang, but I should like to. I think we ought to have a get-together soon. A lot of the questions you raise take too long to spell out on paper. I'm in the last two weeks of readying a novel for shipment to a publisher so I wont propose a date till that's over with. But maybe then we could extend this discussion over a beer wherever you like drinking beer, if you like drinking beer. Meantime, a few haphazard reactions to your joint assault.

First of all, if you'd been quite sober you wouldnt have called me a great poet, because on sober thought I'm not. I doubt I'm any better than Smith, Klein, etc., though I'm certainly different from them. I havent the bulk of Pratt, and I'll never be the personal legend he has been. Sometimes I think P.K. Page is a much better poet than I am. And I wouldnt be surprised if Jay Macpherson and Phyllis Webb[1] turned out to be the best Canadian poets yet. But all that's just Canadian poetry anyway—not that I want to condescend to ourselves—leave that to the Americans and the British—but I do want to keep a perspective. I think there are half a dozen of us in Canada who are as good as hundreds of American poets who get published and praised, while we cant even get published in London or New York. (But that's nobody's fault very much except the people who caused boundaries and help to preserve them.) But there aren't and there never have been poets in Canada in the same street with Dylan Thomas or Auden[2] or Eliot or Browning or Emily Dickinson or or etc. Let's keep those names in mind when we use the word "great." Occasionally some of us put up a good poem; it seems hard to put up enough to make the sound of a poet. Frankly, of the poems of mine you were kind enough to list as good, I can stand only "Mappemounde" now. Chicago *Poetry* turned "David" down as "melodramatic"; I was sore at the time, but now I think they were right. It's well-constructed, it's metrically sound, it tells a story, etc. But it's two-dimensional where it should be three. Most of my stuff that's got into anthologies and school texts is in them precisely because they are secondrate. My best stuff continues to be misunderstood or ignored, even by you two (except, I'm glad and grateful to see, "Mappemounde"). My best poems, I'll tell you what they are—and dont tell me I dont know because I wrote them. I've had to live with them as well as write them, recite them from platforms, revise them, etc. You know what I mean. "War Winter," "Introvert," "The Road to Nijmegen" (these last two rejected in Canada, by the way, and published by John Lehmann[3] in London, despite what I said about English publishers). From *Anian* volume, beside "Mappemounde," I'll stand on "Montreal," "From the hazel bough," "The ebb begins from dream," "Pacific Door" (first published in *Harper's* and I think a solid poem where "Slug in the Woods" is only a tour de force), "Young Veterans," "Ulysses." (Not "Vancouver Lights," which is faded with its own topicality, and not "Reverse on the Coast Range" which had a merely pretty and sentimental ending). However, I'm willing to throw all those away if you'll let me keep the *Trial of a City* book, esp. "Bushed," "Images," and "St. Valentine" and certain sections of the title-piece. The whole book represents for me a deepening in meaning and intention and a widening of technique. It's still not a good book, but it's the best book I've done yet.

Of course it's unfair of me to grope in cold sobriety with phrases you two struck off in moments of winy rhetoric. So I take your disapprovals at the same discount as I took your praises.

Curt Lang trots out the old bugbear used so often to discourage a poet when he's no longer "young" (what the hell is "young"? I'll bet Lang is older than Denys St. Garneau[4] was when he died, or Chatterton or maybe even Keats—but I dont think he should feel his case is hopeless for all that). Well, I dont think I'll ever improve enough to be a great poet, but I'm quite sure I go on improving, in my little way, just as Yeats did in his big way, and Chaucer in his. Chaucer's finest work he did in his fifties, Spenser in his forties, Shakespeare between 35 and 50, and Herrick perhaps also. Milton *began Paradise Lost* when he was fifty, Browning wrote *The Ring and the Book* in his middle fifties. Hardy was in his sixties before he learned how to write good verse, Amy Lowell wrote juvenilia till she was forty, and Frost till almost that vintage, and Robinson Jeffers. Ransom didnt write a good poem till he was 36. Housman—some of his best stuff in his fifty-first year, de la Mare in his forties, D.H. Lawrence likewise (and dying), Edith Sitwell in her fifties, Robert Graves likewise.[5] Jesus, you fellows have it all ahead of you, barring radioactive fallout . . .

So you can "talk to anyone" and I cant. Because I'm a professor?! What a quaint Victorian concept of a professor. Of course if you are "too lazy to come out to UBC" and drop in on my creative-writing class, 3–6 Thursday afternoon, that does erect a minor obstacle. And I *am* busy, but at a lot of things, radio, tv, public lecturing (I've just got back from talks at the Universities of Oregon and Washington, and some good stag parties thrown in), square dancing, studying marine shore-life, starting to get up some Spanish for a trip to Mexico this summer, gardening, writing letters, working on the novel, on articles, playing table tennis with my kid, partying with my wife and friends, just going on living like anybody else. And when the novel is over I'm getting back to verse and I hope to write better than I ever have, again without too much hope that I'll ever write anything really first class. But maybe.

I like most of your poems, Alfred W. Purdy, and I'd like to talk about them with you sometime. So I'll drop you a note when, as I said, the bloody novel is off my chest.

Sincerely,

Earle Birney

1. P.K. Page (b. 1916): highly regarded visual artist, novelist (*The Sun and the Moon*, 1944) and poet (*The Metal and the Flower*, 1954; *Cry Ararat!*, 1967). Jay Macpherson, see page 166. Phyllis Webb, see page 160.
2. Dylan Thomas (1914–53): Welsh poet (*Twenty-Five Poems*, 1936; *Collected Poems* 1934–52) who may have been as important to the work of AP's middle period (1947–60) as Bliss Carman had been to his first two decades and D.H. Lawrence would be to his major phase (1960–87). Something of what Thomas meant to him can be gathered from the following vignette: "I have a mental picture of myself at that time, riding the interurban from our small house on Vanness Avenue near Burnaby to the mattress factory on Clark Drive. I am reading *The Collected Poems of Dylan Thomas*. A gangly thirty-to-thirty-five-year-old, hair receding at the temples, and an expression of mixed interest and puzzlement flits across my face while reading. And glancing around self-consciously at other early morning travelers to see if anyone has noticed these intellectual proclivities, and again to see if there are any good-looking girls on the interurban. A poetry-writing factory worker with pretensions to culture" (*RBS*, 134). W.H. Auden (1907–73): despite some occasionally negative comments in the early letters, AP considered Auden, after Yeats, to be the most important English poet of the twentieth century. He could quote several of his poems from memory, and "Musée des Beaux Arts" and "In Memory of W.B. Yeats" were in his personal anthology of favourite poems.
3. John Lehmann (1907–87): founder and editor of *New Writing* (1936–41) and *The London Magazine* (1954–61), Lehmann also wrote studies of Edith Sitwell, Virginia Woolf and Rupert Brooke and a three-volume autobiography.
4. Hector de Saint-Denys-Garneau (1912–43): one of the major figures in modern French Canadian literature, he published only one book during his lifetime,

Regards et jeux dans l'espace (1937). *Poésies complètes* appeared in 1949, *Journal* in 1954 and *Oeuvres* in 1971.

5. Amy Lowell (1874–1925): popular American poet best known for her imagistic verse (*Sword Blades and Poppy Seed*, 1914). Pound referred to her branch of Imagism as "Amygism." John Crowe Ransom (1888–1974): influential teacher, critic (*The New Criticism*, 1941) and poet (*Chills and Fever*, 1924). Walter de la Mare (1873–1956): popular English poet (*Collected Poems*, 1979) and prose writer (*Memoirs of a Midget*, 1921). A.E. Housman (1859–1936): English poet, best known for the perennial favourite *A Shropshire Lad* (1896), which he published at his own expense. As with Carman's poetry, AP knew much of Housman's by heart and often quoted it in his letters, prose and in conversation. He recognized that neither was among the best poets in the tradition, but in his personal pantheon each was among the most loved ones. Edith Sitwell (1887–1964): English poet (*Street Songs*, 1942) very popular in the 1930s and during the war. Leavis dismissed her work as belonging "to the history of publicity, rather than that of poetry." Robert Graves: (1895–1985): English novelist (*I, Claudius*, 1934) and poet (*Collected Poems*, 1975). His autobiography *Goodbye to All That* (1929) is a modern classic. AP knew his work well. (For Frost, Jeffers and Lawrence, see below.)

To Earle Birney (Vancouver), from Vancouver, March 17, 1955

Dear Dr Birney, (I mean Earle)
I stand corrected on several counts. But I will not retract on the poems of yours I like. Incidentally, I'm sober now, worse luck; just got home from work which makes it difficult to get out to your class 3–6, just a working stiff, 3 years high school and lots of reading, and varied other experiences. Europe: Spain, Italy, France etc. next Sept, along with Curt and another chap. Curt is 19 by the way. Dunno how old Denys St. Garneau was when he died, don't know him either.

Incidentally, I'm very glad to hear from you. I remember reading about Dylan Thomas being surrounded with worshippers in the Van. Hotel, and being a little bored with it all. I don't at all feel like that, but I still regard your stuff as the best Canadian poetry written, Pratt or no, and the hell with what the author thinks (if he thinks they are not).

Ever read Cary's[1] *The Horse's Mouth*? The phrase "stabbed awake" comes to me recurrently because up till a year and a half ago I didn't like any of your poetry, even though I had *David* (did like that title poem). Then I discovered your stuff. Life must be a continual growth and widening of horizons. At one time I could never have liked Thomas. I do agree with you about Thomas. There was only one Dylan Thomas, and when we have a few drinks we read "Lament" aloud or "Fern Hill," and others;

just about drive my wife out of the house. She mentions feebly from the bedroom that the youngster has to sleep.

So "Vancouver Lights" is topical: admitted, but it is conceivable that much the same circumstances could occur again; beyond that there are few endings that stick in my mind like "There was light." I can read that too! I have read *Strait of Anian* from the library, but don't remember "Now is Time" at all. I'm still growing despite my 36 years, and I have no doubt that when I read "Now is Time" again I shall appreciate it much more. I shall particularly look up "From the hazel bough / The ebb begins from dream." *Trial of a City* I read cursorily and you shame me a little. *Turvey* I thought magnificent; perhaps comedy cannot be more than two dimensional. Do you think Leacock's[2] stuff is? It swims back from childhood now that it is two dimensional. That doesn't matter. I am a solemn person while reading, but in *Turvey*, especially in the part where Turvey was getting an anima [enema]?, a hypodermic? I forget, I roared. But "Flight Across Canada" in *Trial of a City* left me cold.

I have a confession to make. Before I read "Mappemounde" I wrote a poem with the cumbersome title "For 'Richard Hakluyt and Successors'" which depicts somewhat the creatures on the old ocean maps that you described in "Mappemounde." It was taken by *Sat. Nite*[3] and will appear shortly. As I said, this was BEFORE I read "Mappemounde," and I thought I had a theme no one ever had written about. But when I read yours I felt like tearing up the poem, almost. This is it:

From the whales broaching on the stenciled coast
Of Terranova, cherubs with puffed cheeks
Blowing, and coloured cormorants like spikes
Of malachite balanced thoughtfully, on a ship's mast:

These were voyages conceived in queens' bedrooms,
Mentioned in old documents and discussed
By doubtful ministers with stiff perukes pressed
On furrowed brows. The awkward captain comes,

Bows, hesitates and opens in the slow, warm fall
Of words; fingers a black eye patch perhaps;
And pours a fervoured flood on the still
Listening ears, on the held, momentary lips.

Saliva ran in the captain's mouth, and spilt
Over his gold moustache; and the tall
Candles guttered. Dolphins intoxicated by a richer salt,
And birds sang on the antique coast of Hy-Brasil.

As you see, this poem differs materially from yours, and I have a sanctimonious horror of being imitative. Although I have been. I'll enclose a few of my later poems for your cursglance.

Do you mind my thinking you've written better stuff than Pratt? Do you say "he has not reached the stage of proper appreciation for Pratt, the fact that he likes me (Birney) denotes a shallowness and lack of insight; no doubt he is a half-boiled pullet's egg, not yet turned over." You may think that. But I stick to my opinion. Birney: my hero. Pratt wrote "the grey shape with the paleolithic face / is still the master of the longitudes." That's great! Also, hell I've got to look it up:

But in the sound of invisible trumpets blowing
Around two slabs of board, right-angled, hammered
By Roman nails and hung on a Jewish hill.[4]

Magnificent. No one ever wrote any better. But the fact remains that Pratt is stiff, perhaps a concomitant of his style and verse forms. Not in the *Cachalot*, and a few others. But I can't read him as I do Birney. So I'm a moron. Don't get me wrong, to coin a cliché; if I didn't like Birney I'd say so. In fact I wouldn't bother writing him. The little of P.K. Page I've read I've liked, but admit I cannot fairly judge on that amount. But Finch[5] judged on "Scroll-Section" and "The Statue" and a few others is better than Page. That's a bad way to judge, I know: say one poet is better, not appreciate each on his merits. As a matter of fact I like Malcolm Lowry[6] better than anyone but Birney. Again I am prejudiced. I spent two drunken evenings at Lowry's on the north shore along with Curt Lang, drinking gin and orange juice, eating anchovies and copying Lowry's stuff by damnable lamplight. Lowry knew Thomas as did his wife, repeated some scurrilous gossip about Thomas' wife being Augustus John's[7] mistress at one time. And we chuckled at the vitality that must reside in the unwithered frame of the old boy (John). Lowry was glassy eyed and imitated Roy Campbell[8] outside the Oxford Hotel playing the barrel organ and Lowry did a clog dance on the wooden floor "dee, dah, deedle de dah etc." and later went swimming like

Proteus with massive belly thrusting aside the water, and no doubt scaring all marine life for miles.

I've been writing all this on memory from your letter and now will have to look at it. Quite agree there's never been anyone here like Thomas, Eliot, Auden, Dickinson, Browning etc. But you know Auden's cold, too damned intellectual. Poetry needs more than that. But how many of the aforementioned poets are there? It is no disgrace we have none. Of course publishers are blind idiots most of the time. "David" should have been published anywhere it was sent with the exception of *The Ladies Home Journal.* You would have to elaborate on that two-dimensional idea re "David." As I see it, your use of the phrase means that David was not a fully developed character, nor the poem itself. No, I'm wrong. But you couldn't see all of the man in the poem? Even if you were right I wouldn't care. But I wish you'd elaborate. "Slug in Woods" has a shining end "So spends a summer's jasper century" which Joan Buckley also thinks water soluble. "Eagle Island" is not great poetry but it gallops; it can't be read aloud (by me) but it chuckles in the mind. [. . .]

As you say, Curt and I were both quite high when we wrote the letter, and the "old" was meant to be insulting. It's like saying hell to old ladies which is not a good simile. But we both said Birney will throw this in the wastebasket, so what? Well, he didn't. But you see our feeling? Speaking of juvenilia, I wrote a verse play for radio about childhood called *A Gathering of Days* and sent it to CBC a month ago. They received it Feb. 18. No word yet. Say to myself, they're sure to reject it. Is that the attitude to take? Graves, you mention. He's a peculiar poet (and novelist) I'd like to know something of his philosophy, and yours.

About "we can talk to anyone," well I can't. I'm liable to be tonguetied sometimes, not often, but once in a while. I might with you, but not on paper. But give me a few drinks and I'll roar with anyone. The idea of you not being able to talk to anyone is more difficult. Can you talk to laborers, some are intelligent and can be talked to. Of course it doesn't matter. I'm being very diffuse and cloudy. You're busy as hell, no time to breathe, and you don't want to talk to anyone at all. Let's just drop it.

Curt is studying Spanish for our trip to Spain this summer. Picked up Smith's latest. Couldn't resist. Disappointment. Reprints "Plot Against Proteus" but not "Like an Old Proud King." He should be better. I hope you do improve, muchly. And I hope you can find time to come along to my address and drink beer (love it) or wine (love it) even rye or Scotch (don't like em). Here I have 50 odd books of poetry, plus a first ed. of

Godwin's *Lives of the Necromancers* I picked up at the Antiquarian book-shop on Broadway where you go sometimes. Don't expect a reply to this what with tv etc. I might say that I expect to be a better poet too. I have no greater interest in anything unless it is finding out what makes these odd two legged creatures act as they do, and getting my own idea where they're going to end up. Present time I think they'll end up next to a dead dog in an unmarked grave. I've got no phone. Curt's is De 5287 R. But I disagree with "without too much hope that I'll ever write anything first class." A poet should always think he will, so long as it doesn't dull his critical faculties. What else keeps him writing? I expect to write some-thing first class, and I will. Advice to Dr. Birney: go ahead and think you will. Sound like Edgar Guest?[9] Sure, I've many faults, much to learn, but to offset that I know damn well I'm going to write something good. Good to me, anyhow. Is that enough? I've written verse since I was 12, a mat-ter of 24 years. And I've been very slow in learning, but it's a continuous process. If I sound like a braggart, I'm not. But anyway . . . We'll buy some French wine anytime (weekends preferred but not mandatory) you have free time.

Sincerely,

Al Purdy

P.S. Curt has written only two good poems in my opinion, but I think one of them very good. He is being very obstinate about one phrase, "one is dead" I say it should be "one dead," adds force etc. I mention this since if we do meet you and he or I read this poem, you might deliver a pontifical opinion. AWP

1. Joyce Cary (1888–1957): English novelist, best known for the trilogy *Herself Surprised* (1940), *To Be a Pilgrim* (1942) and *The Horse's Mouth* (1944). He served with the Red Cross in the Balkan war of 1912–13 and was decorated by the King of Montenegro.
2. Stephen Leacock (1869–1944): prolific humourist, internationally famous dur-ing his lifetime. Best known today for *Sunshine Sketches of a Little Town* (1912).
3. "For 'Richard Hakluyt and Successors'" appeared on March 19, 1955 in *Saturday Night*. He doesn't mention that "Flies in Amber" was published in the previous issue (March 12).
4. The first quotation is from *The Titanic* (1935), the second from *Brébeuf and His Brethren* (1940).
5. Robert Finch (1900–95): a professor of French at the University of Toronto (1928–68) and poet. Though neglected today, it is worth recalling that Finch's work appeared in *New Provinces* and that he received the Governor General's Award for *Poems* (1946) and *Acis in Oxford* (1961). He also had a distinguished career as a literary scholar working on seventeenth- and eighteenth-century poetry.

6. Malcolm Lowry (1909–57): lived in Canada from 1939–54. Best known for *Under the Volcano* (1947). AP's account of the "two drunken evenings" spent at Lowry's in *Reaching for the Beaufort Sea* has the following description of his first encounter with the English writer: "The man who emerged from the driftwood shack looked short because he was so heavily built. Sporting several day's beard, pants held up with a piece of rope, bloodshot blue eyes, face nearly beet-red, he seemed a drunken bum. And I wondered: how can this guy be a great writer?" AP wrote two poems about him, "Malcolm Lowry" and "About Pablum, Teachers, and Malcolm Lowry" (*The Crafte So Longe to Lerne*). He also wrote "Dormez-vous? A Memoir of Malcolm Lowry" (*Canada Monthly*, July 1963), "Lowry: A Memoir" (*Books in Canada*, January–February 1974) and "Let He Who is Without Gin Cast the First Stone" (*The Montreal Gazette / Weekend Magazine*, August 17, 1974).
7. Augustus John (1878–1961): the best-known and most successful British painter of his generation. Caitlin MacNamara, who married Dylan Thomas in 1936, had been his mistress.
8. Roy Campbell (1901–57): South African journalist and poet, notorious for joining Franco's army during the Spanish Civil War. His *Collected Poems* appeared in 1950, an important study and translation of Garcia Lorca in 1952. AP refers below (summer 1955) to his translation of Baudelaire, *Poems of Baudelaire: A Translation of Les Fleurs du Mal* (1952).
9. Edgar Guest (1881–1959): English-born American journalist and writer of verse. Guest wrote a daily poem for the *Detroit Free Press* that was nationally syndicated. The very popular poems were collected in *Just Folks* (1917) and *Life's Highway* (1933).

To Earle Birney (Vancouver), from Vancouver, March 1955

Dear Earle Birney,
I find I disagree with your judgment of "Pacific Door." "Atlantic Door" is better. Certain lines, of course, are the same, but it is the differences that do it. "Whalehalls" for me is the perfect name for the sea. It at once limits the picture and widens it. "Lymph" meaning the poetical clear water and also the clear fluid from a human body fits exactly the lines that follow about the red infusions of sailors and lascars etc. that still make no difference in the hue of the waves which "fracture white as a narwhal's tusk." You'd better revise your judgment. Of course, I don't suppose you will. I realize that a philosophy is wrapped up in the sentence "that there is no clear Strait of Anian to lead us easy back to Europe" and it's good. But nevertheless, that single idea is all that is really added to the poem. Whereas in "Atlantic Door," many images are added, "scattered twigs on a green commotion." What about it?

Your letter has aroused my interest in your poetry; I suppose it is natural that if you have even a tenuous knowledge of a writer, a papery echo of himself, then the more human interests are aroused. I've been reading your stuff several times and find much missed previously. Some people might read and find all on first reading, but one of the delights of poetry to me is the continual discoveries bobbing up over the worldcurve. Your "dazzle of folders" and the simple uncomplex image of "brown as whiskey." What makes a poem race like "Quebec May" is more than I can tell, except perfect iambic. It sounds incanted. "Eochromes" leaves me a little puzzled. I had to look it up separately: "eo" having to do with early geologic ages: "chrome," yellow and other pigments from lead compounds. But again mental stirrings give me an idea, but am still not certain where "eochrome" fits in. Unless it is that these early pigments and mineral formations might have told a story rowelled away by icecap and snowwild wind? "Scylding boaster" is mythology of course that I am too lazy to look up. And "provender the luminous young" is a particularly felicitous description. You, I suppose, have only one language, in the sense that you speak the words you write in classroom. That is an advantage perhaps. But I have two languages. In most company I would not use such words as "paresis" or "pelagic," since they would not be understood. Hence I am familiar with many words pronounced seldom, which makes emphasis difficult at times. In "Winter Saturday" I have not seen anywhere a better phrase than "hatch from their car like trembling moths," but on reading it alone, the phrase must be in context. Then the magic is complete. Also "they trip two tittering girls in their whistle's lasso." I am knee-deep in Ezra Pound at the moment; but his images are literary for the most part. An odd blend of simplicity and erudition. But at the present time I simply cannot read *The Cantos*. They are not coherent enough or continuous. But I revel in the Faber ed. of *Selected Poems*, the one with the Eliot preface. A friend is sending me *Strait of Anian* for last Christmas and when it gets here (she's taking a helluva time) I shall probably try and get out and get you to place your signature, also to mark the changes in "Mappemounde." I don't mention that poem because it's perfect of its kind. You say you haven't written anything first class. Which means that you think the subject has much to do with its "first classness." I don't. Eliot or no one else ever wrote a poem like "Mappemounde" and can't now because it's been written and cannot be bettered. I am perfectly subjective in this statement as I must be. I am not a critic but a poet, and do not hold it up beside other great poems. This is not necessary. It stands alone without company, beautiful-odd, old-Saxon-jargon that is queerly imminent as death. It brings all the old maps and youthful stories of explorers floating back on your tide to emplume the present with Tyrian purple. Extravagant? Can't I be? "Fardel" is an archaic word meaning burden, but I can't find "farded." I suppose it means impregnated with the remains of a man's body in "Invasion Spring."

Al Purdy

To Earle Birney (Vancouver), from Vancouver, April 1955

Dear Earle Birney,
I knew about "whalehall," having been curious enough to ask a lot of questions of various people about the language used in "Mappemounde." The thing absolutely fascinated me when I first read it, still does. Have also read Pound "The Seafarer." He calls it the "whale-acre," also I suppose swiped from the old boys. But some of your words, most of them, I would judge, were personally invented. "Heart's land trace" is peculiarly magic. I could wait no longer for the Christmas laggard and bought a copy of *Anian*. Have read the poems in *Trial* only a couple of times, but imagine it is myself at fault. Generally I do not have patience to go over and over a thing, push myself till I'm word weary. But so often I have to make a re-assessment of poetry once disliked, and since your own letters have roused a good deal more interest than normal, I shall get a copy and try again. You may say, or I say, "Bully for you." I realize that sounds as if I were in such a position of eminence myself as to be giving you special treatment, almost condescending. I assure you it is not. All your discussion of sources and special words brings several to my own mind. Those in skiing, of which you have used "herringbone," but "Christiana," "telemark;" bullfighting, "veronica" and "media veronica." Also came across a lovely word in Joyce "pavan" or as I prefer the French version where the accent is on the last syllable "pavanne." It could be used in countless ways. Your own grounding in words and literary references is an enormous leap ahead of me in writing poetry. I got out the encyc and looked up Laurentian Shield. You will think me a collector of coloured words, and I am, but "plumbage" is good. Curt Lang came across "phototropic." The advantage of education is you know such words ordinarily on sight. I should think one disadvantage would be that it is more difficult to be in the mainstream of life and not an observer. I am told by a friend that Thomas was a participant and I am an observer. That's arbitrary, but partly true, I think perhaps you're in the same neat pigeon-hold. Disgusting, isn't it? I presume you are not writing poetry now from your

letter. I'm sorry. But you will. If you're like me you can't help yourself. In poetry as nothing else the sense comes on rare occasions when your mind feels projected beyond its own capabilities, some *rara avis* of thought, some exultation of words, that says what could never be said in prose. I work away at prose occasionally, but I am very bad. Paradoxically, I feel that prose has too many limitations that I lose in poetry. Most people would say otherwise. I hope you don't stay at UBC too long for the sake of your writing, that is. I think the mind settles comfortably into a groove as mine has here. Mexico should help. Who was the eastern Eng-born prof-poet who went to Malaya to teach Lit. and came back with some records for CBC about adopting a monkey? Looked him up. Patrick Anderson.[1] I think I should have written much from that experience. Some critic said Anderson was much affected by Dylan Thomas and copies his rhythms. Can't see it. Ever read Irving Layton[2] whom Smith reviewed last Sunday? "In the Midst of My Fever" is a beautiful evocative title. And the absurdity of "The Long Peashooter." When I was a kid I used to fire peas across the wide road onto a Biblical neighbour's window, frantically stubborn, and day after night. Dunno if he ever heard the hard dry sound of peas but he must have . . . Layton sounded good in Smith's excerpts. Privately printed, though, and hard to obtain. Here's my last verse:

TO CANDACE
   (Which is not her)

She hath placed sandals outside her door,
So that the heart clenched at seeing them,
Moving apart aways, and there
Considereth a rarity without name.

She hath plucked flowers in Landseer
That lieth under the mountains of Ale:
And seemeth by ordinary to smile
For sadness like blue larkspur.

Let no more be said but must fade
Beyond traverse the part that is her.
Wall up with silence this certitude.
Add nothing, not argent nor vair.

That poem is about a girl who may or may not have committed suicide. You might be interested in hearing the story. Loretta had a sister who was divorced from her husband and committed suicide. Loretta herself grew ill as a result and was sent to a sanitarium. A friend tells me she died just two weeks or so ago, and the implication was that she probably took her own life. Her sister shot herself in the head with a revolver. Loretta had been married herself but was divorced in 1946. Her husband was a sports fan and she was a writer, fiction and undistinguished poetry. Loretta was a peculiar person, difficult to talk with and impossible to penetrate very deeply. But she was deeply sensitive, and my friend tells me she found a man necessary to direct her life for her. I don't imply she was a nymphomaniac which was my first thought. But in this day and age it is vaguely moving to come upon a person who is dependent and still intelligent. About a year ago Loretta and I walked in Stanley Park looking for the emu,[3] while I tried vainly to penetrate the aforementioned shell. I talk in an ambiguous manner sometimes, and it seemed to me that she purposely drew the wrong meaning from the things I said. In the end I was frustrated. I drove her home and reduced my conversation to monosyllables. Yet she was a person of some physical beauty, intelligence, sensitivity, (which I have not at all illustrated). She wrote me a letter later in the form of a poem (now lost) calling me "the searcher for the emu." I think now that letter was one of her rare efforts to a greater understanding. My friend tells me that if she had known Loretta longer "it would have been only to learn the sum of things she could not know about Loretta." And I say to myself, if I had answered the letter, what might not have happened? If you are a fatalist, she would have died anyhow. But then I might have penetrated that carefully erected defence against the world, that private universe. But she had no means of communicating her feeling at the death of her sister to anyone. Her husband was a sports fan. She died. Is that too cut and dried? Dependency in a self-sufficient world. Or rather, a particular and definite sort of dependency. I tried to put that in a poem without saying it, but probably I failed. But I try. I hope you'll write again.

Best wishes,

Al Purdy

1. Patrick Anderson (1915–79): English-born poet who lived in Montreal during the 1940s and was associated with the *Preview* group. He taught at the University of Malaysia from 1950 to 1952. He writes about Canada in *Search Me: The Black Country,* and *Canada and Spain* (1957), and about Malaysia in *Snake Wine: A Singapore Episode* (1955).

2. Irving Layton, see page 45.
3. The search for the emu lies behind the poem "Emu, Remember!" in the 1956 volume with the same title.

To Earle Birney (Vancouver), from Vancouver, April 1955

Dear Earle Birney,
Strait of Anian makes me wonder where you got the term, if you read Howay and Scholefield's *British Columbia*, but I suppose it recurs in all writing on the subject. Have read *Trial of a City* twice since I wrote the letter to you. Aside from comments on another page it is difficult to place this play in the category of Fry, Sinclair[1] etc. And not alone because it's Birney. Only nominally is it a play at all, and I notice you do not call it a play. The reader or listener cannot make the customary identification with any of the characters in *Trial of a City*; perhaps you feel they should do so through Mrs Wuns, or Powers. This reader-identification business you may or may not agree with, but generally the reader must fasten himself to a sympathetic person in the play. Of course qualities of you and I and all of us are scattered through all characters in *Trial*. Therefore I suppose it is a cross section of human qualities and characteristics. But I will not regard it as a play . . . it's poetry. Legion[2] (who was one of Lowry's characters in "Sestina in a Cantina;" and please don't tell me that of course Legion is not only one character) has the trite rhetoric of a car salesman and a bad preacher which is what you intended, Mrs Wuns is a hedonist, an idealist and a materialist all in one, Long Will of Langland (lovely name) saw only the bad things through the eyes of his own era; Gassy Jack I loved stranded in his saloon in the past; the Salish chief had the sadness of his race and the world-view of the Indian in regard to other people. Is it a good thing or bad thing that the Salish blood, the blood of the chief goes careening and singing down the years in white veins? I think you said something in this verse drama that you wanted to say, and felt needed to be said. Have read the poems you mentioned as being your best. "From the Hazel Bough" reminds me of the early Yeats "I went out to the hazel wood / Because a fire was in my head." I know, I know . . . It is unlike but it pleases me to think so . . . I admire your knowledge of words, specialized words. "The ebb begins from dream" is a beautiful poem. I had to look up "pelagic" in Oxford, as I did "paresis" in another poem. Ever think of bull-fighting terms, veronica, and media veronica, muleta etc? Notice "Mappemounde" is revised to the extent of two words from the first ed. in Smith's anthology. Deleted "all" in "hems

heart's landtrace." Much better. Also approve "towards" instead of "to" in last line. "War Winter" has the same modern-archaic language as "Anglo Saxon Street" which you should have included in your best. Poems can be panorama without obvious "message" and still be very good???? Where'd you get "peltwarmer"? "Introvert" is not a success to me, although the lines—"Some float like sloops of all his wish, / flow and flower his lost delight"—read the mind of a man while I think of Thomas' "Hunchback in the Park" which portrays with words. "The Road to Nijmegen" is magnificent. Some of the thought in Spender's[3] "I think continually" but "we remember the gentle and true as trees walking, / as the men and women whose breath is a garment about us." A poem like this says things that cannot be analysed or even thought of except in another poem. The strong sense of belonging to a good race who "left the vivid air signed with their honour." "Pacific Door" does not reach the greatness of "The Road to Nijmegen," but "The Strait of Anian" motif about there being no easy road to Europe I like. "Bitchy" is a lovely word in a poem, belongs no other place. Of the poems in *Trial of a City* I liked "Bushed." Have more difficulty understanding them than earlier poems, and I fear my own limitations stand between myself and the poems. Have read so much of your poetry lately I'm a bit dizzy.

Best Wishes

Al Purdy

1. Christopher Fry (b. 1907): best known for his plays written in verse (*The Lady's not for Burning*, 1949). Lister Sinclair (b. 1921): wrote many plays for stage (*The Blood is Strong*, 1948) and CBC radio. Though he has no entry in *The Oxford Companion to Canadian Literature* and a very short one in the *Encyclopedia of Literature in Canada*, he is a much more important cultural figure than most of the contemporary (post-1980) poets, playwrights and novelists with more substantial entries.
2. "Sestina in a Cantina" is a four-page poem set in "A waterfront tavern in Vera Cruz at daybreak" in which several characters, including Legion, deliver monologues. AP probably first read it in *Canadian Poetry Magazine* (September 1947).
3. Stephen Spender (1909–2003): critic (*The Struggle for the Modern*, 1963), autobiographer (*World within World*, 1951) and poet. Spender's reputation has never been quite as high as it was in the 1930s and 1940s when he was associated with Auden, MacNeice and C. Day Lewis. Roy Campbell referred to them collectively as Macspaunday. "I think continually of those who were truly great" is typical of his often idealistic poetry of the 1930s.

To Earle Birney (Vancouver), from Vancouver, summer 1955

Dear Earle Birney,

Sorry to hear about your physical condition, hope Mexico will help. I saw you when you were reading poetry at the art gallery several months ago, and thought at the time that you needed something, whether a woman or a rest I couldn't say at the time. Very probably I will have left by the time you return. I shall probably leave Vancouver at the end of August and damned if I know whether I'll come back. Unless my judgment changes in some respects I won't. But in any case I am glad to have heard from you by letter. And your poetry will go with me wherever I go. *The Strait of Anian*, that is. Reminds me of Roy Campbell carrying Baudelaire through Provence and Spain. Campbell must have been a romanticist and may even have liked Baudelaire. He translated him anyhow, but it turned out to be more Campbell than Baudelaire from my reading . . .

> O worms! black friends, who cannot hear or see,
> A free and joyous corpse behold in me!
> You philosophic souls, corruption bred,
>
> Plough through my ruins! eat your merry way!
> And if there are yet further torments, say,
> For this old soulless corpse among the dead.[1]

Isn't that a cheerful quotation to speed a poet to Mexico. Shall take beside *Anian*, Pound, Eliot, Dylan Thomas, *Oxford Modern Verse* and perhaps Yeats. Notice an article in Van. *Prov.* about Granville. Think you called it Gastown in *Trial*, but forget. Will rip out article in case you're interested.

Drink enough not to stay entirely sober, sleep enough to be rested and fornicate as occasion offers. And I shall not be forgetting "Mappemounde." Please write more poetry.

Best wishes for renewed health on your part.

Al Purdy

1. The lines are from Campbell's translation of "Le Mort joyeux" in his volume *Poems of Baudelaire* (1952).

To Earle Birney (Vancouver), from Vancouver, summer 1955

Well, here I sit solitarily drinking the last of the home made wine, poems copied, nearly ready for bed, a six foot, 200 pound splinter of discontent. What do you think of Curt's poetry? I think if he keeps going, which is problematical, he will be far better than I. Who is to say? Now that wine has removed inhibitions it has produced a lethargy that will end in sleep. Tell me, how do I write better poetry? You can't? I'm not surprised. You can write it yourself but damn if you can tell someone else how, your classes to the contrary. All this white paper to use and I don't feel like using it. I could talk now, but no one's here. But what could I say? How can I say. Ah, the uses of wine, which leads one naturally to the uses of cocaine and heroin. Would I then write better. We are great readers Curt and I, under the influence to paraphrase the WCTU, come along and let us inflate your ego by our rendition of "Vancouver Lights," "Mappemounde" etc. See you, perhaps.

Al Purdy

Irving Layton (b. 1912): a poet and teacher whose books of poetry of the 1950s and 1960s, as well as his public championing of poetry constitute a major episode in our cultural history. He was a one-man delegation for poetry and, as his letters (*Wild Gooseberries: The Selected Letters of Irving Layton* [1989]) indicate, for Irving Layton. AP's meeting with Layton in Montreal in 1955 was, as he has repeatedly acknowledged, a decisive moment in his evolution as a poet. Though AP was often openly critical of Layton's later work, they remained competitive friends, each seeming to recognize the other as the only serious challenger in the game of who is king of the castle of Canadian poetry.

From Irving Layton (Montreal), to Vancouver, June 8, 1955

Dear Mr. Purdy,

Thanks greatly for your kind note and order. I have frequently seen and admired your pieces in the *Canadian Forum*. There are things you do that no one else in Canada excepting yourself seems to be doing. Thank goodness, there's no library smell about you.

You're damned right, and a whole lot more perspicacious than Smith—to my own knowledge I don't derive from any particular poet, but then I don't read enough of any one of them to know for certain. In any case, I leave such useless inquisitions to the profs & academics whose bread and butter all such departmental dust and owl-hooting finally add up to. Nevertheless, on the whole, Smith did a good job as he's the first academic with guts enough to say some kind things about my poetry. [...]

Irving Layton

From Irving Layton (Montreal), to Vancouver, April 13, 1956

Dear Al,

[...] I say again I liked yr. last poem. Let me give you a tip. Never depre-cate your own work. You'll never get very far that way. If you write poetry, you must believe in your self. In a poet, arrogance is a more *communica-ble*, certainly a more useful virtue, than humility. You've got all kinds of talent, Purdy; what you need is a bit more confidence in yourself. If you write poetry give her all you've got. Like a woman, faint heart never won her citadel. [...]

Yrs/Irv

From Irving Layton (Montreal), to Vancouver, July 1, 1956

Dear Al,

Your two friends were here this afternoon and Kurt left with the poems you sent me. He said he wanted to study them before writing you his opinion of them. I thought them the very best things you've done up to now, though you may not agree with me. I think you've at last found the form suitable to your free-swinging imagination. Not only that, it permits you to comment as well as to imagine. What you need is a form that al-lows you lots of elbow room, to slide in and out of your many moods and complexities, your passionate uncertainties. I enjoyed all three poems, though I think I would award the prize to the second one where comment and imagination slide into one another like two shadows mingling in a kiss. I'm sure you can write many more like that one; you've got the in-vention of the novelist or playwright and now that you've alighted on the mould to pour that into, you ought to be writing some of the best stuff of your career. I tingle with excitement when I think of what these latest poems of yours lead me to expect from you. Just have faith in yourself, and don't let anyone or anything make you lose that. A poet, a real poet, is worth a million of the damned useless carcasses that litter up this world. Their passing is of no more account than yesterday's wind or barleyleaf. But the loss of a single poet is irreparable. I would like to see poets more arrogant—and more ruthless. Especially today, when everything conspires to kill or still the creative spirit are ruthlessness and arrogance needed. It's a question of survival, and as always the weak go to the wall. And it won't do to mistake the hyena's sniffs for sighs of compassion. Damn,

Yrs/Irv

From Irving Layton (Montreal), to Vancouver, after July 1, 1956

Dear Al,

All this week I have been busy packaging books and sending them out; more and more I'm beginning to feel myself a publishing firm rather than a poet. There used to be a time when the free moments I had or could snatch went into the composition of poems. Alas, that happy time now seems far far away. Orders come in for my books; they must be filled; bills must be made out and mailed—what a business! My correspondence has continued to grow—this one writes she read a poem of mine and fell in love with the fellow who first showed it to her; that one that . . . It all adds up to hours at the typewriter, bills, letters, statements. Still I derive some consolation, I tell myself it all goes towards helping me develop a prose style! I plan to write short stories for the next year or so, and when I think of that I envy you your fluency. How do you do it? Turning out all those plays, etc. You might give me some pointers when you get here for the summer. I suppose you know I've written about a dozen short stories, three or four of them not half bad. I don't know whether you've ever read one of them, but if you can put your hands on *Now Is the Place* you'll find it contains two short stories of mine that I'm reasonably happy about though many years have elapsed since I wrote them.

I liked your line-by-line reaction to my latest. That's the only kind of criticism I value and I usually end up by judging my critic by the lines he picks out for mention and approval. You've got a perfect score. If my correspondents are to be believed *The Bull Calf* is my best book to date, though my own vote goes to *The Cold Green Element*. But who am I to say? I'm only the author of those blasted things. I think the *BC* will grow on you if you stay with it for awhile. It's the most organically integrated of my books; the death of the bull calf is my symbol for tragedy and I consider the various answers that man may make to the mystery of death—religion, history, sex. I reject the first of those answers along with mysticism (Disunity). Sex, life, creativity are for me interchangeable. History is what man makes of himself; the accumulation of knowledge, tools, is what confers dignity on man. Read "One View of Dead Fish" and "Boys Bathing." In another poem "Boardwalk in Verdun" I picture the possible routes that man can take, the different philosophies open to him, myself opting for the audacious and creative in the poem symbolized by the Nietzschean Übermensch.[1] In the end however he becomes something too exotic to be supportable by brute nature, he dives down and cuts his own roots—he destroys himself. Nature throws up all sorts of forms, the NÜ although the most attractive is only one of many. The tragic sense lies in the joyful acceptance of our destiny.

Don't worry about my ever becoming academic. No chance of that at all and if you saw my recent poems you'd soon realize how groundless all your fears on that score were. If I had the money I'd bring out *Music on a Kazoo* (over 50 poems, some of them masterpieces of ribald obscenity) but I haven't and will therefore leave that for the following year or the year after.

Yours/Irv

I've taken the liberty of mailing you some parcels of books. Anything you can do to sell them would be warmly applauded by me, and would be a real help in keeping me out of debtor's prison. Yes, you may allow 40% discount on the retail price. The following are the retail prices.

The Long Pea-Shooter (HardCover)	$2.00
" " (SoftCover)	1.50
The Cold Green Element	2.00
The Bull Calf and Other Poems	1.50
The Blue Propeller	1.00
Origin	.75

I liked your poem tremendously. One of the best things of yours I've seen. Betty was also greatly impressed by it. She sends you her warmest love, and so do Max and Sissyboo. They want to know when Uncle Al is coming!

1. Nietzsche's "overman" or " superman" is the individual who rejects conventional morality and, using the will-to-power, chooses or wills a way of life that

engages his whole self and produces a free, undeluded individual capable of responding to the tragedy of human existence with a "joyful wisdom." The concept
is central to Layton's major poems of the 1950s and 1960s. "NÜ" in the next sentence stands for "Nietzschean Übermensch."

To Earle Birney (Vancouver), from Trenton, February 1958

Dear Earle Birney,
Many thanks for your letter and kind words. I should like to think I was
getting better myself, instead of perhaps merely changing and becoming
more complicated. The stuff in that chapbook [*Emu, Remember!*] is all at
least two years old, written just after the Ryerson one.

I am amused by your description of the Centennial. Is it as bad as all
that. Actually I have some right to be classed as a BC-er. Spent part of
the war there and then from 49 to 56, and will likely go back sometime.
I gather from a bookseller friend out there that they're spending lots of
money on culture. Wish I could get in on it, but understand they commissioned [Lister] Sinclair to do a play about BC. I admire Sinclair (at
times) but rather think it should have been an open competition. I'd
have sent in an entry myself. I'm writing doggedly and persistently for
CBC now, with poor to fairish luck. Had four plays on since '55, two this
last year, but adaptations. However, have two tv deals ready to go ... The
thought occurred as soon as you mentioned this Centennial business,
what about *Trial of a City*. Why couldn't it be expanded, adapted to another medium etc. Generally a courtroom drama, in the ordinary *Caine
Mutiny* sense of the word, has a lot of inherent drama. I do not compare
Trial with that, please believe me, but ... here's a radio drama on a BC
subject, a courtroom drama, which sort adapts readily to tv ... I'm probably way off base, but still ... My own last was about Spartacus and the
Roman slave rebellion of 73 BC. I hope it takes, but some bad spots may
kill it. High drammer and tragedy.

I'm sorry we didn't have a beer myself, or several. Curt Lang, a friend
of mine, said he had quite a chat with you at the art gallery about two
years ago. He's been sort of a catalyst for me. His character is such that
people are liable to be fully occupied liking or disliking him, and I sneak
into the conversation when it's fully developed, like making a contribution to a snowball ... I spent a year in Montreal recently, and the writers
who can write, intend to write and will write some day are all over the
place. Of course Layton and Dudek[1] make quite an atmosphere all by
themselves; you've probably seen the diatribes in the *Forum* and those in

Dudek's new mag. *Delta*. Layton and his wife just separated, by the way, and now I read his erotic poetry with a chuckle, being well versed in the situation . . .

Chap named Acorn[2] and I have a book coming out with Contact Press, the Dudek-inspired outfit. 20 pages apiece. Will send along a copy . . . Two titles; Mine: *The Crafte So Longe to Learne*. An open invitation to anyone who reviews it, but what the hell.

What about your own stuff? Dried up or still dribbling. Acorn tells me your "Anglo-Saxon Street" is shit, and I tell him he has no critical sense for a poem except his own narrow point of view. But then paradoxically, he thinks you're one of the top poets in the country . . .

You still think Pratt is the legend you thought he was at one time? I'd disagree now, even more strongly than then, despite Sutherland's[3] attempt to ascribe religious motifs to Pratt's poems . . . Someday I'm going to dramatize *Down the Long Table* for CBC if you don't do it first . . . also interested in Winnipeg General Strike, march on Ottawa in '32 or '33, but damned if I know how to do those for a visual medium.

I enclose a couple of poems with this, later stuff, though not the latest. "The Great Man" is, of course, Layton.

I'm building a house at Roblin Lake near Trenton, doing it myself for monetary reasons. Between that and writing I keep busy. Acorn, who is a communist carpenter and poet, is here with me for a while. (I hope he can put in window sashes and doors.)

I'll look you up for a few beers and jawing session when I go back to Vancouver. I'm noted, by the way, for my beer consumption. For some reasons it seems to strike lesser mortals (i.e. two beers and sick) with awe. Address 134 Front, Trenton, Ont. if you find time to write.

Al Purdy

THE GREAT MAN

Wife

Five minutes once in the early morning
Under the words was someone—
Before and after even the discerning
Saw no one . . .
When outside opinions reached him
He altered and became them.

Only words reached and touched
On my life—and the children,
Not finding him anywhere but
In poems, must soon have known.

Friend

Sure, I praised him in the journals.
I think he deserved it.
But I became part of his furore
And poet's equipment:
One of the eyes that upheld him,
Raised the scaffold for
His footing on clouds that seldom
Have a good anchor.
Paradoxically, I talk to him, his voice
A sonorous echo among the galaxies.

Critic

Sex among the first editions,
Advice to the sick and childless . . .
I must admit
He's almost a Canadian Catullus
With Freudian guilt. I'm convinced
His supersonic voice
Conceals a child in time once
And still afraid of noise . . .

Himself

I am that Prince from Serendip
Who was what his mind held:
An Asian goddess, the Greek in Kishinev,
A conservative in Montreal.
Fifty years into the future
My poems will be read and loved;
Among the old books and authors
I shall sin-metrically live.

Pay homage (girls) because of this:
I am that Prince from Serendip.

Not published, of course.

1. Louis Dudek see page 279.
2. Milton Acorn, see page 157. AP edited and introduced Acorn's *I've Tasted My Blood: Poems 1956–68* and wrote the elegy "In the Desert" in his memory.
3. John Sutherland (1919–56): editor (*Northern Review*), poet and critic. AP is referring to *The Poetry of E.J. Pratt: A New Interpretation* (1956), which reflects Sutherland's recent conversion to Catholicism. A selection of Sutherland's writing is available in *John Sutherland: Essays, Controversies and Poems* (1972).

To Earle Birney (Vancouver), from Ameliasburgh, June 30, 1959

Dear Earle Birney,
Good to hear from you, and about your bustlings hither and yon in the culture soaked little isles.

Amelia was probably some sprig culled from the root and branch of English nobility back in the days when the United Empire Loyalists were being loyal. Place used to have the honest name of Roblin's Mills for an old small-time capitalist here. He died at 97 just after the turn of the century and his sons rapidly dissipated his substance. There is a fine old five storied stone mill in the village with walls two feet or so thick which I've explored betimes and searched out history. Built in 1842 succeeding another mill. Will Roblin (grandson) rented the mill before 1st war; got dissatisfied with his earning and demanded more. Miller refused and mill closed, village declined all to hell as a result. Interesting little capsule portrait of life and death of a village which I've explored etc. (Place used to be 500 pop., now 200 or less.)[1]

I get lonesome for BC sometimes. The place-names you mention are all familiar and nostalgic to me. Did you ever go to a place called the New Station café? The police go through there by twos every hour on the hour. I heard they discontinued the ferry service to North Van. Too bad—it was the best dime's worth I ever got. Wenner-Gren will probably be next premier of BC since he's the biggest property holder, and Robert Summers (spelling correct of last name??) will handle his timber interest.

I know just enough of James Bridie[2] to be interested, but that doesn't take much—just a few reviews in the *New Statesman*. And that's some time ago. If I could get to London I wouldn't be very critical of what was offered at the theatres, not for a time anyhow. Very interested in Ustinov[3]—have book of his called *Plays for People*, but it's early stuff.

Curt Lang passed through here on his way to BC. He had a guitar and a fund of Rabelaisian stories. Once we were sympatico, or so I seem to remember. But gone now I'm afraid. How the hell does it happen? But I mourn the past. He was sent back at the expense of the government because of some contretemps or other. Smuggling on a boat in the Med., ball bearings and so on, he said. Also skin-diving for an archaelogical expedition and coming up with amphorae of wine from old Roman ship. How did a Roman ship have Greek containers of wine, the name I mean—or do we call all such containers amphorae?

I think poetry here is in danger of being taken over by the Macpherson–Hine[4] school. The latter writes about original sin and makes me sick to my stomach. The former about Jung mythology and archetypal myths (whatever they are), but she has some passion, I think. Met her once—an exceptionally nervous and learned young lady with a tic.

Glad to hear you're writing—no poetry I suppose?? Why the hell not? Another book of poems and you could get a Canada Council grant to explore the BC forests, Driftwood Valley etc. I wonder if they give grants to go to Tahiti.

Have you met Christopher Logue[5] and the H-bomb disarmament boys in the London pubs, or are they too serious to frequent such places? English verse as exemplified in the *New Statesman* doesn't appeal to me at all right now—or is it just *NS* type verse? Doesn't seem any guts in it at all. Or is it me?

I'm marooned here in the bucolic countryside for the last two years, but with occasional expeditions to Toronto and Montreal in search of work. Without success.

Has compensations, of course. At this time I'm making strawberry, dandelion, orange, rhubarb and pineapple wine. Drinking the dandelion at this moment. Fairly powerful too. The exotic (for wine) ingredients of the others came via my brother-in-law who delivers for A&P store. Last fall I made about 150 bottles of wild grape wine and managed to maintain a slightly pickled state for the cold months. But the dandelion wine I make offends my pretensions to dilettantism . . .

Yes, I'm writing too. Have a book out with Ryerson this fall called *The Crafte So Longe to Learne*—ought to be an invitation to critics. It's 26 pages, but still a chapbook I'm told . . . I'm still changing and watching myself change, like diving into successive pools of water and seeing your own reflection in each. But damned if I know where I'm going, or whether my stuff is any good. I can see some difference in what I write now and what's in the Ryerson book, and that's just 2–3 months ago.

Did an adaptation of Peter Freuchen's book, *The Legend of Daniel Williams*. On suggestion of CBC producer John Reeves I wrote ballades (to be sung) for between scenes instead of music (radio of course), and "based" it on the book. That means I used the characters, but rewrote the story. It's corn, but may have some merit.

I still own a house (with mortgage) in Vancouver, so will have to go back there some time. My wife is in Montreal supporting me very inadequately—so I wouldn't be sure what address to give as home residence. Anyhow, I'm bound to be out in BC sooner or later and I'll hope you have time for a beer. You pedagogues are always so damn busy.

Best

Al Purdy

1. AP wrote about the mill and the Roblin family in several lyrics ("Roblin's Mill," "Inside the Mill") as well as in the long poem *In Search of Owen Roblin* (1974).
2. James Bridie (1888–1951): pseudonym of Osborne Henry Mavor, Scottish dramatist (*The Anatomist*, 1931; *Dr Angelus*, 1947).
3. Peter Ustinov (1921–2004): British actor (*Spartacus*) and dramatist (*Romanoff and Juliet*, 1956).
4. Daryl Hine (b. 1936): Canadian-born editor (*Poetry Chicago*) and poet (*The Carnal and the Crane*, 1957; *Postscripts*, 1991) who has spent most of his life in the United States. Both poets write in traditional forms.
5. Christopher Logue (b. 1926): playwright, journalist and poet, best known for his remarkable free translations from the *Iliad*.

From Earle Birney (London, England), to Ameliasburgh, August 20, 1959

Dear Al,

If I don't answer yours now, god knows when. Am pushing out the last Chaucer article for a journal, and getting ready, as well as I can, for Vancouver again, the academic squirrel-cage, bigger and noisier than ever. It's sixteen months since I was in Canada and though I've by no means become English, I'm in some pleasant limbo of just being someone who lives in London—and with this supernaturally sunny summer, it's hard to leave. Also the plays, museums, parks, pubs, and even some of the people.

I have your reactions to the Macpherson–Hine stuff. Hine, I hear, is in hospital here; has a book of poems he's been peddling unsuccessfully so far. I saw some of it—trying to be "beat" all of a sudden. The only smart one hereabouts is Christopher Logue, who recites his new English beat verse with four jazzmen over BBC for a fat fee and publishes the most synthetic tripe I ever read, all over the place. I knew him in Paris six years ago when he was writing more "difficult" poetry than any other expatriate, and a great snob. Now he is the new English Man of the Peepul, full of shit (asterisked in the better journals only) and libertarianism. But when you meet him he is as limp handed and uppish as ever. The only one who outsells him is that royalist Edgar Guest, Betjeman,[1] who has never looked back since he was photographed with Princess Margaret in the *Tatler*. I've been buying or reading all the British poetry mags, and I really think we're doing as well in Canada these days. The liveliest stuff is still American, though, as Graves says, most of it is written for an expendable economy.

Glad to hear you have a chapbook coming out. Will look forward to a copy. My *Selected Poems* should be out next year—Abelard–Schuman here & possibly New York, & McC&S in Toronto. Will have some new ones. Have done a few out of travelling in Asia last summer. One coming out in *London Mag*, a Mao translation in *New Statesman*, and something last week in *Times Lit. Supp.*, but an old one. Trouble is I keep revising old stuff when I should be trying new ones.

Maybe I'll see you in Vancouver this winter. I'm flying back via the pole so won't be stopping in eastern Canada. Phyllis Webb is back in Toronto; a good poet, though not much of a producer yet. And a nice girl. Do you know her? Give her a ring at WALnut 5-2913 when you're next in Toronto and say hello from me

Your title—Robinson's edition spells it "The craft so long to lerne"— anyway I don't think Chaucer ever spelled it "learne," but a small point. You know, of course, he was talking of Love not Art. Maybe you are too. It's a toss-up which is the more "dredful joye."

Cheers,
Earle

1. John Betjeman (1906–84): English poet (*Collected Poems*, 1958). He published a blank-verse autobiography, *Summoned by Bell* (1960).

To Earle Birney (Vancouver), from Montreal, October 1959

Dear Earle Birney,
Greetings—on your return to mountains (overlooking the city) and mud flats (False Creek & environs).

Look forward to your collected ed.—but hope it is no signal to cease and desist—

Logue comment interesting. His verse is crappy jingle—but I do endorse the anti-H-bomb testing—for which I understand he and Priestley and Russell[1] etc. are the main props—

Oct. 21 my first play re-broadcast on CBC Wed. Night. About childhood . . . if you listen—Sentimental shit in spots too—I have to admit. Originally done Sept. 3, '55—The money I can use.

Regards,
Al Purdy

1. J.B. Priestley (1894–1984): once popular English playwright (*Time and the Conways*, 1937) and novelist (*The Good Companions*, 1929; *Lost Empires*, 1965). Bertrand Russell (1872–1970): Welsh-born mathematician and philosopher (*Principia Mathematica*, 1903). T.S. Eliot described *Principia Mathematica* as a work "of inestimable value to culture." His *History of Western Philosophy* (1945) was an international best-seller. A pacifist during World War I, Russell became increasingly concerned with nuclear disarmament after 1949.

To Earle Birney (Vancouver), from Montreal, November 1, 1959

Dear Earle Birney,

I'd like one of these Arts Scholarships from Canada Council. Would you write me a letter of recommendation?

I'm asking E.J. Pratt and Milton Wilson[1] for the other two, and with a lineup like that (if they come through) don't see how I can miss. Jay Macpherson says Pratt is always generous with people who want recommendations, and I hope his health is good enough in this case.

If I get a scholarship I intend to go to the upper Skeena and see what I can find out about the Tsimsyans there, and perhaps from thence to the Queen Charlottes and the Haidas. I can't help writing poems—but I'd like to do some more plays for CBC, or what the hell. Then I'd like to go to Mexico when the cold weather hits, and do my writing there. Live as long as I can on the money I get (if I get it), then get a job as night watchman for BC Forest Products in my old age.

I've got a play with CBC which they contracted for right now. About an American negro, Daniel Williams, who came to Canada's Peace River country after the American Civil War, lived with the Beaver Indians there, killed two Mounties and was executed for murder in Mar., 1880. Songs between scenes instead of the conventional music. I'd like to do more about the Indians, Tsimsyans, Salish, Haidas, or any of them that take my fancy and will make a play. What are they doing now, how adjusted to coeval Canada . . . You know . . . you did it yourself in *Trial of a City*.

May have a chapbook with Jay Macpherson, recent poems in Montreal . . . title I think, *Montreal Poems*[2] . . . enclose the best of them here to give you the idea I'm worth voting for. But of course, for Christ's sake don't vote for the candidate unless you think he'll do something about the present corrupt administration . . .

I enclose a poem by Logue which surprises me. First one of his I've liked. Does it support the character of his you know? Bit like Reaney[3]? Most of his are chopped prose made to look more than it is. Is he changing and becoming more (or less) than his clammy handed self? Or is this the mark of an unhinged mind? Send it back if you have a copy. I haven't.

Anyhow, I'm sending my application forms to Canada Council within a week, and I think supporting letters are supposed to follow as soon as possible. So if you think CC should squander its money on me give me your vote: a laudatory letter. If not, what the hell. Maybe I can get one later. A scholarship that is. But anyhow, please let me know if you can or cannot write this letter???? I'd like to get out to BC again and will if I get this thing . . . rather lonesome for the smell of Hastings St. and False Creek and mountains over all . . . was stationed (in RCAF during war) in upper Skeena country, but didn't have brains to take advantage of opportunity at the time.

Please drop me a line. Sometimes I think of the Birney of "Vancouver Lights" and wonder where he is. The same? No, of course not. Or *Trial of a City*, or "Mappemounde"? All the goddamn Birneys wander over the globe looking for poems as I do . . . Do they?

Layton here is selling in the stores like Billy Graham or Norman Vincent Peale.[4] 5000 copies of this ed. of *Red Carpet* . . . Christ, the stuff'll be popular next. Ever meet him? Wonderful experience to see the naked ego like an unruptured maidenhead floating in the living room void . . . and he knows, he just knows, that he is the great one, the poet who will top Milton and Blake and Yeats and who do you like? He said so . . . and there you are. But in a sense I love the guy, so improbable, grotesque, and despite his ability somehow wrong. Why? It's all too bloody trite and rehearsed . . . so much assurance and so little doubt . . . He says to himself, this is what is popular so I go dead against it. He looks in the mirror and what does he see? Not a little fat man who will die soon, but a bloated haloed and immortal genius . . . and this precludes searching and looking and wondering to my way of thinking. Or does the opinion of self detach, and look dispassionately at the poems? Somehow I think the opinions of self and poems are cut from same cloth. "The immortal claptrap of poetry" is too designed . . . but I assign him a large status in my private Tussaud's, and think to myself I should not bloody well have this uncertainty. I should know he's good (as I know he is) and great . . . well . . .

Ever see Lowry's wife out there? I'm told the chap who translated *Under the Volcano* to Fr. is thinking of writing some bio. stuff on Lowry . . .

Run out of words.

Regards,
Al Purdy

AND WE SHALL BUILD JERUSALEM
—in Montreal

From the factory at noon with fifteen minutes
in my pockets to spend:
the Church of the Nativity at St. Germain
and Ontario (not listed in Betjeman's parish churches);
the streets full of school children,
matrons and tradesmen and traffic continuous . . .
Standing under the giant stone-grey
monster, looking upward till things blurred.

The white marble virgin benign and vacuous
(no strain or effort required for blessings),
treading out the life of an evil reptile
with its red mouth gaping (which I took
to be a harmless lizard). No doubt it's impressive,
has even a gathered crushed beauty
caused by so much weight falling into the sky.

All afternoon,
among the monotony of doing meaningless things,
my hands kept up their industrious trivialities—
I thought of the tawny

sunlight on temple roofs in the Land of Two Rivers,
stood on a jungle delta
when the priesthood originally
and willingly forgot their own clever origins,
as the land grew fat with waste gold.
But I could not forget myself
and the centuries' umbilical cord
that binds me to a fat imaginary god
with a seven day epic creative itch
that shrinks to a jingle my last best poem.

But I forgave him at five o'clock
the weariness of my limbs, the castrated
effigy of myself in a window—because
I saw between pale faces of travellers
going nowhere forever in buses
and motor cars, the tall church tower!
toiling into the sky its human filigree,
permitting the heavy bells to blaze
over the old town their passionate cries
of jubilant silver hypocrisy—
a tawdry embroidered magnificence.
Almost I forgave him the pale travellers
on buses, hid from the light a long time
between the sweating breasts of their women.

1. Milton Wilson, see page 69.
2. Macpherson's Emblem Books published the collection under the title *The Blur in Between*.
3. James Reaney (b. 1926): a playwright (*The Donnellys*, 1983) and poet (*A Suit of Nettles*, 1958), Reaney has won the Governor General's Award three times.
4. Billy Graham (b. 1918): very popular American evangelist whose books include *Peace with God* (1952) and *Angels* (1975). Norman Vincent Peale (1898–1993): American Christian Reformed pastor and writer, best known for the best-selling *The Power of Positive Thinking* (1952).

To Earle Birney (Vancouver), from Montreal, November 17, 1959

Dear Earle Birney,
Many thanks for the recommend . . . If I get this award I should be looking you up next summer for a beer, maybe . . .

At the moment I am afflicted by that bane of poets, namely work, physical, comparatively unremunerative, monotonous in the extreme, and with the added danger: I may get used to it. Helluva thing!

Note the piece in *Sat. Rev.* by Ciardi.[1] Cites you and Layton . . . Doesn't seem to like Pratt. So what about your "Pratt as legend" thesis—and "Birney will never be the legend Pratt is" . . . ? No, I don't think so either, but why the hell should he? I mean, you lose sight of the poetry in the legend. Wade through *Brébeuf* (or however you spell it) and find that beautiful ending. But is there anything else but? And: "the grey shape with the paleolithic face / was still the master of the longitudes" . . . with the one or two preceding lines . . . and a few others. Apart from your own personal friendship with him, do we need someone like Pratt in our past (for that's where he is)? I always have the feeling he's slightly inhuman, his poetry, I mean. What about Reaney's dictum that we start with a clean slate, that Can. poetry is all to be written—or something like that?

Just sent *Turvey* to a friend of mine studying medicine in Geneva. When will you write another? Not necessarily like that, of course. What about the bum who gravitates from one job to another, is a catalyst in every situation . . . goddamn it I'll be giving you plots if I don't shut up— and that's an old one.

Best,

Al Purdy

1. John Ciardi (1916–86): American poet (*The Collected Poems of John Ciardi*, 1997) and translator (*The Divine Comedy*). The October 24, 1959 issue of the *Saturday Review* was devoted to "The Creative Arts in Canada." Ciardi's column, "Sounds of the Poetic Voice," offered a one-page overview of the current state of Canadian poetry based on his reading of Ralph Gustafson's *Penguin Book of Canadian Verse*. After dismissing nineteenth-century poetry and the poetry of Pratt as based on "the mistake" of "thinking that poetry resides in its subject matter rather than in its poetic performance of itself," Ciardi goes on to praise Birney, Scott, Smith, Watson, Dudek, Reaney, Klein, Everson and, especially, Layton.

From Earle Birney (Vancouver), to Montreal, December 1, 1959

Dear Al,

Hope the Can. Council thing goes through. Hope also you're getting some time free for further poetry. I'm not. Last thing I wrote was on the island of Porquerolles off Toulon, in September—perversely a poem about a Himalayan dancing bear in northern India[1]; anyway the *New Yorker* have surprised me by taking it; maybe this means I'm slipping, but at least it's nice to slip on a fifty dollar bill rather than a one dollar; actually I don't know what they pay, never having tried them with a poem before except once unsuccessfully.

Things are looking up a bit on this coast so far as poetry readings go. There's a Vancouver Poetry Centre, very indigent and inefficient but still willing to sponsor George Barker[2]—we had him all last week—and soon Richard Eberhart.[3] Robt. Duncan[4] is coming up from S.F. in a couple of weeks and will read somewhere. I found Barker a complicated guy; Chelsea veneer over a wild Irishman. Drinks as hard and morosely as Dylan but manages to get sober again for appointments and readings. Like Dylan, his innate fertility in image-making is a curse as well as a strength and leads him to theoretical insistence on the absolute value of form in poetry which his own poetry only exemplifies occasionally and after enormous struggle; but perhaps it's the struggle that makes even his bad pieces interesting. He had along a copy of his *True Confession of George Barker* (published only in England in a limited edition, after Sir Geoffrey refused to include it in the Faber Collected edition); it has some of his best satirical-autobiographic writing; a pity it isnt circulating over here.

I'm going to read my own stuff in Seattle, at their Poetry Centre in February and go on down from there to read at Reed College, Portland, and at the San Francisco Poetry Centre—first time the latter has ever asked a Canadian. I think there is a definite upswing of interest in Canadian poetry below the line, at least on this coast. [. . .]

I'm afraid I think Ciardi is right about all the Pre-Pratt stuff and partly about Ned, though my own article in the new *Our Living Tradition* makes me look inconsistent. The trouble is that article was written as an address at Carleton on the occasion of Pratt's 75th birthday, with the expectation he would be in the audience, and though I didnt say anything I didnt believe, I left out a lot of things I'd rather say after he's dead, since he's stopped writing and nothing said critically would do anything to him except make him feel unhappy and betrayed by an old friend. The truth is none of us who write poetry should allow ourselves to make public critiques of the others, not in a small country like this where we know each other too well. [. . .]

Wish I'd heard your play. Had to go to a goddamned psychiatric lecture at the Arts Club—Madness & Poetry or something. [. . .]

Phyl Webb lives here now, and I find her a welcome variation from the almost unbroken non-poet front of Vancouver. All the rest of you have abandoned us.

In my letter to the Can. Council I stressed that Mexico was a sensible part of your plan, since I'd lived there & knew it was cheap, etc. Do you know Mexico? I have a lot of theories about how and where to live that I can bore you with sometime.

If you work on Indians out here, you should get to know, if you dont already, a couple of the Anthropology profs here—Carl Borden, who has made some spectacular carbon-datings and archeological finds and pushed back the early Indian dates in BC several thousand years. Then there's Suttles, who is a Salish authority. Also there's Bill Reid,[5] a Haida himself and a sculptor, totem pole re-carver, etc. He's in charge of the setting up of a set of Haida poles on the campus at present.

I share your contradictory feelings about Irving; I think he's heading for some enormous gloom if ever he faces the possibility that poetry, his poetry even, may not be the answer to everything after all. But meantime he's a shot in the arm and very necessary to have in Canada.

Margerie Lowry, about whom you asked, is in California so far as I know, though havent heard from her for a couple of years. I heard a rumour she was bringing out a second novel from the manuscripts. There was masses of unfinished stuff left at his death and I think much of it could have been published as fragments or even as short stories—but it's her problem and not one I'd like to have to decide. Malcolm scarcely ever wrote an undistinguished sentence, but the connections between them is another matter.

Let me know when you hear from the CC.

All the best,

Earle

1. The poem is "The Bear on the Delhi Road," one of Birney's finest and most often anthologized.
2. George Barker (1913–91): English poet (*Poems*, 1935; *Collected Poems 1930–1965*, 1965). He is a central character in Elizabeth Smart's *By Grand Central Station I Sat Down and Wept* (1945).
3. Richard Eberhart (b. 1904): American poet (*Collected Poems 1930–1960*, 1960).
4. Robert Duncan (1919–88): American poet (*Ground Work II: In the Dark*, 1987) with a Black Mountain inflection, influential on the Tish group.
5. Bill Reid (1920–98): Haida jeweller, broadcaster, writer (*Indian Art of the Northwest Coast: A Dialogue on Craftsmanship and Aesthetics* (1978) and sculptor.

To Earle Birney (Vancouver), from Montreal, February 14, 1960

Dear Earle Birney,
Greeting. I hope you received the mimeo thing I sent.[1] No cover, had
trouble with an artist who changed his mind. But we're getting Betty
Layton and a couple of others to do something for future issues. Mimeo
work is also terrible, but will do better with that too. Anyhow, object, if
any, is to get away from deadly dullness it seems to me pervades most
mags, with possible exception of Dudek's. Also no US stuff unless we
think it's wonderful and can't be ignored. But the *Fiddlehead* is a horrible
object lesson in that regard. I notice Acorn spelled metaphors metaphores
and made a mistake in my piece on Lowry—but what the hell.

Anyhow, have you got anything, article, poems or what have you,
pontificating on the Canadian scene? Article ought to be two full length
foolscap sheets or less, but could run up to three if you need more
space. I'm thinking of something along the lines of say, RELATION OF
POETRY TO THE TRENDS OF THINKING—I mean, does it have any
influence on people. Or RELATION OF POETRY TO POLITICS and
THINKING BEHIND POETRY—I mean philosophy there. Those titles
are bad, but you get what I mean. Layton makes claim to Nietzsche,
Macpherson, Jung. Yours is a more personal way of thinking, to me anyway, that aims at a deeper fulfilment of the individual, a breaking out
from national boundaries, a sadness at our violence etc. Anyway, that's
part of what you are to me. However, I don't suppose you enter into
what you write about others. Another title: DO CANADIAN POETS
(ANY OF THEM) DESERVE A WIDER WORLD CIRCULATION
THAN THEY GET? Or THE PRECIOUS AND INGROWN IN
MODERN POETRY. One thing about the poetry we're writing now is
that it has nothing in it (or I don't think so) that bespeaks the feeling
and longing of your *Strait of Anian*—there is no clear and easy road to
Europe—I know that's a misquote—I should have said back to Europe
even in a misquote.

So are we always longing for the Good Land of Temlaham that lies
behind in the past? Umbilical cord to Europe? I suppose . . . There ought
to be a positive virtue in living in what is still really a new country. But
we make all the old mistakes here and some new ones. What about THE
CLIMATE NEEDED FOR POETRY . . . ? Eliot says a poet should be a
bank clerk or something similarly sedentary. Does this mean they should
take no part in world events and express no opinion in their work? I think

not. I mean, the poet is a whole man and has an opinion (or should) about nearly everything.

Anyway, I expect you'll have ideas on the things that interest you, without my suggestions. But it's my nature to do that anyway. I'd certainly like something from you if you're so inclined, in the mood now or in future, have time in the midst of students crying for knowledge and enlightenment, . . . AT WHAT DATE DOES CANADIAN POETRY BEGIN, SHOULD EVERYTHING BE DISMISSED BEFORE PRATT? OR CARMAN–ROBERTS–LAMPMAN? WHERE IS POETRY GOING IN THE MATTER OF FORM AND INTELLIGIBILITY? IS THERE A MAJOR FIGURE IN THE WORLD TODAY? And etc.

All the best,
Al Purdy

1. Acorn and AP's magazine was called *Moment*. When I asked him to talk about it, he said, "It was called Moment and that's about how long it lasted."

John Glassco (1909–81): poet, memoirist (*Memoirs of Montparnasse*, 1970), translator and pornographer (*The English Governess,* 1960). His letters to AP are among the most stylish he ever received.

To John Glassco (Foster, Que.), from Montreal, January 24, 1961

Dear John,

We've now got a time set and date for this "party"—at Ron Everson's[1] apt., which is at 4855 Côte St. Luc. Time 8.30 or thereabouts. Date: Feb. 1, Wednesday. Can you make it? Thought of phoning you, but Eldon Grier[2] thought it might be better to write. However, in case of need, my own phone number is RE 9-8912 . . .

Eldon Grier is going on Feb. 3, so the whole idea I guess is there should be some sort of do before he goes. And if you have a few recent poems how about bringing them. I think most will—then we all have ammunition.

Leonard Cohen[3] has promised to be there. Expect Mike Gnarowski[4] will also. You know him? Pat Waddington, everybody we can get except Layton. He and Everson don't get along as you probably know, same with Layton and Dudek.

Eldon Grier tells me you gave a good reading that I missed, must have left too soon. Hope you can do it again. As I intimated gently and quoting L'l Abner you're one of my poetic "ideals"—enough to make you vomit, eh? Now I hope your rural mail route won't interfere with culture, but maybe you can get a good hearted neighbour to feed the horses and cows and take over other connubial duties, eh? I understand there are nothing but good-hearted neighbours around Foster, Que.—right close to Noyon, isn't it?

Your next poem ought to be "Notes on the Cremation of Abel Vosburgh"[5]—since you're so close to the scene of burning. Or maybe I'll write it myself, for I have been thinking about it a bit—perhaps on the lines of Robinson Jeffers'[6] philosophy. But will the white mare and chestnut gelding miss their customary lumps of sugar for this one night? I'd quote you here about the chosen instruments of God's punishment, but can't remember that bit exactly. Anyway, come. You might even enjoy yourself, and anyhow Everson generally has lots of liquor.

By the way that reverse stain is not menstrual fluid, it's homemade wine. Do you suppose sediment in wine is like afterbirth? Make a note, please. The image might come in handy for your next rural poem. Shall we expect you? No—that's like a second coming. Anyway, please come.

Best,
Al Purdy

1. R.G. Everson, see page 391.
2. Eldon Grier (b. 1917): much-travelled painter and poet (*Pictures on the Skin*, 1967).
3. Leonard Cohen, see page 258. AP both admired Cohen's talent and was bemused by his "various positions."
4. Michael Gnarowski (b. 1934): professor of English, publisher, editor and poet (*Postscript to St. James Street*, 1965). With Louis Dudek, he edited the important anthology *The Making of Modern Poetry in Canada* (1967).
5. Abel Vosburgh was a Doukhobor involved in the burnings of houses to protest government policies.
6. Robinson Jeffers (1887–1962): California poet (*Tamar and Other Poems*, 1924), with a tragic view of life. Though AP never wrote about him, references to Jeffers pepper his letters.

To Earle Birney (Vancouver), from Trenton, October 5 or 6, 1961

Dear Earle Birney,
Have been talking with a Mr. R.S. James at CBC who is ass't supervisor

of radio drama re possibility of dramatizing "David." The CBC series "Cameo" "did" Pratt's "The Cachalot" recently, and Mr. James tells me it came off well.

The idea is to add dialogue and music to the poem which a narrator reads. I happen to be quite fond of "David" as a poem and would like to dramatize it. Would you be willing to negotiate with CBC script dept concerning the poem?

In case you are willing for me to go ahead with it, would you send along a short analysis of what you were trying to say in the poem? I don't mean to sound like an undergrad here, but I want to see how it jibes with my own ideas. I see "David" and "The Finger on Sawback" as similar to your theme in "Bushed"—and I think you read my perhaps inept analysis of that poem when I was in Vancouver last year.

Up till two months ago I was writing poetry frantically and almost compulsively—but now I seem to have stopped. Have about 50 pages if I could find a publisher who doesn't mind four letter words which, I assure you, are necessary in their context. J.R. Colombo[1] says no "reputable" publisher would take a chance on it. However, I suppose this is irrelevant—

So anyway, could you let me know about "David"? I can assure you that I'd like to dramatize the poem in a manner of which you would approve—but apart from you, the indubitable author, I'd just like to do it. What else can I say?

Sincerely,
Al Purdy

1. John Robert Colombo (b. 1936): well-known and prolific anthologist, editor, compiler, poet ("found poetry" and collage) and man of letters.

From Earle Birney (Vancouver), to Trenton, October 13, 1961

Dear Al,

I'm complimented that you would like to dramatize "David" and I wouldnt think of telling you how to do it. It has already had at least one musical setting.

I've had to "expound" this poem on too many occasions, some of which probably got into print here or there, but I think it's better for you to set down what you want to do with it, send me a copy, and I'll tell you if I think you've really got off the track. And you can stay off it still, if you want. Seems to me you would have to write your own "David" in a way, to do this job, and the more you do that the better it will be. So far as the extremely simple structure of the poem is concerned, and the meaning of technical words (which you would know anyway), I've talked about them in a series of questions directed to high school students in the back of my *Twentieth Century Canadian Poetry*. But I was also fumbling with a much larger and cloudier symbolism which I'd rather not talk about since if it isnt there it isnt there, and if it is you'll have seen it.

Everything of course is subject to CBC willing to pay a decent permission fee. They gave Pratt quite a sumptuous one some years back, but I won't hold them to an equality with Ned, bless him.

Hope you get a publisher for your fifty poems, four letter words and all. Would it help if you made them five letter, say by spelling fuck phuck and shit schit or even schitt; looks more learned and cosmopolitan that way don't you think?

All the best,
Earle

To Earle Birney (Vancouver), from Trenton, October 19, 1961

Dear Earle Birney,
Got your note today, and will tell CBC in another letter this evening to start negotiating with Dr. Birney. That was the phraseology used by R.S. James in the radio drama dept.

I have your *20th Century Canadian Poetry* by the way and will look at the back. Milt Acorn was here for two weeks recently and read it. He hadn't before. Said there were poets in it he hadn't seen.

I'm a little afraid of what you'll think of anything I do with "David" since it's your baby, but I've loved the poem since I had enough sense to do so. About 1950, I think, before that my own ego stood in the way. Much more difficult to do than "The Cachalot," and a much more sensitive poem in all ways. No, I'm not worried about technical words. My grasp of language is probably a strong point. I think intuitive as well as lexicographical if there is such a word. I'll get your notes right now and read them before I go on. Okay, I cry quits, "bergschrund" and the accented "névé" are outside me, but I'll look em up. But I see you've provided definitions . . . That business may be hard to get across in drama; the ordinary listener won't know what they mean, unless I provide very graphic descriptions and action—

Certain bits of dialogue in the poem I would delete, because they would duplicate the dialogue in the descriptive drama.

I'm scared to hell about not pleasing you, because I'd feel I'd in some sense ruined the poem if I don't make it come across clearly. About the symbolism, I want that to be more explicit than in the poem, and hope you agree. One simple thing the poem does is replace David with Bob in the living world, perhaps giving the world many of David's qualities, the best ones.

But I can't get away from "Bushed."[1] However, I don't want to go into it too much right now or I'll lose something that I intend to store up for the actual writing, if you and CBC agree to terms. I don't want to trigger ideas now, and uselessly, since I have a sieve of a memory unless I get ideas on paper right away. Reading "Bushed" at this moment I'm rather awestruck at this poem, pay you what I think is the ultimate compliment: I'd like to have written it. Tho I'm so different I never could in a million lifetimes. Also, I suppose you know the revolving sun in "Dusk on English Bay" is mindful of MacLeish's[2] poem or vice versa—"You, Andrew Marvell"—I've always come under the spell of your poetry (in the last ten years or so) in a way I never could with Layton's. Why, I wonder. I guess I think of Layton as a marvellous virtuoso but I can never believe, not quite, that he really felt that way. And hence I can't either, not quite. By the way, I'll enclose one of Acorn's that I also envy. I'd like to have written it too, but there again Acorn is alien to me.

I'm getting a bit incoherent I see, drinking wild cherry wine while I type. Acorn incidentally, has a social sense unmixed with sadness, that is fierce and unrelenting. The poem I enclose is a marked exception to this fierceness. You, to me, have a social sense that includes sadness and history. Queer as I think of it. Time will have a stop for you and I, but never for Acorn. I don't think he'd admit it even if he knew for sure. That indomitable quality I admire. But he's naive in a way I have never been, nor yourself I suspect. He still isn't sure about the sexual behaviour of homosexuals, for instance. I gave him Havelock Ellis[3] to read. And yet he writes SUCH poems. If you do another anthology—Oh well, I suppose you won't. Why don't you edit one of the series Ryerson is putting out? Smith wants to hear from Colombo. I wish you would.

Best,
Al Purdy

1. There is an unpublished essay on "Bushed" in the Purdy papers.
2. Archibald MacLeish (1892–1982): American dramatist (*J.B.*, 1958) and poet (*Conquistador*, 1932). Only Auden's "The Musée de Beaux Arts" is mentioned as often by Purdy in his essays and letters as "You, Andrew Marvell."

3. Havelock Ellis (1859–1939): English writer on sex. His major work is the seven-volume *Studies in the Psychology of Sex* (1897–1928).

> **Milton Wilson** (b. 1923): professor of English at the University
> of Toronto, editor of several anthologies, literary editor of *The
> Canadian Forum*, and author of books on Shelley and Pratt. AP
> always spoke warmly of Wilson's responses to his early submis-
> sions to *The Canadian Forum*. Layton's letters show that he had an
> equally high opinion of Wilson's critical acumen.

From Milton Wilson (Toronto), to Ameliasburgh, November 10, 1961

Dear Al,

I haven't much to say of a concrete critical nature about this collection of poems except that I agree with you pretty exactly as to which the best are and also that they're among the best and most characteristic things you've done. My only real difference is that I don't think the second half of "Negroes on St. Antoine" really comes off, whereas I think "The Widower" is a fine poem with a deceptive hovering lyric movement that I find very effective and beautifully suited to what the poem is saying. I'd like to substitute the latter for the former. The group would then consist of "The Widower," "For Norma," "Poem for One of the Annettes" and "Collecting the Square Root." (By the way, I first intended to include "The Listeners" as well, which works up to a powerful climax-cum-anti-climax, but considering the size of my backlog of accepted poems, I guess I'll stick to the above four. About a full page's worth.[1] My only problem is that much as I like the "Square Root" poem, its long lines and our narrow columns are not going to present it looking at its best—there'll be lots of tucked-under lines and maybe misprints from a cursing lino operator. Oh well. As for "For Norma," fortunately the *Forum* isn't reputable in Colombo's sense of the word anyway. And of course it wouldn't be the first "offense" (the third I think). Colombo's advice about off-rhymes etc. reflects his own development. He tends to go through contrasting phases, and he seems to be in a formalist one at the moment; certainly his recent poetry seems to be moving in that direction.

I gave your revised text of "Biography" (née "Doggerel") to Jay Macpherson a long time ago in case she wanted to use it for the pamphlet of poems she was preparing for you. I presume the book isn't out yet—so perhaps the copy is still needed. Or maybe she has just forgotten to return it. I'll inquire. Or if you have a spare carbon, send it along and I'll get it into the *Forum* right away—i.e., January. I do have the unrevised text at hand. The group of four may have to wait till spring.

As for "David," I agree with everybody else about its being a fine poem (I also agree with you about "Bushed"), but I haven't thought about it much and couldn't give a considered reaction. However, I just sat down and reread it, and roughly speaking, I'm struck for the moment like this: if David himself were the centre of the poem, it would be little more than a poem about euthanasia—whatever the large scale heroic trappings as we move from robin to David—or (equally) a man-vs-elements poem in which nature the competitive friend-enemy turns monstrous and ogre-like (from the Gleam to the crooked Finger, or Goliath gets David in the end). But David doesn't belong in the centre. Bobbie is the "tragic" hero as well as the speaker, and it's a kind of initiation poem, a coming-of-age sacrifice, even (excuse the exaggeration) a puberty rite of sorts. Bobbie kills David and thereby comes of age, their pupil-teacher, blood-buddies, romantic friendship (male division) relationship ("matching stories from school days") has got to turn into a Cain-and-Abel one way or another. Or to put it less questionably: it isn't just the initiation into the fact of death in the wild that makes Bobbie come of age (this is a common Canadian theme—see Weaver's Oxford story-collection[2]) but Bobbie's sense of guilt and responsibility for it, however accidental it may have been. He began it and he is forced self-consciously and in cold blood to finish it off. (What do you think of the image of the broken doll, by the way? it's a striking mo-ment, and I think it has affected my feeling about what is going on in the poem.) The scramble down from the high ledge of the living immobilized hero to the plain of the crushed and defaced body below is a wonderful passage. The Furies are in pursuit—the Finger's lengthening shadow—but it isn't just fear, it's the sense of disgust, contamination, a revulsion almost sexual in its effect in the toadstools obscene and the squelched slug. But the sudden change of tone in the last stanza moves suddenly beyond all that. I don't see the end as purely negative and fatalistic, although the age of romantic heroism may be over for Bobbie. The last mountain is the first something else, dwarfed as it may be in comparison, and the tone of the end seems serene even confident, partly no doubt because of the sud-den contrast. You mention the Cambrian waves and the geological side of the poem. In a sense David remains embedded in limestone—the real David not the pulp in the valley, and he liked to spend moments of danger naming strata in the rock beside him. He is a primitivistic figure embedded in remote history, as well as the lost state of Bobbie's youth. When I began I didn't intend to go on at this length; I guess I've let my critical imagination wander a bit; but I leave it as it came to me, and you can take it with as many grains of salt as you like.

Regards,
Milton

1. The poems appeared in the February and April (1962) issues of the *Canadian Forum*.
2. The reference is to Robert Weaver's *Canadian Short Stories: First Series* (1960).

To Earle Birney (Vancouver), from Ameliasburgh, December 3, 1961

Dear Earle Birney,
Just got a letter yesterday telling me you'd come to terms. I thought the thing had fallen through, and Mr. James at CBC apparently thought he'd written before to say go ahead. But he damned well hadn't. They tell me it's scheduled for New Year's Day, so I am working like hell this week. Through their own failure to communicate with me in time there won't be opportunity to even ask you any questions and consult you before the thing goes into rehearsal.

Have written the first scene, which comes after the first two verses of poem, and it's GOOD—I made David centre of a humorous incident to take off the curse of philosophy later. Also, I intend to give it an upbeat at the end, tho of course your verses will end the play. Way I'll do it is anticipate the ending in a prose dialogue scene. So if you have one single word of advice please send bloody quick.

Tonight is Sunday, oops, early Mon. morning. I expect to be working most of the night. Have a wood fire in my Quebec heater here and water boiling for coffee.

By the way, Milton Wilson and Louis Dudek kindly gave me short analyses (is that plural correct?) of poem. Wilson says the ending does have an upbeat despite the words, partly due to change of tone. Dudek calls it "flunked Nietzsche" and a "Canadian failure"—I disagree strongly, at least, why the hell bring in Nietzsche? And I just can't see it as a portrait of a failure. Maybe I WON'T see it that way.

Any final word?

Best,
Al Purdy

To Earle Birney (Vancouver), from Ameliasburgh, February 1, 1962

Dear Earle,

Pleased you liked the script in general, and of course keep the carbon. I had made up my mind, re the "possible addition," not to use it on discussion with CBC people. Would have been just too too—

Didn't wish to imply homosexuality at all—tho it certainly had occurred to me. Can't there be a male relationship without that getting into the act? In my experience there can, and I don't think it's necessarily in the interest of "reality" to push sex into a poem like yours. One or two people have said there is homosexuality implied in the poem itself, but I don't see why. Anyhow, it could have no bearing on the story itself as you told it in the poem. Male friendship or male "love" certainly can exist without having that in every case. Sometimes I think Freud's influence has got us hypnotized as hell.

Why don't you make a tape of the tape before you have to return it? Set up your two recorders in an empty room and close the door on it for half an hour. Extraneous sounds ought not to be too bad.

Looking forward to your book—Hope new poems go into it, and *Trial of a City* is not deleted because it's a play.

The older Bobbie, to my mind and thought, was to make the separation between "now" and "then" more pronounced. I guess I made Bobbie a somewhat stronger character than the poem did, but if Drainie[1] read the poem like I think he may have (I didn't hear it) he made the younger Bobbie much too smooth and strong. Oh well—

Very best to you,

Al Purdy

1. John Drainie (1916–66): Orson Welles called Drainie "the greatest radio actor in the world." His career is commemorated with the John Drainie Award presented annually to an individual who has made a significant contribution to Canadian television broadcasting. Bronwyn Drainie's *John Drainie and the Dilemma of Canadian Stardom* (1988) is an informative biography.

Gwendolyn MacEwen (1941–87): Toronto novelist (*Julian the Magician,* 1963) and poet (*Afterworlds,* 1987): one of the most original writers in the Canadian canon.

From Gwendolyn MacEwen (Toronto), to Ameliasburgh, March or April 1964

Dear Al,

No, I didn't employ "archetype" in the previously derogative sense . . . but archetype as embodiment, yes, of course. Manifold also. Manifold so that each person can choose whichever personality within another he likes. Asimov[1] or somebody has a magnificent story about the martian boy who was doomed to adopt the image of each person's need . . . every new person he encountered transformed him into the object of their desires . . . he was a chameleon thus, very tragic also . . .

Saw *Becket*[2] last night . . . Jesus what a film. Women are redundant in a film like this, like in Lawrence . . . I come away with furious jealousy for the full-blooded relationships men can have with *men*. [Peter] O'Toole portrays this excruciatingly. Not really homosexual, but passionate and agonizing. Becket and the king have a deeper love between them than either could have achieved with any woman. If they whored around, they always did it *together*. Christ.

Stein[3] kept a little woman in her Paris apartment who used to sit and knit doilies and stuff . . . when guys like Hemingway etc. would come to visit, Stein would point to this dame, saying: She's for the wives to talk to. Then Stein would converse with the men. Christ.

I'd better leave off before I get rampant. The only real women I know are women who have something of a man in them . . . and the only real men are those who have something of the woman. You might say that this is universal, but it isn't. Only some, I think, know what it means.

It's so easy to play the feminine advantages. But they exist only by virtue of the male ones . . . as vice versa. Things like loyalty and honour exist, oddly enough, between men. Women together are a dead loss of subtlety and evasion. Women with men have relationships charged with sexual tension. Men with men seem to have something else. Something most enviable it makes me green. Green. I gotta go; will probably see you some time. Stupid letter.

g.

1. Isaac Asimov (1920–92): prolific Russian-born American science fiction novelist (*I Robot*, 1950; *Foundation*, 1951).
2. Since *Becket* was released in North America on March 11, 1964, I'm assuming that MacEwen wrote the letter in March or April; based on the 1959 play by Jean Anouilh, the film starred Peter O'Toole as Henry II and Richard Burton as the

eponymous hero. In *The New Biographical Dictionary of Film*, David Thomson dismisses it as "what passes for a film of ideas." It won the Academy Award for Best Screenplay.

3. Gertrude Stein (1874–1946): American art collector and writer (*The Autobiography of Alice B. Toklas*, 1933). The woman who took care of the wives is probably her long-time companion Alice B. Toklas (1877–1967).

George Woodcock (1912–95): a prolific literary critic, biographer, historian and travel writer, Woodcock was also the founder and long-time editor of *Canadian Literature* to which AP contributed essays, poems and reviews. Though Woodcock and AP corresponded frequently, their letters are marked by a curious reserve that prevents discussion of personal issues. The letters were published as *The Purdy–Woodcock Letters: Selected Correspondence* (1988).

To George Woodcock (Vancouver), from Ameliasburgh, July 30, 1964

Dear George Woodcock,

I write this rather hurriedly to let you know that I just got a letter from you today, dated April 24. Explanation? I was 5 weeks in Cuba, and my wife sent all my mail there in direct contradiction of all instructions. Among this mail was your letter and a cheque from CBC for $250. I've spent the intervening weeks since I got back in bawling out my wife. She seems, however, to remain remarkably unchastened. 2 weeks ago I just made a statutory declaration in Toronto to the effect that I had not absconded, et, digested or regurgitated said cheque. They are gonna send me another. Since I just got mail today from Cuba when I get their cheque I will then have (presumably) 500 skins. Problem: should I own up and admit, or just go meekly to penitentiary?

Of course I'll let em know, when the other cheque gets here. Just the same it's a chortleable problem.

Re Souster.[1] I expect you've long since farmed this one out.[2] I've also already done a review of this book elsewhere. However, I'd like to do others; since I can't always afford to buy the new books I'm getting em lately thru reviews. For instance, Cohen has a new book coming in Oct., I believe. I'm particularly interested to see what Cohen is like since *The Spice-Box*. I've already done Layton, and feel Birney is a subject for someone like yourself or Smith. Incidentally, just met Smith again after nearly 10 years at poets' conferences at Stanley House in Gaspé. Also Frank Scott, Gustafson[3] etc. Just about everybody but Layton. Was soused for a week. Which is an exaggeration, but not all that much. Phyllis Gotlieb[4] also has one coming on same date as other three mentioned. All the above should be two paras, but please forgive me.

John Newlove[5] is another I'd like to review, since I think he is a bright new emerging talent. I've already done his *Elephants, Mothers, Etc.* for *CanFor*. But he has another coming in April called *Moving In Alone*. I'm very enthusiastic about this boy. I think with very good reason.

You mention something longer. I suppose you must mean an article. I have none of those. However, I think the immediate poem-scene is more interesting with MacEwen, Kearns, Newlove, Bowering, Nowlan, Moskovitch, Mayne and Hertz[6] than it has ever been in my memory. Therefore, I could write one if you are interested.

I think I've seen poems in *CanLit* only once, one of Watson's pieces. If you are even mildly interested I'll send along a piece called "Mr. Greenhalgh's Love Poem, (or: passion among the ESPers)" which is both facetious and serious. It'd be nearly 2 pages in *CanLit*.

My sub must have run out, since I note the last ish I have is #19. Could you renew it with #20, please. Will send along m.o. when I hear from you. Apparently we have both been wandering, I hope you enjoyed yourself as much as I did.

Best Wishes,
Al Purdy

1. Raymond Souster (b. 1921): influential Toronto editor (*Contact* 1952–54) and poet much influenced by Imagism and William Carlos Williams (*The Colour of the Times*, 1964; *Collected Poems*, 1981 ff.).
2. AP refers to Souster's *The Colour of the Times*, which he reviewed in *Canadian Author & Bookman* (Summer 1964). The review is reprinted in *Starting from Ameliasburgh*.
3. Ralph Gustafson, see page 369.
4. Phyllis Gotlieb (b. 1926): Toronto poet (*Within the Zodiac*, 1964), dramatist and science fiction novelist (*O Master Caliban!*, 1976).
5. John Newlove, see page 260.
6. Lionel Kearns (b. 1937): West Coast poet (*Practicing Up to Be Human*, 1978). George Bowering (b. 1935): a prolific West Coast novelist (*Burning Water*, 1980), essayist, critic and poet (*Kerrisdale Elegies*, 1984), Bowering wrote the first monograph on AP (*Al Purdy*, 1970). Alden Nowlan, see page 153. Henry Moskovitch (b. 1941): Montreal poet (*The Serpent Ink*, 1956; *New Poems*, 1982). Seymour Mayne (b. 1944): professor of English at the University of Ottawa, translator, poet (*The Impossible Promised Land: Poems New and Selected*, 1981) and critic.

From John Glassco (Foster, Que.), to Toronto, September 5, 1964

Dear Al,

Let me offer congratulations on your "Country North of Belleville" copping the President of Western Ontario College medal. In this case I feel it *is* the best poem of 1963, and even said so at the time. Reading it the first time I felt it was something I'd like to have written but couldn't and never would, and kept muttering the lines over for some time. But God knows I'm no critic, I just have prejudices and undefinable attractions—and this landscape and mood came through to me as no other poem has done for a long time. Perhaps I just like decreptitude, desertion, the encroachments of woods and weeds, lost fences and savage stubborn marginal farming; but no, it's not just that, it's the perfection of its form after all, the deep breath and the sigh which make it *move* and which one keeps hearing in alternation all through. The bit from the top of the page (in *Tamarack,* page 65) to "with his own brain—" is wonderfully beautiful.

Apropos, I'm probably the only person I know who *likes* car-cemeteries. I always stop on the highway and admire how well they fit into the landscape hereabouts: they're beautiful, suggestive and highly moral, I don't mean the ones that have been mashed in head-on collisions, it's the ones that just wore out and are still above ground that appeal to me. And the ones that have been turned on their backs and de-wheeled and gutted. There's an early cemetery near here where the models of the 40s are actually sinking into the ground, like the first stone fences, with their old bathtub shapes half buried. These are the kind I like best of all. Probably something subjectively wrong here.

Do write when you can,

Automorphically yours,
John

To John Glassco (Foster, Que.), from Ameliasburgh, September 6, 1964

Dear John,

Thanks for letter—Now I remember that "automorphically"[1] stuff again.

Agree with the picture you give of cars, and not the wrecked (entirely) ones. Why not a poem?

It gets revolting to go on like this—but as I said, along with Scott, your *Deficit* deserved what it didn't get. However, nobody even remembers who the hell did win the GG that year. Somebody told me, but I forgot immediately. I even wrote you a letter at the time. Did I ever tell you I stole that book from a Montreal store, on accounta I didn't have much money at the time? First time since I was a kid, or nearly, since I stole a book. Kept me enraptured off and on for a year.

Had meant to write you before. But we didn't talk much together at Stanley House (tho I was talkative enough), such occasions being or seeming almost accidental. I mean: the occasions when you burst out with words and enthusiasms etc etc.

Don't want to steal your decayed thunder but, if you have *Annettes* look up "Remains of an Indian Villiage." [. . .]

However, all that sort of thing is a danger, don't you agree? You could get like Housman or Jeffers. Both of whom have a high magnificence on occasion. As in the latter's "Hurt Hawks" and the former's

> The King with half the East at heel is come from lands of
> morning.
> His fighters drink the rivers up, their shafts benight the air.
> And he who stands will die for nought, and home there's no
> returning.
> The Spartans to the sea-wet rocks sat down and combed their
> hair.[2]

(that's stuck in my mind a long time)

I suppose it will be a long time till I see you again, and even then— One perhaps senses or even knows more than the occasion will ever bring forth. About people I mean.

Does the sadness of decayed things also stand for people, whose bones don't lie around on the surface? I would think so. I'd like to deceive myself about that as long as I'm able tho; to say I still have some vitality and lust for life remaining—and yet paradoxically appreciate ruined things. The best of both—

I'd like to see a poem from you on "their old bathtub shapes"— Dripping with old fenders, magnetoes, kidneys and grey weathered human guts.???? Which is a pretty good indication of how I might do it. A hospital with blood bank (oil) and possibly eyes (headlights) etc. is a further parallel. I expect this sort of thing will be carried much farther in the next 50 years.

Wife's asleep, so I'm condemned to pen. Just reading [Edmund]

Wilson's[3] *Letters* and Gus [Ralph Gustafson] gets plenty of attention.
Understand he's a friend of yours—so good.

Yours Glasscomorphically,
Al

1. AP quotes "automorphically" from Glassco's previous letter where Glassco had
described seeing abandoned cars being slowly absorbed by the fields in which
they stood.
2. AP quotes from memory Housman's "The Oracles" (*Last Poems*, XXV).
Characteristically, he makes a couple of alterations, "come from," for instance,
should be "marched from."
3. Edmund Wilson (1895–72): influential American literary critic (*Axel's Castle*,
1931; *The Wound and the Bow*, 1941), he wrote for *New Republic* and the *New
Yorker*. In response to requests from strangers for books, autographs, etc., Wilson
sent a card which listed all the things he could not or would not do because of
the pressure of work.

Margaret Atwood (b. 1939): best-selling poet, critic (*Survival*,
1972) and novelist (*Surfacing*, 1972, *Oryx and Crake*, 2003), and the
dominant and most influential Canadian writer of her generation.
AP's admiration is obvious both in the letters and in his tongue-
in-cheek poem "Concerning Ms. Atwood" (*Naked with Summer
in Your Mouth*) in which he imagines her winning the Nobel Prize
and meeting with the universe's First Cause.

From Margaret Atwood (Vancouver), to Toronto, September 16, 1964

Dear Al Purdy,

Thanks for the note. Take it you got the message, either from R Souster
or bookstore, that I'd heard you were in town & had tried to get in touch
with you. Thought we all might go up & heave a few beer bottles off the
top of the Park Plaza[1]—but I missed you.

I had a most euphoric ride across Canada—saw the sun rise over the
prairies, a most frightening sight—the Total Canadian, I discover, has
vast empty spaces outside him, as well as between his ears—& in Calgary
someone dropped a suitcase on my head (accidentally I like to think)
which may have made the mountains seem even more hallucinatory to
me than they really are. I was most impressed—think I'll ship a few of
them back east—Toronto needs them.

Right now I've more or less dug myself in—have a vast place, top of a house on one of the hills, with several large rooms, none of which have any furniture—so I rattle about in them like the proverbial P. in a pod (or like A. Purdy's brain inside his head)— but I have the best view in the whole world—right over the city, across the harbour, with lots of mountains. Love it.

The university is another story. The professors all think I'm a graduate student & the graduates all think I'm an undergraduate—& when they learn the Horrid Truth they all utter little shrieks of dismay, and blush. I shall have to paint my wrinkles grey, I see, before they'll treat me with the respect that someone who makes as much money as I do (!) is entitled to.

I haven't yet located Milton A[corn]—he doesn't seem to be in the phone book—but I'll get him sooner or later. Vancouver swarms with people I've known (actually about 2)—one a great friend who went to the States 4 years ago and has come back with a hillbilly autoharp and a psaltery—when he plays them he looks like a piece of Victorian pre-Raphaelite outhouse art. The other is a kind of mountain climbing lawyer with asthma. [. . .]

It will doubtless be a peculiar year for you, too; but you must keep calm. Whenever I become exasperated with Toronto I like to remember that it was once at the bottom of a shallow prehistoric swamp—& perhaps still is. [. . .]

Hullo to Eurithe,

Yrs, Peggy A.

P.S.—I thought I had the prize for the WORST HANDWRITING IN THE WORLD—but you win.

1. Situated at the corner of Avenue Road and Bloor Street in Toronto, the Park Plaza had a roof-top bar popular with writers and publishers, many of whose photographs were on the walls.

From John Glassco (Foster, Que.) to Toronto, September 18, 1964

Dear Al,

Hugely flattered to hear you stole my book.[1] This is fame. I used to steal a lot of books myself, mostly from libraries: my method was to look at the little card in the back envelope and if it hadn't been taken out more than twice in the past year I would figure I needed it more than the public.

You're right about this attraction for decay going too far. One could end up all misty-eyed fondling a farmer's old rubber boot. Which is why

I'm not going to write a poem about a car cemetery, though your images of old fenders, magnetos and smashed headlights are tempting. Why don't you do it? The backward look on ruined things I have eschewed. I just look at them now, sigh and turn away.—By the way, I think the emotional value of ruined and abandoned *things* was first grasped by Wordswords [sic] in poems like "Michael" (the part about the unfinished sheepfold, right at the end) and the beginning of "Hart-Leap Well": for me, it's still a spring of the purest and best romanticism, something that Irving, Arthur, Frank, Klein[2] and almost all our contemporaries have passed up: they have other springs, a few a little better, some worse, but all of them subjective rather than projective. But, as you say, with Jeffers and Housman it sometimes becomes a kind of wistful or petulant nostalgia, and could well end up in a love of "the picturesque" and even in Goldwaterism.[3] I think the same thing goes for dead people too, buried or unburied: that's where one could become really automorphic. One has to speak for oneself, in the end.

Enough of that. I sent off for your *Annettes* to Toronto last Friday. Arthur Smith said it should have got the Gee-gee prize—I think that was the year Prof. Finch got it with his well turn'd versicles, or was it one of Reaney's books of needlework?[4] I was tremendously impressed at Stanley House by your poem about the man in the belfry,[5] with its tight structure and the freezing dramatic last line, "I think he will fall." You know how a poem should end, *always*, and that the end grows out of the beginning.

Of course we're going to see each other again. The last letter I had from you was in 1961, an invitation to a party at Everson's, and I remember I had what I thought was a bad cold and couldn't come. It turned out to be t.b., and I spent the next 9 months in a blue funk and a sanitarium, so now I've only 3/4 of a lung, which is however enough, they say.

How did the project of your anthologizing the little magazines come out? I'm quite out of touch down here.

Yours,

John

Just saw your review in the *Forum*[6] this minute. You've pinpointed the exclusive and (to me) deleterious influence of Williams on young Can. poets. The depressing thing about it is that they are writing just the way he did in 1917, which is a little backward, even for Canada.

Your surmise of how Wms.[7] wd. have written Blake's "The Tiger" has aroused my Muse.

THE TIGER

The tiger is an animal
    with black and yellow stripes
Black and yellow—remember that, O my townsmen
    It is of the greatest importance for you to remember
That the tiger
        has
                black and yellow
Stripes.

                      Williamorphically,
                      John

1. *The Deficit Made Flesh* (1958).
2. Irving Layton, A.J.M. Smith, F.R. Scott, A.M. Klein.
3. Barry Goldwater (1909–98): A Republican senator from Arizona, he ran against Lyndon B. Johnson in the 1964 American presidential election.
4. Robert Finch won the award in 1961 for *Acis in Oxford*; James Reaney won it in 1962 for *Twelve Letters to a Small Town* and *The Killdeer and Other Plays*.
5. "Wilderness Gothic." The last line is "Perhaps he will fall."
6. In the September issue, AP reviewed John Newlove's *Elephants, Mothers & Others*, Roy Kiyooka's *Kyoto Airs*, and Gerry Gilbert's *White Lunch*.
7. William Carlos Williams (1883–1963): American pediatrician, novelist and poet (*Paterson*, 1946–58). Though Louis Dudek, George Bowering and David McFadden tried to interest AP in Williams' work, he remained unimpressed.

To John Glassco (Foster, Que.), from Ameliasburgh, September 22, 1964

Dear John,
Since I have applications in sextuplicate versus triplicate to make out for Canada Council I'm doing more pleasant things first. Esp. since I find your verse of William Blake by Williams cum Glassco as suggested by Purdy so amusing. Of course my review broke down because I rather dragged Williams in without sufficient cause, and finished by saying rather lamely that the 3 poets concerned had adapted W's idioms and hence were safe. But I'm pleased you agree that he (W) can be deleterious. Some of these kids worship W. literally worship—young Vic Coleman[1] of Toronto is one in that category. And I've never seen a best or exclusive way to write poems yet, tho you'd think the Tish-boys and Cataracters[2] believed they had an exclusive pipeline to the wine vats of Parnassus.

Didn't know about that 3/4 lung business, not exactly anyhow. Knew you'd had some trouble, but was vague about it. I suppose things depend on how well you get by with what's left. Did the sanitarium by any chance overlook a cemetery? Or a wreckers? Migawd, can't you work something in there?

No, old cars are not for me either. I really don't know how to write a poem before I write the damn thing. Talk about it is fine. George Whalley,[3] for instance, talks a fine poem, and is a nice guy. But doesn't write poems for my money. I can yak about the stuff all night and still have no plan of procedure. Which point irritates me about these young guys. Here I've been writin all my life and don't know, whereas they know all ALL I say at the age of 18 more or less.

Annettes has been sold out for a year. Sorry. Reaney got it that year (62), and tho I didn't expect to see a Contact Press book in the running it would have given me a boost ahead if it had. Those things do, you know. You find yourself in a euphoric fever, at least I do sometimes, as a result of a word or a prize or whatever. Actually pushes me on, I believe. However, I'll have another candidate in spring of 65.

In a way this is a bad year for your own book to be coming, on accounta everybody looks at Souster and says look at all the books that guy has written and isn't it about time—? You know. Whereas *Deficit* should have had it—when?—in '58 or '59 I think. The injustice of that was somewhat remedied (tho not enough) by a CC thing that year I believe. Just the same, it bloody irritates me to see some of the crap getting prizes.

Yes, I hope we'll get together soon again, all of us if possible, and perhaps more too. I'm especially sentimental in retrospect about such affairs. Everson sent me a photo of that group he took, and Dudek looks like a country bumpkin sneering at somebody. I look drunk (I am), Cogswell like a lady boy scout gone pregnant, you like a kindly old aunt etc etc. Only Gustafson looks so non-affected that he has to be affected. If you haven't this photo why don't you write Everson. Incidentally, I thought he was the funniest thing I ever saw falling off that log on the beach—and stiff as a staring-eyed corpse when I picked him up. And asking Madame what'shername for her room number so he could sneak in for a little lovin later.

Why don't you send that W. verse to *CanFor*? Reading in Toronto this Sunday along with Souster, Avison[4] and one or two others. [Milton] Wilson mceeing. Will try to remember and show it to him. The first two lines are not good because so damn iambic. I'd like to see the poem with another verse. "O my townsmen" is priceless in this context. Couldn't you get *Paterson* in there too?

I'm not too crazy about the little mag project, feel much as Scott said he felt. Anyway, I hope to get a CC thing without offending Dudek. I should never have got myself hypnotized like that. But I like Dudek a great deal, always have. Hence when he comes up with something like this maybe I get sentimental, or maybe my unstable enthusiasms get the best of me.

What I really want to do is go travelling next year thru the Canadian north, from Yukon to Ungava if I can manage it. And write poems. I hate to anchor myself in one place like I have for the last few years—even tho I have had frequent trips here and there. I get sort of desperate and feel time and circumstance are closing in on me, maybe like you in the tb joint. Only time I'm more or less content lately is when movin and goin somewhere—Flaw of character I suppose. Domestic life begins to bore me—

Just stopped off to get a drink . . . Also to watch the Br. tv "The Planemakers"—one of the two programs I have any use for. Tonight's was a doozer. Guilt guilt guilt. And you could believe it.

Anyway, I better get to composing a short squib: why the hell do I need a CC grant, and what immortal works shall I not write if I do—

Incidentally, used to steal library books myself. You check your books out, then go get the book you want to steal and walk out. You just forget to check the extra if they finger you. So drop me a line eh, maybe not as quick as this one, but still when you get a few minutes away from whatever the hell you do there. Which I've never figured out, on the odd times it's occurred to me: water the horses, feed them, plow a field, have a drink, shovel (oops, I mean pitchfork some) hay down from the loft?

Do write.

Best

Al

THE TYGER (by Glassco, Williams, Blake & Purdy)

Yes—yes
        my fellow townsmen
you will not see that fellow on the streets
        of Paterson NJ
the Tyger I mean

                     his stripes and tail
          lashing lashing lashing
                 in pediatrics
          where I sit scribbling on a prescription blank
          or in my shabby office
                          I think of him
                          the Tyger
          & speculate about his origins
          walking home on a tree lined street
          after delivering without much difficulty
          (some women have damn wide cervixes
          and you know that my fellow townsmen)
          Mrs. What's her name's latest
          thinking how well fitted and happy I am to
          deliver Tygers
                          I mean babies of course
          whose symmetry is exactly like a sentence
          by a judge ending with a preposition
                   And who's responsible
                          that's what I want to know
          I ask YOU that
                 my fellow townsmen
                 who's responsible
                 for all the Tyger babies
                 in the public wards of Paterson NJ
                 depending on public charity
                 that they may grow tall and not possess rickets
          Look into your own hearts for the answer to that question
          people of my town
                          who's responsible
          for all these striped babies?
          Who's been fuckin around?

1. Victor Coleman (b. 1944): a one-man avant garde, closely associated with
Coach House Press as editor and author (*One/Eye/Love*, 1967).
2. *Tish* (1961–69): a mimeographed Vancouver magazine founded and edited by
Frank Davey, George Bowering, Fred Wah, David Dawson and James Reid. For AP
it represented a branch plant of Black Mountain and was therefore suspect. For
Layton, the *Tish* poets' "only originality so far consists in the novel spelling of a certain four-letter word" ("Forever Honeyless," *The Telegram*, October 8, 1966).

3. George Whalley: (1915–83): professor of English at Queen's University, critic (*Poetic Process*, 1953) and poet (*No Man an Island*, 1948). He supervised Michael Ondaatje's MA thesis on Edwin Muir; a translation of Aristotle's *Poetics* was published posthumously. During service as a navigator with the Canadian navy (1940–45), he designed a marker buoy used in the invasion of Italy.

4. Margaret Avison (b. 1918): Toronto poet, highly regarded by AP, even though he often admitted that he couldn't claim to understand her stylistically difficult early poetry (*Winter Sun*, 1960; *The Dumbfounding*, 1966) and was put off by the Christian orientation of her later work (*Sunblue*, 1978; *No Time*, 1989). Still, he quotes the opening couplet of "Snow"—"Nobody stuffs the world in at the eyes / The optic heart must venture"—in his introduction to *No One Else Is Lawrence!* and adds the comment, "thus saith Margaret Avison, and she speaks true." She was awarded the Griffin Prize in 2003.

From Margaret Atwood (Vancouver), to Toronto, October 4, 1964

Dear AWP,

There may be a certain significance in the fact that I can read your writing but you can't read mine. [...]

As for my temper: I'm afraid it's a figment of your imagination. I don't have one really. If you are still worrying about whatever-it-was that went on at Doug's,[1] I think we can regard it as an expression of a) the fact that I was rather sick and very tired, and b) that, given a choice between a hen yard and a thunderstorm, I'll choose the latter most of the time (which is a way of saying that I don't like being pecked at; if you must behave like a chicken who's just found a worm, get yourself a new worm). Besides, don't pretend that you don't like anger. You love it, especially other peoples' anger against you; I suppose it affirms your identity or something. At least when you're being kicked in the shins you're not being IGNORED. (I repeat, I haven't any temper I HAVEN'T ANY TEMPER you hear.)

As for where I'm going etc. (a popular song echoes from some cave of my childhood; when I was 8 or 9 and you were ...? So you must remember it; I think it was a Wild Goose song, sung by Frankie Laine?[2] Is that a real person? And the chorus went something about where you going What're you gonna do, Answer: We're on our way to nowhere ...) The trouble with you is you think of EVERYTHING in terms of poetry. I don't want to be "A Poet": it's too much of a racket these days (writing poems is something else again). To be "A Poet" you've got to get an image, as the ad men say, and as far as I'm concerned once you get too definite an image it sort of screws you as far as writing poems goes. Unless you are very good

85

indeed you start writing to measure; you don't want to do anything that contradicts the image. So I would rather be an amoeba. Don't laugh, but instead consider the essence of amoeba-ness. They're transparent, & thus hard to find. They change shape by sending out pseudopodia (e.g. conversations, letters like this one & poems etc.) and encounter the universe by flowing around it; when in hostile environment they encyst by forming a hard shell, & hibernate till coming out again is worthwhile; they are unicellular & primitive. (Of course one kind causes amoebic dysentry but we won't mention that.)

As for York U and you: I know little about it, but I expect that the university will get more out of you than you will out of it. I've always thought that most people go when too young: this is trite & rather wrong, but at 18 you usually don't have enough experience to bring *to* university. Of course you'll be able to steamroller over all the other students & perhaps the profs. as well. I wouldn't want to have you in MY class!! You'd be too much of a shit-disturber. And we all know that university induces conformity.

Let's, by the way, take a small look at the word "academic" before we start flinging it around. It seems to connote (besides just "association-with-a-university"):

    a) being esoteric, obscure, pedantic

    b) belonging to some kind of established in-group or "academy"

    c) in writing (as well as the above), writing according to a rather
       set or prescribed form & ideas etc, or excluding all other forms.

(I don't attach much value-judgment to the word; you and most others give it a negative one.)

So next time you call me academic, please indicate which connotation, so I'll know exactly which nasty name I'm being called. Perhaps it might even be possible (sometimes on count a), and if you regard a certain group of American writers as established, on count b); not, I think, on c), espec. after your *Forum* review) to return the serve.

Meanwhile, I feel I ought to be working like a bugger (buggeress? buggerette? or Germanic buggerlein or buggerchen? suppose though technically buggerliness in all its adjectival forms is forbidden to me forever); but mostly I just cram my lectures the night or the hour before, & spend the rest of the time looking out my windows, fiddling about, writing some, & exploring the city; which is indeed strange; a very wide unfinished place.

Recently also I heard Alfred Deller (Consort) sing Elizabethan madrigals & other goodies; but suppose you'd consider that an academic pursuit, so I'll say no more about it.

Sinc.,

Peggy

P.S.: On the identity question: You'll be amused to hear that I'm down on at least one Departmental list as "Mr. Atwood," and that one of my students handed in a paper inscribed "Miss Atwort"—which is so lovely I think I'll keep it for my real name.

—Kindest to Eurithe.

—P

1. Doug is D.G. Jones. AP and Atwood met for the first time at Jones's cottage at Paudash Lake. When AP teased Atwood about being an "academic," she retorted by shaking a bottle of beer and letting it "swizzle" (AP's word) him "full in the face."
2. Frankie Laine (b. 1913): singer popular in the 1950s and 1960s. He sang the theme song of the popular television western *Rawhide,* which starred Clint Eastwood before Sergio Leone made him a star with spaghetti westerns. "The Cry of the Wild Goose" was a number 1 hit for two weeks in 1950. A competing version by Tennessee Ernie Ford peaked at number 15.

From John Glassco (Foster, Que.), to Toronto, October 15, 1964

Dear Al,

Glad you liked the Tiger parody, but it's not good enough for publication, just a 3-min. postscript effort! Your own "Tyger" is much better, but it's not the good midwife Williams, it's pure Purdy. Mine is a snide criticism (parody is a nutshell form of criticism) inspired by the suggestion in your review, and is meant to pinpoint the weakness of Williams' whole method and attitude, his affirmation of the unadorned *thing*, of "the importance of the red wheelbarrow and the white chickens"—those now-sacred lines in which the faultiness of his whole poetic vision is (for me) concentrated: his flat announcement of the beauty and *flatness*, his *pride* in being a Peter Bell looking at a yellow primrose and that's all.[1] I think his influence has been wholly bad. But no wonder he appeals to all our budding bearded bardlings: he has a recipe for Instant Poetry. Because that kind of stuff isn't really very hard to write. His *own* work I quite like: it reminds me nostalgically of the twenties. But this isn't the twenties. What I mean is, his warp was worse than his woof.

Everson sent me a print of the Stanley House photograph, which I value for sedimental reasons. Don't we all look awful. You don't look drunk, but rimbaldian (this is a favourite *mot quebecois*: by the way, did you know your profile is pure Egyptian, ca. 3500 BC: check with any tomb-painting!) Oddly enough, I look more professorial than any of the professors, which worries me. Frank [Scott] looks like a professional boxer.

If you ever have time look in *Tamarack Review* No.23, for "A Season in Limbo," by one Silas N. Gooch. This is my t.b. sanitarium journal. The phony name is because I might have had to go back to the place: making up the anagram amused me for 2 whole hours up there: time hangs heavy in a sanitarium ... For God's sake don't you get run down and get this bug: it's the poet's occupational disease.

It's highly instructive to think of this malady in its historico-medico-artistical context. I have a spare demi-john in my bathroom of para-aminosalicylic tablets that could have saved the lives of Keats, Chopin, Mozart, Jane Austen, Katherine Mansfield or D.H. Lawrence. Too late, too late, for all those poor bastards and bastardesses, terrified, coughing up their lungs, hoping against hope, doomed, just born too soon. The pills are made out of coal-tar or something and cost about 2¢ a pound. Souster[2] could write a poem about this.

At the risk of seeming impertinent or officious, I beg you not to bother too much about the paltry encouragements of fame. Fame has a way of carrying a terrible backlash. It's better to be obscure and unrecognized: one writes better. At any rate, it's a good thing not to get into the rat-race of public acclamation, like poor Daryl Hine or Leonard Cohen or Odets or Mailer or Capote, *âmes damnées* all.[2] I was so glad you decided against the little-magazine assignment. Not your dish, Al. You are the best poet of your generation in Canada. I hope you get to the Yukon: I never will.

I keep running on, here it is 3 a.m., and I am plastered as usual.

Winter coming on, and that means no more birds singing. I've been thinking, our feathered friends had the right idea when we all evolved from the reptiles. We moved towards intelligence and stayed on the ground; they moved straight into joy.

Yours,

John

1. Glassco refers to Wordsworth's "Peter Bell," a poem parodied during the poet's lifetime by J.H. Reynolds and Percy Bysshe Shelley ("Peter Bell the Third").
2. Clifford Odets (1906–63): American naturalist playwright, best known for *Waiting for Lefty* (1935), a play about a taxi drivers' strike. Norman Mailer (b.

1923): American novelist (*The Naked and the Dead*, 1948; *The Executioner's Song*, 1979; *Ancient Evenings*, 1983), probably the best living writer not to have won the Nobel Prize. Truman Capote (1924–84): American novelist best known for *Breakfast at Tiffany's* (1958) and the non-fiction novel or "faction" *In Cold Blood* (1966).

From Earle Birney (Vancouver), to Ameliasburgh, c. October 15, 1964

Dear Al,

Havent had a chance to answer yours of Sep 24 till now. However, I did send a chit to the CC. I hope it helps. I thought you might like to see what I wrote, and attach a copy.

The Poetry Ed. liked "Mr. Greenalgh's Love Poem" which you sent on Sep 15 but wasnt too happy about the way in which the associations get so loose at the end; most of the way, he says, they're exciting and free; at the end, for him, just free. Well, it's a criticism, though I suspect if the poem had been shorter it would have passed more easily through his needle's eye. There wasnt time for it or the other one, for this *Prism* anyway, so I'm returning them both so that you can feel free to get them in somewhere else earlier than we could now plan for. You ask me whether I think "On a Park Bench" is a poem. Of course I do, though for me an incomplete one, one that leaves the essence unexplored, the mysterious moment of communication between poet and mother-on-bench: what happens to it? how did it start, finish, or didnt it happen at all, didnt her nerves quiver at all in the poet's? I want to know more, and a poem for me isn't just a titillation, it's a satisfaction, an orgasm not a belly rub.

You have a review in the Sep *CF* containing, in the opening of its 2nd para., one of the more remarkable misstatements of the year. "Twenty years ago young poets," you tell us, "imitated Bliss Carman[1] (in Canada anyway), Eliot, Auden and the 19th century romantics." Jesus! What "young poets"? Name ONE in Canada (you certainly couldnt outside of Canada) who was imitating Bliss Carman in 1944 or indeed in 1934 or 1924, anyone who was, is, a *poet* by any honest definition, and who was young, or even not really young, say under forty. NAME ONE! Do you know who was writing poetry in 1944 in Canada? I'll tell you, and I'll tell you who I think they were imitating, insofar as they were imitating anybody:

Anderson at age 29: Dylan Thomas
Bailey at age 39: Eliot, Pratt
Avison at age 26: Marianne Moore? Yeats

Daniells at age 44: Eliot
Dudek at age 26: Pound, Auden
Finch at age 44: French Symbolistes
Gustafson at age 35: Hopkins
Klein at age 35: Eliot
Le Pan at age 30: Lewis
Livesay at age 35: Auden, Sitwell, Symbolistes
Lowry at age 36: Aiken, Melville, Elizans
MacKay at age 43: MacNeice, the Greek poets
Page at age 28: Anderson, Thomas, Barker
Wreford at age 29: Auden, Lewis
Whalley at age 30?: Lewis
M. Waddington at age 27: E. Sitwell
Souster at age 21: Whitman
Wilkinson at age 34: Dickinson
Smith at age 42: Yeats, Eliot

There isnt one damn poet, old or young, worthy at all of the name, none writing & appearing in the mags and anthologies, who was being influenced 20 yrs ago by one damn nineteenth century romantic or by Bliss Carman. No nor 25 or 30 yrs ago. Forty years ago, yes. Man, dont think everybody a little bit older than you is CGD Roberts vintage. You're half right about Eliot & Auden, if you have to make superficial generalizations, but the real truth is more like this column—all over the place. I left myself out because I KNOW how scattered & unconcentrated my influences were. Sure, they included Audenspenderlewis, & Eliot whom I always despised, but these influences were no more important than those of Cynewulf, Chaucer, John Skelton, Herrick, Homer, Hardy, Robinson Jeffers and Wilfred Owen. And of all these only Chaucer seems to have been abiding within me, and yet led to little I could claim by kinship with him. [...]

Earle

1. Bliss Carman (1869–1929): with Roberts, Lampman and Scott, one of the "poets of Confederation." A prolific poet with over fifty volumes to his name, Carman was the Leonard Cohen of his day. The majority of AP's poems of the 1930s and early 1940s are strongly influenced by his work.

Alfred Bailey (1905–97): New Brunswick historian, university administrator and poet (*Miramichi Lightning*, 1981). Roy Daniells (1902–79): professor of English at the University of British Columbia and poet (*The Chequered Shade*, 1963). Douglas LePan (1914–98): diplomat, novelist (*The Deserter*, 1964) and poet (*Weathering It*, 1987). Dorothy Livesay (1909–96): feminist activist, editor and poet (*Collected Poems: The Two Seasons*, 1972), with a wide influence on Canadian female writers. L.A. MacKay (1901–92): Canadian professor of classics at Berkeley (*The Wrath of Homer*, 1948) and poet (*The Ill-Tempered Lover and Other Poems*, 1948). James Wreford (b. 1915): a Scots geographer (*A Social Geography of Canada*, 1991) and poet (*Of Time and the Lover*, 1950), lived in Canada from 1945–54, then returned to Scotland to teach geography and Canadian studies at the University of Edinburgh from 1954–82. Miriam Waddington, see page 222. Anne Wilkinson (1910–61): poet (*Collected Poems*, 1968) and biographer (*Lions in a Way*, 1956); she makes an appearance in Michael Ondaatje's *In the Skin of a Lion* (1987).

To Earle Birney (Vancouver), from Ameliasburgh, October 19, 1964

Dear Earle,

That's a blockbuster of a letter. Before I get nasty want to thank you for CC missive. You hit what's nearly the crux of the whole thing in your comments about the travel allowance. On accounta I don't suppose very much "lateral" travel is possible in the north, and I'd likely have to go back south in order to go east or west. By plane anyway. Tho of course I'll take whatever transport is available. Anyway, it's a good letter, with, I think, very accurate judgments and estimates throughout. [...]

Anyway, you challenge me to name a poet who was influenced by Carman. That's easy. ME. He was the first reason for my writing poetry, and no snide comments please. I got over him eventually as you know, but "Arnoldus Villanova, 600 years ago [not 20] said peonies have magic and I believe it so."

Your list is damn impressive, and gives me info I didn't have before. I could have guessed some of it, but not nearly all. However, one of the things it demonstrates very strongly to me is that the poets with good models improved, and those who imitated (or were influenced by) Carman didn't. Moral: Imitate the best. I may say (modestly) that Birney too at one time was one of my influences. Still, despite this severe handicap, I survived. No kiddin tho, there is a point here. And don't you remember Carman's vogue at that time, and earlier?

You say none worthy of the name was influenced. Of course you're right. Except me. And I wasn't worthy the name at that time. But there were also the CAA [Canadian Authors Association] type (generalization) of poets who go nowhere. You know damn well they were influenced. Carman was worshipped among some of those people, just as Williams is now, he and the BM boys.

Still, I'll give you best somewhat, since it isn't a precisely accurate generalization. If I'd written 40 pages tho would have done better. But I will not agree when you say that Carman had no influence. 20 years ago and farther back.

I went thru most of the influences you name in that table, except Eliot. But I went from Carman to Chesterton, W.J. Turner,[1] Hardy to Yeats. Then Dylan Thomas. The Americans I didn't even know about a few years back.

Among your particular influences, Auden and Jeffers have been strong. Hardy a little less so. The others not at all. Donne and Marvell to some extent. Even Kipling at one time. Yourself and Layton tho, in Canada. Eliot, beyond admiring somewhat "La something or other"[2] and "Prufrock," not at all. I can't even understand "The Waste Land," nor very sure there's much to understand.

Interesting to me that Jeffers is included on your list. In the last five years I've developed a helluva respect for him. "Hurt Hawks" for instance. That image about eagles wings as "folded storms at their shoulders."

Next day—and where the hell was I?

Anyway, I find your graph damn interesting. For instance, whatever happened to Wreford?[3] Or did he ever happen in the first place?

I see you have left out Pratt, perhaps thinkin he didn't imitate anyone.

What a nasty question. Do I know who was writing poetry in '44? I've written the stuff myself since I was 13 years old, and I've heard of or known most of them, including many who never got anywhere. Who weren't as you say "poets"—depending on the level of merit you have to achieve to deserve that epithet. But why worry about nomenclature, let the old ladies have their magic occupation. "Honest definition?" I've never seen a valid definition yet, one that would hold up, either of poetry or poets. Lots of stop-gap ones tho. And nearly everyone I know (who writes poems) just loves to make such definitions.

Anyway, before I stop, thanks again for your letter. Really, I should think anyone who was so sharp and perceptive in such a letter wouldn't be the opposite in the accompanying letter. I'll give you about 50% of your points tho. Will you be that generous/dishonest??? No. Anyway, if I get this thing I hope to see you in Van, for I'll be out there before leaving for the north.

Best

Al

1. G.K. Chesterton (1874–1936): widely read man of letters, writer on religious topics (*Orthodoxy*, 1909), novelist (*The Man Who Was Thursday*, 1908) and poet (*The Wild Knight*, 1900). AP could recite most of "Lepanto." W.J. Turner (1889–1946): Australian born, emigrated to England at 17. He was a music critic (*New Statesman*), drama critic (*London Mercury*), novelist and poet (*The Dark Fire*, 1918). In "Touchings" (*Naked with Summer in Your Mouth*) AP quotes a favourite verse from his "Epithalamium for a Modern Wedding," and "In the Caves of the Auvergne" may have influenced "In the Caves" (*Sex & Death*).
2. "La something or other" is "La Figlia che Piange."
3. Wreford returned to Scotland in 1954. He probably caught AP's attention by winning the Governor General's Award for Poetry in 1950 for *Of Time and the Lover*. His poetry does not appear in Margaret Atwood's *The New Oxford Book of Canadian Verse in English* (1982).

To John Glassco (Foster, Que.) from Ameliasburgh, October 20, 1964

Dear John,
Drunk or sober you write an interesting letter. I'm in the same condition at this moment. In fact not too sure how far I'll go with this. But I do note that your typing is better than mine. However, that may be due to soberer recessive genes. Or something.

I never thought of Williams' pride in his flatness before. Of course it's true. Unlike you tho, I don't like his stuff at all, tho Dudek has been trying to shove him down my throat every time I see D. I don't even like much the red wheelbarrow etc. bit. Tho when I read Woolf's toy can (or whatever it was) filling with rain in the night and no one seeing or noticing, it sends me out in all sorts of directions.

Yes you do look professorial. Helluva thing. Re the 3500 BC Egyptian: some guy in a St. Lawrence/Main poolroom slugged me on the nose in 1960, no doubt sending me back 5500 years.

Frank a pro boxer reminds me: I was down in your neck or cocyx of the woods last weekend with him, and put my arms around an ex-pro boxer's wife in drunken euphoria and nearly got my profile altered to 7500 AD, Ron Sutherland,[1] English Dept at Sherbrooke. You probably know him. Anyway, after crude threats I wandered drunken in the night rain thru North Hatley until Frank picked me up in his car. He wouldn't mention it either, even when I did next day in sober contrition. I could tell from his silence on the subject that I was in disgrace. His unspoken thought was: I might be a poet but I mustn't put my arms around other men's wives. [. . .]

A few hours later. Re your comments about fame. Unusual, to me, to rush off to Europe on a grant as so many do; for it seems more pleasure-seeking than a genuine desire to write. Which is possibly unjust to people like Cohen and Hine. Still. I do feel that way about such jaunts; not all of them, but some must be like that. Those who have very specific things to do in Europe maybe okay . . .

And oh yes, fame as the spur—When you are expected to write poems, when writing them becomes so ambiguous you don't know if you are doing it because you are supposed to or because you want to . . . I get a helluva kick out of writing a good poem, one I think is good. Right now I'm not writing much. I COULD write some mediocre poems now, but don't want to. I mean, once you have the craft and practise in you, then you can use it practically any time. But some other ingredient is needed than technical ability to write the good ones. I don't suppose I can lose that now. And I hope not, decidedly.

I suppose writing poems has become my marihuana any more, raison d'être . . . And they say that poetry can't be life, but it certainly does become such a large part of life (to me). It blends in with living very well much of the time, since all my stuff is very biographical. But you're liable (me or others) to want and to have an experience for the sake of writing a poem about it. Possibly that's okay about some experiences. But one has a myth in the mind about emotional experiences that induce guilt if your motives are too ambiguous. And mine are. I've become so self-aware in the last few years as to see several motives for every act, and as a result become unsure of any of them. Also likely to choose as valid the least self-complimentary one.

Re my tiger parody, of course you're right, and I knew that when I wrote it. Got carried away somewhat . . . You have the only copy, so it won't get around . . . And re Williams, I believe I rather dislike him for living such an ad agency admirable life and giving his all to others. As if to say to other people (like me and you): this is what you must do with your life, and I have demonstrated it for you. Ughh! But all heroes have this quality, don't you think? At least those who touch the fields that interest you. The "Dr. Livingstone, I presume" bit (for instance) I find silly. Tho that "field" isn't close to me. Maybe, tho, Williams didn't MEAN to be such a revolting archetype. And I can't can't get much from his poems. Dudek practically bombards me with Williams and Pound every now and then—tho not in a thrusting-it-upon-me way—and I feel oh so bored.

When is your book out?

Birney assailed me for review—for saying poets 20 years ago imitated

Carman in Canada. Challenged me to name one. I did. Myself. Perhaps I was the only one who escaped (eventually) his influences unharmed. Birney had a graph made out with all the 20-years-ago poets, giving their ages then, and their influences. Made a good case too. And I grant him much validity, but I still think the old-lady poets, those who submerged and were never seen again, that many of them at least, were Carman worshippers. But he, apparently, will give no ground . . .

Re W. again: yes, the horrible thought of him admiring flatness for its own sake, as apart from its effect. Like isolating some part of the body, letting it function islanded . . . Yet he, W., takes pleasure in flatness, and thereby gives it meaning—to himself, of course.

I quite see why you're somewhat alienated by that book clipping thing. Art becomes a prey to technology etc.—is that what you mean? Next: the electronic orgasm. Reminds me, I wanted to take my stolen book along to Stanley House and get you to sign it—but felt that would look kinda— well, not natural somehow. But I LIKE signed copies. So I wanta send it along to you for your John Henry Glassco. That too is my sedimental side.

The bit about the pills that could have saved Keats, Chopin, etc.—Of course I know modern medicine could have saved those guys, but it never occurred to me to think of it quite so specifically. You have more reason to do so. Of course, Souster probably would. Shall I break up that paragraph of yours into an instant poem? Could probably be done. Don't you see the enormous obligation you've put upon yourself to send this info to Souster? A great poem remains unwritten while you remain inactive. Ow!

I am at the moment in a helluvan embarrassing situation. Some guy in Vancouver has sent me his long prose-poem entitled "War-Cry," wanting advice where to send it, comment etc. I don't feel competent. Hey, bright idea. Wanta look at it? I suppose you don't, but still . . . This guy has a reasonable amount of talent (Red Lane[2]) in ordinary poems, and I've tried to encourage him or—what does one say describing one's activities when they sound objectively condescending? Anyway, it fucks me up a bit, having this big poem sent to me. He asks me if it should be sent to *Maclean's*—and that's ridiculous to me. Poppa, what shall I do? I suppose, send him some euphemisms.

Am getting a little drunk again myself, after having recovered during the break in this letter. Tryin to keep my weight down allows me to get drunk quite easily. [. . .]

I think probably I will get to the Yukon or wherever. All the currents seem to be running my way right now. And I say this despite the risk of

95

misjudgement. But why the hell should you? I'm not ever very sure where poems are. You've found them around Foster, and they lurk still microscopic and macrocosmic around you, I would think. But I suppose it's personal boredom that drives me north. Besides, I've written about the immediate rural vicinity here until the name of Roblin Lake makes me shudder.

Re the Everson photo, have you seen that grotesque face peering over your left shoulder in it? The MUSE? Migawd, the look on Cogswell's[3] face! A sweet fat boy pleased with himself and acknowledging posterity's plaudits. Oh how nice it is to be a poet. Send me one dozen roses . . .

You keep running on . . . ? What about me? Tell me, despite the good sound of it, why do you think the birds moved straight into joy?

Best

Al

Do write some more.

1. Ron Sutherland (b. 1933): professor of English and comparative Canadian literature at Université de Sherbrooke, novelist (*Snow Lark*, 1971) and critic (*Second Image*, 1971; *The New Hero*, 1977).
2. Red Lane (1936–64): poet and elder brother of Patrick Lane.
3. Fred Cogswell (1917–2004): professor of English at the University of New Brunswick where he edited *The Fiddlehead* and inaugurated Fiddlehead Books. He has written more than two dozen books of poetry.

To John Glassco (Foster, Que.), from Ameliasburgh, November 1, 1964

Dear John,

Fuck being forgiven for anything, especially trivialities. It doesn't apply except obliquely, but I'll quote the Yeats verse anyhow—

> To many women I have said, "Lie still,"
> And given everything a woman needs,
> A roof, good clothes, passion, love perhaps,
> But never asked for love; should I ask that,
> I shall be old indeed—[1]

Glad to hear you got *Annettes,* which is the only one really worth having to me. Tho perhaps *The Crafte So Longe To Lerne* Ryerson '59 has some stuff in it. It's 23 pages, a buck at Ryerson. If you don't have that chapbook I'll send along one, tho I think only two poems are in it—If you haven't *The Blur in Between* Jay Macpherson still has a few copies I think, at 15 Berryman St. Tor. Tho actually, *Annettes* is about all—

I knew, of course, that birds evolved from reptiles; but not the singing for joy bit. Ya, I guess we went whoring after god (a good phrase) I completely agree with you we got on the wrong track, and that "joy" bit is very crucial—Tho on the other hand, would we change places with birds despite said joy? Very doubtful. We want to have it both ways. [. . .]

Most things I write about did happen in some sense or other, and I suppose you write the same way. Your writing on the four stages of despair particularly interesting. The bad tidings bit—I suppose you know Frost's poem, which I've always remembered in part—"Why hurry to tell Belshazzar, what he soon enough would know"[2]—My mother paid me 5¢ a book to read Dickens when I was a kid, which is almost Dickensian itself. But tempted to go to library and read the parts you mention. But how the hell could you manage to read detective stories, unless there was nothing else? Migawd, you must have been bored to death. As a kid of 17 riding the freights, my mind used to exist in something near desperation. Like: what sort of agony is this to be going nowhere with no end in sight. The present to be so dirty and ugly and the future to promise nothing better. Of course I didn't actually think those thoughts, but felt them. And yet, many years later, I look back on that time with pleasure and enjoyment. One of the qualities of being human I guess, you make your tb interesting and pleasureable. Me the same. As I remember, I disliked being a child immensely. Yet I write an idealizing play about it in 1955, with nostalgia pouring into all the sluices. It took you less time tho in this instance. The vision-chart in optometrist's window also anomaly in this world of sharpers and executives.

Do you know A.E. Ellis' book, *The Rack*? Dull in spots, but utterly absorbing in others. About a tb hosp. Send it along if you haven't.

Best,

Al

John: I'd like to see more of you. Please let me know when you're gonna be anywhere, like Toronto, Ottawa or my neck of the woods. As you know, it's so very hard to know people, or catch them at the exact moment when both can be interested. Almost an accident. Let me know. I'll do the same.

1. The lines are from Yeats's "In Tara's Halls."
2. This is from Frost's "Bearer of Evil Tidings."

To Charles Bukowski (Los Angeles), from Belleville, late 1964

Dear Charles Bukowski,

Enclosed the review[1] of your book I just did—No guarantee Alan Bevan will use it in *Evidence* but I think so—sorry the first page carbon is dim. As you may gather I like your stuff. First guy I've seen since Layton I had much use for. "Same old stuff?"?? Maybe.

I was gonna say, hey, let's start a new school, but I'm a little overwhelmed right now at the uselessness of writing anyone—I think in many ways I'm a great deal like you or vice versa—but like I say, I'm overwhelmed at the moment—Drinking wine: and I hear steps of the golden men who push the buttons of our burning universe—No kidding, I am drinking homemade wine, I make wild grape stuff that stains your mouth and makes your shit look like the oily blackish grease inside auto wheels

[Fingertip-size stain follows. Typing resumes below it.]

Sample above. Sometimes I'm so conscious of the futility of doing any damn thing, like writing to somebody whose poems I like—Take a look, by the way, at mine. Have about 8 or 9 in coming ish of *Evidence* with maybe this and a coupla reviews.

Come to think of it: I must be just writing you because I don't wanta work on a play I'm doin for a Montreal CBC producer about Helen of Troy's lipstick—I'm writing the goddam thing like a short order cook in a hash joint—wrote most of it longhand in a night and now lengthening and revising as I type—And don't wanta do any more so I'm writing you. That's complimentary eh? Not entirely the truth tho. I do admire and all that shit. But I've been admired a few times myself and I know what it sounds like. Like I also say in review: I think it's a one-sided picture of you, but then I expect you'll change. Unless you wanta stay the same, same tone, same idiom eh? That might make you mad for me to say that, but I believe it strongly so I say it anyway. Just the same you have a lovely lovely line of shit. [...]

If you feel like writing write—The piece below may have come from you, at least partly, tho I pledge my bones I talk that way part of the time anyway. And these people do live and did say what they say in the poem.

THANK GOD I'M NORMAL

From the west coast X writes
"someone at CBC is trying to block me."
In Toronto W says, "I want him to die,
if he'd just die—
Then I'd have enough money to publish my poems."
Only the guy in Montreal says nothing,   (This gal's husband
having gotten all the awards going already.   is a dentist)
Besides, he's so neurotic he's written
a handy literary guide to the bughouse.   (That's Layton)
From Calgary: "They won't publish my poems.
They're afraid of me, for I tell the Truth.
And They can't stand Truth!"
From the Maritimes: "We've got a tradition behind us—"
(Ya, it's what they sit on.)
Me, I'm like all the rest. I wanta be famous!
But I'm not gonna be paranoic
        I'm not I'm not I'm not I'm not—
Anyway, I don't know how to end this.
But the morning mail drops in the slot
and a letter from the scholarship people says,
"it is with regret that we inform you—"
        Why—why, the sonsabitches!

1. Purdy's laudatory review of *It Catches My Heart in Its Hands* appeared in *Evidence*, no.8 (n.d. [1964]). The issue also featured a special section of nine poems by Purdy. The review is reprinted in *Starting from Ameliasburgh*.

To Charles Bukowski (Los Angeles), from Ameliasburgh, late 1964

Dear Charles Bukowski,
I do not agree that your life, as you imply, is little enough (no typewriter here). You're the only poet in the States I have much use for—your poems have already loosened up a friend's verse so he's written a fairly good poem—

Of course re history etc.—no man eventually looms very large. But myself, I still get a kick outa life, and until I don't I'll go on—

Canada? ya, a lotta Canadians conspire to give that impression— However, I'd no more judge the US by Sen McCarthy & Edgar Guest than I would by Wernher von Braun or Fermi or Chaplin[1]—All you can see at one time is an aspect. Canada has quite a few good poets, damn few novelists etc. Tho no poets much like yourself. By the way I've picked out about six names, among them yours, I'll list as dedications in my book coming in about a year.[2] Hope you don't mind. The others are A.E. Housman ("Could man be drunk forever"), Auden, Jeffers, Catullus & Callimachus of Alexandria—Quite a combo—Sure, disregard reviews—if you can. Sometimes I've learned something from them tho. If I believed everything tho—Yes, schools I agree with you.

You think of Burroughs[3]—I don't want to. You & I about same age— me one year older—I wrote to show off when I was 13 at school. Now I can't help it. So help me, I can't help it.

Tough? Well, let's say instead no one writes like you. I'd lost hope of seeing somebody I like in totality over there until you—Of course, 3–4 poems by Corso, Leroi Jones[4] etc. Very few. I kid you not—Tell me to fuck myself or don't even bother thinking. Really doesn't matter. Poems do. So write you bastard—write.

Al Purdy

1. Senator Joseph McCarthy (1909–57): described by *Chambers Biographical Dictionary* as "American politician and inquisitor" and by Harry S. Truman as a "pathological character assassin," he was responsible for the McCarthyite era (1950–54) in American politics. Wernher von Braun (1912–77): German and American rocket engineer, instrumental both in the German V2 program and in the American satellite program. Enrico Fermi (1901–54): Italian-born American nuclear physicist, awarded the Nobel Prize in 1938. The element fermium was named after him.
2. *The Cariboo Horses* (1965) appeared without a dedication.
3. William Burroughs (1914–97): Beat generation novelist, best known for *The Naked Lunch* (1959).
4. Gregory Corso (b. 1930): one of the Beat poets (*Gasoline,* 1958; *Bomb,*1959). Leroi Jones (b. 1934): radical African-American poet (*Selected Poems,* 1979) who changed his name to Amiri Baraka.

To George Woodcock (Vancouver), from Ameliasburgh, November 13, 1964

Dear George Woodcock,
Do you know if there'd be any chance of doing a reading at the university in, say, January? I'm homesick for Vancouver, and plan a month or so visit. George Bowering is talking about lining up a reading in Calgary to help pay expenses, and I wondered if the same thing might be possible in Vancouver. I don't know the people to whom such an inquiry might be addressed, and thought you might. Would Earle Birney know anything, do you think?

I was interested in your "Earliest Voyages"[1] review, especially this passage; "—while the hybrid Metis society which actually appeared in the prairies showed regressive tendencies that might well have led to its reabsorption into a modified Indian society had the link with European civilization been broken, as it was in the case of Greenland toward the end of the fifteenth century."

In other words, even given complete isolation, as in the case of the Eskimos, you don't think Riel could have (for instance) headed a country that might have eventually achieved some sort of progressive technology. Of course Riel is not a good example, since his presence presupposes the factors that made him viable for a short time—

In science fiction there is a type of writing which places H-bombs side by side with sword and dagger, tho I've forgotten the explanation given for this if there was one—But I find it a fascinating idea—that the Norse explorers are actually responsible for much of the culture of present day Eskimos. Of course, it's only a theory. Still, if comparative studies of Eskimo society were done, taking in all of them from Greenland to the Aleutians (and I think there are some in Russia?) wouldn't this tend to prove or disprove the theory? If Norse influences can be identified as such, then there might be some Eskimo communities who show no such influences.

I read recently quite an entertaining book called *Northern Adventure* (fiction) which mingled anthropology, archaeology, botany and zoology of the north. I take it that mention of earlier cultures in this book was authentic, despite the book being fiction. Curious also to think that now the deadly successors to the Norsemen are actually in process of wiping out Eskimo culture as it exists at present. All pockets and isolated minorities are being eventually swept into the human mainstream, which tends to homogenize and wipe out all traces of the past.

Gwyn Jones[2] apparently holds the view that encroaching Norsemen had little or no effect on the Eskimos. I find that hard to believe. In fact I don't wish to believe it. I prefer to think of the human race as eminently teachable, continuing to change thru adaptation and adoption of new devices—Said new things tho are generally material and physical; attitudes of mind change much more slowly, it seems to me.

Harking back to those "regressive tendencies" you mentioned—I wonder what they signify. Even if the Metis had such tendencies, would they have retained (in case of isolation) many of the grafted new things, weapons, etc.? Also, what effect on a backward culture mentally, consciously or no, does a superior culture have? In any such cases, whatever such mental effect might be, I think it would result from superior technology and not philosophy. All of which seems to me quite pertinent concerning our reservation Indians today.

One might regard the area of highest technology as a vortex (the US) toward which even the remotest regions are drawn—One has a picture of Eskimo gangsters and civil corruption, the Beatles, and Dean Rusk[3] and Kennedy as folk heroes. With climatic modifications, I suppose.

Anyway, as you will gather, I was interested in your review.

Best,

Al Purdy

1. Woodcock reviewed Tryggvi J. Olson's *Early Voyages and Northern Approaches 1000–1632*, Gwyn Jones's *The Norse Atlantic Saga*, and *John Ledyard's Journal of Captain Cook's Last Voyage* in *Canadian Literature*, No. 21 (Summer 1964).
2. Gwyn Jones (b. 1907): Welsh historian (*A History of the Vikings*, 1968; *The Norse Atlantic Saga*, 1964).
3. Dean Rusk (1909–94): Secretary of State in the Kennedy and Johnson administrations, he retired in 1969.

To Charles Bukowski (Los Angeles), from Ameliasburgh, late 1964

The reason I included Callimachus is for one short verse beginning "They told me Heraclitus, they told me you were dead" which you probably know.[1] I also include Catullus, or did I say. Well—I have no inferiority feelings about these guys, including you. But I learned from them all (including you) and owe them that much homage. And like I said, you're the only one over there I have much use for—I mean sure, I can even read Wilbur[2] and get something: "like palaces of patience in the grey and changeless lands of ice" is a helluva good line. So is "all that ragged, loose collapse of water" referring to fountains. What I don't like is these bastards' sweetness and iambic smoothness and their too-too thinking. I don't like some of the guys in *New AmPo*[3] for an opposite reason: they think all they have to do is cuss a bit and act mysterious or whatever, and they have a poem. Which is a lotta shit. I like cuss-words, they're natural talk to me, and I use em. But I don't like the togetherness let's everybody pat each other of the Duncan-Creeley-Olson bunch. And I don't like their so-called poems either. And I don't like the holy attitude *noli me tangere* (whatever that means) of their awed disciples.[4]

So do I like anything? Sure. "Ballad of Despairing Husband" of Creeley (that's about all tho), much of Corso, Jones and one or two others. Most poets think they're great and that too is a bit disgusting unless I agree—but then I think I'm pretty good too, so who am I to kick? If you think so about yourself I sure agree, as I said. You ought to. But it gets to be a chickenshit sort of attitude anyhow—

You ought to see me here at Roblin Lake: dressed in shorts, drinking coffee, (on account I gotta stay sober to write a "poem for voices" on comish for CBC re D/Day—about war, really) and the old kitchen woodstove goin like hell, papers all over—Snow outside, rabbits shitting on the lawn and eating afterbirth of grape wine I threw out 2 weeks ago, lake cracking a bit from cold, and myself here banging away—I don't work, by the way, just try to write and live off my wife. Never much money—

When you get a copy you don't hafta type, send me your piece on poems today if you think it's any good. You don't think like Hemingway, just Buk, and that's enough. I should say being prez. of GM or bein Buk is to some degree a matter of choice eh? I mean, you can say you can't help it, and you can't, but it's still a matter of some choice.

I have just read *The Bracelet of Garnets* by Alex Kuprin, and the damn thing threw me. Really did. Nice romantic antidote for Dostoievsky. Also, *The Land of Rumbelow* by Carlos Baker, which is a good well-written academe book about evil and violence. If you're interested that is—

Ya, I guess we want to LOOM LARGE. But hell I gotta live my life moment by moment, and it gets too much trouble after a while to keep thinking how your literary life is gonna look—how do I say it? I mean, I gotta live now too, and that's what's important to me—I gotta write my poems and do my fucking now. And while I am also aware of being dead in a sense, being 200 pounds of dead genius can also look after itself—Original? Ya, only I have no one style, I have a dozen: have got to be virtuoso enough I can shift gears like a hot rod kid—So I doubt that my exact combo ever came along before. Unlike some, I have no ideas on being a specific sort of poet. I mean, I don't make rules and say this THIS is what a poet HAS to be. I don't know what the hell a poet is or care much. I do know what he isn't sometimes. And don't think it's very important to make definitions, like some of the culture bugs in Canada who want a lit and a culture etc. Couldn't care less. I'm me, right now, and I'm writing, and that's enough. Fuck everything else. This is difficult to say: for you're right in some ways with the non-original bit, but only in some ways. Besides, if we ever get together over a bottle of whatever is the only way to talk of some things—For I'm rambling too.

The hell I'm funny with my dedications. I admire these people, and why shouldn't I say so?

All is shit? Well, shit! All is not shit. I don't know what all is, but if I ever find out I'll send you a night letter. Sometimes I think I'm 100% mood, meaning 100% down, depressed, shitty—then I get drunk on a poem for a week, but damn seldom. Got a little drunk on some of yours—"the golden men / who push the buttons / of our burning universe /" Ya—youth—you I guess are the same as me, you still wanta fuck the sexy lookin kids—at least I do sometimes—but I mourn the fact even that's wearin off and I hafta put it in a poem.—

I now gotta write this "poem for voices" 4 men and 1 girl on their way to a battlefield, but arrive too late. Battle's over. They fall asleep on battlefield. Happens about 6 times. Girl is a whore, hasta be. Nice parody of Oklahoma to include before Hiroshima—

> HIRO///SHIMA//—
> where the sun shines
> nearly every day
> and the fields of rice
> they don't taste nice
> but everybody's happy and gay
> Hiroshima—every night my geisha girl and I—

Include a piece coupla years old I still like—And book'll be along as the mails take it in your fuckin backward country—Now hafta start on wine, been sober too long, so with customary sign off—

Also gonna be in play: (parody of Wizard of Oz) Idiot farmer's song:

We're off to make our fortunes
from apples and pears and plums
of purple and gold and yellow
to be sold for very large sums—
We're off to make our fortunes
and we'll never come back till we does—does—does?

Hey, poppa, does does rhyme with sums somewhat?
[Thumb-print size stain follows.]

1. "They told me, Heraclitus, they told me you were dead" is from "Heraclitus.
Paraphrase from Callimachus" by William Johnson Cory (1823–92). The poem is
collected in *Ionica* (1858).
2. Richard Purdy Wilbur (b. 1921): urbane and stylish American poet (*Seven
Poems*, 1981) and translator (Molière).
3. Donald Allen's influential anthology, *The New American Poetry*, was published
in 1964. It helped introduce the Black Mountain poets, the Beats and other less
well-known poets to a wider audience.
4. Robert Creeley (b. 1926): edited *Black Mountain Review* (1954–57). His
Collected Poems 1945–1975 appeared in 1983. Charles Olson (1910–70): the leading theorist (*Projective Verse*, 1950) and poet in the Black Mountain school (*The
Maximus Poems*, 1983). "Noli me tangere" ("Do not touch me") is said by Jesus
to Mary Magdalene after the resurrection.

To Charles Bukowski (Los Angeles), from Trenton, Ont., January 9, 1965

Dear Chas,
Glad you got the Layton book, which is a sorta collected poems of his.
Incidentally, I disagree a bit with your review of him for *Evidence*, on accounta I think his real good stuff is in *Red Carpet*, and just the odd one
since.[1] However, it was a good review as a piece of writing: by which I
mean I liked it on accounta a picture of Bukowski came thru. But I figure
Layton is pretty well washed up, mostly on accounta he believes his own
somewhat parochial Canadian publicity. But these poems, in *Red Carpet*,
had one helluva big effect on me when I first read them, which was in different books before *Red Carpet*. About 10 different small books, in fact.
And Layton himself is an impressive bastard, even in private he talks for
publication, if you get me. But I really weep real tears when a guy like
that, who has said so much, and COULD say much more it seems to me,
succumbs to his own goddam pr crap. He's 52 or 3 now, and I maintain
his mental attitude is all wrong for writing poetry. He thinks he's the

purest transcendental genius—which doesn't explain it exactly . . . What I mean is, anything he writes he feels this way about. It was written by him, Layton, therefore ipso facto it's great. Like Cassius Clay. Me, I know I'm good—but that isn't really the point. The point is I haven't even touched the things I think could be said, even if I don't know what they are. I think that should be his attitude too, for his own mental outlook to me means he'll settle for less every time. However, he has the remains of a lotta talent left . . . as you know—

Re your comment, sure the univs are dead, but that doesn't concern me much. I have only so much time, and I don't wanta waste it on trivialities. Maybe that's the wrong way to think, but I'll stick to it. I have my own way to go, whatever that may be exactly (I don't know). I figure I'm a neurotic and physically worn out man at 45, and I intend to spend what time I have writing about what interests me or not writing at all. Which last I find to be rather inconceivable.

Ya, I agree with you completely about Le Metro. Even in ordinary readings I feel afterwards as if I'd wasted my time. Here (Le Metro, I mean) let em have it (Corso, Ginsberg[2] et all—tho I didn't know Ciardi was one of them). In the first place I don't agree at all that a poet or painter or whatever has to or should live in a segregated area in order to study his own navel. Like Greenwich Village I mean.

Tho I didn't "hang around" Metro, only there for one evening as a sort of rural visitor.

Agree also with your comment on Jeffers. Tho I don't necessarily agree (which you didn't say anyway) that Jeffers should have isolated himself the way he did. But, if that was the only way to write the poems he did, then yes, sure, isolate yourself or himself. To me he's one, or perhaps the only, great poet in the last American 50–60 years. Who are the others? You tell me. For when I think of a poet, I think of one who has something to say to ME, no matter what his time period was. And none of them mean a goddam thing to me except Jeffers. Lots of small talents, tho I suppose I should except Dickinson from that, but no big ones who open up things. Tho I'm not sure Jeffers did that. Why then? Just because I feel the same way as he did very much of the time. Robinson,[3] at the end of his life, wrote some poems of a very similar way of thinking. Pure pearly pessimism. And I'm thinking of "As It Looked Then," which you may or may not know. Since I'm inclined to believe that all peace and content are momentary illusions for people other than vegetables, pessimism with alternations of self-forgetfulness seems to me the most I can hope for. Which is a pretty grim outlook, and my poems don't support such thinking all the time. However, here's the Robinson poem at the beginning of next page just in case you're not familiar with it.

AS IT LOOKED THEN

In a sick shade of spruce, moss-webbed, rock-fed,
Where, long unfollowed by sagacious man,
A scrub that once had been a pathway ran
Blindly from nowhere and to nowhere led,
One might as well have been among the dead
As halfway there alive; so I began
Like a malingering pioneer to plan
A vain return—with one last look ahead.

And it was then that like some spoken word
Where there was none to speak, insensibly
A flash of blue that might have been a bird
Grew soon to the calm wonder of the sea—
Calm as a quiet sky that looked to be
Arching a world where nothing had occurred.
                                        —E.A. Robinson

[...] I'm goin out west at end of this month where I have readings and interviews etc. Sometimes think it's the equivalent of pickin up stuff in bars, reading I mean— [...]

In New York we stayed with this negro painter in his one room studio in the Bronx, almost got to meet Paul Robeson whom he knew, which would have been better'n Metro to me. Incidentally, if you have any copies of earlier books of yours I want em, send me quick please. Either for money or for free, but send em if you have em eh?

                                        Best,

                                        Al

1. In his edition of the Purdy-Bukowski letters, Bruce Whiteman suggests that "Purdy has evidently read the manuscript of Bukowski's review of Layton's *The Laughing Rooster* . . . which was later published in *Evidence* no. 9 (n.d. 1965)."
2. Allen Ginsberg (1926–97): closely associated with the Beat movement, he wrote *Howl* (1956), one of the poetic anthems of the 1950s and 1960s.
3. Edwin Arlington Robinson (1869–1935): New England poet; AP memorized

several of his ironic, objective and often dark lyrics. His later long narrative poems (*Merlin*, 1917; *Tristram*, 1927) have not lasted as well as the lyrics in *The Children of the Night* (1897).

To John Glassco (Foster, Que.), from Trenton, January 11, 1965

Dear John,

I was thinking of Glassco and his "better not to have been born at all"[1] and wondering if you felt it all the time. Probably not. I do sometimes myself, especially as I get older and my body gets stubborn when I want it to do things. Makes me wonder if I've burned myself out, as if life were a disease which some get a more virulent dose of than others.

Got a letter from [Maurice] Girodias,[2] the Olympia Press guy, a while back, which I didn't expect. I remember your remark that he has a martyr complex. Fun to go thru agony I suppose, for those people. You didn't feel that way about your asylum incarceration I guess tho—But I think we all enjoy defiance as long as it doesn't make things worse, cf. Silas Gooch.

I meant to ask you, since you know him well: what do you think of Eldon Grier now? I mean, is he getting any better or staying the same? I was amused by someone, I forget whom, telling me he was writing a story and entitling it "A Shameful Story" or something like that and including "shameful." The story didn't sound that to me. He interests me, but undoubtedly we'll never be particular friends, because I am sure he thinks he detects condescension on my part. ESP you know. Everybody maybe knows what you are and there ain't a damn thing you can do about it. Maybe the "shameful" bit IS a criterion. But he does interest me. Some of his poems sort of hint at a "breakaway"—

Take you: I'm sure you're so selfconscious you know what your shadow is doing when you're asleep. You also interpret the slightest twitch of lip or inflection of phrase. Or am I wrong?

Now what the hell was it you remarked about enjoyment of past agonies? Have to look up that other letter of yours.

Going out west at the end of this month, readings at Calgary and Vancouver, enough money and perhaps a little more to pay for the trip. Eminent literary guy and all that crap. I asked George Woodcock if there was a chance of anything like that on accounta a friend of mine is getting married in Vancouver, and also because I wanted to go for I know so many people there. Incredibly he dug up some things to make money from—

I had hoped to have a drink with you somewhere before that, but apparently no. After then. I think we could talk real well sometime if circumstances and mood and inclination are all right. What airs I give myself saying that tho. Talking is so fortuitous and happenchance. I remember once 3 of us talking in Vancouver, and Doug was expounding some subtle points to somebody named Dave, who was rather obtuse about them. Later Doug said I understood his subtle points (which I did, for they weren't hard) and it gave him a warm feeling. Yet, at the time, I felt no more than mild amusement for the points Doug was making without getting them across to Dave at all. (Perhaps incredibly, to you—I just listened.) But what I mean, or am trying to illustrate: good conversation must be something in which the participants feel they have understood something, and also contribute themselves, like holding a ball poised in the air on a fountain. Is that true? Possibly. I'm sure you understand what I mean generally anyhow.

I am presently getting a little high on wine, this being Sunday and I just having worked about 2 hours (hard) pouring cement to make piers to bolster a rotten timber in the cellar of this house. Then crawling into the 3-foot-clearance cellar to place the goddam stuff. I really am getting old if I can't take that much work, also down to about 194 pounds, lowest since I went to Cuba. Maybe that's it.

So how are you and why?

Best,

Al

1. The line is a free translation of one of AP's favourite lines in Sophocles: "Not to be born is, past all prizing, best" (*Oedipus at Colonus*, 1225). He quotes it in "Rodeo," "My Cousin Don" and "On Being Human."
2. Maurice Girodias (1919–90): legendary Parisian publisher (Olympia Press) of pornography. He brought out Nabokov's *Lolita* in 1955. His essay "*Lolita*, Nabokov and I" prompted "*Lolita* and Mr. Girodias," a tart disagreement from Nabokov.

To Charles Bukowski (Los Angeles), from Ameliasburgh, Ont., April 1965

Dear Buk,
Helluva cold last two–three days—and reading Baldwin's *Giovanni's Room*[1] and wondering about people just wondering—

You must have got my stuff by now, and hope you like it. In some way I haven't entirely figured out my identity depends on my poems and so does yours on yours—I mean this is me, and like me like my poems. I don't mean the phoniness of patting each other on the back, but like said once or twice, if you didn't you'd say so. I guess you would too. Dunno if I would or not if I didn't. Probably wouldn't bother . . .

But I look at my own poems, and say, did I say that, did I feel that?? "Percy Lawson" poem for instance. I must be a phoney sonuvabitch, because I don't really feel that now. But did I when I wrote it, or was I merely writing a poem that way because I knew how? Just the same, in some way I haven't figured (like I said) whatever I am is in my poems. But any number of my own poems seem alien to me now, in feeling as feeling corresponds to my present feeling—Yet I wrote them. Didn't I feel them then either? Christ yes, I know I did, for I've got such a thing about authenticity and verisimilitude that I even use people's real names in poems and take a chance on being sued by people like Art Watt in the Lawson poem. Course that's ridiculous anyway.

I must say tho, that I do value your opinions about poems. I'm very like you in poems in many ways, and very unlike you in others. My so-called world-view is close to yours, tho at the same time has variations. But yours is only what I see in poems. Tho I think that must be, has to be, authentic.

Incidentally, to change the subject a bit, nabbed a Fellowship for four grand plus travel from Canada Council—got turned down by Guggenheim. Leaving for Canadian Arctic sometime in May.

Anyway, talking about feeling as above, bothers me. I'm so fuckin self conscious I doubt the motives for shitting. In anything I figure is important enough to think about it, that is. And maybe the reason I doubt the past tense feeling in poems of mine is: they now have a separate identity from myself. There they are, and they say I felt that way. I think I want to quarrel with them and say: "To hell with you, poem. You're a bloody liar! I did not!" Ever feel that?

Change subject again: lookin forward to your book. I'll try to keep you posted as to peregrinations. Incidentally, hope to lower the whole moral tone of the true north. That's the stock line I give people. Actually tho I feel pretty scared. I mean, here I am a pretty old bastard, 200 pounds of soft gut and flabby muscles, heading off where danger and death are real things. Besides I'm much too lazy to exert myself the way I'll have to. Besides, no women around except Eskimos probly. (I wonder if blubber is fermentable?) Anyway, I want your book when available . . .

You could be right re the long distance thing—I've been a quarrelsome bastard in a lifetime myself. Sometimes people get mad at me and I can't even figure out why. Other times I know damned well why, which is much less frustrating.

Anyway, when I say I will not NOT (repeat) say if I don't like your stuff, important as I know that is, it's because I have some precedents to go on. Like I know a few poets up here I think are pretty awful. But why the hell should I tell them that? No, I haven't said they're wonderful either (tho in reviews I try to say kind things that won't discourage young poets, and don't agree at all with the sweeping condemnation sort of review in the case of youth and possible development)—but try to stay off the subject altogether. Ya, it's tough. What I mean is tho, I'm sort of sentimental about some people and like them apart from poems. You know, people who invite you to dinner and have a drink or what the hell—And I think of one guy in particular. If I say the truth he'll hate my guts. Should I do that? Even if he asks me, as he sometimes does? Course I can never get down to this level of communication with people whose stuff I don't feel somewhere—Well, better stop, drink wine.

Al

1. James Baldwin (1924–87): African-American novelist, long-time French resident: *Go Tell It on the Mountain* (1953), *Giovanni's Room* (1956).

To Charles Bukowski (Los Angeles), from Pangnirtung, Baffin Island, August 19, 1965

Dear Buk,
Have written you a coupla letters afore this, but not since I remembered your right nr. on De Longpre. So will hold this one, which is just to bring you up to date and to hope you have more access to alcohol than me. In 6 weeks I've had 1 40 ouncer, which doesn't seem much rum over that time. Enforced sobriety doesn't appeal. Of course the odd few drinks from other sources, me never refusing an offer—

Ya, 6 weeks in the Arctic. 24 poems, about 10,000 words of prose I hope to work into an article for coin of the realm—

Pang is right on the Arctic Circle, about 200 people, mostly Eskimo. About 30 whites. I spent 2 of those 6 weeks in an Eskimo camp living in a tent on the Kikastan Islands in Cumberland Sound, which is on the Japan Sea. Damn near froze to death. Went out hunting with Jonesee (the Eskimo guy I went with) once only. Must be gettin too old—just can't take it. Dogs all over the place at that camp. Great brutes between 100–150 lbs. They have a taste for human shit, and they won't let you shit in peace, keep dashing in tryin to get a mouthful while it's hot. Finally ended up usin a biscuit tin, in the tent, then takin it out to the dogs for their breakfast. I could pick and choose the lucky dog that way. Of course I wrote a poem about that, you can imagine maybe—[1]

Right now—I'm waitin to grab a plane south (been waitin 8 days now) on accounta I get a trip to Cardiff, England as a delegate to a Commonwealth Festival or some damn thing like that. I mean a free trip, 6 days & transport. Dunno exactly how I got it, but don't care much. Intend to go thru London bookstores & pubs for a week. Feel like I could drink beer 24 hours steady I'm so dry right now.

Yah—got an Eskimo to do some drawings, & Alan Bevan of *Evidence* wants to do a book of northern poems using your 2 books as models (more or less) on which to take off with his own ideas. I am all for it, just so I can wriggle out of a contract with last publisher. And think I can. Yah—this Eskie did one of the guy tryin to shit & surrounded by dogs. Has the shit droppin right outa the guy's ass—Doubt if that sort of realism will go—But Christ—it sure gives you the feelin, with those dogs nearly right up your ass—

Anyhow, I got to get south and fill out papers for this trip, which is for Sept. 16. Right now I'm sick to death of the Arctic, but can't get out. Can't afford to charter a plane ($550.) so hafta go along on somebody else's charter to Frobisher Bay. Thence to Montreal.

Trouble with this whole biz tho, is here I am writin poems I'm not really involved in—I mean, this isn't like writin about a union or a woman I know etc. etc. I come up here to get material like a goddam phony reporter. So I look at what I see then write poems. Had a kinda fever, I guess. For a while I wrote a poem every day. It's the wrong way around. The material should come to me naturally, not me to the material. No more will I do this sort of thing. I'll back away from the temptation to write one about tyin my shoelaces.

But then—the Arctic did interest me at first. So maybe the poems aren't completely phony. Still, I won't do it again.

Will mail this in Mtl.—take a chance on yr. address. You want any books in England let me know at 435 Sackville St., #20, Toronto, where my wife is.

Just the same, quite a place here, mountains hulking around, some with large brown patches of iron deposits—like bloodstains from a giant's battle. Icebergs drifting by in the fiord,—they've disappeared since August, but are still in Cumberland Sound. The sunset stretches a gold bar across the fiord mouth to the west. Nights now about 5 hrs. Was only twilight in early July. See if I can copy a poem on the back of first two sheets.

Best,

Al

1. See "When I Sat Down to Play the Piano" in *North of Summer: Poems from Baffin Island* (1967). The Eskimo guide's name is given in the book both as "Jonese" and "Jonesee," but most commonly in the latter form.

To George Woodcock (Vancouver), from Frobisher Bay, August 21, 1965

Dear George,

Got word a week ago—should say my wife phoned me a week ago at Pangnirtung that I'm selected to go to this Commonwealth Festival thing at Cardiff, Wales. There being papers to sign etc. I tried to get out of Pang right away. However, weather was bad and so on—

Anyhow, I'm quite elated at the prospect, as much for the idea of rummaging thru London bookstores as the Festival, not being sure exactly what the latter consists of—

Re the Arctic, have written 24 poems here, 22 of them about the north, and revised 2 others. I enclose the last revision, not about the north; but I've been working on it the last two days, and therefore it's on my mind. There are weak spots in it yet, but I'm beginning to run short of patience. The last line implies solid ground, whereas the preceding lines have to do with the contents of a millpond, and the two don't jibe too well. However, I think the idea comes across. Very pleased with first 9 lines:

> and the wind-high ships
> that sailed from Rednersville
> to the sunrise ports of Europe[1]

If you take it apart for analysis it doesn't mean much, but the way it's said gives me a certain feeling of uplift—or call it "uplift." Or maybe it's the Haig and Haig scotch I'm drinking—damn good stuff.

At Pang I had an old Eskimo do a bunch of drawings with the idea of including them in a prospective book of northern poems, called: DOGSONG—Poems from Baffin Land. I prefer "Baffin Land" to the customary "Baffin Island." Also written 10,000 words or so of prose, notes etc. for an article. Hope to incorporate poems in with the prose, an "Arctic Diary" sort of thing.

Incidentally, Rednersville is a tinytiny village on the Bay of Quinte that used to be a port for the old sailing ships that took grain and squared timbers to Europe from the surrounding countryside, including Ameliasburg.

Heading now for 435 Sackville St., #20, Toronto, where my wife is. And thence to Wales Sept. 16. With a feeling of expectation, that interesting things are going to happen—

Thanks for your large part in this.

All the best,
Al

1. These lines are from "Roblin's Mills [II]."

To Charles Bukowski (Los Angeles), from Toronto, October 5, 1965

Dear Buk,

Another letter back which I misaddressed.[1] Helluva bad memory. Won't even open this to find out how lachrymose I was that time.

Just got back from England and a rather drunken three weeks. Week at Cardiff Wales at a poetry conference which was a kinda shambles. Egoes underfoot all the time. American beat expatriates there too, and three or four of em took at least half the talking time. Petitions to the queen, open letter to Mao—that sorta crap. Fortunately there was plenty to drink, and some half decent women around whom I pursued desultorily. Once or twice getting quite close and hot.

Now busy seeing how I can make some money from that Arctic jaunt. Lotsa poems of course, of whose merit I blow hot and cold. My wife is goin to teacher's college here, and being nervous as hell about it. She should be nervous! I mean she manages me, why not a buncha kids between 6 and 13?

Back to Ameliasburg this Fri—hear the wild grapes are ripe, and oughta make at least one batch of wine—Not usta seein my hands white and not purple. Searched the book shops there, bought about $150 worth, which is quite a lot. Plans for a fairish-long poem on something I uncovered about the north. Seems at Ellesmere Island, farthest north of any human occupation, coupla Eskimos went there from Etah in Greenland 600 years ago. Man and woman. Lived in a house which an archaeologist uncovered in '58. Man died for whatever reason. Woman covered his body with stones to keep off animals. She went into stone and skin house, ate the last of her dogs and died herself—presumably of starvation. Her bones were found in '59. Immediate question is Why?

Why go to Ellesmere, which is damn grim and desolate. Eskies are gregarious anyway. Why why why? Oughta be a poem anyway . . .

Lovely stroka luck re money. Get $450 for reading (supposed to be speaking but to hell with that) for a univ. students' union, plus expenses. Wow!

Enclose a clipping, the script part of which I think is funny as hell. Makes me wonder if some of these people undress in the dark and whether they indulge in immaculate conception.

Best,

Al

1. Bukowski lived at 5124 De Longpre in Los Angeles.

To Charles Bukowski (Los Angeles), from Ameliasburgh, October 1965

Dear Buk,

Good to hear from you again, and also about this new book of yours. After reading these deballed English poets especially, I'm looking forward to yours—

I guess I'm a year or more away, unless I do one with just arctic stuff. May have to, even tho I know it's not as good as the mill run; but it doesn't mix with mill-run. So what the hell. I'm dry anyway right now, not in the liquor sense, but writing good poems. Haven't done what I consider a good one in a long time. Scares me a little.

Trouble with people sending you flattering inscribed books is you always WANT to believe they're good, even if they're shit, and they almost always are. You can't just come out and say a guy's stuff is shit—or can you? I'm in much the same boat, for it seems a lotta people want to show me their poems and sit back and wait for the praise. It makes me realize how I did that myself in the past, and embarrassed a helluva lotta people who didn't wanta say how bad I was— [. . .]

Layton just came out with his collected poems, mammoth, about 350 pages. $3.95 softcover. I figure I've read most of his stuff anyway, and he won't surprise me much, even tho I do think he's good. But he doesn't have that quality to me, surprise I mean. And I'm sad about him, for he oughta be a lot better. However, he thinks he's terrific, and I guess that's what's important to him. Can't think that about myself, just feel washed up.

I do the same thing with your book, by the way, and get many different reactions. Mostly good, very few bad. It bothers me if I meet a guy
who doesn't like what I consider your best stuff. As if his dislike is aimed
at me and my own choice of what's good. Because most poetry *is* the oh
and ah stuff, and gee whiz look at my shiny new emotions, and ain't I sensitive!

Re Layton again, he certainly was the best thing that ever happened
to Canada tho—until he came along everyone sounded like your aunt
Martha—I guess I ask too much of him—it oughta be enough that he's
good without me wanting him to scrape the skies every time he writes a
poem. And I guess I want you to do the same thing, without doubt I do.
And it's humanly impossible to pull out all the stops every time. Unfair to
ask it. But the hell with that, I still ask it—of you and Layton. Especially
now I think I'm writing crap myself.

Funny things are happening. Some guy wants to set my stuff to electronic music, this having been commissioned for radio. I suppose there
is a few bucks in it, and I always go for the bucks. I mean a buck is a buck
even if a woman isn't always a woman. By the same token a drink is always drink tho a man is not always a man. How far can that be carried?
No farther please jesus.

Running outa beer, but thankfully I have halfa bottle of Napoleon
brandy I snuck back on the plane from England. Planned to attempt a
seduction with it, but fuck that. Better to drink it.

Selah (whatever that means)

Al

To George Woodcock (Vancouver), from Toronto, April 6, 1966

Dear George,
So you haven't vanished off the face of the globe—Merely India—and I
thought I was doin a lot of travelling! (Oops, should have put in address:
435 Sackville St., Apt. 20, Toronto)

Re Davey and McNamara[1] books, fine if you like. Should say I'm not
generally very "taken" or enamoured of the particular style of writing
Davey and his boys espouse. They know how they're gonna write a poem
before they write a poem. And I'm afraid my antagonism to this and other 2nd hand ideas of theirs will show in any review. If you don't mind this
pre-judging on my part fine, send along books. I don't mean McNamara
here.

I didn't do any more on the Birney.[2] He's very busy—has a book of prose coming with CBC pub. A thought on that: why not review both his *Selected*, which is due shortly and the prose articles in the CBC book at the same time—One ought to throw some light on the other. And seems to me Birney deserves large treatment. Don't know exactly how you feel about his work, but I'm admiring, with a few reservations. Seems to me also the prose book would do away with any need to tape record anything and the whole call for a full-length article. I doubt my capability in any such assessment, and maybe one of the more prominent critical figures like Smith or Milton Wilson would be better. As you know, they have far more all-round erudition and general knowledgeability of such things as literary inter-relations, influences etc.

Re myself, been pretty well stuck in Toronto, and getting damn sick of it. Not the idea of Toronto itself, but staying in one place without much physical movement. Been working on Arctic poems which are to be pub by McStew either next fall or next spring, title: *North of Summer: Poems from Baffin Island*. They're using repros. of A.Y. Jackson's paintings to illustrate. But I've been working on these pieces quite steadily for 8 mos, not every day, but in spurts and spasms in bursts and intermitent scraps of energy. Not for the last two weeks thank god. Been doing fair amount of reviews. Like to do them, yet obscurely resent the energy required to smooth and refine the reviews after first writing. As you likely know, Birney says he won't do reviews because he has to live with these people. Which is true, and I may be storing up resentment. But when I look at some of the axe-to-grind people (well maybe we all have) then I think it's a good thing to write them—Who knows.

Expect to go to Newfoundland this summer, in camper and pickup truck. To NorOnt. for week April 24 to read poems in 5 high schools. Wanted to see country round Kapuskasing and thought this good opportunity.

Anyhow, I suppose you're glad to be back, and Inge is too, at Van. just with the onset of spring—and a few walks in Stanely Park which I'd like to take with you—Lotos-land stirs from somnolence at this time, from the horizontal posture nearly achieves the leaning, by which I mean I'd like to be there at least briefly. Maybe I'm just bored with Toronto. Should go stand in front of the new city hall and deliver a short prayer to Henry Moore ghost statue.[3]

Best,

Al

1. Frank Davey (b. 1940): editor (*Tish, Open Letter*), critic (*Surviving the Paraphrase*, 1983) and poet (*Selected Poems: The Arches*, 1980). AP's reservations about the poetry of "Davey and his boys" have their origins in their admiration of the Black Mountain poets. Eugene McNamara (b. 1930): professor of English at the University of Windsor, editor (*University of Windsor Review*) and poet (*In Transit*, 1975).

2. AP spent some time working on a book-length critical introduction to Birney's poetry before giving it up and handing over his taped interviews to Frank Davey. As later letters indicate, Birney was upset that AP gave tapes with some potentially embarrassing revelations to Davey, a relative stranger if a former student.

3. AP is referring to Moore's "The Archer" whose installation in Toronto's Nathan Phillips Square was being delayed by public controversy and hostility. Not Toronto's finest hour as a budding cultural capital.

To Earle Birney (Vancouver), from Ameliasburgh, July 11, 1966

Dear Earle,

Nothing much to say. Just got back from Trenton last night, after having meant to sleep there, but too damn hot. And how's that for inconsequential yak—

Have been writing poems pretty plentifully here in the last few weeks, but don't have a very high opinion of what I've written. I suppose I channel what vitality I have into poems, which means that I'm not doing things that provide more grist—Of course not doing things is money too, for I'd be in Greece or Rhodesia if I'd got that Gug. Add gossip: Colombo says in a note that Atwood got the centennial poem contest, but that I received honourable mention. He ends the sentence with an exclamation mark.

I suppose what I'm writing is more or less passable, but I think either you or myself would want to feel when we write the sort of lift and air bubbles in the veins that make it worth while—Incidentally, I took your suggestion re the Nor/west Passage poem, and interjected three quatrains with the third line of four stresses having a double rhyme. However, I don't think that does it either. Came across some good prose by John Ross, the old captain (1777–1856) who commented:

> "—let them remember that ice is stone
> a floating rock in the stream—"

It's not verse but it oughta be.

Also by Ross:

> "—being informed
> that we were Europeans
> they answered
> that they were men—"

Of course Ross finishes the last word of that quote by adding "Innuit" after, but it's better without.

I think I'll give the poem ("Passage" poem) one more try, with a different rhyme scheme in the middle, I should say different metric scheme, because I don't care whether it rhymes. Point about it is: if I could get one good thought in any damn rhythm at all, then I think I could carry that on thru—But jesus, it has to come out of my blank blank mind!

Have you heard of what Doug Jones calls a Frank Scott "love-in" later in the year? Almost sounds like a free whorehouse.

I'm beginning to feel exiled here, cut-off, trapped by wholesome womanhood in the shape of my wife. She probably feels the same with the proviso, male. The currents of life are elsewhere from me right now, tho I hope to locate them again, or what I think they are for me. In the meantime I type here with Eurithe in the other room looking at a crappy tv movie. Last night tho, we saw *Who's Afraid of V. Woolf*, which was not crappy. All Eurithe's brothers, sisters, relatives of any kind, didn't like it, so I was almost sure it would be good. How's that for snobbishness? But god, something to see the snarling snappy stuff of a bad marriage whipping into your eyeballs like healthy poison—If I didn't think such plays a dead end I'd think Albee was the next Williams or Miller.[1]

When you have some idle time let me know what's going on—

Best,

Al

1. Tennessee Williams (1911–83) and Arthur Miller (b. 1915) were the dominant American playwrights of the 1950s and 1960s. The former was best known for *The Glass Menagerie* (1944) and *A Streetcar Named Desire* (1947), the latter for *Death of a Salesman* (1949) and *The Crucible* (1952).

To George Woodcock (Vancouver), from Newfoundland, August 1966

Dear George,
Soon be leavin here, courtesy of the CNR I hope. Haven't got the Ingstad book yet, which I want badly in order to check it against what Mowat says, esp. the Carbon-14 datings. Mowat[1] sorta gives Ingstad the literary

brush-off, and implies strongly that he (Ingstad) even found the site under false pretences. i.e. that Geo. Decker, the farmer who owned the site-land, thought Ingstad was Jorgen Meldgard, a Danish arch.

Anyway, I think it's really not giving Ingstad a very fair shake. For Carbon-14 tests prove the charcoal at the side is pre-1000 AD.

Got your Birney review in *Forum*[2] along with other mail at Deer Lake, where it was sent on. I'm rather fond of Birney personally, but apart from that I do agree with you. Particularly on the point: (paraphrase you) he doesn't reveal himself. He doesn't even if you know him well either. But then, the person you can figure out really well is a distinct minority. A unicellular creature maybe, and there do seem to be such in the world.

Rain rain rain here. I'm so sick of scenery I'll never say a word about nature again, if I ever did before—I did see one solitary maple among all the spruce, poplar and birch. It was blazing red. Make you feel like waving it in Joey Smallwood's liberal face and saying "this tree is NDP, not Red, just socialist"—or some such foolishness.

I'm supposed to be meeting the students at UBC Nov 16–18 courtesy Canada Council, at which time we shall break some bread or a bottle—yes?

Yes, at this moment I am sick to death of Newfoundland. To write a play would call for at least 6 mos residence. Not me, I can't stay that long here. 5–6 poems so far, and I'm ahead of the game. J.M. Synge[3] must have been a hero to write *Riders to the Sea* if Ireland was like Nfld. That's extreme, of course, but like the Beothuck skeleton in St. John's I need a change—

Incidentally, I've reached the point where I will now enjoy writing this Mowat review—and hope you don't mind the delay.[4] But after reading Mowat my own ego shrinks in shame. But then, what is the right amount of ego suitable for a human being, let alone a writer? Not as much as he has anyway. [...]

Best,

Al

1. Farley Mowat (b. 1921): very popular, prolific and controversial writer, particularly on the Canadian north. His books include *People of the Deer* (1952), *Siber: My Discovery of Siberia* (1970), *Canada North Now: The Great Betrayal* (1976).
2. Woodcock reviewed Birney's *Selected Poems* in *Canadian Forum* (August 1966).
3. John Millington Synge (1871–1909): between 1898 and 1902 spent portions of the year on the Aran Islands off the west coast of Ireland. His experiences are

described in *The Aran Islands* (1907), and they also influenced *Riders to the Sea* (1904).

4. AP reviewed Mowat's *Westviking* and Helge Ingstad's *Land under the Pole Star* in *Canadian Literature* (Summer 1967). The review is reprinted in *Starting from Ameliasburgh*.

To George Woodcock (Vancouver), from Ameliasburgh, October 12, 1966

Dear George,

Inge wrote and said you'd had a bad time, but are recovering well etc.[1] I hope this last is true, and that you're able to rest without worrying about things, particularly writing. I don't know what to say in such situations, so after expressing my concern, and hope you'll be around soon, I'll leave it at that. Will call Inge when I get to Van. next month, and see how the nurses survived your visit to hospital. (I remember one when I was in RCAF hospital who used to rub my belly with alcohol—my feelings were mixed to say the least.)

Bryan McCarthy[2] just spent 8 days at the house here. He's writing a book on CC Fellowship, about CanPo. We spent two days consuming beer and the rest yak-yak, which consisted of 18–20 single-spaced pages of question and answer by the time he finished. Then off to area around Bancroft in camper to look at some tax land, to be sold at sale today at Belleville, the County Seat. About 70–80 miles north, same areas as in a poem of mine, "The Country North of Belleville." Place all lit up with autumn, red leaves and yellow, plus evergreen. That's what you poor westerners miss—for about one week one can believe God is a frustrated housepainter. Anyway, we acquired 124 acres at the tax sale, for slightly less than $1200. The original owner has the option of buying it back for the next year and a day, then title reverts to us. Roblin Lake is now surrounded by cottages, water-skiers in summer and roaring motor boats. So we decided to sell here, if and when we get final title to this land, and move north.

It seems I have a radio play coming Dec 23, a half hour piece on a program called *Introducing*. History of this piece of some interest: wrote it in '64 when Robert Weaver wanted a piece for D-Day, and took 5–6 weeks to do it, just before I left for Cuba. Then, 3 days before departure, neither Weaver nor Frank Willis liked it, so I had to write another play in those 3 days. Migawd I sweated blood for a while. Anyway, I wrote *Dormez Vous*, which they approved. And now, or I should say this last summer, while reading scripts for CBC they asked for plays for this new program. I gave em the one Weaver had turned down. (Not mentioning that, of course.) A really far-out piece, about a group of people on their way to a battle, which has already been fought and they arrive too late. This happens three times, and the dialogue and action has slight variations each time, tho the characters are basically the same. An apple tree with poisoned apples is tree of life, add symbolic stuff—All my interest in the piece has long ago disappeared, but it's nice to get paid for it at this late date.

Another visitor Friday, woman who's writing a children's novel, also a history of Prince Edward County.[3] Wants me to write her a letter on behalf of former project. Has one children's book coming with Peter Martin Associates in Toronto. Very interesting woman, sort of late-blossoming writer, since she has five half grown kids.

Introduced me to E.B. White,[4] whom you likely know, but one line of his is great: "And the geese cheered." What I started out to say was: all this activity and visitors has kept me way from Mowat's book. But a coupla more poems on the "Viking Coast" theme, with which I am pleased and also greatly discontented.

I'll copy the last one out, and also one of Kennedy I wrote a day or two ago. The last needs a line somewhat like Eliot's "some infinitely gentle infinitely suffering thing"[5] to make it work. But how the hell do you come up with a line like that unless you do? Also dissatisfied with the Birney piece, which Inge mentioned you had. It doesn't really get at Birney. But I'm sure there's another Birney, very different than the one in his poems and these essays on writing. The submerged Birney that I get hints of every now and then rouses my extremest curiosity.[6] [...]

Hope to see you in Van. I hope you won't be confined to coffee only. One develops these alcoholic tastes at great expense, seems a pity not to use them. Now maybe that's the trouble with growing old—one develops tastes in women and is either forbidden or can't use them. What was it Shaw said about the young? Something about youth being a wonderful thing and what a pity it's wasted on the young—only he said it better. You know the one.

Best,

Al

George—when I start to copy those poems I start to revise—and revise—and revise. I'm still doing it.

1. Inge Woodcock had written that George had suffered a heart attack.

2. Bryan McCarthy, see page 223. As with many other younger poets, AP often helped him by reading and commenting on his work.
3. Janet Lunn, see page 431.
4. E.B. White (1899–1985): American essayist, associated with the *New Yorker*, and children's novelist, best known for the classic *Charlotte's Web* (1952) and, perhaps, "Across the Street and into the Grill," his parody of Hemingway.
5. The line is from the fourth of Eliot's "Preludes": "I am moved by fancies that are curled / Around these images, and cling: / The notion of some infinitely gentle / Infinitely suffering thing."
6. AP's review of *The Creative Writer* appeared in *Canadian Literature* (Winter 1967). It has been reprinted in *Starting from Ameliasburg*.

Margaret Laurence (1926–87): best known for her Manawaka novels, *The Stone Angel* (1964), *The Jest of God* (1966), *The Fire-Dwellers* (1969) and *The Diviners* (1974). AP's friendship began with her when he and his wife stayed with her in England during Eurithe's convalescence after surgery. They corresponded regularly and at some length for nearly two decades. Each read the other's work and wrote more supportively than critically about it.

To Margaret Laurence (Elm Cottage, Penn, Bucks., England), from Ameliasburgh, December 10, 1966

Dear Margaret Laurence,[1]
Bob Weaver said I was going to meet you when I came back from Newfoundland this fall. However, you were in Manitoba at the time. Perhaps later.

I am just another admirer, and you have those ad nauseam I suppose. Went so far as to buy your books tho, and that's goin pretty far for me—I generally try to wrangle used or reviewed copies or some damn thing like that. Must admit tho, I intended to get you to sign them if I ever caught up with you personally. Incidentally, I hope you bawled out someone at McStew for the paper they used in *Jest of God*.

All best wishes,
Al Purdy

1. Purdy typed this as "Lurence" and corrected the misspelling by adding the missing "a" in ballpoint, followed by the hand-printed comment "AINT THAT AWFUL?"

From Margaret Laurence (England), to Toronto, January 16, 1967

Dear Al Purdy,

I was really glad to get your letter. Owing to one of those ironies of life, you were the person I most wanted to meet when I was in Canada this summer and the only person in the whole country (almost) whom I didn't meet. Actually, it was owing to a line from a poem in *The Cariboo Horses* that I went back to Canada at all last summer.[1] It wasn't exactly one rural winter—more one rural spring, when I sat beside my wet-beech-log fire, surrounded by nothing but beautiful trees, reading your poem and thinking at that moment with both amusement and rage that I also hated beautiful trees. The next day I walked into the CBC office in London and said "I'm homesick, and I'm going home," and my friend Ken Black there said "Okay, you can—let's see what we can do," and from that beginning sprung Bob Weaver's miraculous work in getting a Canada Council grant for me, including a travel grant which allowed me to go to Canada for the summer. Naturally, as soon as I hit Toronto I discovered that I didn't hate beautiful trees at all—what I hated was Avenue Road and the everlasting traffic which makes sleep impossible unless you are half stoned or preferably more so. It was good to see people like Bob, but otherwise I couldn't wait to get back here to my kids and this house which must have the frailest plumbing in the world (the tank on the toilet says charmingly but with vast inaccuracy, Pontifex's No-Sound). I guess I like this place because it doesn't claim perfection—it just staggers along somehow, with damp walls and other blemishes but it has elegance and warmth (spiritual; the physical warmth you have to work for constantly). I find it reassuring. Those beautifully appointed houses in Toronto give me the creeps. So I'm stuck here, and at the moment I have to buy this house, because it has to be sold, and either I buy it or I move out, and I can't bear to move out. Thus it was that I have spent the last month in Egypt, on an assignment (this sounds professional—but I've never done this sort of thing before) for *Holiday* magazine.[2] I am hoping to raise some money thereby. I took my two kids along (daughter 14; son 11) and we had a terrific month, so it wasn't wasted even if the magazine doesn't buy the articles. As it turned out, the Egyptians are very fond and sentimental re: kids, although they were a little uncertain about my nubile daughter (marriageable age in the UAR), but in general the presence of the kids paved my way considerably. I think they also believed that no one travelling with 2 kids could possibly be a spy. What I really want to do is to get these articles written and get started on another novel. A lot of life seems to be the process of clearing the decks, or maybe it only seems so to me because I only started earning my own living when I was 36 and that is probably leaving it a little late.

I didn't bawl out Mc & S for the paper (and, I may say, printing, binding, etc.) of *A Jest of God*, because I think they wanted to bring out their fall list of novels in some kind of uniform form and anyway what's the use. Also I dearly love Jack McClelland,[3] although we fight quite often.

You were in England about a year ago, I think, re: the Commonwealth Arts Festival[4] (what a fiasco), and I wanted to go to the evening which ludicrously combined Canadian poetry with W. Indian poetry, but unfortunately had to go to see a Yoruba opera that night. A friend of mine at Macmillan's told me about driving you and some other Canadian poets home that night, and thinking "My God, if we crash, Canadian poetry is finished."

If you can ever get to England some time, please phone and perhaps we can meet. Phone—Penn 2103

> Best Wishes,
> Margaret Laurence

p.s. have seen your Eskimo poems in *Parallel* and *Tamarack*,[5] and think they are—what? Difficult to say without sounding phoney. I like them. The people come across. And so do you.

1. The lines "surrounded by nothing / but beautiful trees / & I hate beautiful trees" are taken from Purdy's poem "One Rural Winter" in the collection *The Cariboo Horses* (1965), which had won the Governor General's Award for poetry.
2. The articles that resulted from this assignment, "Good Morning to the Grandson of King Rameses the Second" and "Captain Pilot Shawkat and Kipling's Ghost" were not published in *Holiday*, but appeared later in Laurence's collection of essays, *Heart of a Stranger* (1976).
3. Jack McClelland (1922–2004) had been president of McClelland and Stewart Publishers since 1961.
4. The Commonwealth Arts Festival took place September 16–October 2, 1965. The Cardiff conference of Commonwealth poets was part of the festival.
5. A bi-monthly journal of opinion and the arts, *Parallel* published in its second number (May–June 1966) three of Purdy's Arctic poems: "Canso," "Looking at Swinton's Book of Eskimo Sculpture," and "What Can't be Said." In its Spring 1966 issue, *The Tamarack Review* had published as "Arctic Poems" the following: a prelude poem, "Dead Seal," "At the Movies," "Metrics," "The North West Passage," "The Country of the Young," and "When I Sat Down to Play the Piano." This selection was preceded by Earle Birney's poem "in purdy's ameliasburg."

To Margaret Laurence (England), from Toronto, February 2, 1967

Dear Margaret,

Hadn't realized you were already flitted back to England. Bob Weaver had said by letter that we were all to have lunch together—

Just as well you didn't get to the Commonwealth Arts thing at the Royal Court—Was a shambles. And the thing at Cardiff was far worse. Bunch of American expatriate beats there, only a few, but they brought to my mind all the American articulateness of their State Department and public relations people, as poets, tho bad ones. The Africans, who didn't know English too well, couldn't keep talking pace with them. As you see, I am extremely anti-American, a Canadian trait said to be predominant.

Yeah, the ambivalent bit about "the beautiful trees." Of course maybe it's the soggy sentimental associations and heritage that one dislikes. Many poets have raved over nature, and the tendency still exists. But if you're marooned among the damn things by lack of money you don't appreciate nature quite so much. One always (I think) wants to reserve the power to say, "to hell with this place"—always a matter of money.

Your Egypt trip sounds good, and the idea of using kids as a front—! And I would love to go thru the touristy places, pyramids etc. Which I did last time in London, with John Colombo. Birney was busy keeping social engagements.

Your house sounds attractive etc.—tho from my point of view in order to write I have to go out and look for things I want to write about, i.e. put myself in a physical position where I'm enough involved in strangeness and the strands of an existence outside my own norm (never finish this sentence) so that I both want to and have things to write about (what a tangled sentence). Anyhow, maybe you're the sort of person who can hibernate in a cottage and write like hell at the same time, I suppose about past experiences filtering into now. I do that too, but generally feel like litmus paper about to change colour. (Violent purple?) Incidentally, have just written a piece about the house at Roblin Lake, which I'd like to copy, but it will take all the space. Will anyway.

INTERRUPTION[1]

When the new house was built
callers came:

black squirrels on the roof every morning
between sleep and wakefulness,
and a voice says "Hello dead man."
Chipmunks look in the windows
and you look out,
but neither moves
for their lifetime and half yours.
Orioles, robins and red winged blackbirds
are crayons that colour the air;
something sad and old
cries down in the swamp.
Moonlight in the living room,
a row of mice single file
route marching in the silver shade
until they touch one of my thoughts
and jump back frightened,
but I don't wake up.
Pike in the lake pass and re-pass the windows
with clouds in their mouth.
For 20 minutes every night
the sun slaps a red paint brush
over dinner dishes and leftovers
but we keep washing it off.
Birds can't take a short cut home
they have to go round the new house;
and cedars grow pale green candles
to light their way thru the dark.
Already the house is old:
A drowned chipmunk in the rain barrel this morning,
dead robins in the roof overhang,
and the mice are terrified—
We have set traps,
and must always remember
to avoid them ourselves.

Anyhow, I see there is extra space. Re Jack McClelland, I feel under the skin we don't like each other much. More feeling than anything. Incidentally, the same paper was used on Layton's new book,[2] and Irving is steaming a bit. Thankfully my own new book (May) is a sort of art book, with both Arctic poems and A.Y. Jackson repros,[3] so they can't very well use anything but good paper.

I hope you can finish articles and necessary money-making and get back to novels, your strong point—I suppose I'm doing an equivalent of articles in CBC work, couple of plays, hour long program of poetry and prose, also reading scripts to pay the rent.

In the event I get my fellowship this spring,[4] I will be in England on the way to Greece, and we shall have a drink or meal or whatever.

Best,
Al Purdy

1. The finished version of this poem was published in the collection *Wild Grape Wine* (1968).
2. *Periods of the Moon* (1967).
3. *North of Summer: Poems from Baffin Island* (1967) with illustrations by A.Y. Jackson (1882–1974), one of the Group of Seven.
4. AP had applied for a Guggenheim Fellowship.

To Margaret Laurence (England), from Ameliasburgh, April 20, 1967

Dear Margaret,
Thanks much for the Plath[1] books (didn't know she'd written a novel and curious about it), and let me know how much please.

Re Tutuola,[2] I picked up a couple of his in England in Faber softcover, started to read *The Palm-Wine Drunkard* but never got far, started to do something else probably. (Incidentally, William Golding[3] is another of my enthusiasms, I have all his books.)

Yeah, the bit about "who is less sincere than I—and who are the sinners?"—Some less perceptive, yes, for you don't expect a guy working in a factory etc. to be appreciative of the same things you are, and the guys I know could hardly think of anything but new cars, women and getting drunk. Of course money too. They spend their lives that way. But doubt if their lives are as much mixed up as my own.

Could be Plath decided not to survive because she saw what you say she saw, and perhaps also because she didn't satisfy herself in her own writing and her own life. Of course it sounds puerile when you put it down on paper, and I can't get around that. I think I used to feel and believe that a corner would be turned in my own life and I'd find the answer to things, the key, a flare would light in my head and my life would change—Rather silly, for it never happens. I guess some, maybe Bertrand

Russell, pick some "cause" and fulfil their life that way. Anyhow, it's the sort of thing you can sometimes talk personally about if the other person can talk on a discussion level. Yet, I'm a kinda combative conversationalist sometimes. Met a guy yesterday, should say I talked to him for the umpteenth time, and it always ends the same way. He goes on advancing his rigid fact-theories, I pay little attention to them and think they're mostly silly, and he does the same thing re what I say. Most frustrating. Enemies are never wholly enemies or friends friends—

Ottawa is 180 miles from here, Mtl. 250. I shall try to get to Ottawa when you're there, likely drive. Will try to catch your eye when you curtsy to Michener.[4]

I knew about your award beforehand, but was supposed to keep my mouth shut. However, I couldn't resist intimating you'd get it.

I hope you're writing like hell, because I'm not. Haven't written a good poem since that one I sent you (no connection) and dammit that irritates me tho I can't do a thing about it. I get the *Beaver* mag (HBC) yesterday with a poem of mine and the A.Y. Jackson repros that are to be used in my own book. I think they're terrible, and Jackson is a study in retarded development. I sure stuck my neck out re those paintings. Always do that tho, pull some enormous blunder—enormous to me anyway—then cuss my own stupidity. So Jackson will sell a few books of poems, but his paintings look like geriatric vomit done from habit. One step above "Autumn Woods" if you ever saw that abortion on suburban walls.

I think I've worked myself into too depressed a mood to write a letter. Be sure and let me know when you'll be in Ottawa and Mtl., and will see you then.

Best,

Al

1. Sylvia Plath (1932–63): American poet who moved to England in the early 1950s, married Ted Hughes in 1956. *The Colossus* appeared in 1960, her only novel *The Bell Jar* in 1963. She committed suicide in February 1963. The publication of *Ariel* in 1965 "established her reputation with its courageous and controlled treatment of extreme and painful states of mind" (*Oxford Companion to English Literature*).
2. Amos Tutuola (b. 1920): Nigerian novelist (*The Palm-Wine Drunkard and his Dead Palm-Wine Tapster*, 1952).
3. William Golding, see page 280.
4. Roland Michener (1900–91): Governor General of Canada from 1967–74.

To Margaret Laurence (England), from Ameliasburgh, July 8, 1967

Dear Margaret,

The way you seem to be feelin a long quiet drunk with a friend, someone you can talk to, would be a good idea. Universal panacea, they say, but at least it does bust your life into before and after. However, it must be fun burnin all that money you coulda had for the typescript. Anyway, I recommend a drunk, tho I ain't qualified to prescribe—that or twenty four hours fucking.

My book[1] is on the way to you surface mail. I suppose it takes weeks.

I sometimes, rarely, feel the same way you describe, tho maybe I am too lazy to take desperate measures. In one way I have an idea that, pleasant as it may be, that England is wrong for you as a writer. Nice pleasant cocoon alright, but what very close relations do you really have with people over there? And really, do you care very much either way? Burning one's bridges by selling one's cottage is just as violent a measure as burning immortal prose, besides you retain the cash deriving from figurative flames, and can use it to move around. In Africa I would think you lived emotionally off the people around you, but are not doin it now. Of course I'm givin you pretty simple answers to problems and it ain't that simple I know. But in a way it's a good thing that you can have such violent reactions (to the English desert I'd say), and can realize something is damn wrong.

Yeah, the goddam antho [*The New Romans*] is hovering over me all the time. To say the least, I don't like it. Why the hell did I get into it? Dunno, tho I thot it a good idea at the time. Still is, but wish someone else would do it. Deadline is, say, end of Oct. Lotsa time.

BBC says they won't send the money to you taxfree the bastards. I'll take em into small debts court or something?

Still, there must be something purifying about burning a novel. Can't imagine doing it to poems. I now staple all the hand-written work sheets and then staple a typewritten version to them, so that it must look like twentieth century dead sea scrolls. I can imagine some poor bastard trying to figure out what I'm like from reading them—so many contradictions nobody could do it. Especially me. So anyway, I cheer your pyromaniac self, while my scotch blood boils sympathetically for all that money up in the clouds mingling with Strontium 90.

Now hafta get back to antho, goddam it. One real sizzler, poem, makes US sound like a decadent Assyria over-running the Children of Israel.[2] I hope you get paid at Oxford, which gives me a vision of a lot of old men running around in black night gowns.

Best,

Al

1. *North of Summer.*
2. Perhaps Eric Nicol's (b.1919) "Dat ol' man river," which appeared in *The New Romans*, although many of the poems in the anthology could be described as "sizzlers."

To Margaret Laurence (England), from Ameliasburgh, August 22, 1967

Dear Margaret,

First congrats on the movie sale, and this should give you money to do what you like and live where you like. The tyranny of money lifted, or I suppose so and hope it's into large enough figures to do that.

Second, I've been looking at *Chatelaine*'s on the newstands, and can only find Aug. and Sept. and your story in neither. As well, I seem to know no one who subscribes to the mag. So I'm writing the publishers and asking for that copy.

Thank you for your reaction to the book. It's probably as good a description, and flattering to me, as I've seen. Even if poetry isn't your specialty you could still review the stuff. I had the idea when I went north, that no book I'd read had given me the feeling of what it was like to be there, the colour, smells etc., just the reality. The authors would describe, but they didn't make you feel the place. All travel writers, just about tho. The way you put words down on the page I envy, and doubt very many novelists can do it so well. I'm often stopped in attempting to describe feelings and have to do it by eliminating the false ones to get at the real ones, those that strike me as right and true. But in a letter your prose still looks good, as if you said exactly or very nearly what you were getting at—Different sort of mind from mine, I suppose—Damned if I know the difference between a poet and a novelist anyway, this ability with words is certainly superior to mine.

Kabloona[1] is by De Poncins, which I have but haven't read. And yeah, the pictures are not exactly crap, but they seem very old-fashioned to me. But a lot of older people and art addicts may buy the book because of them. I shouldn't complain—Coupla reviews, three—two quite favourable, and one favourable with reservations. The writer picked out the poem "Innuit" and said I didn't see the old man at all but "merely some vague person of my own" and how distasteful that was. In a way he's right, since I didn't treat the old man as other than a focal point for my "race-soul" idea, especially since I didn't know the old man. But I don't think the idea of a "race-soul" is vague, although it might be hard to express in concrete terms, since who the hell has a touchable soul anyway. But Eskimo sculpture, and I suppose African sculpture, is much more representative and typical of those cultures than white sculpture is of white culture, especially since the physical medium of soapstone and ivory is more limited than material available to white sculptors. Anyway, re the book, I like indulgently to think that I did something re the north that hadn't been done (other than by Robert Service[2] who is so different from me), treat the north as a real place with real, tho different people. This is pretty egotistic on my part, but what the hell. When all the reviews are in I'll find out what the consensus is. My idea is that the big weakness of the book is that it didn't treat the lousy dirty side sufficiently. But much of the time up there I was in a state of mild euphoria at just being there. The Eskimos at Frobisher Bay, for instance, are in a helluva bad situation, belonging to neither world, white or Eskimo, drinking and the occasional murder. But I didn't see any of the murders and drinking, I did see what I wrote about. And reviewers are bound to ask for things I didn't see. Anyway, glad you enjoyed it.

I don't think that's bad, wanting to be other than where you are, so long as it isn't a continual psychic state. Personally, I get sick of most places if I'm there long enough. I go on these jesus reading tours and drink too much and eat too much and come back perfectly content for a while, then get restless again. But I guess we're all peripatetic travellers over the earth—no, not all, but many of us. That bit you mention about "values and loves here"—one doesn't lose them by going away (or am I being trite and obvious) doesn't one set them in another perspective, perhaps a clearer one? One realizes the value of things gone after they're gone—And I keep thinking I'm speaking crap, and I guess I am. Obvious things.

Yeah, Ludwig's[3] charm—it's undeniable, tho when I met him I had the idea he didn't really see me at all (just as the reviewer thought of me and the Eskimo carver), but likely didn't think of a Purdy race-soul. Very confident and sure, so much so that he seemed not to [make more] than the obvious cordial gestures, and was more curious about you/me than anything else, and quite a mild curiosity. He also strikes me as the professional academic and speech-giver, at gatherings of students and profs, rather than the pro. novelist. I am envious of his ability to talk on his feet, which I have not got, and yet feel this quality detracts in some way I don't know. It over-balances him into being more a public personality than anything else.

Why don't you get a job as a script writer for your own film? That would pay all expenses, give you a trip somewhere in the US and time for Canada too. If you get enough money you can hire a girl to do the dishes etc. and you can write. Does that sorta thing work?

If you are in London and feeling good-natured can you get me some more books? Don't repeat don't, go looking for them if you aren't in book stores anyway. But if you are, and the Hakluyt Society's books are there gettem to send me Vol. CXIII *The Troublesome Voyage of Cap. Edward Fenton*, ed. Taylor, and Vols CXIV–CXV *The Prester John of the Indies*, ed. Beckingham and Huntingford. No idea how much money. I have a passion for authentic sea stuff, partly because of the archaic language and Coleridge, I suspect. For chrissake don't go to any trouble—but can't resist taking advantage of a willing woman????? I paid ten bucks for one of the Hakluyts in a Mtl. book store, which is six bucks over-price. I resent that slightly.

Personal—I am goddam sick of poems and poetry, ALL poems and poetry, even my own. Tho did write one I like ["Joe Barr"], which I copy on reverse, first one I liked of my own in mos. Anthos are awful. Nevermore quoth Poe. Least not till I'm dead broke. Off to Expo as an observer next month, where Pound and Neruda and lesser lights hold forth.[4] I shall get their books autographed to ride my hobby horse still farther. Possibility of short term grant to live three mos in Ottawa and look at the House of Commons, CC of course.[5] Another crazy idea for poems. Culture is for non-writers. Wouldn't mind talking of books and poems, particular ones, but not god save us culture. See I'm ended.

Best,

[unsigned]

1. *Kabloona* (1941) was written by Gontran de Poncins in collaboration with Lewis Galantière. It describes the fifteen months Poncins spent with the Eskimos in the High Arctic in 1936–39.
2. Robert W. Service (1874–1958): popular novelist (*The Trail of Ninety-Eight: A Northland Romance*, 1911) and poet (*Songs of a Sourdough*, 1907; *The Spell of the Yukon*, 1907). Though he arrived in Canada in 1896 and is now part of the Canadian canon, it is worth recalling that he was born in England, grew up in Scotland, settled in Paris after the the First World War and died in Monte Carlo.
3. Jack Ludwig (b. 1922): novelist (*Confusions*, 1963; *Above Ground*, 1968). With Saul Bellow and Keith Botsford, he founded and edited the magazine *The Noble*

Savage. It has been suggested that Valentine Gersbach, one of the characters in Bellow's *Herzog*, is a portrait.
4. Pound and Neruda (1904–73) took part in an art festival held at "Expo '67," the international exhibition held in Montreal from April 28 to October 27, 1967.
5. AP received the grant.

To Margaret Laurence (England), from Ameliasburgh, September 16, 1967

[Salutation missing]
Hey, you comin back to Canada! I shall burn a candle for your arrival at the H-bomb factory. Or re-invent the heliograph to signal Aldebaran[1]. Always wanted to signal Aldebaran anyway.

I have got your mag, Chatelaine sent *Chatelaine*, shall roll it up tightly to cut down air resistance and throw vigorously east.

Have just got back from Expo World Po., Toronto tapings and script judgings, reading at Queen's, and just writ 19 (nineteen) letters tonight, this being the 20th and longest and last. I'm dizzy! You figured that out anyway, of course.

You describe a complicated mental and physical situation in your letter. Migawd. "cats and roses"! Of course, there is the perhaps point, if you get back here all your best friends might be English. I doubt that tho. There is also this: you can go to any damn place in Canada and write about it if you're able to. I doubt like hell if you can do that in England. Course I could be terribly wrong. But I, me, self, do feel this way. I could only write about England from my Can. point of view. Okay, I'll try again. I mean, suppose you take a shack near Toronto, and if things are right there you'll write about it. As a comparison, HAVE you already done this in dear old Bucks? Sure you'll find a shack. Tell Jack McClelland you want one of his smaller outbuildings (say seven rooms) moved to the beach past Scarborough on LakeOnt. Perish the goddam cats and roses. What a title! Makes me wriggle to think of it.

Yeah, moving is terrible. I'm just doing it by the way. Goin to Ottawa on a short term CC grant. After Oct. 1, plan to attend House of Commons and make a fool of myself writing about the other fools. Address: 173 Waverly, Apt. 1.

If you can drive and pick up a car then a city is easy to reach. At least some are. Toronto especially. Of course you'll perhaps get tired of that too, but so what—there are more good places to go. I'm being glib here, for maybe you're not the same as me in that. But if I could write like you I'd wander to all the Can. places and write a book about em. George Woodcock did about BC,[2] but you bein you I expect you'd want a thick gooey theme to hold it together. [...]

Oh, Ludwig meant what did you think of me personally—Isn't that strange. We all do it, ask people what they think of other people. I think of people who I'm sure had several different sets of thoughts which they could think simultaneously. Some people can talk about one thing, think another, and have still another in their mind, and maybe some of these thoughts merge around the edges and we're liable to get sunset all over thoughts of our friends.

It never occurred to me about Ludwig protecting himself in his novel. Of course he isn't straightforward in his story, which as I recall seemed to slide one way and another. No, you couldn't put your finger on the author till the end, when he came out with his "life philosophy" or something. I thought it a failure, but an interesting one, good in spots. I don't remember what I meant by that sentence you quote. I sometimes forget the beginning of a paragraph at the end of it. [...]

Okay, if you can get books will send money to acc't you let me know about—And thanks. Books are comin outa my ears and nostrils. They tickle too. House is fulla them, on the floor, all tables, shelves, open, shut, half-read, never read, never will be read, blue orange scarlet beautiful beautiful. [...]

The reading at Queen's was pretty good, Layton and I, about 500 people there, mostly freshmen, some sitting in the aisles. Very seldom get an audience that large or as enthusiastic. I went to the hotel in Kingston, met Layton downstairs and arranged to meet him shortly after washing up. So I went to my room, but it turned out to be Layton's room, and my key surprisingly unlocked his door. I hadn't looked at the number on my key. Anyway, I looked around and saw all Layton's poems ready for him to read that evening, and I said gleefully I'll never never get a chance like this again. So I put all Layton's poems and briefcase under the bed, went out and locked the door and went to the right room. Layton and my wife and I went to dinner and came back. Then I went to Layton's room to get him for the reading. He looked at me grey as a faded maple leaf and said "Al, I left my briefcase at that restaurant and it has all my poems!" I couldn't keep my face straight and told him he hadn't left it at the restaurant and confessed. But I could see a whole train of happenings, Layton and I back at the restaurant asking about his briefcase, the worried arrangers of the reading, myself perfectly innocent but struggling inside. Must stop I see. Thanks for book. *Chatelaine* on the way to you.

Best,

Al

1. Aldebaran is the brightest star in the constellation Taurus.
2. *Ravens and Prophets: An Account of Journeys in British Columbia, Alberta and Southern Alaska* (1952).

To Margaret Laurence (England), from Ottawa, November 26, 1967

Dear Margaret,

Reading your letter again about writing this novel, have decided I never want to write one, not unless I have everything in my head and the thing absolutely demands to get out. I am slightly familiar with this idea of evasion, since I used to write plays for CBC, or perhaps should say I tried to, since I had about fifteen accepted and produced of the more than hundred written. I used to try to get to work every day on the play I was writing, after having presumably got the plot complete in my head (tho it never was complete), and before I'd settle down at the typewriter I'd do all sorts of silly things, like making coffee, washing dishes (I was alone most of the time), just walking back and forth back and forth thinking about the damn thing. Does all this have a familiar ring? I would get the mail first, I'd do any damn thing before getting to work, and when I did get to work I'd work all sorts of odd times, some days for only a few minutes, others for hours and hours. I had the idea then, and I probably still have it, that I ought to feel absolutely mentally alert and bright, that I ought to have had a good long sleep the night before, and that this sharp edge obtained would only last a short time. Therefore I had the readymade excuse to stop whenever my head so much as nodded. And I believed I had some sort of God-given right to go off on tangents whenever I felt like it, to write poems etc. etc. It's a wonder I ever got any work done.

If you're right about assessing your own difficulties, they are much more complicated than mine. You believe most of your difficulties unconnected apparently with writing, are actually and really connected with writing. You'll be having your husband and cottage and kids in the next novel (not that I suppose they aren't in the previous ones somehow as well as yourself) and the whole structure of your life. The trouble is that one sees thru one's own self-deceptions in these matters, but just being cleverer than one's non-clever self doesn't enable

136

one to surmount it. There must be yet another self that observes, cynically or otherwise, that sees the two selves struggling with each other and the physical world of writing and non-writing. We don't know about the third self, and the proposition that "it" is there at all must be arrived at like astronomers predicting new stars and comets and such on the basis of the way the solar system acts (that's the first two selves), and some hunk of rock behind Jupiter is causing a hitch in its orbit. Therefore, I wonder if I still do want to write a novel, just because I say I don't? The bastard me is watching the first two me's, and I don't like being manipulated by another me because I don't like outside interference even tho it is by me, if you follow this which I'm beginning not to—

I seem to be doing a lot of different things, and if I could split up the work among my different selves I'd be willing to pay myself union wages. Writing reviews and coupla short pieces about poetry for local paper, anthology, readings at Carleton, talking to creative writing class and denying the necessity of being a prophet (they all want you to be that, and it irritates me) reviews for lit mags. Bob Weaver asked me to do about a dozen poets for a coming ish,[1] and I couldn't refuse Weaver very much, and ambiguously not sure if I wouldn't want to anyway. Also writing poems. Meant to include a short one here if I can find room. The hell with the Birney book, their "advance" is not really an advance, and the money comes only when the book is done and accepted. Besides, I'd like to get Birney's love-life and everything else in such a book and he and they wouldn't like that—Wow! Always, or rather used to, tell Birney if he died before me I was gonna grind him up and marinate him for an aphrodisiac. I like the guy, but could never figure out his apparent attraction to women. He uses his poet-self of course . . .

IS THIS THE MAN?[2]

When I see the cabinet ministers rising
un-Venuslike from the sewage
of words and one particular old
buffalo assumes by accident a pose
of statesman delivering cost estimates
like a police lieutenant I say to myself
"Is this the man?"

Or the member left over after redistribution
rises during the question period
to say we stand on guard and how
patriotism swells the bosom and the member
rises for royal commission to investigate same
again Mr. Speaker I question myself
"Is this the man?"
No doubt the Minister of Trade and Commerce
and the Minister of External Aff. & Transport
and the Minister of Economic Integration with the US
are all honest and some bilingual
but the cost in time and money
comes high to find the man I'm looking for
and none here seems remotely capable
of running the affairs of my small
village of Ameliasburg
when the reeve retires next month

These goddam air mail letters are a fiendish business, since you either have too much or too little space and can't feel comfortable knowing the sentence is gonna end with a whimper and all the meaningful and delightful things you mighta said can't be goddam said because a word from a poem (in this case) projects like a phallic whatever into your thoughts—Which gets silly, but the blank space below irritates me, but it irritates me more to say silly things to fill it. Of course another air mail letter right now, but that's cheating, must be concise etc. I was never concise, always shapeless, formless and blundering off outside the edges of whatever it was.

                              Best,
                              Al

1. Purdy's review appeared in *The Tamarack Review* (Spring 1968). Entitled "Aiming Low," it commented on new collections of poems by George Jonas, D.G. Jones, Roy Kiyooka, A.J.M. Smith, Dennis Lee, Raymond Souster, P.K. Page, Lionel Kearns, Dorothy Livesay, George Woodcock and Alden Nowlan. Also included in the review was *The Making of Modern Poetry in Canada* edited by Louis Dudek and Michael Gnarowski. It is reprinted in *Starting from Ameliasburgh*.
2. The poem was published in *Wild Grape Wine*.

To George Woodcock (Vancouver), from Trenton, March 1, 1968

Dear George,

Expect you're back in Switzerland now, and thought I'd send a thank you note for your supporting letters, since I just received word of getting the CC Fellowship, and now await the Guggenheim results. I am very grateful and all that sort of thing for your help. Let it go at that, for it can never be expressed anyway.

I'm definitely, now, doing a book on Birney, and looking toward it with foreboding. Have made tapes with him, but got nowhere close to what I was looking for. I wanted to relate changes in his own life with his poems—you know, suddenly he discovers Sartre[1] and how does this affect his poems? But like I said, got nowhere on this tack. There must be another Birney somewhere, dammit, for if there isn't I'm chasing nothing. Of course he's a damn impersonal poet, says really very little about himself, only gives his reactions to situations and conditions.

Final manuscript for *The New Romans* (the US book) is nearly finished and wife and myself off to Mexico (driving) for a month. In fall to Greece, Italy, and other archeaological places, possibly also Rhodesia and S. Africa if I have enough money. We hope to get away south in perhaps ten days.

I hope Sicily was okay for you. Incidentally, enjoyed your piece on the McCarthy book in *CanFor*[2]—thinking: Vietnam is one place I don't wanta go. For myself, been so wrapped up in this antho haven't done enough writing and will soon forget how. Week or two ago tried a Vietnam poem, trying to keep away from the blood and guts stuff. Will copy it.

OVER THE PACIFIC[3]

I do not know very much about Vietnam
except that death happens there quite frequently
    (happens?)
I am ignorant of the birds
and small animals they have there
but can easily imagine the Canadian robin
arriving every spring among the rice paddies
and Canadian blue jays fly thru the jungles
whip-poor-wills in the uncertain dusk
wondering whether to sing or not
maybe even the northern loon

with his cry like a newborn ghost
of lakes and rivers and evergreen forests
hovering over the marshy distances
the voice behind the many faces of the north
which is the inarticulate essence of Canada
Of course it is impossible
but I would like to send our birds there
the singable ones that is
or even small animals with a comic growl
who could never hurt anything
as ambassadors to the Vietnamese

                              Best to both of you,
                              Al

1. Jean-Paul Sartre (1905–80): novelist (*La Nausée*, 1938), philosopher (*L'Être et le néant*, 1943) and political activist, as central to the intellectual and political life of France in his day as Victor Hugo was to his.
2. Woodcock reviewed Mary McCarthy's *Vietnam* in the February issue of *The Canadian Forum*.
3. The poem was published in *Wild Grape Wine* (1968).

To George Woodcock (Vancouver), from Athens, January 13, 1969

Dear George,
Greeting—Everywhere I look in mags I see George Woodcock has another book out or coming soon, and I'm so damn jealous I can hardly stand it—I also note your piece on the true north in *SatNite*,[1] and look forward more to the book on Canada in general than, probably other things—

I am writing like hell here, but poems, not the book on Birney which I am supposed to do. Have written 5–6 thousand words of that and when I look at it it disgusts me—I will face it then turn my back on it, I am not a critic!

But I am very pleased with the poems, some 16–18, I've written, particularly one, which is fairly long (two pages) or I'd send it along.

Incidentally, I've forgotten what I was supposed to write about myself, something to the effect of myself at age 25 and on or something: great philosophy I have regurgitated ass-backwards into poems—Something like that I think—however, letter from Gary Geddes[2] says you're using an interview he did, so therefore you won't need another piece from me—The interview probably says things I'd say myself anyway—I've noticed I repeat myself when talking about such subjects, harp on the same themes etc. i.e. I stress variety monotonously often and have none thru said stressing—

As I write this I'm just told there's a letter from you at the first address I had in Athens—Incidentally, I hope no small cheques or large have been sent for anything I've done for *CanLit*, since I believe a batch of letters sent on to me some time ago from Belleville are now definitely lost, which gripes me somewhat—

Anyway, we are settled in a three room suite in Athens at five bucks a day, which undoubtedly would cost $20 in Canada—10-year-old brandy is $1.50 a bottle, and I read the *Herald Trib*, *New Statesman*, listen to football games on US Armed Forces Radio and sometimes go to US movies which are generally bloody awful—If it keeps up my paranoia will take a dangerous turn—I had some hope for and from Trudeau at first, but seems not likely now—

I note Ernest Buckler[3] has another novel out, which I also hope to read soon—His first was great I thought, his second an ambitious flop, and this one—? Also William Golding has had a new one[4] for a year now—Later, I'm looking forward to canvassing London bookshops at some length—I know enough about older Canadiana to know bargains when I see them—

We shall be taking off for Crete in the next week or two, in meantime I enclose a verse for Inge—

ST. PAUL to the CORINTHIANS[5]

We decided some time back that
we were stuck with each other more
or less when I said "You bitch" it no
longer meant she was exactly
that but conversely it ain't
no valentine either when she says
"You bastard" it means I may
be one but she forgives me
which is rather harder to bear
And I want the people to know
                                        —Corinth, Gr.

                         Best to both of you,
                         Al

141

1. "The New Arctic White Man" appeared in *Saturday Night* in November 1968.
2. Gary Geddes, see page 284.
3. Ernest Buckler (1908–84): Nova Scotia novelist, author of the classic *The Mountain and the Valley* (1952) and *The Cruelest Month* (1963). AP may be referring to *Ox Bells and Fireflies* (1968).
4. Golding's *The Pyramid* appeared in 1967.
5. "St. Paul to the Corinthians" was published in *Love in a Burning Building* (1970).

To George Woodcock (Vancouver), from Elm Cottage, Penn, Bucks., England, April 6, 1969

Dear George,

[. . .] Re the article[1] I sent, I was very much aware that it was not dealing directly very much—for some reason I found that difficult, though I've been yakking away with Margaret Laurence for what seems days on that very subject. Her idea is that one is visited, in the best moments, with a condition of non-religious grace, and she applies this term to a lot of writers, including Graham Greene and Joyce Cary.[2] My own thoughts are to the effect that while writing the mind will inexplicably take sideways darts and tangents that seem much more interesting than the main theme of what is being written, and that these tangents must be followed and fully explored. Much of the time they will oddly be relevant to the main theme, or even take over from the main theme. This and Margaret's "grace" seem closely related to me. It is not at all similar to what is meant by the term "unconscious writing," since one knows what one is doing, is completely self-aware while possessed by a jubilant feeling. But to go on is to lapse into clichés. Re the article again, I could give this another try if necessary. Try to connect the physical and mental at different times of my life—but then you may have enough.

Somebody told me—I think it was Margaret—that your reputation over here is pretty high, even though you've been away for years. I expect this is true, since the price on that first book would indicate something of the sort. At any rate, those early books are damn hard to pick up. [. . .]

Best,

Al

ANNE OF GREEN GABLES OPENS IN LONDON

The only fly speck on Anne's
epidermal horizon was

the guilty freckle unshaveable
she implored Lucy Maud
Montgomery to remove electrically
in order that she might never
grow up with flawless armpits
queerly attractive to Anne's
one true lover

(last line an echo of Leonard Cohen)

1. AP is probably referring to "Purdy at 25" which he published in *Intercourse*
(October 1968).
2. Graham Greene (1904–91): one of AP's favourite novelists. He mentioned several times in conversations with me that he couldn't understand why Greene was never awarded the Nobel Prize.

To Margaret Laurence (England), from Ameliasburgh, May 31, 1969

Dear Margaret,
[. . .] Have another review that really alarms me. This by Pacey, who has condemned my stuff for centuries now.[1] That he should suddenly like it means I must be finished, the poem I writ this morning has to be shit. I can hear the nasal intoning of "Dearly beloved, we are gathered here to celebrate John Philip Grove and Al Purdy who was not the least of these in life—" I mean Frederick Philip Grove, which mistake illustrates what I mean.[2] Life indeed has its turn-arounds not to mention its upsidedowns.
[. . .]
Hey, did you get Greene's essays?[3] If not, buy one for me, read it to yourself then mail it to me. Let me know cost—which is $8.50 here and hurts. This way looks after both of us, and two birds make better pot-pie than one. Besides, after reading another review I can't resist Greene.
Milton Acorn came down here for a—groan—several day visit. I would have you know that Acorn is not like other acorns, he does not lie still on the forest floor and shut his big yap. He talks. He wakes at 6 a.m. and stalks thru the house reciting poems, all of which sound like the King James version. Luckily Eurithe went north to clean mouse shit from farm, Acorn and my own child went with her, and I am happily free and alone a short time. But my watch stopped, and I phoned to find out the time to find out as well that Eurithe is on her way back down south with a

sick diabetic aunt who refuses to take insulin, apparently visiting woodsy witch doctors instead. So I'm fucked up again. Acorn is the only person I can think of off-hand who won't let me work. Or sleep. Or even sit in silence. He just got sixteen hundred dollars from CC and is happily basking in liquor and contented ego, expecting me to celebrate both. I expect pity by return mail.

Just writ pome called "Astronot,"[4] which I feel will set back space exploration to Jules Verne,[5] if not stop it forever.

Read poems at Albert College—very peculiar biz. Once went to Albert myself way back in Thirties. Figured when I got the invite: old grad returns (I didn't grad—I ran away in the night) to accept honour due etc. Funny thing—I wasn't there because the Eng. Dept. wanted me but because the graduating class did. Very religious school, Albert, god in every classroom and chapel 99 times a day. Hear from the one teacher that arranged it to suit grad. class that I am a stench in the nostrils of religious men which I feel kinda flattering. Anyway, I read, same as always, and hear the headmasters sneaked in and departed quick. No real nasty words in my poems, least not many, but I don't sound cultured I suppose. Anyway, drank beer in this teacher's apt. later after all students under 21 screened out—Peculiar, eh? Also $150. and it makes me wonder how the students dug it up.

You and your talks and lectures. Me, I gotta teach two weeks, believe me baby, no more. Never still not once again more no sir.

No outsider could comment really on this break-up of yours, tho outsiders always do. All one can say if he wants it to go ahead and ditto you, which is heartless nothing. Must admit from you that it sounds like it's gone too far for any mending, the ass being out of the marriage, which I like and is hereby copyrighted. Phone Belleville, 962-7809.

Rather amazingly the Canada Council sent me a copy of Ray Souster's manuscript, asking me if I think it worth publishing and deserves a subsidy. I'm surprised that Souster can't find a publisher and the CC thinks his book needs any opinion.

Have somehow come up with a headache, undoubtedly from the sediment in the last bottle of scotch. I didn't even get the Racial-Rachel bit till after re-reading your letter, so I think you're a bit prejudiced in favour of understanding. The Laurence books are all lined up on my shelves in one spot. Impressive. Did I say St. Martin's Press sent me a de luxe leather bound ed with marbled end papers of *New Romans*? Surprising, but I suppose they must do that for all the books they publish. But if the pub.

binds such a minor book as *Romans* they oughta come up with some good copies, really well-done, of yours.

Must stop, coffee and codeine I guess.

Best,

Al

1. Review of *Wild Grape Wine. The Fiddlehead* (March–April 1969).
2. Pacey had published *Frederick Philip Grove* in 1945.
3. *Collected Essays* (1969) by Graham Greene.
4. Published in *Love in a Burning Building*.
5. Jules Verne (1828–1905): the popular French writer who was the first novelist of modern science fiction.

To Earle Birney (Vancouver), from Ameliasburgh, June 18, 1969

Dear Earle,

Could be you're right that whoever writes the Birney book will do a worse job than me—I hadn't realized this possibility very strongly till I looked at the new McStew series. McLuhan, Laurence, Pratt[1] and some guy named joe. Yes, they are most jesus dull. I suppose also that the book Bowering is supposed to be writing about me may also be this bad, which gives me hernia of the ego or something—

We don't know when we're gonna drive west exactly. I have a stint at Ryerson Polytechnic in August as Colombo's acolyte in a creative writing class or seminar, or whatever it is. Also some CBC work, coupla readings—Re Lowry book, dunno whether to sympathize or not, since sympathy from someone who abandoned a Birney book seems obscurely insulting. [. . .]

I am glad to hear Joe [Rosenblatt][2] is writin good stuff, tho I'm not sure what you think is good and I do too, very often coincide in the case of Joe. As you've pointed out, I'm much too intolerant of poets who write in a way I don't approve. I sometimes even excommunicate them, that is don't buy their books. Letter from Joe re the Acorn book which he'd seen, saying something to the effect that I'd saved Acorn's life, which is a bit much. Acorn was a bit down tho, but he has bounced back since pub. of book, psycho, paranoid and schizoid as ever. He was down here for a week, the first night of which he got up from bed at 6 a.m. and started to recite (loudly) poems. I mentioned in a penetrating whisper that I didn't appreciate his goddam shit at that time of the morning, whereupon he challenged me to fisticuffs which I refused disdainfully telling him to go out and get a reputation. But it was a fairly eventful visit. He just got a short term CC, and we went to a bank and got travellers cheques, which he lost as soon as he came into the house here, which I expected him to do but forgot to expect it at the time he did it. Later (June 12) we read at Classic's Book store, and had to be outside on accounta too many for store. So apt. owner called the police, which made it comfy. Acorn ranted, if you know what I mean. Never heard him do it quite the same before, actually ranted, emphasizing either vowels or consonants until you couldn't tell what the hell he was saying. Ah well—

You must be depressed to quote Chaucer like that—What is it, really, anyway? Age? Hell, I feel the same way a lot of the time, and Eurithe has taken off 5–8 pounds which irritates the hell outa me when I look at her,—and this surely indicates age, when you're irritated that your wife can take off weight and you can't, instead of appreciating the improvement in her figure. That's the goddam trouble with marriage as you know well—You look askance at yourself, as well as others whose condition is, as you say, "the way it should be"—I'm far too self-centred to think everything is as it should be unless everything serves all my needs and whims too—Morning after—Some people showed up from Kingston who'd been reading my stuff and came along to see if the flesh equalled the fictional character created on paper. I don't think it did, since people generally make up their mind what you are beforehand from your poems anyway. Still, it was an afternoon of beer etc. Tom Marshall,[3] whom I like, also came down with the others—Generally have the feeling that I'm expected to perform for such people, as Layton has it in some poem or other. They *want* to be impressed by the flesh, which is where Irving has an advantage, if one thinks it's important to impress them with more than poems.

I continually say to myself that poems are the most important thing, and yet there's a good chance that I'm obscurely and unfigure-outably lying to myself too—One part of one's mind thinks one should be golden boy, having the personality of Trudeau (who even before he got into politics had the personality to make everyone else in a room aware of him). (How did I get on this subject? Must be depressed this morning.) However, in my own mind I think a good poem says "Fuck you" to all the golden boys—

As you probably know, I growl at Eurithe too, having done it so long it seems a natural male condition of existence—generally my growling is not straightforward, has motives she doesn't know about. And to think another person is that important as to keep one's real motives concealed—well, it just proves the basic dishonesty of poets, Purdy in particular. However, I suppose the point of mentioning this is we've been together night and day almost continually for the last year, and I'm feeling very polygamous—either as a result or as a natural condition.

Well, off that subject. I wrote the moon-poem, not the "celebration" poem they wanted, but a rather sarcastic don't-care-much-effort. Didn't like it myself, which bothered me that I didn't, so wrote another—and this too has goddam little to do with celebrating the astronauts landing on the moon and planting the US flag which may wave forever the papers say—Called "Nine Bean-rows on the Moon,"[4] and I give a Chaucer scholar one guess as to where that title comes from. You see how straight forward I am?

Getting too long-winded. We don't know when we're gonna take off for the west. Will let you know tho, when we do.

Best,

Al

1. The McLuhan and Pratt volumes were by Dennis Duffy and Milton Wilson. There was no volume dedicated to Laurence.
2. Joe Rosenblatt, see page 154.
3. Tom Marshall (1938–93): novelist (*Goddess Disclosing*, 1992) and poet (*Dance of the Particles*,1984). AP wrote the elegy "A Sorrow for Tom" on his death. He also refers to his death in "Bits and Pieces" (*Naked with Summer in Your Mouth*) and "Departures" and "The Names the Names" (*To Paris Never Again*).
4. The allusion is to Yeats's "The Lake Isle of Innisfree": "I will arise and go now, and go to Innisfree, / And a small cabin build there, of clay and wattles made: / Nine bean-rows will I have there, a hive for the honey-bee, / And live alone in the bee-loud glade."

To Earle Birney (Vancouver), from Ameliasburgh, August 5 or 6, 1969

Dear Earle,
I'm kinda lonesome for Birney, sitting in the midst of rural Ont. with beautiful trees waving in the breeze etc. However, the delay getting west is for money's sake (not because I want to work at the same school with Colombo—incidentally, there's even a slight double-cross re this last antho he's doing with Hurtig, but then my paranoia and Birney's perhaps cancel out)—I have the last instalment of CC grant, and not a great deal more, since spent so much in Europe. Therefore I am creating a lit agency called "E. Parkhurst Agency" of 91 Cannifton Rd., Belleville. This agency has already written thirteen letters on my behalf to univs in Ont.

soliciting readings at $150. per. More letters to western univs soon when I get all their names and places. Friend who's doing a book in Trenton (unbelievably in Trenton, with a Dutch emigre artist who's pretty good— sorta luxury item with about 15 woodcuts) printed up a few letterheads for the new agency. "E. Parkhurst" is, of course, Eurithe's maiden name. I hope to bring you a copy of this book on the way west, since it will consist of most new poems.

Really tho, the place seems dull here, or else I'm dull—despite a coupla readings at Albert College. [. . .] Also Mtl. at Sir Geo. with time spent at Smith's which was also hilarious. So many things about this trip were funny or sad, it's too long for a letter, Smith really is a goddam square tho, albeit a sad square—

The house here is much changed from time of your stay (no empty wine bottles, all beer now), I use one bedroom for workroom with new bookcases built there, office desk I picked up cheap, and posters all over the wall. Incidentally, you oughta get McStew to do a poster of you for the CanLib ed. of selected. We even have water in the kitchen piped up from lake, electrical appliances humming thru the night—

Bowering says he has 23,000 words done of a book on me, a book which I both welcome and feel apprehension about. i.e. will there be any real insights in it, will it tell me anything about myself I don't know— both of which are doubtful, not to slight George at all. (His new book coming with Anansi, which I read for CC, is goddam good) However, it might help to sell Purdy and thus make me a buck. I thought I had a few insights about Birney while writing his book, but later it looked just bad. I seemed to say all the obvious things, Birney's compassion etc.

See you later,

Best,
Al

To Earle Birney (Vancouver), from Ameliasburgh, August 29, 1969

Dear Earle, (gee whiz a letter) (!!!!)
Before I forget—and Geddes may have already written you—Frank Davey is onto the Birney book now. He was down here copying the tapes I made at Waterloo and seems very enthusiastic. I don't think much of Davey's poems, but he is some kind of pedantic half-assed scholar, and I rather think he will do a good job on my failure. As a person he doesn't appeal to me either, but setting this aside he wants to make a reputation as a critic

etc., which I expect may horrify you. But never fear, he thinks too much of himself to write a book he doesn't believe in somewhat more than himself—He is also very thorough-going, and I think will work hard and I hope quickly; especially since Bowering tells me he has $35,000 (jesus, what a typo!) on Purdy, words that is. And I still feel a little guilty about failure on Birney—

I forbear pointing out that the Lowry book is your own damn fault, and am too kind to gloat at your troubles with it, and editors. It's a bloody hard job, for your kind of writer, needs more of a pedant such as Mandel or Dudek etc.[1] Of course I expect you were fond enough of Lowry to wanta take the book on for that reason mostly, and I strongly agree that the intro you wrote on the human side of Lowry—from what you say it appears to be on that side of him—should be included.

The teaching bit at Ryerson was grisly at first, and Colombo bugged me whether he knew he did it or not, one snide remark about waiting for my drop-out students in his classroom down the hall which enraged me quietly, so that I was waiting for verbal opening with him later. However, I got back any dropouts later and some of Colombo's too when I figured out in the second week some sort of method. I just yakked away as a sort of M.C. about students' poems, got them to comment and set the comment against something else, got rebuttals for opinions etc. I worked it so the people there did much of the discussing. Nights I drank beer and stronger, got home to hotel late several occasions, hangovers in the daytime, tho not prostrating ones. As I did mention before, I believe, money was foremost thing, but I spent most of it on beer and hotel. But the secondary thing was I'd be able to say I taught at Ryerson if need money and the occasion arises again. At the end I felt all fucked out, mainly because my voice seemed to echo in my head, and mere act of speaking was tiring. I find lately that my voice on such occasions has grown much louder than it used to be, losing all my previous genius for sensitivity and delicacy of course, so that I feel like a goddam pipe organ or something. Among the students: an ex-nun, a private eye, and a girl who when I read her poems on request was so afraid of men that I could feel her ass (not really) edge away from me on the studio. Jesus, I thought, hope she doesn't get any friction burns from nylon. [. . .]

Sure I like AJMS myself, but a weathervane in conversation and a square in print. [. . .]

I think I'm joining Birney as a father-figure, since young poets keep writing about their troubles, asking advice etc. So many poets are out and out nuts, not sane sober like you and I, eh? [. . .]

Best,

Al

1. Eli Mandel, see page 286. Birney was working on an edition of Lowry's collected poems, with introduction and annotations. Jonathan Cape, the publisher, decided against publication of the manuscript because the introduction and the notes were too long. Margerie Lowry sided with the publishers in part because Birney had dropped some of Lowry's poems.

To George Woodcock (Vancouver), from Ameliasburgh, September 3, 1969

Dear George,

[. . .] My classes were only two weeks in duration, therefore I had little time to become other than a bit tense, which I was. And I didn't "teach" in any conventional sense, since I initiated discussions and kept them going among the students, switched from one viewpoint to an opposite one that I had noted previously, and made the thing more speculative than pedantic—

I didn't know Mordecai[1] did any actual teaching, thought he was more showpiece and consultant than anything. Had a drink or six with him in Mtl. two mos ago with some amusing aftermaths, sorry I'm not seeing you to tell you about it. The whole trip (a reading at Sir George[2]) had some odd incidents. For instance CBC at Mtl. got both my wife and myself on a television interview together. She'd never been on television before, and the interviewer snuck a couple of fast balls at her she wasn't able to handle—I was mad as hell about the whole thing, but the details require more than a paragraph. Richler, wife and myself went for a drink at Arthur Smith's from the hotel, and almost the first thing Smith said to Mordecai was "Mordecai, I wish you wouldn't write those articles saying nasty things about Canada in foreign magazines, not so bad when you do it in Canada—" He was a bit taken aback (Mordecai), and I said something to the effect that all targets ought to be struck, and claimed Smith's party made an excellent subject for satire not to mention dear Arthur himself. Of course Smith shushed me vigorously, especially when I suggested the *New Statesman* as an excellent outlet for the convivial parochialism of Canadian literary gabfests.

Anyway, see you when I see you,

Best,

Al

1. Mordecai Richler (1931–2002): journalist, script writer and novelist (*The Apprenticeship of Duddy Kravitz*, 1959; *St. Urbain's Horseman*, 1971; *Barney's Version*, 1997). AP argued with Richler and stopped speaking to him after reading his negative and condescending comments about George Woodcock's writing. In the late 1990s, both AP and Richler told me separately that they regretted the argument and wished that one or the other had found a way to patch things up. For AP's version of the events see the letter to Miss Iris Jones, November 5, 1971.
2. Sir George Williams University in Montreal, later Concordia University.

To Earle Birney (Vancouver), from Ameliasburgh, September 22, 1969

Dear Earle,
Nothing specific to say, just wanted to write before leaving for Ottawa, which will be Sept. 30. I think we told you our address will be 173 Waverly, Apt. 3.

Both Scott Symons and Pat Lane[1] descended on me for two days, one of them spent at the lake and the other here at Trenton (where, despite the address, I am writing from). Lane is likeable and unpretentious, Symons just the opposite, I don't mean that he's pretentious, but migawd, how complicated can you get! I believe you know him fairly well—Of course I am now going over his novel, partly as a result of his visit. I am also sick as hell, having slept last night with a cold gale blowing in the open window on me, and sleepily not knowing enough to close the window but shivering and huddling and getting sicker—May I also take this moment to bring up, broach, mention delicate, the subject of an-tho—for which we now have a fine/bad Layton panegyric to the US—and also pieces from Margaret Laurence and George Woodcock—where's Birney?—

Fred Cogswell wrote me a scathing letter about my piece in *Com. Lit.* saying I had neglected to include Nowlan among the poets and list *Fiddlehead* and Dorothy Roberts.[2] Also accused me of being "against" New Brunswick and being a member of the Ont. establishment. I meekly admitted being guilty about Nowlan and *Fiddlehead* (in the list of mags) and that this was a bad mistake on my part. I said it was ridiculous that he should think me "against" N.B. and wasn't he getting a little paranoic to think that? And establishment, me, by God? I suppose my status has changed somewhat in the last few years, but I can't see Purdy being regarded as a suave mover and shaker, recipient of favours from the most-high. [...]

Must stop, but will copy a poem on reverse, since this is the only one

I have much use for lately. Note the strong rhythm, which I don't like but couldn't avoid. Tried to write it in loose speech-rhythms, but wouldn't work that way.

Best to Esther, and remember our address when you're in Ottawa.

Cheers,
Al

JOE BARR[3]

In a grey town of seven-week days
during an eternal childhood
where I was so miserable sometimes
at being me that I roamed lonely
over the reeking town garbage dump
unable to talk to anyone
locked in my own body
captive of the motionless sun
in an eternal childhood

Old Joe went there too
happy as a young dog
pushing the garbage with his stick
grinning like a split orange
telling himself stories all day
the doors of his prison opening
into rooms he couldn't remember
places he couldn't stay
the river providing a green sidewalk
that bore his mind's feet lightly
his days like scraps of colour
and the night birds always teaching
him songs that because of his stutter
he never learned to sing

I could have learned from Joe myself
but I never did
not even when gangs of children
followed him down the street
chanting "aw-aw-aw" in mockery

children have for idiots
In a town that looked like a hole
torn in blue clouds
where I made-believed myself
into a moonlit grasshopper
and leaped the shadowed boundaries
that bore my mind's feet lightly
forty years ago
in the grey town of memory
the garbage dump is a prison
where people stand like stones
the birds are stuffed and mounted
a motionless sun still hangs there
where Joe is a scrap of crimson
when the sun at last goes down

Of course, Trenton is the town meant here, and having called it "that raped that hustled town" you get the idea yourself—I will never get used to owning a house here, intend to sell the place as soon as we can get a price, but in the meantime we're stuck—Joe Barr is the actual name of the town idiot of my childhood, tho I've probably carried the parallel between us farther than it really was—But for some inexplicable reason I remember him, bearded, spittle dribbling on mouth corners, wild look—Poor bastard is dead long since. Trenton itself is a puzzle—why do I dislike the place so much? The obvious reason is association with an unhappy childhood, but I should be past that now, really should. But there it is, the place disgusts me.

1. Scott Symons (b. 1933): former curator of the Canadiana collection at the Royal Ontario Museum, novelist (*Place d'Armes: A Personal Narrative*, 1967). AP probably read the manuscript of *Civic Square* (1969). Patrick Lane (b. 1939): West Coast poet, his *Poems New and Selected* (1979) received the Governor General's Award. Though he and AP met in 1969, they grew closer only after the latter moved to Vancouver Island.
2. The article "Canadian Poetry in English Since 1867" appeared in *Journal of Commonwealth Literature* (July 1967). Dorothy Roberts (1906–93): New Brunswick poet (*The Self of Loss: New and Selected Poems*, 1976) who spent much of her adult life in Pennsylvania. Alden Nowlan (1933–83): New Brunswick writer of memoirs (*Various Persons Named Kevin O'Brien*, 1973), short stories (*Miracle at Indian River*, 1968), plays (*Frankenstein*, 1976) and poetry (*An Exchange of Gifts: Poems New and Selected*, 1985).

3. Published in *Wild Grape Wine* (1968).

> **Joe Rosenblatt** (b. 1933): visual artist and poet (*The Joe Rosenblatt Reader*, 1995) and editor (*Jewish Dialog*).

To Joe Rosenblatt (Vancouver), from Vancouver, December 5, 1969

Dear Joe,

If I could read your goddam writing I'd reply at more length. As it is, all I can gather is you're in France, and that you wrote me a letter that you think I might not like. Can't remember any such letter, so don't worry about it.

I'm here in Van. after paying the way west with univ. readings, now can't make up my mind whether to go to Mexico or teach at Simon Fraser, the last of which has been offered me.

As I look at that awful scrawl of yours, picking out only a word or two here and there, I realize there's little point in me saying anything about your trip, except that I'm glad you're there and presumably not dead. I expect you'll write a poem or two about your experience.

After such a long time away I find Vancouver bores me, especially since I don't try to "make the scene" in the sense you do. In fact I don't give a shit for the scene. I try to go to places where I will feel like writing poems, and this ain't it. And I am also grousing to myself about this Simon Fraser job, since the money would be useful, but it would take a chunk outa my life I'm not sure I wanta give even for money. And this adds to my own depression, a condition of mind in which you haven't found in me very often.

Anyhow, this letter is just to let you know I'm alive, and possibly you are feeling rather cut-off from Canada. Be reassured: it's still here. Good luck.

Best,
Al

To Margaret Laurence (Toronto), from Burnaby, BC, February 1, 1970

Dear Margaret,

Since just talked with you, felt like writing a note. Don't worry so much about the goddam letters. Will give you a contract of non-sale, will make a deal not to sell, you can sue, besides I have enough goddam letters, just won't sell—but in case I do I'll split the money.

Okay the lectures get me down. The kids in class know fuckall about CanLit, or just about any lit, with some notable exceptions. This being the case I feel I should try to *make* them know something about poetry by *liking* the stuff. Which is the way I aim what I say. I don't mean shove it down their throats. I do mean reading a helluva lot of it, also talking about the particular poets, disagreeing with the excerpts of criticism I read to them (almost always) (disagree, I mean)—But it still gets me down. There are some students in class who, from their comments, want great elaborate theories built up, to explain not only CanPo but all. Well——? I mean, I can't. This makes me feel goddam inadequate.

However—however—the money! You know I got a thousand bucks (less tax) for a month's non-work? I mean, show me the ditch where you can do that, even if you write a poem about ditch-digging. Must admit I'd rather do that, write the poem that is. But the stuff I'm writing seems crap. Have to go to the metrical analyst's for an overhaul. This bit about Annette[1] also bugs me. I'm goddamed if I'll give her a pass for a crappy paper, or honors which she says she has to have—if she does nothing as I expect. Eurithe seems to think I'm a cold-hearted bastard about it, which bothers me. Because sometimes I show signs of being that to myself, and how can a cold-hearted bastard write good poems? I ask you—Therefore, because of the lit gain involved, I must not be a cold-hearted bastard. Right? So pass the bitch. To hell with that, I won't, not unless she writes a good paper. But it bothers me. Am I wrong? Anyway, sometimes I think all the poems I would consider good are already written, which is a nasty thought. Then I will have to bone up on Parmenides, Rilke, Coleridge's *Biographia Literaria* (which someone left in my office) etc.[2] And that's hell. I wanta find out things for myself, as I said in the last letter.

Re poems, I once thought of getting/having Eurithe get a job teaching on an Indian reservation and me being an invisible entity nearby drifting etc. That's what I am too. Three/four years back when I thought of that, and still think it's a good idea.

Don't you feel this lit guilt yourself?—writer-in-rez and all that? Or is it the washed-up writer talking? Anyhow, this fucking place is dull, television at night, *walks*, (dunno how Eurithe stands it, and she hates me for not goin to Mexico)—I think there's a pressure on me I put there myself, to write better, to always write better. Right now, I can't. And don't like it.

So what else is new? Birney I sympathize with, for he is a friend, tho

I can't talk to him the way I do in letters to you, or in person. I do agree that he's a phony lothario, whether he realizes this or not. But in a way, perhaps unexplainable, I do sympathize with his wish to stay young thru others. In another way I do not, for it makes him a phony if he knows it, an idiot if he doesn't. I think a lot of men—at a certain more youthful age than him—have the wish to fuck every beautiful woman in the world. Some women perhaps too, vice-versa. It's not altogether silly, perhaps has to do with one world psychologically, one human world etc. But really, the only important women are those with whom there is some kind of rapport, whether instant or developing. And beyond that again is death.

That brought Lawrence to mind, D.H. Since the more I read him the more I know he's the poet that talks in the language and uses the thoughts I aim towards. Not just death, but that too, since it's always so mixed with life—I mentioned his poems to you before, and do now emphatically again. I wish you'd get his two vol collected from library and read quickly quickly, particularly *Birds, Beasts and Flowers*, then return to the poems that seemed good.[3]

I am thinking of all sorts of ways and stratagems to get books and mags I want. You'd be amused. Eurithe says I'm the oddest mixture of ethics and complete disregard for them she's seen—of course her experience is a bit limited. She has been pushed and prodded in the direction my mind takes because of her connection with me, else she couldn't stand me at all. And yet I am quite amoral about some things, material things, a dichotomy she doesn't seem to get. But then why should she? But the dichotomy is not one to me, since I separate all things into compartments—Yeah, and hark back, all women are not symbolic of one world etc.

Love,

Al

Hey—I put the carbon in backwards, so you have the only copy. Burn it? Sell it? Zerox it? Use it for toilet paper? One page at least shall escape the mercantile world—

P.S. A student, who is quite possibly trying to curry favor (I can't tell) has sung one of my poems to me over the phone. Sounds like Leonard Cohen, Eurithe says. I am buying a guitar tomorrow.

1. Purdy's student and one of the women celebrated in *Poems for All the Annettes* (1962).
2. Parmenides (515–450 BC): a Greek philosopher of the pre-Socratic period; Rainer Maria Rilke (1875–1926): a German poet. Samuel Taylor Coleridge (1772–1834): poet, philosopher, and critic, published his *Biographia Literaria* in 1817.
3. D.H. Lawrence (1885–1930): novelist, poet, and essayist. *Birds, Beasts, and*

Flowers, originally published in 1923, appeared in volume II of *The Complete Poems of D.H. Lawrence* (1964).

To George Woodcock, from Burnaby, BC, March 21, 1970

Dear George,
Many thanks for sending the book. It's practically in the coffee table prestige class and, as you said, a picture-book, but still lots of Woodcock prose.

I returned from the east last Sunday, reading at Sir George and the nearly inevitable party afterward. At which I refereed an unscheduled bout between Peggy Atwood and Irving Layton. It seems he had told the students at York (right after her reading) that she was a lousy reader and moreover "women poets were good only for screwing" which remark didn't please Atwood, and I don't blame her much.

McStew has sent along my own collection of love poems called *Love in a Burning Building*, which Harold Town turned down for illustration because it was too hard-boiled! Purdy hard-boiled? I should say: McStew sent it along for revision and additions.

Term papers coming along now, signals the end of my academic odyssey nearing. I'll be in touch with you a little later, with the hope that you can attend a party that has been mentioned by Sandra Dzwa[1] prior to our departure from Vancouver—

Best,
Al

1. Sandra Djwa, see page 396. Just as he always spelled xerox as *zerox*, so AP almost always turned Djwa into *Dzwa*.

Milton Acorn (1923–86): a carpenter and a poet, Acorn was the most troubled and often troubling of AP's friends. The early years of the relationship are captured in the poem "House Guest" which describes a visit of Acorn's to Ameliasburgh during which the two men worked on the house and "quarrelled over socialism   poetry how to boil water / doing the dishes   carpentry   Russian steel production figures." In the preface to his 1986 *Collected Poems*, he refers to Acorn as one of his most important influences, "I learned from him both how to write and how not to write. (Very few people can teach you opposite things at the same time.)"

From Milton Acorn (Parkdale, PEI), to Ameliasburgh, May 8, 1970

Dear Al,

Sorry for no letter. I was (silly) trying to manage the fight all by myself, by phone calls and telegrams. I just couldn't get thru by phone or telegram. Several letters went out; but to those at the heart of things—in Toronto.

I've just been rereading *Poems for All the Annettes* rerereading it with joy and gratitude; which sort of spoils a line in my own poem "On Shaving Off His Beard" which I intend to read at the award ceremony, in Grossman's.[1]

Al, as blood to brother, be there. I consider I have won a much more significant award than the one I lost.

By the way, I made a great pitch for an award when I asked for an introduction from you for *I've Tasted My Blood*.[2] Well, it was a great try, and you made a great try.

By the way, the Indian in me is now authenticated. The documents discovered, on one line (maternal) . . .

It makes me (maybe) one-eighth; but as I've told you, an analysis of physical features makes a much higher content probable. I was *born* with brown eyes! Not a "blue-eyed baby" but a brown-eyed papoose.

I'm still a bit obsessive about this thing, and will remain obsessive til I've comprehended fully what it means and doesn't mean. Hope this reaches you before the strike!!

Love,

Milt

1. The ceremony at Grossman's Tavern in Toronto on May 16, 1970—to honour Acorn after *I've Tasted My Blood* was passed over for the the 1969 Governor General's Award—assumed almost immediately a nearly legendary status. Acorn's biographer, Richard Lemm, describes it as follows: "On that evening, more than a hundred friends and admirers crowded into Grossman's, with a remarkable crosssection of Canada's literary talent, including Irving Layton, Eli Mandel, Margaret Atwood, Dorothy Livesay, Al Purdy, Joe Rosenblatt, Doug Fetherling, Ron Everson, Graeme Gibson, and Abe Rotstein. One delegation had arrived by train, on the 'Poets Rapido' from Montreal's Central Station.

"Layton and Mandel had raised $800—a substantial sum in those days (the Governor-General's Award was $2,500—and the cheques bore the names of writers listed above and others such as Leonard Cohen, Earle Birney, and John Glassco." (To bring the total to $1,000, Layton phoned the premier of Prince Edward Island and secured a promise of $200.)

AP offers another version of the event in *Reaching for the Beaufort Sea* (237–8).
2. The Introduction to *I've Tasted My Blood* (1969) is reprinted in *Starting from Ameliasburgh*.

To Earle Birney (Vancouver), from Ameliasburgh, May 18, 1970

Dear Earle,
Wanted to say hi before the mails get stopped. [. . .]

I went to Toronto for the Acorn shindig, and never saw so many people honouring a poet in my life. People are really friendly to Acorn. And honestly, I think his book does and did deserve the award. Not that I mean to put Bowering [who won the 1969 Governor General's Award] down with such a statement as Layton did with his ("there's more poetry in Acorn's dirty little finger nail than there is in the collected works of George Bowering": Layton) Still, Layton is generous. He phoned the premier of PEI to get money for Acorn and got $200. Nice.

The party was loud, raucous and drunken, with me being not the soberest. Dave Godfrey,[1] Gotlieb, Marty Avenus, Tom Marshall, Mandel, Layton and Aviva, Ron Everson, Dorothy Livesay (all the way from Edmonton), and dozens of others.

I may have had the distinction of being involved in the only overt unfriendliness there (at Grossman's Tavern). Was escorting a Ryerson Press editorial girl (nice and blonde and sexy) to the can, and thru my own silly clumsiness caused her to fall flat among the beer-drinkers. Raised her to her feet apologizing feverishly and confusedly, and proffered her a cigar by way of recompense and absolution. Was about to light it when this guy I'd never seen before heaves in sight six inches from my left nostril and says with unmistakable nastiness: "Fuck off!" Well, heavens to betsey, Earle, you know me better than to think I could possibly have done anything to offend him. Nevertheless the acrimony was strong, and I felt he wished me no peace of mind for the next few minutes. But with the peacefulness inherent in all the tribe of Purdys I questioned him re his intentions, only to have the same instructions repeated. Whereupon I shoved him vigorously around the scapula into a table full of beer drinkers. Then lit the lady's cigar, keeping a weather eye peeled to see his reaction to that. But the waiters, having seen me clasping a microphone previously and thinking I was Mayor Denison, threw the other guy out as a gesture of courtesy towards high municipal office.

It was a silly memorable evening, with Acorn making a speech, Mandel making a speech, and Layton the peroration, myself having said I wanted to drink beer only. Acorn got a large metallic object on a purple ribbon pinned to his throat—and what the hell!—you've been thru those shindigs yourself—

This may or may not get to you for a while. But good health and all that, and wishes etc. Also affection.

Best,

Al

1. Dave Godfrey (b. 1938): member of the creative writing department at the University of Victoria and novelist (*The New Ancestors*, 1970). Godfrey was very active in the Toronto publishing scene during the 1960s and early 1970s; with Dennis Lee he co-founded House of Anansi, and, with James Bacque and Roy McSkimming, New Press.

Phyllis Webb (b. 1927): a still underrated West Coast poet who worked in publishing and radio (she conceived the CBC program *Ideas*). Her books include *The Sea is Also a Garden* (1962), *Naked Poems* (1965) and *Wilson's Bowl* (1980).

To Phyllis Webb (Vancouver Island), from Ameliasburgh, June 30, 1970

Dear Voice,
I mean Phyllis of course—
—what the hell, it is a *good* voice, and you know it!
A trailer? Is that a good idea? You do need a little space, tho I know you figure the whole island will be space enough. Still—
No, I read at St. Lawrence with MacEwen and Waddington, and to be on the same bill with Waddington is always terrifying for me. No, I don't mind crowds any more. Seem to have picked up enough experience at this sort of thing . . .
No good books *lately*, tho, think I mentioned have a book of love poems called *Love in a Burning Bldg.* coming in Sept. Also did write what I think is the best poem in a coupla years called "The Horseman of Agawa," which will be in the mag sec. of *Globe and Mail* in the next few weeks.
I'd like to see more of the Kropotkin poems,[1] esp. when you feel they have integrated and taken shape—Liked the *Forum* one, or should say several (two that is) (looked em up), and know you have some structural thoughts on the whole—Since I expect to do a coupla more anthos in next year or so, interested also for that reason.
How are *you*, Phyllis, as apart from what you're doing? The burst of writing has been good, I know—Again, apart from the merit of poems

themselves, but for *you*. Perhaps I felt something of this when I wrote "The Horseman."

Write me when you are in the mood and feel like it please. Not this one necessarily. I am interested in Phyllis, you know, apart from The Voice. Are the nights still bad occasionally? or not so much now? Is some aim or direction more apparent? i.e., what makes sense? I remember years ago in Mtl. how your nerves barricaded all doors and windows of that apt., tendrils flying from your ears and mind and exploring the darkness outside. Do write when you want to please.

Best,
Al

1. Webb's "Kropotkin" is in *Wilson's Bowl* (1980).

From Margaret Laurence (Elmcot, England), to Ameliasburgh, August 5, 1970

Dear Al,

The poem is splendid.[1] Thought so when I heard it over the phone but only certain now that I see it and read it. It gets across that quality which is in all your best poems, I think—i.e. the sense of the present being part of the past and also of the future; the sense of everything being connected, somehow, so that the ancestors are everybody's ancestors, and we ourselves are ancestors-in-the-making, or something like that. Also some kind of sense of reaching out beyond our planet and yet the acute ever-present and also painful feeling of awareness of an individual's humanity.

—Looking back on that paragraph, I see how right you were in the poem, too, about the translation of feelings and responses into words. It's all I can do, too, but one feels sometimes (most times, I guess) that it's goddam inadequate. And faced with any kind of direct thing—like the rock painting and a person's unverbal and deep response to it—one almost wonders if someday the human race won't outgrow words. Maybe we've had to work, as a species, through all these christly knots of verbalism only in order to get back to something we once had and now only have sporadically, or maybe we never did have that direct response in any very subtle way, in, say, the caveman era, but it's possible to have it. I dunno. Words are very baffling. And yet, on the other hand, it's only your words which can communicate to other human beings the whole feeling of your response to the Horseman, and your catching of Eurithe's response (migawd, that part is lovely!) I sort of catch the (you should excuse the expression) purity of her response to the Horseman, to the ancestors, and I have to see it as something complete in itself, somehow very strong and with great integrity, almost impossible to anyone who is even at the time translating it all into words. (You remember the scene from Brian Moore's *An Answer from Limbo*,[2] where the writer at the funeral of his mother is fictionalizing it all in his mind, already, and sees himself doing it?) I thought, reading the poem, as I've thought before (also with other poets etc.), how strange to be Eurithe (please pass on these comments to her—they're for her maybe more than you, or as much)—like being Sarah, with Gulley Jimson in *The Horse's Mouth*;[3] only a very strong-in-herself woman could be, I would suspect, just because you *do* do most of the talking, but there's another dimension of life where the living is done directly, which is her dimension but also the one you're trying (like all writers) to catch in your impossible net. Jesus. Anyhow, the poem made me think of all these things, which I record in words. We serve an ironic god.

The illustrations were pretty rotten, I thought. Purdy in Mod garb was a bit peculiar, and Eurithe as Sprite-Of-The-Forest was a damn sight too pixie-like. General effect, actually, for most readers, would be okay. But what they should've done was to print very plain that pic of you and Eurithe which is on yr livingroom wall, plus an exact reproduction of the cave painting, very stark, something like that. Newspapers and mags, however, never do these things right. I speak from gloomy experience of having stories idiotically illustrated for many years.

Odd thing—the day after the poem arrived, two dear friends arrived from Canada;[4] have known them for 20 or more years. They are from Toronto; he teaches in Library School, U of T. Said they damn near missed the plane because John at last minute said "We have to take that page from the *Globe & Mail* with Al Purdy's poem; Margaret will want to see it." They couldn't find it. Chris (his wife) is pacing floor while John fumbles through old newspapers and finally they leave without it. Both very enthusiastic about poem, in real way. Relieved when they learned I'd seen it. I pass on this little episode with no charge. Thought you'd like to know. John is great admirer of yr work, and is (unknown to you) a v. good PR man on yr behalf.

House is a shambles. I think I'm running a hotel here. I love it, actually. I hate the thought of autumn, when all visitors will have departed and I will have no more excuses to keep me away from work. I don't want to think of that goddam novel. Dunno how to tackle it. I realize more and more that realism bores me to hell, now. No way I can do it in straight narration. Can't think of any other way. Stalemate. Words fail. Maybe I should take up painting or music? No? No. Anyway, thanks for poem.

Love,

Margaret

1. Purdy had sent the pages from *The Globe Magazine* of July 25, 1970, which contained an illustrated version of "The Horseman of Agawa."
2. Brian Moore (1921–99): Irish-born Canadian novelist (*The Luck of Ginger Coffee*, 1960; *Black Robe*, 1985; *The Statement*, 1995). *The Answer from Limbo* was published in 1962.
3. *The Horse's Mouth* (1944) by Joyce Cary was one of Laurence's favourite novels.
4. John and Christine Marshall.

To Earle Birney (Vancouver), from Ameliasburgh, August 6, 1970

Goddam it Birney,
If I wanta give away a valuable work of genius that will undoubtedly depreciate to miniscule value in near future, stop trying to talk me out of it! You're welcome to say: I'll give Purdy my next hundred buck book, and I will damn well take it. Just try, I say, just suggest it, and watch out for the reflex leap I make in the direction of whatever it is. Okay?

Anyway, it's wrapped, boxed, sealed, fucked but not corded, on accounta I got no cord. Only look, I'm only givin away two, you and M. Laurence, so please please don't show it to anyone who might think they deserve a free copy. Dunno who that would be, unless Andy perhaps (and I'd like to give him one, but one must draw a line or something eh?)— This is, of course, to say forgive me for whatever I have to be forgiven for, to imply that I am a noble character and will not sign my goddam name on Indian rock paintings like you wrongfully stated and I am hurt, my feelings are wounded badly. Besides, the ballpoint I used wouldn't mark the iron oxide. The book box is not as good as I would like, on accounta glue didn't stick perfectly. If you have a bottle of red ink, dab the label's nose like it's supposed to be.

Just came back from Sudbury, Laurentian U, and a nice likeable square conservative English prof who felt he had to keep up with me drinkin, so fed me beer after beer, himself drinkin one for one, then we switched to scotch, and after three drinks he suddenly got glassy eyed, and Eurithe had to drive his car to the reading where 28 people showed up. Weep not, the next highest was 22. I assume the bit about him tryin to be a hippie,

163

as he may have thought I was, and tryin to keep up. But I kinda think it might be true. He got beer in esp. for me (which was nice of him—name of Ron Bates, poet too), soaked me in a Finnish steam bath where we all wore swim suits (that's why he's a conservative)—After the reading Bates is owl-solemn still drunk, but drives his own car, right up a one-way street in Sudbury the wrong way while everyone yowls murder in his ears—At this time I have survival-fears, and a milk shake is suggested for obvious reasons. So we see the red hot slag being dumped from the US mine (for which he has a pome I read of course) (makin noises like they're works of genius, which in a different sense they are)—and go home for more beer, Bates having forsaken scotch. We plight our troth by promising signed books to be sent later on accounta vows made to be broken.

Then drive to Cochrane, ride the Polar Bear Ex. to Moosonee and an Indian boatman from the little sticks (hail to Moose Factory, where it rains and rains and I hate to get my hair wet on accounta then it looks like I got even less than I have and I know no swooning Indian maiden will consent to swoon for me . . .) But I don't write a poem, which grieves me. I don't *feel* like writing poem, and this unborn poem is not to be borne. I alibi I only write about things that are important, thus if I can't write them they're not important; but see thru my own sophistries and the result is hardly satisfying.

English girl here right now, we met in Europe being chased by a love-mad Athenian, and I am intrigued by the way her ass wriggles goin up the loft ladder which I hafta hold on accounta she is more scared of the ladder nor me.

Luv,
Al

P.S. Thanks for character reference!

To Margaret Atwood (England), from Ameliasburgh, October 21, 1970

Dear Peggy,
Okay, you're really fuckin up my future sales—Have also a long correspondence with Margaret Laurence, which she forbids sale of—Must be 50–60 letters, and every now and then mock-threaten her to sell them. She neither quite believes nor quite disbelieves me. When she was staying here once last summer, she checked her own letters in my file to see if they were there—I being out at the time.

Being a simple soul, your whereabouts at any given time bewilders me.

But since any presence of mine does not seem to coincide with yours at any given place, I'll send this to England address. I'm reading in Toronto at York Oct. 27, but you're in Ottawa. The League thing was dull thru the day's business, most of which I avoided, but the party wasn't bad. I'm told I tried to devour Gustafson's tie, and he told me about this somewhat aggrievedly next day while wearing a roll-neck sweater.

The bit about Gwen M. alarms me somewhat. You seem to imply that if I use your poems I'm obligated to use hers.[1] This had not occurred to me. Both of you are in the McStew 20 poets antho, and the people in that are there for somewhat different reasons than the Ryerson one—I am trying to stay away from "well-known" poets such as yourself and Gwen, but thot I could break my own rules if I feel like it. Still think that too. However, I should probably leave both of you out, since the McStew book does what the Ryerson one doesn't: sort of points up the well-known poets etc., etc.

Point about love affairs, perhaps—one sort of digs oneself into a situation where it seems impossible to get out without shaking one's whole conception of one's self and decidedly hurting other people. This apart from possible limitations of lovers—which I note you do not fail to mention in poems, along with some of your own. From another angle: if the love affair were really important, one would say fuckit and take off with the other person anyway. Which leaves the strong possibility that it is one's own self at (possible) fault, that one is incapable of feeling strongly enough. And I'm sure you've thought of all this . . . I suppose the lover is a complete anarchist if he or she has the nerve . . . Or the feeling . . . Or whatever . . . But if so, one cannot be too conscious of the debris one leaves behind; in which case how can one have been sensitive enough to have been in love in the first place? Feelings shoot out in all directions, and does one prune them severely? Anyhow, I hope you're nice and (almost) hard-boiled again . . .

I'm writing fairly heavily, one or two of which poems seem good . . . One of them seems to be much like the Atwood style . . . But I don't write almost continually the way I used to, don't have the impetus continually—I wait until I suspect an opening, whereas before I *made* the opening . . . Dunno if that's good or bad, but it does delete a lot of crap. And that's ambiguous too, since I still grope for openings in any possible poem-situation . . .

Expect to get some money from Ont. Arts Council for next summer. Also hope to go to Hiroshima, which may seem unusual to you. Does it?

But I can anticipate some of the feelings I'd have there, can half-write some poems now, something of the same way I felt before going to the arctic . . . In my mind, I label it the big thing, the place that unites feeling and words etc . . . Trouble is it probably calls for reading Spengler and Toynbee,[2] various histories of the east and west etc. Terrible price to pay for poems . . .

                              Best and write when you feel that
                                      way,
                                    Al

1. AP was editing *Storm Warning: The New Canadian Poets* (1971) at this time.
2. Oswald Spengler (1880–1936): German historian whose *The Decline of the West* (1918–22) was one of the most influential books of its time. Spengler argues that civilizations are subject to cycles of growth and decay, and that Europe is entering a period of decline. Arnold Toynbee (1889–1975): English historian, best known for his once very popular now virtually unread twelve-volume *Study of History* (1934–61).

Jay Macpherson (b. 1931): long-time professor of English at the University of Toronto and poet. *The Boatman* (1957) won a Governor General's Award. Emblem Books, her small press, published AP's *The Blur in Between* (1962).

To Jay Macpherson (Toronto), from Ameliasburgh, November 5, 1970

Dear Jay,
Stop kickin yourself in the pants. I probably deserved all your nasty thoughts and words to your friends.

Re letters sold to a university (Sask),[1] I thought you would remember that neither you or myself had ever exchanged personal letters. However, if there had been anything of a nature you would not wish known, then I should not have sent those letters. Margaret Laurence (now back in England) and I have sent many letters to each other, and she has expressly forbidden me to sell them. Now and then I try to kid her a little about this, never seriously.

Must admit that I had been puzzled by your attitude towards me—at least until Peggy Atwood (whom I like much) mentioned why. And I think your friend, who gave you the information, and whom you say is "without a shred of malice," must nevertheless be convicted of some slight distortion.

You are quite right that permission should be obtained from the writer before selling such letters. I must plead guilty to that, and can only say that at the time I didn't even think of it, being in need of money and it seeming to be a lit custom to sell papers and letters.

Any letters from myself, you are quite welcome to. Do what you like with them.

No, I haven't regretted publishing *Blur*. At the time, my style had changed greatly, and I didn't want the old style to be confused with the new. However, that hasn't happened. *Blur* was a well-produced book, in fact I note its price has gone up considerably in rare-book listings. I wish I'd held onto a few copies.

One of my hobbies happens to be collecting signed copies of books, mostly by people I know. Have some 400 of these now. I got a copy of your first book some time back. If I sent it to you would you say it's for me, please?

I'm sure you couldn't have said anything very bad about me anyway, so please forgive yourself. There's no need of me doing that.

Sincerely,

Al

1. AP's papers are at Lakehead University, the University of Saskatchewan and at Queen's University. The majority of his books were bought by Avie Bennett and donated to University College, the University of Toronto. He was less concerned with keeping the papers together than with getting as high a price as possible for each sale. Most of the papers are at Saskatchewan (1970) and at Queen's (1969, 1981, 1987, 1995, 1997). As John Lennox points out, "his relationship with both parties subsequently went sour because of money and other disagreements."

Angus Mowat (1892–1977): librarian and writer. His books include *Then I'll Look It Up* (1938), *Carrying Place* (1944) and *Conversations with Young Librarians* (1945). He is the father of Farley Mowat.

To Angus Mowat, from Ameliasburgh, November 26, 1970

Dear Angus,
If you get this letter in time, why don't you come down Sunday? Might or might not be one or two other people here, Acorn a poet, and Melady a teacher from Trenton Collegiate. Come and help fill in the silences.

Your letter calls for some cogitation on my part. Okay, Joe Barr. You could say, I learned nothing from him then. You did apparently. However, there's this about our two different but similar environments in Trenton: you were a different person than me. You see what I mean? You *could* be affected by the remark you quote. I could not have been at that time, I was much too stupid. My childhood was miserable, as a result of my character and environment. Yours the opposite.

My life didn't really start until I joined the RCAF. At least not from the point of view of beginning to realize I could affect what happened to me by the viewpoint and stance I took towards it. (Whatever it was.) You, apparently, are a bit screwed up now, in your opinion you can't say things. That's horseshit! You told about the time when you were building this boat with your wife in some remote area, and this to me just cries for writing about. And you're a damn fool if you don't, the exact antithesis of the self you present as your younger self in Trenton. To hell with whether you can or can't! Write it! Or tell it to Farley, eh? Memoirs of Angus, by Farley? Do you hate me for that suggestion?[1]

Re Joe Barr in Trenton, at that time I didn't understand the idea that each town has its idiot-butt, for understanding such things came later. But I don't actually feel a loss, as perhaps you seem to think I should. There has been, and still are, times when I've lived a life that made up for any deficiencies in the past. And now is all-important. I don't feel a damn bit deprived. And referring back to my phrase "feel a loss"—I mean a loss in the sense of being uncomfortable, being miserable in the town where I grew up, whereas I should have met some of the people you met or their facsimiles, and thereby enjoyed life. I'm too different from you for that. You reverence the past you loved. (But not enough to write about it, or feel any confidence that you can get those feelings down on paper—which irritates the hell outa me. It's a sort of death to feel one's self incapable of these things, especially in someone like yourself who has already come up with two novels.) (And look, if you don't write that time down, you'll kick yourself all the way into the grave and spoil your last drink thinking of it.)

To hell with Keats, you read him. I did, at a time when I couldn't appreciate him much. Now, I have little time except for the moderns, and for my own writing. The pastward look is for writing, not for inhibiting now.

Al

1. As AP knew, the relationship between Angus Mowat and his son Farley was strained at this time. In the end, he wrote about Angus Mowat and the boat

twice: the essay "Angus" and the poem "Scott Hutcheson's Boat." The former was published in *Weekend Magazine* (August 10, 1974) and reprinted in *Starting from Ameliasburgh*, the latter in *The Woman on the Shore* (1990).

To Earle Birney (Vancouver), from Ameliasburgh, November 26, 1970

Dear Earle,

[. . .] As you might expect, I'm going nuts with work. Two articles for *TorStar* (the second is much better than the first, which was chopped) and one for *Maclean's*—me complaining like hell, but sorta enjoying it I guess . . . But I sure will be glad to get away. Movement from here will be like mooring my brain and sailing my body—which is goddam poor imagery, but you know what I mean. Not that the body is inactive, in most of the ways a body is active, except for the extraordinary sports of skin and muff diving. (Do you know the last term?)

Yeah, Prince George is extraordinary, I think because of McKinnon and the Eng. Dept. as well as populace. Isn't it really odd to see "a sea of faces" stretched out before you? I read at Loyalist College in Belleville to not more than 40 or so and it disgusted me, well not exactly, but I like an audience whose reaction you can feel when your head is down reading . . . The kid who read before me—from Loyalist—had had a book out by Delta, Wally Keeler, and his poems were mostly sex, tho not bad. At one point, near the end of his period, he said "these poems are for my latest mistress and woman who is sitting in the front row"—and I had seen this modest looking gal before, all alone, who now betrayed no visible reaction to Keeler's words. Still, I had a reaction. I thought: the self-advertising prick!

Earlier I was on some sort of closed circuit tv the college has, wearing dark glasses for defense against the lights, girl student on one side and male on the other. Interviewing, that is. She asking silly questions like: does your brain work when you write poems? (really very similar to that) Or: You're a nationalist, Mr. Purdy, why do you go to Greece? Me saying gravely, sure, my brain works when I write poems. And, I go to Greece cause it's the cradle of western civ. Should I stay in Canada honey? But I sure musta fucked up that interview for her, because she was nearly crying at the end and after. I hafta put my arm around her and reassure her she didn't bloop it up. But I look back at that interview, and see I could have worked harder and answered her questions more irrelevantly (as I did the guy on my right side), and possibly interestingly. Not "a pettiness to expiate" but a thoughtlessness on my part. I probably should try and phone her still to make amends. Amends are always more difficult than the opposite, whatever the opposite is of amends.

Your Basil Bunting[1] sounds like a showman who can't miss on any culture stage in the US. Even a good poet, you intimate. Do think the blaser, creeley, duncan, tallman[2] lineup behind him sounds revolting, not to say throwupable? I applaud you turning down the party invite, even tho you must have thought as I would: who are these pricks turning down me. On the other hand (I would've thought), these goddam in-groups don't know a good poet unless he's an actor like Bunting. Still, I don't think it sounds like a party you need mind missing, with the possible exception of Bunting.

I accept your stern decision re taped Birney with, if not equanimity, at least troubled calm. Knowing, of course, that you'll fuck around and waste all the good stuff on well-shaped, non-literary, but appreciative, feminine ears.

But don't give me that "pathetic little life" bit—At least when you're having me on I can tell once in a while—

Okay, re comments on article: don't we really have different social environments, even if perhaps not greatly different? Re riding freights etc. (which was included so I could talk more easily), sure an American might have done the same in the US. But what citizen of any country couldn't do something similar? And so what if they could? Doesn't it add up, the various parts, to a Canadian whole? You are certainly not going to give me, nor is any one, the components of a unique national identity, other than such memories, history, etc. Perhaps the impression of the whole piece was exaggeration, but name me a specific item which I exaggerated. Oh sure, Mathews manages to antagonize more people than any fifty branch plant managers. He has real talent that way. But on the other hand, he speaks his mind, is not afraid to come out and say things. And there are so damn few people who will stand up and say things, that I admire him for that. Even if he does seem, at times, like something a bit nasty, and I'm afraid he does—at times. [. . .]

Incidentally, the *Star*, Peter Newman, that is, offered me a job in the ed. dept. at $13,000 per. I'm flattered as hell, of course, but think I'd blow my mind at a job like that. What think you? I said I had no time, but was tempted. Newman asked me to write an article a month. In my weaker and more drained (mentally) moments, not sure if I'm capable of even that. I think it'd drive me nuts. Also offered me the book page, five columns a week etc. That too would knock me out, I'm sure. But maybe a column a month.

Earle, be sure and send me a copy of the new book when it comes. I'll drop you word from Mexico where we get to, tho I'm not really sure myself. Eurithe says Oaxaca, sounds like an Englishman saying Oxo. I suppose no chance at all of Birney getting to Mexico—Did I say I got the Ont. Council of the Arts cash? Well, did. Also, gonna try to go to Hiroshima on a short term in spring. Might as well get around a bit, as long as travelling is all downhill. Well, we leave next week, after the last touches of antho are finished. Also a CBC date. Re antho, got the damnedest snivelling letter from Seymour Mayne and Bryan McCarthy wanting in. Makes me wonder if I ever whined like that—

Well, must stop. Work to do. Eurithe comments on your description of her in no very gentle manner, but also laughs. And may I direct similar sentiments to Esther,[3] your "enduring protectress and sybil"—

Best,

Al

1. Basil Bunting (1900–85): English poet, influenced by Pound and influential among poets in the Pound line. One critic called him "a strict experimental formalist." His best-known poem is the autobiographical *Briggflatts* (1966).
2. Robin Blaser, see page 504. Warren Tallman, see page 301. I'm assuming that the lack of capitals in "blaser, creeley, duncan, tallman" is deliberate.
3. Esther Birney, Earle's wife.

To George Woodcock, from Ameliasburgh, November 30, 1970

Dear George,
I think this is the finest writing of yours I've ever seen. Of course, I mean in *Canada & the Canadians.* I've read only the chapter on culture (I would look at that first!) and the Preface, and part of the first chapter. But the Preface is some of your best, probably THE best, writing. I've never seen the status of being a Canadian explained or defined re feeling (etc.) as well.

Inge's photos are also marvellous (excuse the superlatives). Tell her you must have pointed out what to photograph and how to do it, else she couldn't have achieved such virtuosity. Which ought to make her Women's Lib blood seethe a little.

Of course, you mention you're gonna be objective in the rest of the book. Doesn't matter, when you start that well, it's gotta be good.

Okay, me on the borderland between poems and prose. Gee whiz, here I thought I was writing prose all along!

What I should have said re Preface, is that your own feelings come across and transmit so well. Papa's dream of the peaceable but exciting kingdom, and all that. (Did you ever think that period on Vancouver Island might be a good book? The sylvan utopia and all that?) I think it strange that when I wrote a review of your poems in *Tamarack*[1] I tried briefly to imagine your own exile's return feelings.

In the same category, we had some visitors yesterday, among them Farley Mowat's pop, Angus.* He, despite lifelong residence in Canada is emotional about Scotland, wears a kilt etc. I told him he was an emotional dropout and living in the past and that his home was here. I didn't expect it to have any effect tho, and it didn't.

We leave in five days (I hope). Did I say I got the Ont. Arts Council grant? Yes, and thanks. Also applied for short term to go to Hiroshima in the spring from CC (and got that too), so feel mediocrity is incumbent upon me. We both have survived poverty, yourself comparative affluence—but dunno if I can. My wife has decided she loves me as a result of personal changes. How can I surmount my lost selves who were much more loveable?

Will let you know where we get to when we know where we're not.

Best (and to Inge)

Al

*he expected to finish his life in Scotland!

1. The review of Woodcock's *Selected Poems* was part of a group review published in the Spring 1968 issue of *Tamarack Review*. It is reprinted in *Starting from Ameliasburgh*. It's obvious from the review that AP admires Woodcock, but it's not at all clear that he admires the poetry as poetry.

Postcard from Kathy, Paula and Linda, students at the University of Western Ontario, to Ameliasburgh, March 9, 1971. The photo shows Parliament Hill with "the trooping of the Regimental Colour through the ranks of the New Guard."

Dear Mr. Purdy,

We thought about you while looking at native sculptures in this unlikely locale. We enjoy your work immensely. Would you consider ever coming to London Ont. to speak to students, and give some inspiration to us here?—We love your "ballsy" style. If you do ever come to London, we'd like to buy you a beer or two.

Kathy, Paula, and Linda

To George Woodcock (Vancouver), from Ameliasburgh, March 14, 1971

Dear George,
Greetings. Just a note to let you know I'll be here for another month or so. (Before going to Japan, that is.)

Snow over your head along the roads here, which is not a very cheerful homecoming. Also word McClelland and Stewart may be sold. If to US, I don't see how Jack McClelland can justify this, he being co-chairman of the Canadian Independence thing.

I finished the bio-crit thing I was doing. Also revised it. 33,000 words. Visited Ron Everson on the way north, and he went over it and made suggestions and corrected mistakes. Now it will take much more work to consider his suggestions and correct mistakes. (Dammit!) will send you a copy after finally finished.

Interested in your remark on Callaghan and MacLennan[1] as writers likely to fade as their own time passes, i.e., some of the experimenters are likely to survive, while the conventional naturalists will probably fade. I suppose the same applies to poems, that each generation breaks with the past to the extent that it comes up with a form and mode suitable and popular in its own time. Perhaps a few, or one or two, of these may last longer thru the passion and excellence of their work . . . Interesting to place this critical grid atop contemporary poets . . . If you class such people as B.P. Nichol and Victor Coleman and the B.M. people in the class of experimenters, I would still argue that they don't rise above process itself. But that is possibly a man rooted in his own time speaking. And I should dislike to discard realism completely, which I don't think you meant anyway . . .

Best to you and Inge,

Al

1. Woodcock's prediction seems to have come true. Morley Callaghan (1903–90) and Hugh MacLennan (1907–90) were the most highly regarded Canadian writers of fiction in the 1940s and 1950s, but they are little read today except on introductory courses on the Canadian novel. Callaghan is best known for his stories, the novel *The Loved and the Lost* (1951), and the memoir *That Summer in Paris* (1963) which should be read with one eye on Hemingway's *A Moveable*

Feast. MacLennan's *Two Solitudes* (1945) is probably more often referred to than read, and *The Watch that Ends the Night* (1959) has its admirers. AP's admiring poem, "Letter to Morley Callaghan," is in *The Woman on the Shore* (1990).

To Margaret Laurence, from Ameliasburgh, March 15, 1971

Dear Margaret,

Greetings and all that—after the silent interlude of mail strike. I wrote you a long letter just before [we] started from Mexico which came back to me—Won't send it now, since it was mostly about Geddes, who seems a bit irrelevant after two mos.

I returned, with Eurithe of course—*we* returned—to find snow up to the hubcaps of a brobdingnagian chariot (always knew I'd use that word sooner or later), and Jack McClelland issuing statements that he must sell the company, perhaps to an American firm, imminently. Guess it's not sold yet tho. But it would be very odd to say the least if he sold out to a US outfit, he being co-chairman of the League for Canadian Independence. How could he justify that? I'm sure he would, but how?

My much bashed-about Purdy-edited book, *Storm Warning*, about to be published (unveiling in Toronto Mar. 22), myself going to Japan in early weeks of April. Will send a copy along to you before leaving.

We are staying in a friend's house near Belleville, on accounta the snow is too deep at the lake, and besides there's inadequate heating. He (the friend) is in Florida. My own mood is ghost-like, for unknown reasons—All the landmarks—my own and physical ones—seem to shift so constantly, that in some ways I scarcely know I'm back in Canada or that this is a familiar world. The strangeness of Mexico might even be more appropriate to existence.

How is your novel, which in fiction-reality must cling to compass points? I say no more than ask the question, because if you're not writing and working at it, even the query is dangerous.

I wrote 33,000 words of bio-crit prose in Mexico, got up every morning for three weeks and coffee and typewriter, banging out two-three thousand words a day, then revision and re-typing. Ron Everson went over the manuscript in Florida—where we stopped at his place on the return journey—and now the damn thing has to be done again. Also a few poems, only one seeming much good to me. Which is a fairly shoddy poem-result of the trip. But then, it never really was an enthusiasm of mine when we left, but Eurithe's. She'd like to be there still. I was sick to death of the place when we left. The prose mentioned is a personal autobiography of 1950 to '60, living in Mtl., etc., verging into criticism by discussing Lowry, Layton and Acorn as I was involved with or knew them. Dennis Lee at Anansi talked about such a book from me before I left, and I thought it a good enough idea to go ahead. But Anansi had a bad fire at their warehouse a coupla weeks ago, and I guess it makes their situation pretty shaky. Seems also they are backed by new Canadian money, in the form of the Walls, two US emigres.[1] Seems Dave Godfrey made a point of saying this to the press, causing Dennis Lee to issue a statement explaining the Walls—and I would guess there is now an acerbity between Lee and Godfrey.

Have just read a new book of poems by Ramon Guthrie, *Maximum Security Ward*, a 73-year-old US poet, which is very fine. Good review in *NY Times* caused me to buy it. Pick it up if you see it. $7.50 in US (Jesus!). Re books, I paid $1.50 for *Lady Chatterley*, at used book store in US. This no cause for comment, except, "Privately Printed, Florence, 1928." Know what that means? Not sure I do myself, except that I think it's one of the most valuable of modern first eds, and guess anywhere from $50 to $200. Got on the ordinary fiction shelves by mistake—in Philadelphia—and I paid for it while being careful the cashier or owner didn't examine it at the time. Regard it as something like picking up Hemingway's *Ten Stories*, for $1.50. Quite a number of good buys, cheap, like Klein's *Poems*, 1944, for 25¢. Callaghan's first book, *Strange Fugitive*, which is worth around forty bucks at Canadiana prices. And four or five Groves. The Groves seem to me crap, but their price has gone up fairly high. And this is the side of my character aborted by the 20th century, when I might have been a gold-seeker in the Yukon in '98.

Love,
Al

1. Ann and Byron Wall. Ann Wall became a major shareholder and president of Anansi Press.

To Earle Birney (Toronto), from Ameliasburgh, March 20, 1971

Dear Earle,
I am feeling sad—which is perhaps not a very good reason to write you another letter so soon after the first one. Also feel ghostlike at the moment, nearly invisible to others—which will pass, of course. (The goddam tv shows in Toronto won't help tho.)

To another subject than myself, I liked the Town portrait that is now postered; you're fading out of life and into death, and death to life, dunno which. (Eurithe hates it.) There is a grisly horrible quality about that poster, totally unlike you, which yet hints at all of us . . . The picture in the Geddes book is Moses of course, and the past several pictures of you have all been pretty different, which I like too. Fading from metamorphosis to metamorphosis . . . all any of us see is a stir in the spring air . . . (If this goddam letter depresses you, throw it away!)

Have you ever read *Adolphe*[1] by some obscure Fr. writer at the beginning of the 19th century? I feel like him too. Except I also feel very strongly me, which I always have. (None of this fuckin no-identity stuff about Purdy, but ghostlike at the same time. How do you figure it?)

I'll have to read *Adolphe* again to verify how silly I am. My memory of the book ten years ago is much like the guy in Proust, chasing a woman thru the labyrinths of his own mind.[2] Also a physical chase, by stage coach and other ways . . . Queer thing about love is that the mind is aware—or thinks it is—that there are certain ways to act and modes of conduct that give a certain appearance to the beloved, and which will ensure reciprocal feelings. But these rewarding ways of acting and conduct are impossible to discover, and one falls back on being one's self. Mostly a very unsatisfactory self too. But what is one's self? I find myself colouring myself to others—or at least one or two others—and can't be sure if the colours are real, or have become real because I used them.

Well, love calls me to the things of this world (Wilbur) or something . . . Guy coming out with a battery cable to start the car, battery dead now . . . Snowed six inches, and have to go to Toronto . . . Take a train I guess, for hear the roads are bad. Hope to see you before we both wander off to the opposite ends of the earth and Moses swims to Hellespont with an aqualung.

love,
Al

1. *Adolphe* (1816), by the Liberal political theorist Benjamin Constant (1767–1830), is a love story notable for its psychological perception. Though not directly autobiographical, it has its origins in Constant's complicated relationship with Madame de Staël. Its last chapter has one of the most poignant sentences in European literature.
2. AP is referring to the eponymous hero of Proust's *Du Coté de chez Swann* (*Swann's Way*) who becomes obsessed with and finally marries the courtesan Odette de Crecy.

Dennis Lee (b. 1939): editor, anthologist and poet. Lee was one of
the co-founders of House of Anansi Press and has served as literary
consultant and editor with Macmillan and McClelland and Stewart.
The esteem with which he is regarded as an editor is attested by the
fact that Michael Ondaatje's *The Conversations* (2002) and AP's *A
Splinter in the Heart* are dedicated to him. He is the author of several volumes of poetry (*Nightwatch: New and Selected Poems*, 1996)
and well-received books of poetry for children.

From Dennis Lee (Toronto), to Ameliasburgh, May 2, 1971

Al,

I don't imagine you want a reader's-report-style comment on *Square
Zen*.[1] Let me make a few remarks on it and shut up.

I meant what I said about it being too first-drafty now; that is, I think
there are some really splendid things in it already, and if you feel the
interest there's no question that you could turn it into something ener-
getic and glowing. Just to cite a few of the things I really like: Nostalgia
and Layton's poem (9–11); in fact, the thing lifts and crackles whenever
Layton gets onstage; the first winter at Trenton (36–39); a magnificent!
3rd paragraph on p. 45; the poolroom fight (52–55); Layton again (55–
58); the Annette section (60–62): the Lowry visit, the writing on the ma-
chines (72–73), what-people-read (75–78) ... those are just some of the
places where I turned on muchly.

I was puzzled, to stay at a mechanical level first, by the three sections the book is in: pp. 1–65, which are chronological pretty much, then
65–84, which goes back to the same starting point and does Lowry, then
85–97, which goes through it again with Acorn. I also wondered about
the relation of those last 13 pages to the form it appeared in *I've Tasted
My Blood*—is this the earlier draft, or a later expansion? I thought the
Ryerson piece had more sheer energy, was less diffuse and carried over
much more of the spirit of Acorn (or of Acorn-and-Purdy).

Also made me think that—if you do want to pull this out again sometime after you're back—the kind of interleaving of prose and the poetry
you wrote from particular occasions that is done in the Acorn introduction
might be a really good tactic throughout. You do just a little of it in this
draft; but it could be really strong if you did it 8–10 times, n'est-ce pas?

Beyond that, I think a quick re-read might leave you feeling as I did: that the notes and spadework are all there, but too often there are pages that are merely a string of anecdotes, with no focus beyond the fact that they happened to you in that order. They don't rise into tales, the way they do sort of in the Acorn intro; or at least they do sometimes (like the marvellous Annette tale, and many others), but when they don't it seems awfully disjointed—seems like quickly sketched vignettes and recollections, from which you can make a superb memoir if you choose to, leaving a lot out in places (like on the European tour), burnishing other places, maybe including more of your present rumination elsewhere. Plus poems you wrote later about the events. (Maybe a few sample poems of the kind you were actually writing during the period covered in the book too?)

This is all I want to say, Al Purdy's imagination can make this incandescent, without faking it—if that takes hold of you when you're back.

I'm as violently interested in it as ever—there *are* a couple of structural problems to be solved, and then the burnishing—but there is stuff in it that will be magic, several places where it already is. As you guessed, I feel embarrassed at saying to you, Hey, this is a first draft. But that's all I'm saying, no more no less; I'm grateful you've stayed as easy as you have, and hope I can nudge you—don't say yes or no now—since the mixture of affection & respect-for-craft I feel is still itching for the memoir this is halfway to being.

Out of my embarrassment, can I lay on you half of a poem I wrote back 3–4 years ago, as one of my civil elegies? I left it out of the book, because it didn't work terribly well; but I'd like to show you the last half of it which does work better and also has your name in it. Conveys anything else I've got to say, only tangentially, but conveys it.

Dennis

1. An early draft of *Reaching for the Beaufort Sea*.

To George Woodcock (Vancouver), from Japan, May 24, 1971

Dear George,
Thanks for the letter, esp. since I'm going a bit nuts not hearing any English. I think the antho. of "the Canadians abroad" is a marvellous idea. It's also amazing to me that anyone can come up with an idea that seems new to me, for an anthology. I suppose it must have been done, but I haven't heard of any. Okay, I think the idea is great for two reasons, first for the actual writing about other countries themselves, which are

presumably both subjective and objective; and second for the idea of a silent Canada, implicit in writing about other countries. I haven't said that well: but writing about other countries only leaves a stillness at the centre, defines an emptiness if you like (and I don't like), perhaps better than a direct approach.

(Sure I think you're perceptive, also logical and instinctual.)

How could this implicit definition be taken advantage of in a book such as the one you outline? Title: *The Rest of the World.* No, that's obvious and proud proud. But it's "nice." Feelings are bound to come thru about home base anyway, but still it seems there ought to be a way of turning this interior thing to advantage. Of course it would be mentioned in intro, but still . . . (I am pleased you thought of me for junior ed—tho not that much chronologically junior—for this antho. I'd love to help.) (I'm writing Jack McClelland next, and will mention you feel you might do an Intro.[1] I'll also say you have an idea for a book—the antho—and then leave it to you to outline details.)

I sometimes describe myself as singleminded (re poems), but think this term might be altered to laziness sometimes, in doing anything else but write, that is. I've wandered around Hiroshima, being alternate baffled by the language and physically tired by the effort. I'm not really at all interested in seeing Japanese architecture etc. etc. I'm interested in whatever provides me with poems (viz singlemindedness). And I have difficulty explaining myself to myself in this: am I interested in what I see apart from poems or not? I am interested in what provides poems, but certainly only from that angle. This sort of thing would be too damn self conscious for many "love life" and "enjoy everything" purists. It troubles me a little too, except I think life for me is wrapped up in poems, which is the way I discover what I think and feel. All the genuine emotions and feelings etc. other people have felt have also been wrapped up in poems for me. Incredible selfconsciousness I guess, probably common to most writers or all. Also a beforehand thing. I make up my mind previously (sometimes) what will provide poems, and then aim directly for them. Not always, but fairly often. In any CC fellowship, tho, you have to do this.

Probably anything I ever thought was important got into a poem sooner or later. And I *discovered* what was important thru poems.

I've written six here, and started four more, all of which failed. I take that last to be a signal I've written enough here. So I'm leaving.

I'm curious about the reasons for Inge's feelings about Japan—feelings easy for me to speculate about, like "westernization" etc. But that's too simple, or may be. Hiroshima is 2 1/2 million people, and it's easy to feel here that this is just one segment of a vast megalopolis (please, the dictionary), humanity living in little cubicles etc. Also, I feel there's something deadly about this bloody outright imitation of US "culture" and technology. After a particular point (not the GNP), the necessary minimum standard I suppose, it leads to the same thing the US stands for, if it stands for anything. I prefer the "standing a little apart" countries, those that still have a chance of going in a surprising human direction. Of course that's idealism. But, if anything, to be human is not to be categorized, to be pegged as this or that, Darwinian-cum-human offshoot oddballs . . . "old civilizations put to the sword . . . " But maybe I'm deceiving myself here, for I like the old Japan now vanished, and haven't the energy to search out traces now, and aim directly at what I thought of beforehand, bomb poems, human poems too I hope . . . Contradictions . . . So I'm interested in Inge's thoughts on Japan . . .

I leave here tomorrow—three weeks are enough! Six poems. Three others on other subjects, one a little surprisingly (no) on Mexico. Please write me at home address . . .

Leave out the States? Hum—mm. Token only? Been done so damn many times, or so it seems. I don't think I could possibly write a poem directly about the US myself, which might be some sort of criteria . . . I'm sick to death of talking and thinking about the US.

The *Selected*, I think, will now be (then) in fall of this year. An English agent is trying for pub over there; and I had originally said spring '72 to give her (them) a chance to find one. But I now have enough poems for a separate book besides the *Selected* as well. Call it "The Horseman" (too much like Richler?), for convenience. If the *Selected* appeared in spring '72, "The Horseman" would have to wait another year, according to Jack McStew. (Two books the same year are a bad thing, he says.) So I think definitely the *Selected* in fall of this year. That means an Intro by you sometime this summer. I hope this would not screw up plans for the score or so other books you're writing. Tho I think you must have levelled off a little now. (You know my thoughts about your prodigious output.) I'll be "most pleased," in fact damn gratified if you can do something . . . I say now: no particular length, whatever suits you.

Yours (and to Inge),
Al

1. Woodcock wrote the introduction to AP's *Selected Poems* (1972).

Dennis Duffy (b. 1938): professor of English at the University of Toronto and author of *Gardens, Covenants and Exiles: Loyalism in the Literature of Upper Canada/Ontario* (1982), *Sounding the Iceberg: An Essay on Canadian Historical Novels* (1987) and *A World under Sentence: John Richardson and the Interior* (1995).

To Dennis Duffy (Toronto) from Ameliasburgh, after May 1971

Hi Dennis,

I was surprised to see your piece on my pastness in the *Can. Studies* mag. Surprised probably because I attributed to you a remark in the *Canadian Forum*, which was contained in an article about Robert Lowell reading in Toronto. Something to the effect that I had no "depth"—[1]

After reading this piece I can never say that you have no depth. I do not want in any way to put down George Bowering[2] (apart from this note), but I think his book superficial compared to your article. You deal with ideas and concepts and their relation to feeling: he dealt mostly with emotion and my "picturesqueness," which I am exceedingly tired of—Please don't mention what I say here about Bowering, since he is a friend, and I don't wish to alienate him completely. Not that you're likely to anyway. Of course, admittedly, 30,000 words requires more than logical analysis and something about the subject of the words.

Perhaps the sentence I find most interesting is this one: "To invite callers that one originally snubbed when they first appeared is not always pleasureable." A sister-in-law of mine is right now having her insides probed by a Kingston psychiatrist. (She is the "Norma" of "For Norma in Lieu of an Orgasm.") And she is an exceedingly intelligent and sensitive woman, and I think this very intelligence militates against the psychiatrist, since I think she is very well aware of the reasons for her "illness," and they are real reasons, for I probably know most of them. But mere knowledge of reasons alone doesn't help much, at least not in the case of someone like her. In other cases, where the reasons are an immediate discovery to the person, then I suppose their reaction to the knowledge might be good.

Of course the parallel you were thinking of was not strictly psychiatric, but might be instanced in the probable general refusal of explorers, pioneers and settlers to think of Indians, whose lands they were pre-empting, as real people. But the descendants of these explorers must think of them (Indians) as real people. I think of Leslie Fiedler's[3] books in this connection; you undoubtedly know them. In any war, I expect the opposing sides have this feeling about the other, to some extent. viz atrocity stories etc.

You mention the line about one of the Dorset's thoughts which "turns to ivory."[4] I've just finished typing a *Selected*, and changed this line to something like "fused with ivory." What is the difference? I think the "fused" bit indicates rather more that the Dorset's brain still exists.

Obviously your mention of the minor and major themes that intertwine is also accurate. I've been aware of this as a prison for myself for some time: i.e., one may never entirely abandon some of these themes, but on the other hand they can begin to seem too prevalent, too omnipresent. I wrote seven Hiroshima poems in Japan, and six of them appear in the August *Saturday Night*. I regard those poems as extremely objective, with perhaps one or two minor exceptions to that "rule"; and I am only personally involved as just slightly more than a spectator and observer. I try to balance my own reactions (which is craft, I suppose); not to be sombre; tho I may not succeed in that. But you might be interested in your own opinions of those Hiroshima poems. I used as epigraph Jarrell's line: "They said, 'Here are the maps'; we burned the cities."[5]

In connection with revision, which you mention also, you might be interested to see a different ending to "At Roblin Lake" which was in the '68 *Annettes* (the frog poem), the ending being now:

> And, wondering at myself, feeling
> in this little green god of the flesh
> the same moment of elation
> I have when mind joins the body
> in one great leap beyond the universe:
> and stars shine thru his polka dots
> as he escapes back to the lake,
> and death no doubt from other monsters.

In typing the *Selected* I've been unable to resist revision here and there. But I do resist the temptation to continue on and on in this letter, based on your article. I'm sure you would also find the anti-American theme good for another article. I mention this because of the article in the same mag as yours, in which the anti-nationalists seem to me reactionaries from Mathews and Steele,[6] just as the latter are from their bête noir. Reaction produces reaction which produces reaction etc. just like on the corn flakes box. An exaggeration of feeling produced by an exaggeration of feeling.

But in reading your piece particularly I wish you were doing one of these short books on me, because then I would be able to find out more of myself. Don't you think so, doctor?

Best,

Al

1. AP is responding to Duffy's "In Defence of North America: The Past in the Poetry of Al Purdy" in *Journal of Canadian Studies* (May 1971). In 1969, in the March issue of *Canadian Forum*, Duffy, in the column "Thammas," had written: "Two English Canadian poets now write as citizens, Al Purdy and Dennis Lee. The first has not yet acquired that depth and thunder this country needs. The second is learning his craft. Many more must, if the present statelessness is to end in anything other than absorption into that Great Babylon which Lowell goads and immortalizes" ("Hearing Lowell Read").
2. Bowering had written the monograph *Al Purdy* (1970).
3. Leslie Fiedler (b. 1917): one of the best-known literary and cultural critics of his generation, the prolific Fiedler wrote *Love and Death in the American Novel* (1960), *The Return of the Vanishing American* (1968) and *What Was Literature: Class, Culture and Mass Society* (1982).
4. "After 600 years / the ivory thought / is still warm."
5. Randall Jarrell (1914–65): American critic (*Poetry and the Age*, 1953) and poet (*Complete Poems*, 1969). AP admired Jarrell's poetry and criticism, and at least one of his poems ("Red Fox on Highway 500") is somewhat indebted to one of Jarrell's ("Field and Forest"). The line quoted in the letter is from Jarrell's "Losses" (*Complete Poems*); AP used it as the epigraph to his *Hiroshima Poems* (1972).
6. Robin Mathews (b. 1931): poet, critic, and professor of English at the University of Ottawa. Mathews' polemical *Canadian Literature: Surrender or Revolution* (1978) is nationalistic and neo-Marxist in orientation; *Treason of the Intellectuals: English Canada in the Post-modern Period* (1995) is a sequel of sorts. James Steele (b. 1936): co-edited with Mathews *The Struggle for Canadian Universities: A Dossier* (1969). AP refers to Mathews' article "US Expansionism, Canadian Literature, and Canadian Intellectual History," which appeared in the same issue of the *Journal of Canadian Studies* (May 1971) as Duffy's. Mathews argues against seeing the Canadian and American intellectual traditions as based on "a shared North American tradition."

Michael Ondaatje (b. 1943): editor, poet (*Secular Love*, 1984) and novelist (*The English Patient*, 1992). Ondaatje and Purdy met at the cottage in Ameliasburgh in the mid-1960s, and though they exchanged few letters, each had a high regard for the other's work. In several letters to different correspondents, Purdy describes Ondaatje as perhaps the best poet of his generation, while Ondaatje describes him as a "great poet" in his "Foreword" to *Beyond Remembering*. AP is a presence in at least two sections of *In the Skin of a Lion* (1987).

To Michael Ondaatje (Toronto), from Ameliasburgh, June 22, 1971

Dear Mike,
Please write and give me your phone and address this summer. Your handwriting is so bad I doubt you can read it, so I'm hoping you'll tell me what you said in a letter a coupla mos ago. Mine is just as bad, hence the typewriter. Say hi to Kim.[1]

Best,

Al

1. Kim Ondaatje (b. 1928): visual artist and writer (*Old Ontario Houses*, 1977), Ondaatje's wife.

To Northrop Frye (Toronto), from Ameliasburgh, July 5, 1971

Dear Northrop Frye,
It was pleasant seeing you in Ottawa last Tuesday. You looked a bit absorbed in reverie at that table, so I hesitated for a moment to interrupt, but finally as usual plunged in. Hope no trains of thought were derailed.

I've sent along two books to you at the Massey College address, which I hope is the right one. Postage for return is enclosed here.

I just returned from Japan about three weeks ago, Hiroshima to be more exact. Wrote some poems there. Six of these will be appearing in August *Saturday Night*. I'll try to get some extra copies and send one to you.

Also have a *Selected Poems* in January, which will send then.

I may also ask you for another letter of reference, which task I expect you're sick of. For myself, whenever a young poet is especially admiring, I expect this request to follow in due course. That's cynicism, and when so many people have written letters for me I shouldn't feel that way. I do think there's something wrong with the system when such requests must be made so continually. Of course, if someone would give me an honourary degree then I might get an honourary pay cheque for doing an honourary job. This seems unlikely, however. I've had two short terms and two seniors thus far. I fully expect someone to point an index finger at me sternly and say, "Purdy, you owe the Council x dollars."

I enjoyed *The Bush Garden*, which is both a suitable title and also unsuitable. I think it no longer applies as fully as it once did. Personally, I've never felt cut off from any centres of culture or chit-chat with artists etc. There are always books, and I don't like in-group movements. I'm talkative enough via letters, as you will no doubt have noticed.

Best Wishes,
Al

David Helwig (b. 1938): editor, poet, short-story writer (*The Streets of Summer*, 1969), novelist (*Jennifer*, 1979; *Just Say the Words*, 1994).

To David Helwig (Kingston), from Ameliasburgh, July 28, 1971

Hi David,

[. . .] Re you being all your characters, you might be interested in my impression of M. Laurence's feeling about *being* her characters. She says they take on an independent existence in her mind. I interpolate here and say that she seems to feel this is uncanny, and that their conduct is inevitable, they make their own lives. This is alien to me, for I share your feeling that I project all characters, tho not necessarily all feelings. (And that is ambiguous.) But they are an extension of me, my poems are me as well. Anyone who does not know what I write does not know me. Do you feel this about your own writings? It's not like having once run a four minute mile and that fact being part of you, which of course it is if you did: but the fact that I have these capabilities and thought and accomplishments etc. etc., all the way along the line . . . i.e., I am not a face value person, whatever I seem is not so, not without other considerations. Of course, I guess most people might feel this if they thought of it.

Re the feelings of something wrong reading WGW [*Wild Grape Wine*], George Grant[1] once was embarrassed because he enjoyed *Cariboo Horses*—which I find interesting. Can't one enjoy what one disagrees

with? I don't mean burning babies or torture, the obviously sick things—
Much better to talk in person (if possible)

Al

1. George Grant (1918–88): very influential teacher and thinker whose nationalist *Lament for a Nation: The Defeat of Canadian Nationalism* (1965) reached a
very wide audience. *Technology and Empire* (1969) offers a conservative critique
of modern civilization that draws on the Judaeo-Christian tradition and the
work of Jacques Ellul, Martin Heidegger and Leo Strauss.

To Margaret Laurence, from Ameliasburgh, November 2, 1971

Dear Margaret,
You really are a home for dis-homed authors. Janes, yet.[1] I can well imagine you're different. Also you and your goddam articles, and me in the
same boat.[2] One more for Newman, and he wants me to go to maritimes,
which I do in another week or so, and so busy I can't think, talk, etc., but
I'd better be able to write.[3] Eurithe and I ended up the trip hating each
other's guts, she particularly mine.

The selling reviews bit is finding money, which I always like the feeling
of[4]—No, never thought of that, since I sell all my crap in one place so long
as they don't double-cross me (you recall the U of Sask bit) . . . Besides, I
could never keep any one thing or many things in good enough order to
find them when needed. Anyway, articles weigh on me, but poems don't.
Simple or not. I look at these enormous piles of books around me and
think how nice to sell em all but a few and go live with a nutbrown maiden
somewhere or something—impossible tho, they're all millstones.

Birney telling me he sends his books to the US mag hoping for a
review, finally gets the mag and thinks AHA, this is it. Then sees a review of Purdy and thinks Oh shit what do I hafta do?? The review ends:
"These are the two most essential Purdy books to own & Purdy, whether
he is Canadian or not, it doesn't matter, is a most essential poet to read."
Now isn't that sweet? Makes me feel great, read me because the curse of
Canadian might never have descended and I might even be American if
no one says different.

Well, I wrote eight poems on the way west, a couple not much good,
four–five a little better, and two–three *might* be good. One was a five page,
single-space poem about dinosaurs yet![5] I should say *one* might be good.
About the battlefield at Batoche, but even then I dunno.[6]

Selected comes in Jan. or Feb. and McStew (Jack, I suppose) having hassle with potential Br. publisher. To hell with it. *Storm Warning* sold 2234 copies in first report, which is pretty bad. But my own books sold much worse.

Well, if this seems unadulterated gloom I don't mean it that way. Fuck book sales! I wrote some poems, and there may be some merit in them. Which is important to me. I felt good when writing two of them, felt there's something. They will be a long time coming in books, since *Selected* has nothing but poems already in books.

Talked to Layton on phone last time in Toronto to see Peter Newman. Told him his *Nail Polish* was terrific—which it is. Not all, but much. You see it? Also reading Atwood's *Power Politics*—migawd, it's good! Also monotonous if you read right thru. Same tone, same woman, same feelings mostly. But jesus, does she get it across! But I must admit that she strikes me as inhuman in some way, tho I like her personally much. The woman bit is carried too far in her, just as the man bit is in others. Male and female just cannot react against each other that hard, and still remain real people to themselves and others. We're all fallible whatever the gender. Maybe your bit about being forlorn and bereaved because a woman writer etc. is true. Neither man nor woman ought to have to somehow compete on the same ego trip as writing. Or any other way, I expectoo. (Take your tweezers and separate those words.)

I really don't see why I'm dividing this into paragraphs, because there isn't a genuine paragraph in the letter, only a kind of pot pourri, a pot pourri being something like an omelette upside down in a pot.

I accepted a job for two weeks teaching (creatively, of course) at Banff next year, and they sent me some literature on the place, one bit which is a scream, pleasurable or tortured.

"THE BLISS CARMAN AWARD FOR BALLAD OR LYRIC POETRY

"This award was established in 1956 by Edith and Lorne Pierce[7] in memory of the Canadian Poet Bliss Carman (1861–1929). The award will be for the best example of ballad or lyric poetry submitted by a full-time student of the Banff School of Fine Arts.

"All entries must be submitted to the Director, Banff School of Fine Arts, Banff, Alberta, and must be received not later than July 23rd, 1971.

"Entries may be ballads or lyric poems of not less than 30 lines. Alternately a competitor may submit two sonnets. Entries must be typewritten on one side of the page only.

"The award will be made by a panel of judges appointed by the Director of the Banff School of Fine Arts.

"If no poem of sufficient merit is received, an award will not be made.

"The winner of the award will receive a ring once owned by Bliss Carman and now the property of the Banff School of Fine Arts. The ring will be presented on a suitable occasion and a replica of the ring will become the winner's personal possession."

(No comment by me!)

REMEMBERING HIROSHIMA[8]

In the darkness is no certitude
that morning will ever come
In dawn spreading pink from the east
is no guarantee that day will follow
nor that human justice is more than a name
or the guilty will ever acknowledge guilt
All these opinions arrived at in years past
by men whose wisdom consisted of saying things
they knew might be admired but not practised
arrived at by others whose wisdom was silence
And yet I expect the morning
and yet I expect the day
and search for justice in my own mind
abstracted from mercy and kindness and truth
become a much more personal thing
I search for it in myself
with a kind of unbearable priggishness
I detest in other people
And yet the I/we of ourselves must judge
must say here is the road
if it turns out wrong take another
must say these are the murderers
identify them and name their names
must say these are the men of worth
and publish belief like fact
must say all this in the absence of any god
having taken a gleam inside the mind
having grown an opinion like rings on a tree
having praised quietly the non-god of justice
having known inside the non-god of love

as our peers did once in the long memory of man
Self righteous and priggish of course
not humor will save it from that
nor the laughter of clowns
but it is all a man can offer the world
a part of himself not even original
the strength he uses to say it
the time spent writing it down
the will and the force of solemnity
are his life tho his life ends tomorrow
and it will and he's wrong

—Ameliasburgh, Ont.

Margaret: the line, "become a much more personal thing" is added in this typing.

Yours,

Al

1. Percy Janes (b. 1922) had published with McClelland and Stewart his second novel *House of Hate* (1970) for which Laurence later wrote a critical introduction when it appeared in the NCL series in 1976. He was staying at Elm Cottage and working on another novel.
2. Laurence had promised Newman an article for *Maclean's* "My Canada" series, and "Where the World Began" appeared in *Maclean's*, December 1978. In addition she had contracted for six articles with the *Vancouver Sun*.
3. Purdy's account of his trip to the Maritimes was included in "A Feast of Provinces."
4. Laurence had sold to York University for $800 all the reviews of her books from 1961–71.
5. Probably what was eventually published as *On The Bearpaw Sea* (1973).
6. Probably "The Battlefield at Batoche," included in *Sex & Death*.
7. Lorne Pierce (1890–1961) was editor of Ryerson Press (1922–60) and a Canadian nationalist who published, among others, F.P. Grove, Earle Birney, Dorothy Livesay and P.K. Page.
8. A revised version of this became the concluding poem in *Hiroshima Poems* (1972).

Iris E.T. Jones: unidentified

To Miss Iris E.T. Jones (Villanova, Pa.), from Ameliasburgh, November 5, 1971

Dear Miss Jones,

Thank you for sending me the zeroxes. I feel much the same as you do about them. I've been away on a ten weeks tour by trailer of western Can., therefore didn't get your letter and the zeroxes until just a few days ago.

I feel somewhat violent about Richler, whom I have met once. I've written a nasty letter to the editor of a mag called *Books in Canada* (6 Charles St. E., Toronto, Ont., Can.), finishing with: "I fully agree with Richler that ice cubes are always ice cubes—just as a prick is always a prick."

You will note that I prefer personal attack in this matter—principally because in an earlier article (on which the NY one was based) Richler said that because George Woodcock preferred to live in Vancouver, he was a mediocre writer who mined in memoirs the lives and work of more talented writers. (Words to that effect.) Now I really don't give a damn for his comments about my Arctic comments, but the Woodcock bit was entirely malicious.

I do hate to get involved in these personalities, but see no way out in this case. I do applaud your own efforts in publicising the fact that Canada is not the 51st state. But I am a writer, already involved with the Committee for an Independent Canada. If you take *Maclean's* magazine or read books of poems, you will have seen my work. I am involved in all this very definitely, but I have to keep my involvement at a level where I can still write, still function as a writer.

Richler, as I said, is a prick. However, I would rather that fact were known in Canada than the US.

All best wishes,
Al Purdy

To Margaret Laurence (England), from Mexico, February 14 or 15, 1972

Dear Margaret,

We are now camped in a sort of cottage by the sea, great waves roaring in etc. Hoping to rent a house for a month tomorrow. If we do will say so on outside of envelope, and you can write to us c/o American Express, Merida, Yucatan, Mexico. We are now at Progresso, which is 20 miles from Merida. Just came from Valladolid, where there was a Mardi Gras that kept us awake most of the night, and feel blah. Night before at the Isla Mujeres (Isle of Women).

Well the beer is great, ditto the people, but Mexico is not my bag. That is, I cannot write poems here. Wrote three or four last year, but things turn into crap in 1972. I should, of course, be satisfied with 1971, which was a very productive year (and I am), but still wanta write wherever I am. It isn't a dry spell so much as just writing badly here. Just not interested enough, I guess. I hope you are not the same. Knew this would happen before I came, which may have helped it to happen. Of course, some of the archaeological stuff is great—old cities spreading for dozens of acres. The big swimming pool at Chichen Itza is worth anybody's time. 140 feet wide, 65 feet below the surface of the ground, black and ominous, with a big stone platform where the priests hustled in virgins and children without soap. It really does look like an evil place, and one might think so even without knowing its history. The sort of spot where your backbone tingles on accounta that watered down Keltic blood.

But Palenque was the spot that impressed both Eurithe and I most. A city in the jungle foothills, where a huge tomb was discovered inside the pyramid in 1951. Middle aged man buried, or rather entombed there, fancy sarcophagus of stone, his bones smothered in jade and gold— shades of Tutankhamen. And the city of old grey stone spreading for acres and acres, abandoned by the builders long before the conquistadores came, which gives it a sense of mystery. The big pyramid has 120 steps leading to the top, a wee bit tiring at the end—Still, I don't feel like writing poems about these things, as I would in Canada, or as I would any- where that I was certain of—For instance, I know I'll write a few poems in South Africa next winter—(I have an application in for another CC, which I'll probably get—)

All the area around here, as well as farther north, is where Hernan Cortes and his men finagled the Indians out of the country—I'm read- ing a book by Bernal Diaz del Castillo,[1] who was a conquistadore under Cortes, and one can marvel at the two-facedness of Cortes. He told so many lies to the Indians (hard to think of the Maya as Indians) that if you took the opposite to what he said he would always have told the truth. Bernal Diaz wrote sometime around 1560, and died about age 90. One gathers that Cortes conquered the country mainly by using the Indians against each other; if there were any natural enmities he simply enhanced them, using one side against the other, and actually [had] some hundred thousand Indians along who were hostile to Montezuma when he took Mexico City.

When we first got to Merida we were trapped in a toilet factory in a hailstorm. Big bullets of hail enough to kill a bald man. Then a coupla inches of rain in an hour or so and a big wind. The sewer system couldn't handle it, and water roared down the street outside the toilet factory, running downhill, six and eight inches deep. Inch thick boards floated past the window. We priced the toilet fixtures and tile—very high, don't buy your toilet in Yucatan. The people seemed to think the storm was a great joke. Afterward, I went to a bar for a drink, stepped thru the door into eight inches of water—Incidentally, Eurithe tells me it's Sunday. I'm a day older'n I thought. In Merida we kinda marvelled at the Montejo house, circa 1549, built by one of Cortes' men's sons. Bearded Spaniards in grey stone carved on the front, and unless I'm mistaken some of the smaller carvings have their balls showing. Could I be mistaken? Not like Louis Riel in Regina, no cloak to cover these boys.

I'm down to a svelte 190 lbs, face like a hot dog with highlights of red, whereas Eurithe has gained a pound or two from eating the bread. All I do is drink beer and throw in a bun once in a while to soak up the moisture.

Eurithe has blown fuses with her electric frypan all the way to Cape Horn. Very embarrassing sometimes, to look at the motel lady with innocent face while she searches for a new bulb she thinks is burned out and apologizes to you. But here, in this cabin-motel, we hafta use sterno, since even the coffee pot makes the moon go dim when we turn it on—the coffee pot I mean, not the moon. Address: Me, c/o American Express, Hotel Panamericana, Calle 59, Merida, Yucatan, Mexico. IF IF we get the house. See outside of envelope.

Love, from both,

Al

1. Diaz (1492–1591) wrote *The True History of the Conquest of New Spain* (1632). There have been numerous English translations, among them *The Bernal Diaz Chronicles: The True Story of the Conquest of Mexico*, translated and edited by Albert Idell (1956), and *The Conquest of New Spain*, translated and introduced by J.M. Cohen (1963).

To Irving Layton (Toronto), from Ameliasburgh, early May 1972

Dear Irving,

I'm doing an anthology for McStew, choosing the two poems I like best from each of some twenty Canadian poets. Harold Town is doing "portraits" of each of the poets. Therefore, I hope you can make an appointment with Town as soon as possible. A followup letter from McStew will advise you further on the portrait business.

I should explain that the twenty poets chosen are those I believe the "most significant," my choice of "the best poems," those poets whose work will survive them for at least a few years, as I believe your own will. I'll also write an intro explaining my choices and lauding these particular poets. All of them now living.

The two poems of yours I want for this book are: "The Birth of Tragedy" and "Composition in Late Spring," these illustrating, as I believe, two distinct aspects of your own work.

Sincerely,

Al

From Irving Layton (Toronto), to Ameliasburgh, May 14, 1972

Dear Al,

Our letters must have crosst. Glad to hear you're doing a book[1] for McStew, and I hope it turns out to be a money-making success for you. It's doubtful if poets can be marketed like lust and love, but maybe H[arold] T[own][2] can make his portraits into erotic thrillers à la *Love Where the Nights Are Long*. F'rinstance he can have you going down on Milton Acorn, or vice versa or present Scott and Smith with fingers up each other's arseholes. I can give him some beautiful suggestions, but he's inventive enough to come up with a few of his own. [. . .] Get McStew to give Town a free hand, and I think you'll be in the money for the rest of yer life . . . as miserable as it is.

You might have chosen two other poems of mine, but I make it a policy never to quarrel with an anthologist's choice. As long as you cover them with enough laudatory lard, I don't really object too strongly, tho' what the hell you mean by "two distinct aspects of my work" I don't know. Two? But then you're a dropout and probably never learned to count beyond that.

Much love

Irving

1. Layton refers to the anthology of love poems that AP was editing for M&S. Harold Town was to provide portraits of the poets. The project fell through when AP and Town couldn't agree on how the royalties should be divided.
2. Harold Town (1924–90): one of the best known Canadian painters of second half of the twentieth century. See David Burnett's *Harold Town* (1986).

The following letter marks the beginning of a lengthy disagreement, carried on primarily through the mail, over an anthology of Canadian poems and portraits of Canadian writers that Purdy and Harold Town were supposed to work on together. The main and perhaps only reason for the failure of the project, though it's worth noting that the two did not get along, was a disagreement over how the royalties were to be divided: Town wanted 75 per cent for himself, while Purdy wanted an equal division. Purdy's autobiography, *Reaching for the Beaufort Sea* (1993), offers another account of the incident (pp. 245–7). McClelland, while trying to placate Purdy, supported Town's position.

To Jack McClelland (Toronto), from Ameliasburgh, May 1, 1972

Dear Jack,

Thank you for taking the time to set out your position on the TOWN/ purdy book at some length.

Recently a friend passed thru Toronto on his return from Florida. Ron Everson, whom Town had portrayed some months before. He phoned Town, as he had apparently been invited to do previously. Town said on the phone: "It's my book, not Purdy's." Now Town knew Everson was a friend of mine and would repeat this to me, so obviously it's a message to me. His attitude, as yours, is pretty clear.

However, friendless as I am in the places of power, I must reiterate one or two things, even add a point or two. In the first place, no contract has been offered me, and this three years (since the summer of '69) after the book's inception. After the said three years, a financial arrangement is proposed that is definitely to my disadvantage. I feel this is an injustice, and feel wounded that my own publisher, who has always had first refusal of any books I've written, should now be asking me to accept an unfair arrangement.

You mention that for a time Town felt strongly that an anthologist should not include his own work in his own book, but that you explained the matter to him. I've only one comment on that: it was and is none of his business who goes into that book. He is the artist, and I the editor. Of course it is obvious to me that he wants to be more than artist as per his comments to Ron Everson.

You say we're dealing with a black-and-white situation, and that Town is inflexible. So, it appears to me, are you.

What Town does and says really doesn't concern me a great deal. I remain indifferent to his opinions in every respect. What you say and do concerns me a great deal. I had not expected this attitude on your part, and it leaves me with a depressed feeling.

Best wishes,

Al

From Jack McClelland (Toronto), to Ameliasburgh, May 5, 1972

Dear Al,

Your letter is one that I can't really deal with. You say that mine "leaves you with a depressed feeling." I am sorry about that, of course, but you have not really come to grips with what I said in my letter. Let me restate the position.

Town's position is inflexible. The right or wrong of that position is totally irrelevant. He is inflexible, and based on my knowledge of him, there is no possibility of his changing his view. My attitude towards his position is also totally irrelevant. I can't change his view. I can't force his view. You have no contract—well, neither does he. Contracts, as it happens, are to me one of the least important aspects of book publishing. I deal in good faith. I stand by any commitment I make. I simply don't feel that contracts are any more than a necessary evil. Admittedly, had we had one in this case, no problem would exist now. There would be no book. But such an occurrence is so rare that it's not worth talking about.

You seem to resent my black-and-white attitude but damn it, Al, it is a black-and-white situation. All the talk in the world, all the opinions in the world, are not going to change this one. What I am saying is—you can talk to Harold Town, if you wish, or I will meet with you and Harold, if you wish, but I don't think it will change anything or help.

I am truly sorry about it, but that's the scene. The options I set out are all open, but if they don't appeal, then there is no book.

Sincerely,

Jack

To Jack McClelland (Toronto), from Ameliasburgh, May 8, 1972

Dear Jack,

You say I have not really come to grips with the situation, said situation being that Town is inflexible. You also say that Town has no contract, which seems to be unimportant in his case, and that you deal in good faith.

Well, cast back your mind to the time when this book was conceived, when it was suggested that I edit the book and Town do the portraits. In good faith I accepted; in good faith I took it for granted that the eventual contract would call for a fifty/fifty division of whatever money derived from the book. It never occurred to me that suddenly—after three years—Town would suddenly—no, not suddenly, but after three years—say he wanted most of the money. I don't think your good faith is involved in this situation at all, since there is no contract: my good faith is, for exactly the same reason. I have worked on the book, off and on, for three years, without a contract, which surely calls for a modicum of "good faith" on my part. I had to have good faith in the absence of a contract.

Yes, I have a very depressed feeling about this whole business. Principally because of your attitude. Town's doesn't surprise me at all. Even tho it was unexpected. I think that Town's ego demands that he be the whole show with this book, and that you support him in this. Which is why I say your attitude is depressing to me.

You say you are contending with a situation "in being" so to speak, things as they are, rather than harking back to a contract that should have existed but does not. Surely you must be aware that I took this book on the aforementioned "good faith," are you not? If it had occurred to me that such a situation would arise, then I would have asked for a contract at the book's inception. Isn't that *good faith* on my part?

Isn't it also good faith that you have had first shot at any book I've ever written? You have not been interested in any book I edited—with the exception of *Storm Warning*, for obvious reasons—only in those I wrote directly. My point here is that a contract would have been handy as well as good faith in this instance, the latter being insufficient.

So all right, Town is inflexible. I don't feel very flexible myself either. I think you ought to arbitrate with Town on my behalf. But you don't think I have any case, other than the fact there should have been a contract in the first instance. You don't feel that my own *good faith* has been in any way betrayed by Town. You don't believe that in a case like this, where there is no contract, that I am justified in thinking all along that the fifty/fifty split was natural and inevitable.

I don't want to meet Town any longer. Re taking this demeaning and unjustified short end (very short) of whatever there is from the book, I won't. This in all good faith.

Best Wishes,
Al

From Jack McClelland (Toronto), to Ameliasburgh, June 16, 1972

Dear Al,
There are some letters to which there can be no adequate reply. Yours for me is such a letter.

You suggest that I should arbitrate with Town on your behalf. Arbitration implies power or the ability to influence. I have already pointed out that in this case I have neither. Town's position is inflexible. He is clear, totally clear, on this point. In fact he feels the proposed split is more than generous.

You feel aggrieved because you assumed in good faith a fifty/fifty split. Town feels equally aggrieved in that he assumed in good faith that you would accept that his contribution in terms of time and nature was substantially greater than yours. Were your contribution previously unpublished Purdy poems, I believe he would have made no such assumption. As I have said, arbitration is of no avail. One party is inflexible and adamant. Now it seems so is the other: both in good faith.

Because your goodwill is important to me, I suppose one course would be to argue on your behalf with Town, or even to suggest that I have done so. Truthfully I haven't. And for two very good reasons. The first, to repeat again, is that Town has made it clear that nothing will change his position. The second, unhappily for me in terms of my relationship with you, is that in all good faith I agree with his view.

You attribute it to his ego. I don't. I attribute it to a straight calculation of the amount of work and creative effort in the contribution of both parties and the fact that he originated the idea. Let me try to take an unbiased look at the relative contributions and suggest that you check my summation with some other people.

The first contribution of both—and not the least—is your names. Here it is even. You are one of Canada's leading poets. Town is one of Canada's leading artists. As I have suggested earlier, if you were contributing new Purdy poems to go with new Town drawings, then a fifty/fifty split would be mandatory. No argument.

Next let's look at Town's additional contribution to this book. He was asked to do twenty original portraits. What does that involve? As I understand it, it involves a minimum of two, and sometimes many more, concentrated sessions with each subject—some lasting six hours or more. Then many hours of additional refinement, trial and error, all at a concentrated pitch of creative involvement. Plus the use of costly materials. Then the finished work emerges. Sometimes it is easier than that, of course, and sometimes it isn't. It is because of this that a commissioned Town portrait starts at about $2,500. It is because fees of that sort are charged that very few portraits are commissioned from artists of his standing. I know you are aware why artists like Town can't charge less without destroying their reputation in the art market.

So, in fact, Town is contributing about $50,000 of work to the book, less agent's commission, so let's say about $30,000. Okay, you can argue, if he is going to get $30,000 out of these portraits, what the hell is he worrying about? Sadly, Al, the fact is that he isn't. Who is going to pay $2,500 for a portrait of Earle Birney, Leonard Cohen or Al Purdy? I'm damned if I know. I sure as hell am not. Town can give them away, but he can't sell them at bargain rates, not only because it hurts his established market but because his dealer bloody well won't permit it.

An artist, like a poet, has only so much creative energy and can only do so much first-class work. It is much more than a question of time. Why, then, is he doing this? He is doing it because he believes in Canada and is interested in Canadian poets and because he thinks it is worth doing. The sacrifice is considerable. The contribution is considerable. The amount of return he will get from the royalties on this book, no matter how many copies it sells (and it won't be that many, in any case), ain't going to be much of a return on this investment. If the book sells, it is surely going to sell largely because of the portraits, which is another aspect of the contribution that must be considered. I don't here denigrate the Purdy name but there are already Purdy anthologies on the market, and there will be others, and in addition to that there are countless fat anthologies on the market that are better bargains, so why is this book going to sell? This book will sink or swim largely on the quality of the portraits. It will be an expensive book.

So then we come to your contribution. The first chore was to select the poets. Were you a neophyte coming new to the chore, were we asking you to evaluate Italian poets, Russian poets, Chinese poets, then that's one thing. For you to make up this list (or for somebody equally familiar with Canadian poets), it's only a few hours' work. In any case it didn't take you very long to prepare the list of poets. You were asked to do the book because of your existing knowledge. So the big contribution in compiling the list was really your expertise or, to put it differently, the contribution already enumerated—your name.

We come to the real contribution (other than your name and reputation), the selection of the poems themselves. You did it honestly and conscientiously. You reread and studied all the poems of all the poets involved. You did an honest and conscientious job but you were hired because of expertise and knowledge. The hours that you expended on this were really of your own choosing. The time was not wasted. It adds up to cumulative knowledge that will be valuable to you in many ways in the future.

Well, that is enough summation. There is nothing further that I can do. I think you should consider this evaluation. I think you should discuss it objectively with others. If you still reach the same conclusion, then that's the way it will have to be. I can't change Town. If I can't convince you, then all I can do is offer you a fair financial settlement for time and effort and cancel the arrangement for this book. There is no other way. I am fresh out of miracles. I sincerely believe that nothing can or will change Town's position, but anyone is welcome to try. Sorry about all this.

Sincerely,

Jack

Purdy's response to this letter repeated that he was unwilling to accept any terms other than an equal division of royalties. With neither Purdy nor Town willing to accept the other's stance, the book of poems and portraits was dropped, and McClelland was left with the job of cleaning up. Despite the serious disagreement, Purdy continued to publish with M&S until 1990, when a dispute over *Reaching for the Beaufort Sea*, his autobiography, resulted in his transfer to Harbour Publishing.

To Robert Fulford (Toronto), from Ameliasburgh, July 12 or 13 or 14, 1972

Dear Bob,

Who the hell is this guy [Dennis] Lee is talking about?[1] Am I really like that? How come I don't wear earrings, or why doesn't he who can't possibly be me?

Thompson and Brule?[2] Well, the parallel is a bit remote in time and possibility, but perhaps a bit accurate too. Physical poetry that maps a country can't possibly do that unless it also maps the human interior.

But Whitman? I detest Whitman! He bores me terribly, I won't read him. The parallel Lee makes is that by not being like him I am like him, to the extent that both wrote about their countries. At home, yes. But then, where the hell else should one be at home? Which is not a rhetorical question at all. In the US or England, which are the only other places open? Would you, Bob Fulford, be at home in either place? I doubt it. The implication in Lee tho, is that if I am at home at home then others are not. Which I guess is true enough. But despite A-burg, I regard home as no one single place, having grown too restless from travelling—which somehow expresses the essential lonely state of a human being—and expect and perhaps need to be somewhat alienated wherever I am. This so-called "alienation" does not mean lack of identification or affection, merely that as human beings we are always always cut off from other people because the self-conscious person is always aware of this separateness. So that perhaps I find an echo of myself in all strange-familiar landscapes.

Incidentally, I certainly deny that I am the "common man"—I think that's shit! The common man as I see him, almost always, is still interested only in sex, money, success, a new car and death. But then so am I, so where is the difference? But you go into a pub and talk to the habitués, they don't talk either your language or mine. With very rare exceptions, of course. So I'd rather let Ray Souster claim the title of common man, and even re him I'd give you an argument.

The business of having "opened room"—well, with shameful egotism,

I must admit that has been in my mind always, always being the last few years. On the other hand, isn't that what poems do anyway, re the interior being? Still, no one else has said that, and I hope it's true. Norman Wells is a strange place in the newspapers, for instance, and the newspaper stories or the articles or even novels will not change it from that . . . i.e., is Norman Wells a place to live for you, where people fall in love and die and do all the things people do? I don't think so. But I think it's mostly in the minds of the young that these things are important. If one writes about the Yellowstone National Park then young students will, to a degree, identify with that place . . . And this is a peculiar business, eh? I mean, your immediate backyard is your own body, then flaring outward to the areas for which you have feeling, and interest. By that token, we have always flared outward to the US. But I think this is really against whatever Canadian nature is, and that their very likeness, in language and ways of thinking, is a measure of how different we are. Because there is always one human boundary we cannot escape or pass: self-interest. Their interest is themselves, as ours has not been in the past but is now becoming because of people like Mathews. (I read your piece and liked it, and think it takes a guy like him (who I may or may not like) to make us realize we are not Americans.) The definition of Canadians has always been easy for me to make, because I have always felt it. But not easy for some others, as I also know. Canadians have been disguised as other people for a hundred years, or so I think, and suddenly are beginning to realize such disguises are useless. One world is a fine good thing, but before it always is the self, the self pre-eminent.

As a modest boast, I never expect to be anything but myself, in some ways certainly like Mathews. Warts and all. i.e. this business Lee talks about, of "making room"—has become a bit of an obsession with me. And I think of an audience of the young, without glossing over or talking down or making things other than they are. Migawd, I really do sound like Mathews to myself sometimes, times like now. Forgive it, please.

Best,

Al

1. Lee's "Running and Dwelling: Homage to Al Purdy" appeared in *Saturday Night*, July 1972.
2. David Thompson (1770–1857): English-born Canadian fur trader and explorer. His travels and surveys in the West were the basis of his important map of Western Canada. Etienne Brulé (c. 1592–1633): the French-born Brulé was one of the first *coureurs de bois* and the first European to live with the Huron.

To Dennis Lee (Toronto), from Ameliasburgh, July 18, 1972

Dear Dennis,
A few lines before going west next week. Re your piece in *SatNite*, I mean.
Whitman? I can see one point in that, I mean the being at home bit, in
a country rather than a backyard. Tho your point about writing unlike
Whitman—(his stuff bores the hell outa me) holds, your bit about opening up the country thru poems—if I agree with that I'm egotistic, but
I do. And I do like the idea of playing five musical instruments at once,
literally as to device and techniques—And I seem to myself to be, lately,
using less and less technique, or perhaps only depending on what's most
natural to me now, generally one technique, rather than the several I'm
sure I used previously.

I certainly reject that "common man" bit—come on, Dennis! Really.
Tell it to Souster. I make no claim to be extraordinary, an intellectual or
what have you, but whatever sensibilities I have are not at all similar to
those you find in a pub.

Yes, I do have this sense of "opening up" the country, writing about
places in a way that has not been done here before. But that's rank egotism, which I detest. (I've seen too much of its destroying qualities in others.) But I don't feel half-at-home, any more than all human beings are
forever alien wherever they are. I mean they are forever alien. The Camus[1]
sort of alienness, the outsider sort. Not an outsider meaning you can't
feel what others feel and do, but that you examine your own feelings and
reject many that you are supposed to have. Not mere acceptance of all
things, but rejection, acceptance after feeling and thinking about things.

As Plantos[2] in his expressed credo wishes to explore his immediate
natural environment (Parliament St. in his case) (in the same issue), I've
done that so much, or so it seems, around here, that I dislike the objective
thought of writing any more about A-burg, yet I'm bound to do it again I
suppose.

Did you notice Plantos' comment about academics going to Baffin
Island? Lit parties and back-patting friends and so on? Incongruous to
me, never thought of myself as being party of any of that activity. After
Mtl., and the Layton-Dudek axis, of course.

Anyway, it's a good piece, tho the Whitman parallel still astonishes me.

But I don't agree at all that the *Selected* is a con job. I selected the poems myself, picked the ones I liked best in the compass of 128 pages. You
mystify me when you say that. What other poems should I have chosen

in place of some that are included? Many of the poems in *Burning Bldg* were omitted—tho others included—because of the time proximity of that book to the present one. It had occurred to me that I needed, on balance, some poems from that 1970 book, and did include a few. Surely you didn't think Jack McClelland or John Newlove made that selection?

I leave for BC and Alta next week—hopefully to ride a fishing boat in the Gulf of Georgia and write at least one poem about it. Ostensibly, I'm there to do a piece for *Maclean's*,[3] since I couldn't get onto a fish boat to write poems. And of course I will write the mag piece. Also two weeks at Banff in a creative writing class. (If you snicker, I'll piss on you!) Money to go tho.

Incidentally, Neruda already has the Nobel Prize. I don't know Canetti . . .[4] Just got a book called *The Splendour and Death of Joaquin Murietta* by Neruda, and overblown, grandiloquent to a degree I should have foreseen. Neruda piles up the images and metaphors—still, I've liked some of his stuff a great deal.

We seem to have gotten out of each other's orbit, as does happen . . . Note you are now an editorial advisor or something. I had heard you were being "pushed out" of Anansi, which the communiqué from Anansi might seem to substantiate. I hope not, if it is true. My own warfare with Jack McClelland—and principally Harold Town—approaches climax and denouement, and I am depressed about it.

Al

1. Albert Camus (1913–60): French dramatist, essayist and novelist, best known for the novel *L'Étranger* (1942) and the philosophical essay *Le Mythe de Sisyphe* (1942).
2. Ted Plantos (1943–2001): Toronto editor (*CrossCanada Writers' Quarterly*) and writer of fiction and poetry (*The Universe Ends at Sherbourne and Queen*, 1977).
3. AP published "Caught in the Net" in *Maclean's* in May 1974. It is reprinted in *Starting from Ameliasburgh* as "Lights on the Sea: Portraits of BC Fishermen."
4. Elias Canetti (1905–94): Bulgarian man of letters, probably best known for his novel *Auto-da-fé* (1935), his study of mass behaviour, *Crowds and Power* (1960), and his love affair with Iris Murdoch. He appears in her novel *Under the Net* (1954). He was awarded the Nobel Prize in 1981.

From Dennis Lee (Toronto), to Ameliasburgh, July 24, 1972

Dear Al,
Felt really grouchy on the day your letter arrived, and had a bad time with it (along with everything else that was happening). Have re-read it, and

don't feel so shitty . . . maybe will try to get into the points you raise, but I don't presume it matters all that much.

No, I'm not being pushed out of Anansi, or if I am it's being done so subtly I'm not aware of it. I want to write more, is the main part—I'm going to edit only new books by our existing authors. And I'm not very good at the kind of tougher financial management that we need to do to make sure we don't go bankrupt, so I'd rather not bleed all over the carpet daily by being in the thick of them. Sometimes I dunno really what *is* happening, at Anansi or anywhere else where people are very very closely involved with each other: you know the events that have taken place, but what it is that they mean seems to change from day to day. [. . .]

"Running and Dwelling" was super-condensed in its expression—it has already drawn one letter from Robin Mathews to *Saturday Night*, coming at me for colonialism (guess what?) over the piece; he distorts everything in it, [. . .] but I guess I shouldn't have given him any openings to begin with. You have to read it 3–4 times, I think, before some of the qualifications and proportions in what I said come clear. For what it matters:

- You got me right on Whitman—I said you and he were alike in only that one respect, otherwise different. Seems to me worth pointing out because I see each of you as having done something for the first time—embodied deepseated attitudes in your poetry, making it a voice for people who have those attitudes but may never read poetry, in your respective countries. If people were accustomed to thinking of poetry that way in Canada already, there would have been no reason to pull in Whitman; but they don't, generally, and I didn't think I could get the drastic nature of the claim across otherwise. Apart from that, as I agree, Purdy and Whitman write different, think different, feel different.

- I didn't say you were an alien here; I said there was a fairly complex pull of tensions in different directions, and the sense of not knowing how our being-at-home-here is to find expression is one of those tensions—there are completely opposite ones at the same time. I don't think people can ask poets to resolve those tensions, if they're present in a widespread way; I think they can only ask them to get them on paper in a superb way. I don't see that anyone here has done it previously to the degree you have.

- Don't fuss about egoism, man—I did all the heavy declarations for you, you didn't put the ideas into my head or use me for a ventriloquist's dummy—why not lean back and enjoy some honest praise? Especially since it's accurate.

- The thing I object to in *Selected Poems* is the title, *Selected Poems*. One by one, the poems inside are super. But a "Selected Poems" it ain't, except in the sense that you selected some poems and put them in it. Any reader that sees the title, though, is bound to anticipate something very different—a winnowing of Purdy's best. There are so many of your best poems that aren't there, that someone who buys the book with that expectation—which 90% of the buyers will have—is getting led down the garden path. But I really dig the poetry itself, and think the arrangement etc. is very cunning. (I know that *Love in a Burning Building* complicated the whole thing; but that is a professional, intra-publishing screwup which the general public can't be asked to sympathize with; I just think that to have the country's best poet available in such a strange mixture of forms—a hardback selection, more or less of love poems, a paperback *Selected Poems* which isn't, but has alot more good poems in it, and alot of fine things (like "The Horseman of Agawa," I believe "The Beavers at Renfrew," etc.) available only in other, earlier books, or magazines, or wherever—I find all that a weird situation, and I don't think M&S, who have the final responsibility for the tactical planning of this kind of thing, have handled it all well. If you start from a reader's end, who hasn't read you yet but would like to find out what all the shouting is about, and would also like to get to all your best work as easily as possible, then maybe you'll see my point. What a lot of words about a draggy matter.

Yeah, we do seem to be out of each other's orbit. I can't sort out just what orbit I *am* in right now, I guess for obvious reasons. I've decided to live up at my parents' cottage in Sept-Oct-Nov, come down 2 days a week to teach at York—I hope I can get my head emptied up there more successfully than I am down here, every time I start something here, something else interrupts it and has to be written. There's something called Zeno's Paradox—you walk half way to your destination, then you have to walk half the remaining distance, then half the remaining distance, etc.—the thing keeps subdividing and he proves that you can never arrive. That's what I've been living over the last couple of months.

Sorry for such a spooked letter. Oh, one other thing—the "common man" bit. Again I don't think you read the section quite closely enough. I didn't say you were a common man; I said that the necessity of keeping that way of perceiving things present in your poetry was one necessity you feel, and it co-exists with the necessity to see things from very opposite ways, and that tension embodies larger tensions in the country. That strain in your writing is exemplified by stuff right in the poem you sent, like "It's downright unwomanly / and unnatural in fact / it just ain't nice." That's a "common-man" voice being used, and being spoofed at the same time—but the perspective on it is double, you're not *just* twitting it, you've got some investment in it, *and* in its opposite. Is all I said.

Aw shit, would enjoy drinking beer with you sometime. Ciao for now. Hope this reaches you.

Dennis

Pierre Elliott Trudeau: (1919–2000): prime minister of Canada 1969–79 and 1980–84. AP went to Cuba in 1964 with a group that included Trudeau. He sent Trudeau copies of several of his books, and the latter acknowledged them with brief letters. While AP admired Trudeau, the late poem "A God in the Earth" (1990) places him among "men who accomplished little / and latterly failed / without even knowing they failed / What shall we think of them / these small men / who cannot lift the heart / or stir the blood with visions."

To Pierre Trudeau (Ottawa), from Banff, August 2, 1972

Dear Pierre,

It was most pleasant to see you—and your wife—again after what seems a long time. Your comment about myself not seeing you because of your office—altho I said not at the time—is probably true. After all, having a sandwich with the justice minister is a bit different from the same sandwich with the P.M. And it did occur to me that you would be much too busy—and important, I must admit—to have any time. This is not just humbleness, I hasten to add, since I'm not a particularly humble person. I thought it was being realistic. But after seeing you briefly here in Banff I realize I must have been wrong. Your well-known personality—and I am not being sardonic—always did exert a slight spell over me as well as others. (See the poem in *Wild Grape Wine*.) (The one about the Liberal leadership convention, that is . . .)

As mentioned when you were here, I'm going to South Africa this winter. With odd feelings about it. As if I've pushed my luck about as far as it can go, and something is bound to happen to me. Dunno if you have such premonitions or not.

I am, as seems usual, somewhat depressed about Quebec. Last year I talked to René Lévesque re separatism etc., and wrote a piece for *Maclean's*.[1] Just a few days ago I wrote a short poem on Lévesque,[2] which I copy on the reverse side of this page. But despite this feeling, I can't think anyone else could handle the whole de facto situation as well as you already have, and will probably be called upon to do again in future. I went to Ottawa during the FLQ crisis nearly two years ago, feeling that even civil war might not be a fantastic outcome. And of course, wrote a poem on those feelings at the time. And I've asked the CBC at Toronto to send you a record I made last year, called "Al Purdy's Ontario" . . .

I'd like very much to have a sandwich, coffee, or whatever, before I leave for South Africa via England this winter. And will drop you a note c/o Miss Viau. Incidentally, I went to Japan, Hiroshima, that is, last year, and the poems appeared—six of them—in *Saturday Night*. I'll try and dig up a copy of that issue and send it to you. Please say hi to your wife for me, in case she remembers the somewhat ill-at-ease poet when you were both in Banff.

Best Wishes,
Al

1. "Lévesque: The Executioner of Confederation?" *Maclean's* (October 1971). It is reprinted in *Starting from Ameliasburgh* as "Bon Jour?"
2. "A Handful of Earth."

To Earle Birney (Vancouver), from Banff, August 2, 1972

Dear Earle,
Eurithe didn't make it this time, she deciding that the house being rented in Trenton (now empty) more important than coming. I am of course desolate.

I have managed to annoy my US students, one in particular, with anti-US poems, she saying twice she had no intention of going to bed with me. I really think she must have it on her mind at that rate. Indulged in a nose to nose shouting match with her. Also have offended the sensibilities of several others, to the point where I am now taking in my own poems for criticism since they're so delicate about their own. Not as hard-boiled as I sound however. It is tough to have your poems pulled apart by some guy with a loud voice.

Met Trudeau in the Alpine library Sun. Surprised he remembered me after so long . . . I had kinda backed off from getting in touch since I thought he'd be so busy and important etc. To my surprise he said he hoped it wasn't something like that. By god, I have never found him as arrogant as other people say.

I will need you badly in Vancouver. This woman is writing me love letters, and has formed an undying attachment etc. Normally I would not object to this, thinking such admiration well-founded and deserved. But I don't like her looks (met her spring last year), and she may figure out what hotel I'm in—If I grow a beard do you think that sufficient disguise? Or maybe a trench coat and jodhpurs? May I enlist your help for male lib?

Come off that crap about McStew not wanting your poems! I mean I may be dumb, but not that dumb. [. . .]

Anyway, introduce me to the various "friends-of-my-wife" in order that I may have protective coloration and suitable bodyguard in case this woman catches up with me. (By the way, I have writ a pome on this situation. Me blushing shyly behind my modesty and protesting coyly. Hey?)

I too have no contact with McStew, having had a falling-out with Newlove, and only the p.r. people as dry grapevine.

As I may have mentioned, gonna go fishing on a fish boat in [Gulf of Georgia] there. (I like "fish boat" instead of gillnetter or seiner, sort of more Purdy colloquial!) Seems that this Jack Ferry Associates is eager to show me the fishing industry. It's like the Martian who landed atop the Vancouver Hotel, didn't have to say "Take me to your leader" Bennett[1] was already there to get his vote as a landed Martian emigrant. (All right, go ahead and kill me for that!) See you in Van. around the 19th.

Luv,

Al

1. W.A.C. Bennett (1900–79): long-time Social Credit premier of British Columbia.

To Earle Birney (Vancouver), from Ameliasburgh, November 9, 1972

Dear Earle,

Your notepaper is making me envious. Have decided to lead with my ace-gunfighter I guess.[1] Top this one, unless there's a motel in the crater of Vesuvius.

The ills the flesh is heir to have sorta got me lately, so doing little but drink beer and moan about my sorry fate. Well, a little more. Arranged the African trip today, Dec. 11, with stopover in Rio. Come back more or less when I feel like it. Movie named *Black Orpheus* was made in Rio years ago, and I hope to tromp over the poor section overlooking city where that was made. [...]

Of course I see your point about readers. Large countries, as we both know, tend in some ways to be even more insular than small ones. They believe the sun rises and sets on their own productions, for instance, associating art and literature with great power, and using the same adjective. Or so I think. Perhaps at least part of the time, the kinda manifest destiny sense a big country may have actually does help in the arts, just as ego is necessary for a writer to write well—Again, so I think, and these are not profound thoughts.

Still, when I think of your poems and you, and Layton and his, apart from nationality, particularly your best, I don't feel in the slightest bit that these are inferior. One can't permanently remain interested in inferior literature, can one? Anyway, one part of the mind leaps the picket fence of nationality, decides these are fine poems whatever their origin. Except I don't think of origins at all times, only when it's necessary. And whether your poems or my poems ever get published elsewhere or not, I can't think yours are anything but good, and don't feel any inferiority in myself either.

I'm not at all sure mine will ever get published elsewhere. And while not precisely satisfied with this outcome, it's still too much trouble to worry about it or make more than a somewhat lethargic effort. I realize I'm taking the stance of an old lady in full flush of euphoria after having written a poem, and she believes it to be the greatest ever—all her friends tell her so. Perhaps we are like that old lady in a way (altho I doubt it), our friends (fellow Canadians) saying we are great etc. But you can make an argument for either side here, Rod McKuen[2] or Emily Dickinson ...

Before I forget (now we're in Mexico), Atwood's book [*Surfacing*], I agree, very fine. One thing troubled me, the complete switcheroo at the end. After heroine is back to nature, she suddenly turns round goes back to city and her lover. That wasn't led up to far as I could see. There is a very shifty centre in a woman like that. Doesn't one want a modicum of persistence and permanence in the self?

Haven't read her handbook on lit [*Survival*], but hear the title is the key, and she takes poems of ours (yours, mine, Layton's etc.) to demonstrate that theme. Good enough, but at this point I've no doubt about survival, and doubt also I was thinking of it the way she seems to . . . If I worried much about that it would be like worrying about death etc. All of these things have their place in a life, and we are preoccupied with all of them, more or less at one time or another.

Incidentally, re death, many years ago in Vancouver Curt Lang tried to get my poems published there, the publisher turned em down, saying they were about sex and death. Which I agreed with then and do now. Any writer worth his salt has them for subject matter, of course in degree. They also involve love and life. Anyway, thinking of using SEX AND DEATH as title for book, with a note about that little anecdote above. Have a nagging thought tho, that Berryman used something similar before he said farewell cruel world. [. . .]

Again reverting to ego-boosters like US publication, I'm one down to practically everybody on another ego aspect, the writer-in-rez bit. Never had an offer in solid terms, tho U of Man. did nibble last time thru . . . I could use the cash as apart from ego-support.

But I gnaw away on this US pub bit—I really think one can't waste time moping, you know the poems are there to be written, and it seems like hardly anything has been already written that cannot be bettered. I say that not as boaster or braggart or in excessive self-confidence, but as what I regard as simple fact. Every time your mind stretches a bit at some euphoric written instant, you realize this is so. Despite all the great things, very little comes within your peculiar orbit and registers as something you would like to have done . . . Or so I feel. For it seems to me the best stuff is yet to be written, and while I may never even come close, no inferiority is gonna stop me from having a shot at it. Which is a kinda manifesto, except not so thundering, nor sad as all manifestoes are kinda sad . . .

Jesus, we go far back in time, when you resurrect those old letters and poems. I remember only "Night Errant" or was it with a "d," Errand, or is there such a word? That other self, so far back, and your other self . . .

I've been tinkering with "Joe McLeod"[3] with your letter beside me, dunno if it's better or worse yet, but will be different. You have an eye for that sort of thing, whereas I was only uneasy about the poem. I'm really talking about myself in it, the business of gods and idols. One always expects too much of one's friends or women, the sandpapered burglar's fingers encountering an abrasive alien soul under flesh. Not only iconoclasm re Sadler's idol, but the fact that McLeod himself could probably never feel those things . . . And it gets a bit similar to Hemingway I suppose . . .

What is Faust to me,
in a fairy splash of rockets
gliding with Mephistopheles on the celestial parquet!
I know—
a nail in my boot
is more nightmarish than Goethe's fantasy!
                              —(Mayakovsky)[4]

Surprised as hell you don't know him. Also came across this re sculpture of Aphrodite:

Aphrodite gazed down upon Cnidus, and said,
"Where on earth did Praxiteles see me naked?"

That written 2,500 years ago! Or did the translator write it? But I'm
reading Mayakovsky again as a result of this exchange, and more than
ever enjoy him. Will send the book along to you if you want it, but quote
some from "Cloud"
    for myself as well as you . . .

                              Al

1. AP is writing on stationery from the Desert Haven Motel, Lovelock, Nevada;
the letterhead has a drawing of a cowboy leaning against a fence. He looks more
like a cowhand than a gunfighter, though his right hand has formed a mock pistol.
2. Rod McKuen (b. 1933): minor American songwriter and lyric poet (*Listen to
the Warm*, 1967), very popular in the period.
3. See "Beat Joe McLeod" in *Sex and Death* (1973).
4. Vladimir Mayakovsky (1893–1930): playwright and poet who saw himself as
the voice of the Soviet Revolution. Disillusioned with the Soviet Union's turn
to Stalinism, he shot himself in 1930. AP refers to his "The Cloud in Trousers"
(1916).

To George Woodcock (Vancouver), from Ameliasburgh, November 25,
1972

Dear George,
Leave for Africa Dec. 11, feeling sentimental, wish you were in the east
so could have a drink and yak a little . . . Everything gets a little frantic
around this time, as you know well. Busy, jesus! But I suppose I like it, or
wouldn't take it all on.

Sorry I didn't see your book before leaving—altho may yet—will certainly on return. Mail gets held for me in Belleville, since I've had sad experience of mail getting lost when forwarded.

I don't remember you mentioning *Who Killed the Empire?*, but I'm liable to miss things when drinking anyway, or even when not. Good title. You make me curious about it.

Have you got any news of the Atwood resurgence there, I mean principally in *TorStar, Globe,* and *SatNite* . . . *Surfacing*'s very sharp and good, tho I wanta punctuate it for her, and she'd kill me if I did. The switch at end doesn't seem quite prepared for to me. Nor does the central theme of *Survival* seem to hold, because survival is practically the spine of worldlit. And yet, despite all strictures, Atwood seems to me the white light of writing in Canada right now. Did you see anything of the feuding of K. Dobbs[1] and the Anansi-New Press nationalists? Letters in the *Star*, and answers in Dobbs' column . . . Dobbs is sad re Macmillan sale, yet Macmillan remains a minor item, hardly affecting matters one way or the other—unless Maclean-Hunter mushrooms into it and changes the picture.

Best,

Al

1. Kildare Dobbs (b. 1923): editor, essayist and travel writer, won the Governor General's Award for the autobiographical *Running to Paradise* (1962).

To Margaret Laurence (England), from London, December 12, 1972[1]

Dear Margaret,
Tried to phone you on arrival this morning but operator couldn't find your listing despite my detailed & intricate etc.—So what the hell—! Eurithe and I will be over in late March I expect—

Got your letters yesterday—didn't write after arranging passage (your reservation helped) in the end I had *two* reservations. BOAC at Tor. told me.

Any way, tumbled into bed here round 9:30 after abortive phone call. Dead weary, etc. Now 3:40, my flight at 7 pm.

Yeah, read Atwood's *Survival*, think it's admirable. Creating a lot of arguments, too, which is good. Of course the victim bit is true, but you can't make as much of it as A. does, because it's one of the major themes of world lit—The part about five obscene sexual positions is also relevant, altho she's making political awareness perhaps a larger part of Canlit than it is. Best part of book is impression here's a sharp mind that read & thought & decided—One doesn't have to agree with her all the time—Anyway, what such a book does is tend to create a critical climate for one's own work, viz Eliot—Any poems or fiction Atwood writes now is liable to be measured with her own yardstick. She is, in some ways, saying: this is how poems & fiction should be written—

I would find it difficult to think of Hagar as victim despite her being trapped & dead at the end. Or Duddy Kravitz. David what's his name in Buckler, yes[2]—Nor do I think of my own poems as a whole demonstrating the victim thesis. So much one could say—but too long & tiresome. I'm in a fair state of malaise right now myself. The point of grimness where you say, what do I really want to do next & how important is it? This is where the Zorba-thermostat[3] ought to cut in. But it ain't up to now. Will write you from Jo-burg.

love

Al

1. Purdy was on his way to South Africa.
2. Hagar is the protagonist of Laurence's *The Stone Angel* (1964), Duddy Kravitz of Richler's *The Apprenticeship of Duddy Kravitz* (1959), and David Canaan of Ernest Buckler's *The Mountain and the Valley* (1952).
3. "The Zorba-thermostat" is unclear, though it must have something to do with *Zorba the Greek* by Nikos Kazantzakis (1883–1957).

To Earle Birney, from Coatzacoalcos, Mexico, February 27, 1973

Dear Earle,

Mexico is getting to be a habit with me—us, for Eurithe is here too. Driving to Yucatan—Ron Everson will join us in Merida Mar 20 for a coupla days, then we head north. Stopped at San Miguel for a night and cordial visit with Leonard Brooks and Reva.[1] We're supposed to call again on return trip, but dunno. Eurithe wants to go via Tampico—

Road death today a hundred miles north of here. Truck took a turn too fast & somersaulted over & over, hit a kid too—All this seen thru rear vision mirror, or so it seems now—Truck & cars stopped behind us. Don't think driver could possibly survive—Eurithe kinda went into shock, doesn't wanta talk about it—Very grim business—[2]

Did some writing in Africa, but not satisfied, never am I guess—Stayed a week at Margaret Laurence's in England. She's just finished another novel. We had a few drinks before I left, in fact quite a few—

Hear from Leonard Brooks you're dissatisfied with reviews of your new book—there aren't enough of them—Sorry to hear that—I enjoyed it.

Hope to see you in Toronto this summer. Our address until Mar 23 will be c/o American Express, Hotel Panamericana, Calle 59, No 455, Merida, Yucatan, Mexico. We'll be home about mid-April.

Love
Al and Eurithe

1. Leonard Brooks (b. 1911): English-born Canadian painter who has been a longtime resident in Mexico. His work hangs in the National Gallery (Ottawa) and in the Art Gallery of Ontario. He has also written several books on painting, including *Watercolour . . . A Challenge* (1957).
2. The accident is described in some detail in the poem "In Mexico" (*Beyond Remembering*, 560–72).

To Margaret Laurence (England), from Florida, February 11, 1973

Dear Margaret,
Great news the novel [*The Diviners*] done. I hope it comes fairly close at least to your own difficult original vision, so like turning yourself inside out and then finding what you were after has reversed itself. [. . .] You know what I . . . Secondary wish, I hope it's a novel others also think is fine, deleting the word "great" and Barry Callaghan chokes when he reads it as he must to verify his own mistakes. I am personally pleased to see you get into something that, while it includes the personal vision, also moves to a greater degree into objective narrative. Obviously you were not with the Selkirk settlers, except in the sense that a novelist is always with his or her people, therefore it gives you a different kind of creative scope. As you may have guessed, I have misgivings about the accompanying song bit and all that, but regard it as unimportant window dressing. I guess you don't. Well, the spinal cord is the writing, just as it must be in this picture book McStew projects for me next year with photos etc. à la Farley.

Reverting to that project, it's been decided that *In Search of Owen Roblin* shall be the poem, and not "country" or "rural" poems for the photographer. You remember the garbage dump bit that's part of the longer poem. It's probably the best part, incidentally. I wanta do more on that poem (*In Search of . . .*), but can't now. Fuck being objective too. Perhaps like a novelist in this instance, I wanta get everything about me into this, obviously ego eh? If I inhabit those goddam early settlers then they are me and I am them. I'd like to get a farmer in there who's a failure, can't keep up with more successful ones, dies trying and knows his own failure. How in hell do I do that? One poem would do it if I can write it. You'll have to see this one of mine. It both fails and succeeds in different places . . .

We went to Cape Kennedy the other day, on accounta I wanted to see the rocket graveyard, now called a museum. Read a book in Africa that made me think a poem possible re the graveyard. Outmoded rockets and all that, now mouldering into rust. But they're not mouldering, painted and trim as new corsets or working model of a ballista. Had to take a two hour tour by bus of the whole shebang, bored the hell outa both Eurithe and me. Some 120 people in two buses. Two tours of places, rest of time in bus. Eurithe got out first time, viewed computers and lunar modules like a cynical martian housewife and got out first of all the 120. I was second. Second out-of-bus was for the biggest building in the world, the rocket assembly building, which has weather of its own, huge big large monster great heaviest farthest most wonderful—she stayed in the bus, wouldn't budge, all alone. I too all alone among the 120 and bored. The poem reflects my boredom, just lousy. Maybe I oughta turn it around that way, to boredom of the big and wonderful wow explosions. Makes me think of north poem I wrote in the arctic with me in a boat and all the world south, so that for the first time in my life I could piss on the world.[1] Metaphorically of course. Before going there I had visions of whole city blocks of black rafted into the sky and burning to ashes, meaning the money spent on rockets that would not be spent on slums. And two terrified little monkeys (Able & Baker) in 1959, clinging to each other in outer space, and wondering where are they now? Buried among the poisonous snakes and alligators of Cape Kennedy. Human graveyards at Cape C. too, those of the earliest settlers, not much attention paid to them of course when astronauts are there for autographs. (Hey, Dr. Laurence what about your auty-auty-graph?)??) (??) (go ahead and say it, I dare you).

The hero-worship letter, not important really, as you know. I *don't* think it makes you look ridiculous, no, what the hell, part of this age like others, and it influences one other person to read your books great eh? Look at me being Walt Whitman to Canada according to Dennis Lee . . . Walt Whitman Purdy aha aha . . . As you know I don't agree that when the Manawaka circle complete that you're complete. You can always collaborate with Simone de Beauvoir on how awful it is to be a woman.[2]

215

But the old sausage-grinder doesn't stop that easy. You're thinkin of the vital things like sex and children and all that. "An aged man is but a paltry thing / Unless could clap its hands and sing / And louder sing / For every tatter in its mortal dress . . ."[3] Why the hell not? Up to you to find out how. And I don't mean Ayn Rand.[4]

Do read [Ramon Guthrie's] *MAXIMUM SECURITY WARD.*
Probably good to get away so you can be miserable in comfort.

love
Al

Leave here in three days.

1. "South" in *North of Summer* (1967).
2. Simone de Beauvoir (1908–86), French novelist, philosopher, feminist, and political activist.
3. From "Sailing to Byzantium" by William Butler Yeats:
    An aged man is but a paltry thing,
    A tattered coat upon a stick, unless
    Soul clap its hands and sing, and louder sing
    For every tatter in its mortal dress.
4. Ayn Rand (1905–82), American novelist and champion of individualism, known for her two best-selling novels, *The Fountainhead* (1943) and *Atlas Shrugged* (1957).

From Margaret Laurence, England, to Ameliasburgh, April 21, 1973

Dear Al,
Thanks for letter, just received. I wonder if you got mine (probably crossed with yrs) saying Elmcot now sold? Very relevant to what you said in yr letter! Actually, I could have (probably) made about £5 thou more if I had sold to a developer. But I would have felt like hell about it. As it is, it has worked out (unless any snag develops) very well for me in ways other than financial, as well. Mr. Wilson, the buyer—the "squire" across the road at The Beacon—will not tear down Elmcot nor cut down the trees; he will rent it to a couple or a family for a pretty low rent until such time (if ever) that one of his sons wants the place. Anyway, as long as he or his sons have it, the house will remain. He's giving me the price I wanted for it—that is, the price I reckoned I could reasonably expect from a private buyer, not a developer, namely £25,000. Well, that is 3 times what I paid for the house; even reckoning the money I've put into it, it is twice the total amount of my investment in the place. Who needs more? More than that, and one is really getting greedy. I'll have had 10 good years here, very

productive re writing and a very good place for the kids to have grown up, and the house will now provide me with considerable more £££ than I put into it. The great side-effect of all this is that Ian and Sandy Cameron will be renting the place for the next year, from Wilson, which is good in itself, and which also means David can stay on for awhile, until he decides where he wants to go. So—I'm not complaining. I *was* determined not to sell to a developer, and as luck or chance would have it, it's turned out well for me, which is gratifying, as doing what one considers the right thing to do very seldom brings any kind of bonus! This house has always been lucky for me.

I've sent novel to publishers now. I'm not exactly pacing floor, but nearly. During this past week, I've re-read my manuscript copy twice, trying to see if the damn thing is any good or not—how crazy can you get? I've got twenty million things to do, re clearing out house, but can do nothing until I hear about novel. I know that the editors are going to ask for a lot of cutting on the manuscript, *if* they accept it at all. I just don't feel like going back into it, Al. What to do? I don't even think it can be cut all that much. Well, we'll see.

Have bought myself a cassette tapecorder and am fascinated by it. Am going to go in for cassettes and not bother about a record player when I get to Canada. Will just get some of my favourite records put onto tapes. It's really marvellous. And so simple that even I can work it without difficulty.

I'll bet anything that Eurithe wouldn't sell the farm to an American, when the chips were really down.[1] And I know damn well you wouldn't. This "highest bidder" bit is such a specious argument, isn't it? It's why we now don't own large amounts of our own country. No point blaming the Yanks for that. It was all sold by Canadians.

I should be back in Canada by July 23 or around there. Oh heavens, how will I ever get everything done here by that time? I will, or course, but I do panic a bit sometimes.

Love,

Margaret

ps. it may be quite true that everybody has their price—in fact it probably is true. But it isn't necessarily in monetary terms. It depends on what one wants the most, which isn't always money, given a certain basic coverage in that area—I mean, if one was starving, naturally one would do almost anything in order to eat. I guess we all have areas of vulnerability—I'm not sure what mine are; it must be something to do with either writing or my kids, or both. If I *knew*, absolutely for certain, that *The Diviners* would *never* be published, by anyone, unless I cut out several scenes which I consider essential—would I do it? I think now I wouldn't, but I can't be sure.

1. In an earlier letter, Purdy had described how his wife had said that she would sell her land to the highest bidder, whether or not that person was American.

To Margaret Laurence (England), from Ameliasburgh, April 30, 1973

Dear Margaret,

Okay, congratulations and apologies. I probably said you'd sell to highest bidder. Maybe Eurithe wouldn't sell to an American when chips prone, but she says she would. But she won't get the chance.

Of course it's our own damn fault for selling out, whatever—(*interruption*) it is: but what happens afterwards, how the people act who do the buying, is only indirectly the fault of the sellers. i.e., the buyers have a vested interest, a power lobby both in US and Canada if there are enough buyers (and there are), an effect on their employees (Canadian, that is)—"We won't sell to such-and-such, our worse mousetraps or our better detergent etc." All sorts of ramifications, as you know. Anyway, I wronged you, and I hate to wrong a woman let alone a man, altho if it comes to that I'd prefer to wrong a woman, and wouldn't you prefer to wrong a man?

What the interruption was: Mel Hurtig in Edmonton asking me to write a history of Ontario, 150,000 words, taking two years, with an advance of living expenses for that time.[1] Jesus, did he take me aback and forrard. Phone call that is. I'm too shell-shocked at this moment to pursue any line of thought. It would call for intensive research of all kinds, interviews—I should say "popular history"—since his *History of Alta.*[2] sold 140,000 copies, which is the reason he thinks Ont. might do much better. Again, i.e., money. I am happy to sell out for money, unless . . . On the other hand I'd wanta do a good job by my standards—which is liable to take a goddam lifetime.

I'm sorry, when I began begun started incepted took off with this letter, meant to say hell it's gotta be a good book. I mean, didn't the great Laurence write it? Else what's that ink-stained gremlin wound up with typewriter ribbon doin in the corner looking cowed and four ounces underweight? What it amounts to is: you can't do fuckall until you know do they like it—The writing itself has gotta be good (since that's you), but what you wrote about: does that hold together? (I feel the same way

218

when I write an article, and hearing your outraged snorts, say humbly that this is a matter of personal insecurity about creativity: it may have left us and we don't even know it or feel the departure of what we didn't know we had when we did have it except for smug pride that's all in the past and memory being what it is may never have existed except as smug pride now that we once might have been writers. (Commas, where you want em.) I mean, this is the visceral disease of writers; is what I write any good? I don't think you could now write anything really bad, not as to the prose style etc. . . . . Subject matter and a sort of overall thing—that's what you're worrying about I expect. How well do the style and the inner feeling of this-is-right meld in with the structure, so-called plot etc. God, I hope it does.

I am still thunderstruck by the Hurtig proposal. It's too big a thing to glibly say yes I will or no I won't. I doubt my own capacity, by which I mean vitality and energy to do all the research etc. required. More specifically, I get tired—my eyes do—after a certain amount of reading (which calls for an eye doctor of course) . . .

What do you want most, since you say either writing or kids—no, that's wrong, those are your areas of *vulnerability* you think . . .

And yet, they're gone eh? The kids I mean. They're not really yours, except in a kinda loving memory sense. They don't need you as they did. What remains? Something apparently. Maybe, for a woman, and perhaps some men, a clinging to a different kind of life, when one "was needed" when the juices all flowed at a different rate etc. That's kinda simple, I guess. Writing: the writer normally says he/she hates it, but loves moments of it (or is that normal?) . . . But I look back, think, did I ever really love it that much? Dunno. Might well have hypnotized myself about it somehow. I mean about the good moments. Were there any. Sure, I know when I write a good piece, you do too. But doesn't one idealize and romanticise that, in the past, into something more than it is? Is it all that great, really? Or is it the capacity itself rather than the moment of doing it? Dunno, again. I love the ability and capacity that I sometimes think I have to write well, but the subjects I'm interested in grow less and less, i.e., I write about the blacks in S.A. from my own cynical no-purdy-won't-be-a-guerilla stance, instead of stirring saddle songs of revolution and the bro-hood-of-man.

Hurtig has really fucked me up, the bastard. After being lost about writing, my thoughts inevitably go back to his offer. A "popular history" (his Alta history sold 140,000,* or did I say that?) is one thing, the way I'd wanta do it is another. He knows my prejudices and would expect em, but I'd also wanta do a factually accurate book, but an artsy one as well—by that last I mean not just a personal recital of fact and interpretation. I'd be liable to shave dialogue between Tiger Dunlop and John A.[3] into the section on the settlement of Upper Canada. Well?

love,

Al

*yes, I did—

1. The sentence following the italics was typed in red.
2. James Grierson MacGregor (b. 1905) was the author of *A History of Alberta* (1972).
3. William "Tiger" Dunlop (1792–1848) was a journalist, politician, and an official of the Canada Company, whose *Statistical Sketches of Upper Canada* (1832) was designed to bring settlers to the province. John A. Macdonald (1815–91) was the first prime minister of Canada.

Jean Woodsworth Ross (1913–95): one of AP's favourite cousins.

To Jean Woodsworth (Toronto), from Ameliasburgh, April 5, 1973

Dear Jean,
(I almost said "Jean Ross" above). Good to hear from you. Bad to hear the news about Don.[1] I had, last Sept. or Oct. or whenever it was called at Don's farm to visit him, and the guy there said he'd bought the farm and also that Don had had a fall from a horse and was in Kingston. I'm ashamed to admit that, altho I meant to visit him, I left the country for Africa before I got around to doing so. (I've just returned from Africa, and then Yucatan) . . .

I agree with you completely that Don had a tragic life and tragic death—But tragic to whom? I guess not to himself. But to you, to Claire, perhaps to Rusty, and yes, to me. When we were youngsters I liked him very much, but after the war I thought he was guarded, suspicious and defensive. While, perhaps, I had lost those same qualities in myself. I'd rather remember him on the farm when we were kids, and accused of putting eggs in the horses' water trough, and both guilty as hell.

I had been in BC until sometime in Sept. doing a story on BC fishing, so you couldn't reach me at that time. I am as appalled as if this thing had just happened, and it does "make very little sense" as you say. Unless one is religious (I am not) life tends to make little sense. It appears that something might have happened to Don during the war that sent him into that drinking frenzy and its death culmination. I am deeply sorry. I wish he could have had a more satisfactory life. To me, that "good life" depends on both personal and altruistic (still personal I guess) accomplishment, or what the individual thinks of as accomplishment. Again, I am deeply sorry.

Jean, I'll phone you when next in Toronto, which should be in next few weeks. Eurithe and I just drove some 4500 miles in ten days, and boy we're tired. That address in your letter is 207 Ellis Ave., which should be in phone book.

Until then all good wishes,
Al

1. See the poem "My Cousin Don" in *Piling Blood*.

To Pierre Trudeau (Ottawa), from Ameliasburgh, May 1, 1973

Dear Pierre,
Greetings and salutations. I'm just back from Africa and after that Yucatan and Quintana Roo. The black/white thing in Africa is even worse than I thought, merely reading about it in Can. Br. and US newspapers. I mean, separate entrances to urinals, liquor stores, separate buses etc. You'd hear screams in the night and breaking glass in the hotels I stayed at in Cape Town and Johannesburg. Not crummy hotels either, middle-class places like Claridge's in Cape Town. After three weeks of it, I got depressed. Drinking brandy in my room with a black houseboy made me think I was making a flaw, a slight chink in all the monolithic apartheid laws. Of course I wasn't, but it's a nice fantasy I got into a poem.

And in Quintana Roo, driving close to the Br. Honduras border, a flock of green parrots shat on the car. One hasn't lived until shat on by green parrots. If you haven't been there yourself, I'd recommend it as a marvellous place. Cozumel, an island in the Caribbean, for instance. Pre-Columbian ruins there, and five of us drove a rented jeep up a little rocky jungle path until we had to park, and went the rest of the way afoot. All sorts of water sports from Cozumel, the sort of thing you might like.

Congrats on still being the P.M. Much more exciting, I'd think, teetering on the razor's edge of the NDP. If you have any spare minutes I'd love to have that lunch mentioned in Banff. In 1967 I sat in the visitors' gallery in the House, and wrote some poems. Was disappointed in them then, but might try it again for a coupla days. With you there, maybe I could do better.

Enclose a coupla poems from *Queen's Quarterly*.[1] The one with the four-letter word caused a lady to write to the university prez complaining that times ain't what they used to was, when dirtyminded writers can get away with that stuff. I'm sorry to have insulted the lady, but think she's lived a sheltered life.

Hope to see you in Ottawa.

Best wishes to yourself and wife,
Al

1. "Sizwe Bansi Is Dead" and "Melodrama" appeared in the *Queen's Quarterly* (Autumn 1973).

Miriam Waddington (b. 1917): short story writer, critic (a study of A.M. Klein) and poet (*The Glass Trumpet*, 1966).

To Miriam Waddington (Toronto), from Ameliasburgh, May 7, 1973

Dear Miriam,

Thanks for your note. Of course, pleased to sign yours any time or place. I get this off to you fast before you go to PEI.

Haven't seen Jean in some years. She's probably told you her brother died. I grew up with Don more or less, he on the farm and me in town. Difficult to know what turn he took that made him into a quarrelsome drunk. But I prefer to remember him as a kid—

Jean was always my favorite cousin, tho probably she didn't know that. The Rosses then seemed such an ideal family, the beautiful people before I knew the full implications of that phrase. You know the sort of thing, born to be handsome and successful, and they had no doubt and neither did anybody else. Some kind of native aristocracy, such were probably my unthought thoughts then. And Jean is the only one among them that seems to be just that sort of person today.

Of course, as mentioned, I haven't seen her in years. Mean to look her up. Some kind of strong core in her that made only her own kind of life possible. I mean, thieves and murderers are beyond her understanding, she couldn't get into their heads or feel their thoughts. Or is that exaggerated? But you try to put your finger on a particular quality in people and perhaps only touch a general area in them and not the specifics.

Best Wishes,

Al

Say hi to Jean if you see her before you go.

> **Bryan McCarthy**: (b. 1930) Montreal poet (*The Bad Book*, 1972). AP reviewed McCarthy's *Smoking the City* in *Evidence*, No. 10 (1967).

To Bryan McCarthy (Montreal), from Ameliasburgh, May 12, 1973

Dear Bryan,

I got to work right away on your poems when they arrived, on accounta I expect to be away a week or so.

I've entirely omitted poems from *Smoking the City*, because hell you oughta have lots in the eight years since that book. If you are, after 15 or 20 years, editing a selected, okay include those.

Re "A Night on the Town," it's a good poem, but much too long. The first two pages oughta be cut to half a page. Cut the bit about crossing the street to six or eight lines at most. Begin again at "She comes in in the evening—" A line or so to intro that, to the effect you are thinking of this while at the movie. Then back to the reality-irreality of the movie. You may feel you've done this already, but I think it could be done more tersely. Admittedly you are rarely terse.

I've some general comments on your poems after reading them quickly like this. I doubt you'll like my comments, but you can always go back to Russo. I'm also a little leery of expressing them, since most are critical. I think you could write much better if you could only get your mind off yourself and your own opinions. Fuck your opinions about how bad the world is! We all know it's bad, or if we don't we're blind, deaf and dumb. The effect of talking continually about the badness of the world is the boredom it induces in a reader, an effect of sameness. And while the world may be fucking bad it is not always the same. Many bad moments, some good moments—and you don't have to dwell at length on either. If you have no good moments, by the way, then you oughta knock yourself off. I recommend sleeping pills, as supposed to be nearly painless.

My point here is you've got a brain and some large ability, but I think you're wasting it, or rather both. "On the Town" is a damn good poem, for many reasons, but you seem to have no idea of what to cut and what to leave in. The first two pages that I recommended cutting to half of one are really irrelevant to what you're getting at in the poem: and that is a counterpoint of the movie, plus a blood fantasy and your own life. Trouble crossing the street is a mere incident, and should be left at just that. Apparently you admire Fraser [Sutherland], whom I regard as rather simplistic. Something odd about that, on accounta I think you should be more simplistic, and drop some of that verbiage. How? Well, one suggestion, write classroom poems every day of not more than 15 lines, confine yourself to two adjectives, at most three, by simply counting them. Is that silly? You think you're an expert? None of us are fucking experts. If one thing doesn't work, try another.

In many ways I don't think you're writing what you're really thinking. Also, your ranting is much the same as Acorn's ranting. What about that slight smile, or even that whole-hearted grin you bestowed grudgingly on some large or small gal? Isn't that worth a poem too, without getting in also a condemnation of entire western, eastern, polar and extra-terrestrial civilization? What I'm talking about here is: you gotta change your style, and hence your life. Of course you may think I'm fulla shit. But so what? Point is you're not getting enough attention. And why not? Because you're not saying it. Whereas you do have the brains and ability to say it, and your truth is certainly not my truth. Your world is not the one I see. The one I see contains what you see, and much else besides. For chrissake, I'm not tryin to put you down, I'm just tryin to talk about your stuff the way I see it.

The poems I've picked out are those in which there is some human feeling, either express or implied. I don't mean either you nor I should or could be boiling with treacle old lady tenderness and that crap. Just that there are moments in your life when you're entirely defenseless, for whatever reason. You may think you've written about these. I don't think so. There are moments when you think of someone else, at least I would hope so—and if you write about em do so without intruding yourself at all.

When I first selected your poems I wasn't aware that I did so while looking for the aforementioned "human feelings"—But I realize that I have a basic antagonism to many of your poems simply because they're so one-sided. And you might quite easily say here, at this point, that I too am involved, shit blood and fuck saliva. In a way, but only in a way, that is true. But your blood and shit are surrealistic, not real blood and shit. On accounta they too go along with the world view, which is how bad things are.

I think there are no poems in the world of blackness and condemnation which do not also include an urgent feeling of tenderness and pity. I cite Jeffers and Housman particularly. I realize "tenderness and pity" are lousy words to use. But many of Jeffers poems—which contain a very black view of the world—hold a feeling of magnificence, of terrible pity because this is the way things are, like Greek tragedy if you like . . .

I don't want to lecture the lecturer, and that's what you are most of time. BUT BUT BUT . . . You might cast it thru your mind that I have no earthly reason to pick up your poems, select some, reject others, and then criticise you like this. Except good will. Or friendship. Take your pick. My point is you oughta be writing better, and I'm trying to look at the reasons why I think you're not.

All of this may seem confused, too confused for you to pick out what I really think, tho I assure you I've tried to make it clear. Okay, one, you admire Acorn and Layton, but what you admire in their cases is parallelled in yours by a similarity to their rant. Your good stuff is overwhelmed by rant sometimes, not always. You admire Fraser, I should think his seeming simplicity. But you are not simple. At least not in use of language. You have this tendency, in fact downright overboardness to pile words on words, regrettably words that say much the same things as those preceding.

I can't, of course, tell you how to write poems. I don't know how myself. I can only say what I see in your poems. And I would think you might suspect that other readers—perhaps without analysing why—might feel the same. You want fame. It sticks out over you like a stiff prick in a girls' school. Okay, why aren't you famous? Could any of the reasons I've mentioned be a reason?

This gets long. Pay no attention to it; go your own way like you've done. Ascribe my opinions to my shortsightedness and fat cat attitudes. Or that having "sold out" as per your Bukowski quote, then I want you to do the same. It's nice and easy to think that.

All the best (whatever that is)

Al

To Bryan McCarthy (Montreal), from Ameliasburgh, May 25, 1973

Dear Bryan,
I call your attention to issue #2 of *Booster & Blaster*, manifesto by McCarthy & Russo in rear:

1) Discontinuance of Canada Council grants to writers, editors and publishers. The Canada Council has, unwittingly, fostered a "quantity" literature and apathetic anxiety among writers to produce for the sake of production.

If you want me to write a letter I propose a complete turn-around by yourself, saying in effect, that the Canada Council is a fine institution and that you believe in it wholeheartedly—now that you want some money yourself. Of course you also accepted it in the past, but didn't produce the books you said you were going to do.

I don't believe that one should reverse one's self on moral principles like you came out with in that magazine, especially not almost imme-diately after such principles are formulated. If you think the Canada Council is the shits you shouldn't expect to be a beneficiary.

I spent some time on your poems, making a selection of 18, and doing so while I was in the midst of other things. I'll still write a letter on your behalf, but only after you reverse yourself on the previously expressed opinion about the Canada Council, in either *Booster & Blaster* or any other magazine with some small public circulation. Which strikes me as a fair offer.

Best Wishes,
Al

To Milton Acorn (Toronto), from Ameliasburgh, June 6, 1973

Dear Milt,
Good to get the long informative letter from you. Also good you don't find my poems completely bad. Incidentally, after a reading at Kingston the other night, a guy about 70 with a grey fringe of hair walks down the aisle and says, "Very amusing, but not poetry." One gets this sort of thing every so often, from complete strangers who feel both competent and need no invitation for such gratuitous comments. I really don't care what such people think—unless they thrust their views on me without neces-sity or invitation.

No, I hadn't been aware that the 1837 rebellion also occurred at PEI.

Very interesting that your own ancestors were involved. Re your comments on the English, it's odd that while the English have committed some of the most treacherous and cunning acts that, in many ways, we (you and I and others—and I do suppose you too) have much respect for them. For instance, Shaw went there for recognition. Others go to the US for the same reason. We can't put down many things about England. They were and are a centre of culture, and even their ridiculous claims to having civilized savage colonies, as in the manner of Rome perhaps, are not entirely without foundation. Obviously, we can't put down Blake, John Donne and many others. The British colonized, economically exploited etc. etc., but they did leave some small legacy behind them. It's only when they make large claims that absolve them entirely from doing damage that they are ridiculous. I'm not sure what marvellous benefits the Soviets have given Czechoslovakia for instance, but Soviet imperialism in that country has certainly been the reverse of Karl Marx and bestowed a legacy of hatred for many years to come from the Czechs. If the claim is made that the Soviets inculcated communism in Czechoslovakia, then I would say it is the Czechs who should have adopted those politics without outside interference. As the world is constituted, the Czechs would have decided themselves whether they wanted to embrace such politics.

But back to your own ancestors, and the pride involved in having them. My own are UELs as you likely know, landed at Adolphustown in the 1780s. But I distrust the pride involved in having such ancestors. I'm perfectly pleased to have them, of course, but think I'd be just as proud if they'd been dirt farmers also, which they were also among other things. Pride ought to devolve from your own accomplishments principally. Of course the tradition means something, especially when you look at your own activities. You seem to continually mention your Indian ancestry, Milt, beginning to seem a bit like Grey Owl,[1] a full-blooded Englishman who claimed to be Indian. My point being that whatever virtues Indians have—and they have plenty—you must have your own. And you were brought up in PEI with an ordinary education in the midst of ordinary culture. You have written fine—sometimes I think great—poems. These poems coming out of what you are yourself ought to be the reason for pride. You've accomplished nothing else, no matter what your claims, not really. Such things as the Allan Gardens [Toronto free speech demonstration] episode and your Indian blood—these ought to be taken for granted. They're part of your life as an ordinary individual with particular political and personal beliefs. My parallel to these would be, say, installing a union in a factory and pulling a book away from a publisher who's acted contrary to its own country's interests. Many others have done less, as much, and many much more. Other people seem to attach interest and merit to such things. I don't—apart from the fact that I could act no other way in accordance with my beliefs and what I am: i.e. I take no credit for doing what I couldn't help doing anyway. Incidentally, I'm told some of my ancestors were also sheep-stealers on the Scots English border, and were hanged by the English. Which sounds too picturesque to be true.

Re Cuba, you are a black and white guy in regard to anything at all. Cuba is a marvellous place in some respects. It also has the large virtue of standing up for its own rights in the world, which Canada has not done. I applaud them for that. However, I do not believe that Cuba is a model society because they happen to be communist (small c, for communism doesn't belong to one country only) . . . There are many faults and injustices in Cuba. I could go into these but won't. There's little point.

You completely misunderstood "the small dead animal" in the Cuba poem.[2] Besides politics, that poem was about the transitory nature of human life, and the dead animal was meant to convey our own (all of us) transitory lives.

Sure, we, all of us here, write in the Canadian idiom because we're Canadians. Except possibly the Black Mountain people. I would feel extremely phony if I didn't. I should not have said I'm not part of English lit, since I think we all are by reason of writing in English. And we all have that litlegacy behind us. I'm sure you'd agree with these points. As I agree, that my poems would be "largely incomprehensible to Englishmen," tho I'd hope some small emotions got thru.

The bit about Castro jumping up and saying "We're going to take over" was not meant to be literally true. How in hell could I know that anyway? I was dramatizing in the way that seemed best to me at the time, something that was, from what you say, quite mundane. Like Paul Martin being appointed to the Can. senate. Of course I'm sure you'll deny that Castro being elected senator was mundane. My point is, that, in a poem, I wanted his (Castro's) feelings to be felt in such a way that the reader would feel them too "when first putting on his pants in the morning." Get away from the literal. I shouldn't have to explain to you that poets aren't always literal, you should know damn well they aren't.

And I am not you, no matter what points we have in common. I do not intend to sit at your feet and learn politics or anything else from you, which you appear to expect. You have a talent for misreading my poems completely, or almost, sometimes. And I think it's a very nice thought, Castro jumping up at some student conclave.

Still, despite disagreements, we do have points in common. Yes, I tend to mythologize you in reviews and comments. So do most others. There's always a solid basis of fact behind the mythology. I don't make you into something you are not, or intend to do that. Nor, probably, do I always interpret your poems correctly, and it would be extraordinary if I did. And you have the same trouble with mine, it seems. I'd distrust any review you'd write of me, simply for reasons of black and white excess in any direction. At the end, you'd be liable to change me round to something I'm completely not, just as you did in that Souster article some years ago. For you have such belief in your own rightness no matter what that you can conceive no other interpretation. You've changed your mind completely on Souster from what you tell me, and yet in that piece not too long ago he was the common man, the god you espouse and believe in. Now he is not. There has to be some balance in these things. Souster is a damn good poet, who does write of ordinary things and people, but by writing about them makes himself not quite ordinary. Just as you are not a carpenter and too damn lazy to ever be one again. You expect more from Souster, both in his political views and poems, than he is able to give. And you do the same with me.

I write in my own way toward a society that will probably not come in my lifetime, perhaps never. I regard myself as being a man of the left, with the NDP in this country as my hoped for vehicle toward that end. But neither do I always agree with them. And I certainly want no part of the Russian brand of communism. If this country ever achieves some form of socialism, then I hope we can finally do away with regionalism, racialism and all the other isms, and perhaps be a world community. But that is far off as I see it. In the meantime, I hope for what is immediately possible, with the farther steps going on after that is achieved.

Please please don't write a review of me Milt. The book was sent to you as a present to a friend, and not a review copy.

love,

Al

1. Grey Owl or Archibald Stansfield Belaney (1888–1938): born in England, emigrated to Canada in 1906 where he became a guide and trapper and over the next decade assumed an aboriginal identity. He became a well-known woodsman, lecturer and writer (*Pilgrims of the Wild*, 1934; *Tales of an Empty Cabin*, 1936).
2. The line, "a small dead animal" is from "Fidel Castro in Revolutionary Square"

(*Cariboo Horses*): "And back at the shining Cadillac / we came in (Batista's old car) / under the side where I hadn't / Noticed before the body / of a small dead animal—".

To Jack McClelland (Toronto), from Ameliasburgh, June 29, 1973

Dear Jack,

Thanks for your letter and good wishes re the History of Ont. being projected. The terms are that I will receive $500. a month living expenses (against royalties) while the book is being written. 10% royalties for the first printing (I forget how many that is) and then the royalty rate jumps. Mel believes that such a book will sell well. He is working out a contract to this effect on his return from holidays.

No advance has been paid re *In Search of Owen Roblin*—At the present time I'm satisfied that there hasn't, because I'd like the terms to be pretty well worked out first. Waller[1] wants royalties instead of (possibly in addition to—) flat payment. I'd prefer he took the flat payment. Altho I haven't said this to him up to now, merely that he has to decide for himself. [...]

I talked to Bob Weaver last Monday, and he still sounds agreeable to the record being done. But again, his conversation was vague, nothing definite was really said. It would take you talking to him to obtain any definite yes or no arrangement. Could you do that? I mean on the phone, which ought to be sufficient. Rightly or wrongly, this Roblin book is important to me (sure, any book is), and I want to get it settled.

I have an offer to be writer-in-res at Loyola of Mtl. for this year, but at this point will likely turn it down. But if I took it, it would be difficult to have the editorial meeting with myself, Newlove, Waller and yourself after the end of August.

Previously I had cited the A.Y. Jackson illustrated *North of Summer* as a reason for the royalties being 15%. But I accept that this was a special case, and also because of your own long letter written when I was in Yucatan. Therefore, can we drop the royalties to 12% in your estimation?

Why don't you drop down here and have a drink, as I am doing now? No business, royalties or any of that crap—which can be looked after at other times and places. Okay, sit with a drink and watch me work—: I am building an outside work room, 12' X 13', diggin up the whole earth to make a foundation. Of course you're busy, but what the hell—John's ankle getting busted was an accident, sure it was an accident. Christ, I sat in that hospital lobby at emergency for five hours thinking poor Newlove, I woulda been screaming with pain.

I'm told Birney has a new girl friend (add gossip): so I wrote to Earle and said please, boy, give me some hint how you do it. Can I put a bug in your foreskin, Earle? May I marinate you for an aphrodisiac?

Okay, I'll bring a bottle next editorial meeting?

Al

1. Bob Waller was the photographer whose photos illustrated *In Search of Owen Roblin*.

George Bowering (b. 1935): a prolific West Coast novelist (*Burning Water*, 1980), essayist, critic and poet (*Kerrisdale Elegies*, 1984), Bowering wrote the first monograph on AP (*Al Purdy*, 1970).

To George Bowering (Vancouver), from Ameliasburgh, September 26, 1973

Dear George,

Why do I detest Whitman? He's monotonous, long-winded and fulla shit. Sometimes, rare, he can be good, as in "When Lilacs Last—" (tho it's too long if I remember rightly) "Whitman made me"? Well, you amaze me. I learned much more from Thomas, metric people like Chesterton, Hardy esp. D.H. Lawrence, Layton (whom I loved around 1954–1955), even Bowering, which last perhaps you will say is like learning from Duncan, Creeley, Williams etc. It ain't to me. But figure I can learn from anybody I like. That doesn't include Whitman. He's boring to me. I'm intolerant of personal bores. But I resent that bit about "Whitman made you"—I dislike his repetitions, his philosophy of good fellowship and the common man, all the clichés used about him—

What's the reason for all this crap between you and Acorn? I think you're both indulging in trivialities, in fact I think it's beneath you to join in that silly chit-chat. Acorn is a good poet and so are you, but it doesn't help your reputation to do that sort of thing, and you are concerned with reputation . . .

I'm at Loyola (or did I tell you?) two days a week . . . Commute back and forth, sleep one night at a friend's in Mtl. then train back. We're also building a 28' X 14' addition to the house, as my work room. The latter is all my own work, now the walls are up but no roof yet. Former is supposed to be contracted by E's brother, but I seem to be involved in some of the work anyway. Down to 195 lbs. I claim the Loyola bit is so I'll have a free year next year, but still feel a bit guilty about it. I've never gotten trapped for this long before. Nor do I feel didactic as I think academics usually are about creative writing.

Al

From George Bowering (Vancouver), to Ameliasburgh, November 11, 1973

Dear Alphonse,

Just because yr saving carbons of yr letters, that dosnt mean you have to type my name at the beginning. Shit, if theyre going to be in a library anyway, let some poor creep figger it out textually, that's what theyre sposed to be doing there, anyway. They certainly arent keepin and readin the letters to find out what we think or say to each other. Or maybe to just find that out, but certainly not to act on it, not to change their lives. They weep rather than rejoicing when the library burns down.

I dont know what all this is between me and Acorn. At first I decided not to answer any of his uninformd blatherings in public. Then when he attackt friends of mine I descended to trying to explain things to him logically, but he persisted in not understanding, and when it became too clear not to understand, lying about what I had said. I then returned to an earlier position and said forget it. He's hopelessly incapable of conducting an honest and intelligent discourse, and that is too bad. It makes me sad to see a guy who was once considered or considering himself a leftist, getting in with the redneck crowd. I think he has been a good poet, writ good poems, and sd so in public. I spose he hates me for that for some reason. I will never understand that kind of person.

I didnt understand yr suggestion that academics are didactic about creative writing. I dont know how can be such a thing, tho I am willing to believe it. However, most of the academics I have heard talk on the subject are against creative writing courses. Thank god that I havent had to teach any for about 4 years. Tho it is laughingly easy work, it does get under my skin when I think about how little is being done in that expense.

It now shapes up that my eastern readings are from Jan 28 till abt two weks after that. Why dont you get me a hundred and twenty five to come to Loyola and talk to yr class?

and give my love to those doxies at that bastion of larnin

George

To Jack McClelland (Toronto) from Montreal, November 14, 1973

Dear Jack,

The party was great. I was a little surprised that it was. On the face of it, if you bring authors and booksellers together it doesn't guarantee a free and easy and enjoyable party. But I thought it was just that. Odd to be asked for so many autographs. I must've signed the McStew catalogue at least six or eight times, as well as many books. I had been drinking rum most of the afternoon, then tapered off with beer at the party—maybe that was why it was enjoyable—

I'm pleased, naturally, that the *Selected* sold so well, or at least 3,100 and some copies till June seems not bad to me. Titles seem to make a helluva difference. *Wild Grape Wine* is not selling well at all, but I will lay a bet *Sex and Death* will.

I'm sorry Farley Mowat wasn't there. I killed Angus Mowat's dog accidentally a while back. Turned into Angus's drive at about ten mph and the dog ran right under the wheel. Bit Eurithe and Angus, the latter badly. We drove thirty miles to Napanee to the vet and then hospital for tetanus shots. Too late for the dog. I dug his grave under an apple tree, Angus being too old for that. Very odd feeling, in my shirtsleeves, wind off the Bay of Quinte, digging a grave. And even if it wasn't my fault, I was still the one who shoved grief into another person's life—and I like Angus much, as well as the dog.

This letter is not apropos of anything in particular—except to say I enjoyed the party and thank you for it.

Best,

Al

To Earle Birney (Toronto), from Ameliasburgh, December 23, 1973

Dear Earle,

It's a damn fine book [*What's So Big About Green?*]. Just got back after very short ten days in Yucatan to find it. I pick out "Small Faculty Stag" as I did once before; regret using the word poignant re ending, but it is . . .

Also the book has a vitality in all its poems . . . Dunno what to say about those Fiji cockroaches, except I'm jealous. Good to find a villanelle too. You're probably the only live man writes villanelles now. It's a triumph, Earle!

How are the memoirs? I tried that for thirty thousand words and didn't make anything of it. Difficult to say everything, tell everything, so many people you might hurt or . . . what the hell . . . But you look at Garner[1] and see one way of doing it—which is okay, but I'm sure it's not your way. At the moment, I can't write poems, only reviews. Editor friend in Mtl.—as I mentioned—has me doin a long piece on Lowry.[2] And I'm getting damn sick of Lowry.

Joe [Rosenblatt] and Susan Musgrave[3] made it to Merida where we got together. She being quite a skittish lady, as Joe may tell you if you see him. Both Joe and myself spent some time calming her. I liked her but didn't at the same time if that's possible, and it is. Joe is doing some quite marvellous drawings. I'm convinced that's where his future lies, and expect you to disagree. But the essential naivete of his poems is not present in his art; the monsters are thurberish[4] as well as rosenblattish. Kinda sly monsters, so blatant they oughta be ashamed but aren't and brazen it out. When we left, Susan planned to go back to the Charlottes, and Joe to Vera Cruz and then Acapulco, or maybe it was vice-versa in Joe's case. Was interested in Susan's saying Harlow[5] was writing her a supporting letter, she afraid he would go into detail about her instead of just marking her in the slot supplied as "exceptional"—She did say that, and of course she may be exceptional, to some people. But it's interesting she thinks so too.

Have had the worst review in my life from one G.S. Kaufman in *Chevron*, Univ. of Waterloo. I do hope he's American, since he has no good word at all to say for me, and it would've been much more believable with one good word added for slight contrast. You might be amused by the beginning of review, (which McStew sent me):

"Al Purdy is one of the Canadian poets, right? And good old McClelland and Stewart are the self-proclaimed Canadian publishers, right? Then a new book of Al Purdy poems published by M & S must be the thing to get, right?

"Well, *Sex and Death* may be something but it's not good poetry, and the political and social insights contained here are too often embarrassingly shallow. Purdy is undoubtedly one of the most self-indulgent 'poets' publishing on the commercial market today . . ."

Etc. Please mention this to David Bromige if you're in touch.[6] If he thought I murdered him, I've undoubtedly been drawn and quartered, vivisected, and rejected as mulch for any self-respecting garden. I feel as if I'm getting what I deserve, only a little too much at once from one source.

Staying at a friend's apt in Belleville, since A-burg an icebox inside a frig inside a cold storage locker. Drank a great deal in Yucatan, seem to be continuing here—having my own sense of failure I suppose, as apart from Lowry's. Altho what strikes me as Lowry's terror, I do not have. (We all transpose such feeling and situations from others to ourselves, at least I think we do, and I do) . . . More a physical failure, as I think of it—than a literary one—A slow running down of the body, the impossibility of excellence other than momentarily; a feeling of futility that destroys even some of those moments; and being trapped by everything I say or do or even feel . . . Shit . . . That's getting depressing. When we got back from Mexico, Eurithe's family had heard Trudeau had been trying to get in touch with me. Everyone very curious. Why was Trudeau etc. I told em he'd intended to offer me the ambassadorship to Mexico job, but I meant to turn it down on accounta I wanted Brazil. They didn't know whether I was saying true or not. Actually, it was a party with that Russian poet Yevtushenko I believe.[7]

love,

Al

1. Hugh Garner (1913–79): Toronto writer whose realistic fiction deals with working class life (*Cabbagetown*, 1950; *The Silence on the Shore*, 1962). *One Damn Thing after Another* (1973) is his autobiography.
2. This appeared as "Let He Who is Without Gin Cast the First Stone" in the *Montreal Gazette*, August 17, 1974. It is reprinted in *Starting from Ameliasburgh*.
3. Susan Musgrave, see page 277.
4. James Thurber (1895–1961): American humorist whose sketches, essays and stories appeared in the *New Yorker*.
5. Robert Harlow (b. 1923): BC novelist (*Royal Murdoch*, 1962; *The Saxophone Winter*, 1988).
6. AP reviewed Bromige's *The Gathering* and *The Ends of the Earth* in *Queen's Quarterly* (Winter 1969).
7. Yevgeny Yevtushenko (b. 1933): very popular and much-travelled Russian poet (*The Promise*, 1957; *Babi Yar*, 1962). He has also published a novel (*Berries*, 1981) and an autobiography (*Precocious Autobiography*, 1963). AP considered him a less substantial poet than Andrei Voznesensky.

To David McFadden (Hamilton, Ont.), from Ameliasburgh, December 29, 1973

Dear Dave,

The gallstones operation seems trivial besides the boredom. So here's my story of being sick, long ago in the air force (just one, I have others): about 1943, I was sick as I've ever been, temperature, couldn't walk, some kinda arthritis, then got pneumonia atop that—Had a nurse from my hometown in hospital in Vancouver, one of those snooty bitches who thinks she's better than you are (we all run into that kind at some time or other in our lives) . . . Anyway, there I was with a temp of 104–5, and she wouldn't do anything for me in hospital at Kitsilano at RCAF base. I thot I was dyin, and came damn close. But did recover, then had this angel called "Sammy" for a nurse, she used to rub my belly with alcohol under the bedclothes, and I'd get such a goddam erection I was practically under a tent. Usta plan and plot how I could get Sammy alone on a night shift when she worked, but never did manage. Always wondered how the other patients stood those belly rubs without getting outa bed and chasing her into the snowy rainy Vancouver winter. Occasionally she would "accidentally" brush against my prick or slide over pubic hair, and my expression musta been a real study for her . . . And she was attractive, breasty little thing . . . Was I the favoured patient, or were there others getting those nice belly rubs? Who knows. Does that cheer you up?

I have the same spells of boredom, lethargy and the works. Got a line in an arctic poem about that, hearing the desolate cry of old squaw ducks alone, tho with Eskimos who spoke no English, so lonely suicide would've been exciting—the line: "I think to the other side of that sound"[1]—Which is about all anyone can do . . . At least, for me, periods of really black depression seem to have stopped. Shoulda said I was on a little rocky island in Cumberland Sound, Baffin.

Aiken bores me, but dammit I like some of Jarrell.[2] Read "Losses" and several of his war poems.

I was away for coupla weeks in Yucatan, just got your letter. You must be either dead or human again now. I'm writer-in-rez at Loyola, Mtl., Mondays and Tuesdays. Start again Jan. 14. Any chance of seein you?

Al

1. The poem is "Metrics" (*North of Summer*).
2. Conrad Aiken (1889–1973): once prominent American poet (*Preludes for Memnon*, 1931) and novelist (*Blue Voyage*, 1927). *Ushant* (1952) is a psychological autobiography with portraits of Malcolm Lowry and T.S. Eliot, among others. Randall Jarrell (1914–65): American poet (*The Lost World*, 1966), novelist (*Pictures from an Institution*, 1954) and critic (*Poetry and the Age*, 1953). Several of his poems were among AP's perennial favourites: "The Death of the Ball Turret Gunner," "Field and Forest," and "Losses." He paid Jarrell the fine tribute of borrowing from and alluding to them in his own lyrics.

James Wright (1927–80): American poet (*Collected Poems*, 1971).

To James Wright, from Montreal, March 9, 1974

Dear James Wright,
This is a fan letter, so be warned. I hope it doesn't go to the wrong Wright, since there are two in *Contemptible AmerPo*. 1969.[1] I've been reading your stuff since you collaborated with Robert Bly[2] in some translations of Neruda some years ago. In anthos entirely. Have no books. (Intend to get a collected or selected if there is such) Point is: I've enjoyed the poems in this uncurrent antho very much, particularly the last part of the one about Harding (which is beautiful-ugly), "Before the Cashier's Window" and "In Response to a Rumor."

When I read the Harding poem I wrote one about the "Fixer" in Belleville (Ont, that is, where I come from—I'm writer in rez at Loyola, Mtl.) Saying that, should also say I've pubbed some fifteen books myself. "The Fixer" in Belleville was a guy named Mackenzie Bowell who got to be P.M. here in 1895, was Grand Master of the Orange Order then, which helped him with votes.[3]

No matter. Are you still writing as good as that? Beautiful technique, mournful and sonorous, intensely grandiose and marvellous? Shit—you must expect that sorta thing from anyone who likes your stuff! (Don't cringe!)

Poem I read of yours several years ago was about the sound of miners underground, their iron carts rumbling etc. That was you?? One about horses too? (This other Wright[4] fucks me up somewhat.) It had to be you, because these later poems have the same feeling about them.

I liked some of James Dickey's[5] stuff a while back—until his last book or two. I still like that mid-point stuff of his, but disappointed in his later work. What I meant to say after that intro to it was: despite all poems being in a sense a tour de force (plural), yours are real. Comparisons are awful! Shouldn't've started the para. that way. I mean, I believe and feel that stuff of yours. Which is praise, I think.

Best Wishes,
Al Purdy[6]

1. AP is playing on the title *Contemporary American Poetry* (1962, edited by Donald Hall).
2. Robert Bly (b. 1926): American poet (*The Light Around the Body*, 1968) and translator.
3. See "The Statue in Belleville" (*Sundance at Dusk*).
4. Charles Wright (b. 1935): American poet, won the Pulitzer Prize for *Black Zodiac*.
5. James Dickey (1923–97): American poet and novelist (*Deliverance*). AP admired his earlier work, and wrote him a fan letter.
6. The letter was returned by the post office.

To Margaret Laurence (Lakefield, Ont.) from S.S. *Golden Hind* in the Gulf of St. Lawrence, June 5, 1974 or damn close thereto—

Dear Margaret,

Well may you ask what the hell I am doing here? (Margaret: "Al, what the hell are you doing there?" Me: "Uh, well, I think I'm gonna write a piece about life on the ocean wave in the River and Gulf of St. Law.")[1] It's now Monday, and I've been here six days, going by bus and train to Toronto and St. Catherines, catching the ship at Thorold, then riding the thing to a spot a few miles from the Gulf, where we have been anchored for two days. There's only been three days of travelling time outa that six on the non-briny. Seems there is labour trouble at Baie Comeau, also ships ahead of us to get unloaded, so we're stuck out here in a thirty mile-wide river or gulf, just waiting. Another ship has been waiting about three miles away (parked there) for eleven days.

I hope you're slightly interested in all this, because it's about all I have to talk about. I probably mentioned this trip to you before, but it finally was arranged quite suddenly. Sheena Paterson (who may have gotten in touch by now, I think she said she wrote you or was gonna visit you at Lakefield) was supposed to send a photographer aboard at the Beauharnois Locks, but it was night when we got there. I phone her from below Montreal, on a gadget where you say "Over to you" and things like that. I felt like a grounded or watered-down Spitfire pilot. Anyway, the ship is 620' long and some 68' wide, with cabins and things like that at either end, so you have to walk seeming miles to get meals in the Officer's Mess (where I eat, naturally). I kept going to the crew's mess at first, because I thought it would be more interesting, and would show my democratic nature in the story I wrote. (see next page for continuing this interesting story) Then the captain kept calling at my cabin for meals, and I think: is my aristocratic lineage and upbringing apparent in my face? Does blood call to blood? Anyway, when it's rain you damn well get drowned going from the forward cabins to aft dining rooms. I've talked to many of the crew, decided they lead a fairly dull life, and they think so too. I'm well aware you can go into their lives intensively, and find out more about them personally and then they ain't dull. However, I can only treat them fleetingly in a piece like this—for instance the 2nd cook from Barbados was torpedoed off Cape Hatteras in WW2 on a CN ship, and his brother died in the same life boat. The man who hauled him into the lifeboat, Luther Beckles, also survived, but died on a lake boat a few weeks ago near Rimouski. His body was sent back to the West Indies by Air Canada, but the authorities sent it back because the Canadians hadn't made out a proper death certificate giving the cause of death. Beckles wife accompanied the body on its flights back and forth. That seems a bit horrible to me. Two of the 18-year-olds on this ship went to a whorehouse in Baie Comeau a few weeks back and the Fr. girls thought they were English cops and wouldn't serve them. Of course the kids were drunk. Does this strike you as interesting?

You are a last resort. I must talk to someone (having drunk the two bottles of Scotch I brought along and made as many notes as seems worthwhile). Like I say, we've been parked, uh—I mean anchored—in this goddam gulf or river for two days, and I may be here for weeks. If we finally do get to Baie Comeau, I shall quickly jump ship, and take a train back west if there is one. Incidentally, a guy named Parker in April went to the mate to get paid off at 4 a.m. in the morning (you can get paid off in any port in

Canada), but mate rightly refused to wake the captain. So he left the ship, stole a milk truck and drove it to Forestville 70 miles asked for directions there. But people got suspicious, called provincial police and they nabbed him. He got 15 days, which ain't bad for car theft. Once he would've been strung up to the nearest tamarack for stealing a hoss, or drawn and quartered or something. Anyway, meals are great, three choices of meat noon and evening; room is about 12' by 14' with big bathroom and shower. Television in rec room which you can only get the Rimouski channel (near which town Beckles died. I think it was his heart). And there is something frantic about sitting in a ship doing nothing. I've finished my wine-making article, at least the draft before the last, drunk 65 ounces of Scotch in six days, exercised at night by doing a hundred toe-touchings (and gotten a blister on my ass as a result, and now bandaided, can't do any more) . . . Incidentally, I wrote near 4,000 words of the wine piece, and it will have to be cut. There are some damn interesting things in wine history. I feel like quoting you one paragraph, in which, tongue firmly in cheek, I am talking about women related to wine. It's expressed in such a way that no doubt the piece will get a reaction from every women's lib devotee in the country. But I hope it's amusing. You might like to see 2–3 paras.

"In 1955 my first play was accepted and produced by the CBC,[2] so we moved to Montreal so that I could reap the rewards for my genius. And my wife went to work to support me, as any well-behaved wife should and must. I wrote. And made beer with a couple of friends, one of whom was the same Doug Kaye mentioned previously. His marriage had foundered on alcoholic shoals. Henry Ballon, a third member of the trio, was a pharmacist. His job enabled him to buy health malt wholesale, also a supply of returnable mineral water bottles. We then scrounged a fifteen-gallon oak whiskey barrel and were in business.

"Over the winter of 1956–57 the three of us had fifteen gallons of beer brewing in the barrel, the same amount maturing in bottles, and fifteen gallons that was ready and had to be drunk every five or six days. We had to drink it because the batch in the barrel had to be bottled, and there weren't enough extra bottles in which to store the stuff. We brewed ourselves into a tight alcoholic circle from which escape seemed impossible. We drank beer for breakfast, beer for lunch and beer for dinner. I was coming out of our ears. We gave the stuff away, with strong injunctions to return the bottles by, say, Friday, when the next batch was ready to bottle. I began to smell of malt; dogs sniffed me suspiciously on the street; I crossed the road to avoid policemen. Friends began to drop away . . .

"There were other handicaps as well. The bathtub was filled almost continually with mineral water bottles being washed in advance of our deadline for the next batch of maturing beer. My wife couldn't take a bath for weeks, months even. She complained bitterly and I think unreasonably about this. After all, we had to wash those bottles somewhere. It would have been unsanitary to do otherwise.

"Women are sometimes very intolerant creatures, while at the same time possessing many good qualities. My wife kept on complaining. If I had been aware at the time of some of Pliny's writing in ancient Rome, I would have mentioned them to her. Pliny says that Roman women were forbidden to drink wine (I've never forbidden my wife anything), and that Egnatius Maetennus' wife was clubbed to death by her husband for drinking wine from the vat. But I didn't know history was on my side in 1956. Nor was I aware that in 2000 BC the Code of Hammurababi says no priestess shall open a wineshop nor enter one for a drink: if so she shall be burned. In a matter related to alcoholic consumption an interesting Syrian law states that if a woman perpetrates certain sexual transgressions on a man, then both her nipples shall be torn out. Of course those dark days are long past, as witnessed by my own enlightened attitudes. Anyway, women's lib obviously didn't exist in ancient Rome and Babylon. But it's well to remember that the state of women is always reversable."

So there. Do you pulse with righteous indignation, or just feel it's trivial? I was somewhat amused at first, but then wondered about it, begins to seem worse and worse the more you look at something like that . . .

Like I said, we've been here two days, and may be here much more. When we finally get to Baie Comeau, I shall jump ship, fly or bus back if there's no train. I've written about six poems here, one of which might be okay, another can't be published because of personalities, finished article, read some Rilke poems from a Penguin (I'm sure the translation by a guy named Leishman is awful, because they're metric, stilted and words shoved in to fill a metric space like mortar)[3] and getting depressed about life . . . Times like that one should be with friends and weep together and drink to make up for dehydration. You talk about *The Diviners* being your last novel, and I think lately I haven't been able to break thru to another stage another thought I might flatter myself is original, either in saying or meaning. I wonder if that's what you mean—the feeling you've absolutely said all you can, and there's nothing left in you. The feeling your brain has discovered as much as it can discover. I can't figure that out entirely. Can only speculate: if I had more vitality would content matter less and form more, could I then deceive myself that I was having brilliant ideas, or else would the less-brilliant ideas be expressed so well thru the afore-mentioned vitality that their less-brilliance wouldn't matter? I seem to grow less and less sure of my own philosophic (to make it sound more dignified and impressive than it is) base sometimes: i.e., is all worthwhile, or nothing worthwhile, or just some things worthwhile. There is a feeling in Rilke that all, any situation, is worthwhile if you can manage to extract or appreciate. I'm much too fallible and human to feel that myself. And yet, I write six poems in a boring situation, writing a boring letter to you as if I were talking (tho I'm not sure I'd talk like this, some things can only be written) . . . Writing has always seemed worthwhile to me, and yet does mediocre writing, is mediocre writing still worthwhile? Goddam Rilke! There is one passage tho, in which he and a companion are looking at some Egyptian ruins, I think near Akhnaton's hangout (wasn't he the boy-king who started a new religion in Egypt?) which is meditateable on:

> Man and beast appear
> to keep at times some gains from god's eyes.
> Profit, though difficult, can be secured;
> one tries and tries, the earth can be procured,
> who, though, but gives the price gives up the prize.[4]

These clever paradoxes! Very rational, but Rilke conveys emotion or feeling badly, does it through exclamations, oh and ah. Yet I'm sure some would say the opposite. Emotion, rationality both must be fused in a natural language. Here something jars, perhaps because of Leishman.

Two stone castles in the Thousand Islands, one of them Pickford's, "America's Sweetheart"[5]

> Time that with this strange excuse
> Pardoned Kipling and his views.
> And will pardon Paul Claudel,
> pardon him for writing well.
> And indifferent in a week
> To a beautiful physique . . .
> Worships language and forgives[6]
> Everyone by whom it lives . . .[7]

And yet, in some ways the world has not quite forgiven Pickford, has it? The absolutes and exaggerations of poems and prose do not always hold. Must stop. This letter is getting out of hand and envelope.

love,

Al

1. The piece was published as "The Rime of the Fledgling Mariner: Retracing the Route of Canada's Early Immigrants Along the St. Lawrence." *Weekend Magazine*, August 10, 1974.
2. Probably "A Gathering of Days," produced by John Reeves.
3. *Selected Poems by Rainer Maria Rilke* (Penguin, 1964), translated and introduced by J.B. Leishman.
4. From "From the Poems of Count C.W." by Rainer Maria Rilke.
5. Mary Pickford (1892–1979), stage name of Gladys Mary Smith, famous Canadian-born star of silent films, who became known as "America's Sweetheart" because of her innocent film *persona*.
6. In the space to the right Purdy had typed "(Worships language and forgives. W.H. Auden . . .)."
7. Purdy re-arranged lines from Auden's "In Memory of W.B. Yeats." The pertinent stanzas are:

> Time that is intolerant
> Of the brave and innocent,
> And indifferent in a week
> To a beautiful physique,
>
> Worships language and forgives
> Everyone by whom it lives;
> Pardons cowardice, conceit,
> Lays its honours at their feet,
>
> Time that with this strange excuse
> Pardoned Kipling and his views,
> And will pardon Paul Claudel,
> Pardons him for writing well.

To Earle Birney (Toronto), from SS *Golden Hind,* in the Gulf of St. Lawrence, June 5, 1974

Dear Earle,
I may quite possibly be going west near the end of this month without seeing you again before leaving. I may have mentioned that *Weekend* is arranging for me to talk to Dave Barrett[1] in Victoria, and his press sec. wrote me to find out if I actually was a suitable character to talk to Barrett. However, it will probably come off.

I've now been parked on a 10,000 ton freighter in the Gulf here off the Quebec North Shore for the last four days. Total time from Welland—I mean since Welland, eight days—five of which have just been sitting. Anchored. Seems there's a strike, or a work-to-rule thing among the longshoremen at Baie Comeau—where we're bound with soy beans and corn—and we just can't get there, what with a coupla ships ahead, plus the workers' slowdown policy.

This is another *Weekend* article, of course. I figure on doing three or four more for them and maybe one for *Maclean's*. Sheer greed on my part, altho I like doing these things for *Weekend*. I guess you haven't seen either of the two already published, but will try to remember and send you a zerox of one—I've written four so far, the last mostly done on the ship here, about my wine-making experiences and the history of wine and beer. Fascinating, some of the history. Did you know, for instance, that the priests in 16th century France brought down a curse and anathema on insects to prevent them ravaging the vineyards? Or that at the time of Classical Greece drinking postures changed from the vertical to the horizontal, i.e., everyone lay prone on couches to drink around 500 BC?

That Persians and Goths discussed and argued questions when sober then again when drunk, to get both angles? And you might be amused by what B. Franklin said about the human elbow: "If the elbow had been placed closer to the hand, the forearm would have been too short to bring the glass to the mouth; and if it had been closer to the shoulder, the forearm would have been so long that it would have carried the glass beyond the mouth." Don't ask me what use such facts are beyond writing this article. I have also written eight or nine poems while parked here, of which one or two may have some merit. Since I haven't written many poems lately, this seems good. Also read the Penguin Rilke, and think Leishman must be a lousy translator, words shoved into slots to make all things metrical. Still, I had neglected Rilke, and find some of him impressive. Also more than halfway thru *My Life and Loves* by Frank Harris,[2] which is surprisingly interesting in spots . . . I am beginning to go quite frantic from just sitting here tho. Of course *Weekend* is paying expenses (nine bucks a day, minimum rate, arranged by my wife's cousin), but that's not the point. Days drag by. It's 325 paces around the ships deck, some two miles or so in twelve circuits, which I did last night. Ship 620 feet long. Relevant but irrelevant facts, I'm getting smothered by them right now. I now see why medieval seamen jumped ship. It wasn't because the world was flat at all. But the sea certainly is "hight time," haven't seen any flame-fanged bale-twisters tho. No nadders either. I haven't been so bored in years. Hope to escape in the next day or two. There sometimes seems no end to this sort of thing—the ordinary tissue of life is permeated with boredom, then unexpected bright places difficult to predict. I was highly interested the first day or so of this trip, now phut! Sure, I should be able to extract and feel maximum enjoyment from all situations, but reality is somewhat different than that rose-coloured philosophy.

I suppose one's ego should be large enough to say that what one has written is important, therefore one is justified, and that the bright places make things worthwhile. But I'm not at all sure that I've written anything very important, just human stuff locked in physical and temporal strata. Perhaps that should be enough. And the "bright places" are only worthwhile at their occurrence, so that one feels on a ski jump from high to low and back again. The existentialist business of inventing the world and oneself each day easier said than done. Rilke kinda puts me off in that respect. And after you've written poems for years, you see that many of the things you write fall into a "knowing how" category, this way will make a poem and another way won't. So you take the way that will because your mind works naturally in that direction. Rilke is sort of "accept, accept!" which I don't like. (I'm fucked if I'll accept a lot of things.) A kind of roseate look at depression and death. One accepts, but dammit one doesn't have to like it, stoicism is too damn Greek for me. I want to be the cat yowling on the backyard fence sometimes. In fact I ought to write some of this in a poem.

Love to both of you,
Al

1. David Barrett (b. 1930): NDP Premier of British Columbia from 1972–75.
2. Frank Harris [James Thomas]: (1856–1931): editor of several newspapers and reviews (*Saturday Review* [1894–98]), journalist and autobiographer (*My Life and Loves,*1922–27).

To Angus Mowat, from Ameliasburgh, June 17, 1974

Dear Angus,
Got back Sunday to find your two letters. Leave again Monday for Banff and this year's teaching stint. Won't be seeing you this time, not till late August or so.

I move to your own letter to me: does happiness come from all these inconsequential things, you ask? I'd like to think it's a little more basic than that, and involved in personal character. You must remember that my personal circumstances, family circumstances that is, were very different from yours. Son of a widow etc., and perhaps what they call recessive genes mean that I was a shy, awkward and sometimes much afraid small boy. My memory now (whether accurate or not) says I was also a bewildered kid, out of place wherever I was and whatever I did. It took me until the RCAF before I developed a natural manner (the kind that says you don't give a shit even if you do), whereby girls didn't seem so inaccessible. You know sex does have a lot to do with this, as well as personal character. I felt deprived of the possibility of anyone else ever liking me as a child, and other children always seemed so natural to me, whereas I was not. Now that may be normal in a child, I don't know—since most of them probably go through hells adults are not likely to guess. Anyway, I didn't begin to live until the age of 21.

Yourself, by environment, family that is, genetics, and any other words you want to throw around, were very different. I didn't, for instance, develop a capacity for love and affection (always supposing I have that capacity now) till I became an almost-adult, meaning that I'm still an almost-adult. (And it would be entirely regrettable I think if we ever grew up completely, and lost the traits we think of as childlike.) Whereas you did, for some of the reasons mentioned in the first sentence of this para. You fell into things. I wasn't able to—and struggled, until my character must have really turned ass-backwards. I wanted affection, then despised it, hated it, then reversal when not caring came to care; and finally came to think that I could actually do anything, achieve anything I wanted to do enough. Some of this was subconscious, some was not.

When I say I believed I could do anything, I mean I could write anything, say anything that was real and important and which I was able to think of in the first place. And there was a feedback from writing to life. Because maybe writing enables you to glimpse some of the important things about living, and these are seldom glimpsed wholly by anyone. They are a system of values which you can't put into words at all, but only act on them in your life by segments, and write about them in segments, incidents, happenings that interest you by reason of the aforementioned values. Which you can't even name.

But latterly, I begin to switch around again. I can't achieve anything, not just *anything*, because some of the values you subconsciously acquire prevent this. And when I can figure out some of this, in actual living colour, then maybe there's a poem.

I hope all this doesn't sound stupid or merely confused. I attempt to describe the mind process whereby you became what you are, and I became what I am. And I haven't doubted what I am for years, not in the sense of my own capacities, which I think are such that when I get a hint of something in the mind I can follow it through sometimes to what's valuable. Which is also ego. I think you describe the physical processes of why you are you, and I try to do the same mentally. I'm bound to fail a little, as think we both are. But it's an interesting, fascinating, marvellous puzzle, and I mean living.

Can I keep that letter until late August? I'd like to—possibly—write something based on it—not prose tho, but whatever I think a poem is.

I'm tangled up now in these articles. Among the three I took on on my western trip is one I'm not interested enough in. I think that therefore I will have to write so well, line by line, that even tho my interest is not enough the writing may be. Which might mean that I'm fooling myself. But I took the thing on, and will carry it thru.

Must stop, have work as apart from the pleasure of writing to you and Barbara.

love,
Al

Roderick Haig-Brown (1908–76): Brown lived several lives in his sixty-eight years; he was a soldier, trapper, tourist guide, magistrate, chancellor of the University of Victoria and the author of more than twenty-five books. In the letter AP refers to an article he is writing about him for *Weekend*, "In the Shoes of the Fisherman"; it is reprinted in *Starting from Ameliasburgh* as "Cougar Hunter," and, together with their correspondence, as part of the volume *Cougar Hunter: A Memoir of Roderick-Haig Brown* (1992). The following passage from the preface to that book captures something of AP's attitude to him: "H-B had assurance without it being in any way offensive; an orderly mind, one to which I began to attribute some varieties of wisdom. I felt he knew much more about life than I did."

To Roderick Haig-Brown (Campbell River, BC), from Ameliasburgh, September 1, 1974

Dear Rod,

Thanks much for your hospitality and all. I enjoyed talking to you, and certainly hope to see you again. If you get to Toronto I expect you to come the rest of the way to A-burg (12 miles from Belleville) . . . Bed, board and whatever booze there is, will even get a bottle of good wine if I know you and Ann are coming . . .

What does a member of the International Fisheries Comish do? I mean at the Adams River? Do you stand on a river bank and count fish until you run out of fingers?

We talked about you being an authority on fishing, me saying you were the foremost "writer-authority" on fishing, or words like that. Is that true? If not, how would you express it?

I would like to know about one occasion on which you had a bad time, when you were not, as you mentioned, a pretty cocksure and self-confident kid. Any of those? I mean, were you always always sure of yourself in the bush and mtns? I probably asked you that before; still, I'm asking again because I haven't typed those notes yet, having only got home two days ago. I want a balanced picture to go with the self-confidence. You see what I mean? There was the occasion when you and your friends were raising that ship, ice and cold and all that—but it isn't quite what I mean. There was also the time when you were hanging onto the boat and near to drowning—was there a moment of terror there? In my opinion it makes a person more attractive to have a few moments when he is quite unsure of himself, even tho he recovers shortly.

When those devil's club thorns came out of your arms while scribbling away in London in '31, did it make you feel homesick for BC? Of course I'm likely to say that it did, but I'd like to know anyway. How big were the thorns. I know what devil's club is by name, but never ran into it myself. A kind of cactus, I would suppose, tho not cactus.

I must have been the opposite to you as a kid, since I remember riding the freights to BC at age 16 and being slightly scared most of the time, the world not being too much with me but not enough.[1]

I'll have more questions later if you're good-natured enough to answer. But that's probably enough for now. I've caught up with correspondence (twenty pieces of mail going out tomorrow), and will shortly be getting down to work on the Haig-Brown saga. Oh yes, I meant to ask:

do you have any favorite passages in your books? I'd like to know, even tho I expect to rummage through them and hope to find some myself. I'll undoubtedly quote from them here and there, at least the ones I have—and do suppose I have enough . . . to do that . . . Picked up another copy in Vancouver, forget the name, but a nice d.j. copy with drawings, pubbed by Morrow, four bucks.

I expect you're back to work judging by now—but do hope you can get back to writing as well. I agree with you re not having written a book in some time. I don't like to say that's what you do best, but it's one thing you do very well. I don't like to see you stop doing it.

Best to both of you,
Al

1. AP is echoing Wordsworth's well-known sonnet "The World Is Too Much with Us."

To Kenneth Glazier (Calgary), from Ameliasburgh, September 1, 1974

Dear Mr. Glazier,

Thank you for your letter requesting my thoughts as to what elementary and high school English should be about.

As I understand it, most provinces have a compulsory Canadian Studies program in secondary and high schools. This consists of geography and social studies and history. However, it is left up to individual teachers or school boards as to whether Canadian Literature should be included in Canadian Studies. In very many schools it is not.

Canada is one of the few countries in the world, perhaps the only one, where a study of the national literature is not required and absolutely mandatory. For no other literature can take the place of a country's own—the feeling of identity, placeness (which is to say, neighbourhood) and feeling for what we are depends on creative writing. Not solely, for radio, television, newspapers and movies all contribute. However, legislation makes the Canadian element in those last media mandatory and integral.

It strikes me as disgraceful that we have permitted the literature of other nations to dominate and predominate English courses in our secondary and high school—to the near-exclusion of our own.

Sincerely,
Al Purdy

To Mike Doyle (Victoria, BC), from Ameliasburgh, September 4, 1974

Dear Mike,

A little surprised to see your piece on my writings in *CL*.[1] But it's a good article. I'm liable to be prejudiced tho.

Might be interesting to compare Bowering's review in the same issue with some of the things you said—for instance, you rather disagree on the technical quality and ability of said writer. You mention Louis Johnson of New Zealand as having written a comparably bad book to *The Enchanted Echo*. I think mine must take the palm for badness merely because of Johnson's title, *Stanza and Scene* which obviously indicates more intelligence than I possessed. Alliteration in both tho.

Re W.C. Williams, I was never under any influence of his at any time. That's the only definite error I can see in the article. Louis Dudek kept urging me to read him at one time, but I merely glanced at Williams' stuff. In fact, still haven't read it with an assiduity. The date on "At the Quinte Hotel" is in error. It was written in '68. Several of the dates were made earlier on those poems in *Annettes*, for the reason that Jack McC had given me permission to publish the second ed and including poems before 1965 (when *Cariboo Horses* was pubbed), but not later ones which were slated for McStew. Since I always wanted to get my latest stuff into a coming new book, I changed the dates on that later stuff (about five or six pieces) and included it.

Your point about there being too much Al and not enough Purdy in some poems is well taken. Of course it's obvious that I am a character in many of my own things. Such things as "The Runners" and "In the Foothills" in which there are other—personae?—are fairly rare, altho some, like "The Athenian Market," don't get noticed because not good enough. Most objective things change colours for me and become at least partly subjective. The horse's head is his own but his ass is mine—something like that?

I expect that sooner or later the idea of a *Collected Poems* will come up from Jack McC., and wonder how in hell it can be done. I mean, do you mix all your stuff together and shake well? Or do you try to do it chronologically, or else become cunning and try to orchestrate the book according to some plan of your own? I think perhaps chronologically proceeding backwards might be one way? But I dislike ending or starting with poems I don't think are my best. Which is an argument for the "shake well" method.

The business about changing—my own, some of them, have undoubtedly occurred from reading other people's poems, and thereby taking a new look at some of the people I knew and realizing they were more complicated and simple than I had thought them . . . One does not simply "take thought" and thereby change, but must change naturally in response to external stimuli such as poems and people or whatever. Of course one is also self-conscious about these things, since we live in a hall of our own mirrors. If one tries to force change, then gimmicks are liable to intrude into your work for their own sake rather than the poem's. It becomes the old argument about form and content, which I dislike, but which is nevertheless valid somewhere in the mind. One might say that content is conscious and form ought to be subconscious. I can remember trying to write a poem whose final title was "The Madwoman on the Train" in a free form, trying and trying, but the thing turned out shit. So I switched to one of the most difficult forms there is, the sestina, altho I varied it at the end as I remember. At least I could actually write that sestina, but not the free form poem.

What I'm getting at, I suppose, is partly the Donne[2] thesis ("I am a piece of the main"—altho I think more than a piece, and partake of all things), for obviously one may get inside other people but nevertheless remain oneself. I am very wary of change for its own sake, and yet all of us must change, move or die, whether artistically or actually. There is no easy answer to these things, since the degree of will affects the personality and vice-versa.

I expect you'll see *In Search of Owen Roblin* which just came out—a radio piece that is, in some sense, a psychological self-examination as well as other things. I think it doesn't come off completely, tho perhaps partially.

I enclose a piece that might interest you, I think certainly one of the better poems of the last few months. In my own view, it seems to change from being a poem to something that allows you to forget it being a poem. I hope so anyway, altho that may be only in my own own mind.

It will probably go to *Queen's Quarterly* with some other recent things which they've asked for.

Anyway, it seems a good article for me—since I too find the contrast with that first book with later ones a bit puzzling. I have some specific reasons for the change—early models of form and rhyme seemed too simple and I grew dissatisfied with myself. I wasn't either lucky or unlucky enough to emerge fully formed from the mental egg, as some seem to do. And yet after whatever changes did occur, I found myself still in possession of some of the earlier traits and abilities, for instance the business of rhythms, iambic or otherwise, that may make a poem come off in three or four different rhythms. And I can't dismiss many earlier writers, Turner, Chesterton etc. as some do. I suppose I retain them forever. Whereas some young kids writing poems do not seem to read anything at all, except, say, Olson, Creeley and Pound and those allied to B.M.

Must stop.

Best,

Al

1. Doyle's article, "Proteus at Roblin Lake," appeared in *Canadian Literature* (Summer 1974).
2. "No man is an *Iland*, intire of it selfe; every man is a peece of the *Continent*, a part of the *maine*." This is from Donne's seventeenth Meditation. It's likely that AP, like most of us, first read it as the epigraph to Hemingway's *For Whom the Bell Tolls*.

To George Woodcock (Vancouver), from Ameliasburgh, September 6, 1974

Dear George,

Thinking about my last letter to you: I don't really want to review Birney's *Collected*. I'm by far the most interested in young poets, whose talent you can't entirely predict. I'm editing another anthology of them [*Storm Warning 2*], collecting the material now. I guess the deadline will be about April of next year. I might write a piece on all these poets later, at least the most interesting ones? I suppose a thing like this is bound to reflect my own tastes, as such books always do. And I have no defense for them at all.

Jack McC., incidentally, wants me to do a handbook for teachers, along the lines of Atwood's *Survival*—He's irritated by that book a little, says he wants something a little less biased to come out. The obvious answer to that might be: do you want it biased toward McStew. I guess this is confidential—from what he said, he didn't want his attitude toward Atwood noised about. But I think yours is rather similar, except that his is a publisher's attitude and yours a writer's.

I suppose you'll have the copy of *Owen Roblin* I sent you from Toronto by now ... Bob Weaver is really responsible for this one, having in some sense conceived the idea himself—altho I don't think he expected it to turn out as it did. The original plan was that it should be a verse history of Roblin Lake, sort of: which, when I came to write it, seemed very confining. So when the end product arrived, Weaver was a bit non-plussed. He said: (whether thinking of its implications or not) "How much research did you do on this?" (I had read eight or ten books only, and had a vision of the dozens I hadn't read and perhaps should have—) So when the thing was published, Bob was kinda stuck with it. There was a play, verse-play I should say, which he may not have particularly liked, but which he was identified with through having asked for it and having his name on the dedication. Therefore it's being re-broadcast this Sunday and also the Friday after that. Now I may be misinterpreting all this, but it strikes me as amusing.

The poem, I feel, is somewhat and largely flawed, perhaps because I flit around in time from myself to Roblin and my grandfather and the UELs. Still, as I look back at my own attitudes as expressed in the poem, I think I did feel that way (jealous of better writers) without knowing it at the time I'm writing about. Which is nothing very extraordinary, but it does give me a feeling of involvement later in what I'm writing about, the sense that earlier these people were in some sense antagonists whom I had to turn into something else.

I'm getting too involved here, since you haven't read what I'm talking about.

Best,
Al

To Robin Mathews (Ottawa), from Ameliasburgh, September 27, 1974

Dear Robin,
Good to hear from you.

Re Birney, I didn't do the book on him because I was in Greece on a CC award at the time, and it would have been too much work. I didn't read the book Davey did until I started work on an article for *Weekend* about Birney. (It's now finished and ready to go.) I don't have a very high opinion of the Davey book, on accounta when you start to do a book of this nature on a Canadian writer it isn't worth doing if you intend to make it partly a put-down. I know Earle feels this very strongly. I've recently seen some of his letters (carbons) to Davey, and if I'd gotten letters like that I'd probably shrivel into the size of a coconut.

Whaddaya mean am I Black Mountain enough so that he would give me some justice? You're supposed to know something about lit yourself. Have you never read my stuff at all? If so, you ought to realize it has no resemblance to BM. If you don't, take another look. Re the Bowering book, I disagreed with many of the things he said, but it isn't generally my policy to take up public cudgels on my own behalf. I've done it once or twice on behalf of both Birney and Layton, but unless a review or book gets too personal the author is entitled to his opinions. But like I said, I don't feel that books on well-known writers should be put-downs to the degree that Davey made his.

I'm swamped with work here, including the Birney article and two others, so I haven't read your poems. You're not the only one who can be too busy—jesus, the stuff piles up on me. Even if I'm not teaching. And I really object to your suggestion that I might be enough like BM so that Bowering would go easy on me.

Best wishes from my annoyed
stance,
Al

To George Woodcock (Vancouver), from Ameliasburgh, October 5, 1974

Dear George,
Recently Jack McC. wanted me to write a handbook on CanLit, since he doesn't like Atwood's. I put him off. Delayed a decision, that is. But I couldn't get as complete an overall view as you, and you have all the equipment to do such a book. You also have much of it already written, if you wanted to use such essays as those in the *Globe*. It calls for the overall view as well as the particular, theorizing as well as concrete evidence direct from the writers talked about. I wish you'd consider such a book. Atwood's was much slanted, towards Anansi writers, towards bending everything to her particular theories. That was natural in someone like her, who couldn't be as—not neutral in likes and dislikes—but sort of over-seeing from merit and above all, the sort of book that says: what

does it all mean, this literary stuff, to the guy or gal who doesn't read much, at least not beyond the newspapers.

I believe there's much very fine writing appearing in this country. Not "great" writing, and I can't think of any great writer right now in the world. But there's a whole country-wide "school," because in one sense Canada is a huge ten-acre region—or maybe a little larger than that. I'm not really sure it's important that a so-called "great" writer should emerge, when we have so much stuff just under that category. Of course I mean poetry, since I don't think the country's prose approaches it. It's probably the era of a high level of poems and poetry—not just here, but in the US too. James Wright and Robert Bly strike me as best there. However, at Banff this year I "found" several good poets (which is why I mentioned writing a piece on the interesting young poets for *CanLit*), and feel sure there are others I don't know about. I did mention editing an anthology of young poets for Jack McC. didn't I? I'm a little terrified to mention this very much to other than friends or poets I like, because I'll just get drowned in the stuff (and all without return postage). In your essay, you talk about the "emerged" writers, altho just slightly emerged in some cases. Newlove and I have been trying to have McStew publish Trower, his best stuff since he's very uneven. And Suknaski[1] definitely ought to have a book out by some publisher who would showcase his best stuff. Lane already has, at Anansi—altho I have the feeling that Lane won't improve much, will stay just as he is in the "Oh what a terrible world!" genre.

Anyway, what you get across to me in your essay is this elegiac sense of mourning in Zieroth—altho not so much in Marty—for a time passed away.[2] But to experience the past fully enough nostalgically enough is a triumph in the present. Altho—think there is a little too much of that, that terrible nostalgia we all feel for lost youth, lost happiness and all the rest of lost things.

But I don't want to go on speculating like this—since the reason I started this letter was to say your essay was good and to urge you to con-sider writing more along these lines.

Best,

Al

1. Peter Trower (b. 1930): BC logger and poet (*Ragged Horizons*, 1978) and novel-ist (*Dead Man's Ticket*, 1996). Andy Suknaski (b. 1942): visual artist and poet. AP edited his *Wood Mountain Poems* (1976).
2. Dale Zieroth (b. 1946): poet (*Clearing: Poems from a Journey*, 1973; *Mid-River*, 1981). AP included his work in *Storm Warning*. Sid Marty, see page 295.

To Earle Birney (Toronto), from Ameliasburgh, January 3, 1975

Dear Earle,

—Wonder if red is plainer nor black? Yeah, think it is. Anyway, I already writ you and sent article I wrote. I did not write the title, which I thought after seeing it was exactly the sort of thing you were peeved about. I really do sympathize with that feeling on your part now, and would feel like hysterectomizing D. Livesay if she could stand it. And then to have me—supposedly—do much the same damn thing! Anyway, the culprit for that title is one Sheena Paterson, mg-ing ed. at *Weekend*.[1]

What the hell colour eyes do you have if not blue? Have noted the other info, since I may reprint that piece somewhere. It was cut rather badly here and there. Re the two "best poets," I don't include myself in any such assessments, hell I'd be silly to do that. Let others make judgments about me—which is why I was so damn annoyed with Lane.

I'm sure I told you about that in my letter, which you may get, have got, will get etc. Anyway, here's the story. Lane, Alan Safarik (the guy who printed *Bear Paw Sea*) and Doug Brown (editor of *Copperfield*) drove down from Toronto to see me. Being somewhat stoned they took six hours and ended up six miles down the road. I drove there, found them comfortably ensconced at a neighbour's drinking his beer. I kidded them about that, mock apologized to the guy who was their temporary host for my sponging friends . . . Then led them back to the house here. When here, Lane got mad at me for what I had said, walked out, followed by Safarik. Brown and I followed a minute later in his truck (he drove), since it was 3 or 4 a.m., tried to get em to come back. They refused. I said the hell with it, so we went back and kept on drinking ourselves. Where they got to at 3 a.m. I dunno. However, I hear from Annette later that Lane, in Vancouver, is saying I turfed them out at 3 a.m., boasted I was the poet laureate of Canada or would be after death. Which is bullshit. In the first place, I don't boast like that, in the second, I didn't kick them out, they went themselves for very flimsy reasons because they wanted to be angry at me, apparently. I had already gotten the rubber mattresses from the trailer we have in the backyard, so the three could sleep on them. To say I'm annoyed is very mild.

Reverting to my story, I think there's no doubt I made it plain that "David" was fiction, even tho, as you say, it derived from a newspaper story. I didn't expect it to have a title like "The Man Who Killed David" tacked on. Nor did you.

I've heard nothing of your *Coll. Poems*, except did see their listing in McStew Cat.

Eurithe has abandoned me for the sweet south—or did I say that in the letter you ain't got? She's in Granada, I supposed to go there too later this month, but it will be Feb. before I go to Peru. Did I say I had a short term CC? Well, it's for Peru, but so much to do can't leave.

That bit about me writing so many poems is absolutely inaccurate. I don't. Three or four in past several months. I expect you are much more prolific. Re you being "properly grateful"—shit, I expected you to be mad as hell when you saw that title. With some justice too. I talked to Sheena Paterson and said that was just what I was trying to convey: that Birney was sick to death and annoyed with being accused of murdering David. Her answer wasn't very satisfactory.

Guess I gotta call Lily "Wai-lan" now[2]—is this the Manchu or Hindustan usage? Anyway, I'm writing a film script, articles, editing book—and making money therefrom of course. Come up with mucho poems on this trip—if you feel like it! There are times when it feels like a "duty" to write poems which is all wrong. Don't you think? Christ, I remember Peter Stevens[3] saying something to me in a letter after I'd sent him some poems, words to the effect of "You've recovered your form" or "At your best again" or shit like that. Makes you feel like a sausage machine, writing for writing's sake, rather than the thing's sake, whatever the thing or feeling is.

> Okay—love to both of you,
> Al

1. "The Man Who Killed David," *Weekend Magazine*, December 14, 1974. Birney had sued Dorothy Livesay for libel after reading the following passage about his poem "David" in her article "The Documentary Poem: A Canadian Genre": "Birney's companion on that fatal mountain climb was a *real* David. His death was due to a rock slide." (*Contexts of Canadian Criticism*, 1972). For the full story see Elspeth Cameron's *Earle Birney: A Life*.
2. Birney was living in Toronto with Wailan Low.
3. Peter Stevens (b. 1927): professor of English at the University of Windsor, biographer (*Dorothy Livesay: Patterns in a Poetic Life*, 1992) and poet (*Afternoon: New and Selected Poems*, 1992). His essay "In the Raw: The Poetry of A.W. Purdy" (*Canadian Literature*, Spring 1966) is one of the earliest appreciations of AP's work.

Leonard Cohen (b. 1934): poet (*Selected Poems*, 1968), novelist (*Beautiful Losers*, 1966) and singer, Leonard Cohen needs no introduction. He declined a Governor General's Award for *Selected Poems*.

To Leonard Cohen, from Ameliasburgh, July 2, 1975

Dear Leonard,
I have nine of your books—: if I send along postage will you sign them for me and return?

I believe I have all of them—no, haven't got *Parasites of Heaven*. But will pick that up later.

Have two different editions of *Spice-Box* and *Favourite Game* . . .

Haven't seen you in years, but read where you are from time to time. I've wandered a bit myself, and every now and then someone will ask why I don't get a guitar. If they ever heard my non-singing voice they'd know why.

At one time my opinion of *Beautiful Losers* was that it was a good book, but not original or some such stricture. I've come to change my mind about that in the years since it was published: now believe it's up there among the three or four best ever published in Canada.

Incidentally, when I was at Loyola a year or so ago, Elspeth Cameron[1] (then Buitenhuis) showed me the proofs you'd signed for her along with Harold Town. Nice gal—she ought to be the heroine in a gothic novel. Were you at the party at which Peter Buitenhuis took a punch at Harold Town?

I see Layton seldom, about two years now. The last time has what I think is a hilarious story behind it, involving Hugh Garner in Los Angeles. If I ever see you will tell you. Doubt Irving knows it the way I do.

> Best Wishes,
> Al

1. Elspeth Cameron, see page 401.

To Jack McClelland (Toronto), from Ameliasburgh, July 9 or 10, 1975

McClelland had asked AP to edit a second anthology (*Storm Warning 2*) of contemporary poetry. Because M&S wanted the book to include at least four more women poets (it was International Women's Year) than there were in AP's proposed manuscript, the publisher sent out a press release asking women poets to send their work to him. This letter deals with the resulting situation.

Dear Jack,

I suggest you issue another press release immediately: pleading with all the women in Canada to stop sending poems. Roblin Lake is nearly filled with poems, the village of Ameliasburgh is threatening court action.

Of course they won't stop, but it'll serve the purpose of giving the book still more publicity. I now have some 250 pieces of mail (rough estimate) and presumably there could easily be a thousand by month's end. About fifteen of those were registered. What think you about another press release?

There are obviously two ways of making room for four women. One, cut out individual poems by those writers that have several. Two, cut the three or four least promising people in the book.

I object to the first method strenuously, since the really good poets deserve more representation. And one of them, incidentally, is a woman. (Erin Mouré, whom I mentioned to you earlier.) The second method is embarrassing as hell. I've already picked these people. The only suggestion I can make here is that both of us write to four poets to be knocked out later—altho do it later when we're sure we have four excellent women poets. Say to the rejected four that we had to make room for women, since this is whatever the hell year it is—and their names came up. Phraseology of this important. The best-known of the four is Peter Van Toorn,[1] who is an excellent poet; but the two poems of his I've included are from a book published by Delta Canada, a book which received excellent reviews. There's a fairly convincing reason for knocking out Van Toorn—since he would be the best-known poet in the book if he were included. I say the phraseology is important by which the other three are told they will not be included—because they must not think they are necessarily knocked out *because they are the worst poets*. That's too hard on a young poet's ego. What do you think?

I would also recommend that you pay each of the knocked out four fifty or seventy-five dollars, else a number of books from the McStew shelves? What about that?

Possible the best thing would be to simply say they were knocked out because we had to have more women?

If this method is adopted to make room (knocking out four poets already accepted), then the utmost tact will be required. [. . .]

I'm not sure more women than men write poems, in fact I've known some dogs who could come up with a decent quatrain. However, that's partly irrelevant. As you may know, I avoided the public appeal for poems method while editing this book, mostly because I thought searching out the poets was best, and secondly because of the work involved in answering the results of a mass appeal. But given hundred to a thousand female poets, chances are we actually will come up with some decent stuff. [. . .] I haven't read a single lousy poem yet.

Desperately,
Al

1. Peter van Toorn (b. 1944): teacher at John Abbot Community College in Montreal, poet (*Mountain Tea and Other Poems,* 1984), and editor (*Sounds New,* 1990).

> **John Newlove** (1938–2003): editor, anthologist and poet (*Apology for Absence: Selected Poems 1962–1992*).

To John Newlove (Toronto), from Winnipeg, January 7, 1976

Dear John,

I hope you don't hate Trudeau after that encounter with him and the Great Bore. The only reason he remembers me is three weeks together in Cuba, plus the fact that I generally send him my books.

I'm obviously back in Wpg. It's 30 below Fahrenheit, and all male foreskins have fallen off and blow dessicated and forlorn in the howling gale. Syphilis is rampant, cold pricks common. A-burg was terrible, I quarrelled with Eurithe for a solid month between hauling loads of limestone from Point Anne quarry in a borrowed pickup. We are probably finished for the nth time.

Reading Livesay is too big a penalty for doing your antho. The only really good woman poet I know is Atwood, and she is possibly repeating herself as we all tend to do . . . But I think that most of the poets who inspire awe because of their reputations, inspire it in other people—finally come to a more accurate assessment. I mean, I grew up with Carman, Roberts, Lampman, D.C. Scott etc.[1] I think now that all but Scott are shit. Just a mass murderer, that's me. Smith and F.R. Scott will stand up to a degree, without being extraordinary. I respect Pratt, but his goddam rhythms bore me. They don't talk to *me*. Layton is good, but over-inflated both as to reputation and self-opinion. Cohen has been washed up for some time, but at his best pretty good. Nowlan is too sweet, Souster bores me . . . I feel pretty bad myself.

I'll buy the lunch, you buy the booze. I can't lose on that arrangement. You can't blame me for hoping on that book of articles [*No Other Country*, 1977]. I'll never write a porn novel ever. Either can't or won't. But if Eurithe takes most of what I have, I'd like to re-coup somehow. Anyway, without thinking those pieces genius, I do think some of them as good as I can write prose.

Dennis Lee sent back zerox of my love poems with his comments scribbled all over them. Seems he thinks I'm too obscure in a few places, which is probably true, but obscurity is necessary for me even if I don't know it, in order not to be obscure and to say something. If that sentence is obscure it's your eyeglasses. I mean, your obscurities often lead to clarities, even if that sounds like an excuse. I have Dennis's long poem to Sonny Ladoo,[2] who seems to have impressed him much. Good but over-long and redundant. He's probably franker with me on me than I'll be with him on him. But I think he's a fine fine critic, a frightening appellation.

You've been a good person? Jesus . . . You're a porcupine most of the time, didn't you know? Elspeth Cameron tells me (some time back) that you took a chunk out of her shoulder. She likes you incredibly tho. I agree Acorn postures, but I like some of his attitudes even if I know he doesn't know they're phony, because some ought to be real. Okay, I mean there are genuine parts to him, and you have to ignore the rest, try to; paraphrase bissett,[3] we forgive each other all the time. Of course we don't all the time, but do make concessions for particular people. Huh?

You're a kind person? Bullshit! You're a human being, which can include damn near anything. Alternately or simultaneously.

It's a new typewriter, the other got mad at me. I'd send you the love poems if I had a spare copy, which Newlove curse I avoid by not having copy.

Incidentally, I once started to chew off Gustafson's tie at a League meeting, and hurt his feelings as well as tie, which didn't taste good. Friend at Univ. tells me we both sat on platform while stripper disrobing at local bistro, refusing to leave despite management request. I don't remember this incident, but obviously the bouncers didn't get us. Friend is about 215, ex-footballer, now prof and novelist. We do some drinking.

Hope to see you at Harharfront[4] evening of Jan. 15.

Best,

Al

1. The poets of Confederation and the fathers of Canadian poetry: Bliss Carman (1861–1929), Charles G.D. Roberts (1860–1943), Archibald Lampman (1861–99), Duncan Campbell Scott (1862–1947).
2. *The Death of Harold Ladoo* (1976).
3. Bill Bissett (b. 1939): visual artist and experimental poet (*Nobody Own Th Earth*, 1971; *scars on th seehors*, 1999).
4. Harbourfront in Toronto.

To Jack McClelland (Toronto), from Winnipeg, January 29, 1976

Dear Jack,

[...] What I'm saying is that what you're saying is fine with me. It's just that at some not too distant date I'd like a larger Selection or Collection or whatever. I had gathered that the Layton *Collected* was not a roaring success, and obviously if Layton's isn't mine would not be either.

Yes, re *Storm Warning 2*, it's the best damn book of its kind to come out in this country. Of course there have only been two, since others were not wide open to everybody under a particular age. I mean, I did them both. And I'm really proud of this one.

Winnipeg is hell! Can't go outside without freezin your balls. I have to venture out now and then for booze. I drive, of course. I mentioned my story about Wpg., didn't I: in January in Wpg. all foreskins fall off, so there's all this protein on the streets. The snowplows get most of it. Everybody is Jewish willy-nilly. In May they grow back on again. Nobody knows this but wives and girl friends.

Best,

Al

Adele Wiseman: (1928–92): novelist, best known for her first novel, *The Sacrifice* (1956), which received a Governor General's Award.

To Adele Wiseman (Kleinburg, Ont.), from Winnipeg, March 8, 1976

Dear Adele,

I never did expect to meet you somehow, and had conceived quite a different picture of you than the actuality. Yes, I hope we meet at Margaret's this summer to talk about broken marriages and sex as sublimation for deep-sea divers.

What can I say about the writer-in-rez job you don't already know?

I had some personal reasons for loving Loyola in Mtl., but which had only borderline connection with the job. There I had a creative writing class, and was supposed to give students grades, which I didn't like. Many people came to see me. My duties were two days a week, 10 a.m. to 3 p.m.

I suppose I conceive of the writer-in-rez job as some kind of a reward for writing, and to write. Obviously, the CC asks that writing come first. The question arises that if writing is too much the preoccupation of the writer, what then does the university get out of it? People like Laurence and Birney have been very conscientious in their w-in-r jobs, others less so. At U of M here, I am not. I have two hours a day three days a week, altho I generally come in the other two for mail. I've given one reading and been in two classrooms, managing to avoid entrapment from a degree of low cunning and absence at the right time. However, they've caught up with me lately, and I have three classroom appearances before I escape. It's been an easy job here, with not very many students coming to see me; those who have have remarked that I am difficult to catch.

I have a good apt. near the univ. and have done much reading and writing in Wpg. And I prefer to look at it from that viewpoint: that the job is valuable to a writer (depending on him or her of course), replenishes their wallet, gives them time, prestige and etc. All these would be usual responses to the job, with which you would be familiar from your own viewpoints.

I doubt that my own conditions could be improved on, in other than a salary direction. However, this is the last year U of M will have such a post open, since funds are supposed to be very sparse next year. I've been left alone when I wanted to be, but given sufficient attention to prevent my ego collapsing detumescently. And I should stress that I have no duties as such, I merely keep office hours three days a week. When someone (a prof) wants me to come to class and talk or read, it's my "duty" to do so. And if I hate duty I can reflect on a pretty good yearly stipend complacently. Which has been augmented by some thirty readings at other univs.

I've even learned a few things I would not have learned elsewhere, matters that have to do with a new book I intend to write.

The only thing I dislike about Wpg. is the climate. This is not for humans. One avoids it as much as possible, and anti-freeze in quantity makes it more congenial.

Al

Patrick Lane (b. 1939): his *Poems New and Selected* (1979) received the Governor General's Award. Though he and AP had known each other since the 1960s, they grew closer after the latter moved to Vancouver Island.

To Patrick Lane (Pender Harbour, BC), from Ameliasburgh, April 11, 1976

Dear Pat,

I was pleased to talk to you in Windsor, and pleased that we are no longer on bad terms. I am sometimes cursed, or blessed as the case may be, with a sense of humour that can be quite outrageous and sometimes is not appreciated by others. For instance, among the more alarming times for me lately, was a party at the U of Man's chairman of the dept's apt., in which I drank so heavily I lost track of where I was. Now that, admittedly, is not evidence of a sense of humour, but it remains strongly in my mind since it's the first time I lost track of where I was. It seems I was wolf howling in the female guest's ear, and attempted to remove the wig of the chairman's woman (I say woman, because not wife). So I was out on my ear from that party, which makes me a little wary of future incidents.

I do get into these hassles sometimes, and so apparently do you. However, if we both take it for granted that good will is also present, we might avoid furture incidents. I don't mind chairmen of depts., but prefer better relations with poets (except for one or two I could name, but won't).

I'm just looking over your *Unborn Things*[1] which Howie—White isn't it?—sent me. I think they are good poems, and I feel like re-writing a couple, which has been Louis Dudek's revolting habit. At least that impulse indicates interest. What I mean is: I'd like to see at least a poem or two from you in which you wake up in the morning (in Peru or wherever), and feel good, and the poem reflects it. You know? The grisly side of your nature is amply demonstrated, but I'm saying that all of us laugh once in a while, all of us feel good—even John Newlove. The poems from the black side are fine, do make anyone consistent (as Atwood, say, is—altho she had one or two more cheerful ones in *You Are Happy*), re the critics. It's just that real life is not quite so one-sided. I'm saying this not in criticism, but with the thought that it might just possibly help you.

I hope you don't have to go to the Q. Charlottes to work. Several years ago George Woodcock advised me against climbing a ladder to paint my house, said I'd fall off the ladder. I painted the damn thing anyway, but he was still right. There's a time to work and a time not—and I mean you become something other than a house-painter or a lumberjack. Obviously, if you don't that means another source of income. I have no suggestions about that, but I know that if I ever went back to work (which I never will), I'd get sick of the foreman or boss and get fired pronto. Okay, one suggestion: what about your work sheets? I mean all the crap you've accumulated over the years. I sold to Queen's last time, and could inquire if you have enough to make a bonfire.

Best,

Al

1. *Unborn Things: South American Poems* was published in 1975.

Gabrielle Roy (1909–83): one of the major Canadian writers and one of the few popular both in French and English. Among her novels are *Bonheur d'Occasion* (1945), *Alexandre Chenevert* (1955), *Cet Eté qui chantait* (1972) and *Ces Enfants de ma vie* (1977).The "cover portrait" described below was pinned to the wall above AP's desk. The photograph is by John Reeves and can be found in François Picard's *Gabrielle Roy: A Life*.

To Gabrielle Roy, from Ameliasburgh, May 2, 1976

Dear Gabrielle,
I feel like writing to you because of that piece in *The Canadian*, but more than anything because of that good cover portrait of you. (You may remember Ron Everson, myself and wives visiting you last year, and you signing your books for me in a continuing series—)

It's a good face, I think not necessarily wise as such, but perhaps a face that knows. Having met you, I think you have a proper assessment of your place as a novelist, not small that is—but I do not see in your face the large conceit and arrogance of, say, Robertson Davies[1] or Irving Layton. It isn't humble either, and shouldn't be; a face that seems to say yes, I'm me, without being blatant, or self-conscious, but nevertheless with tremendous surety.

It probably sounds silly, but it's a face that could easily be bronze or whatever they use to make public park statues. Except that this face is much more human than such effigies, and all its lines testify to that. It's a face that I'm slightly in love with, or perhaps more than that, because I wish my own face had some of the cynicism and knowingness erased in order to achieve a little of that clear simplicity.

I hope the brain behind the face will write more novels. And I do not think it/you ought to be worried about joining the latest (even if it's 200 years old) wave of politics, because a writer's most single moment is much more important than a mere two centuries. (Of course I write myself, so possibly my opinion on that point may be suspect.) I mean the deep unconscious things that well out of those depths to join now, things of value, of guts and heart and mind.

The lines in that face are the tic-tac-toe of a life, and they move in all directions as experience does. At right and left angles, curves and triangles of mathematics, but move where mathematics cannot. For science is rules and law and controlled experiment; that face adds an intuitive direction that can't be calculated.

They say: never judge by appearances. To hell with that: I do, I do!

Do you remember saying, "We are the people"? I'd disagree with that to the extent of saying, "We are the writers"—and that is saying a great deal. It adds nothing and subtracts nothing, and all its meaning is what you read into it. We are human and mean and small sometimes as people; but as writers we know that, and that writing is the written dream that forgives us. And your face has forgiven itself. I haven't reached that point yet, altho I know it's possible.

Write some more.

Al

1. Robertson Davies (1913–95): man of letters, playwright and novelist (*Fifth Business*, 1970; *The Rebel Angels*, 1981). It's worth noting that his plays are not mentioned in the essay on drama in the *Cambridge Companion to Canadian Literature*—victims of critical presentism.

To William French (Toronto), from Ameliasburgh, May 4, 1976

Dear Bill,

I read your column this morning re the awards system of CC and it brought several thoughts to mind. But first, let me agree with Jack McC. when he says that the voting system should have a much broader base.

In that connection, I was one of the three judges on the poetry committee several years ago, whose other members were Ralph Gustafson and Wilfred Watson.[1] This was the year John Glassco received the poetry award. However, the committee of which I was a member voted for Irving Layton's *Collected Poems*, altho Watson was not overly eager to support Layton. But he was chairman of the poetry committee, and when the final decision rested with the chairmen of all three committees, Watson obviously must have changed his selection, voting for Glassco along with the other two chairmen.

Which brings up the point that the three men on the poetry committee probably had slightly more knowledge and ability to select the poetry winner than the chairmen for fiction and nonfiction. If not, why would poets be used on that committee and not on the others? Nevertheless, Glassco won.

Now I am not suggesting that Glassco isn't a worthy poet. He is. But the point I make is that Layton, in this case, was selected by all three committee members; and then the final committee turned him down.

Re academics on these committees, I agree that this is a bad practice—but only bad given the narrow base of the selection committees. If you had 30 or 40 or more who voted for winners in various categories, it would scarcely matter if some were academics.

I do not agree that three poets or three novelists should select winners in these categories. For one thing, these writers are in some sense competing with each other, if not at the moment of selection then certainly they will be later or have been earlier. No matter how one natters that writers are not in competition with each other, in some sense they certainly are.

In addition, there are liable to be personal likes and dislikes that the selection committee has about some candidates for awards. Certainly they should rise above such personal feelings, but I don't think they always do. If the selection committee was a larger number of people this problem would not arise. But obviously, academics are not in competition with poets, which is why I say like should not judge like.

There have been quite a number of boobs made in the selection of the GG winners. Of course Acorn should have received the award when he published *I've Tasted My Blood* several years ago. My own opinion on that may be suspect, however, since I edited the book for Acorn. But another that comes to mind readily is the Miriam Mandel[2] award for a book that has deservedly slipped into oblivion since. And I would agree that Peter Newman, who undoubtedly needs the money, should have received the award this year.

One of the most obvious faults of the awards is that when a writer should have received the award one year and does not, then he is liable to be given it in a later year for a book that doesn't deserve the prize. And there is also some evidence on the basis of past selections that judges wish to spread awards around, make sure that all writers of a sufficient level of excellence shall sooner or later receive an award. Collected or Selected works are not ineligible, but in my case on the selection committee I was given to understand that completely new work is preferred. And yet Glassco was given the award for his Selected Poems.

I hold no brief for either Glassco or Layton in their respective merits: but in that one year when I was on the selection committee (I resigned next year because of being in South Africa, and also having a book out myself), Layton's *Collected* should have won.

What I want to suggest very strongly, is that the selection methods for GG winners is very faulty. The committee should have a very broad base, composed of both academics, book editors (you too) and writers, and from all provinces.

One objection to such a committee would be that all its members couldn't possibly know and read all the books out in that particular year. A valid objection. I suppose that prior to the broadly-based committee's final selection, a prior committee would have to select a list of, say, ten eligible books in each category.

Committees, committees, committees! Bureaucracy triumphs, etc. In any case, the present system is, to say the least, imperfect.

Best wishes

Al

1. Wilfred Watson (1911–98): professor of English at the University of Alberta, playwright and poet (*Friday's Child*, 1955; *I Begin with Counting*, 1978). He and his wife Sheila founded and edited *White Pelican* (1971–78).
2. Miriam Mandel (1930–82): poet. *Lions at Her Face* (1972) won a Governor General's Award.

To Earle Birney (Toronto), from Ameliasburgh, July 30, 1976

Dear Earle,
Mistake about the date I'm in Toronto It's the 16th of August.
   Got your book [*Alphbeings and Other Seasyours*] in this mail. It's handsome. Like the "Six for Lan," also "Shotgun Marriage" and others. [...]
   The "Six for Lan" are the best love poems I've ever seen of yours. As if some bars to being personal had dissolved in yourself, and I think you have had such bars. But these, now, are lovely and delicate, they care about what they say.
   I am struck by the differences between my own love poems and yours. I am wildly romantic, at least to myself; but you are delicate and tender, with an overlooking sort of love.
See you on the 16th.
Al

From Earle Birney (Toronto), to Ameliasburgh, August 4, 1976

dear al
your praise of the Lan poems is very generous & warming to me it's so easy to muff any kind of love celebration, and seemingly impossible not to be laughed at for claiming mutual love, when the age difference is 46 years (not to mention the presumed race-gulf) it's only because it's really true, this relationship, that i can get up the nerve to write about it at all—& of course i'm just writing around the rim of it you're right that ive had personal bars, but really more in relation to *publishing*, rather than to writing love poems i wrote a lot of them during the war, & published them in Canada under a pseudonym, which only one reader ever guessed, (Pat Waddington, & he's dead) (no, they wernt to Miriam!) i wrote a lot of stuff too about Ikuko, but was so disenchanted with her treacheries that almost none of it has been published [...]
Earle

Joyce Marshall (b. 1913): Montreal-born translator (Gabrielle Roy's *Enchanted Summer*, 1976), editor, short story writer (*Any Time at All and Other Stories*, 1993) and novelist (*Lovers and Strangers*, 1957).

To Joyce Marshall (Toronto), from Ameliasburgh, August 23, 1976

Dear Joyce,

Thanks for your letter. Hadn't realized the price was now so high. I saw another copy of your book a few days ago, at an antique place on the Trent road. I didn't pick it up because I already had two. If you like, I shall—?

Yes, I'd love to have a copy of the Oberon book if you have a spare one. Ah-um-ahem—how much is it?

I like Gabrielle Roy—when I saw her picture on—was it *Weekend*—I wrote her a letter about it.[1] She signed six or seven books of mine, and did it in a unique way: she signed the first (*Tin Flute*), and said *to be continued in next book*. All the lines in that face tell separate stories of her own life—which I guess most lines do. They always tell you never to judge people by appearances, but I always do, appearance, mannerisms, speech and the works. Don't you?

Would think I now have the largest collection of signed books in the country, some 1,200, about 95% Canadian. But I wasn't able to resist a Yeats and Wyndham Lewis signature, even Mackenzie King, Diefenbaker and some letters from Trudeau (since I know the latter slightly). But they're mostly poetry and fiction, since I know many writers in the country. I'm told by Canadiana dealers the collection is worth some $10,000.

How are you? Writing?

Al

1. The lyric "On My Workroom Wall" (*Naked with Summer in Your Mouth*, 1994) begins "Photo of Gabrielle Roy with her much-lived- / in face a relief map with all the wrinkles / like badges of honour / her face a banner in the wind / Two of Margaret Laurence whom I love dearly."

To Earle Birney (Toronto), from Kiev, September 21, 1976

Dear Earle,
I am writing a poem about Kiev watermelons right now. We got a ticket
for overstaying parking limits two minutes to buy melons & grapes today
in Kiev. The cop timed us.

Yesterday from Samarcand & Tashkent & Uzbek tribesmen outside
Tamerlane's tomb; three days before that in Moscow at the Writer's Union
(they talking about translating *The New Romans*)—(I am still winding
down from writing my watermelon poem!)

About a dozen time zones are screwing up my sleep here, & we drink
boiled water from our electric coffee pot. This is the Hotel Moscow in
Kiev, and let me tell you the Kiev cops are tough!

All the best & see you and Wailan in Canada in Oct.

Al

To Earle Birney (Toronto), from Ameliasburgh, October 18, 1976

Dear Earle,
Back from the Sovietskis. Marvellous time. Maybe I shouldn't say that,
since you couldn't get there yourself. But having seen all the things we
did see, I'm very sorry you couldn't make it. We landed in Moscow of
course, then to Tashkent and Samarcand, then Kiev, Riga, Leningrad
and again Moscow. With sidetrips to Yasnaya Poliana, Tolstoy's estate
and Novgorod.

Gustafson saw dozens of operas and ballets, which I generally avoided (Gus being much more cultured than me), and he had more energy
than I had too, despite his operation of a while back. Anyway, I came
out of it with eleven poems, including the enclosed plus one called
"Colombo Was Here"—It seems he was Voznesensky's guest in Russia,
having been Voz's host in Canada. At Riga, at the Writers' Union there,
a woman named Lalla said to me, "Colombo is a better poet than you,
Purdy. He wrote a poem just for me." Well, I couldn't resist that one, so
dashed off a long poem which I gave to Voznesensky when I met him
in Moscow. Not very flattering to JRC, but he is not one of my favourite people. But the cordiality (for whatever reasons) was great; Eurithe
(who came too) and Betty Gustafson got flowers on arrival and departure; we were wined and dined etc. Rode around in CanAmbas's great
Lincoln, to be the cynosure of the local peasants and burghers—if they

have any of the latter left. Damn thing must be sixty feet long—the car, I mean. Otherwise drove in a big Cheika, used habitually for diplomats etc. Never been treated so royally by non-royalists ever, and left with a good warm feeling for our hosts. Despite that, one poem I wrote (which won't be sent to SU) called "At Lenin's Tomb" is not one they would like. Me bein kinda anti-US tho, my feelings fitted in fairly well with those of our hosts. But the vodka toasts to everything but the kitchen sink began to wear on me, and the flowery speeches! and Voznesensky[1]—well, I love his poems, despite them being in translation. He's a good likeable guy, which I hear (tho didn't meet) Yevtushenko is not. No matter, Voz was the guy I wanted to meet, and we had drinks (all of us) at the Hotel Russia for an hour. One of those trips that leaves a great impression. I think you should try to get there if you possibly can, even yet. I think you'd love it. Please try. You'd come out with some great poems, that I know.

love,
Al

1. Andrei Voznesensky (b. 1933): Russian poet (*Antiworlds / The Fifth Ace*, 1966). AP often contrasts Voznesensky and Yevtushenko. He tended to agree with the Polish critic who referred to Yevtushenko as one of the ten greatest fakes of the twentieth century. (He did not specify the other nine.)

To Earle Birney (Toronto), from Ameliasburgh, November 14, 1976

Dear Earle,

Sorry didn't make it to Toronto after Sudbury, but had much work here as I told Wailan on the phone. For instance, 2,000 words on the *Lit. Hist. of Can.* for *Books in Can.*, eight or nine hundred on Everson for *CanLit*, and some 3,500 article on the Russian trip. To top off all that, Arlene Lampert[1] asked me to go to the prairies for three readings, since the woman scheduled for the trip had gotten sick. Therefore, I had to delay my coupla days in Toronto so I could catch up with all this. I said most of this to Wailan on the phone, but doubt if she remembered it all.

Anyway, I leave Tuesday for three readings out west.

It didn't occur to me when I sent you that poem that it might have a personal application; rather stupid on my part, I guess. My own legs and general physical condition are giving me some trouble. I don't think that doctor in Toronto did any good at all, so I probably won't go back. However, I did want to talk to you about the Soviet Union—and

I think the chief difficulty for you would be boarding and de-boarding aeroplanes. Still, it's a very worthwhile trip, and I'd like to see you take a chance and go over there. People get these chances once, generally, and I remember I felt the same way about going to Cuba. Some photographer backed out, afraid he'd be blacklisted. I think he never made a bigger mistake in his life. I am damn sure you'd write poems if you went. Why not ask Ford[2] about it? Or just take a chance and go, then carry it as far as your physical condition will let you. I've no idea about Wailan, but agree that she ought to go with you. When I say no idea, I mean no idea how the Russians would go for a Chinese gal with you. But to hell with that, take a chance and go. You'll be royally treated.

I've been sawing wood and banging the typewriter here. The wood is for the fireplace, of course, and up to a foot in diameter. Christ, I forget what diameter is: around or through. But I mean through. Shows you you were right about alcohol destroying brain cells, I just lost a dozen or so.

I really will be getting to Toronto—sometime after this next western trip. Incidentally, Eurithe's father has cancer, and is in Kingston Hosp. Eurithe wants to go south and buy a trailer there, one of those big things that's permanently anchored somewhere. But she can't until her father has his operation. Also incidentally, my son just came back from Thunder Bay where he spent several months and had a job that paid him over $1,100 a week—as a steamfitter!!!!! The labourers shall inherit the earth? Let me excerpt a line or so from Voznesensky, change the sex of the subject and make it male:

> You—people, locomotives, germs,
> Be as careful with her as you can—[3]

I mean, be as careful with yourself as you can.

love,
Al

1. Arlene Lampert: organized readings for the League of Canadian Poets at this time.
2. R.A.D. Ford (1915–98): poet (*Coming from Afar*, 1990) and diplomat (ambassador to Russia during the 1970s).
3. The quoted lines are from the fourteenth section of "Oza."

To Earle Birney (Toronto), from Ameliasburgh, November 28, 1976

Dear Earle,

Your Cuba trip sounds fine. How come you use the English "fortnight"? Is that a result of Chaucer?

Okay, the bit about boarding and deboarding planes: they don't have that inflated bicycle tube we have in North America, whereby you can walk on and off planes. You get into a bus that's generally crowded, then you climb the steps onto plane. Reverse when deboarding. Having been part of the sardine-mob in that bus made me think that might be tough for you. However, the translator who accompanied us everywhere, could easily ask that you be allowed to board first, therefore it would be a matter of all those steps only. But we can discuss any questions you might have in Dec.

Yes, *Sundance* [*at Dusk*], —thanks much for the good word on that book. I had such a hassle with Newlove and Avery over that book that the memory still leaves a sour taste. Both wanted to drop a lot of poems that are now in, including the first poem, the tobacco spitters' lament thing ["Lament"]. It was a matter of fighting both of them thru the book's production, and I did give way on some poems that I now regret, which last accounts for the slightly sour taste. It began to sound like a favour if they allowed me to keep some particular poems. Finally I simply made out a contents list of poems and said that's it, and I meant that's it. But I had deferred somewhat to their opinions, which I now regret in some instances.

Praise? Two reviews thus far, that I know of, both favourable. But as you must know, you, Layton and Atwood get much more attention than I do from the media—what the hell is plural of media, or is it plural? But I get as much as I deserve, and mind you I'm not complaining. I ran into the awfulness of someone complaining with Gustafson in Russia, and it made me sick. Will tell you about that when I see you. But what I meant to say is: thanks much for the good word on the book. I probably need some praise for this book more than others, both because of Newlove and Avery and because I felt at the end of my tether as far as writing was concerned. See "Ritual" when I was at a very low point. I was dubious about "Inside the Mill," which is, yes, lyrical, but I was afraid might be sentimental or too easy. I can adopt almost any rhythm—or conceitedly think I can—which made this poem seem a tour de force to me. I'm sure there's Birney in some of those poems, impossible not to be after knowing you and poems of yours such a long time. Think I read "David" not long after the book came out . . .

Only met one Cuban poet, and can't remember her name. I wanted to meet Jorge Guillen[1] at the time, but didn't manage. Incidentally, have I recommended Voznesensky to you? If not, I do—think he's one of the most impressive poets I've read. Try to pick up *Antiworlds* and *The Fifth Ace*, two books in one, Schocken Books, NY. *Don't get the Grove Press Selected, trans Anselm Hollo. Antiworlds* was pubbed originally by Basic Books, and later reprinted in the double volume, in paperback. This has Auden, Kunitz[2] and others doing the translations.

Eurithe's father's cancer now being treated with some sort of radiation, periodically. It's in his face, and possibly that and his neck is a bad place to operate.

Yes, back from prairies a week, and quite a good three readings. Altho the Sudbury ones were more interesting. I went into a classroom before my scheduled appearance, and told the kids I was Layton, and not to come to Purdy's reading, that he was a half-assed poet etc. Then read one of Layton's poems with some panache. I guess a few saw thru the imposture, but Layton was supposed to be in Sudbury at the time; so I got a kick out of being Layton.

See you later—

Al

1. Jorge Guillén (1893–1984): Spanish poet whose fame rests on one book, *Cántico* (1928) to which he has added further lyrics over the years. There is a possibility that AP is confusing Jorge Guillén with the Cuban poet Nicolas Guillen (1902–89) author of *Man-Making Words: Selected Poetry of Nicolas Guillen* (1972). The poetry of the former is "delicate, luminous, sentimental and hypersensitive" (Willis Barnstone), not qualities that AP usually admired. Nicolas Guillen's poetry, by contrast, is engaged, realistic and political.
2. Stanley Kunitz (b. 1905): American poet (*Selected Poems 1928–58* was awarded the Pulitzer Prize). He taught at Columbia University.

To Margaret Laurence (Lakefield, Ont.), from Ameliasburgh, February 18, 1977

Dear Margaret,

Thanks for the good word on poems. And yes, the point about a country is it means a lot more than economics. Many people don't seem to realize that. I've written other poems besides those three, but they seem to me much the best. And maybe you're right about the date of "Starlings," but sometimes the past seems to become the future indefinite, not lost but floating in a place without time, and all three tenses are applicable. And this is a peculiarity about time for me, that apart from definite dates which rarely seem very important, I seem to become a compendium of both past and future. All things have such varied aspects and facets that I see them from many viewpoints. For instance, I'm going to the Yukon shortly. And just looking at a photograph of the thronging main street of Dawson, when the town and area had a pop. of 25,000, later down to a little over 700, and thinking I will write a poem about that, contrasting it to now.[1] Which doesn't sound very good, but the point is I hold both that past and present in my mind, also the possible poem, plus unrealized things that may happen. Probably unfigureaoutable. [. . .]

The Diviners? I have all sorts of feelings about the book, one of them being one you perhaps don't prize as much as I do: the fact that you seldom or never write a line that isn't, of itself, interesting. I mean in a surface way, apart from whatever the total book adds up to. And I think that is damn rare. There are things I did think about the book, as I remember: that the earlier years in it overmatched the other sections in some degree. But the best part of it was what I talked about in the first para. of this letter, the homogeneity of time and what happens, how incidents float in time. Or am I being obscure? I do think it's one of the three top novels written in/of/about this country. And when one develops the ability to do this, I think one should go farther. Always farther, exploring, developing etc.

I doubt that people think you're "in a state of despair" and "bowing out of life." That's a wild exaggeration. And people who keep pestering you to do this and that, well, one learns to dispose of those things in order to do the important things. I am saying: a talent is to be used, even if you let it lie fallow for a time. If you never write another novel, you won't think you're useless in this life, as you say. Of course not, and that's not the goddam point. Because neither novels nor poems are entirely gifts, only in one sense. The qualities that enabled you to write your novels are still there, and one owes both one's self and other people. Don't tell me that's shit either. And life is only partly what you are given to do, which is carrying fatalism to its absurdio. To have written what you did changed you, gave you tools and equipment in your mind to do other and different things. I don't say one should drive and push one's self into those other things, I do say one should not seem to bar them out with fatalism. i.e. they were gifts, I'll wait and see if there's another gift. That's passive and inert. Of course it's not what other people want of you either, but what you need from yourself. But we are liable to miss each other's point if I continue like this. What happens in the mind is so damn mysterious anyway . . .

Incidentally, I don't think "A Handful Of Earth" is as good as the other two, but since it's about the subject it is, perhaps for that reason . . .

I'll see you at this coronation or whatever it is, the Mohawk College thing.[2] Which will be a lousy place to talk, one can't. I may go to Mexico after the Yukon trip, dunno. But maybe we can drink some wine in Hamilton. And hey, I think you're a pretty nice person, if I haven't said so lately—much larger than you know about.

love,
Al

1. Possibly "Hail Mary in Dawson City" in *The Stone Bird*.
2. The annual Canada Day seminar.

From Pierre Elliott Trudeau (Ottawa), to Carcross, Yukon, March 16, 1977

Dear Al,
I received your poem "A Handful of Earth" and found it very touching and beautiful. It is that beauty and emotion which Canadians must feel surging within their hearts, if we are to will this country into its future.

Thanks.

Sincerely
Pierre

Susan Musgrave (b. 1951): West Coast novelist (*The Charcoal Burners*, 1980), journalist, and poet (*Tarts and Muggers*, 1982; *Things That Keep and Do Not Change*, 1999). She and AP became close friends when he moved to Vancouver Island. Her poem "Twenty-Eight Uses for Al Purdy's Ashes" (1999), written before AP's death, is one of the most memorable tributes ever written by one writer to another.

To Susan Musgrave (Sidney, BC), from Ameliasburgh, May 7, 1977

Dear Susan,

[...] I dunno when you'll get back to Sidney, maybe June if that bit about last yr's Collingwood is accurate. But if I don't reply now, it will be a little out of date in my mind, and probably buried under a stack of mail.

I have four books coming this year: three small books of poems, and a big book of essays from McStew. (Will send em along to you as they appear. I don't have that *Wild Grape Wine* I was gonna send you, at least if so I dunno where).

No Other Country (essays)
At Marsport Drugstore (luv luv luv)
A Handful of Earth (new, used and forgotten stuff)
Moths in the Iron Curtain (Russian stuff)

[...] Migawd, what a lit letter you write!

I feel a bit guilty about Vernon, despite managing to stay three addresses ahead of her letters at all times. I'm afraid I hurt her feelings at the Westbury, with my fairly vigorous and slightly unsober non-declarations, like "For chrissake stop sending me luv letters." Can't remember what I said to her anyway. But no, my lack of salutation may have been a subconscious remembrance of your marriage. And it (the marriage) stands out as a bit incredible in my mind. You realize what it does to your reputation? The Siren of the Charlottes is no more, the mermaid has acquired a hairlip?

Another reason I'm writing now is: I hafta do the final piece for the essays in four days, then shove it on a bus to Toronto. I also have to write a piece for the *Financial Post* inside a month (1,500 words) on the "mood" of Ontario. Jesus, don't ask me why they picked me, but $500 I hate to pass up. Anyway, you see if I don't write now, my gravestone will be a rejection slip. And I am now Purdy Industries, Inc. [...]

May I brag a little modestly? There's an academy of Can. writers. Some sixty thousand people voted for three best poets, novelists etc. Voting figures weren't released publicly, but my intense ego made me ask. I came in 7,000 votes ahead of Atwood. Then I go to Coles and see eighteen thousand of her books there and none of mine. But novelist Mowat (who doesn't write novels) was ahead of M. Laurence. And that ruins my ego completely. If voters don't know the difference between Laurence and Mowat, how the hell would they know a poet from Rod McKuen? Which leads me to: what shit it all is! [...]

I won't ask about the novel, but I am curious. I've now forgotten what it was all about, about a tin mine on the Celebes where the action takes place in a pub in Merida?

> Near Boadicea's ruined wall
> the Bearpaw Sea is over all
> and dinosaurs across the way
> release a yip of yea and nay
>
> —Anon (attributed to an 18th
> century monk in Ireland.)

[. . .] I may be seeing you about Aug. if you're back from travels. Reading there. And I will take a few days off to rent a car and travel up the coast to see Jack Jackovich, and Haig-Brown's widow. Jackovich is an ex-football player, now painter, and fishing guide and school teacher, beer drinker, and weighs 265. You know Haig-Brown died, I guess. Wrote a piece about him in *CanLit*,[1] and note from his wife, and hafta see her. (I'd invite you to come if you weren't married.) I'm sentimental about Haig-Brown, and you'll see the reason for it if you read *CanLit* or the piece in *No Other Country*.

Love—for your own sake,

Al

1. "The Death of a Friend," *Canadian Literature* (Spring 1977).

Louis Dudek (1918–2001): professor of English at McGill, editor (*Delta*), publisher, critic (*Selected Essays and Criticism*, 1978) and poet (*Collected Poems*, 1971). Of the writers AP met in Montreal in the 1950s, Dudek is the only one with whom he doesn't seem to have gotten along; the cause may have had as much to do with personalities as attitudes to poetry.

To Louis Dudek (Montreal), from Ameliasburgh, May 20, 1977

Dear Louis,

I was just talkin to Peter Brown, and he says you hate me. And I replied, yes, I know. But then I think, that can't be true. What a waste of time to hate anyone except those really worth hating. And I doubt that I am for you.

Of course we don't get along too well at times, do we? I lash back at people, and you do too. But I'd hate to think either of us had any very lasting feeling of even dislike. I certainly don't. I don't agree with you part of the time, as you don't with me, but surely that isn't very important in the long run. I've always felt I owed you much from just knowing you in Montreal, and still feel that way.

Best Wishes,

Al

William Golding (1911–93): English novelist, best known for *The Lord of the Flies* (1954). Awarded the Nobel Prize in 1983. AP admired his work, and on at least two occasions borrowed from it.

To William Golding (Bowerchalke, Wiltshire, England), from Ameliasburgh, July 26, 1977

Dear Mr. Golding,

My friends, Bob & Donna Macdonald, gave me your address. I believe they are also friends and/or acquaintances of yours.

I enclose a small book of my own as part Intro. (I've written and edited some twenty-five over about the same number of years.)

The reason I write is that I'd like to have you sign your books for me. I have all of them except the play, *The Brass Butterfly*, I think the title is.

The additional reason is: I think Golding is a marvellous writer. That's liable to be embarrassing as hell for you, to be told that flatly, as it has been for me at one time or another. I just shrug and say "That's nice" or some such silliness.

However, to explain slightly, I picked up *The Inheritors* for fifty cents not long after it was published, and got lost in prehistory. Then *Pincher Martin*, and spent some time discussing with friends whether Martin was drowned immediately, or whether he actually did cling to a rock in mid-Atlantic for hours and days. No doubt you are familiar with such discussions. Then I was completely bewildered by *Free Fall*; altho I read *Lord of the Flies* somewhat before this.

Margaret Laurence, a novelist friend of mine, thinks you and Graham

Greene the two top novelists. I plump for Golding, with Greene a distant second. Again, I apologize if this is awkward for you.

I picked up a first ed of *Flies* only recently, and not a real good copy. But it completes my Golding collection, which I cherish. A couple of the later ones, I think *The Spire* and another, are US eds. Anyway, this bibliography is probably boring you.

I came close to meeting you in Greece in 1968–69 when you visited the Macdonalds. Incidentally, I wrote a poem based on that piece of yours in your essays, *The Hot Gates*, with the same title as the essays. That is indeed true love of a writer. Altho I should mention that I wrote another poem based on a piece by E.M. Forster, "Dindia Macolnia Is Shopping."[1]

Anyway, if I send books and international postage, could you sign about ten books for me and return?

I regret not seeing any recent book of yours. I hope it indicates slow gestation.

Best Wishes,
Al Purdy

1. E.M. Forster (1879–70): English novelist (*Howards End*, 1910) and essayist. The poem "Dindia Macolnia is Shopping" is based on Forster's essay (1903) "Macolnia Shops"(*Abinger Harvest*). AP's "Voltaire" is based on the first part of Forster's essay on the French writer in the same collection. In a letter to George Galt (January 11, 1983), AP mentions that reading Forster's *Pharos and Pharillon* prompted him to reread Homer's epics, a rereading that led to the writing of several poems on Homeric themes, including "Menelaus and Helen."

To Brian McCarthy (Montreal), from Ameliasburgh, September 8, 1977

Dear Brian,

The bit about not enjoying anything without wanting to write a poem: I don't think one needs to justify this. It's self-dramatism of course, but quite true and factual—in my case too incidentally. Altho I wouldn't have said "can't enjoy" . . . The mind works rationally for the most part, altho a poem isn't always rational. I mean one starts with rationality, but allows irrationality to enter at times. "Allows"? One can't help it and shouldn't try.

There is a point that occurs to me about your prosody, which is that in some poems, especially, there is a "method" evident—if not method then call it a particular verse form, a way of writing. Since I think you do it well at this precise point, I expect it's best to continue, with the proviso that you're entirely aware of what you're doing. If you break out of that method before breaking out comes naturally, then you take the strong chance of failure. But sooner or later, one must break away from any form. Some don't, some can't, some never will. I think this point was mentioned when talking, that you wanted to write entirely different poems, of a particular kind. Different kinds of poems allow you to say entirely different things, break loose from many constrictions. But still, I think each plateau has to be explored and colonized, as you're doing now.

And reverting back: I expect there's a slight guilt at the rationality of being aware that you'll write a poem if you can, since the poem itself is many times an irrational act; but could never begin without rationality in the first place. (Stone fireplace poem is in *Sundance at Dusk*.)[1] However, when you see the effects of the other people's rationality and irrationality, both, and the apparent uselessness of all our efforts at anything, then poems are harmless enough. And no matter how much time you appear to have, you actually have little time to do anything at all.

"The Nightshift Nurse" poem ending? You need some kind of insight there that quite reverses the flow and even meaning of the poem itself. There is no surprise, no insight, nothing in that last line as it now stands. Something "positive"? Perhaps, but one way to make what actually becomes your last line more striking, is to break the rhythm of the foregoing poem at the end. So that it isn't quite so much a "well-made poem" at the end. That isn't a very easy thing to do, but it's something one is faced with in every poem: will I go on the way I'm going on and have been, or will I gamble on something else? And this harks back to what I said about method: the method you're using is one you're exploring now, but it's certainly possible to break out for one line. And when I say break out, I mean break from the previous form, which breaking may do something surprising.

Of course the above ways of changing the last line are sheer rationality. And thru rationality you dispense with rationality sometimes. The poem as it stands is good, and you take the chance of fucking it up by changing. But I think that's what a poet does, takes chances.

I have to go—take the car in for a grease job shortly. Enjoyed your visit. Next time you're at this cottage, come down and we'll drink wine and play records.

Al

1. The "stone fireplace poem" is "Place of Fire."

To Margaret Laurence (Lakefield, Ont.), from Ameliasburgh, August 23, 1977

Dear Margaret,
Take a look at this Graham Greene.[1] I think it's possible you haven't read it. He saw a much different Mexico than I did, and hated it, detested it. All possible generosity was gone from him when he went there. The book starts a bit slowly, and he's definitely padding it here and there, since I gather it's a commissioned book, or was years ago. I've had the book a long time, but never read it until I went west and took it along for casual reading.

It was strange for me to read the book, and see how he disliked everything he saw and some things he didn't see. I think it the book of a recently converted person to Catholicism, who has to some degree let religion take over his good sense. And yet his acute observation remains; some of his descriptions are marvellous. Hope you enjoy it.

Al

See Page 157 for his description of Palenque—

P.S. I wrote William Golding, asking him if he'd sign his books etc. He wrote back, sending me twin signatures like a crossword puzzle, that I could clip and, as he said, "deface his books"—It broke me up to see those signatures; I chortled for half an hour. Like Gabrielle Roy, who wrote "to be continued" in each book.

1. *The Lawless Roads* (1939).

To Jack McClelland (Toronto), from Ameliasburgh, November 15, 1977

Dear Jack,
The newspaper reviews have begun to come in—some six or seven of them—for *No Other Country*, and I'm left rather disappointed. Particularly so when I remember your own previous good opinion of the book. Only two of the reviews have had much good to say about it.

However, some of the headings are funny: PURDY HAS COME TO SAVE US and PURDY SHOULD STICK TO POETRY.

On the other hand, all the television and radio people I talked to liked the book, some apparently a great deal. But then you'd expect them to, else why should they interview this guy who wrote a terrible book?

Only journalists have reviewed the book thus far. It may be that they think I'm invading their territory, and if they do think that I take small comfort from it. A remark of Earle Birney recently to the effect that Pierre Berton[1] and Farley Mowat write this sort of thing "better than we do" may be more relevant. And perhaps you will do as one reviewer suggested as being legitimate after this book, publish the Collected Poems of June Callwood.[2]

Anyway, this is not an apology for the book, but some rueful comments on reviewers of same. There were so many good opinions after the pieces were published in magazines that I'm taken aback at what the journalists think, and wonder how the literary writers will treat it.

However, writing those pieces (for which I had a book in mind all along) originally was a lot of fun and I felt satisfaction with some of them. I regret neither them nor the book. And I hope the sales figures later will not make you regret it.

All the best,

Al

1. Pierre Berton (b. 1920): popular and prolific broadcaster, journalist and historian (*The National Dream: The Great Railway 1871–81*, 1970; *The Last Spike: The Great Railway 1881–85*, 1971).
2. June Callwood (b. 1924): social activist, broadcaster, journalist, writer (*Trial without End*, 1995).

Gary Geddes (b. 1940): anthologist and poet (*Light of Burning Towers*, 1990).

To Gary Geddes (Montreal), from London, Ont., November 25, 1977

Hi Gary,

Gawd, you have a problem, re adding five more poets.[1]

I think your selection of my stuff is probably the best in any anthology. The only poem I might drop would be "Detail," and possibly a later poem there would be better. Say "Alive or Not" from *Sundance*. However, even that change is not very important, since, as I said, I think it's a good early selection. Unless you change it completely for later stuff—which I don't think you want to do—it should probably remain as is.

As I undoubtedly mentioned to you when you were making your poet selections, I would not have included Coleman, and perhaps not Doug Jones, both of which I regard as "unimportant." However, Jones has a bit more substance than Coleman. As for additions (and that is damn tough!), how about Andy Suknaski, Frank Davey, and leave it at that while I think. I believe you didn't include poets like Scott, Smith and Klein for reasons which still stand? If so, there's nothing to be said. However, I would find Scott particularly hard to leave out. And oh yes, this time you should definitely include Acorn. I don't know how you feel about him, but he's a GG award winner now, which ought to change something.[2] I happen to think he's good. I don't mean always, but part of the time, and you have to select carefully.

Okay, here'd be my five additions: Acorn, Suknaski, Dennis Lee, Davey and P.K. Page. The latter may be in the same category as Scott, Klein and Smith with you. In which case, you might think of Bill Bissett if you can get enough intelligible stuff. Also, you should probably consider Joe Rosenblatt, with same proviso as for Bissett.

Yes, I stick to my original opinion re your "essays"—One way of doing it might be to do only the poets you include in the new book, that is, twenty. Which would give you a companion book to your *20 Canadian Poets*, a sort of handbook for the larger book, and therefore Oxford might be interested. I'm sure you see the point. I do think that's a good idea. And why not drop those you don't think have stood up? Coleman and Jones have not, in my opinion, and were not important in the first place.

I know this is much more work for you: to write about those poets in the book whom you haven't already written about: but there are many advantages to that plan.

And yes, I know the bit about writing too many reviews. It has helped you personally and literarily (both to get your poems published and for personal prestige, as I mentioned to your chagrin?) . . . And since I've written many reviews myself, I know the feeling. Also, it's tough to say hard things about people you know and may stab you in the back in turn. But if you take these things on, you have to say what you think, influenced as little as possible by enmity or friendship.

Yes, I'm writer-in-rez at Western. Nice soft job, no teaching, good money. But shit, I wanta use my time to travel and write poems! For that I hafta have money tho. So Western provides some. Some of which will be used for about five weeks in Mexico beginning next week. We'll drive south to the sun, and I feel like a goddam albino frog under a stone at this moment, pale that is.

Okay, a final suggestion: give up poems completely for the length of time it takes you to do the antho, and also to write the additional essays you need for a companion book to *20 Canadian Poets*? Then fuck criticism for a coupla years, completely. Give it up and write poems. What about that? Your sense of amour propre and need for prestige and money demands both these two books (I shan't mention artistic considerations), but then you must write poems. Each will help the other, both with you and your prestige with publishers.

Al

1. Geddes was revising his popular anthology *Fifteen Canadian Poets*.
2. Acorn won in 1975 for *This Island Means Minago*.

Eli Mandel (1922–92): professor of English at York University, critic (*Irving Layton*, 1969) and poet (*Dreaming Backwards*, 1981), long overdue for a major reassessment.

To Eli Mandel (Toronto), from Ameliasburgh, June 8, 1978

Dear Eli,

Would you still be interested in editing a book of the critical stuff I've written over the past few years—a dozen years, I guess?

I do think it takes a good editor for something like this (that's you if you're interested). Dennis Lee edited a 200-page Selected of mine called *Being Alive* for McStew this fall. And I think Dennis was invaluable for his pointing out poems that might be changed and revised, and for his selections as against my own preferences, and general expertise. However, after all the work he did on this book, I can't ask him to take more time from his own work.

Of course you may not wish to either, since you must be at least as busy as Dennis.

And there's an additional thing to consider: you may look at all the articles and reviews and say: there ain't enough good stuff, it's terrible. That, of course, will be up to you.

The publisher could be McStew, Marty Gervais at Black Moss or Peter Brown of Little Press & Gallery Editions. Both the latter have done or are about to publish books of mine. I think the edition would be quite small, perhaps 26 copies of a special ed. and the others—about 300 hardbacks. McStew would not be interested, I think, in such a small edition. Incidentally, I haven't mentioned this to either Marty Gervais or Peter

Brown, but think both would be willing to do such a book. If not, it's no great matter. And I'm not very sure about much of the critical stuff I've written anyway. But you would have a better idea about it than me.

Anyway, drop me a line here if you're interested.

What do you think of the Jones GG?[1] It seems to me he tries to carve his poems into understated immortal lines, and sometimes comes close. I think he's too goddam arty at times tho; I don't mind reverence for the word, but it shouldn't be that evident. On the other hand, the book is pretty good on first reading. I suppose I have some dislike of a basic philosophy, more evident in past books than this new one, of accepting things as they are rather helplessly which I might call a defeatist attitude not to say decadent (allied to Cohen in this), and making a virtue of it. Of course personal, for things churn in my insides, and I want to rage at least a little. Perhaps close to Layton in that. It's been mentioned to me that Jones is close to a particular kind of French poetry. I dunno. Sure, it's a good book, I say—with reservations.

How are you?

Best,
Al

1. D.G. Jones, see page 312.

To Margaret Laurence (Lakefield, Ont.), from Ameliasburgh, July 6, 1978

Dear Margaret,

I'll try and answer your questions first: I don't know where I am; I don't know what I've been doing. I'm not being ambiguous, because I doubt that I've been doing anything, except the usual readings and writing a few poems. Not many of the latter. Guy wanted me to write the libretto for an opera, which idea I toyed with for a coupla weeks then decided against it. Referred the composer to Newlove, which no doubt he will thank me for. It boiled down to: why the hell would I wanta write an opera? Of course Norm Symonds[1] had a great basic story, a factual thing, which a small part of my mind regretted abandoning.

About the film people asking questions about you: do you really care what people say? You've undoubtedly changed to a degree that any possible answer about you old acquaintances or friends might give could come as no surprise and only a larger degree of indifference. If they read your books, it will be out of curiosity as to what makes you tick. The real audience is somewhere else. I can't imagine Eurithe's family reading anything

I write for any reason but curiosity about me, certainly not for what I might say.

Western? More or less usual, I guess. Did meet a guy, one of the univ. governors, whose name I seem to have forgotten already, whom I went to school with, and who had kept those school mags you get. Therefore I was able to gaze with horrified eyes at the first poems I wrote at age 13. They're just as lousy now as then. Odd that this old schoolmate should become an army colonel then a univ gov.[2] We went to dinner there one evening, and he had assembled any literary people he and wife knew. The intention was good, but the only way to endure such gatherings is imbibe as much as is enough as quickly as possible.

I think there's a fine line between writing a poem and not, and suspect it might apply to prose too. If I have some sort of thought or idea, it's a question of whether I do or do not write some of it down. If I don't I might have lost a fine poem; if I do I'm pretty sure to have lost it anyway, because it's almost always bad. But I have to write a little to find out if it's gonna be bad, or if I get no more words arriving from nowhere. I suppose the comparison with prose falls down, because a novel needs so much more planning? You don't just write a novel from the top of your head, the way I can sometimes write a poem, when conscious and subconscious merge and flow together. But I do think there's a *right* time to write a novel, when all the omens are propitious and the entrails read go, the lares and penates grin at you approvingly etc. As I think I've said, a novel is such a huge job, so much bloody work, I'd only try it thru ambition which is the same case with the aforementioned opera. Still, there's gotta be a parallel with poems in all this. I suppose the real question is (which leads to the novel): what is the most interesting thing in your life right now, what preoccupies you the most, etc. etc.? Even if this subject doesn't connect directly with a possible novel, there are certainly ways of making it connect. Being a surface dilettante of life, I flit from subject to subject mostly superficially. But I think ageing and the changes I see in myself and my own attitudes are probably foremost. And it's tough to make poems from that. Of course there are other things that interest me, but it's an interest strongly tinged with indifference. As long as other people's opinions (unfavourable ones) aren't overt, I couldn't care less. And "caring" is one of the necessary ingredients of poems in most cases, as of anything. In some sense, I think a poet writes one long novel all his life, just as the novelist . . . Now what the hell was I gonna say there, something philosophic and profound no doubt.

Incidentally, I've a 200-page selected called *Being Alive* to differentiate coming this fall. Dennis Lee edited for this one book with McStew, and several poems were changed and revised at his prompting. He really does have a keen eye and perceptions. This will be the longest and best book I've published. Other books no doubt have themes that predominate more, but if there's any mood or area in which I wrote best, that must predominate in a book like this. I mean, other books undoubtedly had more poems written in other countries or love poems or whatever, but if those poems weren't what I do best, they won't be in this book. Therefore, in some ways a Selected is liable to be misleading. Must stop.

Yours

Al

1. Norman Symonds (b. 1920): jazz musician and composer.
2. Colonel Charles F. Way, at this time Secretary of Western's Board of Governors, was born in Wooler, Ontario, and had attended Trenton High School.

To Jack McClelland (Toronto), from Ameliasburgh, October 4, 1978

Dear Jack,
I'm sorry you feel so disturbed over the review I did of [Leonard] Cohen's book [*Death of a Lady's Man*].[1] I should mention: I did not write the headings for the review, and those made it seem worse than it actually was. Actually, I paid Cohen many compliments for his earlier books, and even one or two for the present book. However, I do not think it a very good book, and being so honest yourself, I am sure you would want me to say what I feel and think.

What? Do I hear you say you don't want me to say what I feel and think? I must have heard wrong. Surely you don't want me to be a yes-man, somebody who always agrees with you? I know you have a special feeling for Cohen, and believe he is a special human being. I can understand that, and hope you can remain feeling that way. It is a good feeling, this admiration of "difference" in someone else, and I'm sure that Cohen welcomes it from someone in your position: his publisher.

However, and it's a big "however," I calls em as I sees em, and I don't intend to be influenced by anyone either way. I thought you knew me well enough to know that.

The Cohen reviews I've seen have been interesting: one in the *Vancouver Sun* was a pretty flat dislike; Geddes in the *Globe* thought *Lady's Man* was a comic book, one which ridiculed itself; another review apparently didn't care for it much; and mine, which said that Cohen had written much better previously, and that this book was not up to his earlier standard. I haven't seen any raves yet and don't expect to. *It is not a good book.*

Again, I'm sorry you feel so personally affronted, as appeared when I met you briefly at Hollinger House. Whether you know or believe it or not, I have quite a lot of admiration for you—for reasons I don't intend to specify. And I do hope we can be more or less civil to each other most of the time. If not, well—I accept that too, and can get used to it.

Best wishes,
Al

1. The review appeared in the *Toronto Star*, September 30, 1978.

From Jack McClelland (Toronto), to Ameliasburgh, October 16, 1978

Dear Al,

For years I have been told that few people can tell when I am being serious and when I am not. It has even been suggested that I should carry a sign in my pocket which I could hold up and which would say something like, "I'm only kidding." I would say this to you. If you were not an old friend and had I been in any way serious, I would not, even for a minute, have considered assaulting you in such harsh terms. Had I been serious, it is conceivable that I might have ignored you, more likely that I would have written you, but the last thing I would have considered would be a performance of that sort.

In my trade, reviews are of little significance except for any effect they may have on the psyche of the author. But that's the author's problem, not the publisher's. I don't think reviews, pro or con, have any profound effect on the immediate or future sales of any book. In fact, I would prefer a negative review with a lot of space to a short positive review. I measure the value in column inches. The only type of review that irritates me is the lightweight, silly review. A case in point would be Barbara Amiel's spoof of the Merle Shain[1] book in a recent issue of *Maclean's*. I don't know whether you saw it or not. Instead of reviewing the book, Amiel wrote a piece in the form of a confession from Merle Shain as to how she put the book together. It was a silly review. Yours was anything but silly and, of course, you had some kind things to say about Cohen.

It is true that I don't agree with your evaluation of the book. So what else is new? I seldom agree with other people's opinions anyway. I happen to think this is one of the finest things Cohen has ever written. One thing I don't understand, however, is why, in the very small literary community that we have in Canada, important writers like yourself risk their own personal relationships—and here I am thinking of you and Leonard, although Leonard would be one of the last people in the world to harbour a grudge because of a review—when it would be so much easier to read the book and tell the paper "I don't want to review it." In other words in this very small community, I think it would be far better for all the major writers to say no—considering the pittance they get for doing a review anyway—unless they can be positive about the book by one of their peers. So why should I single you out for this comment? Everybody does it. It is just something that I don't understand. Life is too short.

Cheers!

Jack McClelland

1. Barbara Amiel (b. 1940): journalist and columnist with *Maclean's* (1976–), *Toronto Sun* (1983–85), *London Times* (1986–90) and *Sunday Times* (1991–94). Merle Shain (1935–89): author of *Some Men Are More Perfect than Others: A Book about Men, hence about Women* (1973), *Love and Dreams* (1973) and *When Lovers Are Friends* (1978).

To Jack McClelland (Toronto), from Ameliasburgh, November 22, 1978

Dear Jack,

I'm pleased you're not angry with me, and you really should get that sign you mention.

You must know that I have the highest regard for Cohen. I think that, at times, he's an authentic bloody genius. But I also have less flattering thoughts about him.

I'll never know why I write reviews of people I know, tho in Cohen's case only slightly. You're quite right: it does endanger friendships etc. Perhaps the reason is that it's always difficult for me to turn down a dollar or a writing job, having once been so broke so long that it may still affect me in aftermath. Like some people who went thru the depression, and remain scarred by the experience the rest of their lives?

Incidentally, I do respect your feelings for Cohen: to feel that strongly about someone else is similar to falling in love. Some people in all their lives seem never to feel anything very strongly.

However, allied with his great abilities, I've always thought that Cohen partakes of the egotistic juvenile, balanced on the fountain jet of self-applause. That may annoy you, well, sorry, but there it is. He is also like so many who blossom early, and cannot ever repeat that earlier success, and are completely aware that they cannot. As Cohen is aware of course. But I would much rather think of Cohen at his best, the times when I think he was unparalleled, that he was a magician with words. For *Spice-Box*, for *Beautiful Losers* . . .

Anyway, you can be sure that I did think of risking any relationship with Cohen—which I don't have anyway. Still, I don't *like* antagonizing people, at least only very rarely. Certainly not you, even tho I'll probably never know you very well because I always have the sense that you have feelings and opinions that you're not expressing, however verbal you may be at any given moment. In many ways I think you're a politician in the wrong profession: in fact, I'd like to see you in politics, something un-likely to happen I guess.

All the more prominent writers should say no to reviewing books by one of their peers? Of course that's Margaret Laurence's feeling too. Damaging as it may be to friendships, surely one must say what one thinks and feels about other writers. In fact there's too goddam much mealy-mouthing as it is now anyway. If those so-called major writers do not say what they think about other so-called major writers, then are we to rely on aborted-writer-critics to do so? Critics who are only critics may be more objective, but surely writers have duty to both yea and nay. [. . .]

All the best,
Al

To Dennis Lee (Toronto), from Ajijic, Mexico, January 17, 1979

Hello Dennis,
Perched on the edge of Lake Chapala (fifty miles long and thirty wide), in a cottage rented for $75 a month, all found. 80 degrees every day. A hiatus, a pause? I dunno. Whatever your life is, this place is in between the muscle part of it.

Went to see where D.H. Lawrence lived in Chapala in 1923, and where he wrote *The Plumed Serpent*. Missed it the first time and had to return with more explicit directions (from the local English-speaking library). Two-storey peeling yellow stucco house, with ceramic tile depicting a plumed serpent, the Zaragoza 4 number now changed to a 300 something one. The two-foot tile being implanted in the wall of the house. Nothing to indicate Lawrence ever there but that ceramic tile.

A crazy likeable friend of mine, Wayne Thompson was here in Chapala a coupla years ago with his girl friend. Went to a posada with her (hotel) for booze and dancing, saw an old woman on the other side of room with dog in her lap. Wayne, being crazy (he tells me the story) goes over and asks her if he can have the next dance with her dog. She says yes, so he ups with the dog and sways back and forth cradling the dog in his arms then returns to his gal friend. Then decides it was a good experience and does it again, thanking the old woman (she covered with flashy jewelry) profusely. She takes off a red stone ring and gives it to him. Next morning Wayne wakes up and says to his girl friend, "She was drunk, else she wouldn't have given me the ring. I gotta give it back to her." She says "You crazy bastard, that ring would pay for our whole trip to Mexico." He says, "Don't matter, gotta give it back." So he does. She accepts graciously in her big house, and says, "Why are you here? What made you come to Chapala?" Wayne says, "Well, I heard D.H. Lawrence once lived here." So Wayne goes back to his girl friend, and a day or so later this big black car pulls up where they live. Wayne knows then he is about to be repaid for his honesty and generosity—of course we know too. The rich old woman's flunkey gives him a book. It is a Spanish-English dictionary, used, signed, and annotated by D.H. Lawrence when he was in Chapala. Said dictionary is now one of Wayne's most cherished possessions. He told me the story for the fourteenth time when I was in Vancouver last fall. I believe him too, implicitly. Wayne only lies to his enemies, and he has none.
[. . .]

What are you doing? When I hear from you, you're almost always talkin about *Being Alive* and not yourself. Except for wearing yourself out with your duties at U of T.[1]

I managed to forget my tweed jacket in a motel at San Luis Potosi, it containing address book and passport. Jesus Christ, what old age does to the memory! San Luis is about three hundred miles away across vampirishly horrible roads. So I wrote instead of going. Eurithe has comforted me tho, she leaving the car ownership card at the Mexican entry point in Matamoros. So we're even, almost. Damn near stateless persons. Incidentally, there are several towns along this big lake, including Chapala and Ajijic—the latter our roost.

When you have a moment, write.

Al

---

1. Lee was writer in residence at the University of Toronto.

To George Jonas (Toronto), from Ajijic, Mexico, February 4, 1979

Dear George,
Seems a good time to write when I'm three thousand miles away . . . How
is your quest for fame going? Barbara[1] said you'd done two novels, the
second of which was good. And I believe your joint venture about the
presumed murderer—forget his name—did well. But how in hell did each
of you decide what to write of that book—this is mine—this is yours,
on accounta I write that kind of thing better than you . . .? Anyway, I'm
pleased you seem to be doing well.

I'm amazed that I've seen you so little—since I enjoy the occasion
each time we do meet—or else have I forgotten that too in geriatric
somnambulism? However, I claim it's your fault I've seen so little of you:
you being wedded to the CBC and Barbara (in that order?) and never
achieving the short hundred miles to A-burg. But then I suppose you're
so city-slick that rurality gives you a skin rash and the prevalent hay seed
interferes with your thought processes. Incidentally, on the phone I asked
Barbara how the two of you were getting along, did she still adore the
ground you had yet to walk on: and there was a long silence, as if I had
invaded some region of her soul in which there should be no echoes or
untowards probing. Interesting. Especially since I think most writers of
any quality strip themselves naked, even when they disguise said strip
act as you customarily do. A quality of conservatism and reticence in B.
I hadn't noticed before? No rude hands or questing mind shall sully this
little tendril of purity? Incidentally, how is the poem-piece she was doing
for *Maclean's*?

We're about three thousand miles distant from you in near Ajijic
(pronounced Ah-hee-heek, if you're interested) (something like triple hiccups), on Lake Chapala, the largest lake in Mexico—about sixty miles long
and ten or fifteen wide—estimates vary according to rum consumption.
Surrounded by gorgeous flowers, temperature a steady 80 Fah. or higher
daily. But actually, apart from these felicitous surroundings, there ain't a
damn thing to do. You can't swim in the polluted lake; the geriatric tourists
(they're all at least 80) arouse profound disinterest; in fact I am bored and

reading novels in the absence of television and Toronto Leafs' latest losing streak. However, D.H. Lawrence once lived in Chapala, a town nearby, in 1923, and worked on *The Plumed Serpent* there. Now I have a feeling you might not like Lawrence (for one thing, I think he's a bit anti-Semitic, altho not in any blatant way), but if you do I can only instruct you to read *Birds, Beasts and Flowers* immediately. Anyway—visited his house in Chapala, wrote a coupla poems on the subject. Another poem which I may copy on reverse if I have the energy. And that's it for poems. Not another lousy pome. (Could triple hiccups be something like Triple Sec?) Our ancient car which has laboured long and nobly for 112,000 miles and shows signs of weariness has quite a bit of salt corrosion, so Eurithe has arranged that it should be given new metal petticoats for about $130 American—it would be about $800 Canadian back home and out of the question, since it's a '71 car. So we are to be bereft of Ford for a week: Eurithe won't let it die a natural death and subside with full peacetime honours.

I have a small spurt of energy left—like a 30 degree parabola orgasm—which will use to type poem on reverse. And urge you hereafter to ignore the negligible skin rash and floating hay seed around A-burg which is the penalty all ex-Hungarian streetfighters and elderly guerrillas must dare in pursuit of their art—and visit us if not feeling too snobbish.

In April & after—

Al

1. Jonas was married to Barbara Amiel at this time. They co-authored *By Persons Unknown: The Strange Death of Christine Demeter* (1977) which dealt with "the murder of a Toronto woman and the conviction of her Hungarian-born developer husband." AP's reference below to "ex-Hungarian streetfighters" is an allusion to the fact that Jonas was born in Hungary and emigrated to Canada in 1956 after the failure of the Hungarian revolt against the Soviet Union.

> **Sid Marty** (b. 1944): park warden in Banff National Park, conservationist and poet (*Nobody Danced with Miss Rodeo*, 1981).

To Sid Marty (Banff), from Ameliasburgh, March 23, 1979

Dear Sid,
Of course you were right, we were in Mexico when you wrote that letter; just got back. Hardly any snow here now, generally six feet of the stuff.

Enough outa the book to support you for a year? Migawd, that's a winfall.

We were at Ajijic on Lake Chapala, had a three room apt. for $65. a month American, all found. Temp a steady 80 Fah. daily, smothered in flowers and garbage. That is the place for you I think.

You should question your sanity—tryin to live on the avails of poems. Go duck your head in a snowbank. What avails?

Never met Bukowski—corresponded only. Stopped that when he wanted his letters back to sell somewhere and I'd already sold em for the same reasons: profit. Just like mine to you are your property to sell tho not to publish. Anyway, Buk was mad I'd sold his letters.

He mentioned me several times in his pieces in a prose book, damn flatteringly too, helps to quote him. If he gets better known somebody might believe him about me.

Of all the goddam optimists tho, you really take the arsenic frosted fruitcake. To live on poems! I starved to death on em myself, accounts for my stunted growth.

Drop me a line before you commit suicide and leave all those orphans in Banff and elsewhere.

Best,
Al

To Earle Birney (Toronto), from Ameliasburgh, March 25, 1979

Dear Earle,
Thanks for your note and the new book [*Spreading Time: Book I, 1940–49*]. (I hope to be sending *Moths in the Iron Curtain* to you in the next few weeks.) Dunno when you sent it, since no date on letter and I threw away envelope. I'm enjoying it, having read some before and others not. Esp. "Queen Emma." I can't write prose like that. Enjoyed also "Leavetaking," assume autobio.

Tom Marshall was with us in Ajijic briefly with your book, and I read some of it then. Didn't expect him down and was away when he arrived. We drove him to the plane at Guadalajara a few days later, and had an engagement at Ajijic, so just left him and hurried back. Turned out later his flight had been cancelled because he hadn't phoned to confirm, and had to stay in Guad. a night. Now I feel guilty about it.

I wrote seven poems in Mexico, now dried up completely again. Drove to Florida afterwards, stayed with Ron Everson a week. E. and I sat in the back seat of his Cadillac one day while other drivers cussed his bad driving, one yelling "Get offa the road, you old asshole!"—we trying to conceal laughter and embarrassment in the back seat. Migawd tho, he's good-hearted: wanted to loan me money when we were leaving New Smyrna, said he had a coupla hundred dollars not doing anything! E. and I were a little deafened from his flood of words, some of them damn interesting. I think he's a bit lonely in Fla. tho . . .

Didn't run into anything like your liquored Mexican waving a pistol, thank goodness. We were in Patzcuaro at one point, not far from Morelia, visited a volcano near Acuapan: Paricutin, and wrote a pome. (Send you a couple herewith from Mexico.)

Yes, I think the Nerja caves have been opened only in last ten years. Did I send you my prose pome about them?

I have readings in early April out west, but hope to see you both after that. I see we are both among Amiel's choice of five.[1] When I talked to her she wasn't gonna include Layton; musta changed her mind.

love from Eurithe and me,

Al

1. Amiel's article, "Poetry Capsule Comments on Canada" (*Maclean's*, January 15, 1979) named Margaret Atwood, Irving Layton, Earle Birney, Alden Nowlan and AP as Canada's major poets. She describes AP as "too wise, shrewd and goodhumored for sentimentality. It takes rare reservoirs of rage, love and common sense to capture the contrasts and contradictions of a country as strong and weak, as ultramodern and prehistoric as Canada."

To Louis Dudek (Montreal), from Ameliasburgh, April 27, 1979

Dear Louis,

Thanks for having the book sent to me.[1] I expect to read and enjoy it.

About the Lane–Gatenby reviews: of course both Lane and Gatenby are very much as you describe them.[2] I've said much the same thing to Lane personally, in the past, not lately. But if one wishes to be on good terms with anyone, it isn't very tactful to say such things to the person, or even in a review. As I recall, Newlove hasn't much straight violence, but is also very depressive. As for Gatenby, he wouldn't be worth discussing at all if it were not for the various awards you mention.

I do agree that what Lane–Gatenby exemplify is a coarseness, sometimes of a revolting nature. But Lane has some talent, I think, which makes it a little sad that he's been this way most of his life. As mentioned,

I pointed out to him that his own life hasn't been altogether without joy or some kind of happiness, and that this side of himself should be portrayed as well.

Unless you are being more ambiguous with me than I think—unless you are playing some kind of puzzle game—your point in these reviews doesn't seem to me at all obscure. However, the violence which you rail against doesn't seem to me to be present in all poets. Not, for instance, in Gustafson, nor Everson, etc. But your point is still valid—this violence and coarseness does exist in many writers. I'm sure you'll include Layton in your list; and I believe Atwood essentially a cold writer, however brilliant. And Ondaatje—one of the most interesting lately arriving poets—is soaked with it.

Violence is, of course, a device to gain attention—at least it is sometimes. I think Ondaatje has somehow concealed his own violence from himself, does not even realize it. I say this having in mind some comments by others about him, and believe myself he is the most brilliant of the younger poets.

But it's impossible, I think, to make Lane or Gatenby realize that gentleness also exists in the world. The former is steeped in it, and the latter uses it for his purposes. Or so I believe.

As I probably mentioned, I think it's tragic that Avison, one of the most formidably equipped poets in the country, should become a gospel singer.[3]

But one should stress that the violence we are talking about has always been in existence, and many of the very best poets have used it and portrayed it, and a few have fallen victim to their own predilections and inclinations to it. It does exist, tho obviously we should not be coarsened by it, and should in the totality of our writing take some kind of moral stance. Isn't that more or less what you are saying?

I don't think the pebbles you've dropped in the Grand Canyon (if what you've said can be likened to pebbles) have been useless. However much I like to quote Auden's line ("Poetry makes nothing happen"),[4] I can't altogether believe it. Whatever you may have thought, I have a high opinion of you and a strong respect for you (and goddammit, I am not licking your ass either), and much affection. I expect to both agree and disagree with you in future. In the present case, it's mostly agreement.

When you are talking about this quality of violence, I fully expect you to include me in such opinions. And if so, you must expect me to deny it. As stated, I think violence is present in all of us—even in gentle Louis

Dudek. And enclose some of my recent stuff herewith. Not for the sake of refuting such a possible accusation, but just because you might like to see it. At least I hope you might.

Yes, I think some of your own writing provokes—not hatred, but a dislike of the selfrighteousness some people see in your critical views. Don't you think that's possible. For god's sake, not hatred tho.

About Musgrave—whom I didn't mention before but meant to: I think she's almost completely a mystic, a confessional mystic. The violence in her comes from her subconscious completely. I know the lady slightly, and think very little of this mysticism in her exists on the surface. Will you then say that poetry is being taken over by such people? That's a fairly drastic conclusion, despite the instances cited.

Three of the poems I enclose were written in the Soviet Union. "In the Garden" is from Mexico, a kind of Eden poem (I have an anti-Eden poem as well) (it too from Mexico). The piece about Lawrence is, of course, because I admire him greatly. "Norma's Poem" is about my sister-in-law, who had a nervous breakdown that was very traumatic. The first few lines are a quote from her really, and I turned them around at the end. I'll type that here, since I have only one copy of it and "In the Garden."

NORMA'S POEM

All my life I have been
my father's daughter
my mother's daughter
my sister's sister
my husband's wife

Now I am trying to find
the me who belongs to me

Only the sun and moon
are witnesses
only daylight and darkness
have taken my hand

My father the sun
my mother the moon
my sister the daylight

my husband the darkness
they have given me an old compass
I have entered into their safekeeping
I am becoming the earth

Incidentally, Norma left her husband some time ago, and is now living in Victoria, BC. And incidentally, I've taken a Lawrence quote and placed it out of context completely.

I hope we meet again not too far ahead in time and can talk—since you are one of the people who are at least partly responsible for what I am.

love,

Al

1. Dudek's *Selected Poems*.
2. Dudek reviewed Lane's *Albino Pheasants*, Gatenby's *The Salmon Country* and Len Gasparini's *Moon with Light* in the *Globe and Mail*, January 27, 1979. Greg Gatenby, see page 440.
3. The reference is to the Christian turn in Avison's poetry.
4. The line is from the second section of Auden's "In Memory of W.B. Yeats."

To Earle Birney (Toronto), from Ameliasburgh, May 22, 1979

Dear Earle,
Especially glad to hear from you right now, since I thought I had offended you somehow at your place and didn't know how. If so, you oughta hear Acorn on that subject: he was down here, dogmatic and thundering as usual. I said at one point, "If I break the law and they catch me I gotta go to jail. So why shouldn't Claude Parrot go to jail?"[1] he says "I won't listen to you making slaves of the workers." I says, "When did I say I wanted workers to be slaves?" He says "I won't listen to you makin slaves of the workin class." So we thundered at each other for hours.

Anyway, sorry if I annoyed you. I do that to people at times, viz Acorn. Don't tell me what it was about if I did, then I'd have to explain and you'd have to explain and the conversation would be nothing else but that.

My mesmeric powers—in a word, Shit!

I never bait Birney—wouldn't dare!

I forget the mention of your "Leavetaking"????

Thanks for good words about those two poems. No, the others aren't as good. Or as bad or whatever. I did like "In the Garden," thinking that's the way I do feel about capital L life. But I'm writing so much, so many—and I mean few—things that seem any good to me these days—so little at all really—

Of course Richler gets paid much, Cohen too. I get the CC rate only, surely you knew that. I quite agree that your—500 bucks was it?—rate is justified, but I can't ask that—nobody would give it to me. What does Richler get, $2,000? You're in a different position—apart from reverence from your vast age, and that you managed to survive all those women—having written things like your despised "David," lapped up by so many schoolchildren (I happen to like it much still, despite your sneering remarks about your own wayward child), and the last marvellous piece about falling from the tree while showing off for Wailan ... [...]

My own future activities are fairly limited. Coupla readings near Hamilton in June, a week at Canadore Col. in July (yes, creative writing stuff), in fact damn near anything for money, since I have little comin in this year. I made the mistake of askin for last instalment of senior grant too soon and it was dated Dec. 28 last year, therefore taxable. And last year was my big year for earnings. So I get stuck because of bein stupid. This year, nothin from outside, I mean not CC, and damn little from anywhere.

Yes, Paricutin. I writ a piece in what I imagined might be the words and language of a Tarascan Indian about that—

Odd thing—somehow you and I think alike in many ways (don't ask me how, just feel we do) ...

love to both of you,
Al

1. Claude Parrot was the president of the striking postal workers' union that had defied a government order to return to work.

Warren Tallman (1921–94): American-born professor of English at the University of British Columbia and critic, best known for the "Wolf in the Snow." AP's attack on him is part of his more general criticism of what he saw as the harmful influence of the Black Mountain school of poets (Charles Olson, Robert Creeley and Robert Duncan) on Canadian poetry. For AP, Tallman was their most visible and perhaps influential representative on the West Coast. Of the West Coast poets influenced by Black Mountain, Purdy was impressed only by Bowering.

To Warren Tallman (Vancouver), from Ameliasburgh, July 1, 1979

Dear Mr. Tallman,

As an ex-BC resident, I'd like to comment on your Open Letter to Phyllis Webb in your Vancouver Poetry Centre *Newsletter*. Apparently one of your numerous informants has overheard a remark of hers (which she may or may not have made) to the effect that money spent bringing in American poets for readings could be better spent on readings for BC poets.

Well, HURRAH FOR PHYLLIS, if she did make that remark! Quite true. The money could be much better spent on BC poets.

In your long-winded and badly-written (a creative writer would do much better) Open Letter to Phyllis, you apologize and explain that only forty or fifty American readings were foisted on the long-suffering BC public over the last couple of years. Is that correct? And your excuse is that we all write in English, whether living in the US, in Australia, or Canada, etc. Is that correct? You see, my own comments are written from memory of your Open Letter, since my wife thought your *Newsletter* was toiletpaper and bestowed it appropriately.

I certainly agree with you in one respect: we all do write in English. But lamentably, there is no Canadian citizen at a US university for some twenty years who has ever organized a similar festival of Canadian poets in English in the US. Why is that, do you think? Of course no Canadian prof. at a US university would be allowed to keep his (or her) citizenship for very long. US citizenship authorities would not permit it. Nevertheless, since you are so great a benefactor of Canadian poets in BC, would you consider returning to Seattle, or San Francisco, or Los Angeles (or damn near anywhere else), and organizing a festival of Canadian poets (in English) reading in the US of A? It's a task for which your peculiar cultural talents make you eminently suited.

Sincerely,

Al Purdy

Copies to: Phyllis Webb, Marya Fiamengo, Alan Twigg, The *Vancouver Sun,* Robin Mathews, Milton Acorn

To Frank Scott (Montreal), from Ameliasburgh, August 3, 1979

Dear Frank,
Pleasant to hear from you.

The first two lines of "Spinning" are from a letter from Colleen Thibaudeau.[1] I doubt that her "left" is political, but one doesn't know. Never thought of your own vision, didn't occur to me. Anyway, and as you now know, I suddenly thought "what would happen if you turned suddenly in the other direction, what glimpses of the past would you see?"

I think I understood Ralph much better after that trip. He's a gentle man, as has been remarked by others, even a Russian—should say Ukrainian—translator in Kiev. He is somehow rather naïve, despite his age, and even his indignation is clothed in an odd sort of sweetness. He has the "one world" and we are all brothers feeling more much more than I have, from my point of view rather failing to realize that nations think of themselves first. His ego seems a little insecure (he was hurt that I didn't include him in an anthology I edited, hurt even after nearly ten years). That undeniable goodness he has is almost anachronism in this world or any other. Still, I wish there were more like him, for it would be a better world.

As for *Moths*, yes I do like the title, and there are three poems in it that I would retain for a Collected if there ever should be one. Eurithe's photos didn't reproduce at all well on that kind of paper, and my captions have been called silly. Perhaps they are. But most of the poems don't feel right to me now.

The business, as in "Spinning," of retaining the past. Sometimes it seems that I see a landscape of buildings that aren't there, superimposed on places I've lived, trees suddenly spring green into the air, and people I remember walk and talk as if they are still alive. It's peculiar to be growing older—in fact I wrote a poem about it which I'll enclose. Incidentally, don't feel called upon to answer this letter—not unless you have much time and nothing else to do. Anyway, I'm now thinking of a poem in my mind, about a geologic landscape, a real landscape, as against the different one in my head, the one I mentioned above. Is it gestating? I dunno. I have to find out more about this area's geology first.

I remarked a while back in a letter to Birney that older people were much more likeable to me. He said something to the effect that they learned something over the years. He said "of course—older people, like me, are wiser, better-natured, funnier—there have to be *some* dividends to go with arthritis, insomnia and forgetfulness" . . . Which is partly facetious, but not inaccurate. I couldn't have written "Fathers" a while back. I had this great period where you dash off six or seven poems in a week. Then subside, or lie fallow, or whatever.

I've had a personal horror of certain landmark ages in life, in which you are supposed to feel deprived of so many things you once had. Maybe you did too. Then you realize you haven't lost anything essential at all, and it's the very word sixty or eighty that is synonymous with age that doesn't exist except chronologically. Because all you were is bundled up inside, and you mix it with the present like a green salad. Of course you're much more confined to your body and mind, the latter doing much of the exploring your body did once. (I wonder if Layton ever thinks of that.)

Just returned from Baddeck in Cape Breton, where there was a Scots Gaelic poet gathering, along with some Canadians. I bought all their books and they bought mine. The contrast between them and me must have been striking. I'm pretty loud at times; they are under-stated and non-stressed.

(Just thinking of what Auden did with his limestone landscape, a poem ["In Praise of Limestone"] I couldn't understand very well—I had the sense of people's lives being governed in his landscape by the geology. In all his poems, people and events seem governed by hidden forces, beyond control, as if we were all puppets somehow.)

Gaelic seems to me gargling thru porridge, and finally strangling thru excess of consonance. One Scot, Sorley MacLean, hypnotized himself, and wandered inside a three foot circle of the lectern with his eyes shut. One, Ian Crichton Smith, seemed much the best to me.

Ron Sutherland was there with the pipes, his wife and kooky kids. We got along well, and those precocious little brats of his wanted to cut my hair and thus remove the last hirsute vestige, and the boy wanted to arm wrestle all the time. I explained that I was much too dignified to stand for this nonsense. And I love the pipes, and the whole village was an echo-chamber.

There is something exceedingly precious about Reaney and his wife too. But I read her book, and it sounds like a madwoman with lucid flashes or vice-versa. But some of it was very good, and surprised me, as if I had overlooked some quality in myself I might have explored. And "Spinning" seems to me part of it and unlike my usual self. Not logic exactly, at least not ordinary logic, but eccentric fairyland logic in which yourself is talking to yourself. And you may or may not answer, and the reader may or may not hear those echoes of one part of you.

Do let me know where you'll be reading, and maybe the happen-chance will fall right. Conversations too seem accidents of time and space to me.

Best to both of you,
Al

1. Colleen Thibaudeau (b. 1925): short story writer and poet (*The Martha Landscapes*, 1984). Married to James Reaney.

To Earle Birney (Toronto), from Ameliasburgh, August 3, 1979

Dear Earle,
Since your letter took two weeks to reach me, I'll mail this to Toronto. I enclose the two most recent pieces I like best. The first two lines of "Spinning" come from a letter from Colleen Thibaudeau. I had a week of most intensive writing six weeks back, then stopped completely.

"Fathers" contains a neurosis of mine that doesn't show, but certain ages have seemed to me like deathly watershed, which I contemplated with extreme dislike, didn't even want to mention the possibility of reaching sixty. Then realized that all I was I still am, I contain everything.

Moving around the places I've been and lived in, old buildings spring up in place of new ones, trees leap into the air from their dust and ashes, a phoenix geology joins the present, and people I knew jump from their coffins and walk and talk. Of course this was always so, but never more so than now.

I expect you're enjoying putting this new book[1] together—I suppose connecting the essays with what you feel now as well as the autobio stuff. I thought of doing the same thing myself, then doubted if it'd be worthwhile for me, or that anyone would want to read it, or publish it. [...]

Birney is wiser, funnier—but better-natured? Well, maybe. I prefer to think of you as a bit acerbic, not to be pushed around much. You may have mellowed, but not much. And I just had a letter from Alan Twigg[2] in Vancouver saying he thought I ought not to adopt my "crotchety old man" persona when reading poems. Now am I that? I hope not in either case. But a little acerbic I regard as desirable, it prevents silly questions from an audience. Still, I do find myself growing a bit sentimental in some ways, and maybe "Spinning" is that.

I'm sitting in work room drinking the last of chokecherry wine, and it's so hot you wouldn't believe. In fact too hot to continue.

I hope to see you in Toronto on your return, if I don't melt down into my shoes in the meantime.

Yours
Al

FATHERS

This year I realized my dead father
was sixty when he died and I am sixty
but it's a year like any other year

(The annuals in our garden
are only two months old
just babies in the arms of earth
our perennial peonies are fifteen years
and fifteen years I've watched them rise
in scarlet jets from earth
and still I wonder—what does it all mean?)

He was fifty-eight and suddenly
became an unexpected father
with a look on his face in old snapshots
as if he'd never enjoyed himself much
and two years later he was dead

In 1919 the year after the first war
there must have been several times
when the baby face and old serious one
looked at each other like blank coins
a thought registered a look stamped itself
something now forgotten was interchanged

There is a strength comes from fathers
(a different strength than women)
they are both annual and perennial
but unlike marigold and crocus
they dance under the skin of earth
with a clicking of ancient teeth together
the rattle of bare bones

For Earle and Wailan with all the
best
Al Purdy

SPINNING
for Colleen Thibaudeau

"Can't see out of my left eye
nothing much happens on the left anyway"
—you have to spin around right quickly
then just catch a glimpse
of coat tails leaving the room
(lace doilies on the settee)
light foot rising and disappearing
the last shot fired at Batoche
or maybe it was Duck Lake
—thought I saw someone I knew
and turned faster and faster
said wait for me
it was my grandmother I never knew
before I was born she died
—sometimes I turned fast enough
and nearly caught up with the sun
it bounded like a big red ball

forward and then went backwards
over the mountains somewhere
—thought I saw someone I knew
she was young in an old summer
I tried to remember very carefully
balanced on one foot
but concentrated and concentrated
lightfoot white feet in the long grass
running to meet her lover
I couldn't stop turning then
wait for me wait for me

> For Earle and Wailan
> —a Proustian pome?
> —at any event, a fantasy
> Best
> Al Purdy

1. *Spreading Time: Book I, 1940–49* (1980).
2. Alan Twigg (b. 1952): Vancouver interviewer, columnist and writer (*Hubert Evans: The First Ninety-Three Years*, 1985).

To Earle Birney (Toronto), from Ameliasburgh, August 20, 1979

Dear Earle,

I take it you're home now. Reason I drop you this note needs a bit of explaining. A while back someone sent me a dozen or so pictures of Can. writers, you among them, of which I decorated my wall with four. You, Laurence, Haig-Brown and Berton. I'm just noticing now a peculiarity about your poster which I can only think is deliberate.

There is a mountain climber, presumably you, clambering around inside what looks very much like a woman's vagina. Did you ever really get in that far, is the question I've wanted to ask since noticing? What's it like?

> Most sincerely,
> Al

George Galt (b. 1938): journalist, travel writer (*Trailing Pythagoras*, 1982) and novelist (*Scribes and Scoundrels*, 1997).

To George Galt (Zios, Greece), from Ameliasburgh, August 22, 1979

Dear George,

Well, there does seem to be a mail service between A-burg and Zios! Zion?

Glad you like the poem, but fertility is a myth of your own. I haven't written a decent poem since a burst six or seven weeks ago, in which I wrote half a dozen. Life is static here, not to mention boring. Eurithe is a whirlwind of activity, but I am the still centre. I stay out of her way when I can—since all the building and various activities she engages in do not engage me.

I'm glad to hear you're "busting ahead" with your travel book, and assume *Sea and Sardinia*[1] had some effect on you. It makes me regret that I didn't "write up" some of the places and incidents in Mexico. Once we visited an ancient mountain village—town I guess—that had been deserted for years. Had to travel by bus some twenty miles, under a mountain thru which was a one-way road. An old man at the place we entered either phoned or signalled someone at the other end, to the effect no one should enter from that end. And the so-called road under the mountain was an obstacle course, with half-buried boulders over which we bumped and sway. It was claustrophobic and frightening, perhaps like those caves in Forster's *Passage to India*, in which sound changed to an echo of an echo, and one seemed to be riding the first machine ever built and expect to break down instantly.

At the other end it was some eleven or twelve thousand feet high, and you had to take in huge lungfuls of air, trying to swallow the sky. The old mining town was being refurbished by the Mexican government as a tourist attraction, but not much had been done yet. It dated three or four hundred years old, but I'm not very sure on that point. There were a few hippies from Mtl. living in a house without a roof; a Maori engineer from New Zealand whom I talked to; and several bars. Half the streets were nearly vertical, and you walked them like a sailor on a ship, going zig-zag to cut down the steepness. On the aforementioned bus was a man with an ice cream freezer, an old fashioned one motivated by salt and turning a crank. He expected to sell it to tourists at our destination.

Why I was so afflicted with lassitude that I didn't write about some of these places I dunno. All the good English writers have a book on Mexico—Lawrence, Huxley, Waugh and Graham Greene.[2] Of course things have changed since Huxley and Greene rode muleback over the mtns., but in a way it's still the same; because the contrast with this country is just as great now as it was then. Christ, at least I could write a poem about the place.

Well, the last frontier here is much higher-priced than Greece. It costs you nearly $500 to fly to Vancouver and back. Incidentally, I got something over four thousand to go the Galapagos this winter, and I shall certainly write about it, prose as well as poems. And hafta read Darwin's *Descent of Man*, which I suspect is damn near unreadable. But the whole project *sounds* adventurous, and I need that feeling right now. Whether we get to Easter Island I don't know yet, since I didn't get that much money. Of course Eurithe's passage and expenses are extra, and not taken care of by CC. [...]

I took a typewriter too, when I went to Greece. I cursed the damn thing every time we moved.

Have another story about balls. In Vancouver I had some woody cysts on the scrotum, so I went to a doctor to have em removed. He did, with an electric needle, and said don't move around much until this heals. I paid no attention, went to see a friend forty miles away in Langley, and on the return trip the several scrotum wounds started to bleed. Blood soaked the front of my pants, which I stuffed with toiletpaper. By this time I was feelin a bit weak, so went to hospital again, and fainted from loss of blood on the front steps. My wife had to pick me up and take me home. How humiliating! By this time I was very unpopular at work on accounta the union I'd started in the factory, so quit the job and drove east with all chattels. Never did pay that doctor for his electric needle.

Al

[On the back of his copy of this letter, AP wrote this uncharacteristically revealing self-analysis. It is undated:

> If there is any grandeur, any "soul" in me it will live after I am dead in what I have written. When that dies I will die a second death—All this an assumption built on an unlikely possibility— of grandeur in myself. At this point I have not observed it—]

1. D.H. Lawrence's *Sea and Sardinia* (1921) was among Purdy's favourite Lawrence books.
2. *Mornings in Mexico* (1927), *Beyond the Mexique Bay* (1934), *Robbery Under Law: the Mexican Object-lesson* (1939), and *The Lawless Roads* (1939).

To Earle Birney (Toronto), from Ameliasburgh, September 14, 1979

Dear Earle,

Take a look at that picture of you in Famous Canadians, Writers series thing—you are definitely exploring somebody's vagina, on your way to fallopia.

I was in Toronto Monday, for lunch with Howard Engel,[1] and had to rush right back to have a tooth pulled. Blood didn't clot right after return from Belleville, and I bled profusely. Mouth fulla blood isn't very comfortable or conducive to a serene mind. Had to rush back to Belleville again. Roots of tooth must've been phallic as hell. (See what you bring on with your own explorations?) Coupla days later seem okay, but sure did lose a lotta blood. A gusher, rather terrifying too.

Two–three days before that I had written a poem that keeps quoting itself in my head, at least two or three lines. Very satisfying feeling, to have yourself surprise yourself. Also wrote a short imitation of Gustafson, "Inside Gus," not a parody, straight imitation. Sent it to Ralph, whereupon he immediately sends me one back, an imitation of himself. We really are getting inbred.

Yeah—heard a bit of this Carl Sagan[2]—is he good? Saw him on tv once.

Yes, "Spinning": first two lines were in a letter from Thibaudeau, and since I used em was duty-bound to dedicate it to her. When I read those two lines, immediately thought: okay, can't see much on the left, what if one turned right quickly, what magical things in the past might be seen? And that's the poem, really. What you can't see on the left you can just catch a glimpse of on the right, "of coat tails leaving the room" . . . It's mental legerdemain of course, and also has to do with the feeling sometimes that you just missed seeing something important to you, that if your sight had been keener or you had been more perceptive, you might have seen creation at work, apart from an old girl friend. [. . .]

I'll be in Toronto to tape some poems next month, and hope to see you then. Everything gets sandwiched between readings seemingly, some six or seven this fall. I'm writing very little myself, just the odd poem. All the drive I thought I had seeming to be dissipated in small everyday things, small concerns and uncelestial trivia.

love to you both,

Al

1. Howard Engel (b. 1931): CBC producer and crime writer (*The Suicide Murders: A Benny Cooperman Mystery*, 1980).
2. Carl Sagan (1934–96): popular American television broadcaster and writer on scientific topics (*The Dragons of Eden*, 1977).

D.G. Jones (b. 1929) won the Governor General's Award for *Under the Thunder the Flowers Light Up the Earth* (1977).

To D.G. Jones (Sherbrooke, Que.), from Ameliasburgh, October 18, 1979

Hi Doug,
I expend some of my prized Cuzco stationery on you; hope you feel suitably honoured.

Just heard the word, on radio, *priorization!* What is happening to the language. Little did I think I'd be a purist on the subject, way I use language myself.

I like the poem,[1] one of the two best I've seen on me (why do people write em about me?). The other was by Birney. I suppose that, finally, we do melt into the landscape. Not just me, you, they, all of us. "Not to secure oneself, but the other"—the others you write about, the other self who watches you when you write? In a more public sense, I think writing a poem about Oshkosh, BC is mapping the country, filling in mental spaces, making the thing real by naming and describing it. That's a well-known thought, of course, and similar to what the CBC or newspaper stories do, peopling the void. Yeah, one of your better poems, and I do think you've improved much over the past few years, if you don't mind a compliment. Your stuff is much more actual rather than conceptual, which you may not think a compliment. But if a thing can be both . . . which this is. [. . .]

Coupla weeks ago voice on the phone says, "This is Kim Ondaatje."[2] It's a man's voice, so I think, what the hell, has she got a cold? I say "How are you, Kim? What's up?" Voice says, "Have I got the wrong number? This is Ken Adachi." I say, "You oughta take some Dristan, Kim. That's a bad cold you have." Voice says, "Isn't this Al Purdy. Well, I'm Ken Adachi." "What's that again?" "Ken Adachi." "That's what I thought you said, Kim Ondaatje." "A-D-A-C-H-I, Ken." "Oh. Why didn't you say so?" "gargle-gargle." So I reviewed Lee and Layton. And Mother Goose was happy. [. . .]

Best,

Al

1. AP is referring to Jones's "Welcome Home" (*A Throw of Particles*, 1983) and Birney's "in purdy's ameliasburg" (*rag and bone shop*, 1971).
2. Kim Ondaatje had been the first Mrs. Jones. Ken Adachi (1928–89): writer (*The Enemy That Never Was*, 1976) and book review editor with the *Toronto Star*.

To Earle Birney (Toronto), from Ameliasburgh, November 14, 1979

Dear Earle,

Yes, I'm sorry too that Wailan was so busy.

It bothers me a little that you don't quite get that third verse [of "The Dead Poet"]. Take this proposition: if you have a brother who died before you were born, and whom you say influences your writing, isn't it also (il)logical that he should help you and that you should hear him in your travels?—on the Street of the Silversmiths, in Samarcand etc. ???

Of course Plato's Cave[1] is slightly different: I meant to refer to myself as a shadow of life, without carrying it any further—which I could do. But as the shadow in Plato's Cave, the shadow of his life if you prefer, I do remember "the small dead one." Does that help any?

Of course you have integrity: you are also cantankerous and all the other qualities that I have myself. I'd like to write a poem about you sometimes, but it seems tremendously difficult to me, or else I haven't got a concept that would work.

You are so stingy with your words I'm gonna be too. Incidentally, I'm sorry you don't wanta meet the gal I mentioned, whom I think you'd enjoy. It's your loss and hers too.

You know, for a while I was reading "Fall by Fury" at my own readings? (Credit to Birney, of course.) I still think that veddy English "fortnight" was wrong in the poem—or was it "fortnight"?[2]

love,

Al

1. For Plato's myth or parable of the cave, which illustrates the individual's ascent from the darkness of illusory belief or knowledge into the light of true knowledge, see *The Republic*, Book VII.
2. AP is objecting to the following lines in "Fall by Fury": "Shining ahead was the fortnight / given us here alone by our friends / to swim with the small fish in the pond." The poem describes how Birney injured himself by falling from a tree he was pruning.

From Michael Ondaatje (Toronto), to Ameliasburgh, November 16, 1979

Dear Al,

A fan letter.

For the first time in my life I bought the *Queen's Quarterly*, saw half of one of your poems and bought it and have read it since again and again like witnessing a dream.[1] "In the Garden" is a wonderful poem. All the poems in that group feel so fresh, new-voiced and new-eyed, but especially "In the Garden" and "Figures of Earth." And they have a strange mood. Like those translations by Merwin in his *Selected Translations*[2]—mysterious timeless 14th century Roumanian kind a thing. [...]

Anyway, thanks for those poems.

> See you sometime
> Michael O.

1. Ondaatje is referring to "In the Garden," "Near Patzcuaro," "D.H. Lawrence in Chapala (1923)" and "Figures of Earth," published in *Queen's Quarterly* (Autumn 1979).
2. W.S. Merwin (b. 1927): American poet (*The Carrier of Ladders*, 1970) and translator (*Selected Translations 1948–68*, 1979; *Selected Translations 1968–78*, 1979).

George Johnston (1913–2004): professor of Anglo-Saxon and Norse at the University of Ottawa, translator (*Thrand of Gotu*, 1994) and poet (*What Is to Come: Selected and New Poems*, 1996). Written in black ink in a calligraphic style similar to that of Robertson Davies, Johnston's erudite and considered letters are among the most attractive and interesting that AP received.

To George Johnston (Athelstan, Que.), from Ameliasburgh, December 21, 1979

Dear George,

Good to hear from you. You raise a question re success and the cost of life that I suppose many of us think of. Perhaps you feel the same as me: success is always accompanied by its opposite number, failure. The cost of life is always death. Begins to sound sententious, I guess. Everything contains its own opposite, especially the euphoric and despairing extremes.

Of course, that seems to say nothing in a sense. But we can each of us assess other people's opinions of our own success or failure, and see in either case the opposite, how we should have been much better or that we are much worse. Not that we can be indifferent to either opinion, no matter how much we might pretend to "or treat those two imposters just the same"—(was that Kipling?) for they are not the same.

By my own standards, for instance, I think there are some three more or less successful poems in *Moths*, "On Realizing," "Monastery of the Caves" and "Lenin's Tomb."

I enclose a *TorStar* column which might interest you, by Ron Base,[1] who talks about the self-publicizing people and how we need them in Canada. I dunno if he's tongue-in-cheek or no, but if he is he shouldn't be. So I take it that he's serious. He says David Milne was the non-publicizing sort of painter and says at the end, "Damn him for it"—since the country needs publicity etc. I agree that the country needs some kind of attention that a great artist brings about, but I don't agree that an artist owes it to his country or anyone to be a self-exhibitionist and braggart. (And I glance with distaste at Layton when I say that.)

I'm not at all sure that Milne was a great artist in actuality, altho that is a bit irrelevant to me. What he does seem to have been was someone very nearly utterly absorbed in what he created, and I think that is good. The visual artist, the painter that is, is much more intuitive than the writer despite the example of people like Lawrence. They're lucky, since sometimes I seem to be stalled and frozen into near-immobility as far as writing goes. Whereas a guy like Milne could probably (I say "probably") pick up his brush and let the stuff flow.

Perhaps what we write is a reflection, even if a distortion, of our own lives and our interest in them. If our inner lives are at a standstill, then we do not write much. By that standard the previous part of the year, up until a coupla months ago, has been one of my best. Then hiatus, interregnum, or whatever the term. Wait it out I guess, just as I must wait out lameness in one knee from arthritis. So I enclose a piece that is my favourite from the last few months.

For a while I intended to write Base about his column, then thought what the hell's the use. Let him go to Harold Town or Layton. I cannot think of art as shouting much of the time, nor have much respect for people who do.

Suicide and despair? They're part of life too, and I don't rule them out. Of course I don't welcome either of them either. But I've been close to the first and been involved in the second in my own life at one time or another. At least—and I say this without personal references—those who fall into such categories are not neuter, their gender is life, despite suicide and despair they are able to feel strongly. Vegetables do not commit suicide or despair, they die without a murmur. I prefer to shriek a little.

I read at *To Say the Least*,[2] and seemed to lose interest. But I'll pick it up again on your say-so.

When my knee gets better, we expect to drive south for Mexico, then fly to the Galapagos Islands off Ecuador, maybe around mid-Jan. Have a good Christmas, as we say at this time of year, you and your family.

Al

1. Ron Base: journalist and novelist (*Matinee Idol*, 1985; *Splendido*, 1988). With David Haslam he wrote *The Movies of the Eighties* (1990).
2. *To Say the Least: Canadian Poets from A–Z* (1979) was edited by P.K. Page.

To George Johnston (Athelstan, Que.), from Ameliasburgh, March 28, 1980

Dear George,
I've been away for the last three months, in Mexico and South America—so I'm not sure what poems I sent to you.

We apparently agree completely about Milne. Sure, he had many intelligent admirers, altho it's a human tendency to equate the number of admirers with the merit of the work in question. Taint necessarily so of course. Which gets people like us off the hook, to a degree. Then we look at Eliot or Dylan or Yeats and realize that the equation is not necessarily untrue either.

My own feeling about "On Realizing"—was that I was presenting or writing about the two faces of a poet: the outward face in which he or she aches for success, public success, and the other face which is completely private and aches for excellence. No, I wasn't talking about my own notion of what I would like my public image to be. Whatever that image is, that public image, it won't be me or even close to me. Long ago I realized that, that people, the media in particular, are going to seize on a few things they think they see in you and emphasize them. In fact other people besides the media do the same. All of us tend to associate some particular thing with a person. I, for instance, associate your Icelandic translations with you, also *The Cruising Auk* and a particular poem, "War on the Periphery." However, I mean a physical trait, a stutter, physical size large or small, all sorts of things.

No, I don't think I've ever been in the least danger of being influenced by what people think I am, since I am so completely aware that we and all of us are only one small fraction (perhaps) of what other people think we are. Of course all of us, people like you and I who get interviewed occasionally, tend to talk about what we know interests interviewers and the public. What actually does interest me is in my poems, which they want to talk about and not read. Or else going off on some mental tangent as I'm doing now with you.

No, I haven't tried bee stings, but thank you. Trouble is there are so many goddam remedies and cures, cure-alls should say, that you'd die before you tried them all. But when I have this knee-trouble, I feel old for the first time in my life. Age has never mattered to me much before, but given this treacherous awkward and totally unreliable knee, I think dark thoughts.

However, the gods granted me a surcease for long enough to visit the Galapagos Islands and do a lot—at least a fair amount—of walking there, before the plague's return. And also some poems in Mexico, and elsewhere that I like, and were quite unexpected.

No, I didn't go back to *To Say the Least*, left here in early Jan., and there seemed many things to do. Among those, in Mexico, was reading a book called *One Hundred Years of Solitude*, by Gabriel García Márquez, a Colombian novelist living in Spain—which I recommend to you unreservedly. I think it's a bloody masterpiece, do read it in paperback if you see it, and look it up if you don't. Then I watched the blue-footed booby doing his mating dance, and a whole equatorial island of boobys standing upright to shade their eggs from a tropic sun; when night comes they all sit down at once to warm the eggs on a signal from God; or perhaps one booby says to another, "Let's flop, boys" and they do. Incidentally, the booby's deadly enemy is the frigate bird, a great black shadow of death that robs the booby of his fish. After which I have no doubt the booby says "Friggit" and catches some more.[1]

Al

1. See "Birdwatching at the Equator" (*The Stone Bird*).

To Dennis Lee (Edinburgh, Scotland), from Ameliasburgh, April 12, 1980

Dear Dennis,

Congrats on the Scots thing.[1] Yes, I think it will be good for you, maybe some poems instead of critical prose, and maybe a parallel of the Scots separatist tendencies with the Quebecois ones.

Yeah, it's good Suknaski took your criticism the right way. It might well be that he can write better poems, since he was writing different stuff before all the hoopla about Wd. Mtn.[2]

The change in "Transient" follows:

> (My dove my little one
> tonight there will be wine and drunken suitors
> from the logging camps to pin you down
> in the outlying lands of sleep
> where all roads lead back to the home-village
> and water may be walked on)

Whaddaya mean, where's the last "Stone Bird"? There's only been one, and you haven't seen it. Three page poem to end the book with. I'm gonna keep it down to around eighty pages, pruning out poems and adding new ones if they seem worthwhile. Have about eight from last three months or so, two of which I think pretty good (one of them is the Bull's Horn poem) . . . I think these are the best poems I've written in, say, the last ten years—a lot of variety and much different from earlier stuff (despite the similarity of the bull's horn poem to earlier stuff).[3]

Knee's goddam bad. I guess wet weather is bad for it. In the past it's come and gone, this time here for last six months, with intermittent good spells. Trouble in back is also bad, and the combo isn't pleasant. But I gotta live with it . . . [. . .]

Marc Plourde just sent me a copy of Gaston Miron's poems which he'd translated, called *The Agonized Life*.[4] Bothers me. Those Quebecois look only inward, far as I can tell, and Miron sounds a bit like Cesar Vallejo, the Chilean poet,[5] but lotsa energy. Freedom from English exploitation, etc. etc. I sent him (via Plourde) the bull's horn poem, with a note to get his eyes above his own horizons.

If life is more a case of beer, it's not wine far as I'm concerned. I left two cases of my good wild grape wine with my son to keep for me on departure. He drank all but three bottles, said he was tryin to stop drinkin booze. I castigated him mildly (as is my wont), told him to make his own goddam wine. Luckily I had four more cases stored with in-laws. I didn't tell him that.

It's four years since I had a full-length book of poems, *Sundance* [*at Dusk*], 1976, which wasn't very good anyway. Other new stuff got into *A Handful of Earth*, which wasn't a very good book either. So it takes me a long time too. I don't envy Layton tho nor the stream of consciousness boys. But you, you oughta be writing more. That's the other extreme.

Best,

Al

1. Lee was spending a year in Scotland under the Scottish–Canadian Writer-in-Residence Exchange.
2. AP edited Andy Suknaski's *Wood Mountain Poems* (1976).
3. "Shot Glass Made from a Bull's Horn" (*The Stone Bird*). AP is discussing the composition of his forthcoming collection, *The Stone Bird*.
4. Gaston Miron (1928–96): politically engaged Quebec publisher (Les Éditions de l'Hexagone) and poet (*Deux Sangs*, 1953; *L'Homme rapaillé*, 1970 [*The Agonized Life*, 1980]). Miron was an important figure in the Quebec separatist movement.
5. César Vallejo (1892–1938): Peruvian novelist (*Tungsteno*, 1931) and poet (*Poemas humanos*, 1939). Thomas Merton described Vallejo as "the greatest universal poet since Dante," while Stephen Tapscott has called him "the most eloquently lyrical, personally rich voice in Latin American poetry."

To George Bowering (Vancouver), from Ameliasburgh, April 24, 1980

Dear George,

Yeah, I was on an island in the Pacific, as you mention in your letter. In fact, several islands. How come I am in various places if A-burg is so nice? Well, it ain't very warm in A-burg, for one thing. For another, I get sick of bein in one place a long time, it makes me go to sleep. Besides, outside here and the US I don't get to see television and have to read books without the seducing tube urging me to watch the downfall of the Leafs, Blue Jays or Argonauts. Among the bonuses of this last trip was: I read Márquez's *One Hundred Years of Solitude* in Mexico, and thought it a great book or something close to that. It makes our Canadian novels look pretty sick by comparison. If you haven't read it, do, for the sake of your literary soul if you have one. It's soft cover, written by a Colombian who now lives in Spain, Gabriel García Márquez.

Also among the bonuses of travel, tho perhaps not always directly related to same, I've written more and better poems in the last year than in the last ten years. This of course my personal opinion, as it must be.

I'll be interested in what you do with McFadden's poems, since his faults in my opinion tend to negate his virtues if you take the wrong poems. Said virtue being a tremendous naturalness, if naturalness can be tremendous, and an easy flow of words, plus a lot of other things. The negatives include in many cases, too much length, excessive trivia, the feeling of why bother in many poems. Still, if you've picked (past tense?) the good poems should be quite a book.[1]

How is Kearns doing? You mention doing an essay on him . . . I think he's one of the more likeable people I've met, tho he also seems like so many of the west coasters who reach their level and never exceed it. I'm sure you'll disagree with that, possibly interpret it as a putdown by an easterner (tho I regard myself as a westerner also, having lived in BC a total of nearly ten years), and I regret that very much in Kearns, I mean not having written better.

No, I've never read in Cornerbrook, or Newfoundland at all. Once wrote to the Eng. Dept. at Memorial and said I'd like to read there. They didn't reply. Of course I've been there a coupla times, on my own, and done some travelling up the Gt. Nor. Pen. and up the coast, and ridden fishing boats etc.

Yeah, I agree about all the crap being published. It's never been easier to publish poems or prose in Canada, and a writer really has no excuse if he hasn't attracted much attention. There's more shit being published in Vancouver, Toronto, Montreal and the Maritimes than it's possible to imagine. In a way, tho, this mass publishing makes the better stuff more prominent, and if a hundred cruddy authors publish books and one good one emerges—that may be all we can reasonably expect. Of course the tendency is for all the cruddy mediocre people to get together and slap each other on the back; but I guess this happens everywhere in the world. We all need encouragement, and probably we all need harsh criticism once in a while too to keep ourselves at some level of reality . . .

I spent most of the winter, after the new year, in Mexico, and a coupla weeks in Ecuador and Galapagos Islands. Ecuador and the islands are right on the equator, temp 120 Fah at all times and humid on the mainland. But those islands of Darwin, no rain and dry, dry, and hot hot. No matter how much beer, coffee or anything you drink you hardly ever have to piss, it seeps out the skin always, and you're dripping sweat. But it gets a bit uncanny, that pissing bit, and you wonder what a prick is for apart from the sexual uses. I met a 700 pound tortoise, 160 yrs old, called him Moses, scratched his neck and wrote a poem about him.[2] Met also the blue-footed boobies, who stand around all day in the sun on a mile-long island, shading their beautiful feet from the sun. And three foot iguanas so ugly they're beautiful. None of these critters afraid of people. Very unwise of them, don't you think? [. . .]

Best,
Purdy, his mark
Al

1. Bowering was preparing a selection of McFadden's poems, *My Body Was Eaten by Dogs* (1981).
2. "Moses at Darwin Station" (*The Stone Bird*).

To Jack McClelland (Toronto), from Ameliasburgh, May 9, 1980

Dear Jack,
The Stone Bird has been sent to Linda McKnight, with an extra zerox for you. I'd appreciate your taking a look at it.

Two poems are enclosed. "Country of Losers" is the first poem in manuscript of *The Stone Bird*. "A God in the Earth," the second poem herewith is not included in the manuscript. And it's about these two poems particularly that I'd like your opinion.

Both can be seen as anti-Canadian, altho obviously I personally am not anti-Canadian. However, in "Country of the Losers," I'm using all the clichés about Canada which are current or have been, and are both true and untrue.

"A God in the Earth" is insulting as hell to the last half dozen PMs. I didn't include it because I thought "Country of the Losers" went far enough. However, what do you think?

If a foreign publisher is available for *The Stone Bird*, the arrangement of poems would be different, and possibly "Country of the Losers" would be deleted. However, I don't see why it should be, not if the poem stands on its own as an interesting one.

Whoever wins the Quebec referendum, I think everybody will lose, and hence the turmoil will go on for some time to come: hence also, the "no" reference to Trudeau will still be applicable (when the book is published).

In a way I'm sorry to lay this on you, but dammit, it is your business no matter how much you delegate it. And besides, you have expressed some interest, which I take to be sincere. But knowing all the ambiguities we live by, I expect you to be both annoyed and slightly flattered by all this. Okay.

These are very important questions to me, the ones I ask in this letter, and they do involve you as well. I think I've been pretty acid and nasty in these poems, and there are possible repercussions. Especially if "A God in the Earth" should be included in the manuscript. Incidentally, I've known Trudeau for some years, and met him from time to time, even sent him books. But I think he's done a lousy job with this country, altho I didn't think that some years earlier.

All the best,
Al

COUNTRY OF THE LOSERS

A mythic country
whose runners always finish second
or ninth or twenty-third
when they venture outside
their own borders
(which are incidentally and continuously
violated by other nations)
a country which has never had great men
whose heroes live outside its borders
the closest being a fourth cousin
or fourteenth of somebody who emigrated
somewhere else quite early in life
and wrote a marvellous novel
but never wrote home because he was ashamed to
A mythic country
preoccupied with its own navel
but equally interested in unflattering
outside opinions which some clever
famous author sells back to them
and from which the natives
take enormous pleasure
since it supports their own
worst opinions of themselves
A country in which the best-known

writers are deadly dull
which is the precise reason
why they are well-known
where artists and actors of talent
fled long ago and are struggling
wherever they are to conceal their origins
—the origins of remote forests
rivers and mountains
which the citizens take some pride in
but only because the landscape
is all they have in common with outside
and meeting a visitor they say
"Look at our mountains"
and glance at the other expectantly
waiting for some inevitable comparison
of giant Himalayas or soaring Andes
so that even landscape becomes second-rate
according to eyes of the beholder
lakes and rivers little silver trickles
in the second-rate mind
A country which sells itself shamefacedly
to the highest bidder
but often gladly
to the lowest bidder
whose money flows outward continuously
at the rate of many millions a day
to foreign investors in fact
a country where foreign investment is so high
it buys back its own basic raw materials
in processed manufactured form
with a decorative yellow ribbon attached
at exorbitant prices
and is grateful

From Jack McClelland (Toronto), to Ameliasburgh, May 21, 1980

Dear Al,
I haven't yet had time to look at *The Stone Bird* as a whole. I will in due
course, but for me that type of study takes a little longer. I would also like

to have the opinions of some of my senior advisors before I comment on the complete script. As I have told you more than once, I am not an expert on poetry. I never will be and I am not going to ever pretend to be.

You have, however, asked me to comment on two of the poems. Frankly, I don't like either of them. I don't think you should publish either of them. I don't think they serve any particular purpose. I think what they do—in all probability—is represent Al Purdy in a very negative mood. Let me start with "Country of the Losers." To me it just isn't a successful poem. It doesn't communicate with me because of the hyperbola you have used. God knows there are problems about Canada—and I am the first to admit it—but they don't need to be exaggerated. You don't have to deal with 4th cousins or 14th cousins or whatever. You deal with fact. You don't have to say our best-known writers are deadly dull because that simply is not true. In fact I find the whole poem such a gross exaggeration that it is meaningless to me. It shows Purdy being petulant, negative and making a total hyperbolic statement that bears no relation to what you really feel and I really mean that my friend. This is not a deeply felt poem. It is a superficial poem. I don't think it represents you. I think it is a total unmitigated piece of shit. I don't even believe the last four lines. If you really think that Gerda Munsinger[1] is the least dull corruption, then you know very little about corruption in this country. Al, it was written in a bad mood. Forget it.

As to the poem "A God in the Earth" it to me too is pointless. I don't understand, to begin with, how you could compare all these men. Could you write with any more enthusiasm about the last seven American Presidents. I guess I would single out Kennedy, but then I would single out Trudeau to the same degree that I would single out Kennedy. They have not been successful Prime Ministers or Presidents and I don't really think it is a very good poem.

I'm troubled about your reference to Macdonald, Laurier, McGee.[2] Do you really think these people are that much better? Have you really studied that much Canadian history? I don't think they were.

Frankly, Al, I would forget both these poems. I would tear them up. You complain that Layton doesn't tear up his worst poems. He should and so should you and these are two of the worst I have ever seen from Al Purdy. I am sorry to be so honest but you have asked me to be honest. I would be embarrassed to publish either of these two poems.

The only other thing I can add for the moment is that if I find the rest of the manuscript that bad, I am going to tell you to give up poetry for a year and reconstitute yourself. This doesn't represent the way people are thinking in this country. It doesn't represent the way they should be thinking. Christ, Al, you really are in a foul mood. Forget it. I will be back to you in another 10 days or so. Meanwhile it was great to see you. I enjoyed our meeting. I think you are a great person and I love you dearly except when you write bad poetry. All the best.

Sincerely,

Jack

1. Gerda Munsinger was a German-born prostitute involved with at least one Cabinet Minister (Pierre Sévigny) in the Diefenbaker government in the early 1960s.
2. Thomas D'Arcy McGee (1825–68): Irish-Canadian politician (elected to Parliament in 1867), polemicist for Irish causes and minor poet (*Canadian Ballads and Occasional Verses*, 1858).

To Jack McClelland (Toronto), from Ameliasburgh, May 28, 1980

Dear Jack,
That was a great letter from you, exactly what I wanted. Nothing wishy-washy about it, pure dislike. I had already arrived at that opinion myself, and your feelings support it. Both have been knocked out. And the manuscript is now somewhat different than before, two new poems, two old ones knocked out, the arrangement completely different.

Macdonald and Laurier were at least builders, whereas the modern pms are sellouts in my opinion.

"Country of the Losers" used all the clichés about Canada we have been accustomed to for many years, which are not completely true and yet have a semblance of truth, in fact the poem was partly tongue-in-cheek. And dull writers? Christ, read *One Hundred Years of Solitude* if you wanta make some comparisons.

Many thanks,

Al

From Jack McClelland (Toronto), to Ameliasburgh, June 4, 1980

Dear Al,
I am writing this in haste. I have just received your letter. Christ almighty, we have your book of poetry scheduled for the spring. I didn't like those two poems, but I am really not asking my editors to tell me whether

they like the rest of the manuscript. We are publishing Al Purdy. That's enough. I thought I was making slight joke. I am sorry you didn't read it that way. In any case, I'll be in touch with you before too long, but your book is scheduled. We are going ahead with it and don't be put off by any semi-humorous notes that I throw into my letters.

Best personal regards.

Sincerely,
Jack

To Jack McClelland (Toronto), from Ameliasburgh, June 8, 1980

Dear Jack,
Forget it. We'll both be dead soon.
    I'll attend your funeral if you'll attend mine.

Best,
Al

To Earle Birney (Toronto), from Ameliasburgh, June 11, 1980

Dear Earle,
Didn't see QQ, on accounta Belleville doesn't have it and I don't sub.

I'd never include myself in any H. of F.,[1] up to other people to do that if they think I should be there.

I doubt that Webb, Page or Newlove will make it. Page seems to have written her best before; Webb (and I love her) just seems doubtful; Newlove is paranoid and nursing a broken hip and a bottle out west. Ondaatje tho is writing very well, but is a private poet only. *Billy the Kid* seems a tour de force to me. Mike's private concerns are most important to him, which is fine. But to be a world poet, so-called, I think you hafta come from a country a place and a time, and be somewhat involved in those concerns. Of course you can easily refute that concept, but it's mine and I'm stuck with it. [...]

I have four poems deriving from the Galapagos, none of more than passing interest.

DARWIN'S THEOLOGY

Stand under the great sky round
circling these islands
where the absence of a god

leaves a larger vacuum
than a presence could fill
with a presence
sea and sky completely occupied
by the non-existent monster
—Galapagos Islands

See you in Toronto,

Al

1. H. of F. is probably House of Fame, an allusion to Chaucer's poem with that title and to AP and Birney's discussion of the future reputations of Canadian poets.

To Jack McClelland (Toronto), from Ameliasburgh, June 23, 1980

Dear Jack,

Thanks for your letter.

I didn't think Farley would be anxious to have me writing about his father. And I wouldn't want to do it unless he did favour the idea. I suppose he'd do it himself or will in time, altho he'll have difficulty getting Angus' papers from Barbara. Anyway, I do thank you for thinking I might have a prose book in me at all, even tho I'm sure you say that to all your writers.

Re *The Stone Bird*: I hope this time that more than the two thousand copies of *Being Alive* will be printed, since that book was out-of-print nine months after publication. I'm referring to the first ed of course. Incidentally, I'm still working on the poems intermittently, and sending any changes to Ellen Seligman, the editor.

By the way, I do agree with you about Atwood. At the present time she's the only writer on the horizon here capable of surpassing anything written previously in Canada. Still, I hope you can take a look at García Márquez's *One Hundred Years of Solitude* sometime, and see what it does to your conceptions of good writing.

Best Wishes,

Al

From George Johnston (Athelstan, Que.), July 23, 1980

Dear Al,

You are a good correspondent & worth answering to get another reply. I do like writing letters, but tend to pace a correspondence, partly because I think I write a lot of letters, but probably you write more; I write an average of one a day, maybe more, though some are just notes. But they don't get written in a hurry, for one thing, hand-writing slows me down. But a typewriter seems to put me off. Perhaps one of your Black Mountain bêtes noires (I think that is the proper plural—though I should Anglicise it, shouldn't I?) is Cid Corman.[1] I have been corresponding with him for years. He always replies by return of post, so I have to pace him. I also correspond with Daryl Hine—a much more sporadic correspondent—whom we have known, off & on, since Jay [Macpherson] brought him to see us when he was about nineteen; he slept off his first big drunk in the third floor of our Ottawa house. Cid & Daryl detest one another, but so far they have not expected me to take sides. I have correspondents in Iceland, Faroe & Norway who write me in their own languages. I agree that letters are the best way of getting some things said. As a sort of side-comment, I have allowed my dislike of cassette recorders to harden into a conviction—which is the same kind of thing as a theory, isn't it? Taped interviews seem to have become a blight, they sound unnatural & unspontaneous & I think writers should go back to writing, especially about themselves & their writing. I say to myself that I have permitted my last taped interview: that was two months ago on the subject of Northrop Frye; I talk as much balls into those things as everyone else seems to. I had made this resolution not long before I found out that Samuel Beckett has always refused to give interviews. Well, well, I wonder how long I shall get away with it. So far it has not been hard, nobody has wanted to interview me anyhow. But when Susan Musgrave & Bill Bissett & I go on tour in England & Scotland in the fall, what then? Perhaps you are right about theories; I certainly agree that one should not be trapped by what one says in a public way, but I am not a strong character in this way. How does one answer someone who says, Why do you write this way when in *The Can Forum* (or anywhere) you say the opposite? I suppose I am suspicious of publicly-expressed opinions in the same way that I am suspicious of creative writing sessions. Writing has always seemed a secret kind of activity; I will hardly admit I am doing anything of a poetic nature until it has been well and truly done. An undergraduate friend back in the thirties was much the most useful person I have ever shown poetry to; for a while I tried poems on one or two friends but found the experience unsatisfactory, though for a while Jay Macpherson was helpful, though in fact she said hardly anything. I sent Cid Corman poems for a while, but had to persuade him to stop saying anything about them; he was in fact very helpful on how to be economical, but I was too susceptible to his other comments. And I can see that my comments on your poet brother poem were way off the mark.[2] Except to say that it is altogether a fine poem. You seem to sum up by saying that poetry is where you find it & that I agree with entirely; that is the one important thing to say. However, I have written two things that are going to be published, both in the form of letters to the editor, one to the *Can Forum* telling Louis [Dudek] to quit grading poets (everybody does this, but I pick on Louis) & the other to Cliff Whiten's tabloid [*Poetry Canada Poésie*] saying I wished poets were more interested in language for its own sake. I'll send you a copy of the latter if you don't get it. I am a sucker for subscriptions & ought to quit that. I have been subscribing to *Can Lit* for years, but if I read one item per issue, that's a lot. I have also undertaken to write a technical article for the *Journal of Canadian Poetry* on rhythm. Your comments on rhyme & Pound make me pay attention. You seem to have developed a style without rhyme that is recognizably all of a piece, it is always yours. But a great many people who write in a similar way, even some good ones, all sound like one another. It seems to me that rhymed and measured verse offers more variety, though it has to be very well done. But there is a lot to be said for putting the poetic mind to work on solving a difficult mechanical problem; the effort & sheer drudgery sometimes required have often seemed imaginatively valuable to me. Yet having said that, one comes back to the realization that different things work for different people, there are all kinds of poets & all kinds of poetry. Still, I shy off creative writing writing but am not averse to telling what I know about rhyme, metre & syntax; somebody might pick up something from it. I was agreeably surprised on reading Vol I of Ray's Collected that he wrote some fine rhymed poems & one splendid sonnet. I wonder if any more will turn up in Vol II. Vol I is already an impressive achievement & I am looking forward to II & III. I suppose I share your views about Pound. I don't require to understand him, & parts of the *Cantos* impress me & some other poems but I suppose his Rotarian heartiness of manner & his fascist willingness to short-circuit (if there is such a verb) put me off. But some English critics whom I admire have many good things to say about him & one is given to understand that he was generous. Louis said that Pound had declared rhyme outdated & I reckoned he ought to know. But maybe he was just calling in his big brother. Write again, Al, if you think my answers are worth it (presumably you do)

Yours,

George

1. Cid Corman (b. 1924): influential American editor (*Origin*) and poet (*Aegis: Selected Poems 1970–80*, 1983; *Nothing / Doing*, 2000).
2. "The Dead Poet" (*The Stone Bird*).

Fraser Sutherland (b. 1946): critic (*John Glassco: An Essay and Bibliography*, 1984), journalist, editor (he was a founding editor of *Northern Journey*, 1971–76) and poet (*Jonestown: A Poem*, 1996).

To Fraser Sutherland (Scotsburn, NS), from Ameliasburgh, August 8, 1980

Dear Fraser,
Over the years there've been some thirty or forty poems written about Purdy. This one is the best so far, also the funniest. I dunno exactly why there've been so many (probably the best-known one is by Birney in one of his later books[1]), since I don't seem to myself a particularly picturesque person or whatever provides the grist for poems.

Anyway, I knew you had a wit or three, but you hit your stride here. I'll lose my own patent for humour. Be sure and include it in your next book. I think I'll pin it to the wall here, so I can see myself as others may. Tho if I'm like that, collection is possible by ROM[2] or the Smithsonian.

I don't have anything adequate for reciprocation, but enclose a carbon of a recent piece I liked from Mexico.[3] (I also have one about the blue-footed booby, but not typed in duplicate, which also includes some of my recent themes.) Incidentally, is the "we'll" in "At least we'll needn't flinch" deliberate or just a typo?

The Jim Jones poem[4] is moving to me. In fact I look forward much to your next book, you're getting better.

Best wishes to both of you,
from Al & Eurithe

PURDY IN THE GALAPAGOS: A NEW SPECIES
[by Fraser Sutherland]

The birds are confounded. "What the feathers is *that*?
Is it a man? Is it a bird?

Bigger than a falcon, bigger than a cat-
bird. We won't know till he drops a turd.

"Darwin, old buddy, you'd be confused
At this raucous type of nightingale
Any observations would be unused.
No one would believe that shirt-tail.

"He flies across the sea to gawk
And fashions a curious song
Cigar in beak, auk-
ward, with a voice like a gong.

"At least we'll needn't flinch
From any steps he'll take.
He's second-cousin to the finch,
Nests in an A-frame by a lake.

"He might perhaps be called a roblin
Or more remotely an arctic tern,
A kind of gangling goblin—
bobolink. We'll never learn

"The truth about this birdy.
Darwin, we shall tap a ghost
And ask what of this Purdy
flightless in the Galapagos?"

1. Birney's "in purdy's ameliasburg" is in *rag & bone shop* (1971).
2. Royal Ontario Museum in Toronto.
3. AP enclosed a copy of "Journey to the Sea."
4. Sutherland published *Jonestown: A Poem* in 1996.

To George Johnston (Athelstan, Que.), from Ameliasburgh, August 10,
1980

Dear George,
I've just had guests here for nine days, a Welsh poet and his wife, and
therefore I'm tired. Too much talking, public readings and beer. It's an

exchange thing, whereby a Welsh poet comes here for ten days and a Can. one goes to Wales next year.[1]

If I answer your letter backwards, then it won't seem as if I have the whole letter ahead of me. Does that make sense?

No, I'm not excessively fond of Pound, if I didn't mention that before.

But I think your argument in favour of rhyme just as bad as his against it. Rhyme and metre are not outdated, and I'm sure Pound must have suspected that. Both have lasted a thousand years, and will last many more. And when you say the disciplinary effort required to solve "a difficult mechanical problem" is imaginatively worthwhile, you neglect entirely the basically monotonous effect of iambics (or whatever) and the completely expected appearance of the rhyme sound. However, I quite often use rhyme myself, and metre as well, trying to vary and conceal it within poems where it isn't expected and seems accidental if you do notice it. But I generally let a poem go where it seems to want to go, then touch it here and there deliberately, add metre say, or remove metre, add or remove a rhyme if too close to another rhyme. Perhaps it's not quite as artless as you seem to think? You say rhyme offers more variety, which to me is obviously absurd. How can a dozen poems all written in iambic offer variety? They go dah-dit, dah-dit in your head forever. And why do you think many commercials use some rhyming and metric song or other in order to sell their shitty products? The metrics and rhyme make it easy to remember, and thus the product is too. I could hum you a dozen of these things, whose products I'll never buy if I can help it.

But saying all that is not to say that rhyme is outdated as Pound did. But used wrongly it can sure be monotonous. It also removes all seeming spontaneity as well. Of course I don't expect or intend to influence you in the matter, altho I think it even detracts from the importance of some things one might say. It would have in "The Dead Poet," which by the way is metrical in varied ways. Have you ever looked at the way James Dickey writes poems? He doesn't rhyme most of the time, but almost always has a certain number of stresses in each line that make a constant pattern, even tho the lines do not scan, nor is the number of syllables the same. Nevertheless an effect is achieved that seems metric, in fact is metric if you allow this method. But that's in his early stuff. Later, he went to extremely long lines which I haven't looked at in the same way I looked at his first three books.

If I answer a couple of brief comments that lengthily, I'll never end this letter.

But yeah, I take *CanLit* too, and don't read much of it. Sometimes not even one article.

Ditto interviews, the brain hasn't time to consider things as one does when writing on paper. For instance, I can't and don't write poems on a typewriter, just longhand, then type and scribble up the typing with corrections, then type again, repeating this process as long as seems desirable. But prose and letters seem different to me, and I'd take forever to write by hand. Besides, nobody could read my scribbles. Incidentally, I hate electric typewriters that buzz at you, seem to say, get on with it, you're wasting my time. Imagine wasting a machine's time! But it'd be a real large task to write articles and stories as I've done, longhand. I know that some people do, M. Laurence for instance does her novels in exercise books. While I, by contrast, sat down at a typewriter with one of her short stories in England, and in two days had made it into a play. Of course I scribbled it up, and it had to be re-typed if I remember.

As I said, I'm tired from our Welsh visitors and the three readings I did with him—since Can. audiences didn't know his name I read with him.

Yes, you do have many and varied correspondents. I must average more than a letter a day myself, tho not too many like this one. One does spread oneself more to someone one knows.

Al

1. AP's visitor was Alan Perry, the Welsh painter, short story writer and poet (*Music You Don't Normally Hear*).

From George Johnston (Athelstan, Que.), to Ameliasburgh, August 31, 1980

Dear Al,
Your letter makes me realize that I must do an article on rhyme as well as on rhythm. I am delighted to have you disagree with me, but you must take me seriously. I am aware of what you call "the basically monotonous sound of iambics (or whatever) & the completely expected appearance of the rhyme sound." And if I seem to think your verse is artless I apologize for the seeming, but how could I in fact think so? There are many kinds of art, however, and I am constantly being brought up short by the realization, in my own "art," that I have hardly begun to know what it is to take care. And I have come back to an awareness of the infinite possibilities for variety in measured & rhymed verse. One of my earliest enthusiasms

in poetry was Alexander Pope; I remember being bowled over by "The Rape of the Lock" when I was in high school, & I have kept coming back to him. While I was writing my MA thesis on Blake, right after the war, I realized that there was greater variety & spring in his (Pope's) couplets than—well, than could be imagined. Their variety seemed inexhaustible. Later I came to appreciate the strength of his rhythms & then the assurance with which he caught the rhythms of ordinary speech. He beats Wordsworth hands down on this, except for the *Lyrical Ballads* poems, such poems as "The Idiot Boy" & "The Thorn." Pope is far from perfect, & his couplets are his own, one could not duplicate them—though good twentieth-century couplets would be worth making. Two journeymen poets who worked with him on the translations from Homer made couplets indistinguishable from his, but nobody else could. Some people prefer Dryden's couplets: rather like preferring Haydn to Mozart. For me, Pope shows the many possibilities of rhyme & metre (I mean carefully measured lines), and also the infinite care that must be taken over such a seemingly simple matter as end rhyme. End rhyme must be prepared for; it must not only make sense and be carefully placed in the syntax—and there can be a lot of fun about this—but its sounds must be led up to and followed. I have come to the realization, too, from what translating of skaldic poetry I have done, that vowel sounds are not as important as consonant sounds. They are certainly not as reliable, never have been. When Shakespeare wrote there were as many varieties of pronunciation of English within England as there are throughout the English-speaking world now, & the differences were mostly (& are) in the sounding of vowels. There are many kinds of rhyme, as I say, many kinds of internal rhyming, as you say, but in fact good end-rhyming should do quite a lot of internal rhyming too, & half-rhyming. For my part, I am better satisfied if I am trying to satisfy some sort of arbitrary requirement that won't let me feel that the poem is on its own until I have been over & over it many times. I find this imaginatively stimulating. Not everybody does. And the only final test is, does it work? And the only person who can answer this question is the writer himself (or worse, the critic he carries around with him, who seems to be unwilling to put a conclusive ok on anything). Still, if a poem is well done it's well done, never mind whether it rhymes or measures or not. I don't agree that iambic (or whatever) is basically monotonous, more than any rhythm. It is out of repute now because it is so hard to write well. Shakespeare worked away from it & I don't think Milton ever wrote it, but Spenser did & Pope, & whatever one may think of Spenser his rhythms are no more monotonous than the waves washing on the shore. But I have tried to avoid it, even in ten-syllable lines, where it naturally belongs. I don't know why; I can't help being infected by twentieth-century jadedness, I suppose. Yet it might be worth the effort to try a true iambic ten-syllable poem. It would be an original undertaking, though I am sure Daryl Hine, whose poetry I admire, has done it. Well, I won't say no more on rhyme & metre; I am afraid that what I have said is not very intelligible.

You have a strong constitution to be entertaining a Welsh poet for nine days, & reading with him too. We have had a lot of company during August but it has been almost entirely family; a week from today we shall be on our own again. The young Cotswold stonemason who taught me bell-ringing came over for a fortnight with his girl friend, their first trip abroad. They were away for five days of that fortnight, but we enjoyed the time they had with us. But in general we find company, except for family or very old friends, fatiguing. We have two daughters & the seven-month-old son & husband of one & a seventeen-year-old son with us now. The two daughters, husband & baby are departing tomorrow but another daughter & her boy friend are coming & staying for a week, or until next Sunday when we all drive Mark, the seventeen-year-old, back to school. We shall be glad to get back to our routine, though we have enjoyed the company. But I don't think we could stand a Welsh poet, or any poet, for nine days. I have managed a good routine for a quiet life, though it has taken a while to make it productive; poetry comes slow no matter what I do; but I hope to get more prose written when we are on our own again. Nora, who comes tomorrow, is a Classics student, & I hope to pick her brains again, she is good on poetry, but we are all going to have to devote a day or two to moving firewood. I hope you find this letter worth answering,

yours,
George

I don't know James Dickey's poetry. My ignorance of modern poetry is considerable.

By the way, my end-rhymes, now, are seldom full rhymes; I rhyme the consonants.

To Sam Solecki (Toronto), from Ameliasburgh, November 10, 1980

Dear Sam,
Many thanks for your hospitality. It seemed like a good evening[1] to me.
Thanks also to Ursula for putting up with us afterwards. I hope I see you
again sometime when things seem less frantic to me, and perhaps to you
as well. Webb and Ondaatje sounded terrific to me, particularly the latter. I have much admiration for him right now. There's little doubt in my
mind that he's the best poet now writing in Canada.
     Best wishes again to you and Ursula, and your small daughter.
                                        Al
P.S. If you see Abe Rotstein[2] say hello for me. I met him at party, and he
seemed crippled up some.

1. *The Canadian Forum* held its Sixtieth Anniversary Party on November 8, 1980.
It was hosted by Don Herron, and featured readings by AP, Earle Birney, Phyllis
Webb, Patrick Lane, Gwendolyn MacEwen and Michael Ondaatje.
2. Abraham Rotstein (b. 1929): influential editor (*The Canadian Forum*),
nationalist writer (*Rebuilding from Within: Remedies for Canada's Ailing
Economy*, 1984) and professor of Political Economy at the University of
Toronto.

To George Galt (Toronto), from Victoria, January 14, 1981

Dear George,
It seems I go back east for a promotional reading at Harbourfront, Feb. 3,
but paid by CC. I really don't know how Marta Kurc at McStew accomplished that, except by asking.
     Yeah—"Portrait of M.M." has been called Lawrence's best writing. I
also agree that much of his essay on painting gets dull, but the syphilis bit
sounds so odd![1] And I just got into an argument with Eurithe and Norma
here, me maintaining that syphilis went from the New World to Europe,

they equally vehement that it went from Europe to the New World. I still think I'm right, but a doubt has been implanted.

Have just read *The Old Patagonian Express*, by Paul Theroux,[2] and am saving it for you. I think your book is just as good or better, I think better on accounta you have more imagery, more "good writing" in the way of Lawrence. *The Express* is a trip from Boston to near the tip of South America by train, at least mostly by train. According to Theroux, Guayaquil was crawling with rats; but I didn't see a damn one. He makes it sound like a trip thru the borders of hell at times, especially Colombia and Peru.

Also reading a coupla Lawrence books, rather books on Lawrence: Horace Gregory's *D.H. Lawrence: Pilgrim of the Apocalypse*; and F.R. Leavis' *D.H. Lawrence, Novelist*. I'll be a DHL authority yet at this rate.

Spent some time drinking beer with Joe Rosenblatt, and visiting P.K. Page and her husband (last night). The latter had some Fundadoria brandy, or something like that, of which I consumed a modicum. And you know, on that trip back from St. Petersburg, the drinks were free, and I must've downed about a dozen or so.

It turns out I'll probably have a reading at a Campbell River bookstore, about 180 miles north of here. I've a friend there, name of Jack Jackovich who's arranging it. Ex-football player, painter, high school teacher, fishing guide and housebuilder. Used to be a computer programmer before he got fired, dropped from the Hamilton football team, then divorced from his first wife. Now he's married again with two kids. Forgot to mention, he's a potter as well. Can you top that for occupations?

Good to hear you're doin some work on Pythagoras.

All best,

Al

1. Lawrence wrote a substantial memoir of Maurice Magnus (once Isadora Duncan's manager), which was first published as an introduction to the latter's posthumously published *Memoirs of the Foreign Legion* (1924). The introduction is available in Lawrence's *Phoenix II*. He also used him as the basis for the character Mr. May in the novel *The Lost Girl* (1920).
2. Paul Theroux (b. 1941): American novelist (*The London Embassy*, 1982) and travel writer (*The Old Patagonian Express: By Train Through the Americas*, 1979).

To Heinemann (a rare book dealer), from Ameliasburgh, February 18, 1981

Dear Mr. Heinemann,
Re your inquiry about *The Enchanted Echo*.

I published it myself. The cost was $200 for 500 copies. About 150 copies of that total were sold and reviewed and given away. The remainder stayed with the publisher, Clarke & Stuart in Vancouver.

About twelve or fifteen years ago, when the price was beginning to go up on accounta later books, I went back to the publisher and asked about the copies they had in stock. I'd been afraid to go previously, since I thought the storage charges would be out of sight after such a lapse of time since 1944. Alas, alas! The publisher had thrown out all the remaining copies a few weeks before. And since the inflated price of the book had reached fifteen bucks by the time of my inquiry, and is now considerably higher, I could have doled them out judiciously and lived in comfort on the proceeds.

I doubt that more than a hundred copies are in existence today. The book is a rather flimsy paperback, and apart from that, the poems didn't have much merit. Maybe much less than a hundred copies are extant. I was in the air force at the time of publication, also had some connection with the Vancouver Poetry Society, which helped to sell a few copies. But generally speaking, it was a flop. In fact, it's rather embarrassing for me to read it.

Sincerely,
Al Purdy

From Fraser Sutherland (Toronto), to Sidney, BC, March 16, 1981

Dear Al,

[...] I notice that the April 1 (April Fool's Day) sale of Canada Book Auctions will have the Wilson MacDonald literary archives up at an estimate of $20,000–25,000.[1] Has Canadian literature come to this? The lot includes memorabilia from Bliss Carman, your old nemesis.

You know of course by now that John Glassco died. At the time of his death I was working on his annotated bibliography, a labyrinthine pseudonym-saturated chore I've been working at on and off this past year; had spoken to him on the phone only a few days earlier, and, eerily, received a note from him that arrived in the mail the day after he died. (The biblio's for *Essays on Canadian Writing*.) It upset me a good deal. The week I spoke to him I was researching in the Public Archives in Ottawa, and encountered an affectionate correspondence you and he had—when was that? stupidly, I forgot to take note of the dates, which shows you how far I have to go to be a good bibliographer—including MS. of your poems "Report on Poets Conference at Stanley House, 1964," "The Tyger," and "My '48 Pontiac." I think I told John once that you and he were the two Canadian poets I most admired personally. It's a difficult concept to explain, because though it's bound up with the work you've done, my feeling is not based on that solely. I suppose it's always difficult to explain why a person becomes a writer, in the strict sense that I define the term. A writer for life, I mean, somebody born and made to write, living words. But to me it's uncanny that you and Glassco did, and it's even stranger because you came from opposite ends of the social and economic spectrum. To the best of my knowledge, there was absolutely nothing in either of your backgrounds, ancestry, DNA code to account for it. Yet it happened.

I'll close. I've just gotten a good break. I'll be going to Scotland in October in the Writer-in-Residence exchange,

Best,
Fraser

1. Wilson MacDonald (1880–1967): neo-Romantic poet (*Out of the Wilderness*, 1926; *A Flagon of Beauty*, 1931), whose national tours of the 1920s and 1930s attracted large crowds.

Stan Dragland (b. 1942): professor of English at the University of Western Ontario, editor (*Brick*), novelist (*Peckertracks: A Chronicle*, 1978) and critic (*The Bees of the Invisible*, 1991).

To Stan Dragland (London, Ont.) from Ameliasburgh, May 26, 1981

Dear Stan,

If you don't get down here this summer I'll never speak to you again, especially if I don't see you again for ten years. Yah, I expect to be here all summer, with brief absences for one reason or another.

The book was meant for you, not a review copy. One is never completely sure that a publisher will send to those people one asks them to—Wanted to make sure.

Yah, I think you're likeable too, or I wouldn't bother.

And yes, *The Stone Bird* is a change for me, quite radical if one looks at earlier stuff.

Yeah, those lines of opinion that we cling to, no matter how much the object of our opinion changes sometimes. I wrote an unflattering review of Reaney in the *Globe* a few years back which, among other things, has prevented Reaney himself or admirers who read it thinking I'm anything but a hick. The "among other things" is Reaney's own personality, which I find so guarded as to be baffling. Guarded or shy? Doesn't matter which. Colleen, by the way, seemed almost annoyed with me that I used her phrase from the letter, i.e., "can't see out of," etc.[1]

Okay, how's academe? Yourself? Writing? Difficulty of synchronizing orgasms? Don't answer any of those if you expect to get down.

Me, I wrote two thousand words of autobio stuff (first ten years of life), and working on it between whatever else I'm doing.[2] Only about five–six poems since book, which saddens me.

Dragland a golfer? How strange!

I've been paying much homage to Ondaatje in the last year or so. His stuff seems excellent to me, or better than that. But I have the sense about him that somehow he yet has not found his overriding theme or even voice. If he does, he'll be awesome. As it is, certain poems are almost that now.

See you this summer,
Al

1. "Spinning" (*The Stone Bird*).
2. *Morning and It's Summer: A Memoir* (1983).

Stephen Scobie (1943): professor of English at the University of Victoria, poet (*McAlmon's Chinese Opera*, 1980) and critic (*Leonard Cohen*, 1978; *Alias Bob Dylan*, 1991).

To Stephen Scobie (Victoria), from Ameliasburgh, September 2, 1981

Dear Stephen,

Thanks for book.[1] It strikes me as excellent, something I had doubted before reading it. The only reservation I have is the ending, which has to be down-beat. And yet cannot really touch any kind of grandeur, it seems to me. But [Robert] McAlmon's pride holds it up. Yes, I think the book one of the most deserving I have seen for the GG, and here's Purdy wrong again.

The bit about Purdy being a better poet than before I felt rather insulting, having a strong implication that my earlier stuff wasn't any good. I'm not sure exactly how you meant it, but suspected the worst.

I've read many of the books you read about McAlmon, including the Kay Boyle ed of *Being Geniuses Together*, the Glassco book,[2] Hemingway's *Moveable Feast*, and Williams' autobio several years ago. I presume Williams said something to the effect that McAlmon was a cold fish, and that was the insulting point for McAlmon.

An odd thing you've done in writing this book is: flesh out both the Canadian and American lit tradition. And this is something you say you don't believe in having at all in this country. I believe you said something to that effect (in *B. in C.*[3]) that all poets equalled each other, close to that anyway. Which I thought bullshit, and still do. I haven't got the letter to hand in that particular issue, but correct me if I'm wrong.

There are several poems in this book that I doubt could be any better. Page 9, "Hemingway will tell you—"—Page 10, "My father was a—"—Page 14, "What I learned—"—Page 15, "The pride of my college—" (and I wondered in that verse if it would be better if you'd mentioned the Chi slaughterhouses, which everyone would not know about)—Particularly page 30, "Sir John at the head of—" That is beautifully done. But many others. I'm still surprised on reading the book that you were able to do it so well. If you can do another book as well in a different way, it seems to me the future is open. And there's always that hanging over one's head, the next book, repeat that, do it again, keep it up.

It seems to me also that the book should be issued in the US, which ought to be particularly interested.

Apart from fierce pride, McAlmon's character does seem as he has said and you confirm with the poems, to be peculiarly empty. Apparently he cannot love, is passionately searching for fame (as most people, writers I mean, are), has a large ego (also very common) (which is most unattractive), and is generally not appealing except for the quite penetrating opinions of people and situations which you have given him. (I forget whether his book was very good—but was interested in the comparisons of the same events described by both Boyle and himself) Well, you would have to abandon the first person in order to explain why McAlmon was such a failure, if you believe he was a failure.

Anyway, congratulations.

Best,

Al

1. *McAlmon's Chinese Opera* (1980) was awarded the Governor General's Award.
2. *Memoirs of Montparnasse* (1970).
3. *Books in Canada*.

To Dennis Lee (Toronto), from Ameliasburg, October 21, 1981

Dear Dennis,

[. . .] Of course I'm pleased you think *Being Alive* is good, and that a few others have shared this opinion. But not really very many share it, so my Newlove–Purdy paranoia resigns me to being just under the surface of very much attention. I think people tend to say, sure Purdy's good and so what. Beyond that, they're not much interested. Critical essays on me are rare, in fact there hasn't been one in several years. I have to accept that as disinterest, and conclude that I'm getting the attention I deserve. I will not stand on my hands and perform attention-getting stunts in public. To hell with it I'm sure you feel the same about that last.

I've mentioned in the past that one of the big reasons—in fact the principal reason—that quite a few of the poems in *Being Alive* were changed and revised for the better was you. Going over poems with you, and your comments about this or that, something unclear, could be better, etc., made the difference. This is not mentioned to flatter you, but as a personal fact. Therefore, I can't conceive working on the poems again, at least it's unlikely, unless the same thing happened. And since you'll be busy at the new job and will also want to write yourself, helping me out again would be an imposition. But you did start some kind of fireworks exploding in my brain at the time.

Right now, I've got about ten pages of stuff that I'd consider good enough for a new book, as I may have mentioned to you. So another book will be long in coming.

Jack McC. said a couple of times that he'd be trying for foreign publication, but I doubt extremely that he ever did. I intended to contact a Br. publisher in London, but it seemed a lot of bother if they weren't interested enough to have read the stuff before themselves, or had it pointed out to them. So I did nothing. But I think it's funny to have a Russ. trans. book coming in Moscow just the same.

It's good to see some enthusiasm at McStew, and hope the job doesn't surgically remove such feelings. And of course, any info from you is private. The figure I had for *Stone Bird* (first) was two thousand, whereas they had four thousand of Musgrave's and twenty-seven hundred of Bowering's books in print. [. . .]

I'm off to Ottawa and Maritimes for readings and visit to some friends [H.R. and Vina Percy] in Granville Ferry, NS for about a week.

Yours for 6.5 beer.

Best,

Al

To George Woodcock (Vancouver), from Ameliasburgh, November 26, 1981

Dear George,

Just read your piece in *CanLit*[1] about building your place near Sooke and Kohout and the dynamite. The dynamite bit was hilarious.

Same thing happened to me. About 1958 we had no electricity at the house here. So I cut down one of the big cedars here for a telephone/hydro pole, narrowly missing the house when it came down. I had a rope slung around it to sway it away from the house on the way down, and just managed to avoid wrecking a year's work. Then I dug a hole in the ground for the pole, but came to bedrock about eighteen inches down. So I read up on dynamite from the library, got some advice from someone I forget, bought dynamite and fuse and detonator—at least that's the way I remember it now. Anyway, I tamped in the dynamite and arranged things, lit the fuse and ran like hell. (It too was about 150 feet from the house.) But the dynamite didn't go off. Nothing happened, just like your case. What a quandary. I was scared, didn't know what to do. Fifteen or twenty minutes went by, while I pondered. Then, bright idea, I gathered up a huge bundle of newspapers, crumpled em up, lit them, and threw them into the hole. And again retired in bad order to a safe place. This time it blew, sending burning newspapers high into the sky, while all the world, not to mention neighbours, wondered. (Come to think of it, that's close to Tennyson, eh?)[2]

Never again. No more goddam dynamite for me. To hell with Alfred Nobel, if that's who it was invented the stuff.

Great about your papers. It gives one a nice secure feeling in this insecure world to have a few thousand bucks accruing from wastepaper. And it's very stroking to the ego.

The wind blew and blew in Wales. The Perrys, where we stayed, were very good people. Alan had this peculiar habit of looking at you when you weren't looking at him, I guess to gauge your feelings about anything. I read with R.S. Thomas,[3] the Welsh poet at St. Donat's. Alan had sent him some of my stuff at his request, so he could make sure I wouldn't disgrace him. St. Donat's is about 35 miles from Swansea, and Alan didn't know the way. So we raced thru the dark night over cow paths (yes, literally) and narrow one-bicycle roads, arriving just before. Thomas read first, and turned out he was a vicar or sexton, something religious. I drank the wine Elizabeth Ritchie at Canada House had thoughtfully provided, and pondered. Should I or shouldn't I? I did. (Read poems where my own religious views were obvious.) Alan tried to balance a book on his nose as he did at readings in Canada, but it wouldn't balance this time. No doubt the muggy Welsh air.

Then we drove to Aberystwyth for another reading with both of us later. Nobody there at all, absolutely none. A guy name J.P. Ward, who edits *Poetry Wales* was supposed to arrange it. Ward had published a scurrilous poem about Welsh poets a year or two earlier, implying strongly that Alan Perry (my host) was a homosexual. Alan sued, and won 350 pounds. And had to apologize to Alan in *Poetry Wales*. And this guy was the organizer! Alan dug up someone and we got money for a hotel and retired in disorder.

Eurithe snaps my picture in front of Dylan's house at 5 Cwmdonkin Rd., and we take some more in the hunchback's park. Didn't get to Laugharne, to my regret. Weather too bad. [. . .]

At least your autobio stuff is being published. Oxford turned down mine, and then Peter Brown at Paget Press who claims he wants to publish all of Purdy also turned me down. Which is a blow, a blow to decently covered areas of the anatomy.

Switching to Scotch? Is that easier on the heart? I bought some 86 proof Scotch coming thru the US border, and now feel amply justified despite Eurithe's sour looks.

What but vanity impels us all? (viz Proust) Maybe it's an attempt to justify ourselves to all those 35 billion people who were on the earth before we were and couldn't tell us what it was like. And died landless like the Welsh labourer.

Stay Well,

Al

1. Woodcock's "The Dynamite Man: A Chapter in Autobiography" appeared in *Canadian Literature* (Autumn 1981).
2. "The Charge of the Light Brigade"?
3. R.S. Thomas (b. 1913): Welsh clergyman and poet (*Song at the Year's Turning*, 1955).

To Earle Birney (Toronto), from Fort Pierce, Fla., January 22, 1982

Dear Earle,
Thanks for your letter and invite. I will keep in mind that if I ever stay
with you I'll be smoking cigars in outer darkness. It's good of you, and I
appreciate it.

I had regarded the autobio stuff as rather special, the first ten years of
my life, all those dream-things that happen and which you remember.[1]
Nothing at all to do with the literary life. I stopped at age ten. It doesn't
seem to me that another section about writing and including Can. name-
dropping would meld with that deeply personal first section. Anyway, no
one except me seems to like it—at least no publisher. Basically, I'm interested in nothing but poems (which I'm not writing). I've written prose
mainly because I wasn't writing poems. Although this autobio fragment
did interest me. I had the unlikely illusion that I was saying something,
but turned out to be only talking to myself.

"Old-age-depression"—I know it well. Similar and related to non-
writing-depression and no-woman-depression and not-enough-atten-
tion-depression. Trouble is, Earle, you don't drink anymore. Sometimes
a release and balm of Gilead. And don't tell me it's a weakness. Of course.
So is writing. So is fucking. I think of what a number of people have said,
including John Glassco, that "it's better not to have lived at all," which I
think is shit but can't prove it. Life is largely pointless, even when you're
titillated by flattery or others of the many things that divert one. Of
course these grow fewer with age (wisdom of Purdy), and it seems to be a
matter of trying to outwit one's self.

We went to Yucatan, and I was slightly bored. Maybe been there too
many times. Heat was terrible too. I tried to write some poems, but didn't
like them. Worse, they were bad, and I know that. But there's nothing to
fill that gap in my mind if I don't write, and write what I think and feel is
worthwhile.

Back in Florida, we bought a mobile home. Cheap. We own the home
and rent the land it's on. Run by a power-hungry dictator, also money-
hungry, whom the old people here don't resist simply because of age. I
guess one loses the desire and ability to resist dictators when age comes.
Not you, I think you'd resist. That's a good thing about you. (I can see you
snapping at me when you're one hundred and I'm ninety-nine.)

That was a curious review of Scott's *Collected* by Woodcock. I mean
at the end, where he said mediocre poems were forgiveable if included in

a collected works. Bullshit! Mediocre poems are never forgiveable. But I expect Scott will get the GG this year because he's Scott. I'd rather he got it for his poems. (This in *TorGlobe*) ...[2]

Ron Everson seemed in good form a week ago, altho Lorna is pretty feeble except where food is concerned. Ron looks after her practically hand and foot, I'd say. He must have a tremendous affection for her, not that that's ever talked about. He is writing some too, I guess more than me, which is an indication that blood is flowing. We've invited them down here (New Smyrna is about 140 miles away).

> love to you & Wailan from E & me
> Al

1. The memoir was published as *Morning and It's Summer* (1983).
2. Woodcock reviewed *The Collected Poems of F.R. Scott* in the *Globe and Mail*, January 2, 1982.

To Stan Dragland (London, Ont.), from Fort Pierce, Fla., February 25, 1982

Dear Stan,

Migawd, you do raise questions in my mind. "When you read for themes only, what the hell does it matter what kind of vehicle carries it (?)" Atwood? Yeah, I suppose she may travel well. What has always, in some small degree no matter how much I admire it, put me off in her poems is the goddam coldness that amounts to glacial at times. I don't like a world in which everything is so fuckin cold, nor really believe in it. And since Miss Peggy herself does not impress as a cold person—only a cerebral one—it occurs to me that her writing may be method writing, method in order to be published and popular? But then, all writing is method writing, even if a personal method.

But what I was thinking of re Stan Dragland and his liking for what I write (if I can say that), is that such feeling for writing is a unitary force, we (i.e. the writer and reader) think and feel together: we are not alone, if you don't mind the triteness. The very feeling and concept of the individual mind is that we are alone, which is borne out by all our subsequent to birth experiences (what other kind are there?), with the possible exception of the united feeling in love-making (fucking?) and certain other quite rare, very rare, conditions when we are elevated by euphoria or drunkenness or whatever. [...]

I've always resisted the idea that anyone, no matter who, can hide their light under a bushel. I still prefer to think that way. Emily Dickinson and others like Hopkins come to mind.[1] Both of them, at their best, are so rare and marvellous that I can't conceive them not being found. Of course, most await their day and age. D.'s little gnomic utterances that grow boring if you read too much of her, H.'s word-spinning marvels, how could they ever be lost, unless in a day and age that could not understand, an ignorant age? Most periods and ages in time pay most attention—or so it seems—to their own artists and writers, as is natural. Myself, I look with some awe on the recently dead Auden or Thomas, and cannot conceive how it could be that they were the way they were. Of course this paying attention to the living of one's own age means too much attention is paid to far too many. (As you implied re themes.)

Yes, the streams of time are much too erratic and turbulent to do more than guess what will live. All one can say is that there are basic things of importance; and yet, merely writing about basic things is not enough.

I'm getting longwinded. I hope to get to Europe around next Nov., where I should have gone this year. (Altho, there have been compensations here.) Let me know when we can drink a few beer in London.

Best,
Al

1. Emily Dickinson (1830–86): American poet whose work was known by only a small circle during her life; she is the only woman included in the early drafts of AP's "Bestiary [II]: (*ABC of P*)," his poetic homage to poets he admired. He struggled with the stanza devoted to her but, unable to get it right, dropped it from the published version: "Women? Hard to find any but Dickinson / Emily of that ilk. / Token woman / introvert [indecipherable] / somehow a death-lover without children[,]". Gerard Manley Hopkins (1844–89): Jesuit priest and poet. His work remained unknown until *Poems* (1918).

To Dennis Lee (Toronto), from Fort Pierce, Fla., March 18, 1982

Dear Dennis,
Thanks for your letter and the built-in safeguards re Milton.[1] In your first plan, Milton and I have a round of discussions after selections are made. That is the point at which some disagreement might arise, which is fairly natural after all. I would expect some disagreement, altho hope to keep it to a minimum. I expect also that the discussions with Milton would be in his personal presence, in Toronto, say. And I hope also that you can

be there as well, with your well-known diplomacy smoothing us rough-hewn types into abashed silence.

I.e., I'm saying that we ought to proceed as if everything will be well, while taking some precautions to ensure that end. My own relations with Milton have always been fairly turbulent: but he wants me to edit the book according to his letters, while at the same time castigating me for holding it up . . . But I would like some assurance from Milton to you, in writing, that he'll give me free hand in the selection. Has he done that already?

I'm somewhat intrigued by Milton's $5,000 advance. The most I ever got from McStew was half that. This no doubt is a mark of the forward-looking and innovative policies adopted by McStew since the advent of Dennis Lee.

I do think that you will personally need to say a word or two now and then—to Milton, I mean. He mentioned a title he expected to use in one of his letters. I thought it pretty ordinary and undistinguished. And yet, I regard a title as Milton's province. Nevertheless, a title should help to sell the book as well as being the most suitable and artistic possible.

What kind of agreement has transpired (lovely word, sounds like the last gasp of a goldfish after nuclear war), between Milton and Myself? Only that he apparently wants me to edit the book, in fact is mad to have the book out. As I've said earlier, I'd like some kind of assurance—written—from Milton to you that I'll have a free hand in the selection. Would you attempt to obtain such assurance?

Also, what kind of physical manuscript do you want? For instance, must the poems be typed in the final manuscript? Or can I zerox them directly from the books, while typing those on broadsheets or in Milton's manuscripts? I presume you do want more than a mere list of titles; something that can be looked at and judged as a whole.

Okay, I will write Milton again, giving him an idea of my own modus operandi. And hope that you've made my own independence clear to him.

Departure date from here is only a week or so away. Sun beams down with unremitting fury; my own boredom is unlimited; I can't wait to flee the fuckin place. Will phone you the first Sunday I'm back.

Al

1. AP was choosing the poems for *Dig Up My Heart: Selected Poems of Milton Acorn 1952–1983* that was published by McClelland and Stewart in 1983. Lee was the poetry editor at M&S at the time.

To Anne Goddard (Ottawa), from Ameliasburgh, April 8, 1982

Dear Ms. Goddard,
Thanks much for sending along the Glassco Zeroxes. Reading them, I
think you're right: no reason they can't be released for researchers. I was
also interested to read my own letters, which seem to me more interesting
than those I write now.[1]

Thanks again,
Al

1. AP responds here to a request from Anne Goddard, the Arts Archives Co-ordi-
nator at the National Archives, that his letters to John Glassco be made available
to researchers.

To George Galt (Toronto), from Ameliasburgh, May 24, 1982

Dear George,
[...] I was thinking about that double hook of ancestor-descendant discussion of last night. And I should try to explain my own feelings more
fully. One part of my mind doesn't give a damn and the other part does.
How's that again? Well, I'm a bit put off by all the people scrabbling for
ancestors, genealogies and UEL [United Empire Loyalist] associations,
etc. That part of my mind says: let what I've done when I was alive represent me at any court, celestial or diabolic. What I've done is me, good or
bad and both. There is, of course, another more mystic side, which says
something colourful to the effect that our sons and daughters may reach
the stars or the millennium or a better day, find answers to some of the
questions we have asked. And by them knowing and ourselves bequeath-
ing them the capacity to know *we have in our own lives also known* what
they who are not even alive yet will know in future. We cannot say it, this
thing we know, and which we yet do not know in specific black and white,
but yet we know.
     In my most grandiose moments, I think that it calls for, in both ances-
tors and descendants, people with some sensitivity: i.e., people like you
and I. You will have to forgive that assessment of you on my part as I will
have to forgive my own opinions about myself. And this "sensitivity" will
skip a generation or even two, as we mentioned last night. And I find
it difficult to have any affection for blood relatives of mine who do not
possess this capacity: as you no doubt—or possibly?—cannot feel much
about your own blood relatives. [...]

We must therefore go to work on our own descendants through the medium of ourselves. I'm sure your point was: that is how we influence the future, apart from what we do when alive and leave as mental mementos to our existence. And yet at the point in our lives when we create our descendants, we are incomplete in ourselves, we have not added all the parts, nuts and bolts and genes to our personal selves. The mating urge has fucked us up. The near replicas we create are imperfect, since we too are incomplete until we are able to be and live our fullest lives, the ultimate ripeness. By then, at this ultimate point, our balls are ruined by all the jai alai of youth and lost their perfect rotundity.

This probably all sounds silly, especially when I feel facetious. But anyway, now you know exactly how I feel on the subject. Don't you?

Best,

Al

To Stan Dragland (London, Ont.), from Ameliasburgh, June 23, 1982

Dear Stan,

Thanks for the invite to review. I wouldn't mind at all, except I hate to bother with books I don't like much. Which is most of em, or at least 51%. Old, cantankerous and curmudgeonly perhaps. It would be fun to do someone like this Roo Borson[1] tho. But shit, to look over all the books to find that one. Incidentally, I ordered a book from your reviews (*Brick* ones), the Jeffers one, that is. Not quite so incidentally: I have a used copy of *The Double Axe*, to which the previous owner had attached a review at the time. Unless you know the story of *The Double Axe,* it gets complicated to explain. But Jeffers was a Cassandra, a disliker of the actions and results of the worst side of human nature. *The Double Axe* was a book saying the US was empire at a time when they wouldn't admit that; saying that Roosevelt was a cripple with a power complex as a result of being crippled, at a time when FDR was a hero; Jeffers was a nay-sayer when everybody and his dog was saying whee WHEE WHEE after the wartime victory. Random House emasculated Jeffers' book, (*The Double Axe*, 1948), and Jeffers made little demur. Very odd! The un-emasculated *Double Axe* came out some five years back, which I read on library loan. I now think I shoulda zeroxed the poems not in the first ed. Also, an article came out in some small Can. mag a year or so back about this whole business, which I read at Ron Everson's place in Fla. (his mag).

What I'm saying (and you'll never get another book on Jeffers—or so I think): I'd like to write about Jeffers. He was so mild in his letters (I got the only Jeffers' letters I know of when at Western), which didn't mention *The Double Axe* controversy at all, wanted to make him look good. But *The Double Axe*, in my view, doesn't make him look bad at all.

Or Auden. I regard him as one of the great puzzles: the nay-saying homo, the great poet, (yes, I think so), as an English mag phrased it: Flight of the Disenchanter. I feel close to dead Auden, live one too, and wish I could write as well. Wish I could write at all these days.

I believe there is a life of Auden. Dunno if one of Jeffers. The latter, to me, is the great American poet. A man with guts I'd like to have, alive or dead. Auden the actor-virtuoso. Jeffers a Cassandra. I mention these two as where interest lies re reviews. A man with guts, I say re Jeffers, which I'd like to have: but then, I'd like to feel anything the way he felt things. You give up on finding what life is all about, give up on women, give up on writing, everything all things except life: but those guts those guts. And his letters (his editor) euphemized everything.

Or Lawrence. The Lawrence industry, and The Bible, Lincoln, Shakespeare, Napoleon etc. But the vital blood books, where he was alive tho dead in minds of people who knew him, these are gone. Even his biographers are dead, Harry Moore I'm thinking of. Aldington too. So I think Lawrence is bloodless without Lawrence. Sad.

No hope, after that generous invite. No goddam books. No Borson. All those gorgeous images! She'll probably fall flat on her vagina next one. Or next. That's what happens. Hey: how about a Borson interview? She lives in Toronto somewhere. But aw, too much trouble for all of us, including me. Still . . .

Thanks tho. I appreciate the offer/gesture/cordiality/friendship (etc). Ditto.

Stan, why don't you buy a goddam typewriter? Your letters are too easy to read; I can't stand plain syntax etc. Stan: I hear 25% of what you're writing. Stan: please: buy a goddam typewriter. (My own handwriting is one per cent less decipherable than yours which amounts to a reader's zero understanding) Stan——please?

Al

1. Roo Borson (b. 1952): Toronto-based poet (*Night Walk*, 1981; *Water Memory*, 1996). AP thought highly of her early work.

To George Woodcock (Vancouver), from Ameliasburgh, August 19, 1982

Dear George,

Your account of Giraud is probably more interesting than the book itself. A man sitting in occupied France writing a 1,300 page book about the Metis![1] I expect you'll comment on the racism in your Intro, since it seems impossible to leave it as is.

(I just got this typewriter back after cleaning and repair, and now there's a stoppage when you roll the carriage back, at least a difficulty in the sliding which makes it difficult to think about what I'm writing. May have to change typewriters.)

Anyway, to even read a book like that, despite the information, is a hard task. But Giraud, what an odd bird he must have been! There's the difference between a working scholar like you, or I should say writer-scholar, and me. Years ago, labouring over the long involved sentences of Proust, Dostoyevsky and others, I refuse to read such books. Of course, I'm sure they were graceful writers compared to this guy. When you think of it, it's almost worth a book on other people like Giraud, those people who sat at home, did their research without very much travel in the field. Prescott was another such, I believe. I think of Parkman,[2] but at least he had an initial tour of the west before he settled into pure research.

"—two or three clear Woodcock sentences"! George, do I detect a small trace, merely a smidgen, of ego? Of course, and why shouldn't you have one? But I'm a little amused, since I've noticed few indications before. In Layton, in Clark Blaise[3] (in "Mermaid Inn" column in *TorGlobe*), in meeting writers personally, ego looks and sounds so awful in their mouths and written words. Living near us here, an ex-English employee of the township roads dept. His ego, amour propre or whatever, is entirely wrapped up in the Oldsmobile diesel he owns. Maybe one or two other things too. But things. Whatever the basic person is, the thinking and reasoning and creative man, the mere owning of things is not an expression of it. I hastily add that you are not among such people. Your ego stems from what you are, the creative impulse of mind and brain. Of course, one could say the same of Layton and Blaise: but in them it sounds small and wriggling from under a rock to me. I have heard myself mention things I thought accomplishments of mine, when there was no need at all to mention them. And thought, then or later, that my own accomplishments are really very small. Which places me too low on my personal totem pole, to myself that is, and felt that I have said things in a way unique to myself, and perhaps comparable in merit to others of more prominence than myself.

I suppose it's the small god in people like you and I, the one that says I want to live forever, echoing grandiose down the corridors of time.

As mentioned, I'm sure, writing this autobio, now some 28,000 words, rushing ahead unrevisedly. Seems both good and bad to me, the connectives and background sometimes boring, but places and incidents in which I am enthralled in myself and writing. Dennis Lee, now a McStew culture director of some sort, wants to see it a year or two from now. He's a friend, or I think so, but I mistrust anyone working for McStew. They've fucked me up so many times that, if the book is good, I hate to see any advantage to them from it. And yet Dennis is a friend. How resolve? I dunno. Jack McC. is a sharp business entrepreneur. I don't believe he has a single feeling about good lit. apart from the money it brings him. And despite Linda McKnight being now prez, I'm sure Jack is still the dictator and profiter thereof. My wife is even stronger about this than I am. When I meet Jack I succumb to his personality, then have to remember the number of times I've been screwed.

Yeah, Skelton[4] is admirable in some way. He wears a mask most of the time, but that's common. Yes, he writes "quite good" poetry. I think he misses things that are intangible until you tang them.

Al

1. Marcel Giraud (b. 1900): *The Métis in the Canadian West*, 2 vol. (1986; translated by George Woodcock). The French edition appeared in 1984. Giraud's first publication was *Histoire du Canada* (1946).
2. W.H. Prescott (1796–1859): American historian, best known for the *History of the Conquest of Mexico* (1843) and *Conquest of Peru* (1847). Francis Parkman (1823–93): American historian, best known for his work on the French empire in North America (*Frontenac and New France*, 1877; *Montcalm and Wolfe*, 1884).
3. Clark Blaise (b. 1940): short story writer (*A North American Education*, 1973; *Lusts*, 1983) autobiographer (*I Had a Father: A Post-modern Autobiography*, 1992) and historian (*Sir Sanford Fleming and the Creation of Standard Time*, 1982).
4. Robin Skelton (1925–97): founder of the *Malahat Review* and poet (*One Leaf Shaking: Collected Later Poems*, 1995).

To Milton Acorn (Toronto), from Ameliasburgh, October 18, 1982

Dear Milton,
I'm not sure what's on your mind about me. What am I supposed to have done this time, as apart from old wrongs you have suffered from me?

I am sure that I won't be writing if you keep on condemning me for both the past and present.

Yes, I may have been partly responsible for the publication grant for the McDougall poems, since I recommended it to K. Benzekri at CC.

Your manuscript is now at McStew, awaiting Dennis Lee's reading of it. After that, he and I will talk about it, and you will be given a list of poems or a zerox.

As I said before, I am not your target. If you keep up this condemnation, I won't answer.

Best,

Al

To Margaret Atwood (Toronto), from Ameliasburgh, November 23, 1982

Dear Peggy,

I have to write and say I think you've done an excellent job with the Oxford book.[1] I doubt that anyone else could do as well. And agree also with your use of Smith as the basis or pool of early talent, since he did have good judgment.

Re the majority of poems by males, it seems to me that males just write more poems. Why is another thing.

I am pleased to see Thibaudeau, who has a special magic—or so I think. Regret missing Charles Bruce who wrote of the maritime men: "Forever mindful that something wet and salt / Creeps and loafs and marches round the continent / Careless of time, careless of change, obeying the moon."[2]

The Milne painting, for a book that will represent CanPo in the US and Britain, it seems to me a woman in a rocking chair is not representative or suitable. The choice, I suppose, was William Toye's.[3]

I was impressed with Roo Borson's recent book, and it's good to see her stuff here. It seems to me she has a chance to be very good.

I've seen two typos after a very cursory reading, just a skimming really.

However, at the end, the choice is yours as it must be. I'd make a slightly different choice, but not *very* different. So I congratulate you most sincerely.

Al

1. *The New Oxford Book of Canadian Verse.*
2. The lines are from Bruce's "Words Are Never Enough."
3. William Toye (b. 1926): a founding editor of *The Tamarack Review*, editorial

director of Oxford University Press (1969–91), and co-editor of the *The Oxford Companion to Canadian Literature*. The painting AP objects to is David Milne's *Wicker Chair* (1914).

To D.G. Jones (Sherbrooke, Que.), from Ameliasburgh, December 9, 1982

Dear Doug,

Glad you're not frozen. I was, damn near, this morning. Jesus, this weather!

Yeah, your article[1] reminds me of my brief term as a teacher at SFU, when they gave me a fifteen-word title attached to visiting prof, and a prospective landlady thought I was a doctor, a PhD., and rented us a place she wouldn't have rented otherwise. I thought, in class, that I knew a little bit about lit, and refused as a matter of pride to prepare lessons and lectures. This one time in the middle of a sentence I found I had nothing to say, stopped right there in the centre of four syllables, muttered something, told somebody else to take over, sat down. Your piece reminds me of such limitations. I used to listen to Elspeth Cameron at Loyola, mouth open and amazed that anyone could do this; not dissect, but X-ray.

Yeah, I've always thought of the Fr. Cans as too abstract for me. (How did you know?) But do they think we are too prosey as retaliation? Do they know that we think of them as too poetic and abstract? I still think they're too abstract, dammit; their agony is too agonized, their beauty too fuckin beautiful. Naturally, and with infinite goodwill and condescension, I give them full leave to be whatever they are.

The bit about the poem about the house built from odds and ends: I might have written it. I was writing so much at one time some of them slip my mind. I'm just as liable to forget as you are liable to remember. Now it bothers me, and as you say, if I didn't I should've oughta.

I'm working on four poems at the moment in a transitory renaissance, since my output is down at the approach of death. One of them is entitled "Gondwanaland," which only a full prof of geology is liable to understand enough to disagree with it as a graduate thesis. And another poem of quatrains with rhyming assonance, dissonance and other dances.

I know what you mean re your articles. I was once gonna do it, then reading some of them dismayed me with their non-merit. I couldn't face re-writing them, and couldn't publish as they stood. However, your basic articles won't need it nearly as much as mine. Many of mine were written out of embarrassment at not liking someone's poems and trying to disguise my feelings.

Such dishonesty wasn't always the case, but even apart from that they were bad. Whereas you have the ability to come up with a damned interesting critical book. And you have a feeling for excellence also beyond mine. By the way, I just saw a new book by Robert Bringhurst[2] which I think excellent. I can even forgive him his erudition, which if I were to do the same thing would be pseudo. For instance, he has a suite about the Greek philosophers, both paraphrasing and quoting them. I like this quoted bit because it's as close to rhetoric as he comes (yeah, I like rhetoric sometimes):

> And Parmenides lay in the goat-dunged heavy-stemmed
> grass, imagining things and thinking
> of all of them *there* in the interwoven ply, his mind flying
> and gulping, trying for the whole cascade:
> his brainlobes pumping like lungs, like a muscle,
> the nervecords thundering in the bones' coulisses
> and the heart's whole cargo coming
> tumbling up to him:
> goddesses, girls, white water, olive trees,
> sharks' roe, the sea-haze,
> the migrating eye of the flounder

Well? I heard him read at Blue Mtn. and didn't understand at all on accounta his histrionics, which are like a ham actor in the 17th century shitting Shakespeare.

Glad FRS is surviving. I will always have warm wishes for him among we sad children of mortality.

Thank you again for doing the article, from which I have learned something of myself as well as you.

Best,

Al

P.S. The goddam weather is about minus 20 here. When my wife gets back from nursemaiding her sister, we shall shake the snow from respective posteriors.

1. Jones's "Al Purdy's Contemporary Pastoral" had appeared in *Canadian Poetry* (Spring–Summer 1982).
2. Robert Bringhurst (b. 1946): an authority on books and book design, a

translator (*A Story as Sharp as a Knife: An Introduction to Classical Haida Literature*, 1999), and poet (*The Calling: Selected Poems 1970–95*, 1995). Bringhurst is one of the most original figures in Canadian poetry. AP quotes below from his "Parmenides."

To the Editor, *Toronto Sun*, from Ameliasburgh, December 13, 1982

"—beastliness when inebriated" says Ms. Barbara Amiel, your editor, about me. She also says she has encountered me in "a full state of intoxication."[1]

To my certain knowledge, I have "encountered" Ms. Amiel three times only. First, in her Toronto apartment with her husband, George Jonas (a friend). Second, at Collingwood, when I drove back to Toronto with both of them. Third, at Jack McC.'s Night of a Hundred Authors, when she left the party on the arm of some misguided swain. (On all three occasions I was sobered by the experience.)

However, that business of "beastliness" bothers me a little. *The Oxford Concise* definition of the word is as follows: "Gluttony, drunkenness, obscenity." I have undoubtedly been guilty of all of these at one time or another. But the word also has unstated sexual implications, and I wouldn't want Ms. Amiel to think that. It scares the beastliness right out of me. [. . .]

Al Purdy

1. AP responds here to Barbara Amiel's column in the *Toronto Sun* in which she wrote the following: "As for getting drunk, I can think of no worse drunkards than professional writers. Having encountered, for example, the fabulous poet Al Purdy in a full state of intoxication, I can attest that his extraordinary talent with words is matched only by his beastliness when inebriated . . . No, all things considered, if one must get drunk it should be done with accountants or ballet dancers."

To Margaret Atwood (Toronto), from Ameliasburgh, December 14, 1982

Dear Peggy,
Sorry about your teeth/tooth operation. It's always some damn thing. My leg has been okay for some time now; now it's the back. We should be born with stainless steel bodies, replaceable chassis that is.

I see the sourish Dudek review in *Globe*.[1] The main thing about any book, poems or prose, is how good and how interesting it is. He didn't mention merit at all. You've probably noticed: the salient critical characteristic of Dudek is that he praises young poets, but as soon as they become better-known than himself he tries to chop them down. Some have said that this is a characteristic of many Cancrits, that as soon as a writer gets well known he or she is a target. You've experienced some of that yourself, of course. Dudek is a good (or bad) example of this. His reviews and criticism seem learned and logical with all sorts of critical apparatus, all of which serve to obscure simple jealousy. Or, so I have thought sometimes. The pedant obscures the poet, and the poet's jealousy spoils the critic. I didn't think much of that silly "Margaret Atwood" review either. It was not clever, simply too long and boring at the end. However, it's no use trying to reply to such people; that makes them sound more important than they are. The only thing I would reply to is a personal attack. Barbara Amiel did that a month ago in the *Toronto Sun*; a kind friend sent me the clipping. In case you're interested, here's the paragraph:

"As for getting drunk, I can think of no worse drunkards than professional writers. Having encountered, for example, the fabulous poet Al Purdy in a full state of intoxication, I can attest that his extraordinary talent with words is matched only by his beastliness when inebriated."

That annoys me. Pretty cunning too, compliments along with the nastiness. I've written a letter to the *Sun*, which they probably won't publish, since I understand she's editor there. But it might amuse you, on reverse of this.

> Take care of yourself,
> Best,
> Al

1. Dudek's review appeared in the *Globe and Mail* on December 11, 1982. His main complaints were that Atwood devoted far too much space to contemporary poets—"the older poets (up to E.J. Pratt) are compressed in the first 65 pages, while the rest of the book, about 80 per cent, is mainly devoted to contemporary poetry" and that "her choices are often based on moral and ideological obsessions." He suggested that several of the women poets had been included "because they are female."

From George Johnston (Athelstan, Que.), to Ameliasburgh, May 8, 1983

Dear Al,

Thank you very much for *Owen Roblin* and *No Other Country*. I settled in and read them at once, something I rarely do with books I am sent. I enjoyed them, and that is rarer than it ought to be too, though I always expect to enjoy your books. *Owen Roblin* is a very handsome book; the photographs are good but on one page the text is printed over the photograph in an unsatisfactory way. The poem is very good, true Purdy, with lots of good people and good country and good history. I admire your rangy style which carries so much with so little seeming effort, it can only be the achievement of much hard work. Your rhythms are especially good but elusive of analysis, but I would like to know more about them one day. I think you must know quite a bit though I would guess that you work almost entirely by intuition. You are one of a few Canadian poets whose work I would say I know well—though it is not in me to know anything exhaustively. I have by no means read all your poetry; *Owen Roblin* was new to me. It must be a poem one should hear: do you have a tape? I imagine that I know your rhythms and there were pages here and there—not many—in which you seemed prosier than usual. The opening pages are beautiful, in the conventional sense too, and the portrait of your grandfather is fine. And the closing pages are beautiful, beginning at "The wheels stopped . . ." And I liked the village drunk and the schoolmaster very well. I cannot find the pages I thought might be a bit prosy except maybe the page opposite the map of Ameliasburgh Township. I do not offer this as a criticism, merely an observation; the poem is such a compendium, there are many kinds of stuff in it that every kind of passage seems to be a part of it. Your rhythms are your own, though, I do not know others like them, and it helped to hear you read them, especially that first time in Ottawa. I read *No Other Country* on our way to Toronto by train and liked all of it, though I do have to say that the auto-biographical passages seemed appreciably better than the others. Your autobiography should be very good. You must be the opposite of me. What you say about yourself is straightforward and lively and unselfconscious; what you say about others, on the other hand, is comparatively speaking, selfconscious, not uncomfortably so, by any means, but just enough to lower, or limit, the directness of what you have to say. Your prose is real prose but its virtues are the same as those of your poetry. I am very glad to have these two books, thank you again, and for the friendly inscriptions. What can I send you? Do you have *The Saga of Gisli* and *The Greenlander's Saga*? Perhaps I have already sent you both. I think you have everything else. We stopped off for three hours in Kingston to see George Whalley in hospital. You perhaps know that he was operated on four years ago for stomach cancer, had his stomach removed. He made a miraculous recovery, but this spring he was operated on again, same cancer. He seemed to recover even more swiftly from this operation but that lasted only two or three weeks and then he was in hospital again where he has been ever since, steadily getting weaker. I had a good visit with him and he expected to get better but no-one else expected him to. I did not. But I understand that he is rallying again and getting a little stronger. I shall phone Elizabeth this evening and ask for news. George and I have been good friends, I shall miss him badly. It is hard to see how he can recover, and what can one hope for him if he does? All this to go through again! Yet he has such vitality, it is impossible to say what he may not do. He put me on to reading Edwin Muir's autobiography[1] years ago; have you read it? A beautiful piece of writing. He has a passage about working in a bone-yard which I was reminded of by your dried blood poem. A horrendous poem, and fine piece of writing.[2] I already have "Gondwanaland." I see that I have two Gondwanalands. I was not sure of the first one, though I came to like it & still do. I can see, however, that the expansion is an improvement. The only query I might have is over the two lines "for there was never any purpose / and there was never any meaning."

I hope we may meet during the summer, do not know when. Our summer promises to be full of children and grandchildren. In mid-August we are going to Norway for three weeks; the King has invited me to a workshop at Lillehammer on promoting Norwegian literature in the English-speaking world. It lasts five days but Kurt Ødegård will be there and we shall spend the rest of the time with him and his wife. The plan for a lunch in Montreal seems to be getting nowhere, nobody at this end has any real enthusiasm for it except me. But the Loons may succeed in starting something in Montreal yet; I cannot do much because I live too far out. If you do come to Montreal to see Ron Everson, for instance, let me know, I can come up fairly easily, or if you are driving you might find your way out here. Or we might meet in Belleville. We go to Toronto or Peterborough sometimes; I tend to go by train whenever possible, because I quickly tire of driving. Anyhow, I agree that we should get together.

Yours,

George

I phoned Elizabeth Whalley last evening and George has not rallied, he is just getting weaker & weaker.

1. Edwin Muir (1887–1959): poet (*Collected Poems*, 1963) and critic. Muir is probably best known for his superb *Autobiography* (1954) and his translations, with his wife Willa, of Kafka.
2. "Piling Blood" in the collection of the title (1984).

To George Woodcock (Vancouver), from Ameliasburgh, May 10, 1983

Dear George,

Thanks for the new autobio.[1] I've been reading and marvelling at the difference from me—all those writers you knew, all that litalk etc. Orwell, tho, is someone I'd like to have met. And Dylan Thomas. But I would have been tremendously shy at that time, the Thirties, also far too young. Still, I regret never having met Dylan.

You are/were off to Europe, nearly due back. (The book must've taken some time coming—) I look forward especially to your autobio stuff in Canada. I'm sure it will be different, as you mention, but also a little closer to home and hence more interesting. (To me, I mean—which doesn't mean that England is not—how did I get into this?). Building the cabin, blowing dynamite, etc. parallels some of my own times, as I've said.

I'm pleased you sold your papers to Queen's—as I've likely already said. And I expect they needed a freight car to hold em all. The sale does give one some freedom of movement. I feel almost independently wealthy with that money, of which the last instalment is next year.

This last winter I had a sustained burst of writing poems in Florida, and quite unexpectedly. As a result I have a book manuscript nearly ready, over which Dennis Lee and I are sparring by phone. McStew has fucked me up so often I feel like going to another publisher, and yet Dennis, my friend, is with McStew now. He's also dug me up an appointment with a bone doctor in Toronto, for which I am grateful. Such things matter little and yet at the same time matter greatly, if I can keep them in perspective.

Also, I got stuck with editing Ron Everson's Selected when in Fla. I was looking over his manuscript and said, in a moment of laxness on my part, "I'd be glad to help." Next moment I'm the goddam editor, just like that. If I turn my head in the wrong direction, I'm liable to be editing the *Encyclopedia Brittanica*—the which could not be more unlikely. Still, Everson's is a good book, and I am much too sharp about him grabbing me like that. And last fall I edited Acorn's Selected for money with McStew, and escaped with sanity. When I returned this spring from Fla., Acorn phoned. Eurithe answered. When he asked for me I signalled frantically that I wasn't home. Then later, Dennis Lee tells me he wanted to thank me for my work on his book. So I feel guilty. But Acorn drives me up the wall with his talk about intelligent ravens talking to him metrically. You can't win. Surely Acorn and I must be the most opposite people ever. Have you ever read Joe Wallace?[2] Well, Acorn thinks highly of Wallace's poems, of course because W. was a communist. "Come brother, come sister, let's keep the union strong" sort of stuff. I do like some union stuff, like "Joe Hill," for instance, but but but—

Enough rambling. I hope the flowers are out for you and Inge on return to Vancouver.

Best,

Al

1. Woodcock published three volumes of autobiography: *Letter to the Past* (1982), *Beyond the Blue Mountains* (1987), *Walking through the Valley* (1984).
2. Joe Wallace (1890–1975): member of the Communist Party of Canada and poet (*Night is Ended*, 1942). His 1964 collection *A Radiant Sphere* was "issued in Moscow in three editions of 10,000 copies each—in Russian, English and Chinese" (John Robert Colombo). He toured Russia and China in 1956–57 with Wilson MacDonald.

From Dennis Lee (Toronto), to Ameliasburgh, May 17, 1983

Dear Al,

Beethoven Weeping![1] (Good title, by the way.) Forget about my blood-sugar count; I shall indeed say exactly what I think.

Which doesn't give me any problem, since there's nothing I feel squeamish about saying. First, the book is still in process. And second, it is in process towards being a wonderful, wonderful thing—a work of vintage maturity, full of bittersweet candour and wonder and lostness and roots. Poetically, if I may say it, you are entering your "late period"—and I think you're making all the right moves. Retaining much of what you've done, but also pushing into new Purdy terrain; technically I think of things like the moving in and out of blank verse in "Menelaus and Helen," or the move to quatrains; and in sensibility there are new notes too—which are not some chintzy attempt to be a totally new person, but modulations and accessions of new tone which seem to come organically out of having lived another 5 years, another decade. I don't think the whole book is here yet; but what *is* here is often deeply satisfying, and bespeaks a full book that will be just superb. Lucky fucker!

What did I like particularly? I'm just going to name poems, not linger over particular lines or moments. My Greatest Hits list, this time through, would include these: "Menelaus and Helen," "Lost in the Badlands," "What Is a Canadian?" (though I think it strikes a few false notes, in this line or that), "At Mycenae," "In the Early Cretaceous," which quite took my breath away. "Major" poems and ones on a lesser scale, but each one filling out its own space of existing with a lovely mixture of energy and poise . . . But then, on a different day I might have listed among them "How It Feels To Be Old," "On the Intelligence of Women," "A God in the Earth," "Marvin Mollusc," "Unfinished Portrait," "The Blue City," "For Eurithe," "My Cousin Don," "Birds Here and Now," "Story"—and probably some others. I particularly liked those too; and again, not because all are major, but because each seemed to me to be what it was reaching to be.

In fact, I found so much I enjoyed that it is likely more constructive to come around from the other end, and tell you my particular non-favourites. If that's my Hit List, here is my hit-list. There were a few where I just never felt the Purdy engine kicking into gear at all: "The Mother," "Incest," "Adobe," and "Visiting Tolstoy." (Of those, I thought "Incest" had nice moments towards the very end, though they didn't reclaim the poem; and I thought things in the first stanza, and the entire third stanza, made "Adobe" the most likely candidate for reclamation. I was surprised to find myself reading the whole of "Visiting Tolstoy" without connecting; felt like something that Al Purdy *would* find his juices running in—but I couldn't sense that.)

Then there were some that I didn't just set aside, but that didn't do a whole lot for me (or did much less than I thought they were capable of). "Four Billion Children": I have no difficulty with it being a kind of throwaway or squib; I do have difficulty with the way the imagination feels only half-engaged. "Bestiary": there's something about the form that leads us to expect a series of terse, unforgettable, probably epigrammatic portraits; it's a kind of portrait-gallery, after all, wheeling us past a series of people and summing each one up in 4 lines. So the casual looseness, and the sometimes-not-quite-spot-on phrase-making, seem active defects here, rather than an intrinsic part of the grand Purdy sweep. Just to single out one for instance, not terribly drastic but indicative: "Homer because he was Homer, / but maybe wasn't, or didn't exist." Well, the first line seems to take the easy way out; and the second line makes me feel, "Well, yes, I know it's a true fact—but what's it doing in here? Isn't this a bit like a cough between sentences, while you're waiting to think what to say next? If you're going to 'do' Homer in 4 lines—or even 'do' 'Homer's importance to me,' which is a bit less daunting—surely you can't squander a quarter of your space reminding us that scholars aren't sure whether there was an historical Homer, or he's a composite, or whatever." . . . I linger on the poem because I'd love to see it be really good; could be a super cherishing-of-ancestors poem . . . "At Lenin's Tomb," which feels by the end to be not without a certain lack of point; feels as if the poet felt he'd like to write a poem about all this, but never quite found out what the poem was supposed to be about . . . "Eleanor and Valentina": I enjoyed the very beginning and very end, but never felt the poem hitting high gear—nor indeed any particular gear—between those 2 points.

Those are the ones I challenge, then: 4 that strike me as to-be-lost (unless "Adobe" can go through another incarnation), and 4 that aren't disasters, but seem slack enough that they make the manuscript feel a bit soggy. It'd be interesting to see how the MS would read—what directions it would point in—if you withdrew all 8 for now, and only reinstated the ones that got stronger in another draft. (I think the only existing unit that this would make a serious dent in is the travelling-in-Russia one.) But the overall emphases would likely shift a bit—and some lines of energy in the book might become a bit clearer. Dunno just what.)

Sitting and sniping at those poems, of course, conveys the wrong impression—that the manuscript basically makes me want to snipe. What I said at the beginning is exactly what I feel: the manuscript makes me want more, for it to feel fully achieved—but what it makes me want more *of* is achingly strong and affecting . . . It makes a kind of sense that you should have hit a pause-period, now. Apart from whatever metal fatigue & mental fatigue may have been induced by this great burst, it *feels* like a point at which the manuscript may want to touch down, re-gather and re-focus some of the energies that are propelling it, shed some fat, reach out in some new directions or (perhaps more likely) claim more fully some of the ground it is onto—litanies of things loved & regretted & damned, sparky particular moments from the past (the childhood poems are a lovely group), consolidating for the awesome journey ahead now—with irreverent exasperation about the body's non-cooperation, the loss of friends and so on, and also with this marvellous mix of ongoing vitality, rueful humour, ornery independence, and the plangent hushed resonant full chords of existence that you can evoke like no one else. Lucky fucker!

If it would be of any interest, Al, we could sit down some time and have a go at individual poems. Not, gawd knows, because I believe I know how they should be written. But I've got minor twitches hither & thither, in some, which don't have much bearing on the whole poem, but might be fun to consider, and maybe tinker afterwards. As usual, I'm sure I may

be right often about there being something out of kilter, but way off base
in how I've identified it . . . Anyway, if that looks doable ever and you feel
like it, I'd certainly get a kick out of it. A chance to savour your UN diplomacy sweet reason one more time would be too much to pass by.

(If it's of any interest, I can put my finger on two quite specific things.
I liked "Was It Funny?" I wonder, though, whether putting it through the
typewriter another time mightn't get it internally in synch with itself a
bit more (not sure just what I mean by that, I must admit—it feels a little
blurry around the emotive edges on the way through). And the ending
troubles me quite a bit—I simply can't tell what the last stanza is telling
me. Does the poet mean that maybe he *did* wield the lipstick (and then
suffer from amnesia, till now)? Obviously not; that's ridiculous. Or that
he, like anyone else, had his share of floating aggression and hell-raising,
and would certainly have been capable of lipsticking? . . . Well, I'm sure
it's true; but if that's all that's being said, it's something we all knew to
begin with, and it feels fairly portentous . . . Finally, I get the sense of the
patented Purdy recoil happening at the end of the poem—only this time
with no serious, undercut-or-qualify-or-refocus-everything-that's-come-
before kick to it. Am I missing the point somehow?

(And I'd like to have a bit of a go at "Colombo Was Here." Odd experience, reading it. In the first half or so, I thought, "Well, this is just a jokey
poem, and some of the jokes are amusing and some aren't particularly;
no particular reason to include it." And then I started to feel, "Jeez, this
is turning into a real poem—jokey and mock-lugubrious, fair enough;
but that's the kind of real poem it's *being*." And then at the very end I
felt, "This is a bit extraordinary; the thing is still a burlesque, but Purdy's
wrung a genuineness of feeling out of the whole improbable thing, here
towards the end, that totally transcends what's come before." . . . And now
I wish the first half could be better. I don't mean making it more serious, of course. But tighter, better-paced, funnier—so we don't go from
ho-hum interest (or semi-interest) to feeling oddly moved, but rather
go from smiling or laughing at what appears to be just a comic poem, to
feeling oddly moved. Know what I mean? (It might help, also, to take a
half-step back from the phenomenon of "Colombo," and let the reader
in more fully on something about him from the outset. So it doesn't feel
like just an in-group literary joke—which it's more than, by the end. I
dunno—am I saying anything real? Maybe only that the poem *appears* to
be a bit in-groupy; I think a reader would piece together the basic point
about Colombo, that he's another Canadian poet, a globe-trotter, and not

much respected by this poet, fairly easily . . . Maybe this point should be scrubbed.)

Hi-ho. How I do talk on! Time passes quickly when you're having fun.

You have a wonderful book in hand, Al, and it is probably not that far away from being fully achieved. It's exactly the book you should be writing—still growing, still using your strengths from before, giving us stuff that only you at this point in your life can give us. I'm very much affected. Don't stop (by which I don't mean, "Don't pause.")

Write if you get work.

1. Early title of *Piling Blood* (1984). "Heard Beethoven weeping" is the last line of the poem "Piling Blood."

To Dennis Lee (Toronto), from Ameliasburgh, May 19, 1983

Dear Dennis,
Thanks for the words. Some good, some not so good, but more or less resembling the way I look at some of the stuff—

Yeah, I think it's still in process too. How much longer I don't know, altho I do regard it as a sort of provisional manuscript. As to change and new areas in myself, I don't know that. I do know that I don't wanta imitate myself, seen too many do that.

Incidentally, the chap in "Story" is Norman Levine. I sent him the poem some time back.

Five of those poems will be in *CanFor* and another three in *QQ*. Which is a necessary reassurance, since one part of my mind always feels a bit dubious.

As I may have said, the Soviet poems are included—apart from the ltd. ed thing—because they have a different tone and energy, etc. I'm dubious about the Tolstoy one too, but I like something about it as well. I went over those Soviet poems again, altho with few changes resulting. But some.

And I remain uncertain about "A God in the Earth," partly because of your remarks, partly for reasons I can't fathom in myself.

Yeah, "Four Billion Children" is comparatively trivial.

"Bestiary" I worked like hell on. I'd hate to abandon it, altho Homer is dispensable.

Can't agree about "At Lenin's Tomb." "Felt . . . he'd like to write a poem about all this—" shit, Dennis, that has to be the way you feel about any poem. You just do it, but that sort of feeling must also be there. I was practically writing the damn thing standing in line to get into the tomb, with Gus [Ralph Gustafson] somewhere nearby also writing his mentally.

"Reach out in new directions"—how do you do that?

About "Was It Funny?"—I dunno what it says, but one has to take it or leave it, I think. All but the principal's punishment remains blurry to me. No "patented recoil"—I really can't remember, which is a bad thing to say to you, since I should claim some sort of mysticism. I think tho that I am too easy to understand, and that critics (not necessarily you) need something they can shake and worry and speculate about.

I've worked a great deal at all of these poems, fairly continuously over the last winter. I'd get at them literally every day. Work maybe two–three hours then quit when I felt a bit weary. I'd love to go over them again, but I just don't feel like it from an energy viewpoint. They're too familiar? I dunno. So thank you, but can you wait a little longer when I'm not quite so sick of the damn things?

And yeah, I think you said it: it does seem like a kind of non-Maughamish summing-up, last phase or whatever. I'd like to write more in the How It Feels to Be Old vein, altho not just that—I'm a little afraid the MS is too depressive, but can't be sure. [. . .]

I've just got the Acorn book.[1] I knocked out a poem about Acorn and I calling each other names, petty bourgeois etc., and he saying my line about there being no steel production on Roblin Lake. Do you remember: did he shove that poem back in behind my back? The one with the line "my pal Purdy"![2] Jesus! "In-groupish"? Of course. After I edited *I've Tasted My Blood*, then went to Europe or somewhere, he did the same thing, shoved a coupla more poems in I didn't include. Of course, you will say, that's his right. Everson did the same thing to me so why grumble about Acorn? But that particular poem makes me wriggle slightly, "my pal, Purdy" indeed! But it does seem a very good book to me, much better than I thought possible when I started to go over A's poems at first.

He phoned again the other night. I answered, which is always a mistake. Eurithe should answer, or your phone answering thing, saying dulcetly Dennis Lee is out, I don't know what he's doing but—(Does Dennis know?). Asked me if I thought he'd get the Nobel; I said I hoped so. He always calls while I'm eating dinner, after six for the cheaper rates. We argued about Yeats' line: "A terrible beauty is born" which he said was great and I said not bad but not great. And cited "An aged man—" etc.[3] At the end of the conversation, he asked me if I didn't have to piss, since I'd always ended these interminable gabfests that way before or similarly.

The bastard noticed and remembered. Of course I would myself so why shouldn't he?

My back gets me over a page of typing, so what haven't I said yet? I'm grateful, thankful, etc. I know that we both read each other's minds in some degree, therefore I'm sure you know the good feelings from me. No, your words don't sound "boost the old morale-ish"—they sound Dennisy. In letters like yours, and mine too, one could always add something to alter the meaning of what went before. I do think that about things you say at times, which isn't just a matter of adding something. And, of course, one doesn't set out to antagonize (however much I may have been accused of that in the past, and I have), or to praise unreservedly, just to say as clearly as one can how one feels.

I have to stop; typing does get my back.

Thanks,

Best,

Al

1. *Dig Up My Heart: Selected Poems of Milton Acorn 1952–1983* (1983).
2. In "Knowing I Live in a Dark Age" Acorn refers to "my friend Al, union builder and cynic / hesitating to believe his own delicate poems / lest he believe in something better than himself." "My pal Purdy" and "Russian steel production / at Roblin Lake" are from "A Profound Moment in the History of Canadian Poetry." Both poems are in *Dig Up My Heart*.
3. From Yeats's "Easter 1916" and "Sailing to Byzantium."

To Sam Solecki (Toronto), from Ameliasburgh, September 8, 1983

AP responds here to Sam Solecki's comments about some poems submitted to the *Canadian Forum*. Solecki was the magazine's poetry editor.

Dear Sam,

Thanks for word on pomes. Since I'm in a poem-writing ferment right now, pleasant to think they're not too bad. Friend said too many dates and places about "Death of DHL," whereas I think you need em. I guess you know all the quotes come directly from people involved, some of them I think poignant if not sentimental. And I believe detail is necessary, such as the blue and yellow room at Vence. And yeah, there is danger of depending on the dead writer's own vitality and life. If I ever read the Wms. poem I've forgotten it.

"Gondwanaland" I've been working on again, as you know by this time. I wanted to add more feeling of people to the poem, not just a bunch of rocks on a minor planet in an obscure galaxy.

I hate the idea of "painterly" writing. I was once commissioned to do a review of Joyce Weiland for *Arts Canada*. I thought she was terrible and all the reviews about her shit. They turned down the review when I said so. It's like wine-talk, this painterly stuff, pretension without body.

The "Gondwanaland" poem now ends with the original "Cairn on an arctic island—" but with that new verse added and some condensation— if I didn't make that clear before.

The *Forum* has always been my favourite magazine, in which I published my first half-decent poems. Edited then by Milton Wilson, who gave me the first half-way intelligent review[1] I'd had then. I still regret his complete absence from the magazine, and wonder if his ivory tower is defensible.

"—in the beginning was not the Word, but a chirrup."[2]

Best,

Al

1. Milton Wilson reviewed *Pressed on Sand* in the October 1955 issue of *Canadian Forum*. The best he could find to say about AP's second collection was that "the best poems, unfortunately, exist in the end as little more than collections of loosely related epigrams, so that one is tempted to say that Mr. Purdy's phrases are good, his sentences less good, his paragraphs so-so, and his whole poems not good at all." *Emu, Remember!* was reviewed in July 1957. Wilson closes as follows: "Mr. Purdy's combination of self-educated pedantry and self-conscious Bohemianism is not always very happy. But he brings it off in 'Cantos,' although in a special, unrepeatable way, and in 'Indictment,' which promises well for the future. Indeed, judging from Mr. Purdy's more recent periodical verse, the future may already be upon us."
2. This is the epigraph to AP's poem "In the Beginning was *not* the Word—but a Chirrup." It is taken from Lawrence's *Etruscan Places*: "And in the beginning was not a Word, but a chirrup."

Ralph Gustafson (1909–95): editor and poet (*The Moment is All: Selected Poems 1944–83*). Though AP liked Gustafson, he didn't admire his poetry.

To Ralph Gustafson (North Hatley, Que.), from Ameliasburgh,
September 8, 1983

My Dear Gus,
I suppose Creeley et al (Al?) didn't influence me in an opposite way. Also
writ something called "Ballad of the Despairing Husband" at the time
after Creeley. But those people pounded inconsequentiality into my head
hard, as a means of breaking tension and seriousness.

    I'm surprised Creeley remembered me. I'm also a little surprised I
escaped with my life after a particular evening with Creeley, Bowering,
etc. some 20 years ago. Creeley had insulted Bowering who worshipped
him, and I said why didn't he pick on me who had no such worship.
(Migawd!) When they played a tape of Olson (at a house on UBC campus), I emphasized what a wonderful voice Olson had in such a way as
to make it clear I didn't think much of his poems. Wah (Fred)[1] wanted
to kill me, and I asked him a few times, was he really going to hit me.
We were sitting on a stairway discussing my opinions and his and the
questions seemed to get me off the hook. When I left the place late at
night I had to walk much of the distance from UBC home, quite a distance. There was a big gang of BM people, so I was quite lucky to escape
unscathed except mentally. (Yes, I was more turbulent at the time, much
calmer now.)

    Yeah, Nowlan. In the aftermath, I'm surprised he lived so long. He had
time enough to write most of the poems he could write, and had developed his style into near permanence. Somebody told me—maybe Ron
Everson—they buried him in the "Poets' Corner" at Fredricton and made
quite a to-do of it. I doubt anyone knew him well. He was the sort of person you could drink with, but I think not much closer. Basically a solitary.
But then we all are to some extent. And he left some poems.

    The Moment[2] is not out of sight, a transitory view. Gus/Ralph will be
around a long time, and little reverberations speed into the future. Which
is all any of us can hope for, other than the moment.

Al

---

1. Fred Wah (b. 1939): BC poet who studied with Robert Creeley and Charles
Olson and was part of the Tish movement in the 1960s. He won a Governor
General's Award for *Waiting for Saskatchewan* (1985).
2. *The Moment is All: Selected Poems 1944–83*, 1983.

To Alan Abrams (Windsor, Ont.), from Fort Pierce, Fla., November 26,
1983

Dear Alan,
How are you? And Jean? Doings in the last year? Books? Promotions?
More kids? Whatever?

We bought a mobile here, which is not mobile at all. Some 65 feet long
with room on one side, for which we must rent the lot it's on. Plan to stay
till the snow leaves in Can. I have some four books coming in next year:
Bukowski/Purdy Letters (Paget Press), *Morning and It's Summer* (short
autobio with pictures and poems), Quadrant Press, *At the Quinte Hotel*, a
Selected for US only, then a new book next year. I hope to send a copy of
the first named along to you from here, but may have to wait until return
to Canada.

Spent a week in Spain, returning about two weeks back (we just arrived here in Fort Pierce after driving some 1,500 miles), most of the time
in Toledo, a town right out of the 15th century. At the Parador de Comte
Orgaz(m), an inn on the mountainside where El Greco did his view of
Toledo. I wrote a poem, of course, tho whether it's any good is a moot
point. And we liked Spain much, esp. the booze prices from my viewpoint. Wine so goddam cheap! Only expensive thing is gasoline, which I
only drink from time to time.

I've enjoyed that Faber Muir Selected you got me very much. And got
his autobio to go with it recently. He is definitely the Scots (Orkneys) poet
of whom I have the highest opinion. He was not charismatic and picturesque like Dylan—and there is no Muir industry like the former. Still,
conventional and traditional as he is . . .

The last year has been one of most productive, poems of course. One
looks at the poems carefully, trying to isolate the qualities of lastingness
or brevity they have, and I am still mildly pleased with six or eight of
them. But have to be suspicious of my own attitudes, since I can't stand
on a rock in deep space and look at them objectively. But who can do that
ever? I get ideas and immediately get them into poems (tho not lately, all

the travel has stopped me), or start poems and get the ideas inside the poems. Do you do the same in prose? Get the ideas both outside and inside the writing, both before and after?

Fort Pierce? A dull US city of some 50,000, probably half black, much poverty. We live in a mobile home park, surrounded on all four sides by a wide ditch full of alligators. There is only one entrance not covered by the ditch. Sometimes the alligators sing at night, in warm weather, most peculiar sound. At night one hears from this enclave, cars crashing occasionally on the highway outside. One reads of murders in the newspapers, drug busts, all sorts of crime. But it is relatively secure here, altho it gives the feeling of being barricaded from the outside world. One can't own a mobile here if one is less than 45 years, and a more grotesque collection of dodderers I have not seen elsewhere. It's kinda nice not to be the seniorest citizen in the place, tho that's silly. I don't really give a damn.

As you will guess, I had a letter from England on which the stamps weren't cancelled, which accounts for the enclosed.

Met Ted Hughes[1] in Toronto a month back, got my books signed at his reading. Thought him very likeable, and a damn good poet. Invited him over if he gets back to Can. I mean to our place, since he is a fisherman. Harbourfront, of course. Gatenby having gained another 20 pounds— you remember him? Place was sold out for Hughes, so I had to sneak in by pleading with Gatenby. (I had just gone to Toronto for that day.)

Love from Eurithe to you and Jean, etc. Write if you have a moment...

Al

1. Ted Hughes (1930–98): English poet (*The Hawk in the Rain*, 1957; *Crow*, 1970) and, from 1984, poet laureate.

To Dennis Lee (Toronto), from Fort Pierce, Fla., November 29, 1983

Dear Dennis,
I phoned you before leaving A-burg, but expect your electronic alter-ego was protecting your sleep.

We managed to escape all the sky-shit on the way down here, nothin but a bit of rain. And Fort Pierce is just as dull a place as last year, with my favorite thrift shop for books moved elsewhere. And the weather a sweat bath.

We had just been back from Spain a week, when Eurithe's importunities swept me away here. And Spain *was* enjoyable. Most of the time in

Toledo, a little city right out of the 15th century, surrounded on three sides by the Tagus River, mellow-looking tile-roofed houses, cobble streets, up hill and down, cheap booze, wine works out to 50 cents and up . . . We stayed one night at an inn on the hills overlooking Toledo, the Parador de Comte Orgaz(m), where El Greco is supposed to have painted his *View of Toledo*, now regrettably in a New York museum. Mattress terrible, so I slept on the floor, plagued by a mosquito, which I ushered out the door around 3 a.m. to find El Greco painting on the rocks as if he hadn't died 370 years ago. (Poem, of course.) Then moved back in town, visited cathedral and El Greco's house (where he'd never lived), where the uniformed guards knew less about El Greco than I did and insisted on telling me. Coming back, we flew to Gander first, then down to JFK, then a bus to Newark, then four hour wait and another flight to Syracuse, where we'd parked the car. Pouring rain. Took a motel around 11 p.m., which was 5 a.m. in our real time. All for a cheap flight to Spain. And I buy three bottles of Drambuie at the duty free, and finish em off in the week before we leave for the south. (I do like Drambuie!)

Incidentally, if you see a poem of mine in the current *Sat Nite*, let me know please. I left before I could see the new ish. I should have a coupla things out soon—the *Bukowski/Purdy Letters* and the autobio segment—tho whether I send you a copy here or back home I dunno . . .

Reading Edwin Muir's autobio, Chesterton's essays and science fiction with enjoyment and some boredom . . . Chesterton can be damn good despite his omnipresent Catholicism—

Must get this into mail—

with affection,
Al

To George Galt (Napanee, Ont.), from Fort Pierce, Fla., December 20, 1983

Dear George,

I had already written you at the Napanee address, since I didn't have the Toronto one.

I read *at* one of the Ritchie[1] books, he seeming a little unusual for a diplomat. Re masks, I would rather say that the actual person wears the mask much of the time (not always) and that the writing is closer to the actual man. Second chance and thoughts yes, but sometimes liable to be more accurate and true than the original whatever-it-was. I do like that expression: *les mots escalier* (the French have so many shining little expressions like that) (and I can't even remember most of them, the one about being here before for example) . . .

Yeah, the *Oxford Companion*—pinned like dead butterflies or dung beetles. Reputations, of course. Not in the same sense as, for example, Aubrey's *Brief Lives*[2] (which I am reading), which actually does bring the subjects to life, but rather makes them dead, removing blood from bodies. I had an interesting (to me) thought the other day: the way I regard people younger than me. Here they are, going through all the stages I've already gone through, while I am entering and experiencing a still further stage. It's as if nobody is really ever mature, since there's always something to be added on which will alter the total. My experience is slower and more intensive than it ever was (or so it seems to me); I seem to myself to be much more thoughtful and insightful than previously, altho the bodily functions are less reliable. I see things from a long perspective and in relation to what has already happened. The same thing, of course, happens or ought to happen to everyone, with the difference depending on the number of stages of experience one has gone through. Not superior, I hasten to add; but more amusing as one draws back a little, doesn't care as much for the same things as previously, and just possibly is able to judge and consider a little more accurately. (déjà vu, I meant above) The object and aim of all our thinking and feeling, of course, is to particularize and seize on what we think is important (and I'd cite my Voltaire poem for that).

Landlord problems. Always some damn thing.

John Martin of Black Sparrow sent me 120 more sheets for the hardcover Buk/Purdy letters to sign. Seems Peter Brown has had so many orders he's increased the printing—twice, according to Martin. When I sent them back, I suggested to Martin that he write Brown before sending the sheets, to the effect that I'd had a stroke and Eurithe was nursing me assiduously (as she does anyway), and all I could manage was a feeble X. Gallows humor, and I doubt if Martin does write to that effect.

Re Fort Pierce, we'd love to have you here (bed board booze). Be warned however, the place is deadly dull, and that great events consist of washing the dishes. And garbage pickup was late or early. Christmas party of the Canadians here exemplifies: migawd, are people really like that? Clichés assuming solid material form before my eyes! To grow ancient and brainless at the same time!

Hope you are not the same,

Al

1. Charles Ritchie (1906–95): Canadian diplomat (Ambassador to West Germany and to the United States). After his retirement, Ritchie published several volumes of his diaries. *The Siren Years: A Canadian Diplomat Abroad 1937–45* (1974) won a Governor General's Award.

2. John Aubrey (1626–97): an original member of the Royal Society and an early archaeologist / antiquarian, he is now remembered chiefly for his informal and anecdotal *Brief Lives,* which were first published in 1813.

To Susan Musgrave (Victoria, BC), from Ameliasburgh, April 13, 1984

Dear Susan,

"Receive an embrace from an old and cautious correspondent" is just as bad—or good—as my own salutation. "With cordial greetings" was on accounta I thought you might be too snooty to wanta hear from me at all. Had heard you married into high society and spoke only to the upper classes.

Dear "cautious" correspondent, I love you I love you I love you— please receive an embrace with cordial greetings?

Or how about me bein pleased to hear you're still there and still speak to five-years-back strangers? Warm stuff and all that? Okay? You wanta fine it down to the last decimal point? Pleasure I'm sure.

I didn't know where you were until George Johnston mentioned you were at Waterloo and residencing. I thought you must be divorced by now and married Joe Rosenblatt or someone . . .

Your adventures re money and car sound far too complicated for me to comment about; I just hope you get out of em relatively unscathed and get your car back. Your life is a wild adventure tho; those scary movies you shuddered from in Toronto are pallid by comparison. However, leave me leave your troubles where they are, and let's be more cheerful???

Which is to say, the publisher of those letters [*The Bukowski/Purdy Letters 1964–1974*] fucked me up by leaving in the book a passage I had blacked out from the proofs. So I'm now tip-toeing around the house saying "Shhhh—" to the mice, hoping they won't mention that passage to E. I also had other disagreements with that publisher. He lies to me, or at least he did. Said proofs were sent for a US Selected, to me in Florida, two sets were sent since the first set never arrived. Neither did the second. So I mentioned to him non-sarcastically, "There must be two sets of proofs floating around somewhere in the US mails, eh?" He had difficulty with that one. However, I didn't wanta be too hard on him his wife bein with him at my place where he came to see if things could be patched up. They couldn't. I said no. Next day, Sunday, he phoned me in a kinda weepy voice saying, "I'm sorry, I'm sorry—" I couldn't for god's sake think what to say to him, wantin to get off the phone quick, and finally muttered, "Not at all, not at all," like a goddam Englishman. And hung up. He didn't phone back, thank christ.

By the way, you're welcome to anything you can steal from me, which means of course that it isn't stealing, you can't steal. What about that?

Will send you the Buk/Purdy thing (which I'm tryin to keep secret for aforementioned reasons), when I get an envelope I can recycle to you. No big envelopes. It's not much of a thing tho. I said okay when Peter Brown at Paget (same guy who's "sorry") came up with the idea, as a tossed off thing; I mean I thought it might sell some other books, and I didn't like sayin no to him at the time. I take some joy in sayin no to him now. Anyway, I admired Buk at the time, and still do, altho we've gone different roads. I wish him well on his.

Don't rejoin the League [of Canadian Poets]. Fucked up outfit. Even I, the joiner of all things, had to quit. Much more dramatic to sit in outer darkness and watch them perform without you. I was involved in the start of the league, along with Souster, Birney, Colombo and others. Which was the only reason I stayed so long. The bad poets with bureaucratic tendencies generally get to be recording secretaries on accounta they can't get attention any other way. Fuck em all. What say you from the far reaches of nowhere? [. . .]

How shall I end this? Shall I just say "love" in quotes? Or without quotes? Caps? Italics? Hibernating affection? Lubricious remembrance? (I gotta stop this—it's too hard on my non-inventive faculties.)

Just love then,

Al

To Susan Musgrave (Waterloo, Ont.), from Ameliasburgh, June 22, 1984

Dear Susan,

I'd hoped to see you at that reading in Vic; but there you were, bargaining with gangsters, being a gun-moll and dangerous woman.[1] Do you favour the shoulder holster or a discreet shiv at top of stockings? And there I was, hoping for a gentle smile . . .

Does Paul do all that four years and no parole at any point? Have you thought of writing your memoirs at the early age of 33, or making fiction into truth? Dylan always seemed to me a silly bugger (Bob, that is) . . .

Question, does one want this sense of being all-powerful, which probably comes from killing people too, a pipeline from the immense filtered into the personal feelings . . .

Time at a premium when you hit 33? Come on Susan, that's ahh well, hum—bullshit. You're a young gal, growing younger by the minute while I age rapidly into senescence. No shit either, you always did strike me that way. Comes from avoiding Dostoyevsky and the Greek dramatists.

The line from Camus is hilarious. The kid knew where to hit his old man. Which indicates Camus had a high opinion of himself.

No, I haven't run into the Purdy for Prez bit except by implication in print. It's the sort of thing all writers need occasionally tho, since we are personally surrounded by an enormous silence and a roaring in the ears. But it's not a four minute mile or boxing knockout; then it would be simple. I'm reminded of Layton's line: "Each on the lookout for his admirers" or "their admirers" or whatever. Which is true as far as it goes, but some of your admirers can be unbearable. More likely we look for someone from whom we receive a psychic kick in the guts, as you perhaps do from your gangster.

Re reading—two years back I put my fee up to $500 (after which I became very lonely) to cut down on wear and tear to adenoids. I'd love to read but my goddam fee gets in the way. One can't go up and down yo-yo fashion, can one? (Only in fucking.) Birney kept tellin me I should, and I said no my public needs me thinking of my three faithful listeners at every reading . . . But fuck the reading. I'd like to lift a glass with you at Austerlitz—uh, Waterloo?—well somewhere.[2] Anyway, can they come up with some more money so I won't have to feel I'm cheating anybody—?

We just came back from Spain, fairly boring, at least Torremolinos was. But rented a car and drove to Cervantes country, but of course no trace of him except a few old churches we didn't enter . . . Time scrapes everything away . . . Expected but still disconcerting. Great thing about Spain was flowers by the road, which bare statement says nothing. But they were a wedding gown for the earth, and it was like driving between two comet tails. Red poppies, most of them, staining fields and roads and everywhere, even the crops. Others too, and I knew the names of scarcely any.

And then the trip back took some 13 hours, we fall into an expensive hotel in Toronto, then drive here, and I catch some kinda bug, a cross between flu and cold. Jesus and his child if any! [. . .]

                    With love anyhow,
                    Al

1. Musgrave's second husband was a drug dealer, her third a convicted bank robber whom she had met through a correspondence writing course and married in a maximum-security prison.
2. Musgrave was writer in residence at the University of Waterloo.
3. AP is echoing the last line of Richard Lovelace's (1618–58) "To Lucasta, Going to the Wars": "I could not love thee, dear, so much, / Loved I not honour more."

To Milton Acorn, from Ameliasburgh, June 23, 1984

Dear Milton,
Pleasant to hear from you.

Not much I can say about your mother, except to take the conventional attitude that when anyone suffers the way she did it may be best for them to leave. That's easy for me to say, since I didn't know her. Nevertheless, can I extend sympathy to you without seeming mawkish.

I presume the R you're talking about re anti-life is Rosenblatt. Must admit that even when he was writing about people way back then, I didn't think he was any roaring hell. And I can't get his insects etc. at all. But I'm a little surprised he was able to take them as far as he did, even to getting the GG for his stuff. Still, Joe is appealing personally, even tho I never see him any more. He's again the prez of Poets' League, and I dislike bureaucrats both on principle and personally. Another friend, Janet Lunn, is prez of Writer's Union this coming year. She and some friends were here, and another woman called Janet "head honcho" which made me wanta throw up. How do I get to know so many goddam bureaucrats?

I will not get into an argument with you about abortion. Both you and I should know better than to talk about it, even hint it, mention it or even think it within miles of each other. Okay—spit if you hear me from two thousand miles away and I'll hear you.

Re Khrushchev, I assume you don't believe his statements about Stalin??[1]And that the latter was not such a monster as painted?

I've forgotten most of those long conversations with you re poems and poetry, and let "House Guest" stand for both of us. I did have to tear down and level the cross pieces in the big room after you left, and have been libelling you ever since for a lousy carpenter. At least out of practise? However, poetry is not abstraction to me; but I admit, I was a pretty bad poet at the time of those long arguments. I hope I've improved since. I did learn a great deal from you, which I've never been slow to admit. [. . .]

Eurithe and I just returned from Spain. Too damn many people. Still, we rented a car and drove north from Torremolinos to Cervantes country.

Of course nearly 500 years have razored off all trace of him, except a few old churches he must have known. Even Quixote's windmills are erected and maintained for the tourists' benefit. And I threw my knee out walking, all swollen, so I'm still limping around.

Okay, take care of yourself.

All the best,

Al

1. Addressing a secret midnight session of the Twentieth Congress of the Communist Party in February 1956, from which foreigners were excluded, Khrushchev denounced Stalin's "cult of personality" and discussed openly the crimes of the Stalin era in which he and many others in the Soviet leadership had participated. The speech was leaked and sent shock waves through the communist parties of Europe, some of which, like the French, continued to deny the revelations into the 1970s. William Taubman gives a full account in *Khrushchev: The Man and His Era* (2003).

To Earle Birney (Toronto), from Ameliasburgh, July 10, 1984

Dear Earle,

Thank you much for the sheaf of stuff and poems. I have so many comments and thoughts about it, I'd probably bore the shit outa you if I say it all. (Which I won't) [...]

The new poem is also fine. You're having a renaissance of some kind. I'm sure you know that the cry you heard joins with your own and Wailan's "wanton cries"—But the fear of the cry contrasts strongly with the cries of love and passion. The poem all fits together well, language and incident warm into the cold "brief day."

I always thought that Reaney disliked me too. He's such an odd little bugger and difficult to read—his character I mean, and his seemingly deliberately odd poems too. But I don't think he's a liar, and when he says you gave him the feeling of being able to write about mosquitoes and poker, it has to be truth. Which makes me wanta write a poem about Birney making me able to write poems about all the Birney-mosquitoes and Birney-royal grand-flushes atop Mt. Assiniboine that I almost stop this letter and do it—(just wait)—

"Ellesmereland" has become, in totality, both a moving and chilling poem, and "Case History." What is a "decapodal turkey"? Sends me to the dictionary. Of course, ten-footed provinces. Yes, Uncle has the cutlery.

I'm still annoyed at you making "Mappemounde" so all-inclusive with *all* as I remember. "it hems heart's landtrace" was enough (I had to go back to the poem to quote that). Reminds me of Auden knocking out some of his best passages in his Yeats poem, about Kipling being pardoned by this strange excuse. What was it? "Time what with this strange excuse / Pardons Kipling and his views / And will pardon Paul Claudel / Pardons him for writing well."[1] You're gettin me all literary like. Your own sin was much less flagrant. I was annoyed because I loved/love that poem.

I don't know this Brown[2] guy at McStew. Dennis Lee says he's good of course. I somehow feel that a younger generation is fucking me up with strangers in the metrics. But I give the conventional thought, he must be good or else—Or else what? Of course of course. "Send me your credentials, Mr. Brown."

What was Keats' line, about the oncoming generations which "tread me down"[3]? Or like that.

You wanta echo Housman with "Last Pomes"[4]? The romantic view being that they don't end (and I don't mean Frye), that little trickles of jagged music whisper around gravestones.

I kept lookin for Cervantes' ghost in Spain, but all I saw was Quixote iron-cut-outs pluggin hamburgers. But the flowers, migawd the flowers, roadside red poppies like sunken flags of the Armada.

I have a book myself this fall which, perhaps wrongly, I think my best,[5] and probably also my "last pomes"—

Whyn't you come down here with Wailan and we'll toast Wassail, you in tiffin tea and me in beer? Eurithe has fixed up a room with queen-size bed beneath the garage, and a single bed in my work room. We now have a Belleville cop livin next to us replacing LaGuff. Gives one such a sense of insecurity, when he said he leaves his lights on all night and if I hear a gunshot not to worry, just some revengeful con that he's sent down.

I copy the only poem in the last few weeks below.

ON THE PLANET EARTH

She was lovely as sunrise
meeting sunset at the world's edge
without a chaperone and blushing
I mentioned this to her
mentioned also the Jungian theory
of the unconscious
I said
"All your life there will be

visitors in your mind
you don't know about
and I am there too
when for no apparent
reason you blush
that's me kid—"

                                   love to both of you,
                                   Al

1. AP quotes from the suppressed final stanzas of Auden's "In Memory of W.B. Yeats."
2. Russell Brown, a professor of English at the University of Toronto, took over from Dennis Lee as poetry editor at McClelland and Stewart.
3. From Keats's "Ode to a Nightingale": "Thou wast not born for death, immortal Bird! / No hungry generations tread thee down."
4. In 1922 Housman published *Last Poems*, a collection of 41 lyrics. Though he lived until 1936, the only further volume of poetry he published was *Praefanda*, a collection of "bawdy and obscene passages from Latin authors," and it was brought out in Germany. AP considered *Last Poems* as a possible title for his last book (*To Paris Never Again*), but decided against it because it had been the title of the last books of three of his favourite poets (Housman, Yeats and Lawrence).
5. On his copy of the letter, Birney wrote "It *is* his best! A *great* book!"

To George Woodcock (Vancouver), from Ameliasburgh, October 9, 1984

Dear George,
On the subject of Earle: he's always been so kind and considerate to me in the past that the stories I hear about him sometimes seem rather unbelievable. And then, when I have a few drinks—or quite a few—I say and do things sometimes that also seem unbelievable in sober retrospect. In fact this happened to me recently in Halifax. (I just came back from four readings.) And yes, Earle is getting more likeable the older he gets. (Is this also happening to us?) And I am also pleased that he seems to have found his own peace with Wailan. Which reminds me: when I first knew her, Earle was calling her Lily, which is her name. But Earle must've made her ethnically selfconscious, so now she's Wailan Low, which is properly and orientally mysterious.

Migawd, how could I get in on all this cash you're getting? I feel churchmousy by comparison. People keep rejecting my own prose. However, I get dribs and drabs here and there. I'm not really envious, just a little jealous. What's the difference? I'm not sure, but I think you can confess the latter.

I doubt like hell if McStew could get a proof to you before you leave (of my new book).[1] And I've pushed them so hard over details, such as remainders, terms of contract, efforts on their part to get a foreign publisher (which they didn't) etc., that I doubt if they'd go out of their way to do anything for me. For instance, never in all the twenty years I've been publishing with McStew have they arranged a grant for me from Ont. Arts Council—and these are handed out every year. So this year I write and ask if I'm blacklisted, and equally strong terms. So I get a thousand bucks this year. But I'm still annoyed with them. Maybe it pays to be cantankerous: may I recommend it to you?

This Giraud book sounds awesome, one thousand pages. And yes, I stand by that: one should do the really important things as one grows older. In good health, 72 ain't so old tho.

Yeah, Stendhal's Lottery[2]—and the last word oughta be in caps. I just had quite an argument with Fraser Sutherland, me holding that if a writer has real ability that said ability will reveal itself sooner or later and can't be indefinitely concealed. Unless, of course, an accident happens, the writer's stuff gets burnt or destroyed by a moral relative. Fraser claims—with himself in mind, of course—that a good writer can remain undiscovered. It seems to me that we find our own level in our own lifetimes. I am, for instance, relatively unknown outside Canada. I think it's likely to remain that way. You have an international audience, of readers I mean; and I think that condition will hold for many years. Poetry's something else tho; it's bloody mysterious how readers receive some of us.

Incidentally, good to receive some praise from such sources. Even had a card from Layton in Italy telling me I stink and then saying I'm pretty good after all. I do believe myself that the new book carries the differences of the previous *Stone Bird* much farther, and is a much more personally objective book if one can use that phrase.

Al

---

1. *Piling Blood.*
2. Stendhal predicted that his novels, though unpopular with his contemporaries, would find an audience in the next century.

To Fraser Sutherland (Toronto), from Ameliasburgh, October 10, 1984

Dear Fraser,

Can I talk to both of you, both you and Alison I mean?

On accounta I have to reply to both your letters. First, thank you both much for going to so much trouble, and for having such a good opinion of my stuff, Fraser. And yeah, Alison, let's have an argument—no, a discussion. (I have a sore index finger, which hurts my typing by 50%.) (Hafta use middle finger instead.)

Still on the "do great poems/prose survive, if not burned by moral relatives or jealous friends"? You've both got me so unsure of myself I feel like outright surrender. But it depends on fashion, doesn't it? Largely. I mean if some piece of writing or poem or whatever is suddenly popular. Given some intelligence to the writing in the first place, decent grammar or indecent. But I feel suddenly futile even talking about it.

Okay, take myself. I see myself as someone whose ability has taken him as far as he's likely to go. I am more or less unknown outside the borders of my own country. Deservedly so? I must think so if I stick to my original proposition. But I have the added satisfaction of getting you to argue that I'm a genius, an unknown genius, if you stick to *your* original proposition. So I can't lose either way, can I? Well, can I?

Still, must admit I'm a bit sick of it, in the absence of flesh and blood opposition and mere paper at hand.

Fraser, the poem, my poem, "The Dead Poet."[1] I think you've misread a vital part of it. (And remember, I'm a goddam Ontario Scot—momma's name Ross—and I like sniping too.) There's no pantheism connected with poem at all. It's about a brother who was born and died before my arrival. Keep to the brother. He, and he alone, is the spirit of earth. Is that not permissible in your pantheon, to speak of a dead brother, long buried in earth, as a spirit of earth? The words came from him, the dead brother. Or so I imagine in the poem. And in some mysterious sense, that small whisper of birds nesting and green things growing is his, the brother's own resurrection. Not a religious one, but still a going on and on. Alison, you see what I mean? Leave Fraser outa this. He's bein deliberately obtuse. (Incidentally, Bill Percy said Fraser is the best thing that's happened to *Books in Canada*: thot a wife might like to hear that.)[2] (Myself, I'm not so sure. He gets more reviews by Purdy the mag will fold sure as hell.) Okay, Alison, you see what I mean re the dead brother? You Fraser, a bit behind Alison, on accounta women are more quick witted than us slow ponderous males.

Far be it from me to discuss the poems of a guy who's gonna be book reviewer with the *Globe*. It scares the shit outa me to even be talkin to/with him. Still: I was very interested in them. And cautiously I try to tip-toe around—which is not at all my nature—without expressing an opinion that would leave me vulnerable to an exalted reviewer of the Toronto *Globe and Mail*. I like em. Especially interested in "Imaginary Folksong." Do you know Graves' "Counting the Beats," Fraser? I thought you would vary that refrain—sort of refrain—before the end. And I have a memory of you doing something on Bethune before? In those poets' league pamphlets? Your meat of course, argumentative Scot! It is a kind of lyric—"Folksong"—that I like much. ("Let me not be him.")

Back to my favourite subject, me. Had a card from Layton in Italy, he having just read the *Buk/Purdy Letters* and *MAIS* [*Morning and It's Summer*]. Castigated me for sayin he was washed up in 1965 (if I actually said that), and flattered me for *MAIS* (for which brief cognomen of the book, I thank you), which kinda shook me. Especially after the epithets first, and real strong ones, then addressing me as friend and compliment-ing me. Oh well. Who knows Layton, including Layton!

As for my sartorial style deteriorating—well, you should bloody well talk! I leave it at that. Enough said. Get the point, I hope.

Okay, back to your comment about the ultimate repository of good being the natural world—with which you disagree. Sire. So do I disagree. The comment is a long way from my poem, however. I grant you the Bomb, if you really want it. But as you say, too cheap a crack.

Will you not grant me some emotion in thinking of a dead brother, even if I didn't know him personally? And yet somehow, mystically even if you hate the word, did know him personally. Is emotion only for the liv-ing? He died; he was nevertheless my own flesh and blood; I do feel some-thing, I tried to express it.

In a way, the poem is a sort of lullaby for and to someone who can't hear it and will never know. But I know. And I bequeath that knowledge. To whom? To anyone who will accept it. How about you, Alison? Fraser?

Contemplate nature and stop, which is a lazy excuse for not thinking about God? It seems to me your metaphysical gears are stripped, Fraser? Surely a dead brother addressed in spirit is as real as a humanly invented God? You apparently believe in God, but not the possibility of a brother being a spirit of earth in my mind, as the way I think of him in the poem. Here I say, the concept of a god is fascinating, and the whole history of mankind is filled with references to this non-being. We no longer believe that humanity is a kindly and gentle race raised on milk and loving kindness. But we still—some of us—still believe in the deity trailing clouds of glory thru the universe. And claim that goodness in humanity is impossible without an upper case Him?

As mentioned on phone, hope to see you Fraser for lunch in Toronto, say Nov. 5? With Alison, so we can thrash out the nature of deity, which would undoubtedly bore all of us back to the primordial cave.

My index finger won't index.

Best to both of you,
Al

1. "The Dead Poet" was published in *The Stone Bird*. On September 30, Sutherland had written the following about the poem: "I'm thinking especially of 'The Dead Poet,' which, I hasten to say, is a wonderful wonderful piece of work . . . But when you write: 'Speak softly spirit of earth' . . . It strikes me as a sort of half-baked pantheism. I've never found this implicit idea of a natural religion very convincing whether it's D.H. Lawrence's vision of heaven (a field of waving grass, and maybe a rabbit sitting up) or what we find in Margaret Laurence's novels . . ."
2. Sutherland had become managing editor at *Books in Canada*.

To Irving Layton (Montreal), from Ameliasburgh, October 29, 1984

Dear Irving,
I have your card from Italy. The mixture of invective and praise makes me think of my own opinions of you.

I have always—but especially in the last few years—thought you to be too full of shit to be quite human, else it would come out your mouth and pores, as it does sometimes. You are also a thing I especially dislike in another human being, perhaps because there are hints of it in myself, but only hints: a braggart and blowhard. An old man growing older ungracefully.

However, and I suppose it's a big however: you have also been in the past, but very little in the present, an exceedingly fine poet. I also owe you something personally, for simply being there in Montreal at a time when I needed something like you, a fresh fart (now an old fart) blowing through the so-called culture of Montreal. You were a euphoric shock to me then, and you're a shock of another kind now.

In addition—God help me if there is one—I have always liked you, which I regard as one of my most severe shortcomings in judging human nature. But it is a genuine liking, and does not rest on any opinion of your poems. I think there is a generosity about you, perhaps stemming from the fact that you have had sufficient praise in your life to inflate your ego most intolerably. Nevertheless, generosity in another person is most attractive, and on cloudy nights may even begin to rival truth in attractiveness.

As for your poems, I think they were once marvellous. They are not so any longer. But to me, a poet's reputation and worth does not rest entirely in the present: he is like an iceberg and his worth is 90% obscured and sunken in the past, and the 10% shit of now regrettably visible. Which means, I am happy to say (wallowing in my own generosity), that I think you are still marvellous.

Your friend,
Al

To George Johnston (Athelstan, Que.), from Ameliasburgh, November 21, 1984

Dear George,
I'm so interested—and somewhat bemused—by your opinions about Souster that I have to comment.

It may well be that Souster's voice is anonymous, since he is the complete humanist, always has the right thoughts to fit the liberal definition. You know what those are, anti-bigot, Christmas is commercial but okay for kids, just slightly nationalistic and against US State Dept., against empires, sides with animals against humans, etc., etc. You can name off many more.

And the above are entirely conventional attributes, shared by a great many Canadians. And there isn't a smidgen of originality in the whole lot. He forsakes personality and becomes everyman. Not Whitman's Everyman, which was carried so far in Whitman that it became grotesque.

I can't recall in all my past reading of Souster—and my reading of him is long past—any trace of original thought or a glimmering of even slightly unusual intelligence. Mind you, I do not hold that poets must be highly intelligent or intellectuals (such as one George Johnston), but a modicum adds necessary spice. Souster to me is a slightly superior Edgar Guest.

This may be insulting to you, since you've devoted much thought to the subject on the premise that Souster is an excellent poet. He probably *is* an excellent poet, if your mind turns that way. Your comment about my "seeds drifting away from home" as being too much—as it may well be—applies far more to Souster to my way of thinking: whole Souster poems are both soppily sentimental and completely inconsequential. Many of them are trivia elevated to an artificial importance from being labelled "poem"—"If your mind turns that way," I said above. I mean the judgment of any work of art is mostly subjective, perhaps slightly influenced by the climate of opinion about any particular person and their work.

Souster's reputation is down, I believe, and also believe deservedly. He has no intellectual curiosity beyond what comes to him in the daily newspapers, which newspapers are one of the main sources of his poems. I could not conceive of him reading, say E.M. Forster; Hemingway yes; Proust no. About a poet like Robert Bringhurst, whom I regard as a true intellectual and much beyond me at times: about Bringhurst's excellence, he would have to take someone else's word for it. As he would for many other poets. And if you regard this as a snobbish opinion of Souster, then I think you are missing the point or points. Souster to me is the lowest common denominator you can reach and still be a fairly good—or in your opinion, excellent—poet. *These opinions, incidentally, are confidential.* I would not wish to hurt Souster in any way. He is quite admirable as a humanist and barometer of humanist opinion—But as a poet he is absolutely boring.

I have a Bishop *Complete Poems*, but a Sixth Printing, 1978. It does not contain any of the three Bishop poems you mention. She must've published a later book, or a Last Poems.[1]

"In lyric poetry it is the voice of the poem itself that one hears." Yes, I agree. I've been reading some John Clare, William Barnes and Graves' "Counting the Beats" in a C. Day Lewis book about the lyric.[2] One may feel that these writers write different kinds of lyrics—as they do—but natheless, it is the poem and not the poet. I tried to write some myself, but didn't like them. I can immediately hear you say Aha, he can't get rid of his own voice.

Al

1. Elizabeth Bishop (1911–79): major American poet (*North and South*, 1946; *Complete Poems 1927–79*). The last individual collection published during Bishop's life was *Geography III* (1976).
2. John Clare (1793–1864): English Romantic poet best known for his poems on rural themes (*The Village Minstrel*, 1821; *The Rural Muse*, 1835). He spent the last three decades of his life in the Northumberland General Asylum. AP wrote about him in "I Think of John Clare" (*The Woman on the Shore*). William Barnes

(1801–86): Dorset poet (*Poems of Rural Life in the Dorset Dialect*, 1844; *Poems of Rural Life*, 1868). C. Day-Lewis's book on poetry is *The Poetic Image* (1947) based on his Clark Lectures at Cambridge.

To George Galt (Toronto), from Fort Pierce, Fla., December 21, 1984

Dear George,

I can't think of anything I'd rather do than do the things you're doing at your age. The frantic quality about it would suit me fine, since I've always had the illusion—possibly—that I wrote better under such tension. I mean prose, of course. There's a joyfulness about it, the feeling of being at your best and still improving. Incidentally, how come you never sent along that train piece you did for *Sat Nite*?[1] Ron Everson mentioned it's out, but his copy back in Mtl.

The two most important things to me about the pot pourri book are that you want to do it, as apart from friendship or keeping busy; and that you think the stuff is interesting and worthwhile, as apart from any imagined status of the pot pourri author.[2] Not the date. So if it takes until 1986, fine—so long as you can say yes to the two criteria above.

Must admit, I'm a bit amazed the Woodcock–Purdy correspondence can be interesting. Woodcock is an industry and admirable; but I've never thought of him as especially interesting in his letters. And I shouldn't be a judge as to whether I am.[3]

I had an exchange of letters with Fraser Sutherland a coupla mos back, about his poems and mine that I thought was rather good. I defended the "mysticism" of "The Dead Poet" to him, I thought effectively. He gave an estimate of me that I thought a little surprising. He said that if you searched world poetry you could find the equivalents of Birney, Layton, Atwood, etc., not exactly like those poets but close. Whereas in my own case, Sutherland said I was *sui generis*—which I had to look up as "another breed" and felt suitably flattered. [. . .]

The Wine Book—decided it was too much trouble, and I wasn't interested, despite the undoubted money involved. And that's the same trouble I'm having writing about CanPo[4]: seems a lotta bother unless I can evolve some new opinions and thoughts while writing. And I don't wanta stick with CanPo only, but go into poetry I like, an appreciation of the stuff in my view. And that, me son, is a helluva lotta work. [. . .]

In the sheet sent along with the P-P stuff was mention of possible other inclusions. There were a couple pieces in *Weekend* that didn't get into *NOC*, one on wine that I liked. And a couple of rejections, but those are with the PP stuff I sent you.

No, I didn't realize just how much stuff is at U of Sask. I'm still sore at the librarian there even tho I can't remember his name now, the guy responsible for me going to Queen's afterwards. You may recall or no: I said of a sale to him that I hoped he was satisfied (the sale being consummated by then, and money paid to me), and he said he thought it slightly high (my price). This went on and on until the damn thing was re-negotiated and I had the feeling of being pressured and cheated.

Oh well—

On *Piling Blood* and comparing it to other books. I think *Wild Grape Wine* is the best of other books. But you take the secondary poems of it and compare them with the secondary poems of *Piling Blood* and the advantage is all with the latter. Assuming that the best poems from both books are about equal in merit— [...]

Just occurred to me I could include personal and unprintable anecdotes about Birney, especially, and others in the CanPo piece, which would make it much more interesting to and for me. And some of Birney's own stories about Bliss Carman and Roberts are very good. And he himself is (he himself?) is so prickly and bright that he's better than any character in his writings.

We drove up to Orlando Tuesday (three days ago), stayed overnight in a motel for $21, hunted for books in thrift shops—A few, but the trip was as much an outing as a book search. Altho I have 8 or 9 booze boxes full already as will hafta rent an elephant as return transport north. The car, incidentally, is great. Extremely comfortable, 25 miles per US gallon on highway, air conditioning, etc. Cruises like a dream, on something called "Cruise Control" which you set at proper speed you want, and this is maintained with your foot off the accelerator pedal. And it's almost noiseless inside. Did use a quart of oil, which I'm told is because of rings settling in in a new car.

The area here is just as boring as before. Neither Eurithe nor I are interested in group activities in "park"—bridge and shuffleboard etc.

Did you say that you'd fucked a 43-year-old woman to consider her orgasm(s)?

Eurithe says hi.

Al

---

1. Galt published "Number One Westbound" in the November *Saturday Night*.
2. AP and Galt were discussing a collection of AP's uncollected prose.

3. Galt edited *The George Woodcock / Al Purdy Letters* (1987).
4. AP published two overviews of Canadian poetry, "Canadian Poetry in English Since 1967" (see the letter of September 22, 1969) and "Disconnections," which appeared in the special Purdy issue of *Essays on Canadian Writing*, No. 49 (Summer 1993). *Reaching for the Beaufort Sea*, has several sections dealing with his contemporaries.

To John Newlove (Nelson, BC), from Fort Pierce, Fla., December 25, 1984

Hey John,
Good to hear an all that shit.

Expect you got new book sent via McStew.

AA can't be more boring than this town. Just about everybody in this mobile park is older'n me, which isn't as pleasing as it oughta be. They play shuffleboard and poker and bridge and kiss each other on their porches, which is less revolting than doing it in bedrooms. But I don't play any of those things, nor kiss them. However, beer and booze is cheap and so are used books at thrift shops and the like. But I think we shall find an excursion somewhere and take off from Miami, 118 miles distant from here. [...]

I'm having a bit of difficulty retaining friends and acquaintances. One told me the other day I'd insulted the American flag and started to bawl me out. I told him to fuck off. Rolf Harvey[1] asked me if I thought his stuff was any good. I said no. Our relations have noticeably cooled. If either of us asked the other that last question, we'd know what to expect beforehand and be more cautious.

Must be a bone doc somewhere nearby Nelson? Women docs fine unless you gotta tell her about your syphilis or clap. That hasn't come up yet.

I'm not writing many poems after last push before book, in fact none. So decided to write a prose piece on CanPo, and find it difficult to stay interested. In fact shit, I'll read and write the stuff, but I don't wanta talk about it.

Anyway, since you stopped drinkin, we'll hoist pure spring water if I ever get out there? Did I say I'd upped my fee to $500? Cut down noticeably on my already dubious popularity.

All best,
(and find yourself a goddam bone
doc)
Al

1. Rolf Harvey (b. 1946): Toronto poet (*The Perfect Suicide*, 1972) and television producer.

R.G. Everson (1903–92): lawyer, public relations executive, poet. AP edited and introduced *Everson at Eighty* (1983). The last line of the introduction shows that he was writing more as a friend than as a critic: "The most important thing about him: he is singular and he is original, a poet of high excellence."

To Ron Everson (Florida), from Fort Pierce, Fla., December 30, 1984

Dear Ron,
I've been thinking about you saying you wanted to write a great poem or poems. As I've said, and as you've said (I think you have?), one can't take dead aim at great poems: one must write what one is capable of, what one wants to write.

Every time you write a poem, you're trying to make it as good and marvellous as you possibly can, without even thinking of merit or greatness at all. The poem is in some ways a reverse x-ray of yourself, your mind, what you are. How old you are, whether 81 or 181, doesn't seem to me to make a damn bit of difference. What is important, what is supremely interesting to me or can become so in the course of writing, that makes the difference. Whatever age, I mean. And I think you are lucky to have as much vitality as you appear to have, for this will allow your interest and curiosity to run its course.

Of course I can't possibly say how to write a great poem, as you must know. And these are all personal opinions. And I do not know whether I have ever written, or ever will, a great poem. In fact, I do not know what a great poem is. I am trying to say how not to prevent yourself from writing a great poem. I think that's clear, at least it seems so to me.

Layton once said something to the effect: from now on I'm going to write nothing but great poems. As you would probably guess, I think such a statement is completely ridiculous.

I would think also that mentioning to me that you want to write great poems, with the implication that I have myself done so, or else that I can tell you how—I would think this would cause you to dislike me. I am not a wise man of the east—or west as the case may be. I am personally so ignorant that I have no opinions about a great many things. About a very few things, I do have strong opinions.

Anyway—forgive me if you can.

Al

To Fraser Sutherland (Toronto), from Fort Pierce, Fla., January 20, 1985

Dear Fraser,

I hope I'm not taking time from your work or poems. I feel a bit cut off here. For that reason and others your missives are welcome.

Re the Gus reviews: your lack of enthusiasm for Gus comes through. Suppose I feel much the same about Gus. One says he's worthy and admirable, but adds under one's breath, he's so goddam dull. [. . .]

He uses a kind of shorthand that two people who know each other's habits very well might use. And he is worthy. By merely saying it about him, it makes the speaker (me) seem like a snob. Which of course I am.

I'm a bit flummoxed by G. Galt doing the Woodcock/Purdy correspondence. My memory of the letters is that they are dull. No, not Woodcock as a game bird. Nor are my own opinions of Woodcock's included in the letters. I mean, not all of them. The conventional ones yes, GW as a valuable figure in CanLit, as a phenomena as well, which he certainly is, a bit worthy like Gus as well. Personal feelings, yes, some fondness for him. But the correspondence, to me, never reached the intimate, was always at a distance. That wouldn't prevent interest tho. And GW always seemed to me to be of the generation immediately before mine, more like a respected uncle. But what the hell, if G. Galt thinks there's a book, why the hell not . . .

Your comment re Powe,[1] "An honest critic at last," implies the others are not honest. If you agree with his opinions, he's honest. If you don't, then he's sensation-mongering? Re Powe, I disagree with his apparent thesis that literature should provide us with "strategies for living"—which I think is ridiculous. And think Layton's early poetry was "ringing," not his late stuff. Yes, Cohen is nihilistic, but is so good at times that his nihilism doesn't matter. I more or less agree with Powe about M. Laurence. Powe may be right in saying that Atwood provides "not how to live" but "how to act"—which to me makes her books about the mores of the society in which she lives. I don't believe at all that the writer should tell the reader how to live. Or how to act, other than as a depiction in the writing. Powe would have us believe that writing is a religion, with the answers to

life included if you send two books or twenty (since books have gone up).
I think perhaps the worst fault I could find with Atwood's novels is that I
think they're written to some kind of formula, a fashionable formula, as it
turns out. Only *Surfacing* was not. Well, anyway . . .

Prose pieces on poets, up to now, including Atwood, Layton, Birney,
Laurence, Glassco, and Avison, with some personal impressions and incidents. I suppose related to the "Poets in Montreal" tho. But it's also a general piece, in the beginning, on CanPo, and will need a lot of revision. I'm
some ten thousand words to now. I don't find it easy, and Powe's opinions
(in the review) were handy to push against. But there's no hurry with it,
and I'm just jogging along. And thanks for *The Idler*, which has a BBC
sound to title, and *New Statesman* ring. I suppose deliberate. Johnsonian
connection too, from your comments.

Al

1. B.W. Powe (b. 1955): novelist, journalist and essayist (*The Solitary Outlaw*,
1987).

Brian Purdy (b. 1948): AP's son, has published *To Feed the Sun*
(1976) and *Interloper* (1977).

To Brian Purdy, from Ameliasburgh, June 29, 1985

Dear Brian,
I think you gave up on the novel, *Malevil*,[1] long before page 100 and
therefore missed a great deal.

I am reading it for the second time with equal or more enjoyment
than the first. I hate to see you give up a book I think so rewarding.

The first hundred pages are Emmanuel and his friends, their associations together, Emmanuel's leadership as a child, his mother (much like
your grandmother) and father, his uncle, etc. It ends when he is age 40,
and the bomb falls.

Few at first survive. A dozen or so within Malevil castle, and the society in political terms might be called "primitive agrarian communism."
But that is forbidding, and the story is not. It is told in the first person by
Emmanuel, full of conflict, all sorts of difficulties, sex, and a small war
with a neighbouring tribe which wants to invade. Through all this one
sees Emmanuel developing as a leader and as a person.

One grows to like this Emmanuel, identify with him of course. He leads his regressed "tribe" within Malevil castle, and a form of religion seems necessary to the tribe as a kind of soul. While it is, of course, primitive and regressed, the tribe is not really a tribe but a group of survivors with both emotional and practical connections.

The book is nearly 600 pages, and the ending is surprising; at least it was to me. I will not describe this ending, since you might yet read the book. I don't say it is a "masterpiece" or any such exaggeration: nevertheless, a highly interesting book for my money.

I expect you got my book listing. Any comments?

Al

1. A novel by Robert Merle, published in 1972.

To Dennis Lee (Toronto), from Fort Pierce, Fla., February 5, 1985

Dear Dennis,

I thought I had written you a coupla mos back, and here I am patiently waiting for a reply. But investigation of letters reveals that I likely ain't—written you, that is.

I hope you are moved at this demonstration of patient devotion on my part.

How are you? The state of your health is referred to and requested, as well as all sexual activities which refers back to health. Lit activities may be listed in a separate column.

In short, how are you?

I am grousing not-so-quietly to myself and others that I'm not writing much. Just one poem here that I like at all, which is slim pickins. (So what else is new?) Also some prose autobio-cum-criticism, which I'm not crazy about either. And the weather is a soporific, apart from one cold spell that didn't last. Soothing syrup poured over you, which makes me wanta bite the sun. I'd like to get a reading in Toronto, and that would teach me to grumble! I suppose, basically, what annoys me is the feeling that some kinda electric current that flows thru one in unguarded moments has been diverted to the next generation.

Which reminds me of a card I just got from Layton, who said my "theatrical growling, play-acting, beer-swilling" are bad, then complimented me in order to balance the criticism. I replied that since my mentor and exemplar had always been one Irving Layton I hope and think he oughta be satisfied with the result. Always been difficult to talk to Layton except in a position of profound obeissance.

Just heard Frank Scott died, which stops me in my tracks. He was personally kind to me at various times, and I liked him as much as not-quite-friends allows—or more than liked him. Not in connection with his "position" in lit or politics at all; perhaps as someone who felt in the heart-mind for other people more than he could say in words. I'm in quagmire now, trying to say explicitly what can't be explicit . . . And I don't want to settle for affection alone, which is a cliché and really says lit-tle. Maybe not tho. Just that his absence is as noticeable as a presence, and someone I didn't know at all well has produced a little ache inside me . . .[1]

It sorta stops me writing to think of it too . . .

So you write if you have a moment,
Best,
Al

1. AP wrote "On the Death of F.R. Scott" (*The Woman on the Shore*).

To Dennis Lee (Toronto), from Fort Pierce, Fla., February 22, 1985

Dear Dennis,

You'll get this before going to Cuba, on which trip I hope you enjoy your-self. And Guevara's father—which produces enigmatic feelings. Mine would be: can I get a poem outa this?

Yes, Engel: I've heard since that she died.[1] And of course, as you say, the feeling for another writer; but also as you say, she was a prickly cus-tomer. [. . .]

She sent me one of her novels once, and I reciprocated with a poem called "Separation." She called me up about 1 a.m. on a winter's night. I answered the phone nude since I sleep that way, listened to her moan about the awfulness of marriage breakup standing on one foot in the darkness and freezing at the outer extremities. My poem, apparently, had brought all this on in a rush. And she and Howard once visited me at A-burg many years back, in which she told the story of riding a donkey à-la-Stevenson over the mountains of either Cyprus or Crete, being caught by darkness and rain, taking refuge at a monastery, where the head abbot provided shelter and gave her his own bedroom. After which he attempt-ed to seduce her, and chased her round and round the refectory table. All this while Howard listened and marvelled and I listened and marvelled. It wasn't mentioned which was fleeter of foot the abbot or the writer.

So while she was bristly, a small grin touches my mouth when I think of her. But her novels never made any great impression on me. I suppose one does hope that a portion of one's writing will go on and be read long after personal death. Altho I've always maintained that one has to receive all and any lit awards while alive. Feeling a poem go somewhere in your mind while you track it with your fingers, that's the chief joy. Of course one accepts any and all awards and/or recognition etc., and the present fraction of immortality will not rate highly after death. Of course you mean the strong presumption that a thing is good enough to survive literary senility.

Yes, I sense you howling with sympathy in my dry literary desert where the water table is entirely parched. There's a little quiver in the aether which indicates your feelings. And the book, *Piling Blood*, I find difficulty in thinking it can win anything, since only one review was very laudatory (Sutherland's), and then not evaluative.

No, I hadn't known of your antho activities. I dunno, you're getting a lot of respect in the media, so it may be a few more years till you get really pissed on. At which time someone will want to make a name for themselves by debunking you and your rep. But it sounds a good thing to do, and I've nearly lost track of the young; too much work to buy and read all the stuff that pours out.

Yours stickily with much love,
Al

1. Marian Engel (1933–1985): Toronto novelist (*Bear*, 1976; *The Glassy Sea*, 1978).

Sandra Djwa (b. 1939): Professor of English at Simon Fraser University and biographer (*The Politics of the Imagination: A Life of F.R. Scott*, 1987). In the letter below AP responds to her request for information about his relationship with Scott.

To Sandra Djwa (Burnaby, BC), from Ameliasburgh, April 24, 1985

Dear Sandra,
How pleasant to hear from you!

Of course, glad to help in any way I can. But *pages*? You want pages from me? Is this ten volumes or one?

Incidentally, before I forget: I'd rather you didn't use the letter or quote from it to the effect that "he (Scott) and Pratt had meant more in Canadian poetry than anybody else." Both were enormous influences in CanPo, but I wouldn't want to phrase what I think about them in just those terms.

A complete Pratt coming out; and you, of course, the editor? His poems. And Scott in two volumes? His poems alone, or mixed prose with them?

And re your "I don't think we have ever had a life that is so connected with Canada": you are probably right. One thinks of Mair in the 19th century, but it isn't an accurate comparison. Scott was/is unique among the people I have known; unique for his combination of qualities and abilities; his capacities for friendship; the feeling about him that here was a man whose capacities and talents were enormous.

I met Scott for the first time in the pub at the Ritz Carlton Hotel in Montreal in the spring of 1956. Layton and Dudek were with me. I met him many times after that: at his home on Clarke Ave; at other people's parties; and stayed at his house in North Hatley two or three days.

I suppose I was a little in awe of Scott during those days. A man of great presence; the word most often used is "magisterial"—at least it's the one I use. A very male presence: not a back-slapper as such, but a man seemingly most comfortable in the company of other men; as I think, for instance, that Layton is most comfortable in the company of women. And there was always a space around him. Despite cordiality and warmth in his personality, Scott was always at a slight distance from other people. Perhaps that was because he knew so many people, was involved in so many different things.

I do not believe he ever "talked down" to people; his manner was the same, no matter who it was he talked to or met. Once or twice I saw other people try to get under his skin; he demolished them, cut the ground from under their feet, almost effortlessly.

Several years ago a CBC television play was produced which dramatized the Roncarelli case[1]; and Scott's role in this case, which involved direct courtroom confrontation with Quebec's Premier Duplessis. No, I don't mean that Duplessis was present in the courtroom; his policies were, nevertheless, being attacked. Anyway, I was a visitor at the Scotts in Montreal on the same night the play was presented on television. And practically all the people involved in the court case were also present, including Roncarelli, Stein (the trial lawyer) and several others.

Watching the play of emotion on the faces of these people, that was fascinating. It was impossible for me to form any opinion as to the merit of the play, because I was so caught up with the feelings of these people who were themselves so strongly involved. My wife, incidentally, felt much the same. The whole thing was hypnotic; Scott smiling, avuncular and perfectly self-possessed, almost a public figure in the privacy of his own home. Marian gracious, extremely likeable—

I have very warm feelings about Scott personally: I owe him, for many reasons. He helped me in all sorts of ways: he tried to get me a job at one time when I was nearly unemployable; he wrote letters on my behalf; he believed in me—he had to to act the way he did; and he was a friend.

Scott was such a combination of abilities and qualities that no single one of these says much about him. I doubt much that any one of these qualities would rank first in the world. That doesn't matter; it's the combination of things, the single total that made him unique. From that point of view, I say there was no one like him in Canada or anywhere else. Just knowing him, being aware that he existed in the world, added to my own strength, was a cause for celebration.

As much as one man can be, Scott was Canada. Despite a "one world" concept, this country was the central focus of his life, in both emotion and logic. I've heard him worry about Canada verbally, expressing concern about this or that current happening. And asked me questions about my own feelings in the matter. And any time Frank Scott asked my opinion about anything outside of poetry, he had to be worried.

I said there was always a space around him. Sometimes it seems to me that I was able to cross that space, to meet him as a man and simply that. A man of such strength and character that I can never recall the slightest meanness about him, nothing small or malicious. But human nevertheless. I suppose we all have weaknesses; but his were unimportant.

Every day men die, but this man's life makes dying somehow seem unimportant: all that he was, except his body, still is and goes on and on—

Al

Sandra:

Maybe some of this gets too carried away. You decide that. And let me know if you want any more. I'll be out in Sechelt for something called the Suncoast Writer's Forge in mid-August. But that will be too late for any useful comments by me.

1. The Roncarelli case began in 1946 when Quebec Premier Maurice Duplessis cancelled the liquor licence of Jehovah's Witness Frank Roncarelli, a bar owner,

because he had regularly furnished bail for members of the Jehovah's Witnesses arrested for peddling without a licence or violating Quebec's Padlock Law or for seditious behaviour. Roncarelli's lawyer asked Scott to help in the case. The case eventually went to the Supreme Court, which pronounced judgment on January 27, 1959, in favour of Roncarelli who was awarded $33,123.53 in personal damages plus interest dating from the Superior Court ruling in May 1951. Sandra Djwa's *The Politics of the Imagination: A Life of F.R. Scott* (1987) gives a full account of the case.

To Sandra Djwa (Burnaby, BC), from Ameliasburgh, May 16, 1985

Dear Sandra,
I'm pleased you were able to use those memories of Scott. It doesn't in any sense repay what I owe him, but then one can never really repay kindness or even the memory of it.

I'd be glad to help in any way I can with the book, altho I think you underestimate your perspicacity with the poems. I expect these are the poems you're including in the body of the biography? In any case, sure. Incidentally, did I mention that Scott personally paid my hotel room at Expo 67 when I was short of money; perhaps he paid more than that, since my memory is hazy. And now there's a strong possibility that I'll be working on Expo 86 in Vancouver as a kinda idea man for the company that *may* be doing the "Canada Celebration" . . . If so, mostly in Toronto.

No, I'd prefer to leave out the "most important" reference to Pratt/ Scott. Neither had the slightest effect on my writing. Lawrence, Layton and Dylan Thomas were chief culprits in that respect. Altho perhaps I shouldn't dismiss Scott's lit influence entirely, since I may have learned something from certain free-wheeling poems of his, the one about "La Tarte aux Pomme Profonde"[1] and "The Canadian Authors Meet" and others. But I have certain personal prejudices against Pratt's poems; i.e., nothing of Pratt himself in them, could have been written by a thinking and feeling computer. But that's irrelevant. However, I don't want that remark about "most important" included in anything.

I had a note from Marian recently, more or less in reply to my own to her from Fla. when I heard about Frank's death thru Ron Everson.

The date of my Vancouver descent is Aug. 15—unless I should get out there earlier on this Expo 86 thing. That's still pending, since my company (Holman Production Services) who did Expo 85 in Japan for Canada, is still waiting word from gov't.

Anyway, I'm pleased if I was in any way helpful to you. I hope we can get together for discussion some time soon.

Al

1. The poem "Bonne Entente" ends with the ironic bilingual couplet "DEEP APPLE PIE / TARTE AUX POMMES PROFONDES."

To Robert Eady, from Ameliasburgh, October 17, 1985

Dear Robert Eady,

I seem to have hurt your feelings with my review of Nowlan.[1] I'm sorry for that, and will attempt to answer some of your comments and questions here.

I didn't wait to speak out about Nowlan's work: I have never been asked to write a review of Nowlan before. (Incidentally, Fraser Sutherland also disagrees with my opinions about Nowlan.) In those "thunderous silences"?—it is absolutely gratuitous and uncalled for to criticize anyone's poems unless they ask you about them. I'm sure you know that. Nowlan would have been extremely annoyed with me, not to say angry, if I had criticized his stuff without him asking for it.

"Supposed admiration" for John Wayne? There's not much doubt about that: Nowlan wrote an article about Wayne in the maritimes magazine expressing his admiration. Drinking beer with Nowlan not long afterwards I expressed amazement for his admiration. And that was as far as I wanted to go in the way of criticism.

Please note in my review that I specifically barred "great" poems from consideration. The word is not under discussion.

I agree that Nowlan was better than either Lampman or Souster. I don't like either of those two either.

No, I did not say that Nowlan was "simple," nor do I think of him that way. I believe he did have a large hero-worshipping streak—as most of us do, as I do myself—and those feelings fixed on Wayne. I thought it very odd that anyone as gentle and human as Nowlan should admire an exponent and advocate of violence. When I say "exponent," I mean in his films.

When you bring my poems into it, I have to go a little far afield. Fidel Castro and Che Guevara freed Cuba from the totalitarian Batista. After their revolution Guevara did not remain in Cuba, and died in Bolivia. Undoubtedly Castro has been responsible for executing and imprisoning many thousands of people. I've no idea how many. You say that "may be less frightening" to me than Wayne. I was never frightened by Wayne.

I just don't like him. He was a lousy actor, and his political views were dangerous. It should go without saying that I do not agree or approve of Castro's methods of governing Cuba. But at least he freed Cuba from both Fulgencio Batista and US domination. However, political views seem to me irrelevant in a discussion of Alden Nowlan.

One has to separate personal liking for a person, and one's feelings about their poetry. That is admittedly difficult. Neither Nowlan or I ever discussed each other's poems when we met. Sometimes, perhaps, a third person's poems were mentioned.

What I was trying to say in that review was that Nowlan sometimes wrote excellent poems, and never wrote bad ones (as, say, Milton Acorn). However, he was never the best, never reached above that certain level of excellence. His virtues were that he was extremely human, with all the faults and virtues that term implies.

And I am sorry that my opinions have been hurtful to you. Nevertheless, I stand by them.

Yours Truly,
Al Purdy

1. AP reviewed Nowlan's *Poems: New and Selected* together with John Steffler's *The Grey Islands: a Journey* in *Books in Canada* (October 1985).

Elspeth Cameron (b. 1943): former professor of English at the University of Toronto, critic (*Robertson Davies*, 1972) and biographer (*Irving Layton: A Portrait*, 1985; *Earle Birney: A Life*, 1994).

To Elspeth Cameron (Toronto), from Ameliasburgh, May 30, 1985

Dear Elspeth,
I hear you've dug up another wife for Layton, one who was never completely buried. And that Layton was an insurance salesman and jeweller. And that he is writing his own autobio in order to refute you ...

Well, I wanted to say, stick to your guns. Don't let him push you around. However, I'm sure you won't anyway—won't let him do that, I mean.

Best Wishes
Al

To Darryl Sittler (Toronto), from Ameliasburgh, June 5, 1985

Dear Darryl Sittler,

I'm a writer. I did an article on Brian Glennie some ten years ago, altho I'm primarily a poet.[1] I've received most of the awards going for a writer, just as you have for a hockey player. And the foregoing is to introduce myself.

I'm a Sittler admirer. When I did the Glennie piece in 1974 when Red Kelly coached the Leafs, I knew nothing about you except that you were a very good player. After that awful shemozzle with Ballard and Imlach I admired you a great deal. At the time, I thought both of them (Ballard and Imlach) should be drawn and quartered or the equivalent.

However, it seems to be the way the Leafs of Ballard treat their players, Ullman, Keon, yourself, and several others. But I admired the way you stood up to both of them, in what was probably one of the most difficult situations of your life. And stood up to them without losing any dignity or pride, without resorting to name-calling. And at Philadelphia, adjusted to the new situation well, and went on being what you are.

I'm sure the trade to Detroit was a shock, altho I understand the way it was done was most troubling to you. I understood that Clarke did not inform you of the trade until the newspapers did.

And now, according to the *Star*'s Wayne Parrish, you are again at some kind of crossroads. To retire or not? But that is your decision, of course. I believe you to be a man of integrity, and I'm sorry circumstances have not permitted me to make your acquaintance.

Best Wishes,

Al Purdy

1. AP's piece on Brian Glennie, a defenceman for the Maple Leafs, was published in *Weekend* in 1975 as "Seven-League Skates: A Talk with Brian Glennie." Norm Ullman and Dave Keon were star centres during the 1960s and '70s. Harold Ballard was the team owner. Punch Imlach coached the Maple Leafs both during their great years in the 1960s and later, less successfully, for a short period during the Ballard era.

To Patricia Keeney Smith (Toronto), from Ameliasburgh, June 18, 1985

Dear Pat Keeney Smith,

I'm interested in your opinions of Yevtushenko (and thanks for your June 14 letter). In some ways he seemed to me a talking head, or perhaps a rhetorical head. Peredelkino? Isn't that Pasternak's old home?[1] And yeah, he (Yevtushenko) fascinates me as well, as a cultural phenomenon: one that is only effective in his personal presence, not much so in his actual accomplishments. I read a couple of his poems in translation at Harbourfront last fall. The contrast between voices was extreme. Sitwell said that a poet's voice should be like clear glass through which you see the poem. I agree with that. Yevtushenko's is a distorted glass.

In July, '83, poems from the future *Piling Blood* were published in *CanFor*. None from *The Stone Bird* on that date. Sam Solecki informed me that *The Stone Bird* had been given to a reviewer for review, but the man or woman did not write it.

From my viewpoint a review is a form of advertising for a book, as well as critical opinion for public guidance. Unless the title of the forthcoming book is mentioned when poems are published, such poems are not liable to do much for the future book. Only the 1981 *The Stone Bird* was mentioned in *CanFor*, July, '83.

My own self-love is not so great that I expect any book of mine to change the world or even flicker the traffic lights at a Toronto intersection. However, I've been associated with the *Canadian Forum* for a great many years, while the editorial staff of the magazine has also changed many times. And certain things one writes do become important to the writer, as some poems in *Piling Blood* are for me. But I'm sure you're aware of such feelings, being a writer yourself. And it is odd that the magazine with which I am most closely associated in my own mind should be the only magazine to which I have written a letter asking about reviews. Of course my feeling stems from an earlier age, in which Northrop Frye and Milton Wilson were members of the editorial staff.

Re Voznesensky, I agree. In Moscow in 1977 Ralph Gustafson and I met him at the hotel pub. I enjoyed the meeting thoroughly, and think Voz one of the top poets of his and our time. Oddly enough, when Russian translators did his poems in English, I thought the poems terrible. Only when Auden, Kunitz et al did the translating did they come out with their excellence unconcealed. I'd be interested to see your interview with Voz if you're near a zerox machine. I'll trade you the interview for a couple of old books of mine signed, which you can use to start the barbecue.

Best Wishes,

Al Purdy

1. Boris Pasternak (1890–1960): one of the major figures of twentieth-century Russian literature, Pasternak was both a poet (*My Sister Life*, 1922) and a novelist (*Doctor Zhivago*, 1957). He was awarded the Nobel Prize after his novel appeared. Under pressure from the government, he declined it. Peredelkino was his *dacha*.

To Northrop Frye (Toronto), from Ameliasburgh, June 20, 1985

Dear Norrie Frye,
Just a note to let you know that I was late with my CC application, and it was transferred to the Sept. competition. However, not wasted because of my absentmindedness.

It came into my thoughts recently that you were the first person who gave me any serious criticism. I think it was for one of those Ryerson chapbooks; you wrote a letter saying what you thought. I was pleased, and kept the letter for some years until it disappeared somewhere . . . But I expect you've forgotten all about it. Then Milton Wilson reviewed *Emu, Remember!* and took said emu to be a symbolic bird which it was not. All this in *CanFor* long ago.

Best Wishes,

Al Purdy

To William Golding (Bowerchalke, Wiltshire, England), from Ameliasburgh, July 11, 1985

Dear William Golding,
I'm pleased you're coming to Harbourfront in Toronto in October. I hope to say hello at that time.

I sent you a small book of mine several years ago. I send you another and later book now—in fact my latest. Purpose, both gratitude for books that I've loved and admired (which implies that I must think the book worth sending to you), and a darker more shadowy purpose, on which I will cast some light.

I'd like to write an article about you.[1] But you are a "moving target," altho I am not a "doctoral student out for fresh blood." Quite simply, I'm interested in Golding, both as a man and a writer. (Does each of those two identities, if they can be separated, detract or change the other?)

My qualifications for such an article? The best one would be my interest in the subject. However, I've done some magazine journalism. I've published some thirty books, but only one is the prose articles I did for magazines. I'm not an academic (dropped out of school in Grade 9), and can't spin words the way some of them can. I've received most of the awards possible for a poet in Canada, which is no recommendation whatever.

And if I were you—which I can imagine being in some ways—I would look on me with exceedingly dubious gaze. Therefore, I won't be surprised if you feel that way. Quite a number of schoolchildren have asked me questions also; in most of which I am/was profoundly uninterested. Therefore, this letter may be a greeting only: but a very cordial one.

Best Wishes,
Al Purdy

1. The article was never written.

To Irving Layton (Montreal), from Ameliasburgh, July 26, 1985

Dear Irving,
One is liable to lose track of friends over a period of many years. And you, despite your habit of firing all obscenity guns at me now and then, I've always regarded as a friend.

I knew you so well, for a long period years ago, and have a great deal of respect for you without in any way wishing to sit at your feet—In fact, I'll write you a testimonial at any time, even if you don't need it. I learned much from that two-year period in Montreal in the Fifties, most of it from you. And now, Scott is dead, Dudek has been sour for years (in my opinion), and I believe you don't see Ron Everson—things change beyond recognition.

If you have a moment, drop me a line. Oh, I hear your fartings in the papers now and then, but I mean personally. How are you? I hope well and reasonably content. And writing, which seems more difficult to me as

I grow older. I hope you are writing some really fine poems, the kind I've admired in you for many years.

Are you out there somewhere, Irving?

Best Wishes from your friend,

Al

To Patricia Keeney Smith (Toronto), from Ameliasburgh, July 29, 1985

Dear Pat Keeney Smith,

Thanks for your letter. Books follow separately.

And thanks for the Voz interview.[1]

Yes, I didn't like Yevtushenko's actor-style, and I didn't like him after I had at first. I felt a bit like a flunkey up there, and I didn't like that either. So I gave bad temper a bad reputation. The reasons for dislike of Yev. are too long to go into here, and have to do with personal relations.

However, that's a good turn of the clear glass phrase, the "coloured glass—" and I see you use the Br. spelling of "coloured"—

I get very little when I read Yev. on the page. If he's had a good US translator, a poet generally, then his poems come out as a bit simple-minded but not too bad (he said condescendingly). No, Voz. is much the best. But even there, in my humble (humble?) opinion, and with the best of poets, one is lucky to get 30 to 40 per cent good stuff from their work. I mean stuff that appeals much to one personally. Even in Yeats, who is perhaps my favourite poet, I don't get more than that. The rest of a man's work may be capable—or woman's—but not personally appealing. (I'm getting in too deep here and should leave it.) But there's a passage in Voz. that always appealed to me, I think in "Oza"—"You / People, locomotives, germs / be as gentle with her as you can . . ." That's maybe an inaccurate quote, but certainly tends to demolish critics who think of him as cold.

I don't think you should expect your own impressions of a place, Russia in this case, to match up with someone else's. The divergencies make for interest. My Russian stuff is also very different from Ralph—whom I called Gus in order to relieve the odour of culture—and I also avoided some of the events that were available to us in the USSR. I mean cultural stuff, which I like if I like, and don't wish to be stampeded if I don't.

However, you may have meant something different than the way it sounds. I expect we, all of us, even see colours differently than other people; the stresses of our lives, warp and woof etc., woven differently. I hope so anyway. I'd hate to think of a bunch of manikins parading in similar clothes with similar minds saying identical things.

Yeah, the Voz. interview interesting. And what a great ending for it. His mention of rhyme subtleties—about which (rhyme itself) I have very ambiguous feelings. If Richard Wilbur does it, most of the time okay. But I think many of Auden's are more intrusive, and you're liable to have the rhyme in your head before the sense of a passage. And yet, Auden is one of the four poets—modern ones—I'd name as my own favourites. I know, there are all sorts of speeches, by Auden and others, saying you need a trellis to grow flowers—or something like that. Which I think is bullshit. I think it's much more difficult to write a good and very readable poem minus rhyme than with it. And the weakness of the poem is liable to be immediately visible without rhyme or some sort of formal metric.

I'm going on too long. Thanks again.

Al Purdy

1. Patricia Keeney Smith's interview with Voznesensky was published in *Cross-Canada Writers' Quarterly*, Vol. 5 (Nos. 2–3).

To Irving Layton (Montreal), from Ameliasburgh, August 21, 1985

Dear Irving,

Yeah, without getting sloppy about it, I have strong affection for Layton. And yes, I felt mercurial in those days, and all was possible as you say. And Layton has much to be responsible for, including an unknown percentage of Purdy. Yeah, I did learn something; but that wasn't altogether the point (I mean learning). I said something about it in a fairly mediocre poem I did for Bob Weaver: in which I ascribed various roles similar to the American expatriates in Paris—to Dudek, Scott, etc. That's a lousy sentence, but—I won't explain it further, just send you the poem. I'm sure you hadn't/haven't seen it.

Anyway: hearing from you brings it all back. (Altho it was never lost.) When you arm-wrestled me to a standstill, then took on Mailer, Wallace Stevens[1] and fought a draw with Shakespeare. Remember Dudek looking down on us on the floor while we struggled, he saying: "And these are sensitive poets?" (Greek and Italian papers please copy.)

Change of subject. I just came back from a reading on west coast, and it was suggested that Layton would be great in that setting. (With which statement I agreed.) Suncoast Writers' Forge, Festival of the Written Arts . . . etc. etc. Woman name of Betty Keller runs it. Time: next August, for possible Layton presence. I said I'd write you (to Keller), and thought you might like the setting and things generally. Good motel, meals better than good, and friend of mine (Peter Trower) did enough publicity to ensure I got a fair-sized audience. However: I recommend the setting especially: the sea, the sea ("the blue the fresh the ever free"—or something like that). The other two *known* writers when I was there were Peter Gzowski and Leon Rooke.[2] I asked for more than the CC fee, from which info I'd expect you to do the same if you decide to go. i.e, I asked for $500, and they paid the $300 over and above the CC $200. But for chrissake, don't say I told you that! Anyway, think about it if you feel like it. I'll send the lady your address.

The poems (yours) are fine. Layton at his most Layton, which is the guy I was enthralled with long ago, and remember and remember . . .

Yeah, I know about the autobio, also the Elspeth Cameron book (she wrote me asking permish for some letter quotes).

Possibly non sequitur, but I mourn Frank Scott. I owe the guy. The giants are dying around us . . . I don't mean great poets exactly, for he wasn't that. But a man, a MAN. I shall miss him . . .

I am growing decrepit, but would like to have a flagon or jeroboam with Irving . . . ("Decrepit" means my goddam back is giving me trouble, so I don't travel as much as I did.)

Yours, affectionately & with love,

Al

(Purdy)

1. Wallace Stevens (1879–1955): arguably the greatest American poet of the twentieth century (*Harmonium*, 1923; *Collected Poems*, 1955).
2. Peter Gzowski (1934–2002): editor (*Maclean's*), writer and popular radio broadcaster (*This Country in the Morning, Morningside*). Leon Rooke (b. 1934): prolific and remarkably inventive short story writer (*Death Suite*, 1981) and novelist (*Shakespeare's Dog*, 1983).

To Dennis Lee (Toronto), from Ameliasburgh, August 25, 1985

Dear Dennis,
I think I'd give your antho much better marks than the reviews in *Maclean's* and the *Globe*.[1] And for what they are rather than what a reviewer thinks they should be. (Altho I was amused by Sutherland's review of inclusion as a ticket to D. Lee's establishment.)

However, your antho gave me a much better liking for Don Coles, Lorna Crozier, and several others, apart from those I already knew and liked, such as McKay, Thibaudeau, etc.[2]

Also, in opposition to the reviewers, I think the level of excellence is quite high. It would be extraordinary if there were more than that. But the level of quality is such that it gives one encouragement about the country's poets as a whole. In the US I think there are no supernal geniuses either, whatever that term means. The day of Frost and Stevens is over there, the people who seem to dominate an era, I mean. Perhaps over for good in this time of rock stars and bombs in the laundry bags.

I've been in Victoria and Vancouver for three weeks. But I saw an answer to a Findley letter in the *Globe*.[3] Apparently Findley had said the poets were in some kind of opposition to the government. If that's what he said I couldn't see it in the actual poems.

And I find your Intro interesting, in its mapping the "schools of content" etc. All of them being forms of mental and physical regionalism, narrow spheres of interest which I think writers oughta move from and out of—Ron Everson mentioned to me that the Intro was one of the best things in the book if not the best—

Anyway, it's a good thing to have done, the book I mean. And ought to be done periodically, as it more or less has been. I couldn't possibly do the enormous amount of reading required myself, and suspect your eyesight must be strained. Congratulations on a good job.

As mentioned, just returned from west. Reading at Sechelt, near Van. The place was like living inside a scenic postcard. Short flight to and from Vancouver . . . Place gives me a puritanical feeling, as if I'd not earned all that rich lushness . . .

All best,

Al

1. Lee's *The New Canadian Poets 1970–85* (1985) was reviewed in *Maclean's* (August 12, 1985) by John Bemrose ("An Avalanche of Poets") who singled out Roo Borson, Don Coles and John Thompson for special praise.
2. Lorna Crozier (b. 1941): best-selling poet (*Angels of Flesh, Angels of Silence*, 1981; *Inventing the Hawk*, 1992). Don McKay (b. 1942): poet (*Night Field*, 1991, won the Governor General's Award).
3. Timothy Findley (1930–2002): dramatist and novelist (*The Wars*, 1977).

To Irving Layton (Montreal), from Ameliasburgh, September 9, 1985

Dear Irving,

Thanks for info on back book by Hamilton Hall.[1] It had been recommended to me before, and I got a copy or someone gave me one then. In my own case, trouble seems to hit periodically then remission. Not bad right now, long as I take it easy. And yeah, I don't have a high idea of docs, but you're bound to run to em when something's wrong. Anyway, thanks for info, even if I already had it.

You were born same year as Steve Mac? Eli Mandel once said—on returning from Banff 3–4 years ago, that you were a year older than your advertised age.

And yeah, I look forward to that memoir of yours. I know the gal that's writing the bio, Elspeth Cameron (who's supposed to have found a spare wife of yours tucked away in Halifax, which kinda tickles me true or not).

I am trying to get to Homer's Troy this winter, via a grant of course, which last I don't find out whether I'll get until around Christmas. I may or may not get to Mtl. in the meantime. Therefore, if you eventually have an Italian address, do let me know, and we can sample some chianti and hobble up the Spanish Steps and drink at the Trevi Fountain together. IF IF IF, of course. Who knows what will happen . . .

(I use this notepaper for your possible edification, souvenir of my trip to write Hiroshima poems.)

And no, I'm not happy about your back trouble, even if misery loves company.

> Okay, I wish you many fine poems
> and much happiness,
>
> Al

1. *The Back Doctor: The Doctor's Program for Lifetime Relief for Your Aching Back* (1980).

To John Newlove, from Ameliasburgh, October 2, 1985

Dear John,

Good to get a one-page letter from you, with two-inch margins. Nobody like you in A-burgh, so I treasure your missives. Hope you appreciate the distinction.

As you see, carbon of my publishers piece to you. Far as I know, truth was told, I like Jack McC. despite him fucking me a few times, but don't trust him nearly as far as I could throw him if I had enough drinks. You will remember some of the incidents in the Town episode, you being the grape vine in the matter.

Yeah, when I was at Banff told everyone who mentioned scenery that the whole place was a lot of giant postcards standing on end and facing inward. You're plagiarizing me, but get off the hook with your comment that BCers invented mtns. Maybe we—you, me, whoever—are stuck with the places we grew up in, the beds in which we first masturbated. At my only 500 buck reading this year, the west coast lushness made me feel guilty, I hadn't earned it. Took an extra day in Vancouver on the return trip, intending to see Van. and its changes. Instead, stayed in hotel room most of the time. Went to G. Woodcock's for dinner, met playwright Michael Mercer and his gal, drank too much or too little, flew back east into further boredom.

Yeah, Mtl. poem mag asked for poems of mine years ago. I sent em some; they turned em down, and told me how to write poems, criticizing mine in detail. I told em if I wanted their goddam fucking comments I'd ask, all they had to do is say yes or no. That sorta thing enrages me. I think that feeling did get through to them.

Vancouver is outa my time. I mean the time when I had to buy a cheap bed on Granville with a promise from the store to take it back if I went broke. I did go broke, carried the damn thing on my back for about ten blocks from near Cambie to Granville, then the bastard gypped me outa five bucks (which meant a helluva lot more then) . . . That town is gone.

I would like to write some poems; on the other hand I don't feel like it. I want to want to write. Ya know? But fuckit, has to be strongern that. I may start phony but I gotta find something real or interesting to continue. (To me, of course.) But things die down, and one can expect it. I hope I have enough brains left to know when I'm repeating myself and saying the same things the same way. I hope I can distinguish, but can I?

Nobody but me in A-burg knows that KOK also means cock.[1] Or should I say nobody but me would remark on it—which I did long ago.

Incidentally, re Jack McC., last time I saw him which must be six–eight years ago, at lunch somewhere, he told me a story about how he and this other guy had a bet: this being which of the two could fuck the most women in a 24 or 48 hr. period (I forget which). Honour system of course. Jack told of taking trains, buses, cars, airplanes to get there in time, and said he won the bet—by one or two fucks. I sent him a copy of

Morning and It's Summer mentioning this story in inscription. He didn't reply. Could he be irritated at Purdy?

Letter from Joe R.[2] says the finest thing he did as prez of league was getting me to England. Which flummoxed me, since I didn't especially wanta go, and kinda got talked into it by myself. Joe says also he wishes you'd stop coming up with that story of his fondest ambition to achieve the perfect blow job. I think that's a laudable ambition, a perfect blow-job being undefinable.

Al

1. AP's postal code was KOK 1AO.
2. Joe Rosenblatt.

To Elspeth Cameron (Toronto), from Ameliasburgh, October 7, 1985

Dear Elspeth,

Thank you for the new book. Magnificent looking affair. I hope it gives you credit in all the right places.

I've glanced at it here and there (especially where my name occurs), and it's interesting. (Of course, I'm prejudiced, don't you think?) Irving's life reads much like a soap opera; in fact the parade of women who adored him seems unbelievable to me. However, the most important thing about him is that he did write fine poems—when he was at his best. And a writer should be remembered for their/his/her best. His concern for publicity and mistaking that ability is something else, for which I have distaste.

From what I've read, yours seems to me a fair-minded and excellent biography. I congratulate you. Apart from my personal interest in the book, I think it is the sort of thing we need in Canada: something to arouse more interest in literature here. And saying that sounds like Layton's own predilections for publicity. I don't mean that. I do mean: there's a kind of marketplace in the world, where a country is judged according to what other countries think it has accomplished. I'd prefer a little respect be given Canada, although I really doubt that someone like Layton would bring about that result.

I don't mean to sound like pollyanna or the like. But Irving is just too alive to me in so many ways . . . You remember the old search, when you were a young girl, of looking for someone you could genuinely admire, who could represent all the best things in your own mind? Girls must have this sort of thought as well as boys. In my own case, it's been

a recurrent thought most of my life. And it's probably hopeless idealism. We are all flawed, and must be that apparently. There is no model to
which we might attach such feelings. Which, of course, is a species of dis-
illusionment akin to atheism or agnosticism.

You say something to the effect that Irving never grew up, is the eternal adolescent, with which I agree. But then, I ask, did I ever grow up? Did
you?

There are some mistakes in book. Do you want to know them? I
mean mistakes of fact and figures. I'd think you would want to know
them. I picked up a used copy of the Layton/Rath[1] book recently,
pubbed in 1976 (not '80); the Layton friend, Goodwin (is it that?)
doesn't appear in index; *Transparency* was never an Acorn/Purdy mag;
Layton was an Officer, not Companion, of Order of Canada, and the
book has it both ways. But little things like that don't affect the book's
merit, not really. You mention *Moment* after the *Transparency* mention,
that *was* the Acorn/Purdy mag.

Best,
Al

Congratulations

1. *An Unlikely Affair* (1980).

To Ralph Gustafson (North Hatley, Que.), from Barefoot Bay, Fla.,
November 6, 1985

Dear Gus,
I heard you were ill, but better now. I'd like to express my concern, or
whatever one calls it. Ron Everson is not too well either, and hasn't come
south this year. Eurithe and I are down early to try and sell our mobile . . .

Last month was in Toronto at Birney's and saw a book of yours, a
small book about landscape, I think—Liked it much; read about half between gaps in conversation. Like to get a copy if you have any spares. Let
me know how much money and will send. I really think you're getting
better as you grow older, and not many do that . . .

I'm not writing at all—poems, I mean. Trying to get a grant to go to
Europe next year, but got my application in too late last spring so don't
hear whether I get it until Feb. Several years ago started out for Troy in
Turkey, but collapsed in an air conditioned hotel room (with Eurithe) in
Izmir and had to fly back to England . . . From heat, I hasten to say, which

was gawdawful. I expect we'll get there next year, grant or no, but the grant would make things easier.

By the way, attended the Golding reading in Toronto, which is how come I was at Birney's place. Had exchanged a coupla letters with Golding previously. Before reading a friend says, there he goes now (I was supposed to see him), so I followed, down the stairway at Harbourfront. Caught him halfway down and stuttered something, and he said he had to get to the john. And there I was face hanging out, feeling as if I were on the edge of things and presuming far too much . . . You see, I had offered to drive him around, since he'd never been to Canada. Of course it didn't come off. Gatenby had him booked 24 hrs every day.

Hope you're okay. Regards to Betty.

Al

H.R. Percy (1920–96); Nova Scotia editor, biographer (*Joseph Howe*, 1976), short story writer and novelist (*Painted Ladies*, 1983). He served both in the Royal Navy and in the Royal Canadian Navy. The Purdys often stayed in Florida with Percy and his wife Vina. Though the two writers corresponded often, their letters deal for the most part with everyday aspects of their lives.

To H.R. Percy (Granville Ferry, NS), from Micco, Fla., November 28, 1985

Dear Bill,

Thanks for the Thomas stuff. I think I will have to get the book, forty bucks or no. But doubt if I could plow thru all of it. There are seven vols of Lawrence letters being published, of which I have the first three. But since I have them, think I must get the rest as they are published. But I can only dip into them now and then, so perhaps it's a waste.

Good news about *Tranter's Tree*; but as you say, now wait for publisher's opinions. You are lucky to keep going and improving continually with your writing, as I think you are. By contrast, poets are almost always washed up at my age and yours. The noteable (notable?) exception is Yeats, of course.

Have a book here that will be handy for you: *Fodor's South America* for 1981. That's recent enough to be relevant.

I have to leave for Canada next week and a Vancouver reading. In my absence Eurithe will have a yard sale of all excess stuff. And there's a helluva bunch . . .

It would seem the F.P. mobile is nearly sold. We have a $500 advance thru the bank in Ont., and they arrive Nov. 26. Originally they told us they'd come earlier, which meant we could drive to Canada for my flight to Vancouver, which would have meant a load of books and stuff could have gone that way. Then their plans changed viz the later arrival. Paul Foody and Mim have offered to close the deal for Eurithe, but I think Eurithe must stay and do it herself. She's good at that sorta thing, and we don't want foul-ups.

Yes, I thought Golding likeable in a coupla letters and his appearance on stage. Then I hear from Gustafson that he's feeling his "Nobelness"—which info comes (apparently) from Gus's wife and Robin Skelton on the west coast. I think these people must be wrong. Gus's wife heard a radio program with Golding on it. Dunno what or where Skelton's info came from. But it offends me deeply that Golding should feel his "Nobelness"—and I bloody well don't believe it. I would rather suspect Skelton of nasty gossip, and have some reason to suspect his motives in such matters.

I am not writing poems, some reviews, and previously some prose pieces; one of the latter got into the book section of Tor. *Globe* by failing to get into their Mermaid Inn columns. By default sorta. But prose doesn't satisfy me as it does you. I expect I'd write poems if I went to Ecuador with you (Fodor makes the country sound interesting). However, I think there's a kinda psychic gathering of forces to go into places like Ecuador or Turkey (which latter I think is much more physically dangerous), a needed alertness which is both physical and mental. One is ignorant of language, customs, timetables, every damn thing one can think of—in these foreign countries I mean. So that one is hyped up to a quite remarkable degree—or so I think—abroad in such places. And I'm not so sure I wanta do that—get so hyped up—twice within a short space of time. On the other hand, I would write some poems, I'm sure. Which temps me. Ya see what I mean?

Getting long-winded.

Best,
to both from Al & Eurithe

415

To George Bowering (Vancouver), from Micco, Fla., December 11, 1985

Dear George,

Migawd, I am "always saying" my stuff is better than ever . . . You terrify me, and I sound just like Layton, which I abhor. I now amend that
to say I'm all washed up: haven't written a poem in months. However,
I do thank you, and feel the same about you with the Kerrisdale book
[*Kerrisdale Elegies*] in mind.

Yes, George W. can sometimes be a bit fulsome, and I regard him
as a friend. But then I think of you the same way, so what the hell . . .
I do not think we are liars or even exaggerating very much when it
comes to assessing each other's work. Myself, I generally keep quiet
about it if I don't like somebody's work; and that is my version of
tact.

I don't suppose I've ever said much about you, for instance: but you
seem to me very large out there on the coast, larger than anyone else. The
older generation—Layton, Birney, and that's really all there are unless you
include me as well—has really passed from the scene. And that leaves you
and Ondaatje, as well as Atwood. But I can't regard Atwood the same way,
or as relevant in the same way. She seems to me a sport of the media as
much as a good writer, which last of course she is too. But she is a writer
more than being a poet, if you get me. Somebody invented her, and it
wasn't her.

Anyway, the chief reason for hoping and maybe perhaps believing that
we—you and I and whoever—are good is to feel therefore that we haven't
wasted our lives. That we have contributed something to this country and
the world; and therefore do not feel as Pound was reported to have felt
before he died, that he had done nothing worthwhile (or words to that
effect). And to feel that way we need some praise occasionally from someone we respect, to heal the open ego-wound that never heals . . . For myself, and I expect you'd agree, I couldn't see spending my life in any other
way than I have . . .

Yeah, the eyes, the back, etc. Last summer I had a partially detached
retina; but it healed all by itself. I don't know why. And the back, etc.
Growing older, I will not say, laughingly, old. And yeah, "nothing you can
do about it"—so fuckit, is all one can say . . .

I am nothing like as busy as your schedule sounds. But I don't live
where they can readily get at me anyway . . . Incidentally, my flight back
east was late, and missed connections to Orlando on Eastern, got stuck

in Toronto overnight . . . Readings! I don't mind the actual readings, even like them at times; but the travel . . . ugh.

Okay, gotta write more letters.

Al

E.J. Carson (b.1948): Toronto editor with General Publishing, Random House and Penguin Books (Canada) of which he has been president since 2002. He was also a founding editor of the literary journal *Rune*, and has published *Scenes* (1977), a volume of poems.

To E.J. Carson (Toronto), from Micco, Fla., December 18, 1985

Dear Mr. Carson,
When Elspeth Cameron mentioned to me at the "Night of a Hundred Authors" in Toronto several years ago that Irving Layton had asked her to write his biography, I thought it a good idea for both of them. Irving loves publicity—of any kind, good or bad: in fact I think he has a mania for it.

When I read the resulting book, it seemed to me admirable. And then the various vituperative noises from Layton began. And yes, I think both you and Elspeth are a little naïve not to expect such a reaction. If you look back over Layton's past history, it is studded with such incidents, attacks on one or another person who have either reviewed him or whom he has attacked "just for the hell of it"—including myself.

Layton is a fine poet. I hope his efforts to award himself a Nobel Prize will be rewarded. I wish him well. However, I do not agree with his vilification of Elspeth Cameron, nor admire the motives behind it. In an old fashioned phrase, he "should be ashamed of himself." But there is also something quite humorous about this whole literary comedy. It may be laughed at, then forgotten in the next breath.

Sincerely,
Al Purdy

P.S. But doesn't it help to sell the book?

To Ellen Seligman (Toronto), from Micco, Fla., January 22, 1986

Dear Ellen,

[...] I didn't review Cameron's biography. She asked me if I could say in a letter for publication what I said in a private letter, that Layton has a mania for publicity, that he will in fact say just about anything to secure it. Ed Carson of Stoddart also wrote and asked. I do not believe Layton has any business blackening Cameron's character the way he has with his campaign of vilification.

You ask, is Cameron's book a true representation of Layton? I doubt if that's possible, even by Layton. Incidentally, she didn't "break into the field" with the Layton biography, but had earlier written a bio of Hugh MacLennan. Or perhaps you refer to this new book as being in a different field from the MacLennan book?

I knew Cameron in Mtl. when she was at Loyola (now Sir Geo. W.), teaching CanLit. Apparently I've read her book from a different perspective than yours. In her assessment of Layton she says he's written thirty-five poems of world class, as I recall from memory of the book. That doesn't seem to me contemptuous. However, her description of his (Layton's) life with his various women may be. Still, when you ask someone to write your bio (as Cameron told me Layton did at the Night of a Hundred Authors several years back), then you take your chances. I suppose it's a simple question: did Cameron go too far with what you regard as her contemptuous attitude toward Layton. Perhaps. I hadn't thought of it until you raised the point. It seemed to me that she had a high regard for his abilities, based on that "thirty-five poems of world class" assessment.

I haven't read Layton's own biography.[1] I'm a little tired of all the noise, and prefer to read good poems. [...]

One word more on all the lit. Through all his life, Layton has vilified other people. These include Northrop Frye, A.J.M. Smith, Dudek, and many many others. I can't think they deserved all the shit Layton has dished out, and he deserves some back in return. Despite saying that, I'm fond of Layton. However, I do not think he is God or anywhere near as some people do. Nor do I think he is the equal of the best poets of this century. I would probably estimate his production of world class poems as perhaps twenty—and this I regard as high. Archibald MacLeish, a so-called "world class poet" wrote only one that I find memorable, "You, Andrew Marvell." But nevertheless, all these rankings and screams of rage become tiresome. I am very tired of Layton, despite having some fondness for him. I expect I am on his list of people to attack.

Al

1. *Waiting for the Messiah: A Memoir* (1985).

To H.R. and Vina Percy (Granville Ferry, NS), from Ameliasburgh, May 18, 1986

Dear Bill and Vina,
Some word on our adventures in Turkey—
    We landed in Istanbul after flying all night, in early afternoon. Boy does that knock you out, with eight hrs difference in time.
    Stayed a few days there to get acclimatized. Cab driver charged us twenty bucks to show us the city; usual thing I suppose, blue mosque, Hagia Sophia, Topkapi Palace . . . Didn't thrill me much.
    We caught a bus to Canakkale in pouring rain; the cab drives up a small hill and water coming down almost washed us down with it. We drive in that bus all day by the Sea of Marmora, and it's only 200 miles to the mouth of the Dardanelles, which is where Canakkale is. This was on the European side, Thrace that is. Eurithe wearing her hat with the Canadian flag on it. Everybody, or just about everybody, in Turkey rather small, I mean apart from fatness. Buses cheap too. Anyway, at Canakkale we got a third floor apt. (yeah, apartment) overlooking the harbour, fairly reasonable, about $45. Below us the ferryboats came and went. And yes, we were now on the Asian side, Gallipoli across the water. All sorts of shipping in the straits, including big Russian warships once or twice. I started to write a poem about the shipping once, got to some twenty lines and realized it was an imitation of Masefield's "Cargoes," and quit.[1] (Lose more poems that way.)
    A mile or so away is Abydos, the site of Hero and Leander's love affair in classical Greece.[2] Also the spot where Byron swam the straits. Now polluted as hell. Canakkale a town of about 40,000. Beer about fifty cents Canadian for 16 ounces.

Troy is 17 miles away. We caught a bus. Ruins more or less what you'd think, a jumble of stone, walls sticking up here and there, a little theatre . . . Of course what makes it interesting is Homer. You don't see the ruins only, you see the people as well; you see Alexander the Great visiting and stripped and oiled, running about Achilles' tomb by the sea shore. And Caesar, chasing Pompey over land and sea, stopping at Troy and having some weird experiences. (This is in Lucan's *Pharsalia* in Penguin.[3]) I wrote a poem about Caesar at Troy.

I kept picking up potsherds, one of which I'll enclose here. Must've got a dozen. Who knows how old! Not that many there either, you have to look hard to see them on the stone paths. The poppies just coming into bloom, me picking them and other wild flowers. Met a Swedish couple and drank tea and coffee on their camper they'd driven from Sweden. And mentally started writing a poem about Troy on return. The bus from Canakkale didn't come, so we had to walk to main road.

Anyway, we start out for Pergamum. Eurithe says we get a hotel in nearest town. But the bus didn't stop for us. And we didn't yell in Turkish, Let Us Out, Let us Out! Rode all the way to Izmir, some 240 miles from Canakkale. Took all day. (I am realizing as I write this: there's too much to talk about, I'll never get it all in. I'm writing an article, now at around 5000 words.) I think we'll have to wait until I see you to continue.

My usual handicap, bad back. But I wrote two poems I like pretty well. "Pretty well" meaning they're okay, but not quite the best. The *Collected* has now been upped to near 400 pages, same size as Frank Scott's *Collected*. Dennis Lee said a lot of nice things about it, and will write a short Intro before my own words. I can't say what I think about the book, since its size was enlarged almost in my absence, the poem selection more Russell Brown for the last hundred pages than my own. I feel uncertain about the book, despite Dennis's six page letter of praise. You still have to go on your own feelings, despite other people's input. And you have a vision of your book, rain beaten and warped lying in a gutter somewhere, a thing of supreme unimportance which you always knew . . .

Can't end with me lyin in the gutter rain-beaten and warped. Warped. Can I?

We'd love to get down and see you this summer. Will you be there reaping gold from all the people who wanta hear Vina's lit criticism and Bill's golden words of wisdom?

We are negotiating with a dozen dealers for a new car, since I keep cracking my head on this one, and soon will have no brains of any kind left . . . Oh yes, just the other day I get invited to a poetry festival at Rotterdam. For chrissake—HOLLAND. And we just got back from there, at least Amsterdam on KLM from Turkey. That's last week in June.

This is my five-buck typer, by the way. I like the type size better on the old typer. Ribbon cost almost as much as the typer. And Perry oiled and conditioned it until I feel I musta beat the establishment somehow.

> So okay,
>
> tell us what you're doin . . .
>
> Al

1. John Masefield (1878–1967): best-selling English novelist and poet (*Salt-Water Ballads*, 1902; *Ballads and Poems*, 1910). "Cargoes" was published in the latter.
2. In the myth, Leander falls in love with Hero, the priestess of Aphrodite. He drowns while swimming the Hellespont to reach her; she throws herself into the sea when she learns of his death. AP knew the story from Christopher Marlowe's poem.
3. Lucan (Marcus Annaeus Lucanus) (AD 39–65): Roman poet, the nephew of Seneca. *Pharsalia* is a historical epic in 10 books about the Civil Wars. It is also known as the *Bellum Civile*. He was forced to commit suicide when a conspiracy against Nero, of which he was a part, was discovered.

To Dennis Lee (Toronto), from Ameliasburgh, June 11, 1986

Dear Dennis,

Thanks for the zerox [of the Afterword to the *Collected Poems*].

It's good understandable prose, unlike some academic pieces. (Only had to look up a coupla words, like "quotidian" which I suspected meant what it meant.) (The concept of Dennis as grammarian while writing kids' books instils me with wild surmise!) Among other topics, your discussion of "voice" and "tone" appeals. I don't know if scholarly books talk about that much. Such books are generally so dull I don't read them (only when they concern me, which is fairly rare). And you would almost have to "hear" the poem on the page to distinguish voice and tone. Would you not? And people have told me that they do not *hear* a poem on the page. That always surprises me, since I don't think you can really appreciate a poem unless you also "hear" it simultaneously with reading. I expect you'd agree there.

But the shift of voice and change of tone, both in seriousness and persona, are among the more interesting things while actually writing a poem. I take refuge in that "intuitive" label, and say I've never thought about transitions much. And really, certain things are instinctive. You do them at the time and don't know why. If you did know why and thought about it, your own character would not be what it is. As with you: can you feel your own character changing as you read this on the page?

But certainly, one of the big reasons for me writing as I write is boredom with other writing. That too, you have gone into where I am concerned. (What can I talk about that you have not anticipated?) Familiarity doesn't necessarily bore one; but the impression of clichés non-rampant. (Wouldn't it be great to see a rampant cliché advancing on you at the high port?) And your spatial transitions are exemplified by MacLeish's "Marvell" . . . All of them governed by the turning earth and seemingly descending sun. Anyway, I didn't intend to get into this stuff . . . [. . .]

When I said above "boredom" with other writing, I meant the kinda stuff that has no interest on accounta you've seen so much similar . . . expressed the same way etc. The phraseology and mental content of a poem must sound different, at least one or the other must.

Incidentally, I think strongly your piece should go first in book. Printed in letters of fire of course. But first. It would be "hidden away" in rear, and I do not want that. For double reasons: a. it's about me; and b. it's about you.

Only you and Mandel are intellectual critics. And I can't understand much of what he says. Or don't want to on accounta it's too much trouble for the result obtained. But you are understandable (except to women who don't know what you're after . . . !), have prestige, and to my way of thinking are both popular and intellectual. (This is getting confused!) No, I think your piece and mine make excellent contrasts, because mine illustrates what you are saying, altho in prose. Do you agree that it does?

Again re your piece, some readers are liable to think that you've weighted my stuff with more significance than it can bear, said "significance" being non-existent. To which you're liable to reply, fuckem (I hope). Certain words tho, like "poignance"—"epiphany" etc. do exist outside religion, war and so on, and they express the really inexpressible, at least there are no handy examples here for me to use—and howinhell am I gonna end this sentence?

Bought some more beer, which is very poignant stuff . . . And does in its ultimate aspects produce epiphany . . .

hoping you are not the same,

Al

To John Newlove, from Ameliasburgh, July 4, 1986

Dear John,

I think you may have good reason to be paranoiac, which means you aren't if you have good reasons. Doesn't it?

There is a quality about your poems, lines in them, as if they have been hammered into place and sense, and were then unchangeable. I've just read a Fraser S. review of yours, (unpubbed as yet) which, as I remember, talks about the rightness of syntax etc. Something like that. Saying how you escape mundaneity (okay, okay, I know there ain't) thru this rightness . . .

I met Gzowski last summer in BC and he acted so cold I didn't speak to him again. Wondered what he thought I'd done or said. [. . .]

Wah always seemed like a nothing to me, and a nothing is like a nothing. Some twenty years back I was at his place on the UBC campus and insulted one of the Black Mtn. gods, Olson. I stressed his marvellous voice to the extent that they knew I meant that was all he did have. Wah looked threatening, and I asked him if he was really gonna hit me, a coupla times. Then I had to walk all the way to the street car stop about three miles away.

Did I ever tell you about attending a play reading by Beverly Simon at her house in West Van? The original invite was for Birney at whose house—I mean apt.—I was staying. When they heard I was there they asked me. Way the hellengone this Simon's house was up in the mtns. She read a long play, about 2 hrs., and I thought fine, now I can slurp if I drink and the noise don't matter. But then she said she was gonna read another full-length play. I thought jesus, what did I do, how did I get into this, just for free booze. Besides, my artistic integrity or something was boiling at that point. But I was polite. I did not stand up and say shaddup ya bitch. I just quietly walked out. And ya know, it was miles and miles, mountain lions in the bush growling at me, no street lights, walk with your hands in front it was so goddam dark, and all for artistic integrity. Or something. I must've walked all the time Simon was reading that second play, and looked so beat a kind motorist picked me up not far from the Lion's Gate. And I cursed my artistic integrity. I tell ya, it aint worth it. So hard on your feet. [. . .]

Al

To Dennis Lee (Toronto), from Ameliasburgh, July 5, 1986

Dear Dennis,

Just got back from Holland. In Amsterdam, we found whores' alley. Great fat ugly females with six-foot frontage on street and actual red light bulbs. I was fascinated, keep looking; Eurithe turned her head away, wouldn't look at em. Being a whore demeans females, she thinks; when I can stop laughing I agree with her.

We rented a car on arrival, drove west and north to Apeldoorn etc., over the polders. Dykes interesting, called "sleepers," "dreamers," and "wakers." You can imagine why. The wakers confront dangerous water; sleepers non-dangerous, rivers etc.; dreamers almost entirely outa service. So like humans, eh? It's a poem, but I don't feel like writing it.

Nine days in Rotterdam, and whaddaya know: Gatenby showed up, with a room at the Hilton and air conditioning. Temperature like 90 or 95, free mosquitoes. (I killed ten one night, and no bounty.) And I loved the people, some of them. "My favourite Bulgarian," editor of a Soviet lit mag in Sofia, and his wife. Emotional people. They hug you. Ursula Fanthorpe, a good English poet; the Rothenbergs of US ilk, he a sounder of weird noises; Seamus Heaney, he and I reading together at a pub: me roaring to lift above beer drinkers' noise, he softly so they had to shaddup and listen if they wanted to hear. And Shirley Kaufman, late of Seattle, now of Israel.[1]

Stories in Rotterdam newspapers. Said I read too fast, badly and was a little drunk. Another said I almost stole the show. Take your pick. Well— free beer at all times; should I ignore that? Heineken yet. Has the taste of pissed-in underwear for a week.

In Amsterdam on Amstel river. We visit van Gogh museum. I am impressed as hell. (My back also hurts and Eurithe does all the work, etc.). We ride in a canal-river boat (place is lousy with canals), look at housefronts etc. We search for bookshops; too much trouble finally. And Holland much more expensive than I could've imagined.

In Rotterdam poets all at a good hotel called Central, something like a hundred bucks Canadian. Gatenby at Hilton I suppose thru his deal with Harbourfront Hilton. I do not grouse. I am amused at Gatenby. But we need our Gatenbys and Colombos. They, along with the spittle of Mulroneys and Turners[2] are what sticks the country together? [...]

Oh yes, another guy, one of the festival people at Rotterdam, said he was amazed I could be so sensitive, after hearing "Lament for the Dorsets" in Dutch. (I didn't read it in English on that account.) He was judging by my urbane and sophisticated manner. I told him he was maybe a bad judge.

And the above is probably the only description I'll ever write of our trip. Too much trouble, and where've I heard that said before. Still, I read the above, and think, well, we must've enjoyed it. Me limping around cussing like Richard III for his humpback; Atwood there being cool; the mosquitoes loving it too. (no screens in Holland, incidentally)

And hey, I meant to talk about lit. Not just moderns. Why doesn't Lee like metrics and rhyming verse for instance? I cite your comment on Auden. ("He rhymes—horrors!") And Russell Brown: "Dennis is so sure of himself." Gee whiz, no more space.

Al

1. Shirley Kaufman: American poet (*The Floor Keeps Turning*, 1970) and translator who has lived in Israel for the past several decades. Ursula Fanthorpe, see page 426. Jerome Rothenberg (b. 1931): American poet (*A Seneca Journal*, 1978). Seamus Heaney (b. 1939): Irish poet (*Death of a Naturalist*, 1966; *Field Work*, 1979), awarded the Nobel Prize.
2. Brian Mulroney (b. 1939): Prime Minister of Canada 1984–92, best remembered for his Irish song duets with Ronald Reagan. John Turner (b. 1929): longtime Liberal politician in the Pearson and Trudeau governments and Prime Minister in 1984.

Anna Porter (b. 1947): was an editor at McClelland and Stewart during the second half of the Jack McClelland era and, from 1982 on, the publisher of Key Porter Books. She is also the author of a memoir and several mystery novels.

From Anna Porter (Toronto), to Ameliasburgh, July 15, 1986

Dear Al,
I've been meaning to write to you since I saw the May issue of *Books in Canada*.[1] I had almost forgotten how funny all that stuff was. I still remember sitting on some rock in Ameliasburgh, at dusk, Harold wrapped in a gigantic cape, Jack pouring vodka for everybody. I also remember trying to get some sleep in the loft, while you all kept talking in hushed whispers rising to loud shouts in the living room. Do you still live in the same house?

As for your hiding out in my apartment, for the record: I never kept my underthings in the closet. You were crouched amongst my shoes. From my point of view, one of the small quirky things about all that is that in 1969 I had just arrived at McClelland & Stewart, and indeed a few months before from England. I was a relatively recent graduate from an obscure New Zealand university, suffering from minor culture shock. You can imagine the impression all of you made on me! Obviously, I was sufficiently overwhelmed that I've stayed in publishing ever since.

It would be nice to see you again.

Best wishes,

Anna

1. "As for Them and Their Houses," *Books in Canada*, May 1986: "In the bedroom I drifted into uneasy sleep, then awoke to hear noises I couldn't identify, which seemed to be in the apartment itself. Take no chances, I thought, and dived into the bedroom closet, closing the door behind me, and remained there in the darkness quivering nervously . . . But they never found me—crouched among Anna Szigety's underthings."

Ursula Fanthorpe (b. 1929): English poet (*Side Effects*, 1978; *Consequences*, 2000).

To Ursula Fanthorpe (England), from Ameliasburgh, July 20, 1986

Dear Ursula Fanthorpe,
I bought volume #XVII from an early set of Kipling, dated 1899.[1] It's labelled "Early Verse." I thought of both our opinions of Kipling when I bought it, and had never seen K's really early verse before.

I meant to mention to you when I wrote that Kipling was never personally behind his own verse, not with that first person singular dominating things. And that is unlike both you and I. But in this early stuff K. is behind his poems; he's not prophetic in the dominating sense he later became; under the titles it says, Tennyson, Longfellow, Swinburne, Browning etc. Of course I knew he had to have read those people, but it's a bit of a surprise that he imitated them. And his "School-Boy Lyrics" are included as well, which was a mistake. This early stuff is terrible.

That doesn't make me think less of Kipling, but I'm a bit relieved he didn't spring up full-blown, a great poet as we both think he was/is. "Departmental Ditties" are also included as early poems. His other-poet imitations are labelled "Echoes."

Now that's a helluva way to start a letter to a poet I admire; but this early K. came as a bit of a surprise to me. Later on K's voice was/is magisterial and prophetic . . . But he lost the first person, and judging from those poems' quality it's just as well.

There are maybe half a dozen K. poems that stick in my head. I can't recite em all, just some lines from them. "When I was a king and a mason," and "After me cometh a builder, Tell him I too have known." And "They made Diego Valdez high admiral of Spain." From the same, "The fountain in the desert, the cistern in the waste / The bread we ate in secret, the cup we spilled in haste." And another, "Our Fathers of Old," of which I can't remember much, but it's marvellous. And "Buy my English posies . . ." And "The youth new-taught of longing, the widow curbed and wan . . ." And "All the winds of Canada call the plowing rain . . ." "From heathen tube and iron shard / Thy mercy on Thy people Lord . . ." And "See you the little path that runs / All hollow through the wheat / Oh that was where they hauled the guns / That smote King Philip's fleet . . ." More verses of that last, "Puck's Song." And I find I can remember more bits and pieces and snatches of stuff . . .

Well, enough. I'm pleased I don't write like him, could never come close. That poets really are individuals and have their own virtues and abilities if they can find them in time. As I think you have and have . . .

After Eurithe and I toured Holland in a rented car, we were at Rotterdam where we met you. After R-dam three days in Amsterdam. Got a crummy hotel room by the Amstel River. Visited the van Gogh museum (wow!); went for a boat ride on the canals (disappointing); hunted for antiquarian book stores (found little); found a street that was entirely red light district. The women lounged in front, fat and ugly and lots of time on their hands apparently. I was fascinated, having led a sheltered life and never having seen a brothel. (Yeah, I know, despite advanced age, I never have.) [. . .]

It was a pleasure to meet you and hear and read your poems. I hope we meet again.

Al Purdy

1. Rudyard Kipling (1865–1936): English novelist (*Kim*, 1901) and poet. AP often quoted him in letters, essays and conversation. He also wrote an essay on him in 1989, "Rudyard Kipling" (*Brick* [Summer 1989]; *Starting from Ameliasburgh*).

To Dennis Lee (Toronto), from Victoria, BC, September 21, 1986

Dear Dennis,

More or less settled here now . . . occupying the middle apt. of three. Quite a large house, supposed to have been owned in early days by BC's "hanging judge" Matthew Baillie Begbie. If you don't know him, he was a failed lawyer in England, came to Canada during the Cariboo gold rush and got appointed judge and made a fearsome reputation . . . We bought the place last summer, letting the rents pay for it after a small down payment. (Thus we become slum landlords—tho the place is not that.)

My reading accompli Sept. 12, then Ted Hughes Sept 18. David Day, a friend of Hughes, brought him here on the promise of good fishing. Hughes had 300 at Open Space plus standees . . . He takes a pretty grim view of life, a worser Newlove . . . Also met P.K. Page at reading . . .

Feeling quite displaced and disoriented here, despite relatives . . . And climate is cold despite lush greenery everywhere . . . Trouble is: I have no immediate project on which to focus my miniscule energies . . . There is a book of articles and short things I shall probably work on . . . But the trip out was more interesting than actually being here . . .

And I'm wondering how I shall feel about this Collected when I see it. Don't like the cover picture much, tho I tried to disguise this feeling when I met the book's designer at McStew . . . I look like a character outa the 16th century, not quite real to myself . . .

I wrote a baseball poem when Judith Fitzgerald[1] asked. It appeared in a Can. baseball tabloid. Avie Bennett[2] phoned me when he saw it, said he didn't know I was a "regular guy" and invited self and wife to see a game in his box. I traded Eurithe for her brother and went. Huge box, musta been twenty-five people, with a girl slave serving drinks and food. Among guests Harold Town and Chas. Templeton.[3] Woman I was talking to mid-game says Harold Town said to her: "Purdy doesn't know anything about baseball." I really love that man . . . He reminds me I still have likes and dislikes . . .

Al

1. Judith Fitzgerald, see page 526.
2. Avie Bennett had bought McClelland and Stewart in December 1985.

3. Charles Templeton (1915–2001): a former evangelist, Templeton wrote several popular novels, none of which have made it into *The Oxford Companion to Canadian Literature* or the *Encyclopedia of Literature in Canada* (*Act of God*, 1977; *The Third Temptation*, 1980). He also wrote *Farewell to God: My Reasons for Rejecting the Christian Faith* (1996).

John Bentley Mays (b. 1941): cultural columnist (*Globe and Mail, National Post*) and writer (*In the Jaws of the Black Dogs: A Memoir of Depression*, 1995).

To John Bentley Mays (Toronto), from Victoria, BC, October 14, 1986

Dear Mr. Mays,
I was/am much interested in your essay on Sargent[1] in the Oct. 13 *Globe*. Apart from anything else, it seems to me excellent and enjoyable.

The essay raises certain questions in my own mind. I know that your space in a newspaper is limited; but I am sure you must have considered some of the points for which there was no space to elaborate. At the end you say Sargent's gift was "squandered," and I think you must mean this was because he was rootless and had no centre of being in either geography or philosophy. Altho perhaps the latter word does not apply.

You also seem to imply that Sargent should have stayed in Paris after his *Portrait of Madame X,* despite the outrage of French critics. And that the "lostness" in Henry James' eyes was at least partly due to his being an expatriate. (James has always been much too wordy for my taste, and I've never understood Graham Greene's liking for him.[2]) Re *Portrait of Madame X*, you say it depicted "a fabric of tightly-tuned nerves, ready to tear apart at the slightest touch." But that was not the reason French critics attacked Sargent?

You also mention that Dr. Pozzi inhabits the same world as Sargent, where "pleasure is the only patriotism." That word "patriotism" perhaps refers back to Sargent being an expatriate. And I wonder at your reasons for coupling Pozzi with Sargent, apart from their both living in a world of luxury. Was Pozzi perhaps also an expatriate?

Please understand that these comments are in no way a criticism of your essay. If I were reading a bad essay such questions and comments would not be raised. The fact that I've written this letter at all is indication that I hope you accept it as a compliment. And your essay seems to call for longer treatment, space that I regret you do not have.

Until I read your essay I had coupled Sargent with Whistler as a pair of American expatriates of little consequence. Which shows my ignorance, since Whistler may rank much higher than my small awareness allows him.

I expect to be living in Toronto next winter, and hope I may have the pleasure of meeting you then.

Best Wishes,
Al Purdy

1. John Singer Sargent (1856–1925): American painter, best-known for his portraits of society figures. Rodin called him "the van Dyck of our times." Sargent was born in Florence and spent much of his life in Europe.
2. AP owned a copy of Greene's *Collected Essays* and knew the essays on Henry James: "Henry James: The Private Universe," "Henry James: The Religious Aspect," "The Portrait of a Lady" and "The Plays of Henry James."

From George Johnston (Athelstan, Que.), to Victoria, BC, December 24, 1986

Dear Al,

Thank you for your letter. I did not know that you had a house in Victoria. I hope this means that you are prospering at least comparatively, and being recognized appropriately as one of our country's ornaments. You are not one to make anything of your fame, nor to complain of neglect either, but I hope that you do not have cause to feel neglected. Were you ever a member of the League? I do not remember. I rejoined but cannot give myself a satisfactory answer to the question, why. Your name does not appear on my new list of members. For two or three somewhat separated years I was glad to be a member & to go to their meetings. Well, I am in the Translators' Association now too, I still go to their meetings & enjoy them. Translators are a generous-spirited lot, though they have their quirks and oddities too, but who am I to complain of those? You say you do not get my reference to Gasparini's[1] putting his digestion on the line over you. I remember his review of one of your books a few years ago, in the *Forum* I think, in which he offered to eat his typewriter if you were not the best poet writing in English. Someone else referred to that review as though everyone knew it so I thought you might. [...]

I liked your piece on Milton Acorn in *Books in Canada*.[2] They seem to be making a lot of him now. I liked him well enough what I saw of him and he was always friendly with me but I knew I did not have the patience that I could sense he would call for. And I did not have the patience for much of his poetry. I felt sorry for him & at the same time I knew I had my nerve to be feeling sorry for him, he seemed to be bigger than that. You must have known him well, but I am sure you have more patience & generosity with people than I have. I shall be glad to get your new book & I look forward to reading it. [...]

We cannot stop and have lunch with you when you are so far away, but we send you our best wishes.

George

1. Len Gasparini (b. 1941): book reviewer and poet (*Selected Poems*, 1993).
2. "In Love and Anger" appeared in the October issue of *Books in Canada*. Acorn had died on August 20, 1986.

Janet Lunn (b. 1928): well-known writer of books for children (*The Root Cellar*, 1981; *Shadow in Hawthorn Bay*, 1986).

To Janet Lunn, from Victoria, BC, December 25, 1986

Dear Janet,

[...] Eurithe read your book and liked it, incidentally. I haven't—as yet. Is reading my mind that simple, so that you knew I either would or wouldn't?

I've come across a short review of *Piling Blood* that makes my teeth grind without any muscular effort on my part. Stephen Scobie. He says, "Mmm, not bad—not one of the really *great* years, not a '65 or an '81, but very creditable, should age well." Referring to the vintage. [...] "Very creditable." And "All the familiar Purdy themes and tricks are here, some of them a little *too* self-conscious (if he gives a cute name to another pre-historic fossil, I'll scream) (unquote, he'd scream in tremolo soprano) "some of them sounding suspiciously like what a clever student might write as pastiche Al Purdy." Then says I "get away with it again"—why is it ex-Englishmen are so condescending? He interviewed me before I read this on U-Vic radio, tried to make me admit I nurtured my image deliberately, which annoyed me some. I disagreed with everything he said. And if you laugh, I'll kill you.

We leave for Mexico in four days, another cheap excursion Eurithe dug up at a thrift shop. Air fare and two weeks hotel rooms for $500.

Al

To Dennis Lee (Toronto), from Victoria, BC, January 3, 1987

Dear Dennis,

That's all I could remember. And the damn thing kept running thru my head, and me tryin to think of somebody else in history about whom I could write something similar, if not slavishly copy. All that came to mind was John A., and he's too obvious. Must be somebody else. Somebody you could say the same things about as you did. Beats me.

This was in Mexico, incidentally. There I am in this little tourist hotel trying to remember a Lee poem.[1] Incidentally, we took our little electric frypan and ate steaks at the hotel for around a buck apiece, more or less. The Mexicans charge the same for all cuts of beef including hamburger.

Pat Page phoned yesterday to pay me some compliments, but also to get your address, she admired your crit piece [in the *Collected Poems*] so much. That's kinda nice, I think. Isn't everyone that generous. I asked her if she read N. Frye; she said no. That's comforting, since I can't read his *Anatomy*[2]; I bog down by page minus 1.

In fact most writing is boring me these days, all but Milan Kundera. Layton said the man was marvellous, which almost put me off him, since Layton's recommends are not mine. But he was right. Read *The Incredible Lightness of Being*, (these guys are really dramatists, from Czechoslovakia, I mean, what with *The Engineer of Human Souls*[3]—sounds like God in Science 14) . . .

Seems like I'm writer-in-rez at Toronto this yr; they came up with some bucks for us to rent an apt. Maybe we can have a beer between paydays.

All best,

Al

1. AP may be thinking of Lee's *Civil Elegies* or some of his children's poems that deal with Canadian history.
2. *Anatomy of Literary Criticism* (1957).
3. The title of Kundera's novel is *The Unbearable Lightness of Being* (1984). The author of *The Engineer of Human Souls* is Josef Skvorecky. AP and Skvorecky had dinner together in Toronto in the early 1990s. During a discussion of poetry, they took turns reciting poems from memory, Skvorecky in Czech, Purdy in English.

To Margaret Atwood (Toronto), from Victoria, BC, January 5, 1987

Dear Peggy,

A friend phoned and said Margaret Laurence died today.[1] I feel awful about that. You were a friend of hers, I think. I feel like wallowing in grief—which is silly to say, I suppose—but instead I talk to you.

To hell with it. I will not talk about it.

I've just barely looked at your book, including the one about the ageing poet on the balcony . . .[2] And wanted to tell you: I think you're a beautiful woman, on that book cover, and the woman I saw at Rotterdam. You weren't always, I don't think, but you've become one over the years. Why shouldn't older male writers dream of getting you into bed, and younger ones want to show you their poems? You've become a grande dame as well as beautiful. You actually looked luminous at Rotterdam, or so I thought. Whatever your personal dreams were/are, they must have been realized.

Oh sure, there are always pain and travail, and we all die, as has just been brought home to me once more by ML. Still, as much or more than anyone, you've kept the hounds at bay. And I applaud you for it.

Please don't answer this. The business of Margaret L. dying, it's so awful. And tears come to my eyes, and I say: are those real tears, do you really feel this, or what?

And I say,

CBC National just came on . . .

Well, anyway . . . (As I say, please don't reply to this . . .)

Al

1. AP wrote a brief elegy for Laurence, "Lawrence to Laurence" (*The Woman on the Shore*, 1991). It ends as follows: "And remember a remark by Margaret Laurence / 'I expect to grow old raising / cats and roses—' (but she didn't) / When you dismiss the groping metaphysics / what all this means is a patented / method of jumping from Lawrence / to Laurence and I mourn both / from steel nib pen & ink to cats & roses / Goodbye—"
2. AP is referring to "Aging Female Poet Sits on Balcony."

To George Johnston (Athelstan, Que.,) from Victoria, BC, January 6, 1987

Dear George,

That's a handsome book.[1] Thank you for it. (I will send along my *Collected* as soon as I get some copies.) Carl Schaefer must be a good and close friend of yours; I've just received the book, and no time yet to read it.

I think you might be giving me too much credit for modesty and easy-to-get-along-withness, etc. But no, I don't feel neglected. I've had more attention for this *Collected* than ever before, and superlatives directed my way that seem somewhat surprising. But then Canadians seem to ache for greatness, and do throw around a lot of superlatives for their writers. Reminds one of the Americans talking about their country, which I find a bit sickening.

Yes, I was one of the founding members of the League, along with Birney, Souster and Dudek. But I quit/resigned about five years back, when all that fuss about women poets being deprived of attention by males etc. came up. And Beissel left a bad taste in my mouth after his tenure. The whole thing got to be too much—

Now that you explain it, the Gasparini reference you made is funny as hell . . . Before I forget to mention: we'll be back in A-burg next summer; we're here to escape the snow and because Eurithe has many relatives here.

You seem to have an enormous family. (Mine is all on Eurithe's side; there's none at all on mine whom I have anything to do with.) And to enjoy it. [. . .]

I ran out of patience with Acorn, and now regret it. One had to agree with him at all times to avoid conflict during his last few years. And I got tired of never disagreeing. And yesterday Margaret Laurence died . . . We knew her well at one time. When Eurithe was ill after an operation in England in 1970, we stayed at Margaret's house in Penn for several weeks . . . It makes one feel that life is pretty precarious, your own life I mean, as well as the people you know . . .

Best wishes for yourself and family at this season or any season . . . (Why should good wishes be confined to a season . . .)

Al

1. Johnston wrote a prose memoir of his friend Carl Schaefer, *Carl: Portrait of a Painter* (1986).

To Patrick Lane, from Victoria, BC, February 6, 1987

Dear Pat,
I do appreciate you calling re my *Collected*. It denotes a kind of generosity not everyone has, especially when we're both similarly occupied at Great Literature.

Then I have to go and say I do the same thing, completely screwing my compliment for your compliment by giving myself the same credit. Anyway, forgive me for that. But I've written William Golding several times, before and after he got the Nobel. I had arranged to drive him around Ontario if Greg Gatenby gave him time, but Greg Gatenby didn't. I couldn't even catch up with him at his reading in Toronto, then a friend said during intermission, "There he is going down the stairs." So I dashed after him, introduced myself on the staircase, and was somewhat dashed in turn when he said, "I'm just going to the toilet, I can't stop—" Which stopped me completely. I felt like a teeny-bopper (whatever that is) dashing after her idol and feeling foolish when said idol outfooted me.

And I had this terrific admiration for Golding, still do in fact. Also Ted Hughes. I once wrote a letter to Edmund Wilson; got a card back with slots on it for various comments amounting to the fact that he never answered letters. And also wrote a letter to Roy Campbell in the days when my taste was somewhat different. He answered as well. Ditto Layton, my equipment fortunately not susceptible to the same comment as yours.

The above is prelude to repeating my own appreciation, and confirming that I'm sure Dennis Lee would love to hear from you. Incidentally, I think you and I have interests in common; but somehow the circumstances here don't lend themselves to much social intercourse—very unfortunately for me.

Al

From Irving Layton (Montreal), to Sydney, BC, April 29, 1987

[...] You can understand my pleasure on receiving your latest book [*Piling Blood*]. What can I say? It's a damn fine collection, one of your best. You've stored your mind with fresh images, with a "riot of melons pomegranates grapes." Rhododendrons become "a scarlet jubilee in the blood." I like the fantasy of the fallen petals cheering up the ground.

I don't want to write an essay on your excellent book, I only wanted to let you know how much I appreciate the energy experience and richness that I have found in your pages. My last comment, at least for now I'll let it be my last one, is how wonderfully, how uniquely Canadian I find your poems—especially this collection. I glory in our continued friendship over these many years. With a full heart, thank you for the gracious words you wrote on the fly-leaf.[1]

1. "For Irving with admiration and affection—but not in that order, Al Purdy, Ameliasburg, Ont., Feb. 10, 1987."

To Dennis Lee (Toronto), from Ameliasburgh, June 8, 1987

Dear Dennis,

I feel badly I couldn't say more about your poems that would make you look at them/it differently. That's what you did for me with *Being Alive* and others. I feel inadequate and imperceptive . . .

Of course I know that you have that talent and I don't, your brain can do it. But that isn't my point. I ought to be able to say more where you're concerned because you're you. i.e. you're special for me. Oh I can say things about beginners and neophytes, etc. But that's different.

So I guess this is a kinda apology, but not exactly . . . I leave it to you to assess my feelings.

I'm almost solely intuitive, whereas think you're both that and aware of the intuition that is aware of the mental processes that are aware of etc.

So fuckit.

I have a Lawrence letter (original holograph) on the wall in front of typer, and see where his steel nib pen ran short of ink and he dipped it again, after a faded passage etc. Dated 1922. Las Cruzes, Taos, NM. And how odd to see your own right hand want to reach for the ink . . . Yes, probably a poem, a trivial one tho.

I would like to see what happens to your own poem if you can forgive my own slow reactions etc. . . .

                                    Best,
                                    Al

To Pierre Trudeau (Montreal), from Ameliasburgh, June 16, 1987

Dear Pierre,

Just writing to say hello. In case you don't remember—I'm the guy you drank cider with in Cuba. I think you paid too.

Wanted to say I support your stand on the Meech Lake thing entirely. Received the GG Award in Toronto a coupla weeks ago, and prefaced my thanks for it by saying I hope we recognize Canada a few years from now after Meech Lake and the free trade talks (words to that effect). None of the papers mentioned that, just said I said my wife wrote all the poems and I get all the credit . . .

I can't think of any way to add my two cents worth to the debate I hope will take place. But I hope you'll be involved somehow. I'm sorry Jean Chretien isn't in there too. Turner seems to me a wimp without any program or policy . . .

This may sound a little incoherent, but wanted to wish you well no matter what happens . . .

Al Purdy

To ——, from Ameliasburgh, August 8, 1987

Dear ——,

Sure I know about "these things"—I've been through them. Without names dates and places and people, I assure you that's true. So it's a helluva mess—I know I know . . . But knowing on my part doesn't help at all . . .

I know also, there's a perverse pleasure in your own agony. (i.e. have fun, a grisly kind of fun where you contemplate death and shit and beauty and what the hell all at the same time) . . .

I do feel much the same as you re staying with someone, the near flesh, the loved conglomeration of future dust, etc. Sure. You need it.

Perhaps I haven't made myself clear enough re my feelings of "no advice" . . . I said it was too important, and it is. But more, an outsider (and I am an outsider in this, despite the relationship) is too prone to mistakes. And if I were you (advice?) I wouldn't listen to even the most kindly disposed friends. When I went through all this myself, I didn't confide in anyone; there was no one close.

So the pollyanna approach is to say, you get over it. An awful thing to say! That perverse bit mentioned above says one doesn't wanta get over it.

In case there's the least doubt, I'd like the best for you. You seem close to me not because, but in spite of, the relationship.

No idea what'd be available in grants, apart from CC and OntArts. As I've said, I'm obviously disallowed as a recommendor . . . A jury would laugh and make snide remarks. Seems to me I could say something about that. I'd say, fuck the stripper poems. If there's so much difficulty in getting em published, lay em aside till much later. Write some more. Surely you're not stuck back there among the strippers. How about the present agony? Isn't that much more relevant, both to you and others? Sure it is.

So write some poems about it. Pour out your guts in em. Say whatever. Write all your blackest worstest thoughts and name names even if nom de plumes. Name places. The tape you mention, which I didn't recall. Write it out. Let the old imagination go, in any direction it wants, but go go go. And cry bitter alcoholic tears (if you feel like it) while writing ... It's an escape by going directly into prison and confronting your captors.

I can't write three pages. I'm much too old and decrepit.

Al

Anthony Burgess (1917–93): pen name of John Anthony Burgess Wilson, English composer, critic and novelist best known for *A Clockwork Orange* (1962) and for the dazzling first sentence of *Earthly Pleasures* (1980).

To Anthony Burgess (c/o William Heinemann Ltd., London, England), from Ameliasburgh, November 3, 1987

Dear Anthony Burgess,

This letter is in appreciation of your *Flame Into Being* and its own appreciation of DHL. I've read quite a number of other books on Lawrence, but none have given me quite the same feeling of both interest and affection for a man I consider to have been the best writer of his time. And yes, I agree with you that *Women in Love* is his best book.

I appreciate also that you, a very busy writer, should take time off from his own novels to write this appreciation of Lawrence.

As well, I owe you several bits of information and thoughts that I either didn't know or didn't give them their true importance. For instance, I hadn't been aware that Maria Huxley was so warm-hearted toward Lawrence, and that she had held him in her arms near the end. Or else I've forgotten, since one would think that such info would be included in Harry Moore's book.[1]

I can't agree with you that "it is wrong to judge Lawrence on single works," although, sure, his entire output was "one massive literary utterance." I find his method of writing, repetition of phrases, for instance, both good and bad in effect, depending on individual usage. And certain books, even the much-admired *Sons and Lovers*, I find difficult to read. Other books, such as *Apocalypse*, are too much for me, I don't understand them or am too lazy to keep trying.

But generally speaking, I agree with you when you mention your own favourites. *Sea and Sardinia, Birds, Beasts and Flowers,* and many of the essays. My view of him is undoubtedly extremely romantic, to the extent that I have a couple of his original letters (to his US agent) taped to my wall. Work-room wall, that is. (Yes, I'm a writer.)

The question you raise as to what Lawrence would have done if he'd lived is extremely interesting to me. Yes, I think Joyce had shot his bolt. And I can't imagine Dylan Thomas continuing to write poems in that intense prophetic voice, if he had lived. But you mention Lawrence as a "professional" writer, and I certainly agree. He would have continued writing if alive. And isn't just one more story like "The Man Who Died" very worthwhile? But of course you mean Lawrence's best period was over. I hate to think so, altho it's bootless to speculate. I'm inclined to think that poets, as apart from novelists, have a five to ten year period when they're at their best, and never reach this excellence again. Said period is generally—almost always—when poets are not yet 40. Yeats is the only exception to this rule that I can think of.

If Lawrence had lived, perhaps additional work would have been the result of him being a "professional" writer, rather than the outpouring of "preaching" and things he thought must be said.

I could go on for much too long. However, I enclose zeroxes of poems I've written about Lawrence. Not my best, but written because I loved him.

Sincerely,
Al Purdy

1. Harry T. Moore's biography of Lawrence was titled *The Intelligent Heart* (1954); in the revised edition it was *The Priest of Love.*

To Irving Layton (Montreal), from Ameliasburgh, November 14, 1987

Dear Irving,
Good to see you in Toronto. I'm sorry it was so brief. All my affection for Layton keeps getting renewed, despite the continual risk of sentimentality accusations. And I claim that Layton, despite that brief Hungarian or Bulgarian episode during which you were weaned from mother's milk to Molson's, that you are 100% Canadian, despite your dubiousness about that point in Toronto.[1] Well, 99% anyway. (I'll give you a few pointers on the subject next meeting! Okay?)

But as for my resemblance to Leacock, I really must protest. Unless you intend to write a long academic article on the subject, tracing individual sources etc. in which case I will give you all the help I can. That's the same as saying Layton's relationship to Nietzsche and Milan Kundera is more than kissing kin. And really, I don't think you resemble Nietzsche or Kundera even a little . . . I was once much influenced by Dylan Thomas, but defy anyone to trace that one now.

But Irving, please——Leacock???? And if you must continue this game of influences, would you keep your voice down? I may not be a complete original, but claim natheless that my influences and resemblances are not completely traceable. If there were the vague lineaments of one the country has come to know and love with a wealth of lavished and entirely un-requited affection as—Irving Layton would be discerned: and the tandem known singly and au pair as dirty old men, as you so brilliantly pointed out during your reading.

Yep, the dirty old man himself is certainly partly responsible for Purdy. Howdoya like them apples?

This next one is a secret, so please don't sell this letter for a while yet. Betty Gustafson said to me: could I do anything for Ralph re the Order of Canada? She also said Ralph is 78 and has cancer of the bowels, and such an award would be pleasureable to him. Now, if the Order can go to Fred Cogswell for chrissake, then it sure as hell can go to Gus!

Will you help? i.e. write a letter to this guy with the French name at the GG house (I gotta look these things up) and recommend our Gus? Like I said, if Cogswell . . . Migawd, it does give one pause to fart . . . And I wouldn't want Ralph to hear of this, which is the reason for my injunc-tion to secrecy.

Al

1. AP is either being puckish or he has forgotten that Layton was born in Romania.

Greg Gatenby (b. 1950): Toronto poet (*Growing Still: Poems*, 1981), anthologist (*Whale Sound: An Anthology of Poems about Whales and Dolphins*, 1977) and founder and former artistic director of Toronto's Harbourfront International Festival of Authors. In 1996 and 2000 he organized tributes to AP.

To Greg Gatenby (Toronto), from Ameliasburgh, January 28, 1988

Dear Greg,

Thanks much for all the hospitality.

Re addresses in Toronto, in 1965–66 we lived on Sackville St. in Cabbagetown, just two or three blocks from Riverdale Zoo and the Toronto Crematorium. I used to wander in graveyard and zoo sometimes. In summer of '65 I went to the arctic, returning to work on poems in *North of Summer* at that apt. In fact, I remember turning the light out for sleep in winter after return, and thinking of that title, *North of Summer*, so much like a child's conception of the north. I used to walk to Parliament for groceries, passing the Winchester Hotel at corner of Winchester and Parliament. There was a liquor and beer store close to that corner, and the bums used to hit you up for a quarter to buy something.

In '67 we were in Ottawa, where I was visiting the House of Commons with the mistaken idea that it might provide poems.

For one winter we were in Islington, probably 68–69 or the next winter. Can't remember the street. We'd rented a furnished place from an 80 some years old man named Gatch. Seems he was quite a well-known guy, and I read or heard somewhere that he'd passed his hundredth birthday. That being several years ago. But memory furnishes scanty details. (What writer was first to read at Harbourfront under your regime? I bet you can't remember 15 years back!) At Islington, I'd have been working on *Wild Grape Wine*, and arguing with Jack McClelland.

Now if you ever do a similar book on Vancouver, I can furnish quite a few more details. Re Sackville St., I think we were there at least two years. Eurithe was attending teachers' college somewhere in Toronto. When we went to Ottawa in '67, she had her teacher's certificate and did supply teaching there. Also re Sackville, I found it an interesting area and used to frequent the thrift shops. I recall one night, around 11 p.m. or midnight, I left the apt. to drive to Ameliasburgh. The cops stopped me before I could get in the car. It seems someone robbed a convenience store a few blocks away, and I fitted the description of the miscreant. I wore a brown corduroy windbreaker at the time, which the convenience shop guy had described the robber as wearing. The cops asked me if I minded coming along with them to the crime scene, which I didn't mind but didn't want to say so for obvious reasons. So they took me to the convenience store and I was cleared and returned by the cops to where I was picked up.

And that's it, I guess.

Thanks again for the beer and food after reading. And if you have that Franco-Anglo readings address I'd appreciate it.

Cordially,

Al

To Dennis Lee (Toronto), from Sidney, BC, December 4, 1988

Dear Dennis,

One does lose track of friends and everyone else sometimes. Eurithe and I drove south to Florida, where we roosted three weeks (kindness of Bill Percy and his mobile home). Then drove west thru the US, taking a week to travel nearly 4,000 miles. We turned north south-east of LA, heading for Canada.

But the Californian mtns—migawd the mtns! We went thru 4,000 and 5,000 foot pass(es), snow falling pretty heavily on both. On the approaches to the high one, signs saying don't go farther without chains. Warning, dire prediction, etc. We had no chains. Eurithe happened to be driving then, and she would try for the moon on one tank of oxygen. Me, I'd want a dozen. Needless to say, both of us drove carefully. Me huddled on the seat, hanging onto handles, nails clenched in fingers, blood pressure soaring (had to visit a doctor here for some drugs) . . . Arrived sorta flummoxed and drained . . .

I've been workin at a novel[1] all summer; continued after interruption in Florida; but not yet here. Got to some 50,000 words, with trepidation and uncertainty. About a 16-yr-old growin up in Trenton in 1918, at the time of the big fire and explosion of the munitions plant there. (Second worst or "biggest" in Can. history; and I bet you never heard of it. British Chemical employed some 2,500 men, made TNT and all related combustibles . . .)

Seems hard to get the books I want here . . . Need one on the cholera epidemics of immigrants in early 19th century for instance. My "novel" (must call it that) is partly autobio (of course), but seems to me surprisingly little . . . Patrick's grandfather, age 90 in 1918, was an old lumberjack and backwoodsman, one of those scarey horn-handed old bastards, bull of the woods etc. He dies. Six old men, also lumbermen, come to his funeral, kinda take over the town. And of course the Br. Chemical blows up, with consequent confusion.

Not a children's book, which I meant to write originally. I'm just—

442

goddammit—not a children's writer, I can't simplify things for the lil bastards . . . or think like they do, the way you apparently can. But I forge onward, struggling manfully against entropy. And losing. Notice the sweat on this page?

S. Musgrave and her bankrobber-novelist husband out here . . . Stephen Reid, incidentally, is quite likeable. Musgrave is about as pregnant as possible, due about Christmas. And Linda Rogers, David Day's ex.[2] Eurithe and I both like Linda much. And of course E's various siblings. So we don't lack for people.

The house we bought is across the road from the water that separates us from the mainland. We own the land over there too, about 100 feet wide and say 120 feet frontage. We're a mile or so from Sidney, but within the town's boundaries. I'd say it's 5–6–7000 people.

Must say, I miss the land, water and air from around A-burg (but not the snow). I need all those things to permeate the novel. It's difficult for me, the writing; it's also exhilarating, sometimes.

How are you? That long poem? Back trouble okay? General demeanor and condition? I mean the sorta answer you get when you say to yourself, How'm I doin? . . . How you doin?

Al

1. *A Splinter in the Heart* (1990).
2. Linda Rogers (b. 1944): illustrator, performer and poet (*Love in the Rainforest*, 1995), she edited *Al Purdy: Essays on His Work* (2002). David Day (b. 1947): children's writer and poet (*The Cowichan*, 1976). He has also written *Tolkien: The Illustrated Encyclopedia*, 1991.

To Sam Solecki (Toronto), from Ameliasburgh, August 7, 1989

Dear Sam,

I enclose a new poem.

Also the last part of Akhmatova's long poem, which I found very moving. The A poem you sent is much like Omar Khayyam, eh? Except for last verse. There are other good parts to A's Requiem, but this is by far and consistently the best. Lowell did a great job.

I leave the placement of "The Others" to you, but it'd be good if we could have it on two facing pages, since it would be longer than one. Must be getting to ninety pages?[1]

I still can't read Rilke with appreciation, can't stand those Leishman trans anyway. Mandelstam and Boris P.—can appreciate to a limited extent. G. Bowering wrote saying he couldn't understand why I don't like W.C. Williams: to me the guy is a near-simpleton.

Al

1. Solecki had just taken over as poetry editor at McClelland and Stewart.

To Stan Dragland (London, Ont.), from Sidney, BC, October 28 1989

Dear Stan,

Re D.C. Scott, I see a bit in the *Times Colonist* here that quotes Scott on the subject of Indian schools, to the effect that the object of their education was to make them forget they were ever Indians. Ample room there for a bio.[1]

Yeah, know what you mean about those Afterwords. I just did one for Birney's *Turvey*—and wrote it by centering myself into Birney's novel. [...]

The thing baffled me for some time, since the book seems quite a simple one to me—unless you go all psychological ... Coach House seems to me the opposite of eclectic; they almost strive to be unpopular and little-read and non-bestseller. That's non stuff; so what are they actually? Of course they began with Victor Coleman, who's a non-writer, and fits right in with the non credo. It's easy to say that now they are avant garde or something similar. But unlike, say, Brick, which really is somewhat avant garde in its opinions, Coach House strikes me as too often just quirky. Incidentally, I wrote Brick saying I thought they oughta make a small book out of that Frank Scott issue a year or so back.

The novel[2]—well, I finished it, or thought I did. Then gave it to Dennis Lee for reading. What he said made me realize it was far from finished, so wrote a couple more long scenes for it and deleted one. And just thinking, at one point I talk about the socio-sexual mores of 1918, which is a bad way to do it. I ought to've illustrated that in the dialogue or action: and will have to do so. Dennis Lee also said that my 16-year-old wasn't feeling sex enough. So I wrote a masturbation fantasy-cum-reality, which I dunno whether works or not. Dennis thought it good, but you always read between the lines of what anyone says. There are parts of it that I think good, at least cling to the thought that bits of it have some merit. But I'm sick of it at this point.

I have a book of poems due in March.[3] (I'm about to correct the proofs.) And much other stuff to do ...

No, I never think of my stuff as "bigger than explanation"—However, there is a quality about any good poem, a mystic quality which somehow makes it larger than its author, who may not be very intelligent even. And yeah, I dislike explanations of poems anyway, but if kids are going to read and be interested in them, I suppose they must be explicated. I cannot in my own mind fathom how or why I write poems . . . The reason given in "The Dead Poet" is, I suppose, as good as any, maybe as close as I could come. But all of the reasons I once had for writing poems have changed or been dropped entirely. The basic one is it makes you feel so good to have your brain go drunken, which I expect is what most writers feel. But I'd hate to think that the writers who write purely or impurely for money—I'd hate to think they too had that drunken feeling.

Your horse standing in the shade of a telephone pole: coming from Toronto by train on a hot summer day, I saw a horse shading his head against one upright of a high-power electrical pylon, other horses off to one side in the sun. The first horse didn't get much shade, but obviously relished what there was. He stood with that two-inch-wide shadow on his forehead, almost as if posing. I started to write a poem on the scene, but it failed.

best,

Al

1. Five years later, Dragland published *Floating Voice: Duncan Campbell Scott and the Literature of Treaty 9*.
2. *A Splinter in the Heart.*
3. *The Woman on the Shore.*

To Sam Solecki (Toronto), from Sidney, November 8, 1989

Dear Sam,

[. . .] I suppose I don't give a damn if Kipling's poems are poems or not, altho I think they are.[1] By the time I finished Eliot's long essay I'd forgotten most of what went before the next to last word. But Rudyard slumbers inside me most of the time, until I meet someone who knows not Kip. I think it's frightful ignorance not to know his poems.

I'm reading Robert Lowell's prose off and on. If you haven't seen it, there's a nice passage:

"—I somehow got off on the wrong note about Williams with Ford Madox Ford twenty-five years ago. Ford was wearing a stained robin's-egg-blue pajama top, reading Theocritus in Greek, and guying me about my 'butterfly existence,' so removed from the labours of a professional writer.

I was saying something awkward, green, and intense in praise of Williams, and, while agreeing, Ford managed to make me feel that I was far too provincial, genteel, and puritanical to understand what I was saying. And why not? Wasn't I, as Ford assumed, the grandson or something of James Russell Lowell and the cousin of Lawrence Lowell, a young man doomed to trifle with poetry and end up as president of Harvard or ambassador to England? I have stepped over these pitfalls. I have conquered my hereditary disadvantages. Except for writing, nothing I've touched has shone."[2]

i.e., he thinks he's pretty good. But it's well expressed. One can just imagine Ford guying Lowell.

Have you seen the blooper at the end of my Afterword for Birney's *Turvey*? They omitted the "w" of "now" which fucks up the whole piece. The typesetters, I mean. Who else?[3]

I don't think I can "like" Eliot no matter the bio. You dunno what spats are? Those little pieces of cloth worn on the front of shoes to protect them; the footwear equivalent of a monocle. They kept the feet warm too.

I won't be around when George Galt gets through with me.[4] I wrote Canada Council and told em I have so inhibited GG he can't write till I kick off. [. . .]

Best,
Al

1. Solecki had sent AP Eliot's introductory essay to *A Choice of Kipling's Verse* in which Eliot, an admirer, raises the question "whether Kipling's verse is really poetry," and concludes that Kipling is really a "verse writer" and not a poet.
2. AP quotes from Lowell's "Dr. Williams," the third part of the chapter on Williams in *Collected Prose* (1987).
3. AP had written "Now birds build their nests in springtime. The world renews itself annually. And 'DAH-DAH' goes that music, as it will again and again, as Birney and Turvey knew it would." He also wrote the introduction to Birney's *Last Makings* (1991), Birney's final collection, which had been at McClelland and Stewart since just before the poet's collapse in 1987.
4. AP and Galt had agreed that Galt would write the biography, but only after the death of Eurithe Purdy. Galt has decided not to undertake the biography.

To Sam Solecki (Toronto), from Sidney, BC, December 22, 1989

Dear Sam,
I happen to look in envelope you sent that prose stuff back to me in—and see there was another page to your letter. Already answered that second page, so now I've got the first one to answer . . .

You talk about Milosc—Milosz,[1] that is—who's been interesting to me ever since I saw his photo at a Jeffers memorial or whatever it was . . . There was a look of such absolute cynicism and disbelief on his face looking at Gary Snyder and William Everson[2] it's a wonder they didn't shrivel and disappear. For the first time I could believe in Medusa and her gazers—at turning to stone. But how could a guy like that reveal enough to a biographer?

Apparently disagrees with P.D. Scott . . . [3] You liked that PDS book I believe? I thought it boring as hell. But I agree with Milosz—nothing in Europe would now surprise me, politically that is. Gorbachev as tsar . . . well, why not.

I'd rather have had Sakharov. There was a guy I really admire! He was a big shot already, or he'd have gotten nowhere with all his protests and dissidency. But that takes nothing away from him. He's an example to make one ashamed of not being in the forefront of all revolutions. Like your boy Skorvecky, whose name I'll never be able to spell . . .

But Milosz—I'd love to have met him. That expression in the photo haunts me . . .

Didn't I tell you I read mostly thrillers? You guys in academe hafta read biographies and scholarly studies; all I hafta do is write poems. [. . .]

Cameron-Buitenhuis on Birney for Chrissake. I thought she was already at U of T at New College. Maybe I mentioned: I knew her at Loyola in Mtl. . . . She told me some of her friends called her Becky Sharp. Which is from . . . *Vanity Fair*? Anyway, it's not flattering. [. . .]

I was afraid to say much to Cameron about Birney, after her Layton book. I think she was looking for something disgraceful. Did I mention: George Woodcock wouldn't see her at all.

Not writing much of anything. Started to write a piece on Acorn, realized I wasn't interested. Ditto a poem. Have an admirer out here who bought $350 worth of my early books, left his VCR and tapes here, and has worked a total of four days on first floor where Eurithe is re-modeling the place. But poem-tapes mostly bore me too. Except the Acorn, which I thought marvellous, and the Acorn wake by one Cedric Smith.

How'd it be if I end with Dear Sam? Ain't that switch?

Yours,

Al

1. Czeslaw Milosz (1911–2004): the greatest Polish writer of the twentieth century (*The Captive Mind*, 1953; *The Witness of Poetry*, 1983; *Collected Poems*, 2002). AP's poem "Realism 2" (*To Paris Never Again*) is a response to Milosz's poem

with a similar title that Purdy read in the *New Yorker*. He kept Milosz's photograph on his study wall (see "On My Workroom Wall" in *Naked with Summer in Your Mouth*). Milosz and Peter Dale Scott translated the poems of Zbigniew Herbert together, but fell out over the Vietnam war.

2. William Everson (b. 1912) American poet (*The Residual Years: Poems 1934–1948*, 1948).

3. Peter Dale Scott (b. 1929): Canadian-born poet (*Prepositions of Jet Travel*, 1981). AP refers to his 1988 volume, *Coming to Jakarta: A Poem about Terror*. It's not clear why AP thought that Solecki admired the book; though he was the poetry editor at McClelland and Stewart, the manuscript had been accepted by his predecessor.

To the *Globe and Mail* (Toronto), from Sidney, BC, February 25, 1990

Dear Sir,

Alan Cassels complains that Canada Council subsidies don't produce good literature (letter, Feb. 24), but do "produce a dilution of quality and encourage work, however shoddy, because it is Canadian."

Well, now: do the US Guggenheim Awards result in good literature? Do British Council awards and Booker Prizes produce shoddy literature? And how are these award-funding bodies in the US and Britain different from the Canada Council? Is the Canadian inferiority complex so large we can't have funding agencies for the arts in this country when virtually every other English-speaking nation does? And if not, why not?

What does produce good literature? Ask Vaclav Havel, the new Czech president, who was jailed for years by right wing Communists. Ask Anna Akhmatova, a marvellous Russian poet who spent years in prison[1] (of course that's difficult; she's dead). I doubt if anyone knows what produces good literature, and that certainly includes Mr. Cassels. I suspect he's an embittered writer, recently turned down for a grant by the Canada Council. Or his wife just left him. (Come back, Mrs. Cassels, your husband needs you.) Revolutions, anarchy, chaos, struggle against a huge and impossibly formidable neighbour—do any of these produce good literature?

As for one Crawford Kilian, whose gripe is much the same as that of Mr. Cassels (book page, Feb. 24), I'd like to ask him why the sales figures of his own ten books published in the US are so marvellous? And why does he worry about Canada if he does so well on the US remainder listings?

I suppose I'm a good example of Mr. Kilian's "subsidized amateurs." I apologize to him, and to Canada, for being so terribly dull and unread. I'll try and do better. Living in a garret on bread and water, perhaps I should fly to the US for refuge and succour? Could Mr. Kilian get me a job as an office boy in the United States for Vantage Press, his own publisher?

Al Purdy

1. AP confuses Akhmatova with her husband, the poet Nicholas Gumilev (1886–1921), and her son Lev. She did not spend "years in prison."

Carol Shields (1935–2003): poet (*Coming to Canada*, 1992), short story writer and novelist (*The Stone Diaries*, 1993). The last won both a Governor General's Award and a Pulitzer Prize.

To Carol Shields (Winnipeg), from Ameliasburgh, May 15, 1990

Dear Carol Shields,
Sometimes you read a review that is meaningful to you, and you keep it a long time. I've kept yours of *An American Childhood* in the *Globe* for three years nearly.[1] And just reading it now I feel the same as I did then (without ever having read Dillard's book in the interim) . . . There are so damn many books these days, all days, so few good ones, so many advertised as good etc. that I read few. I mean novels and books like Dillard's.

Anyway, I'm working toward saying that my own childhood was similar—in the coming awake part—to Dillard's, if that doesn't sound like conceit. I came dozedly awake in childhood sometime, then fell asleep again, my life settling into a pretty humdrum existence. I was writing poems, but they were lousy. Then I ran into some people in Vancouver and came rather startlingly awake again. I started reading all the books I hadn't read, I mean the classics, Dostoyevsky, Woolf, Proust etc. And Dylan Thomas on the interurban going to work, and Eliot and the rest.

And changed myself, of course. To forget one's self—or oneself?—I prefer the former—seems to me so rare and precious. And you wake up later and remember how it was . . . So I enclose a recent piece—very damn recent—which is about the loss of self and the finding . . . And with thanks for that old review. I don't think we ever met, altho it wouldn't have been surprising, given my lousy memory, but I'm grateful to you.

Best Wishes,
Al Purdy

1. Shields reviewed Annie Dillard's *An American Childhood* on Saturday, November 28, 1987, in the *Globe and Mail*. If in the following quotation from the review, one replaces *An American Childhood* by *Morning and It's Summer*, Purdy's memoir of his Trenton childhood, Shields might be describing the latter: "*An American Childhood* is about waking up, about the mechanism that causes children in their early years to drift toward consciousness, opening, then shutting, their eyes—dozing, observing, forgetting, remembering, dreaming, staring, then finding themselves (at the age of 10 in Dillard's case) stunningly, joyously awake in a world that is already realized and ready. This awakening, when it occurs, is seldom spoken of, for no adult would understand."

To George Bowering (Vancouver), from Ameliasburgh, June 4, 1990

Dear George,

What kinda bribe would work with you, I mean to make you shut up re Purdy. Ran into Brian Fawcett[1] at Kingston AGM and was reminded of him asking did I have any descendents (this re poems I guess), I gave a smart alec answer which I can't remember. Reminded him of this in Kingston, and he said I'd want to have descendents with this woman he knew and bet me five bucks I would. So he trots her out and leaves me with her. Turns out it's the gal living with D–, and first thing she says is "I'm 40 years old and all my eggs have dried up." I commiserated briefly, but assured her I didn't hold it against her. Must admit she didn't look more than 30 (but that's my own age speaking), and if I'd known her longer I might've wanted more descendents, impossible as that seems to be these days. Anyway, I wandered off when I saw Pierre Berton or someone, and Fawcett owes me five bucks. Please remind him, would you, George. I think one should pay one's bets, don't you.

No, I wasn't aware of what colour I didn't use, and I note you use Can. spelling of colour. Tell me where I've left telltale tracks, please.

Okay, likely I picked wrong poems of WCW to read. Tell me the right ones. I have his *Collected Later Poems*. I will look for yr Asphodel piece.[2] (Do you read yr pieces?) Yeah, I read his autobio, which I thought very good (not to offend you more than I have to), tho I gather his womanizing didn't get into that book . . . And yeah, I have been under the impression WCW was a kinda Souster poet, without many brains behind the unisyllables. I know, I know, all the people who just adore him. But George, you know, you know damn well, ya gotta make up your own mind about things. I'd be glad to like WCW if I could, the wider one casts the net the richer the harvest to misuse a marine cliché. Ain't got *Kora in*

Hell, unless it's in the book I have, but it sounds like a larger book which I dimly remember (no puns on that please).

I came east—at least to Alberta—for reading, then went the rest of the way on accounta a new book. Have a novel in fall, incidentally. McStew.

Olson bores me so bad I had difficulty recovering years back. Maybe you heard the story of that trip to Wah's place (your dear friend) long ago, after you and Creeley had that brief encounter. Wah insisted that Olson was great and I said he had a great voice, with the emphasis on voice. Anyway, these guys are the worst academics I ever saw or heard of, with Olson at the head of the list.

There are many BMs I like much, some that don't seem to belong there like Levertov.[3] But I don't see them any more, maybe they all died off. However, my net of likings was cast pretty widely, and it seemed then that there was little time to linger over things I didn't like. For instance, I hated the translations of Rilke done by a guy named Leishman . . . I still can't appreciate that supposedly great poet if Leishman does the trans . . .

I was pleased to see Edmonton take [the Stanley Cup] this year, and think hockey much more—what?—I mean the form chart runs truer in hockey than baseball. After the Yanks went bad, no team had a dynasty for long, the three-year Oakland stint excepted. Whereas hockey now . . . But that Edmonton combo of the young and the vets, they made Boston look bad at times. And apparently wore out Bourque[4] by the last game. But I'll be surprised if either Blue Jays or Expos do anything this year. It's somehow always a slight surprise when anyone wins, the favourites rarely do.

Al

1. Brian Fawcett (b. 1944): a poet (who has abandoned poetry), short story writer, journalist and writer of books that evade categories (*Cambodia: A Book for People Who Find Television Too Slow*, 1986).
2. AP is referring to William Carlos Williams's "Asphodel, That Greeny Flower."
3. Denise Levertov (b. 1923): English-born American poet loosely associated with the Black Mountain poets (*With Eyes at the Back of Our Heads*, 1959; *Footprints*, 1972).
4. Raymond Bourque: one of the outstanding defencemen of his era.

Steven Heighton (b. 1961): poet (*Stalin's Carnival*, 1989) short story writer (*On Earth as It Is*, 1995) and novelist (*The Shadow Boxer*, 2002).

To Steven Heighton (Kingston), from Ameliasburgh, July 5, 1990

Dear Steve,

I'm sorry to hear about your novel. All that time—if you're quite sure nothing's going to happen—I know it sounds polyanna, but the time wasn't wasted. From my point of view, just doing it makes you know you could do it again. I have another one more or less planned, but hard to say whether I'll finally get down to it. And I assure you, this is true: doing it makes you know that you can do it again. Sure, it didn't get accepted, but fuck that. Doing that novel makes you that much better and more capable and better able to see your own faults.

Course you're writing another on accounta you want to. No other fucking reason. You say it's hard to get started. Well, I think you oughta just jump right into it, not worry very much about plotting or research unless either is so necessary you can't help it. Trouble with delay and with early difficulties is—it removes enthusiasm. And I think that's what you need above everything. To have fun doing it, to enjoy the re-experience, because that's what you're doing, re-experiencing life.

I didn't see the Beardsley review; send it along if you still have it. One in the *Globe* here I didn't like much, oh, favourable in a way. But the woman (Maggie Helwig) said it was partly old poems reprinted and partly new. That's entirely misleading, 91 pages of 111 are new. Price was given as $19.95; price is $9.95. Annoying.

I read at the Musil book[1] years back, gave it up, dull as you say. I've just read a very good Graham Greene just after I'd more or less given up on Greene, *The Human Factor*, a '78 Penguin. And I read his first book, *The Man Within* a while back. It's very flawed as a novel, but brilliant as hell at the same time, quite a feat to be both. I read a bit in one of his essays on Henry James (whom I can't stand—ponderous pretentious bastard), that I thought excellent: "The moment comes to every writer worth consideration when he faces for the first time something which he *knows* he cannot do. It is the moment by which he will be judged, the moment when his individual technique will be evolved. For technique is more than anything else a means of evading the personally impossible, of disguising a deficiency."

Margaret Laurence got this book for me in England, and marked it up before she gave it to me. About the above passage she says, "how can he know so much?"

I don't know Canetti.

I've just written another chunk of autobio for *Books in Canada* and have uncovered a manuscript of Indian myths adapted from Marius Barbeau[2] in 1963. Migawd! I am working on them some, better phrasing, breaking into white space with verses . . . I mean above, *I* adapted it from Barbeau. Free verse. Narrative. If I can get someone to do some drawings of the characters, as on Haida and Tsimsyan totem poles. We'll see. Barbeau has a bunch of books on totem poles, photos and stories. There'd be half a dozen, say, that're very similar; I reduced them, the similar ones, to a single story.

Harking back to that Greene quote, how does one disguise a deficiency? Does one know one's own deficiencies? That is perhaps the key point right there.

Eurithe is still running things and I am as impatient as ever. And yeah, my own novel is due this fall. Galleys next week. It feels odd to me, and it's eligible for first novel award. How strange! Say hi to Sue—Oh yes, I had wanted to write a novel for a long time, but more or less gave up the idea. When I started to write it, I did so more to fill time than anything else. Then got much involved. So it wasn't on accounta I wanted to write a novel so much at first, I just kinda sorta off-handedly did.

if you see my point . . .

Al

1. Robert Musil (1880–1942): Austrian novelist, best known for the unfinished multi-volume novel *The Man Without Qualities* (1930–43) that deals with the society of the Austro-Hungarian Empire during 1913–14.
2. Marius Barbeau (1883–1969): an anthropologist at the National Museum of Canada (1911–49) and the founder of modern folklore studies in Canada, Barbeau was a prolific editor and writer who produced over 600 articles and 100 books. AP's versions of Barbeau's transcriptions of "Indian myths" have not been published. AP describes his 1968 meeting with Barbeau in the poem "Marius Barbeau (1883–1969)" (*To Paris Never Again*).

To Irving Layton (Montreal), from Ameliasburgh, April 18 or 19, 1990

Dear Irving,
Congratulations on the Layton–Creeley letters.[1] Creeley gives you due "provincial" praise, but also more than that. There is an initial similarity to my own experiences with Bukowski, but yours with Creeley goes much beyond mine. And the good thing for you about such books is that they keep you always before the public, a jogging of the elbow, a reminder that we have good writers, and some are more than good.

And thanks for the inscription, which is amusing to me. My impression of AmerLit now is that Creeley has sunken fairly low, and that BM itself is paid little attention to. Its influence in Canada has been nearly all bad, as I gather is your opinion as well. In fact I think we spoke of it once and agreed on the subject.

The opinion of Dudek expressed by Creeley is also one I agree with. No matter how much good Dudek has done as a teacher, his poems have always remained lousy—with a few exceptions—to me. And he has turned sour toward anyone receiving more attention than himself as well. He has become what he describes Leonard Cohen as—a disappointed man. It is sad that this should be so, especially since I owe him something personally, despite all his snide remarks from time to time. He was "kind" I thought at one time.

What I wonder most about your book on cursory reading is: how in hell did Elspeth Cameron get control of all those photos of you?? Isn't it a bit humiliating for you?

love,
Al

1. *Irving Layton and Robert Creeley: The Complete Correspondence 1953–78* (1990).

To Fraser Sutherland (Scotsburn, NS), from Ameliasburgh, September 21, 1990

Dear Fraser,

[. . .] Yeah, they're talkin about a TV interview—so's Adrienne Clarkson,[1] if I'm able to control my eagerness . . . I was at the McStew party in Toronto (Ellen Seligman said I should go on accounta the novel), talked to Clarkson (she's so very well-preserved at age 50 or so!) and Paul Steuwe, new ed of *BiC* (whose first book you once sent me) and Philip Marchand of the *Star*. And discovered—too late—a bad typesetter's error that ruined two lines of novel early on . . .

Oh yeah, Oka etc. Am I the converted? Not exactly. Of course, throwing stones at old women and children in cars. That was awful! No possible excuse. Can understand people bein mad on accounta that barricade at bridge for a month tho.

There are some points about all this, Terry Kelly[2] notwithstanding. At one time, all the Indians in Canada were either conquered militarily or placated somehow. Their land was taken away, then reserves given back to them, obviously inadequate reserves. They are paid, to this day, an average in excess of $8,000 each Indian. Of course they want more. People always want more, Indians or whatever.

However, and a big however, whatever the justice of their case, I do not believe they have the right to take up arms against the gov't and citizens of Canada. Despite once owning all of Canada—even if they did not occupy it entirely and could not because of their numbers—the land was removed from their custody several hundred years ago. Whether right or wrong, that sort of thing went on all over the world, and there is no complete remedy for it now. What are their rights is something to be determined by law, not by arms. Otherwise we have anarchy and rebellion and much bloodshed. Otherwise the Indians would lose much. The situation now is not what it was when the first few white men came. But at the present time, you are not going to displace twenty-six million people, who support Indians who apparently cannot support themselves. No matter how self-supporting and contented they once were, the situation has changed completely. Indians are now white dependents, however little they like that condition. And of course they don't. So what's your solution? Mohawks declare war?

I would've liked to have gone to Oka to see what was happening though, bandwagons notwithstanding.

I've been writing memoirs fairly steadily lately, have some 40,000 words I think. Doing it in the form of episodes, about time periods, such as my air force years, factory years, taxi business and so on. I have about two such episodes to go. And no, I do not go on and on about each period, and the stuff has to be cut down later. Each section is pretty well self-contained, altho leading into the next. And I'm enjoying some of it too.

About half or more of the freight train period was written earlier, and now have to do more. Plus the taxi business, then I'm finished. After that, I'm much more literarily selfconscious etc., getting grants and so on.

How's your condition, financially and psychically I mean? Alison working now, I expect.

I take off in Oct. for three prairie readings; and there will be a lot of huckstering for the novel in Nov., then out to Vancouver late in Nov. I do not look forward to huckstering. Allus figgered if anything was any good it oughta sell itself; course, not true. I have another novel plotted, insofar as I plot anything, but may or may not go to work on it.[3] Too long a job at my age. One can't be very sure of finishing such a project, altho if I wanted to write it enough I sure as hell would anyway.

Al

1. Adrienne Clarkson (b. 1939): writer (*A Lover More Consoling*, 1968), broadcaster (*Fifth Estate*) and Governor General of Canada (1999–2004).
2. Terry (or M.T.) Kelly (b. 1946): Toronto playwright (*The Green Dolphin*, 1982) and novelist (*A Dream Like Mine*, 1987).
3. AP doesn't seem to have gotten beyond thinking about the plot of this second novel. Nothing remains of it in his papers. It has disappeared as completely as the novel he thought about writing thirty years earlier on Spartacus.

> **Don Coles** (1928): Toronto poet (*Forests of the Medieval World*, 1993).

To Don Coles (Toronto), from Ameliasburgh, October 10, 1990

Dear Don,

I think *The Prinzhorn Collection* should've received the GG. It's very fine! I dunno who got it in '83, but . . .

Re *K in Love*, I wanted to have that one of the final three in its year (and this is, of course, confidential), but . . .

Scobie, was it—in '83—Well, I expect it's better not to go into that. However, if I'm ever on that committee at the right time—

Yeah, "write poems as well as he can or she can, and try not to pay too much heed—" Sure, but you're bound to think of "these things" and so am I.

There's plenty of resonance from "Forests" and when I read it (several times), I kept looking for the girl. And whether you intended it or not, that poem is about a girl who gets a fellowship or whatever your "dissertation" means, goes to Europe and leaves her lover behind. And then, "I am going do you realize I am going. And that both of us will survive this?" which fits the love poem completely, and then I am puzzled by which one says "I would take you with me—" So I think it doesn't matter a damn who the people were originally, in the poem they're lovers. At least they are for me, and I think would be for some others as well.

There's a passage of mine in "My Grandfather's Country":

> —there are deserts like great yellow beds of flowers
> where a man can walk and walk into identical distance
> like an arrow lost in its own target
> and a woman scream and a grain of sand will fall
> on the other side of the yellow bowl a thousand miles away

Your shadow reminded me of those last two lines.

Yeah, *Gilgamesh*, but I don't remember the "heifer stirring in the forest far off—" I started to write a play about Gilgamesh years back, wrote quite a bit too before abandoning . . .[1]

Glad you liked "Crucifix,"[2] and I see no reason why people can't admire each other's stuff without thinking the worse, others doing that, whatever "the worst" is . . .

Yes, that's exactly what I intended in that line about "death but lately absent"—[. . .]

I wasn't at all sure about the italics for final verse. I guess my first reason for writing the "Crucifix" is that I admired the essays so much, and thought more people would read it and also admire if they read this poem first. Of course that's very speculative.

My wife, incidentally, is going to drive across the continent in about two weeks, with a friend of mine, driving an old school bus, carrying a huge load of my books. I can't go, and wouldn't want to anyway if there were no novel, driving long distances gets my nerves. Anyway, I have to leave this letter and go help her pack books in booze box empties from Belleville liquor store.

And thanks much for *Prinzhorn*. I'll expect to get back to you on return from west. Do you have *Piling Blood*? My book, that is. I have some extra copies.

All best,

Al

1. AP considered "Gilgamesh and Friend" (*The Crafte So Longe to Lerne*, 1959) one of his first successful poems.
2. AP refers to the poem "The Crucifix Across the Mountains," (*Naked with Summer in Your Mouth*) which is based on the opening sketch in D.H. Lawrence's *Twilight in Italy* (1916), "The Crucifix Across the Mountains."

To Sam Solecki (Toronto), from Sidney, BC, February 27, 1991

Dear Sam,

Yeah, London. Just back here Feb. 22. Got interviewed on BBC, read some bits of novel (to your no doubt great unhappiness if you'd heard), reception at Canada House with Donald Macdonald,[1] a large ex-politician presiding along with assorted guests and lit people, then dinner on Avie, at which a large lady of Russian extraction attempted to hold my hand despite a certain lack of eagerness evinced by me. I had a bad cold the whole time in Fla. and shivery London. Even—God help me—felt I had to return half my living allowance back to Avie on accounta I WAS TOO SICK TO SPEND IT. I did consume a moderate amount of beer at that dinner, principally of course as a partial defense against the lady of Russian extraction. And argued with Christopher Sinclair-Stevenson[2] that lit was not a four-minute mile or a boxing knockout in the case of Yeats and Housman. He argued vociferously *that it was a knockout* etc. in the case of Yeats and Housman. He was 6'4" so I had to shut up. (Yes, it was difficult.) C. S-S is the Brit publisher, by the way. These foreigners!

The Memoir (caps, please) got sent to Ellen. She hasn't read it, of course. Should it have gone to you? I mean protocol?

You're way past me with this "abreast the new European wave" reading. I'll stick to my thrillers. I would like to see a good translation of Mandelstam though. Celebrated and revered Edmund Jabes[3] I don't know at all. I gotta admit, you academics got the advantage of me, sometimes. I would bring up the eunuch in the harem thing if I didn't know better where you're concerned. How is it, by the way? Wet?

These guys you bring up I don't know at all. Zagajewski?[4]—new kinda detergent?

Yeah, Frye . . . End of era, all that.[5] I knew him a very little, probably as much as anyone did. Well, no, I saw him only a few times. He wrote letters on my behalf to CC. I picked up McLuhan's *Understanding Media*[6] in Fla. Yeah, I guess they were giants. Would you add Pratt? I'm always ambiguous about him. Re Frye's feeling the new crit doesn't have much to offer, isn't this generally the attitude of an older generation toward the young? Like me, for instance. I don't even read the stuff, not unless a young sprout like you mentions Zag and Zig between fucks. Was your old man Zdzislaw Solecki? I need new dental work to think of it. Ya know, Sam, there are times when I feel outdated, envious of all the energy needed to even open a fuckin book of this new stuff . . .

Well, I gotta give you credit, you do keep up. (I like your "Maecenas and president of us all" by the way . . . So why the hell aren't you writing more?)

You must have figured out by now, re all my old stuff, I want someone else to do ALL the work, not just some. I don't even wanta look at it.

Yeah, I read the Anansi Frye of his Letters in Canada.[7] Doubt if he ever said anything about me. Somehow I met him a few times, don't remember how. Wrote him on his stuff in *Lit. Hist. of Can.*, where he had the bit about approaching Can. like bein swallowed by whale, and garrison mentality and so on. I was too stupid to feel those things he talked about.

I have readings in March, and a four-day stint in Prince George beginning of Apr. Likely back east end of that month. Incidentally, I can see the advantage of house-watching in your case, multiple advantages.

See you in Toronto or . . . [. . .]

Who was Maecenas?

Al

1. Donald Macdonald (b. 1932): Liberal politician and cabinet minister in the Trudeau era. The reference to Solecki's "no doubt great unhappiness" looks back to a comment he made to AP that the poet should sometimes read more slowly and that he should leave more time between poems.
2. English publisher.
3. Edmund Jabes (1913–91): born in Egypt, Jabes settled in France during the Suez Crisis. Though often referred to as a poet, he is an unclassifiable writer (*The Book of Margins*, 1993) who seems to have invented his own genres.
4. Adam Zagajewski (b. 1945): Polish poet (*Tremor: Selected Poems*, 1985; *New and Selected Poems*, 2003) who has spent much of his adult life in France and the United States.
5. Northrop Frye had died on January 23, 1991.
6. Marshall McLuhan (1911–80): literary critic and media theorist (*The Gutenberg Galaxy: The Making of Typographic Man*, 1962; *Understanding Media: The Extensions of Man*, 1964).
7. AP is referring to *The Bush Garden* (1971), Frye's collection of essays on Canadian culture. During the early 1950s, Frye had written an annual essay on the year's work in poetry for the *University of Toronto Quarterly*'s "Letters in Canada" issue. AP reviewed the second edition of the *Literary History of Canada* for *Books in Canada* (January 1977). In his copy—now at University College, Toronto—there are more marginal comments to Frye's "Conclusion to the *Literary History of Canada*" than to any of the other essays.

To George Woodcock (Vancouver), from Sidney, BC, April 9, 1991

Dear George,

I leave tomorrow—with Eurithe—for a four-day stint at Prince George, the college there, then Apr. 23, fly back east. It somehow seems as if I should inform you of such movements, as if the knowledge of specific geographic locations aids in picturing or imagining another person . . . Maybe it does too. Hard to imagine another person who's nowhere.

I've just been talking, on the phone, with a 92-year-old first cousin in Ont., my father's brother's son. He has a 90-year-old brother. It would seem the family is long-lived. However, Ron Everson's mother lived to be well over 100, after which he seemed to think he was invulnerable, but is now beset by illnesses at 87. [...]

Re Everson, Michael Macklem at Oberon insisted his book title be *Poems About Me*, as previously he insisted that Ron's title be *Everson at Eighty*. I'd been writing him last fall about him possibly publishing my poem-versions of Haida myths taken from Barbeau's totem pole books—Macklem, that is. When these negotiations broke down, on accounta he wouldn't get illos to go with the book, I asked him to send a zerox of a Barbeau letter back to me, because I had no other copy. He said he'd sold it to Queen's Archives along with other stuff. I was quite astounded—to think he'd sell correspondence quite relevant to our negotiations before they were completed. I'm reminded of this by your remarks about Mel Hurtig a few weeks back: but it seems Hurtig is in bad shape, really.

I would like to write another novel at this point, but I'm sure my back wouldn't stand up under the continual typewriter-sitting etc.

Also, just received the Birney *Last Makings*, with my Intro., and feel rather sad about it, Birney, I mean.

Your memory is your identity, at least a large part of it. And it's sad for me to think of Birney in that hospital and not being his acrimonious, combative and charming (at times) self. Wailan was at the A-burg place last summer, with—apparently a boy friend—and said she couldn't handle him any longer and had been forced to send him back to hospital. At 87–88 he is apparently still very strong, but almost mindless. And yet, not an idiot. I remember you saying he didn't recognize you when you visited; I *think* you said that. But he is not there any longer, a ghost inhabits the shell of what he was.

It seems I've "won" something called "The Milton Acorn People's Poet Award"—to which no money attaches. I'm supposed to read six times at Charlottetown this summer—short readings—and wonder if my back will stand that. Also asked to read at Pittsburgh for some international festival there in Nov. (one, Samuel Hazo is the inviter) for a thousand bucks. *That* sounds worthwhile. And perhaps I said already, Howie White is doing those Haida poems at Harbour Publishing.[1]

Which is the news.

Take care of yourself—and Inge. That name follows your own with scarcely a pause when thinking of GW.

Al

---

1. The book was not published.

To George Bowering (Vancouver), from Ameliasburgh, June 3, 1991

Dear George,

[...] Earle was a strange mixture (I must use the past tense), both generous and mean, querulous and hearty at almost the same moment. He once signed a book of his to me using a phrase that might be taken as a bit unflattering. Months later I signed one of mine for him, using the same phrase. He was mad as hell. I had to talk fast to convince him he'd said the same thing about himself.

That's odd—he thinking you were a rival for some baseball job. I had no idea he was ever interested in baseball anyway. And also, had no idea he was capable of entertaining trains of thought like that. [...]

I may have mentioned: finished Memoir, or thought I did, ending at 1965, with not much about writing, just living a life. But Ellen S. wants all my encounters with writers in there. I had preferred to write about the times when I was a more or less *normal* person, and did what I did for reasons of survival only. But she wants Atwood, Birney and probably, god help me, G. Woodcock in there.

Birney has always made me feel slightly guilty about him, even when I was quite annoyed with him. I would analyse my own attitudes toward him, and find great difficulty in making my feelings clearcut to myself. And I felt some guilt over Acorn as well, that I wasn't *nicer* to him. I disagreed with nearly everything about Milton, and yet I sympathized with him greatly. [...]

Chesterton makes great titles!

Al

To Fraser Sutherland (Scotsburn, NS), from Ameliasburgh, July 18, 1991

Dear Fraser,

That notepaper came from Alex Widen, a friend in the west (Van) who works for the postoffice, hence has access to the various gimmicks by which you make up such notepaper. He sent me as well this paper, with the reverse design. Same guy who drove the school bus west loaded with my books (I still have around 15% of them here). I did mention buying the school bus to transport furniture and books west? But I hate to finally abandon this place ...

I phoned Eurithe last night (she's due back here in August), re visiting you etc. She tells me (she made the travel arrangements with the PEI festival lady) that I get one of those special tickets the airline won't let you change or alter without payment of bucks. Maybe you know the kind. The Acorn thing is Aug. 22–28, you had the date a bit wrong. Anyway, my ticket will come from some travel agency in Charlottetown.

I would like very much to get down to your place, with Eurithe, before I dodder too much to travel in the ancient of my age. Ya know? Eurithe right now, as I may have mentioned, is having some alterations done on the Sidney house, and her brother is bossing the job. [...]

Yeah, how'd you guess I get meals the way you mention? I am sick to death of lookin after this place, tell Eurithe a wife's place is with her husband etc. etc.

Anyway: looks like the only way we get to see you is make a special trip. And Eurithe will likely have to have an operation when she returns here next month, hopefully not serious. She retains eastern medicare, since the west makes you pay quite a bit extra. As you see, things get complicated. [...]

Yeah, Gus is sweet and gentle, and also has a monster ambition and ego peering from that inoffensive exterior. I did mention one of my most uncomfortable moments in Moscow was when Gus and I were alone at this restaurant and he says to me outa the blue: "You never put me into any of your anthologies, Al." Kinda sweet and reproachful. Long moment of rather uncomfortable silence while my lightning fast verbal reflexes untangled from the shock. Then he says, "I guess that sounds like whining . . ." In measured tones I reply, "Yes." Then explain that two of the fuckin antho were for writers under age 30. The other, well no defense. But my original "Yes" was the real answer to Gus. And he has Betty and the principal at that univ[1] he was at to write people trying to get him into the Order of Canada. Pat Page said Betty asked her a coupla times to help. I wrote Layton and Atwood asking their help, before I knew how frantic they are. They say to anyone they ask that Ralph is in bad health, implying this is the last request of a dying man, that his country honour him and all that shit . . . Makes one throw up.

Tell Alison to dream on . . .

Al

1. Gustafson had been on the faculty of Bishop's University.

To Sam Solecki (Toronto), from Ameliasburgh, September 15, 1991

Dear Sam,

As my note in previous letters says, those Rilke poems you sent are marvellous.[1] I started to read some mythology after "Alcestis" noting that Rilke changed the story. Of course, quite permissable. In the poem, one can't be sure where the hell the wife comes from, what condition she's in before she goes with the god. And Admetus was a king in the myth I read. None of which matters.

Besides the Penguin, I had read at Rilke many times, but this is the first that does justice to his reputation. There's a Bantam Classic, *Modern European Poetry*, but the translations are unremarkable.[2] From now on I shall certainly give Rilke the benefit of doubtful translations, even if I don't like them.

In "Alcestis" Rilke hit a subject with immediate appeal, since I think one is liable to think: what would my friends do for me in a pinch? (Ever hear Odetta sing "Hangman, hangman, slack your rope" etc. Related.) Most of the time not very much. The "Damon & Pythias" and "Jonathan and whoever-his-was" in the Bible, they are too mythic to mean much. What would [a woman] do for you, for instance? Pick you up if you fell down, bandage your wounds, sure. So would I, and so what? However, there are instances of giving a kidney or whatever; but that's kinda different, isn't it?

One doesn't really really believe in that god stuff in the poem, but somehow Rilke hit it anyway. He made the situation sound so realistic that that old "temporary suspension of disbelief" became actual. And the smile did it, since when we remember someone else we often do so because of one thing, a habit, expression, something they did for you, a smile. You add half a dozen of those things up and maybe you got love, kid.

The situation in "Alcestis" also sounds to me as if Admetus and his wife never quite made it somehow, not together. I mean, there was a lack in that relationship (as there is in most), and there's no one around capable of such selflessness or love. If there is, it generally kills them, as it did the wife. Then we have the memory of a smile. If you have any more by the same translator, send em along.

I'm back at the grindstone memoir. How the fuck did I get into this cyclical shit? Yeah, I know, brought it on myself.

Al

1. Sam Solecki had sent AP Stephen Mitchell's translations of "Autumn Day," "Orpheus, Eurydice, Hermes," "Alcestis" and "Archaic Torso of Apollo." AP then bought Mitchell's *The Selected Poetry of Rainer Maria Rilke* (1980) and read Rilke on and off through the decade. There are many references to the poet in the letters and in the poems. "House Party—1000 BC" (*To Paris Never Again*) recasts the story of Alcestis. Though he knew that he had little in common with the German poet, AP was nevertheless fascinated by him, almost as if he recognized that Rilke was his complete opposite, his antitype.
2. *Modern European Poetry: French / German / Greek / Italian / Russian / Spanish*, edited by Willis Barnstone et al (1966). The Rilke translators in this edition include Robert Lowell, Robert Bly, Vernon Watkins and Michael Hamburger.

To Sam Solecki (Toronto), from Ameliasburgh, October 16, 1991

Dear Sam,
Thanks for photocopy stuff, of which more anon.

With the name of translator, off to library and copy of Mitchell trans of Rilke. Also ordered it at bookstore, since I'm told it's still in print. And much thanks for putting me onto Mitchell. I do think the three poems you sent in photocopy are just about his best. Many of the others are "cluttered" despite their undoubted brilliance, and he leaps around like a mad cricket. That's part of his method, of course, and probably necessary to him. A good example of this is in one of his best poems, the Orpheus one, which is quite chilling. Your own mind has to haul in all the elements of this poem, and in a sense make your own landscape from the materials supplied by Rilke. And his attitude towards sex is highly interesting, seeming to advocate unfulfilled love, and no fucking. Of course if you can say anything as magnificently as he does, even if the sense of what he says is ridiculous, as in seeming to say that a condition of permanent non-fulfilment is desirable, then he sets himself apart from the rest of us sweating copulators.

It does seem to me that Mitchell is his ideal English translator.

What Rilke does more than anything is make me look at myself, both poems and life. I haven't read enough of him to come to any settled conclusion as to what his "message" is, the large import of him. However, I think I both learn and feel something from him; and there are ways in which he makes me feel inadequate. As if I have somehow wasted myself in some areas of writing. Of course my own writing is not nearly so introspective and intellectual, and I have not wanted to go into some of the areas Rilke explores. Rilke seems to me almost entirely a subjective poet, even when writing of something other than himself. He is exploring himself and his life through the medium of others, and I always feel this about him. What the fuck is Keats' line, "Silent upon a peak in Darien" and before that something about the new land or star coming into sight.[1] Well, in some ways I feel the same about Rilke. I didn't expect to discover anyone like that at my age, and I thank you for it.

And your comments on my stuff.[2] Re Sam Johnson, no, birds and flowers don't die. They are eternal in the mind and on the earth; they have no memory, only a circumscribed eternity. The "ancient beaches" bit was going back before I went forward. I didn't adequately say that, of course, and no doubt should have. The trouble is my stuff is so transparent that when you come to the least bit of obscurity it stands out. At least I *feel* it's transparent. The disgust with "man" is disgust with himself in the poem. Not man per se. "trees full of swaying fruit / of hanged men"—that's an echo of Irving?[3] If so, quite accidental. The attitude in this poem is partly just that, an attitude, but more than that too if I'm not into complete contradictions. What you say when something busts up like this is fuckit, and make exaggerated noises. (And it just occurred to me: can you imagine Ondaatje talking the way I am?)

I suppose I didn't want very much to write that last section [of the memoir], and it may be it shows—I mean "Anecdotage." I say what I think are the salient things in my mind, about other people and incidents connected. If I were to go on about them, I would be pushing into other areas of my own boredom . . . And books?—I did mention the poets I liked, and didn't include Rilke, which is now mandatory. I think you approach my mind as if it were close to yours in critical aspects. But *you* are much more the critic than I am. I have "feelings" about poems I read and their authors, and have no interest at all in analysing those feelings. When I do that it will be in poems.

I have very little interest in Walcott. Mahon or Mahan, "Glengormley" is fine.[4] And all this stuff bespeaks the practised poet, and reading them you can't forget that they are practised poets. They are concerned with neatness of phrase, rhyme schemes of all sorts and metrics—balanced against what they want to say. How they say a thing intrudes on my appreciation of them and makes them seem artificial to me. In some of Auden, also a metric measurer, I can escape this, or, as in the last rhyming parts of the Yeats elegy, it doesn't matter a damn and is exaggerated.

It seems to me that one tries to de-emphasize rhyme and metrics in favour of meaning. Surely to Christ the writer doesn't want the reader to be more than slightly aware of his methods. I know, I know, it is taken for granted that there are methods employed, but I don't want them to impinge on my consciousness and fuck up meaning. And when I say this, you should not assume that this feeling about metrics and rhyme is invariable on my part. In old poems, in modern ones by Yeats and others, one is bound to encounter method, which was part of that day and age and methodology. One just accepts it in some instances. However, in Mahon and Walcott these things intrude for me.

I have a reading at the Toronto Skyline Hotel Oct. 24 (that's next week) for a bunch of Toronto teachers, 8 p.m. I think. No, I see it's seven p.m. Then back here. And leave again for Pittsburgh Nov. 5, returning to Toronto airport Nov. 7 en route to Vancouver. I'd love to see you before leaving, and shall miss you when I'm out west. Incidentally, Eurithe leaves here Sunday, Oct. 20. I value friendship, without wishing to get maudlin about it. And friendships as well as loves die, of course—altho the former may last a little longer than the latter.

Had a photo taken of me wearing a Layton T-shirt standing in front of Purdy Lane. Thinking of sending it to Irving. Think he'll like it?

Best,

Al

1. "On First Looking into Chapman's Homer": "Then felt I like some watcher of the skies / When a new planet swims into his ken; / Or like stout Cortez when with eagle eyes / He stared at the Pacific—and all his men / Looked at each other with a wild surmise— / Silent, upon a peak in Darien." Keats famously confuses Cortez and Balboa, the first European to see the Pacific.
2. AP is commenting on "The Poor Bastard" (*Naked with Summer in Your Mouth*).
3. Layton's "The Cold Green Element" shows "a dead poet / out of the water / who now hangs from the city's gates" and the crowds come to see him and watch while "peeling their oranges."
4. Derek Walcott (b. 1930): West Indian playwright (*Dream on Monkey Mountain*, 1967) and poet (*The Fortunate Traveller*, 1982; *Midsummer*, 1984; *Omeros*, 1990), awarded the Nobel Prize in 1992. Derek Mahon (b. 1941): Irish poet (*Selected Poems*, 1991) and award-winning translator.

To George Woodcock (Vancouver), from Ameliasburgh, October 19, 1991

Dear George,
Good to hear. Not good about all the bad stuff. But I guess there's not much to say about it, except that it's no comfort that the same thing is for all of us . . .

Did I mention the sequel to the Trenton Day for Purdy? Kerrigan Almey, who once did a book of mine in Trenton, and did the printing of that poster I sent you: Kerrigan told me the free parking was originally only for the end of 1991.[1] But Kerrigan said he got a handful of nickels, marched into [the] Trenton [m]ayor['s] office, threw the nickels down on hizzoner's desk and said: "How long you think Purdy's gonna live? Here, you cheap bastard, this oughta pay Purdy's parking for the rest of his life."

What I wonder about: how many nickels did Kerrigan expect to pay my parking for the rest of my life? Of course I included that in the memoir.

Which memoir I'm having trouble with, re Ellen Seligman. She wants more about writers. Hafta find another publisher I guess.

No, the Purdy Day was a small affair, only fifty–sixty–seventy people there, but there was beer. And yeah, that's a kinda miserable way to die (re Roy Fuller) . . .[2]

Yeah, Freedom of the City would be some recognition. I'm sorry you turned down the Order of Canada, because you've been very valuable to the country and its writing "community" and have earned it. "Decentralized authority"? (Vancouver) Well—your own influence extends all across the country and is certainly decentralized; "beneficent influence" I should say. It's a small enough token of, what?—"gratitude"? Well, whatever.

I am familiar with the idea that all of these awards, including the GG lit one, mean little as compared to the writer's own lifetime work, spread over many years. They are mere recognition, yep you did it kid, here's to ya . . . But why the hell not? Nobody would ever begrudge G. Woodcock any award he received. Idea being: your country recognized that you've made a large contribution and says just that via its award. Besides, if you get such an award, it makes the rest of us look pretty good too.

(Don't you think that last sentence was pretty cunning of me?)

Proust yet. Reading it was tough enough for me, but to translate it . . .[3]

[. . .]

Looking again at the Roy Fuller bit in your letter: not to see his friends for the last three months!

Yeah, great parties, champagne, bad speech-making, and SEXUAL HARASSMENT . . . Yah can't even admire a nice ass these days . . . I *like* the admiring street whistles etc. Ever hear the Frank Scott story he told of having to arrange a Dylan Thomas party in Mtl. a week before Thomas came and this girl buttonholing Scott on accounta she wanted to meet

Dylan badly? So the party happened, and Frank saw Dylan's and this gal's eyes meet across the room, then he didn't see either of them again for a week . . .

Al

1. As part of the Trenton festivities, AP had been given free parking for life in Trenton.
2. Roy Fuller (1912–91): English novelist and poet (*Collected Poems 1936–61*, 1962; *Reign of Sparrows*, 1980).
3. Woodcock was translating Proust.

To Sam Solecki (Toronto), from Sidney, BC, December 1, 1991

Dear Sam,

I've just finished my Tofino piece,[1] and having difficulty in not seeing money as I look at it. Hope that doesn't occur to the possible reader.

Mentioned I'd picked up a bio of Rilke by one Wolfgang Leppmann, and very good too. What a queer bastard he was, and a basically "poetic" poet, his images marvellous sometimes. Also picked up a two-vol Rilke from New Directions near 30 years old, one prose, the other poems, trans. by Leishman whom I don't like as may have been mentioned . . . Also *Letters to Merline,* 1989. One can't be sure that he didn't get tired of women very quickly, and that he was alibiing himself with all sorts of theories to get himself off the hook. But one can't be sure of that either. Hard to pin down, a guy like that. Can you call Rilke a "guy"? Doesn't seem right.

Of course he was lost, and one part of his mind took pleasure in that, formulated theories to explain his own life and living. All of them unverifiable, since nothing of that nature ever is verifiable. And apparently he had "charisma" or like that, and an element of phoniness. Not handsome either.

And your piece "After Glasnost": seems to me that all European lit in which that was a large factor will have to be re-evaluated.[2] And yeah, I agree about Yevtushenko; he's hardly worth talking about at all except as the pretext for western self-hypnosis. Voznesensky still seems to me a good poet, but not as good as had been thought.

Yeah, I have *Miner's Pond*[3] and reading it at your behest. My jury is still out on her. [. . .]

Yeah, one idealizes friendship, I suppose. But then look back to see how many lasted very long. All the people I knew in high school—every

single one—are alien to me. You meet em, you pick up the verbal pat-
ter quickly. Friendship is a particular virus, unpredictable as love; both
those two words being manufactured to fit feelings we know little about.
[...]

Congratulations on your perspicacity re the GG thing and your pro-
ductivity with articles and litcrit. Keep your mind off or on sex? Bet you
didn't know you had "perspicacity."

Best,
Al

1. "A Place by the Sea" appeared in the *Imperial Oil Review* (Fall 1992).
2. "After Glastnost," *Brick*, 42–3 (1992).
3. Anne Michaels' *Miner's Pond*.

To Fraser Sutherland (Scotsburn, NS), from Sidney, BC, December 31,
1991

Dear Fraser,
I'm puzzled by your article; I don't hear your usual sarcastic, tongue-in-
cheek yet murderous voice that I love so well. Are you in love again? With
M. Strand yet?[1]

Your quote about the unmoved windows and joints and trusses that
are still, I'm pretty unmoved myself. But you get around that very nicely
with "The ground of being may be non-being, but it is demonstrably
earthy."

I once deceived myself that I liked Strand's stuff, but have since reformed, even if he is a Maritimer or MARITIMER.

Andrade[2] says "Poetry leaves out subject and object" which I think is
shit, and am surprised you don't appear to think so. And I note that he
keeps ruling out what poetry is and never gets around to saying what it
might be. I see that sentence is ambiguous. Well, he says what poetry isn't
and never says what it is. Perhaps you stopped quoting at that point however.

"Now you see him, now you don't." May I hope the second phrase is
accurate? I'll take [Elizabeth] Bishop, at least some of her stuff.

But more than either of them, I'll take Rilke. Not all of his stuff either,
just a few. Guy named Mitchell translated Rilke around '82–83, and late as
ever I've recently caught up. One Leishman, whom I don't like at all, had
put me off Rilke completely. But try this one.

AUTUMN DAY

Lord: it is time. The huge summer has gone by.
Now overlap the sundials with your shadows,
and on the meadows let the wind go free.

Command the fruits to swell on tree and vine;
grant them a few more warm transparent days,
urge them on to fulfillment then, and press
the final sweetness into the heavy wine.

Whoever has no house now, will never have one.
Whoever is alone will stay alone,
will sit, read, write long letters through the evening,
and wander on the boulevards, up and down,
restlessly, while the dry leaves are blowing.

Yeah, pessimistic, in the face of Strand's glowing optimism. I was at one time impressed by Strand's honours and credentials. What can I say now—we all make mistakes?

The Pittsburgh reading went okay I think. One college teacher (read high school, I suppose) had his students at the reading write me letters about it. A guy that interested high school students can't be all good, obviously must be simple-minded. Yeah, Cohen is boring . . .

I finished my "memoir" but apparently the powers-that-be at McStew don't care for it, tho they won't come out and say that. Could even be they're right.

The carollers will be certainly here tonight? And mankind has been around two–three million years according to the African paleos investigating various forms of Scipio Africanus.[3] I guess that means forever let alone another 155 years.

Your life sounds full and rewarding, what with exchanging presents and serving meals to friends etc. (I see the origins of your feelings on Oka there.) But Eurithe and I have never "celebrated" Christmas and sent out cards etc. If we feel like giving presents or saying nice things we do that, but not according to calendar dates. For those that do go by the dates—as well as feelings—that's fine too.

I had forgotten about your mother dying, if I ever knew. There's nothing to be said on such a subject of course, except that I know those are traumatic times. When my own mother died years back I could see other people expecting me to feel this and feel that, when I was having a tough time sorting out my own actual feelings. Some, of course, you don't need to sort out. But it certainly is a time of personal assessments and evaluations ...

Glad to hear about the Wpg. job, altho I know the weather there from bitter experience. Remember Pasternak's "To live a life is not to cross a field"?[4] Well, my own death was damn near incurred crossing a Wpg. field. But I didn't realize you'd be giving up your house there. Won't you want to be returning there, perhaps at some future date? [. . .]

And I'm pleased you're doing better financially. Difficult to think of anything else when you're not. Altho, is that really true? One goes on and on, broke or not. I think back to my own—or "our own"—bad times as memorable and productive.

No, I'm writing little or nothing now. Health problem, sure, at my advanced age. To be expected. This last summer Eurithe had her brother work on the house here, adding a new room up top, and hardwood flooring the place. She didn't want me here at that time, since grumbles about noise would've been inevitable. But now—the place seems a mite too grand for one of my basic tastes and needs. I don't use the upstairs room at all, and my work room is downstairs, not up.

Anyway, I'm really pleased you're doing better, and seem so cheerful. I hope your more customary critical nastiness doesn't stay under a bushel forever. Perhaps another book from Gus?

All the best to you, Alison and

offspring,

Al

1. AP and Sutherland had been discussing Mark Strand, and Sutherland informs me that he had probably sent AP a draft of his article about Strand, "Under the Moon's Cold Spell" (*Aloud* [January, 1992]). Editor, translator and poet (*Dark Harbour*, 1993), Mark Strand was born in 1934 in Summerside, Prince Edward Island of American parents.
2. Carlos Drummond de Andrade (1902–87): a major Brazilian poet whose first translator into English was Elizabeth Bishop.
3. Publius Cornelius Scipio (237–183 BCE) was given the surname Africanus after several victories in the Second Punic War.
4. The last line of Pasternak's "Hamlet," one of the Zhivago poems.

To Jack MacLeod (Toronto), from Sidney, BC, February 7, 1992

Dear Jack,

(We did meet one time, did we not?)—

Just recovering from the flu, and a friend sent me your *Globe* article of
Dec. 27.[1] I applaud such articles, of course; would like to see more or related pieces. I mean similar articles, but with different viewpoints.

And yes, I am angry too, about the whole situation. When Mulroney
decided to bring Quebec into confederation via Meech Lake, I am not
aware of any clamoring demand at that time by Quebec people to be included. And I think it's probable that Mulroney simply wanted to show
up Trudeau and make himself look good by doing something Trudeau
couldn't. On the other hand, there *may actually have been a clamor from
Fr. Canada* for inclusion at that time. You're more likely to know the truth
of that than I.

But the economy seems to me of equal importance right now to the
constitution. And despite the recession or depression, in both Canada and
the US, I regard Free Trade as largely responsible for our badly sagging
economy right now. And Mulroney—who again wanted to do something
on a large scale— for his ego's sake, made it happen. So do you believe in
fate or free will? If you voted Tory, well, you see what I mean . . . I'm not
sure I do at this point.

I see no mention of our beloved PM in your article, he with the 12%
rating at last Gallup Poll—at least I think it was Gallup. One question
might be: could Canada stagger out of our seeming impasse with Quebec
if Mulroney were off the stage? Or does that seem irrelevant? Unlike the
US, we seem to have no known legal or parliamentary device to get rid
of an unpopular chief of state. To answer my own question: I believe
it would be much easier to deal with Quebec if the man who largely
brought about the Quebec problem were off the stage. But again, that
may be quite irrelevant at this near-desperate point in our history.

I would especially agree with you in your anger if the break-up does
occur. And much of my anger will be directed at Mulroney, the man I

think very largely responsible. And I agree that Quebec is a "distinct society"—should be recognized as such, although not to the extent of giving them everything they seem to want.

However, we have somehow taken a wrong direction in our efforts to include Quebec in the constitution. I have very little faith in politicians to provide answers. It is from the anger and love of people like you, and others, that the answers must come.

Best Wishes,

Al

1. Jack McLeod's "Canada's Other Revolution" appeared in the *Globe and Mail* on December 27, 1991. It argued that "Since the 1960s, English Canada's world has turned. The changes are as great as those in Quebec. Anglos don't worry much about identity any more—they just want to be themselves."

To Revenue Canada (Victoria, BC) from Sidney, BC, April 10, 1992

Dear Sirs,

My professional income as a writer is slightly less than $11,000 a year. I am told that if your income is less than $30,000 a year it is not necessary to register for the GST. At my advanced age (73) it isn't likely that my income will increase. Therefore, will you please delete my name from your listings. A gross income from writing of the above amount seems to place me below the poverty line, whatever that is. My GST account number is 131371114.

Sincerely,

A.W. (Al) Purdy

To George Bowering (Vancouver), from Ameliasburgh, June 22, 1992

Dear George,

Good to hear from you. You take so long replying to a letter I'm never sure whether you're dead or mad at me for some reason or living with a new woman who gives you no time apart from fucking. Strike out one of those.

Yeah, I agree that most litcrit articles are dull, and yours are not. Or did you say that (hafta look it up)? Reading the Kroetsch one, I rather marvelled how you did it.[1] It's absolutely copyright G.B. I certainly couldn't. I've also looked over your *Curious*[2] and the tone is easily recognizable, which shocks me a little. Except you are much more ambiguous in those poems, as if you really want them to be taken in at least two ways. Incidentally, do you still feel the way you seemed to then about Auden? I really don't give a shit what his sexual preferences are, but some of his poems enthral me. On the other hand, I don't really expect to agree with you every time either; which is okay, I doubt you agree with me all the time either. I think the only fault I could pick out readily is that your writing would be so immediately identifiable, and that may not be a fault at all. Most people work to achieve an identifiable style . . . I'd prefer not to have one myself, and make all poems different. I hear you yell pronto you could pick out my stuff in a dark room wearing ear plugs. But what boots it, this kinda talk. Oh yes, if you have 40 seconds, could you photocopy that Atwood piece for me? Yeah, I'd like to know what you said and how you said it.

No, I didn't do the Gale thing. I did do an interview with both Acorn and Rosenblatt for Gale and money of course. None on myself.[3]

After the Air Farce: got into the taxi business for three years, and it went bust on accounta my father-in-law. He's dead now, so I can say it (I'd say it anyway tho). Then after a year or two of odd jobs at which I was bad at, we went/came back to Vancouver and that mattress factory. Did you see that book Oxford did a while back, places writers lived etc.[4] You must've since you're in it. Anyway, the picture in it of me in a Borsalino hat is from Vancouver, not Trenton. [. . .]

I'm being very inconsequential in this letter, don't ask me why. Glad to hear about the novel. Why don't you quit teaching and write twenty more? Okay, don't answer that.

Yeah, your father 85; mine I don't know how old. At least you knew yours; I was two when mine died. I wrote a poem in which I said he was 60 when he died. And found out later he was only 50, and I don't know how to change the poem anyway . . . [5]

Hope to hear from you in a few months.

Just try and get a few thou from me: it'd hafta go thru Eurithe!!!!

Al

1. AP is probably referring to Bowering's "Stone Hammer Narrative," though Bowering also writes about Alberta poet and novelist Robert Kroetsch (b. 1927) in "A Great Northward Darkness: The Attack on History in Recent Canadian Fiction." Both essays are in *Imaginary Hand* (1988).
2. Each of the poems in *Curious* (1973) is about a poet. The book also has photographs of the writers. The one of AP shows him holding open the door of an outhouse to reveal its female occupant.

3. The interviews were for various Gale Publishing books.

4. *The Oxford Literary Guide to Canada* (1987) by Albert and Theresa Moritz.

5. "Fathers" begins, "This year I realized my dead father / was sixty when he died and I am sixty / but it's a year like any other year" (*The Stone Bird*).

To Steven Heighton (Kingston), from Ameliasburgh, July 10, 1992

Dear Steven,

Better take a chair, this one might go on for more than a page.

Re the story,[1] it scares me a bit to tamper with it. However, suppose we take the line on page 5, second last para., that begins "He told me she died—" Change that to, "He told me she died, my father told me that. He said she had cancer and died quickly." I said, 'You killed her anyway.'"

New para: "His mean face was twisted when I was growing up and avoiding him as much as I could. For I'd made up my mind that this was what the world was like, a place of unexpected betrayal, of unpaid debts, the place where my mother died—a farm woman with a sense of honour."

That answers *how* the woman died, without going into details, which I think are not called for. Of course she ran away with Jacco, that's meant to be implied. Dying of cancer doesn't change that. Since Tim heard this from his father years ago, time has overlaid everything.

I like your "Near Ephesus" a little more than "Graveyard." But I'm not sure what "carcass and fossil" mean—Christmas in Turkey. Good ending. I don't think I can take any credit for that ending. It has clarity, on which I've always prided myself. "the graves sink deeper with time"—"and the spring rain takes their bodies / a little deeper down each year"? Reading "Graveyard" several times I like it better, without thinking it wholly succeeds. It talks seriously about serious things, as Philip Larkin might have said—Did you say you were influenced by him?[2]

I suppose that at the time after *Annettes*—I mean right around then—I was most influenced by Acorn and Layton. Other influences thronged around too, but as I've said, you could learn how to write and how not to write from Acorn. So bright and brilliant, and yet stupid at the same time. The mixture baffles one. I still wish D. Helwig had taken on his biography.[3]

Re "The Runners" and "Cariboo Horses" I've always thought those were about situations just as much as places. You say "love for and identification with cultures—" and that is one of the strong traits of Lawrence. I think of his *Etruscan Places* and so many others.

(I might say, those two poems of yours impress me more than their actual merit impresses. The fact that you write such poems, that these things are in your mind, and you search around the crevices for thoughts that produce the "right" words to say what you mean before you know what you mean. I think that's what I do, or at least did. I can give myself credit for little when I'm not writing much. A while back, nearly any thought produced a poem, I could sit still and a poem would visit me.)

Influences: I was influenced mostly by Br. writers. Haven't much use for American ones, just their language and jargon usage. Jeffers without doubt though. And the aforementioned Acorn and Layton. How humiliating to patronize somebody (Acorn) and then realize they're better than you. I mean patronize for their crudity etc. and in your mind only, not at all verbally, then realize etc. etc. I could never learn from Hopkins or Eliot, the former too radical, the latter too world-weary. Attitude as well as subject.

I've never read much of Wallace,[4] when I did it didn't impress me. It's "nice" that she was impressed by me for the reasons of place and home etc.

As I may have implied above, I think setting and place are secondary to what you're trying to say. They perhaps make you more believable—And my "Country North of Belleville"—the place is damn near the subject matter itself. But these things are not on my mind writing a poem. Landscape alone doesn't induce me to write a poem. I don't in any way dismiss it, but rather take it for granted since it's where we're at, our background which is even close to our foreground at times. I think of my own passage, "—and women with such a glow / it makes their background vanish" which is not a good example of what I'm trying to say. Or maybe it is.

Oh yes, I agree that there are now some quite interesting writers in Canada, proof of this being the increasing attention paid to Can. writers abroad.

If I were you, I'd be getting sick to death of this letter by now.

And yes, the father in this story was just a miserable s.o.b., who changed somewhat later in life. Remember, the boy was a friend of Jacko, and kids of that age (12) sometimes feel loyalty very strongly. There is a matter-of-fact tone through this short piece that I think helps to make it work, at least it does for me. I agree re your suggestion, more info about the woman's death, but think the youngster's hero-worshipping of Jacco (I have to look up the spelling again—it is "Jacco") makes his reaction believable.

476

I've often—well sometimes—been told I've influenced someone. I can rarely see it, but it must be true, since I get it fairly often . . . I would rather say you write with clarity, and learned that on your own. It's such a simple thing, and yet writers want to be world-sweeping and learnedly impressive. Mostly that makes their stuff sound silly.

And Metcalf?[5] While he's doing all his kicking and pricking, he gets quite a bit of attention himself. And most people like attention, and I think he's no exception. This letter is discursive, and replying to yours seemed to call for that. The people he puts down are mostly down already. Nobody reads Grove.[6] Why even mention him? Birney has three or four poems, "Bushed," "David," and one or two others that will live a few years. Pratt I have little use for (does Metcalf mention Pratt?). Wiebe[7] is often unintelligible with his contorted sentences, (less so as time passes), . . . I see the place where Metcalf names names . . . Mitchell[8] wrote one damn good book, *Who Has Seen the Wind*. Tell Metcalf to write one just as good. He hasn't yet. Callaghan's *The Loved and the Lost* is perhaps C's best. Again, Metcalf, go thou and do one as good. Richler, I think, is now repeating himself. He *was* good. But what boots it? I'm too suspicious of any of Metcalf's attitudes to believe him even when it seems he might be right.

Eurithe and I will be in Kingston Aug. 4. Hope to see you then.

—Best to Mary, and tell her Eurithe knows what she (Mary) has to put up with—

Al

1. AP is discussing his story "The Iron Road" which Heighton wanted to include in a special fiction issue of *Quarry*. The story appeared in the summer 1992 issue.
2. The poems are in Heighton's *The Ecstasy of Sceptics* (1994). Philip Larkin (1922–85): English poet (*Collected Poems*, 1988). "A serious house on serious earth it is / In whose blent air all our compulsions meet, / Are recognized, and robed as destinies" is from Larkin's "Church Going."
3. Acorn's biography was written by Richard Lemm: *Milton Acorn: In Love and Anger* (1999).
4. Bronwen Wallace (1945–89): Kingston political activist and poet (*Signs of the Former Tenant*, 1983). She is mentioned in AP's elegy for Tom Marshall "A Sorrow for Tom" (*Naked with Summer in Your Mouth*).
5. John Metcalf (b. 1938): editor, short story writer, novelist (*General Ludd*, 1980) and acidulous and often perceptive critic (*What is a Canadian Literature?*, 1988).
6. Frederick Philip Grove (1879–1948): novelist (*Fruits of the Earth*, 1933).
7. Rudy Wiebe (b. 1934): Alberta novelist (*The Scorched-Wood People*, 1977) whose novels have dealt with Mennonites, the history of the West and native concerns.

8. W.O. Mitchell (1914–98): Alberta playwright, script writer and novelist. Two of his works—*Who Has Seen the Wind* (1947) and *Jake and the Kid* (1961)—are Canadian classics.

To Susan Musgrave (Sidney, BC), from Ameliasburgh, July 27, 1992

Dear Susan,

[. . .] Glad to hear Stephen is busy (tho not about his dad). You people tire me out just listening to your activities. I'm amused by your collecting beer cans. Last fall I walked nearly—say 4–5 miles—every day, and picked up beer cans myself. There's a road near here about five miles no one lives there, and I'd get as many as five–six cans some days. Keeps your exercise interesting.

Yeah, one is always hearing about some prose writer who makes big bucks, the implication being, why don't you? You write what you can write. There is no formula that I ever heard of. Reading a piece by Bev Daurio in *Quarry*,[1] she's got this anecdote tucked in:

An extremely wealthy publisher invites his old friend, a writer, to his daughter's wedding. At the reception, the publisher, resplendent in top hat and tails, takes the scruffy-sweatered inappropriately-trousered writer aside.

"Why don't you write me a pot-boiler I can sell?" the publisher asks. "It'd be easy for you. Just sit down and knock the thing off, get yourself some money so you can afford to do the stuff you like."

"I don't know," says the writer slowly. "Did you ask your daughter to turn a few tricks to help pay for the wedding?"

Which is a bit ridiculous, of course. Seems this was originally told by one Crad Kilodny,[2] the guy who sells stuff on the street and plays tricks on Bob Weaver you likely know about.

Anyway, I re-read a short story I wrote some 25 years ago, and found to my surprise that it's one of the best things I'd ever done. Can't remember writing it at all, had completely forgotten until Alex Widen[3] dug it outa Queen's archives. Hard for me to believe I was that abstemious with words (it's only six pages), and entirely non-biographical— should say non-autobiographical. *Quarry* will run it in their fiction issue. Whyn't you send em some stuff, if you're writing short pieces? Steven Heighton's the editor, *Quarry*, P.O. Box 1061, Kingston, Ont. K7L 4Y5 . . .

Did you hear about Bill Hoffer managing to get a box of Pat Lowther's[4] books and papers etc. at some kind of Sally Ann sale? Seems that Lowther (the husband, now dead) corresponded with Steinbeck years back, and there was a letter or two from him in that box to Roy Lowther. This in Vancouver somewhere. Alex Widen told me about it, he being at the sale too.

My medical troubles? Well, I've been bothered by numbness in the feet for years, and going to a neurological specialist in Kingston. Last year the only thing he could think of was that it might be beer causing the trouble. As a result, no beer. But he doesn't really know the reason, is more or less guessing. When you get away from the obvious medical problems, doctors really know fuckall. Without their electronic gimmicks etc., they're nowhere. However: if this guy comes up with a magic cure for me I'll change my tune. I doubt it tho.

Al

1. Beverley Daurio (b. 1953): editor, poet (*If Summer Had a Knife*, 1987), and writer of fiction (*Hell & Other Novels*, 1992). AP is referring to her article "A Scattering of Observations on Canadian Publishing, Nationalism, and the Writer as Artist" in *Quarry* (Spring 1992).
2. Street-poet Crad Kilodny sold his collections of poems on the streets of Toronto—usually either on Bloor St. or Yonge St.—and submitted pseudonymous manuscripts to publishers that were hoaxes.
3. Alex Widen edited AP's *Reaching for the Beaufort Sea*.
4. Pat Lowther (1935–75): BC poet (*A Stone Diary*, 1977). Roy Lowther was convicted in 1977 of her murder. John Steinbeck (1902–68): American novelist (*The Grapes of Wrath*, 1939; *East of Eden*, 1952).

Alistair MacLeod (b. 1936): short story writer (*The Lost Salt Gift of Blood*, 1976) and novelist (*No Great Mischief*, 2001). AP's letter is in response to MacLeod's article "Remembering Hugh MacLennan," which he had read in *Brick* (Summer 1992). MacLeod describes the novelist as one of the pioneers of Canadian literature: "I miss him as one misses an intrepid pioneer who was among the first to map the rivers and blaze the trails of a new country while suffering great hardship and neglect within that process. 'It is possible to lead a literary life within this country,' this early cartographer seems to have said. 'Follow me; it will not be easy but worthy in the end. Press on. Don't turn back.'"

To Alistair MacLeod (Windsor, Ont.), from Ameliasburgh, summer 1992

Dear Alistair MacLeod,

My Highland credentials are: mother's name Ross; told Purdy was a sheepstealer on the Scots–Eng. border way back, when the English executed him (them?), and two surviving Purdy sisters asked their husbands to take that name so the name'd survive. All very picturesque. Comes from one Bonnie Purdy, who worked for Halifax TV ten years back.

Which is apart from MacLennan, your piece in *Brick*,[1] which I had to comment on. I knew him slightly (who knows another person well?) in the '50s and '60s. I listened to him talk at a Louis Dudek party in Mtl. those days; he showed up at a party at Elspeth Buitenhuis' house in Mtl. to congratulate me on a piece I did on Malcolm Lowry; I listened to him talk in his McGill office, on US imperialism; I liked him.

First major Can. novelist? I'd rather link him with Morley Callaghan,[2] as one of the two prose writers who made an impression on me. I read his paperback *Barometer Rising* not long after its first appearance. And yeah, that one made an impression on me. And how strange for him to find that phrase in Rilke that has gone down and permeated the Can. consciousness, two solitudes. He seems so different from Rilke. But is he, was he really?

"knowing who to write for" in your piece? I always, first and last, write for myself: which accounts for my small readership. If I write for myself, find out thereby what I'm thinking, what and how I feel? well enough, then won't others fall into my mood and feeling and discover what I discover?

"write out of this country"—sure, one must do that. There is no other way despite Claudel[3] and others.

"never to be far from tears"—to be human and to have some small feeling for any damn thing—is never to be far from tears and cussing what needs to be cussed. (Mulroney!)

I wonder: what does the blood do when you're nearly unaware of your own antecedents, as I was years back? Or are the bagpipes so stirring that the soul leaps erect to salute the music and feeling no matter what the blood? When "Amazing Grace" first appeared 15–20 years ago, I had M. Laurence listen to it (her maiden name was Wemys, or similar), and tears flowed.

Thanks for the MacLennan piece, I enjoyed it and you.

Best wishes,
Al Purdy

1. Hugh MacLennan (1907–90): one of the major figures of Canadian literature, MacLennan is the author of realistic novels like *Barometer Rising* (1941), *Two Solitudes* (1945) and *The Watch That Ends the Night* (1959), as well as popular collections of essays. He received five Governor General's Awards.

2. Morley Callaghan (1903–90): broadcaster and novelist (*More Joy in Heaven*, 1937). His most lasting book may turn out to be *That Summer in Paris* (1963), which deals with his 1929 visit to Paris where he met Hemingway, Fitzgerald, Joyce and John Glassco. In September 2003, he was honoured with a commemorative stamp.

3. Paul Claudel (1868–1955): French dramatist (*L'Annonce fait à Marie*, 1892) and poet (*Cinq Grandes Odes*, 1922), one of the major figures in modern Catholic literature.

From Sam Solecki (Toronto), to Ameliasburgh, August 7, 1992

Dear Al,

Thanks for the various clippings. I very much liked Beerbohm's[1] memories of Yeats—he was very good in recreating the visual image (Yeats on stage responding to the crowd) as well as in evoking the voice. It's interesting to see him simultaneously fascinated by Yeats, admiring his genius, and yet having some reservations, some hitch in the feelings and attitude he has for the great man.

Re Pound[2]: I suspect that the debate will go on forever since there are enough people like the first letter writer in the *New York Times*, Dachine Rainer, who insist on white-washing him, even insisting, against the published proof of the letters, broadcasts and memoirs, that he "was not an anti-semite." Just the vile puns on Roosevelt's name alone would have qualified him as one: Jewsfeldt, Roosenstein were two of them. There were also anti-semitic articles in the *British Union Quarterly*. In one issue the four names on the cover were Wyndham Lewis, Pound, Campbell and . . . Quisling. Olson's memoirs are full of references to comments EP made at St. Elizabeth's in 1947 about Jews.

1956 to MacLeish: "Obviously the kikes kept me in here."

1958 to the Italian press: "The fascist dictators made a mistake in the way they persecuted the Jews. The mistake was not in fighting the Jews, but the manner in which the Jews were fought. Rather than attack them as a bloc, each case should have been examined individually."

My favourite sentence in DR's letter is "People who didn't support WWII are frequently deemed anti-Semites." If memory serves me on this one, Old Ez had moments in the late 30s and during the war when he thought the war would cleanse western civilization.

About what happened in Pisa. In the early days he was kept isolated in a special cage with reinforced steel. There were several in a row. Later on he was given more freedom and allowed into the main tent and given access to a typewriter. I think the two servicemen you mention were watching him at *different* periods during the imprisonment. He was there for several weeks, perhaps a couple of months while the government tried to figure out what to do.

About "Archaic Torso of Apollo": I don't have a problem with the final line's insistence that "you must change your life" because it comes from the statue of a God: in Rilke there's often that reminder of ideal states of being—the Angels in the *Duino Elegies*—which we can't hope to emulate, but which we go on striving towards. In your case it would be the perfect poem after which no poetry should/could be written. Compare Housman's "Loitering with a vacant eye / Along the Grecian gallery" (LI in *Shropshire Lad*) where the speaker actually changes his life because of what the statue says!!! "Courage, lad, 'tis not for long / Stand, quit you like stone, be strong."

By the way, I'm reading Williams, Pound, Olson and others in relation to your work NOT because I'm looking for influences. It's more an interest in reminding myself how they solved some problems with voice, the relationship between "breath" / "voice" / "rhythm" / lineation and an entire free verse prosody that each poet creates whether he thinks about it consciously or not. There's also the related affinity of Williams and Olson trying to use Paterson and Gloucester in roughly the same way you relate to Ameliasburgh. Anyway, it's these sorts of billiard ball bouncings of poem off poem that interest me. And Whitman, despite your loathing of all his values and poems is the grand-daddy in so far as he knew where poetry was heading and the possibilities. And like it or not, he's a religious poet, though without your inherent pessimism and doubt.

I like the slightly opaque, paradoxical quality of
"I lessened [lessoned] and grew more"
and the fact that its haunted by an iambic line.[3]
About
"A bird who may have thought
'Oh dear—oh dear—oh dear'"
I like it much, *much* better this way—without the intrusive and too explanatory "the equivalent of". . . but you've already seen that *that* is "too self-conscious."

"off course of course falling" will have a pun even if the first two words are dropped: the "of" will carry the ghost of an "off" and "course" can't help bring in the other meanings.

About a new volume, I see no reason why you shouldn't expect to publish a new book with M&S. I would suggest aiming for the 1994 season. That would be four years between books, and it would give you 12 more months to work on it. Usually the mss. has to be in house by July of the year before the following spring's publication.

Just in my file alone, there must be nearly 20 poems, and you seem to be writing on again/off again. Incidentally, I would be very happy to help you edit it—if you needed help—but the contact with the M&S editors would have to be with you. You know the reasons.

You suggest in passing that I might be interested in doing the ultimate *Collected*. Do bears shit in the forest? Is the Pope Polish? Did Sam Solecki love L– W–? Is Al Purdy one of my favourite poets?

GET YOUR WILL OUT TONIGHT AND WRITE IN BLOOD [TO FOLLOW IN PLASTIC POUCH] THAT IF HE IS STILL ALIVE, PROFESSOR SAM SOLECKI—TO BE FOUND SLEEPING UNDER THE BLOOR VIADUCT—IS THE CHOSEN EDITORIAL VESSEL.

I'm sending you a couple of things.

The first is a compilation of student essay and exam bloopers, some of which should bring a chuckle; they might also make you hesitate about wanting anyone to write about you.

The second is a series of translations and adaptations of Sappho's fragment "He seems a God sitting near you." I've enclosed Sappho (NO, I don't read Greek any more), Catullus's adaptation, Merwin's translation of Catullus, and Bunting's adaptation.

By the way, I'll be up in the first or second week of September—I'll let you know as soon as I get back from visiting my sister's family in Tennessee between August 11th and 21st. By then I'll also have some questions about the poems that need answering—whether you want to answer or not is, of course, optional.

Take care,

Sam

1. Max Beerbohm (1872–1956): English caricaturist, essayist and writer (*Zuleika Dobson*, 1912). His "First Meetings with W.B. Yeats" was originally broadcast on BBC and subsequently appeared in *Books and Men*.
2. AP's reading of Richard Gilman's "Standing Up to Ezra Pound" (*New York Times Book Review*, August 25, 1992) and letters in the next issue resulted in the

poems "Pound" and "On Robert Frost" (*Naked with Summer in Your Mouth*) that
quote from them.
3. The lines "I lessened and grew more" and "A bird . . ." are from "Seasons"
(*Naked with Summer in Your Mouth*).

To Sam Solecki (Toronto), from Ameliasburgh, August 16, 1992

Dear Sam,

Leave tomorrow for PEI, two weeks away, renting a car.

Re Pound, I don't have Dudek's book of letters from Pound any
more, but I'm wondering if any anti-Semitic remarks there.[1] I thought
the Roosevelt background was Dutch. No? I'm so naïve and unthinking
about names generally that I wasn't aware for years that Peter Newman
was Jewish, really not until K– said in a letter that he wanted to review
Newman's HBC book, calling the latter "a Levantine arriviste" . . . Now
that's anti-Semitic.

Sure, I'd love to have you edit final version of Collected, assuming there is one. I'll be watching despite presumed demise. (Thanks for
"Little-Known Facts" etc. in case I don't think of it later) Some of it's
funny, but palls before you finish. And I like that "Mr. Hines says so, and
he's a schoolteacher / he ought to know" . . .)

Re Beerbohm on Yeats: I thought Beer. disliked Yeats and didn't want
to say so outright, but used this method and was very well aware what
he was doing. I didn't like the Yeats portrayed by Beerbohm very much
either, but I'm not really sure he was like that at all—I mean the way
Beerbohm portrayed him. Yes, I'm sure he was snooty at times. Must've
got tiresome so many people being in awe of him. "some hitch, some
reservations"—he sure as hell did (Beerbohm). And if you remember,
so did Gogarty,[2] saying Yeats wanted to be part of the nobility. Lotta
shit. Far as I'm concerned, he was. It's probably a damn good thing he
never fucked Maud Gonne—"consumated" his love if you like. (Okay,
"consummate.")

Yeah, I figgered it was likely two different periods at Pisa [for Pound],
but interesting those letter-writers should be so sure of themselves.

I don't *like* Housman's "Loitering with a vacant eye . . . " etc. This
comes down to the "willing suspension of disbelief" stuff you're supposed to have about persuasive fiction. Something in me rebels anyway
if someone else tells me I must must do this or that. Whether a god or
no, I'm liable to ask the god or goddess to show me his birth certificate.
Nevertheless, "Archaic Torso" is a fine poem, if faint praise doesn't offend

you. But "Autumn Day" hits me a bit harder. And I guess Rilke had the same complaint, a bit anti-Semitic.

I'm sure all these people you mention actually did influence me. But probably only Thomas and one or two others are overt. All that stuff about breath, voices etc. makes me wanta throw up. But probably because of the use the westcoasters made of it, their holier-than-thou attitudes. Not so much because of Olson himself, he was just boring.

Don't get me wrong about Whitman tho: I give full credit in my mind to Whitman, but because of his methods, not on accounta his subject matter. No, that's wrong, not on accounta his attitudes which I think mostly silly. But the way he let himself go, I think quite admirable. And feel a bit similar about Hemingway. But in both their cases, they got hipped on method, and failed to realize "There are twenty million ways / of singing tribal lays" to paraphrase Kipling inaccurately.[3] Of course I can't use em all either, but I'd hate to be confined by "method" and "voice" etc. [...]

"'Roughly' the same way I relate to A-burgh." A-burg was/is the milieu, and you *use* that whether you make a myth of it or no. Pinpoint of the soul, you might say. What fuckin soul? "There are rooms for rent in the outer planets"?[4]

Sure, anyone trying to be intensely persuasive and solemnly important about damn near anything will always seem religious. "The best lack all conviction / and the worst are full of passionate intensity"[5]—are the worst religious?

I am, by the way, composing a short story in my head, adding ingredients and noting them down. About a guy whose wife left him and he's passionate about her, climbs a tree to watch his ex and her new boy friend thru her window, and feels he looks so ridiculous to himself he'd never be able to tell a friend about this in future. Then a tree branch breaks loudly and he has to run for it. Laughing all the time while running.—I'm working it out gradually, but this PEI trip may be an interruption. [...]

George Galt was down Tuesday. Workin hard on his novel and feeling he's written some good stuff. It's a nice feeling.

See you in Sept.

Best,

Al

1. Dudek had published *D/k: Some Letters of Ezra Pound* (1974), and both there and in other remarks made in the period he denied that Pound had made anti-Semitic comments. He changed his view later on.

2. Oliver St. John Gogarty (1878–1957): surgeon, novelist and poet, Gogarty was the model for Buck Mulligan in Joyce's *Ulysses*. Yeats thought sufficiently highly of his verse to include 17 poems in *The Oxford Book of Modern Verse* (1936).
3. Kipling wrote "There are nine and sixty ways of constructing tribal lays, / And—every—single—one—of—them—is—right!" ("In the Neolithic Age").
4. "There are rooms for rent in the outer planets" is from "Married Man's Song" (*Love in a Burning Building*) and its last seven words became the title of AP's selected poems of 1996.
5. Yeats's "The Second Coming."

To Sam Solecki (Siena, Italy), from Sidney, BC, January 22, 1993

Dear Sam,
Hafta send you this *Times* review.

And a quote from another review: "The example of Tolstoy's *War and Peace* has done irreparable damage to Russian literature in this century. Throughout the 1920's, 30's, 40's and into the 50's Soviet writers labored mightily and mostly unsuccessfully (Mikhail Sholokhov[1] and *The Quiet Don* being a partial exception) to emulate the master. Even Boris Pasternak, who should have known better, was seduced into turning out his clumsy Tolstoyan pastiche, *Doctor Zhivago*, and for the last two decades the magisterial Aleksandr Solzhenitsyn, who seems to be suffering from a terminal dose of Tolstoyitis, has been toiling over his multi volume epic on war and revolution, *The Red Wheel*."

(Michael Scammell)

Since I've been attempting *Zhivago*, this seems relevant. I got to around page 300, and gave up. The novel reads to me as if the author is a gifted amateur, disconnected and unintegrated in his narrative. And I gave up on Ondaatje [*The English Patient*] after several attempts at page 100. But just read *Love in the Time of Cholera* and marvel: the guy is a magician. Admittedly, I think there's a slight falling off in the last part of Márquez's novel, but not much. I missed him on tv today, and some people (not Márquez's characters) trying to find the town of Macondo. Márquez saying the mythic has become real, this from Eurithe. [. . .]

All best,
Al

1. Mikhail Sholokhov (1905–84): the most celebrated Soviet novelist (*And Quiet Flows the Don*, 1934–40). He received the Nobel Prize in 1965.

To Sam Solecki (Siena, Italy), from Sidney, BC, January 29, 1993

Dear Sam,

Many thanks for the zerox of the Rilke article. Didn't know Gass[1] was an authority—but how many authorities do I know? Bits of the piece are hard to follow. "Transubstantiate"—yes, substantiate is to affirm, but what does adding "trans" do? I can't find the piece right now, but I recall Gass seemed to think it fell down a bit at the end. I expect you'll be getting the Rilke book he's writing about: can I borrow it?

I recommend highly that you dig up a copy of Anthony Burgess's *Abba Abba*, if you haven't read it already. The first part is about the death of Keats, the second some 40 pages of poem translations of Giuseppe Gioacchino Belli, presumably by Burgess himself, altho he ascribes them to another guy, Joseph John Wilson, presumably his own ancestor, born 1916, died in Manhattan, 1959. Now Burgess's real name is Wilson, as I'm sure you know. And he too was born around 1916, so his sense of humor is getting the best of him. But the Belli trans. are wonderful; you gotta read em. Library there must have the book, if you haven't read it.

Can't you drop that Wellington stuff, or do you think it's a weak spot. If so, you're probably right; but only slightly vulnerable, around the heel maybe. Sure, let's do reading and talk to students.

Howie White gets more and more enthusiastic the more good reviews come in. He now says he wants to do the Collected Prose. I've mentioned to him that I'd like you to edit it, if as and when. I expect your dean-work keeps you too busy right now? But I hope not. Let me know what you think on this.

Incidentally, I've made most of the changes you suggested in poem manuscript. I didn't mention title in sentence above, since Pat Lane, Lorna Crozier, Susan Musgrave, Stephen Reid and David McFadden were here for lunch last Sunday, and I mentioned another title: *Naked with Summer in Your Mouth*. They liked that much more than *To See the Shore*, which admittedly is rather quiet-sounding. And as Susan mentioned, *The Woman on the Shore* preceded it. Only trouble is, *Naked* seems a bit blatant and reaching-for-readers to me. But I like it anyway. That's the one Howie White disliked for autobio.

Gass's essay seemed about as complicated as Rilke's own writing, and yet his prose seemed a bit clumsy here and there. Not like a veteran novelist.

Best,

Al

1.William H. Gass (b. 1924): American essayist and novelist (*Omensetter's Luck*, 1966). Solecki had sent AP Gass's essay on Rilke's *The Notebooks of Malte Laurids Brigge*.

To Sam Solecki (Siena, Italy), from Sidney, BC, February 4, 1993

Dear Sam,

[. . .] It's finally sunk into my head that you're actually working on this Purdy book: I'd had the impression that was for some time in the future. ECW has asked George Galt to do one on Purdy as well, but he can't start until two years from now on accounta his novel, for which he just got a grant in aid of. The ECW book would be 25,000 words. George just broke a finger, so he can't do much of anything for a while.

Trouble with reading my favourite stuff is the univs—or whoever— ask me to read my own stuff.

Yeah, Guthrie is supposed to have written a poem called "The Bear" but I dunno where published.[1] Influences: I once read excerpts from a Guthrie poem about a cave painter, but never did find the book it's in. However, that Guthrie poem probably got me going on my own cave painters poem. Amazing Sartre[2] didn't think his "rewards" amounted to much. Conversely, I think my own life has been pretty good, and the rewards if not munificent have been "satisfactory." But the principal reward of just about anything is in its commission and accomplishment.

Of course Irving was a big influence. It may well be that Irving's air rifle bit connected with my poem, but I've just about forgotten the mind set at the time. Yeah, the "hunchback prince" sounds a bit like Layton as well.[3]

Yeah, I remember saying that about Birney, altho he didn't absorb Joyce seamlessly, and didn't mean to I guess . . . It was probably a matter of pride to demonstrate being influenced by Joyce. I never was, and never could get through *Ulysses*.

Quite agree: I was reading everything at the time of those first few books, "staying stupid," as that Aussie poet had it. Pound did get feeling into a couple of things, "The River Merchant," and "The Goodley Fere," and perhaps some others. But I could never get Olson, however bright and innovative he may have been.

When Jeffers? Migawd, probably the Fifties, but really can't remember. I was reading everyone in that decade. Never written anything about him. DHL? Probably about 1955, when I saw Layton's candle for DHL burning in a niche at his place. Tho it probably wasn't actually burning. And yes,

Layton meant a lot to me in those days. Yeah, the papers at Saskatoon contain earlier stuff than Queen's, but same sorta thing, many drafts of poems. There is also a sheaf at Lakehead U, which are still earlier than Sask.

You have an ability to read which I envy. Livy, Tacitus, Milosz and Yeats' autobios. What a learned bastard you are! These guys scare the shit outa me. I have read Tacitus and some of Yeats' autobio. Trouble with you taking that early stuff as basis for what I think and feel now, you can't. Everything about me has changed since then. Ideas, methods of prosody, everything is upside down.

I've just been reading about William Blake, and came across two–three paras. in one of his letters that might make a "found poem" . . . Seems he threw a guy, a soldier, out of his garden, when the man was there without Blake's permission. Just swung the man around, probably bent his arms back and upward, and frogmarched him away and up the road to some barracks, the soldier cussing away at Blake all the time but unable to do anything about his situation.[4]

okay, better stop

Best

Al

1. AP is being disingenuous; "The Making of the Bear," which influenced his "In the Caves," is in *Maximum Security Ward*, a book he owned and often discussed with friends.
2. Solecki had sent AP an interview with Sartre titled "Self-Portrait at Seventy." AP is referring to Sartre's answer at the end of the interview to the question "In short, so far life has been good to you?": "On the whole, yes. I don't see what I could reproach it with. It has given me what I wanted and at the same time it has shown that this wasn't much. But what can you do?" (*Life / Situations: Essays Written and Spoken*).
3. Layton's "Cain" shows the speaker shooting a frog with an "air rifle." AP's "At Roblin Lake" describes how the speaker captures a frog "With hands—having no air rifle." Layton's "The Cold Green Element" has the lines "and grew a brilliant / hunchback with a crown of leaves."
4. The Blake letter reappears as the found poem "Incident Involving William Blake" (*Naked with Summer in Your Mouth*).

Joseph Brodsky (1940–96): Russian poet (*Collected Poems in English*, 2001) and essayist (*On Grief and Reason*, 1995), awarded the Nobel Prize in 1987.

To Joseph Brodsky (New York), from Ameliasburgh, April 8, 1993

Dear Mr. Brodsky,
I had a street named for me in my home village of Ameliasburgh last year.
It too leads to a graveyard.

I'm referring to your anecdote about "Audenstrasse" in "To Please a
Shadow." My street is "Purdy Lane," which immediately after the street
sign leads downhill to the village graveyard and old millpond.

I am, of course, a writer, having received most of the awards for writing in Canada but little known in the US. And incidentally, visited the
Soviet Union (sic?) in 1977, and met Voznesensky there among others.

I am also an admirer of Auden, but not so fortunate as you I never
met him. I regard him, along with Yeats, as the two poets in English of
this century. As I'm sure you know, Auden scrapped the passage in the
Yeats poem, beginning "Time that is intolerant—" I presume the reason
for that was that he didn't wish to say, "Pardoned Kipling and his views."
Just the same, I mourn that missing passage, which I think one of the
"great" passages in literature.

I won't go on taking up your time. But the business of "Audenstrasse" and
"Purdy Lane" with both leading to graveyards is too odd not to mention.

Best Wishes,
Al Purdy

To Susan Musgrave (Sidney, BC), from Ameliasburgh, May 31, 1993

Dear Susan,
It's a very good poem, and says much about you. But all your poems do
that. Be reassured, you haven't lost a thing, you're even getting better. This
poem is as complicated as any of yours I've ever read.

And I'm concerned about you too. To get both our minds off that,
here's a brief story. David Helwig was down today with his girl friend,
whom I believe he's living with—very nice gal. Anyway, he told me about
meeting Layton in Montreal, not at all sure Layton would recognize him,
but Irving did. And talking together, Layton introduced Anna, his wife,
and said, "Isn't she beautiful?" David said he didn't know what got into
him, but answered Layton, "Like all the others."

Silence fell apparently. I asked what their expressions were like, Irving's
and Anna's. It seems David didn't look, but got outa there as soon as he could.

And talking to David and Judith (Pond), I said at one point: "Every quarrel with Eurithe is a thousand calories." How many calories with you and Stephen?

You have been having a few adventures. Try to keep your spirits up, and remember that these things pass. How can I give you advice, when I've been so vulnerable myself over the years? Still, live through it. When I was on an arctic island years ago, not knowing exactly where, listening to old squaw ducks mournfully saying the world is about to end for ducks and humans, I mentally wrote the poem-line, "I think to the other side of that sound—"[1] You do that too, please. Think to the other side of the bad things.

I thought you had gone back west and were all through at Western. Should've remembered my own stint there, but the times have faded out of my mind. Ask that guy you know and I know, but whose name I always forget, to get me a reading there in early Oct. I had a good crowd there a few years back.

[. . .] Guy in the US at a college, Ken Norris,[2] who used to be in Mtl., asked me for a poem or short piece on Leonard Cohen for his 60th birthday, and book publication. Imagine, Cohen 60!!!! Just yesterday he left a note at a pub for a girl in Mtl., "I'm nearly 30"—or something like that.

You know about Tom Marshall, I'm sure. Died about 2–3 weeks ago. I didn't ever think of him dying, and now think of him often.[3] Steven Heighton (editor of *Quarry*) and David Morley (one of the Brit. poets at Harbourfront), came down here after I got back from Toronto. Before I read there, while standing at the lectern, I said "Greg Gatenby is a genius for getting these readings funded." Pause, then "And he's so shy and modest about it too." [. . .]

My—or should I say, the *Laurence-Purdy Letters* are out—I just got four copies, will likely order more to give away—Editor must get eight, Laurence's kids four more. Oh well . . . Two reviews, one by Marchand negative, another by Rosemary Sullivan (Doug Beardsley's ex) very good.[4] She's a nice gal. She and Sam S. were sorta i/c Purdy when I was at U of T. Call her my fairy godmother, address her as Dear F.G. [. . .]

Met a guy at Harbourfront (poet called M.L. Rosenthal, talked to him about Ramon Guthrie and the latter's *Maximum Security Ward*.[5] By odd happenchance, he at his university had republished that book a few years before and sent me a copy, plus a little book about Guthrie's book. Have I ever mentioned Guthrie and his book to you? Have the feeling I did. Anyway, I left Toronto next day after my reading, tho I coulda stayed three more days for free. Toronto ain't that fascinatin. Sam S. is out west nursing an 80-yr-old sick friend. Jesus, my typing gets worse the longer I go.

Usta do 40 words a minute with two fingers and only 39 mistakes. Did I mention Sam has got some 60,000 words on Purdy? He just came back from Siena, Italy, close to Etruria, on an academic jaunt. I always wanted to get to Etruria in DHL's footsteps.

Do I hafta say again, I'd love to see you here—and Stephen. You get down here you get one of my two copies of the *Laurence-Purdy Letters*, otherwise Linda [Rogers] gets it. That won't do it, eh?

Al

1. "Metrics" in *North of Summer*.
2. Ken Norris (b. 1951): critic (*A New World*, 1994) and poet (*Limbo Road*, 1998). He teaches at the University of Maine.
3. Tom Marshall died on April 28, 1993. AP writes about him in "Bits and Pieces" and "A Sorrow for Tom" (*Naked with Summer in Your Mouth*) and in "Departures" (*To Paris Never Again*).
4. Philip Marchand (b. 1946): reviewer, columnist (*Toronto Star*) and writer (*Marshall McLuhan: The Medium and the Messenger*, 1989); Rosemary Sullivan (b. 1946): professor of English, poet and biographer (*Shadow Maker: The Life of Gwendolyn MacEwen*, 1995). Sullivan and Solecki were AP's contacts in the English department when he was writer in residence at the University of Toronto.
5. M.L. Rosenthal (b. 1917): poet (*As for Love: Poems and Translations*, 1987) and critic (*Running to Paradise: Yeats's Poetic Art*, 1994).

To Sam Solecki (Toronto), from Ameliasburgh, July 2, 1993

Dear Sam,
Yeah, those Atwood letters,[1] hadn't thought of them before. At the time, couldn't imagine anyone being curious about my letters or any to me. Now you make me a bit uneasy. I wonder if a letter from me would put any kind of padlock on them; and here the very mention of them in this letter is a form of publicity for them.

Yeah, I remember the birch bark little book. Was the poem "Reilly"?[2] About riding freights?

Don't remember the large brown scrapbook, but it was likely me that put it together.

Yeah, it was a slow, tough grind, as you say. And I was well aware of what I was doing, changing myself with all the changes in my writing. You're quite right re the plays helping with writing poems, loosening up the voice and diction; and letters to many people filled the same function.

No, I hadn't realized most of the plays about marriages in trouble. Don't remember "The Knot."

There were some Inuit colour drawings from Pangnirtung which I tried to get hold of again from U of Sask. with the idea of re-printing *North of Summer*—but somebody had lifted them. I am, incidentally, doing an article for *Imp. Oil Rev.* on that arctic summer, again. They said 2000 words, but I got it up to 3000, since even then it has to be condensed. But $2,500. which ain't bad.[3]

Come down any time you like. And I think it's a good thing for you to take Andre on a tour like you project. [. . .]

No, didn't know Glassco really well. I must've mentioned the '82 judging for poem award for GG, in which Gus and I picked Layton, then had to talk Watson into agreeing?? But Watson double-crossed us, and went for Glassco, along with the final committee, of which Gus and I were not members. Then Glassco writing me and saying he knew he owed it all to me. I couldn't reply to that letter at all. I may still have it in among some letters I retained for whatever reasons.

The poem you sent, by Mark Strand?—highly interesting. The diction very ordinary and rather talky, understated, kind of, then you come to the end and he sez "It was an angel, one of the good ones, about to sing—" All those words just to imitate Rilke? Of course it isn't exactly an imitation, but you do think of Rainer Maria. Did I ever show you *Maximum Security Ward*, by Ramon Guthrie, because Marsyas is the theme of his book????

But 65 fuckin verses all in that tone of voice!!! It goggles something or other. It calls for you to read Guthrie if you haven't—

I'm now curious about this Purdy book: are you gonna trace the false starts and progressions to where I am now, wherever that is? I would suppose you are.

Those Atwood letters now bother the hell outa me. Never thought of people goin in there to read private correspondence. I knew someone was likely to, of course, but you bring it right home to me. Wonder if I should write to her about it . . .

I'm now trying to peddle papers to Trenton Library, for obvious reasons—I mean obvious apart from money. Queen's will give only ten grand for six or seven years. Yeah, I know the times are tough and people sleepin under bridges, but if ya can get some money outa waste paper why not . . . [. . .]

Waitin for Dean Solecki,[4]
and best to Sam,
Al

1. Solecki had written AP that the papers at Saskatoon and Queen's, which were unrestricted, had many letters both by AP and to him that contained very personal information. Atwood's letters from the mid-1960s were among these.
2. The archives at Saskatoon have many poems from the 1930s and 1940s, including seven hand-stitched booklets containing most of AP's poems from 1936–42. The scrapbook has his published poems from the 1940s. In *Reaching for the Beaufort Sea*, he says that it is lost.
3. "Northern Reflections," *Imperial Oil Review* (Winter 1993).
4. At this time, Solecki was Dean of Humanities at the University of Toronto.

To George Woodcock (Vancouver), from Ameliasburgh, July 18, 1993

Dear George,
Congratulations on this late flowering. Proust alone seems to me enough to keep a team of translators going for at least a coupla years. A team of at least a dozen of them.

Both Marchand in *TorStar* and Rosemary Sullivan in *Globe* said there was a guardedness about the *Laurence/Purdy Letters*. George Galt disagreed with them. You mention she didn't disclose plots. I was never really curious about her plots anyway. And I thought the letters flowed pretty freely, there being very little we didn't talk about. Once, I remember, she was quite annoyed with me because I recommended that she take off once in a while for the experience she'd get doing so. That would've meant leaving her kids in somebody else's care, and she exploded in a letter to me about it. [. . .]

Richler's last novel [*Solomon Gursky Was Here*]? I didn't care for it, thought it sounded as if he was writing for an audience rather than himself, a fantastic story that his readers would gobble up. I didn't finish it.

Yeah, I'd like to see your writing on the ML/AP letters. The comment about the letters being "guarded" disturbed me somewhat. Marchand's comments on Margaret's autobio were also disturbing and unflattering to her. He made no allowances for her closeness to death whatever. His review annoyed people, especially Timothy Findley.

Yes, Tom—It seems like I didn't appreciate him enough when he was here, took him for granted. Now he seems to be in my mind much of the time. I tried to write something about him the other day, but haven't had time to type it on accounta all the work cataloguing papers. So I don't know how it reads. I do enclose a carbon of a 20-yr-old poem I discovered and worked on . . . The piece about Tom is not about his good qualities and lit work, but "A Sorrow for Tom" which is rather less simple . . .

But the number of friends and acquaintances dying is shocking, and all of them younger than me. I wonder if a poem or memoir is in any sense an exorcism. I suppose I've been lucky, in that the people I'd miss most have been "spared." What an odd word is "spared" in this context. Implies deity.

I think all that activity on your part is admirable, and also inspiriting for you. Writing well, one feels that one can conquer the world without bloodshed, a mental domination of things. To feel the firefly sparks whisper from cortex to paper and back again in a mixed metaphor of champagne bubbles. And it must wake echoes in Inge, be cheering for both of you, as your letter sounds.

I'm just looking at the workroom wall here, where I have all sorts of pictures, Gabrielle Roy, Eurithe, Norma her sister (beautiful gal when young), Margaret, but no George W. Have you got a photo you could spare for my wall?

Yes, love to both of you, and keep on doing all these things that give us the possible illusion that we are useful to the world and will live forever until tomorrow morning . . .

Al

To Sam Solecki (Toronto), from Sidney, BC, November 2, 1993

Dear Sam,

Many thanks for all the instructions. As mentioned, I've adopted a couple of them already. The second being to get in touch with McStew, phone Ellen, then phone Avie B. re publishing fall '94. Avie said he'd think about it. Ellen phoned back and said okay. She also said it'd be up to Stan D., if he thought the manuscript good enough. She didn't say good enough, but that's what she meant. I thought it kinda gratuitous. Anyway, I sent the manuscript to Stan last Friday (four days ago). Of course haven't heard if it's good enough.

I arrive in Toronto Nov. 21 via Canadian Airlines, at 9.35 p.m. (supposedly), not sure what hotel yet. Read at Scarborough Nov. 22 at 11 a.m.; St. George Campus, also Nov. 22 in the afternoon; Scarborough Campus again, Nov. 23. 9 a.m. Eurithe and I leave for Orlando Nov. 24. But hope to see you sometime while I'm in TO. At 5 p.m. Nov. 23 I'm supposed to see an Ont. Arts lady, not sure of her name, to get briefed on duties I suppose.

And re Graves: have difficulty making up my mind about him sometimes. His rhymes are so very intrusive! They're so like set pieces, written to order, almost. But that "She Tells her Love" is good. And I always feel that Graves is at least half-phony. But so am I, as Val Ross via W.O. Mitchell quotes me in Tuesday's *Globe*. But Mitchell is really quoting himself. I have the book of his in which he said it—if you saw that Mitchell story by Ross.[1]

The memoir is supposed to come out more or less on time. I spent three days proof-reading, finishing last Sat. Nearly lost my eyes. I just hope they got it right. One short section had me in Mtl. working at a factory, while the longer section in which this was embedded had me in A-burg. I hate fuckin publishers!

I've read very little of Walcott. But the reviews are so near-unanimous I'll have to. And yeah, those autumn landscapes . . . Wouldn't you like to be a painter? No, the only way to say what you feel is with words. Paintings don't nail down feelings, altho "nail down" is bad description.

You'll never get to bed with E–. Poor Sam! In *Beaufort* I describe you as "Casanova in a sport shirt" if they don't edit it out. You like that? Stay on the alert in her company. You do let your tongue go sometimes, somewhat like me, would you say? [. . .]

I hafta go through this stuff of yours apart from writing a letter while thinking about it.

And thanks for your list of titles that might be rewritten. I don't even remember some of those poems—poems?—you list.[2] And it takes a little brain filip worth 90 calories to get me rewriting. They're stuck in the past, those poems, like decayed raisins, and I doubt the seeds would grow grapes. I've forgotten "After Yeats"—but "Non-Poem" didn't seem good enough.

I've read Coles' poem, "Forests of the Medieval etc." and thought it very good, leaves questions in your mind. Been reading Stan D's essays.[3] Stan quotes Dewdney on his methods, something to the effect that there's a barrier in language after a certain point, and this is said in such pretentious terms!!! Writing is a continual mental process of rejection and selection, depending on what the writer thinks to be clichés and what is worth using despite the words' worn-ness. Yeah, Dennis is unrelentingly clever in his *Riffs*. Of course it's good anyway, but I'd like him to relent a little. But I'd never say that to him. After Cohen's second book he bored me, more or less. I know that's lese majestie or something, and there are later lines and passages . . . However, it seems he found a voice and stuck with it forever; and of course that paid off. I haven't read Newlove lately, and we don't see each other. He was so distinctive a few years ago, it's sad he's not any longer.

Did I mention: Eurithe and I plan two weeks in Fla. after Toronto with Bill Percy and his wife. Shopping for bulletproof vests.

Best,

Al

1. Val Ross's piece was titled "Salty Enough to Curl Your Hair," and it closed with the following comment by Mitchell: "Al Purdy once told me that he and I were Canada's two finest honest phonies. Which is a be-yootiful way of saying what we are" *(Globe and Mail*, November 2, 1993).
2. Solecki had sent AP some never published poems and fragments he had found in the archives at Saskatoon and Queen's that had images, lines and stanzas that seemed worth a second look.
3. Dragland's *Bees of the Invisible: Essays in Contemporary English Canadian Writing* (1991). The book contains Dragland's fine appreciation of AP, "Al Purdy's Poetry: Openings."

Val Ross: newspaper columnist and author (*The Road to There: Mapmakers and Their Stories*, 2003).

To Val Ross (Toronto), from Sidney, BC, December 22, 1993

Dear Ms. Ross,

Reading your piece on me in Dec. 21's *Globe*, I come across this passage:

"He doesn't paint a very clear picture of Eleanor Ross Purdy—nor indeed of most women in his life (and there have been many)."

There was nothing in that interview that would lead you to say "there have been many" women in my life.

Nor did I say Peggy Atwood was "too academic" with me. I did say she accused me of calling her an academic, quite a different thing. Nor did I say, "Peggy can't shut me up." A little more accuracy here would not be misplaced.

Nor did I indulge in "boasting about bad behaviour." I do not brag and boast, which is the impression you have left by your article. Perhaps you should invest in a cassette recorder, since your memory seems decidedly imperfect.

Sincerely,

Al Purdy

To Sam Solecki (Toronto), from Sidney, BC, December 23, 1993

Dear Sam,
People write the damndest articles about me! I sent carbons of the enclosed letter to Atwood and Ross. I am a braggart, a philanderer and probably a liar. Same sort of piece appeared in the Victoria paper. I am pissed off.

Best,
Al

To Sam Solecki (Toronto), from Sidney, BC, February 20, 1994

Dear Sam,
Just before or just after I got that Rilke-Rodin from you, I bought two copies of a Rodin book at a Vic. bookstore, one destined for you.[1] Rodin very impressive and good repros. Kinda coincidence these two things— the Rilke-Rodin and the Rodin sculpture book—both coming near the same time.

Reading the Rilke-Rodin, I seem more impressed by Rilke's language than very convinced what a master Rodin is. He seems to hypnotize himself sometimes, Rilke does, with his own talent, as if at will he would write about anything. It doesn't seem chance at all. In a way, the Rilke-Rodin book is a poem that is much too long and does not entirely convince me.

I have by this time gone over all the poems you commented on in your "notes," in only two or three cases disagreeing. The "Lost: One Country" title is changed to "Behind the Rain" . . . And most of the changes have been sent to you by this time. The last verse of the Frost poem—changed from the version sent you recently—is below:

> Musing: that a man (or woman) is surrounded
> by nothingness is undeniable
> the nature of things is nothingness
> —and he must people that space
> all around him by himself
> and the kind of person
> he has become in a lifetime:
>
> unfocus your eyes then
> —the tenants of darkness

shadowy on the periphery
before you finally let go of things—

And the above is slightly changed again. I didn't like to use "him" in line five, but think it necessary. And I used "space" in this version instead of "void." Obviously, when you have a word like "himself," you don't want to add "him" in the same line.

You will not have seen the *Ottawa Citizen*,[2] therefore I quote Geddes: "—he has created an engaging persona and an impressive body of work that have deeply touched two generations of Canadians, embodying both our aspirations and self-doubts as a people, our hard-to-shed colonial arrogance and insecurity."

I reject that bit about "creating a persona"—But I'm amazed that Geddes should come up with that "two generations" comment. You go along all your life without receiving such praise as that appearing now, and when the latter does appear, you find it difficult to believe.

If you see any way to avoid the slight awkwardness of phraseology in those first seven lines . . .

best
Al

1. Solecki had sent AP Rilke's study of Rodin. AP returned the favour with Tim Marlow's *Rodin* in which he wrote, "Do Rilke's words over-describe Rodin?"
2. Geddes reviewed *Reaching for the Beaufort Sea* in the *Ottawa Citizen* (January 27, 1994).

To the *Globe and Mail* (Toronto), from Ameliasburgh, May 23, 1994

Editor,
Globe and Mail
Michael Coren states (*Globe* May 23) that many people during World War 2 believed that George Woodcock was "effectively aiding the Nazi cause" by being a pacifist and refusing to take up arms against Germany. And obviously, Mr. Coren agrees with these nameless "many people": that George Woodcock was a traitor to Britain and the allied cause during the last war. Incidentally, is this by chance the same Michael Coren who made a mint with his condemnation of H.G. Wells in a Coren-authored biography? I really do believe it is the same, uh, person.

The literary and political feuding between George Orwell and Woodcock during World War 2 also forms a large part of Mr. Coren's "case" against George Woodcock. Perhaps he is aware that later on their differences were resolved and the old friendship resumed? And later still, that George Woodcock wrote a biography of Orwell, quite a complimentary one in contrast to Mr. Coren's biography of H.G. Wells.

Of course it was necessary to fight and defeat Nazi Germany, and I spent the war years in the Canadian armed forces myself. However, it never occurred to me then or now that pacifists were/are traitors to their various countrys.

It just happens that Bertrand Russell, the eminent "Lord Russell," mathematician, scholar, and author of *Principia Mathematica*, was imprisoned in England for his pacifistic activities during part of World War 1. Mr. Coren, was Bertrand Russell also a traitor to his country? If so, Mr. Coren, do you intend to write an article about him?

Al Purdy

To Sam Solecki (Toronto), from Sidney, BC, December 10, 1994

Dear Sam,
Glad you're vertical again. Not as bad as Admetus, but perhaps mentally "cut." I think one of the worst things, perhaps, about dying is realizing it really won't make much difference to anyone. Or do you think it will?

Sure, I think we all wish for a quick death, and old age which I am now going through is a slow one. Dying in a lover's arms is fine, except for how that other person would feel. How terrifying for them!

You saw just about everything in that poem ["House Party—1000 BC"], except: there was a suggestion that "Alkestis" (Rilke used Alcestis?) might've had something going with Hermes, the "beautiful god." In Greek myth, gods did mate with humans, read fuck if you like. And yes, I can't imagine a young healthy girl dying without ever having wanted to give birth. Strong instinct. A man could much more easily die without having wanted to be a father.

And I should've said, "after Rilke" . . . But didn't want same title.

(I have, incidentally, just written a three and a half page, single-spaced poem, about the longest I've written that I can remember . . .)

Query: if we make it "Alkestis" don't we have to make it "Kreon" and "Ikarus" and so on? I note that Rilke leaves the 'c'.

The Jeffers reviewer has him casting superstitious spells himself; and has him take a god stance himself (I'm not referring to reviewer's language), when such a distancing is impossible. Yes, we stand on the planet, therefore cannot see it as a stranger might.

In my Alkestis (due deference to Solecki), there is no future Heracles nor uxoriousness on the part of the lady. But "—so beautiful a face it is"—doesn't that infer something? At first the god was like everyone else, but is beautiful at the end of poem. To be beautiful he must change, to "*become*" beautiful, that is.

The "boiling soup" bit takes some consideration. I think "like bubbles in hot soup" leaving out "like liquid in a bowl" . . .

Thanks for critique and review. Comments very helpful.

Do you show red or green now with a beautiful girl?

All best
Al

To Sam Solecki (Toronto), from Sidney, BC, December 15, 1994

Dear Sam,

Thanks for the Alcestis article. I note that the "messenger" in Rilke's poem is "Thanatos" in other versions. Rilke (Mitchell) refers to the messenger as *the god*, and I guess vice-versa.

In my revised version—inspired by Solecki—the messenger has become Hermes. And I'm not at all sure that Rilke didn't have Hermes in mind, not Thanatos. And I prefer to leave the poem that way. Besides every version of a myth—or poem in this case—acts as a variant of the original.

I've just sent along another long poem on "Aphrodite" ["Aphrodite at Her Bath"]—the quotes on accounta Aph. is really the pregnant gal in the poem. No doubt you've already seen what I mean by this.

I'm just thinking of sending all of the new poems along to the CBC-*Sat. Nite* lit awards. Altho not sure that I should be competing with the young anyway. Still, I'm curious about how these things would be received, even if my ego receives near-fatal blows. (Is that possible, I hear you say.) But the typing necessary, migawd the typing!

Best
Al

To Sam Solecki (Toronto), from Sidney, BC, January 7–8, 1995

Dear Sam,

Thanks for review and opera stories.

Too bad we couldn't use a photo of A-burg's one main street for cover.[1] In fact there are such photos. The ordinary non-lit sort of read won't go for all the reviews. So I wonder about so many. And I hear you say there won't be many non-lit kinda readers anyway.

You recall the end of my Afterword for Birney's *Turvey*? There was a bad typo in the last para. Therefore: did you use the manuscript for your copy, or just photocopy the piece from book? I've looked at this again, and have difficulty remembering just what the original version was. But the last para. looks very wrong.

I talked to Howie W. last night, mentioning that you'll be sending info. But you must be delayed, since your letter is dated Dec. 28.

Eurydice tired of Orpheus' "incessant violin-playing" is hilarious to me.

About Akhmatova, "Lot's Wife" is lovely. However: do you read Russian and the original versions, or do you go by translations? I reviewed the recent (fairly recent, anyway) *Collected* published in US (as you know), and thought the translations pretty bad.[2] So on what basis do you have such a high opinion of her? This Roberta Reeder sounds like the same woman who did the bio that was included in the two-vol. *Collected*. I couldn't believe Akh sounded like that in the original Russian. Was "Lot's Wife" included in the US trans.? [...]

Incidentally, I got your letter with the review on a Friday, got the *Globe* next day with the printed review. And I see the bio. is 619 pages, whereas the one in the *Collected* was around 200 pages. So this is a new book.

It's a very good review, incidentally. I mean well-written and interesting. My point is: what poems of Akh's are you talking about—those in the US trans., or the original Russian??? For instance, I think Lowell's trans. of "The Requiem" is marvellous. But there have been many complaints that it isn't what Akh. wrote.???

The trans. in *Poets on Street Corners* edited by Olga Carlisle are by Kunitz, Adrienne Rich, Rose Styron, Richard Wilbur and Lowell, all metrical and rhyming . . . And good. I didn't keep the US Akh. I was so disappointed in it. As a person, Akh was undoubtedly heroic, and of course knew it. [...] And yeah, I've wondered about Edel's five vols about Henry James.[3] I can't read James tho. Even "The Beast in the Jungle" (such an uncharacteristic title for James' tame prose) was nearly too much for me. And yet Greene thought him marvellous.

okay, stay sane,

Al

1. The "cover" is for *Starting from Ameliasburgh: The Collected Prose of Al Purdy*.
2. AP reviewed Judith Hemschemeyer and Roberta Reeder's edition of *The Complete Poems of Anna Akhmatova* in *Books in Canada* (August–September 1990). Solecki reviewed Reeder's *Anna Akhmatova: Poet and Prophet* in the *Globe and Mail* (January 7, 1995). In a telephone conversation about Akhmatova, AP challenged Solecki's description of Akhmatova as "beautiful."
3. Leon Edel (1907–97): literary critic best known for his five-volume biography of Henry James. He attended McGill University in the 1920s and was one of the founders of the *McGill Fortnightly Review*.

To Fraser Sutherland (Toronto), from Ameliasburgh, [after] May 29, 1995

Dear Fraser,
[. . .] Sure, I regretted Gus. He was a "nice" man, crazy for fame behind that calm exterior. A critic in the Soviet Union called him "a gentle man!"

I have to *try* to explain my attitude toward poets, lousy, poor, good, excellent and marvellous. If you write yourself especially, *you cannot take other people's opinions as valid*, or be influenced by them more than reading the stuff and then making up your own mind. And to go farther than that, a poem, a good poem, should stop you in your tracks, it should make you think hard, and you should feel like re-reading it again and again. How many of Gus's make you feel that way? The anthology pieces in books are just someone else's opinion, even if there is a consensus; and the editors excerpt from each other all the time. An antho is liable to be a collection of pieces from other anthos.

Gus was an erudite and mannered poet, and yes a cultured man whose culture mattered very little in the world today—as any culture you or I may or may not possess matters very little. But Gus's less than most. He always *acted* like a poet, as if it really did matter. Which is charming in its own way, even quaint. However, he said nothing ever that I want to re-read. And that is not unkind, it is simply truth.

If you or I had to base the value of our lives on the money we made from poems our value would be nearly nil. We must not have illusions of our own importance. I think the very best poets in the world have each

at most only five or six that I would want to re-read and do re-read . . .
Those poets include Yeats, Auden, Lawrence and a very few others. For in-
stance, I think MacLeish wrote only one poem worth remembering, "You,
Andrew Marvell." And that is something, I think that is much. [. . .]

Best,

Al

> **Robin Blaser** (b. 1925): American poet, migrated to Canada from
> the United States in 1966 to join the department of English at
> Simon Fraser University. His theory of serial poetry has been par-
> ticularly influential. His collected poems *The Holy Forest* (1993)
> was shortlisted for the Governor General's Award. For AP he was
> part of the ominous Black Mountain presence on the Vancouver
> poetry scene.

To Robin Blaser (Vancouver), from Ameliasburgh, Summer 1995

Dear Robin,
I can't remember all I said in previous letter so I'm liable to repeat myself
here.

Yes, I've been pretty hostile to the BM boys, in person and in writing.
I wrote to Tallman when he had all the BM people from US, and said why
don't you get those young geniuses readings in the US? He didn't reply.

However, I've gotta make plain what I meant by the five or six "great"
poems. I meant that over a lifetime, not in one book. Nobody does it in
just one book.

You talk about Lampman and Duncan Scott . . . They were our pioneers, and should be respected as such. But they were not great poets.
They did not compare with Browning, Tennyson and the best English
guys. It does them an injustice to say they can be compared. At their best
they were adequate for their time, but that's all.

The country itself, it's *my* country. I don't give a wet fuck in the Sahara
for all the braggarts south of us and the pompous English either. At the
same time, I gave them credit for what I think they've accomplished. It's
not my country right or wrong, but my country first of all. I suppose
that'd take some more explaining, but you get what I mean. This is where
I live. I could live no place else. [. . .]

Where did I get the sense of who the great moderns are? Christ, you know that as well as I do: over years and years of reading them, with my taste changing over many of those early years. Over years and years of writing, well over sixty years of writing. Almost as long as you are old. I started with Bliss Carman, and he's still in my head, in fact I still kinda like "Make me over Mother April"["Spring Song"]—but it would be ridiculous to call it a great poem. You grow, you change, you move from where you were to where you might reach and what you might become. I've moved. I really doubt you know anything at all about me, after about the 1970s.

I believe we're at the stage now in this country where we have a few good writers. Ondaatje, Atwood and a couple of others. Poetry, our best is pretty damn good; but there are so many just good poets in the world that we don't stand out. In England, I think Larkin was much inflated, since so much of him is mean-spirited and whining. But a few of his things are very good. Hughes, had had five or six years in his beginnings where he was very striking. Not now.

I hope you got my Birney piece, and I'm wondering where to send it next. Any ideas? Have had no reply from *Quarry*. Did you see my piece in *QQ* about Woodcock?[1] But then, I expect you'll disagree with my assessment of him anyway.

Best wishes,

Al

1. AP refers to his "George Woodcock 1912–1995" which appeared in the spring issue of *Queen's Quarterly*. He describes Woodcock as a writer with "a passion about the naming of things" who was important in helping create some of the images of Canada that define the country's sense of its identity.

Lynn Crosbie (b. 1963): often controversial columnist and writer on contemporary issues and poet (*Missing Children*, 2003).

To Lynn Crosbie (Toronto), from Ameliasburgh, August 7, 1995

Dear Lynn,

—Thinking of you, it occurs to me to wonder why you pay attention to old men stunned a little by the way you look—like the old man on the Van. Is. ferry and myself.

I've got your letter in a pile of letters, and because of its lightness or other reasons it's gone roaming thru the whole pile. In short, I can't find it.

I've just written a poem whose ending kept nagging at me for a couple of weeks. It nagged at me when I was thinking of something else, an ending that wasn't good enough, wasn't right, didn't speak to me like a child of mine should. So I've gone back to it several times.

And that brings to mind the great room in my head, the misty room where thoughts are hidden in clouds and I send words seeking them (like egg and darts in human creation), and thus if I am lucky a poem is born. I can visualize this room that's as big as the world, using itself to flash pictures back at me like in-store television. But the words don't always find the right thought, the matching one, which is when revision is called for after the thoughts and words are shepherded into poems . . .

Does this strike a bell in you?—something similar happens in your head. We had some visitors a couple of weeks back. We were all sitting at table in sociable converse, the record player going in the next room with a German baritone singing "Muss i Denn" a good drinking song in German. Then David at the table (an excellent baritone himself) started to sing along with Kunz, (Erich Kunz, that is) but translating to English as he went along, a duet in German and English. The table went silent, fascinated (at least I was) for about a minute.[1]

So much of my poem was exposition, just setting the scene. But the most important part was the ending, which was the effect of this incident. Like I said, what's going on in the great cloudy room upstairs, the prisoners in my mind holding their warder prisoner.

Did I mention our garage burned down? It was a double garage and two storey, huge. It had a room for guests below. (I must have mentioned all this). Now a black scar on the land. Dennis Lee is coming down mid-month, and will be staying in the house. And perhaps you can get down as well?

I've been invited to a daybreak ceremony by a Mohawk friend from Deseronto 18 miles to the east. Eurithe too. He writes poems, which is how I got to know him. But do we want to take part in a daybreak Indian ceremony, will it add to the rich embroidered texture of our lives? Or will it be just shit? I'll probably find out.

Cutting the lawn last evening, thick grass on our little point extending out into the lake. That point is kinda special, since I built it myself. When we first bought the land years back, there was a lot nearby for which the vendor wanted to charge us for the point by the foot all the way round instead of straight across. So we bought a straight-across lot, then over the years I built our own point myself. I lugged wheelbarrow loads of stone and gravel pouring it into the lake. Stones too big for the wheelbarrow I rolled down to the lake pretty laboriously. I suppose that point would have taken me ten years to build. I was kinda scared for a while that the township would say it didn't match the survey and force me to retract it, but they didn't.

Anyway, we now have a grassy point, on which the grass hadn't been cut. Two big willows on it and a coupla poplars.

Trouble is I have a torn muscle in my stomach (which has to be sewn up at Belleville Hosp. Sept. 19), so it ain't easy to mow even with a light electric mower. So I take some pleasure in this point for the foregoing reasons. And the point two lots away used to be wooded, but the owner bulldozed all the trees and brush off before he died a few years ago. So our point fronts bravely into the lake. By the way, don't get the impression we're surrounded by people; we are in a sense only. We have quite a large lot here, and trees cut off others. Only trouble is the black scar of burned garage.

anyway,
Al

1. "*Muss i Denn*" and the event described reappear in a poem with the same title in *To Paris Never Again.*

From Fraser Sutherland (Toronto), to Ameliasburgh, August 25, 1995

Dear Al,

Your letter pre-empted a postcard I was going to send you in the aftermath of your photo opportunity at the Idler Pub: "How dare you try to pass off my poems in *The Idler* magazine as your own! And in the Idler Pub, too, my home away from home!" The waiter took great credit in daring to ask you to sign the magazine: I didn't want to crush his spirit by pointing to our extensive correspondence, signed framed AWP poem on my wall, etc. . . .

Needless to say I look forward to reading *Beaufort*. Having read numerous bits and pieces of memoir in magazines (and even published one—"Poets in Montreal"—remember?) I'm curious about how they all coalesced within covers. I'm sorry you had travails with editors. One of my regrets is not having taken you up on your offer back in 1986 to have me edit your autobiography: I was in a scrambled state then: getting ready to move to Nova Scotia, dealing with the estate of Alison's deceased mother (your girlfriend in Alison's dream), about to take on the book about Canadian magazines, struggling with a new computer etc. etc. Still, a missed opportunity.

I had to learn from the *Globe* review, not having seen George Galt much since we moved here, that he is going to do your biography. I trust he will be suitably indiscreet, leave no skeleton or stone unturned (and even bring in stones when none can be turned over), in fact flaunt all the prerogatives of the modern biographer.

It occurred to me this morning that if you're casting about for another non-fiction book to do, one possibly might be something like: *What's Right and Wrong with Canada* or, more politically, *What's Right is Wrong in Canada* or *What's Right and Left in Canda*. A sort of testament or testimony or summa of all the good and bad about Canada that you see or have seen as the most transCanadian of poets: great mountains but bad roads, great people but godawful politics . . . Think about it.

I was going to quarrel with you about something . . . Oh, yes, I read an interview somewhere in which you disavowed God or religion. God's disappointed in you, no doubt. But He or She will recognize, nonetheless, that your poems are saturated with religious belief, inasmuch as they are perpetually involved in the process of transforming matter into spirit (transcendence), and spirit into matter (immanence) and by implication that to do so is right and proper and part of the divine fitness of things. Yours truly, Al Purdy, servant of the Lord.

Yours e're,
Fraser

To George Bowering (Vancouver, BC), from Ameliasburgh, August 29, 1995

Dear George,
That baseball mania is gonna kill you yet. At least in your case it's only your foot. I've got about six things wrong with me (apart from mental, of course, which I mention before you get to it), the latest being a hernia. They take the knife to me Sept. 19. Dunno how I picked that up.

Eurithe? Fine, but gets tired more easily, and insists on going for a walk in a deserted country area here every evening (unless she's really worn out), which makes me uneasy. Anybody could notice those regular habits. It's not an unknown sort of thing. I've got a little tear gas gun I got in the US for dog protection, which I think I'll insist she carries.

Sure, a lot of people think I should quit, including some of your estimable confreres. However, I enjoy writing poems, which is the main reason I do it. I assume another novel your publisher expects. You must like to write em too, since SFU must give you enough and more to live on. It's an advantage and disadvantage at the same time to have a university education and teach there. As I'm sure you know. I've had to get by on much less money than you, but I venture to say I've had as much or more experience in life as you. And anyway, Eurithe has been such a good manager that after a certain date way back when I haven't worried about money at all.

12 hours a day? You must be kidding. One works when one does work, and it ain't work, as you know. But why talk about it when you know these answers.

That's a quality of your writing, that it's both serious and non-serious at the same time—at least *much* of your writing. And your letter discusses things to which you know the answer as well or better than myself.

And the reasons you give for not writing poems are not the real ones. You're not writing because you don't feel like it; the thoughts aren't coming because you're too busy at other things.

When were we discussing Neruda? When you were in Sidney or at Lane's? I didn't know about any involvement in Trotsky's death. Is that fairly well certain or just a rumor? It's almost as startling as saying Octavio Paz was involved.[1]

I've quit McStew, and will do any future books with Harbour. I'll have another poems inside the next year . . .

I see so little of you for the past years. Of course profs are busy, but even profs have time for their friends.

Best,

Al

---

1. Trotsky was assassinated in Mexico City on August 20, 1940. Three months earlier (May 24), the mural painter, David Alfaro Siqueiros, was part of a group of two dozen uniformed men, all communists loyal to Stalin, who broke into Trotsky's house at four in the morning, sprayed the rooms with machine gun fire, threw a bomb on their way out and escaped. Trotsky survived the bungled assassination attempt, and Siqueiros fled to Chile where Pablo Neruda, also a communist, helped him to stay in hiding until 1944 when he returned to Mexico. In later years, the painter admitted taking part in the attack and that it had been a crime. Octavio Paz offers a brief account in *Itinerary: An Intellectual Journey* (1999) and Dimitri Volkogonov a longer one in *Trotsky: The Eternal Revolutionary* (1996).

To George Galt (Toronto), from Sidney, BC, December 19, 1995

Dear George,

You have been going through some tough times. I do have some feel for that, since Eurithe and my son were both seriously hospitalized.

It's a bit odd to think that the illness of relatives and friends is valuable to you, but it is. The people who cover over their feelings with cynicism (as I do myself sometimes) are not really open to life, which includes literally everything. Vulnerability is something we need in our own lives. Not an easy vulnerability, a tendency to weep over flowers and trivial things, but an openness to life.

But enough pontificating. I don't think you can be entirely correct with your reservations about serio-comic novels. One has to feel and must feel that if it is good enough it will be published and do well. But two months!—for a writer of your "stature" that is too long. Phone the bastards. Perhaps intimate gently that there are other publishers.

In my considered opinion, I am writing better now than I ever have. It is a different sort of writing than previously, of course. It is perhaps not quite so easily accessible as before. I don't mean like Stevens or Avison at their most opaque; and perhaps a little "quieter" in tone. It doesn't "proclaim" itself, so to speak.

I felt badly about leaving McStew. However, Ellen Seligman had mentioned a couple of times that she thought I was the best poet in Canada. I said to her (in a letter) that if that is so, then I ought to be at least as important to the publisher as their worst novelist, who will disappear in a blink of time's eye. But I am sad nevertheless, to be leaving, after 32 years. I expect now that a large Selected Poems will be coming from Harbour, since the nod to publish them has been given me. And I do feel so lucky to be writing well at my age.

The non-hernia bit is still with me. There is something there that drags me down, as a result of some physical exertion last summer. I took some tests in Belleville, which didn't discover it; therefore they tend to say it doesn't exist. But is does exist.

A new book of poems is liable to be delayed by a big Selected. I'm sorry to have seen so little of you over the past many months, actually to have seen nothing. I hope it will be different in the new year.

Take care of yourself

Al

The Editor,
I note that prostitute "The Contessa" was honoured in your "Larger Lives" feature today (Dec. 23); whereas poet Earle Birney was omitted entirely.

Presumably this indicates the *Globe and Mail*'s opinion of Canadian poetry?

Sincerely,
Al Purdy

Cary Fagan (b. 1957): Toronto reviewer and writer of fiction (*Felix Roth*, 1999).

To Cary Fagan (Toronto), from Sidney, BC, December 29, 1995

Dear Cary Fagan,
Your review of John Thompson's[1] poems [*John Thompson: Collected Poems and Translations*] has been sticking in my head.

I met Thompson—probably in the late 1960s or early 1970s—when I was doing a reading tour in the Maritimes. He was either assigned or took on the job of looking after me while I was at his university, I guess Mount Allison at Sackville. We drank some beer together, talked; I was at his house in the rural area he lived in, met his wife, did the reading. [. . .]

His own character—I thought at the time—seemed ill-adjusted to his situation. I thought he did not belong at this university, living in the backwoods . . . and I could see not much "connection" between the man and the woman. And there was a child as well, as I remember. I say all this from my own observations, not from anything John said.

There are lives and occasions when people act a part, something they think fits them, or else imitating someone else whom they admire—for whatever reason. John may have been doing this. He was not enthusiastic about anything during our meeting, did not really "open up" in conversation. I thought he was ill-adjusted and unhappy then, but that is not a thing you're liable to discuss during a fairly brief meeting. He was simply out of place at that backwoods university, living with a woman for whom he apparently had no great affection for, and must have felt trapped. And there must have seemed no way out except drinking . . .

One would need to know more about his life in England in order to say a great deal more. And it's doubtful that anyone will ever do research into his life. His poems, while interesting and meritorious, are not such that anyone will ever dig more deeply into his life than has already been done.

As well, I felt slightly guilty that I didn't stay in touch with him after leaving the Maritimes. I sensed something there, without being able to say exactly what it was. But one meets so many people during readings and elsewhere that faces and names blur.

One does not know *exactly* what caused the John Thompson tragedy. But with S– C– who shot himself for love of a woman, one does know, or at least thinks so. There are not these troubling questions. A woman poet S– S–, supposedly killed herself for political reasons, reasons which I've now forgotten. Another woman I knew of who wrote poems was strangled by her son. (What a horrible way for a mother to die!)

Reading your review I am reminded again of John Thompson, and the feelings I had for him and about him.

Thank you.

Sincerely,

Al Purdy

1. John Thompson (1938–76): a graduate student of A.J.M. Smith at the University of Michigan—his thesis was translations of poems by René Char—Thompson was a professor of English at Mount Allison University from 1966–76. He published two volumes of poetry: *At the Edge of the Chopping There Are No Secrets* (1973) and *Stilt Jack* (1978). Fagan reviewed *John Thompson: Collected Poems & Translations* (1995) in the *Globe and Mail* (December 29, 1995).

Dave Smith (b. 1942): American editor (*The Southern Review*) and poet (*Dream Flights*, 1981).

To Dave Smith (Baton Rouge, La.), from Sidney, BC, January 19, 1996

Dear Dave,

That was most generous of you, to send your book. I hasten to say, I was not hinting that you should do that when I was being a little curious about "southern poetry." And this *is* southern poems (singular and plural) I see from *Night Pleasures*.

I see also that you are a "mover and shaker," an editor, a prof, etc. etc. I am impressed. And wonder where you find the time.

I assume you are interested in my reactions, or you would not have sent the book. I should mention first, being in Nanaimo 60 miles north of here, with Patrick Lane, and a guy named K– R– who had got us there for a reading. We were drinking beer, fairly high, and R– kept asking me, "Al, what do you think of my poems, what do you really think?" This went on for quite a few minutes. Now no one should ask another person that blatantly what they think of his or her poems. It just isn't done; it's an invitation to disaster. Anyway, I stood this questioning for some time, maybe 15 or 20 minutes, then I said, "Well, K–, I don't really have a high opinion of your poems." The atmosphere changed; the climate was perceptibly cold. Then R– said, "Patrick, what do you think?" And Lane said, "I agree with Al." Our later reading passed off without awkward moments.

I like your stuff. The tone and syntax are—I think—my own usages of English. Sort of good English with slang-jargon to ameliorate the stuffiness I'm scared of. I like "A Pinto Mare," especially, the "Hollis Summers" poem, the "Neruda's Memoirs" poem, "Camellias," and others. You have a wide subject matter, which is something I think I have as well. And you are accessible without being simple-minded. Is all this too much? I mean, I get uncomfortable talking about my own stuff or hearing others talk in some circumstances.

I like Buk, but with reservations. In many ways he's a Johnny one-note, with his sixpack and hundred dollar whores etc. But earlier on, he sometimes seemed to hit it. There's a line about Domenico Theotocopoulos, for instance . . . And I once thought that Robinson Jeffers was God, and felt the same about Dylan Thomas. I've changed my mind in both cases, leaving me with a residue of only three or four poems . . . One's early loves are revealing and shameful sometimes. I used to love Chesterton and W.J. Turner, and am left with much residue:

> I have stood up a hill
> and trembled like a man in love
> a man in love I was
> and could not speak and could not move . . .[1]

So thanks for taking the Buk piece ["Lament for Bukowski"]. I hope we run into each other again. It seems likely we could talk, which isn't always a possibility in such cases.

Al

1. The lines are from Turner's "Epithalamium."

To David Helwig, (PEI), from Sidney, BC, February 7, 1996

Dear David,
English hotels sound like an enthralling adventure, League of Nations—
uh *United* Nations, in miniature. Shows you how far back my mind goes.
But I do envy you having had the Br. Mus. for a while. I thought the place
marvellous when I was there years ago. Now I can't even remember why
we went there, as if you needed a reason . . .

Yeah, the Toronto hernia place is the Shouldice Hospital, which does
nothing but hernias. But they won't take me, say I'm too old, and my
hole-in-one is too close to an ancient appendix scar. "Ancient" on accounta I was about 3 at the time. So anyway, I hafta have the operation here,
and the doc who's supposed to do it is in Guatemala, likely plowing thru
the jungle looking for Maya treasure. So I'm getting the runaround.

L–: you mean running *from* Canada and Can. law and his compulsions while here? Yeah, I guess we run toward anything we want, which
I've done unless sometimes I was too scared to do it. And that happens
too. I remember one lady who scared and attracted me at the same time,
so when she was getting coffee I knocked it outa her hand a coupla times
so I could get to talk to her, since I couldn't say why I wanted to talk to
her. I mean to her.

Or do you mean *from* himself? If so, he couldn't escape himself and
his sexual directions. It seems so odd to me that many of these guys—
gays, I mean—are so attracted to "the rough trade"—dangerous other
people. Are they fascinated by danger, by climbing to a volcano's lip, insulting other stronger people? Graham Greene who escaped boredom by
looking for danger? I have, for instance, always tried to treat dangerous
things gingerly and with caution. [. . .]

I hope you'll find yourself reasonably content—if one ever is—in
PEI—I think you said? Depends on the relationship, I guess. I hope it's a
good one for you, and her too of course.

The "Job in Wpg." poem is, of course, exaggerated; but not entirely. I
read a poem by Stanley Kunitz that reminded me of that time, 1965. I had
started "In the Rain" but only written one verse some weeks before now,
and couldn't seem to do anything. Then found it among the litter, and
scribbled away . . .

What beats me about Quebec: they wanta break up the country voted the best in the world to live in . . . I dunno about that, but it's where I live, and I'm beginning to dislike stupid people in Que. quite heartily.

Best to you,

Al

To Greg Gatenby (Toronto), from Sidney, BC, February 21, 1996

Dear Greg,

You're bound to lose money on me, mad entrepreneur that you are. Why not Madonna? I know I know, ya can't afford her.

I do require veiled maidens in diaphanous water-soaked panties, say 40 30 40 or something equally attractive.

I'd prefer you selected the "speakers," these being the guys who talk about me I presume. And I shall be far from the stage when that goes on. They did a kinda seminar on me before I left U of T (to the accompaniment of cheers), and I enjoyed listening to them. Who? I forget. And the occasion had something to do with what they said . . .[1]

I would've much enjoyed seeing Davies attended by scantily clad girls in diaphanous whatevers. I met Wilson MacDonald once when I was at high school in Trenton, a fairly forgettable experience which I've nevertheless managed to remember.[2]

So sure, to all those questions. And incidentally, I have enough poems for another book now, two years after the last one. *Naked* took nearly five years, this one not quite two. It's probably my last one; to be published with Harbour (I've left McClelland).

As I've said before: I think you're doin a hellva good job there and Ottawa is crazy if they short you on funding—or should I say, short Harbourfront?

Best Wishes,

Al Purdy

1. AP responds here to Greg Gatenby's letter informing him that Harbourfront is planning an evening celebrating his work. He refers below to "Al Purdy Day at the University of Toronto." Among the speakers were Russell Brown, Sam Solecki and Rosemary Sullivan.
2. In *Reaching for the Beaufort Sea*, AP gives the following description of the meeting with MacDonald. "In the mid-thirties, Wilson MacDonald, a fairly well-known poet, visited our school to give a reading. I was ushered into his presence and introduced as 'the school poet.' And I didn't even have the grace to do more than wriggle slightly at the description. MacDonald was a gaunt, middle-aged man, with a big nose and dark hair combed sideways across his bare skull. He

looked at me solemnly—I could think of nothing to say. He couldn't either, although he used more words to do it. And I departed the august presence.

"But I still remember his reading, which featured a poem about tugs on English Bay, another called 'Whist-a-Wee' or similar to that, and 'Song of the Ski.' The last named went like this:

"Norse am I when the first snow falls,
Norse till the ice departs,
The fare for which my spirit calls
Is blood of a thousand Viking hearts—

"Now that was more like it, the same sort of heroic drivel I was writing myself with Robin Hood and the Norse myths. Many years later, reading Stan Dragland's *Wilson MacDonald's Western Tour*, I chuckled over the bit where MacDonald locks the doors of his reading hall so that the audience couldn't escape when he sold his books."

From Sam Solecki (Toronto), to Sidney, BC, May 1, 1996

[...] I'll start on the *Selected Poems* tomorrow. I told Howie that given that you've done the selection and that all I'll do is make some suggestions and do a copy edit and check, the only name on the cover and title page should be yours. Similarly, we all agree that there's no need for a critical introduction, though a preface of the kind I suggested to you (made up of paragraphs from earlier prefaces and essays) might be useful for students. I think of it as a sort of mosaic or collage of your comments on poetry, what the scholars would more formally call a "poetics." Howie agrees, but we don't have to decide until the two of you see the selected passages I come up with. Anyway, I'll be back with some suggestions for cuts and additions in a few days.

About the future *Collected Poems*, you know I'd be delighted (a good old fashioned word) to edit the book. The current volume, as I've told both you and Russell Brown, is a very, very good choice, and we could easily build on it. In fact the next edition could be the same size simply by dropping Dennis's essay and using that space for new poems.

By the way, you might want to think of how to publish over the next 5 years:

1996 Fall, *Selected Poems*

1997 Spring, a new volume of poems?

2000 Fall, *Collected Poems*

One other possibility that you and Eurithe might think about: a substantial volume of *The Selected Letters of Al Purdy* after the *Collected*. This could draw on the Woodcock, the Bukowski, the Laurence and the mountains of letters in the three archives at Saskatoon, Lakehead, and Queen's. There's a lot of really good stuff in there both from you and to you. If the volume included some of the letters by people like Bowering, Glassco, Atwood etc. it would have a really good presentation: i.e. the continuing thread would be your voice, but there would be occasional transitional letters by others to show what it is you are referring to in a letter or what the dialogue is about.

Think about a selected letters. I think that in some (many?) respects it would be a more interesting and livelier collection than the ones that have been published. It might also make you some spare cash for a cold winter.

Hang in (as Vanessa, my 4 year old daughter, once said to a gorilla who seemed about to slip from a branch at the Zoo!)

Sam

To Fraser Sutherland (Toronto), from Ameliasburgh, June 12, 1996

Dear Fraser,
I can't think of anything we were wrangling about lately, so what do I talk about? [...]

We (Eurithe and I) are going to your neck of the woods in Sept., first to Annapolis, then to Halifax and Dalhousie for readings. [...]

Anyway, we arrive here and find the raccoons have gnawed out the stove's electric wires, the pumps won't work and we are reduced to the primitive except for electricity. But today we got the stove working on accounta one of Eurithe's brothers does electrical work.

I'm not writing much, and the people I know, friends that is, who're dyin off, are younger than me. Booo-hoo, just gettin ready for the grave myself. But I expect you to tell me I'm too miserable to die and you'll hafta hit me over the head with that rock you mentioned in the *Globe* before I can make it to Parnassus or Olympos or wherever.

I haven't got much to say, as you see, since you stopped insulting me about Lawrence and throwing up Whitman in my face. Title of next book will be *To Paris Never Again*, so you see the way my thoughts are turning.

I thought I was coming to Toronto to talk about three novels with a coupla other people, but they cancelled that for whatever reason. But I wanted to ask you, did you read Anne Michaels' novel? I thought it was like eating/reading nothing but rich dessert and being hungry for a slice of plain brown bread. Fine writing, or course and "a poet's novel," but but but . . .

Dionne Brand depressing and *Night-Blooming Cereus* likewise.[1] You read these?

A building named "The Crystal Palace" in Picton has just been renovated, and they asked for my Prince Edward Cty. poem to print in the booklet they got out. Our beloved Lieut-Gov. Hilary Weston, of the bakery Westons came for the ceremonies, which were complicated. Coupla days before this was to happen, one of the organizers asked me if I'd read the PEC poem if they asked me. Of course, bein a nice sweet guy (who never gets hit on the head with rocks), I said yes. At the ceremony, before Weston and her buns arrived, the guy who asked me to read came by kinda shame-faced and said the program was already arranged so I couldn't read. I wept bitterly, and left the building afore Weston and her buns arrived. Went to Jill Hill's bookstore and bed and breakfast place and looked at books. Jill fed us tea and cakes . . .

She (Jill) has a set of Maspero's *History of Egypt* in 13 vols. Wonderful set. $800. I'm tryin to figure how I can trade for it.

And I went to the banquet at the Kingston meeting, and was somewhat bored (Writers' Union, I mean). Thought I might see you there with a rock in your hand.

Al

1. Dionne Brand (b. 1953): social activist, poet (*No Language Is Neutral*, 1990) and novelist (*In Another Place, Not Here*, 1996). AP is probably referring to *Cereus Blooms at Night*, the 1996 novel by Shani Mootoo (b. 1958).

To Bonnie (?), from Ameliasburgh, July 3 or 4, 1996

Dear Bonnie,
Thank you for the enjoyable poem and your note [about "At the Quinte Hotel"].

Would like to know more about the Quinte Hotel? Going through Trenton, proceeding east toward the bridge, you make a left turn at the light, not at the street that leads to the old marketplace, but the one that angles away from that first street. The place is now called something else, but is still there, half a block down from where the old Gilbert Hotel used to be on the corner.

It was a sort of bucket of blood place; fights broke out occasionally; the surroundings were pretty crude, not shabby, just not pseudo-classy like the Gilbert House pub half a block away. I had a friend named Alan Pearson with me on this occasion (very long ago), and when this little ex-boxer (which I didn't know at the time) started to beat up on these two older guys—I think both of them a little drunk—it made me feel indignant that the waiters did nothing to stop it. And the ex-boxer followed one of them into the john and punched him in there.

It's very unwise to get into a fight in a pub, one is liable to get a knife in the ribs or worse. And I did feel a bit like a damn fool for standing up and challenging the little prick. Pearson just sat there and watched me somewhat unbelievingly, perhaps thinking I was showing off—which in a sense I was. But anyway, as the poem intimates, I knocked him down with my charge and sat on him, and the waiters threw him out to my great relief. The bit about reading him a poem, is of course sheer embroidery. But how else can you write a poem about something like this, except tongue in cheek.

Somebody told me afterwards the guy was an ex-boxer, which made me slightly nervous. I thought he might be lying in wait for me when we left the pub, but no. All this is really extraneous to the poem. However, maybe your students would be interested.

I enclose a notice for a new book of mine that's coming soon. It's a carriage trade thing, too expensive for me to buy if I hadn't written it. But you might know someone with deep pockets. I expect to have a few of these books myself, in Sept. or Oct.

Thanks much for your intro and inexplicable interest.

Al Purdy

To Fraser Sutherland (Toronto), from Ameliasburgh, July 6, 1996

Dear Fraser,

My health, re general-anesthetic, slightly better I guess. Now my eyes are giving me trouble, which I guess is to be expected at my age. An eye doc in Sidney told me I'd have cataract trouble in a coupla years, and his time measurement was pretty accurate. Now looking for an eye doc that won't take forever to get me to a laser beam.

No, in one way I don't look forward to this festschrift, in another way I do—if I can see the goddam books and words by that time. To give you an idea: several people in local variety store the other day, and one says to the people in general, "This is Ameliasburgh's most famous resident." I snarled something like, "Get off that shit," and got outa the store as fast as possible. However, my motto is to accept awards, since they generally pay off one way or another. And advise you to feel the same re your last book, which is liable to get some kinda prize. Books about death are liable to make us take pleasure in being alive.

There is an aspect of praise that makes one feel like a weightless ball being balanced on a jet stream of water, at the mercy of other people's opinions. If I ever write a passage as good as "The best lack all conviction / And the worst are full of passionate intensity" or the "aged man" bit—but no, I still find verbal praise slightly or greatly embarrassing.[1] In print, that's different, and whoever wrote it is stuck with it. I remember Gzowski paraded all the praise on the back of the *Collected*, and asked how I reacted. I said the praise was about somebody else. There is a sense in which that's true.

Much of what anybody writes, no matter how good they can be, is fairly ordinary. Even Yeats and Lawrence etc. I expect you to disagree with that, of course.

> Best to Allison,
> Al

1. From Yeats's "The Second Coming" and "Sailing to Byzantium."

Doug Beardsley (b. 1941): a Victoria poet (*Wrestling with Angels: Selected Poems*, 1995) who collaborated with AP on *No One Else Is Lawrence!* (1998) and *The Man Who Outlived Himself: An Appreciation of John Donne* (2000).

To Doug Beardsley (Victoria, BC), from Ameliasburgh, August 25, 1996

Dear Doug,
Quite right—I *was* pleased with "In Mexico," for somewhat more than thirty seconds. It now seems ordinary to me.

Quite a feather in your cap, whether sparrow or peacock—your poems at the Benefit Concert. I like the poems, the first more than the other two, "Survivor" I mean . . . I hope it went well.

Yeah, *Snow Falling on Cedars* is the best current novel I've read in some time.

Nowlan had a poem about a moose that strayed into an urban area.[1] Crowds gathered (presumably in NB); the animal became dangerous;

it was shot; motorists blew their horns. Patrick and Lorna just edited Nowlan. Patrick has a poem about a cougar in which, when the cougar was killed, everyone lifted their rifles and fired at the sky. The parallel is unmistakeable.

Atwood did that with one of Dickey's poems, following the poem even more closely. I used the ending of a McDiarmid poem: "Audh knew" equals "Frank Scott knew" or something close.[2]

I think it's perfectly legitimate to do this, but it takes away something in your mind from your opinion of the poem in question. Said poem is lessened to me in some way, not perfectly original. We all build and derive from each other; but some methods are better than others. It's the degree of derivation that seems important to me. Atwood's degree was much too close to the Dickey original. Mine derived from McDiarmid in only one phrase, but still owes the Scotsman.

Yes, I'm sure Patrick has been hurt, and badly, at various times. His hardboiled manner bespeaks it. Also, he's told stories, sexual ones, unflattering to himself, as if they remain in his mind and he still feels guilty. I think it seems necessary to him that he "lash out" at people and situations now and then. He remains enough of an enigma that one doesn't get very close to him, and is perhaps "warned off."

best to you,

Al

1. The poems are Nowlan's "The Bull Moose" and Lane's "Cougar" and "Cougar Men."
2. AP ends "On the Death of F.R. Scott" (*The Woman on the Shore*) with "What's right? / Frank Scott knew."

To Margaret Atwood (Toronto), from Sidney, BC, December 4, 1996

Dear Peggy,
How about "Atwood Escarpment" or "Atwood Gorge" or the "Margaret Desert". . . We both could do better, eh?

Thanks for your speaking, which you appeared to enjoy, as you did the section of your novel and question and answer session with another gal. I usta say I wasn't especially fond of reading, but that's not true. It's a challenge to read your stuff and get other people on your side whether they really want to be there or no. And I was *moved* by all those people applauding at the end. Stood there with my face hanging out. You left early and avoided my embarrassment.

And that Mona Lisa photo of you that appears with book ads: Did you mould your face like that, then spray it with epsom salts or some other stiffener. Looks Egyptian. Wonderful what contact lenses will do; but they had a good foundation in your case.

Well, I hope much you get the Nobel; but maybe it'll take another book or two. Both for your own reward and satisfaction, and for the country itself. We need heroes (you'll never be a heroine—they're in old movies), for more reasons than to counter US bullshit. When I was in the Soviet Union in 1977, I told em we didn't have to heat our houses within 200 miles of the US border on accounta all the hot air emanating [from] that direction.

Al

To George Bowering (Vancouver), from Sidney, BC, December 16, 1996

Dear George,

I've had it in mind to thank you for your contribution to the Purdy Harbourfront evening for some time.[1] However, the last two weeks I've had some very painful arthritis. I had to cancel a book flogging appearance in Vancouver when it started, plus a reading.

Before that Eurithe and I were in Prince George and Fort St. John. At Fort St. John we were in a helicopter (both Eurithe and I and a coupla others) following the Peace River, the Moberly and Halfway. Swooping from canyon to valley and river, we were more like a bird than a bird is. Waking up moose and elk in the leafless forest, sending them running once or twice, over cattle ranches etc. We enjoyed the trip thoroughly. I'd be willing to bet you've already had such a flight.

Right now, Eurithe is back east for the funeral of a sister-in-law, someone we were both extremely fond of. That's the worst of growing older, so many of your contemporaries die, some of the best ones.

I was quite emotionally moved by that "tribute" at Harbourfront, as I suppose was noticeable in my voice. I thought a hundred or two hundred people at most, with perhaps a polite round of applause at the end. Instead, well . . . It had never occurred to me that I was such an emotional person.

Best,

Al

1. The evening for AP was held on November 15, 1996 and featured the following

speakers: Margaret Atwood, George Bowering, Patrick Lane, Janet Lunn, Dennis Lee, Sam Solecki and Rosemary Sullivan.

To George Bowering (Vancouver), from Sidney, BC, February 3, 1997

Dear George,

Good to see you so active with both poems and translations. And my own records are unsurprisingly untidy as hell.

A close friend of mine, Bill Percy, has died. And that is the worst of growing old, that your friends die off like that. In Bill's case, it was arranged that an early review copy of a book of mine sent to Bill by Jay Macpherson should be sent to me. He died Dec. 17. The book came from Vina near the end of January. There was a note from Bill on the front endpaper. Leafing through it, I noticed at the end a couple of pencilled lines:

I'll wait for you in the west

Till your own sun comes down for its setting.[1]

—that one hit me kinda hard, written as if he knew he didn't have much time remaining.

I had a reading in Toronto Jan. 10. Then we went to Florida, to Bill's and Vina's place—now just Vina's—where we had often gone before. Of course it wasn't at all the same. I got a cold which I had to shake off, since I had had pneumonia four years back and was scared of it again. The weather cold for Fla. much of the time. [. . .]

Think of Yeats: "an aged man is but a paltry thing / a tattered coat upon a stick / unless soul clap hands and sing / and louder sing for every tatter in its mortal dress." I have got the line spacing wrong, since this is from memory. And the last three poems I've tried to write are lousy, now abandoned.

This is a downhearted letter, and I am sorry. I hope you don't mind too much. It is difficult for me to feel otherwise for a while. Or perhaps I am exaggerating, since I do that sometimes, even when I know I am doing it. It's so difficult to get Bill out of my mind.

And I see I left out a line of Yeats above, placed it wrongly above.

Do keep "pecking away" at your memoir "sort of stuff"[2]—one looks back at one's own life and finds out new things by writing it. I took ten years, actually, to write my own memoir, in bits and pieces until I was finally able to do it more or less continually and chronologically.

I'll try to be a little more cheerful next time. All good wishes to you and Jeanie.

Al

1. AP uses the lines in the poem "Departures" (*To Paris Never Again*), a group elegy for "Enid," "Hilda," "Tom" and "Bill" and again in "Her Gates Both East and West," one of the last poems he wrote.
2. Bowering's memoir, *A Magpie Life: Growing a Writer* was published in 2001.

To Sam Solecki (Toronto), from Sidney, BC, February 18, 1997

Dear Sam,

I think there is no consolation for death, and I wouldn't want any if there was. If you can't feel strongly about a friend's death, how do you know you can feel anything but selfishness? And in the last ten years there have been seven or eight people who were either friends or whom I felt something about. In a way, it's worse than your own death, because you won't know much about it, at least not very probably. And that will be most likely brief; not always brief, of course. But I think of that line of mine: "We live with death but it's life we die with."

I'll never understand how a guy can know fourteen languages like Schliemann.[1] Yeah, I've known the Ceram book for many years. It gives one a head start on archaeology at an early age . . . I read a lot of that English guy's books; can't think of his name, but he wrote about a dozen. Leonard Cottrell. But there's a saturation point, I think; I have the books now, but don't look at em very often.

That's a dramatic title, *The Last Canadian Poet*.[2] Doesn't any other poet think the way I do? Of course Dennis Lee. It's occurred to me often that if it hadn't been for Eurithe I wouldn't have written nearly as much. Oddly enough, I think oddly, she doesn't feel very much gratified personally; and thinks she hasn't accomplished much in her own life. I suppose I shouldn't be surprised at this desire for accomplishment in others, since so many have it. She was moaning low this evening that so many others, male and female, have done so much travelling at a much earlier age than us (she and I), while we were struggling just to get by. True, and she doesn't have the consolation—which is the wrong word for me—of writing. And when I say to her that I owe her much, it seems to mean little since she believes that I am not her accomplishment. Which is only partly true. In a sense I am her accomplishment.

Jack McC's letters to me were often acerbic, and I recall I was slightly the same way with him. Dunno if he has our battle over the poem antho that also involved Harold Town. But the memory of Town still annoys me somewhat. Did I ever tell you about seeing the Blue Jays in Avie B's box, with Town and others. Town says to a lady there that "Purdy doesn't know anything about baseball." I told the lady to tell Town, "I hope he becomes a village." We loved each other.

Yes, I admired Anna's looks. But that bit about her underwear was an exaggeration.[3] I was in her closet, but there was no underwear. I just added that on accounta it made a better story. Don't you think so?

Rilke was very much younger than me when he had his—interregnum, should we call it, without the extra r. Oh sure, the time of silence comes, whether now or later. But I wouldn't include Rilke as someone who should've been very alarmed at his silence. Well, neither am I for that matter. I've always felt that I could write a poem at any time. Point being, is the damn thing any good? Incidentally, I think it's great to take Andre around like that. Stephen Reid took his daughter to Cuba, something she'll remember for seventy years or forever. Which is an odd thing about life, how if a thing happens once it has happened forever; nothing wipes out its reality. Meaning, if you do something you're ashamed of, you're always ashamed because it can't be altered.

Must stop, see you, and watch for traffic lights,

Al

1. Heinrich Schliemann (1822–90): German archaeologist, famous for his excavations at Troy and Mycenae. C.W. Ceram was the pen name of Kurt W. Marek who published several very popular books on archaeology including the bestseller *Gods, Graves and Scholars* (1951). Leonard Cottrell was an equally popular writer on archeological topics. AP paid him the ultimate compliment by using a sentence from his *The Bull of Minos* as the closing line of "On the Decipherment of 'Linear B'" (*The Crafte So Long to Lerne*).
2. The full title of Solecki's book is *The Last Canadian Poet: An Essay on Al Purdy*.
3. For more on Anna Porter's underwear, see her letter of July 25, 1986.

Cathy Ford (b. 1952): poet (*Cunnilingus, or How I Learned to Love Figure Skating*, 1997).

To Cathy Ford, from Sidney, BC, March 26, 1997

Dear Cathy Ford,
I'd like to make my feelings a bit plainer about Dorothy Livesay[1]—as I assume Patrick Lane did, since I know his. Years back I think, when Livesay

was a leftist, took a strong part in political affairs, I think that was a good thing. She spoke up for women, and that too was a good thing.

However, I disagreed with her personally, and thought she was much over-rated as a poet. She did write "Call My People Home," which I except from my general opinions of her poems. It was much more than a disagreement with her where I was concerned: we quarrelled . . .

However, I am sorry not to be able to appear on behalf of the League of Poets. If such a reading were on behalf of almost anyone else, I'd be pleased to be a part of the reading. I hope it goes well for you.

Sincerely,
Al Purdy

1. The celebration of Dorothy Livesay's life and work was held in Victoria, BC, on April 6, 1997.

Judith Fitzgerald (b. 1952): Toronto reviewer, writer (*Marshall McLuhan: Wise Guy*, 2001) and poet (*Rapturous Chronicles*, 1991).

To Judith Fitzgerald (Sundridge, Ont.), from Sidney, BC, December 3, 1997

Dear Judith,
Eurithe and I just got back from Italy, where we spent some time retracing D.H. Lawrence's steps in Etruscan tombs and museums. Hence delay. And jet lag, wow!

Yeah, Eurithe is okay. But we're both feelin awful from being in the sky and in airports for about 24 hrs and losing a day's sleep. I can't type without mistakes.

The docs in Belleville found nothing much wrong or they would've told me: "retention of urine" whatever that means besides what it means. And I'm now back at 195 pounds.

You are so sharp with words that perhaps you don't even know how crisp and accurate you are sometimes. [. . .] When I read your pieces on Lillard[1] and others a while back, and you said something to the effect that he wrote most about himself, that his ego was the subject, I agreed most. I had heard him speak in that defence of the forest affair that took place in Van., and he bragged about having written some three or four hundred newspaper lit columns, and I wanted to gag. Ego is the most and least valuable thing a writer needs. His was overweening. But he died of cancer, and that's supposed to make things right. It doesn't.

I didn't know you were ga-ga about hockey as well as baseball. I grew up on Conacher, Primeau, Jackson, and Red Horner. AND Kennedy et Syl Apps etc.[2] Hunched over the radio and cheering every time the Leafs scored. Haunting the town garbage dump for Beehive Golden Corn Syrup labels for which the company gave you hockey pictures mounted on a piece of cardboard. Big ones too, not like the little things you see today. I practically hauled those labels outa the filthy garbage, and had pictures of the whole 6-team league.

You're talkin about Adele Wiseman[2] I guess, and I didn't know her story. But I did know her, just slightly. Are we on the same beam here?

I feel much the same re Carr.[4] One of the great ones. I dunno if you saw my so-called autobio, in which Eurithe and I went through much of what you're going thru now. Marchand in the *Star* called it one of the worst-written and most interesting pieces of writing he'd read. Maybe. I'm glad to have lived through that time, to know that it did something to and for me altho I don't know exactly what. Eurithe doesn't feel like that at all. It was a horrible time for her. It was for me too. But after it was over, I wouldn't have *not* gone through it (yeah, double negatives) for anything. It was both hell and paradise at the time; and now, I think it gave me something I couldn't get any other way.

I gotta stop. My head is pounding from jet lag and sheer weariness. So take care of yourself. I think you've got guts and courage in equal amounts.

Best,

Al

1. Charles Lillard (1944–97): BC writer (*Warriors of the North Pacific*, 1984) and poet (*Shadow Weather*, 1997).
2. Charlie Conacher, Joe Primeau, Harvey (Busher) Jackson, George (Red) Horner, Theodore (Teeder) Kennedy and Syl Apps were among the greatest Maple Leafs of the 1925–1950 era.
3. Adele Wiseman (1928–92): novelist (*The Sacrifice*, 1956; *Crackpot*, 1974). Her correspondence with Margaret Laurence was published in 1997.
4. Emily Carr (1871–1945): painter and writer of autobiographical sketches. *Klee Wyck* (1941) won a Governor General's Award.

From Judith Fitzgerald (Sundridge, Ont.), to Sidney, BC, January 18, 1998

Dear Al,

I read about your typewriterliness in The *Globe* a while back and just wanted to show off what a computer can do. Actually, I really want to show off probably my one-and-only-ever appearance in *Maclean's*, so, there you go!

Italy sounds like it might have been neat, retracing DHL's steps, especially the tombs.[1] That part of the world, generally, overwhelms, probably, everybody. I always think of the squishedness of everything as opposed to the aired-out feeling here, in this country. Flying's awful, always. I refuse to do it, after coming back from France. (No smoking for a nervous smoker/flyer? No way.)

I did receive a copy of *To Paris Never Again* and found it moving and inexpressibly sad and comforting at the same time. I liked "Herself" and the poem about you and Alden N. and Milton A. I didn't read FS's review (though saw that he'd done it). There's a tone in these ones, especially the second half, a quiet awe that is not naïve, if you know what I mean. I loved a lot of these. The one about the scroll and plywood, that's beautiful. It is an illusion. Time is a human construct. You are not wrong. But, it's not only content, nor thrust, either. It's because it's poetry. Just is.

Yeah, I didn't know Adele Wiseman well; but, I did read the hell she'd been through at Windsor. I would put *The Sacrifice* on my list of best-ofs in the last century. I'd put *Painted Ladies* on it, too. I was thinking about Bill [Percy] the other day, about *A Model Lover*, actually. I have a really terrific picture of Bill and me where I'm wearing his cap'n's hat and he's looking elfishly, almost crazily, ecstatically up-to-somethingish. I liked him very much and I liked working with him which is how I met him but, naturally, everybody who meets Bill becomes his friend and vice versa. I'm sorry he's not with us, one of the good ones. Things nuts here, per usual. Dan has been waging war with the driveway (which is longer than a hockey rink) and, mostly, the driveway wins. See, I think Johnny Bower and Gordie Howe and Dickie Duff, Al. Syl Apps, yeah. All them guys. I loved watching hockey on the tube, then. The long camera shots, the rough cuts and it was so bloody important, eh? Like, really important your guys score so you could gloat about their guys? A win was a win, then, now it's just a statistic. George Elliott Clarke[2] includes a quote from somebody named Bains in this verse play he wrote I'm reading. "The old enslavement was to nature, and the new one is of one individual to another, beginning with chattel slavery and proceeding to the modern kind, where enslavement has assumed the most grotesque form—not only wage-slavery, but also bondage to the financial institutions which, in the present period, hold the entire world in their grasp." (Clarke, by the way, loves Layton.)

You oughta read "Righteous Speedboat," a short story by an up-and-comer, Jarman. It's a stunner. Don't know him nor who he is, just liked the story a lot.

So, Dan comes in, we trapped a mole in the back room in a mouse trap, right? He wonders if we can sideline in mole pelts. Silly guy.

Yeah, I know that love beyond love you describe in one of the poems,[3] I know it exactly and you got it exactly right and I hadn't thought it until I read it. Anyway, I am off to The Big Smoke for a few days and just wanted to check in. Hope you're rested after this latest gallivant and, like, try staying put for at least a week, okay?

On accounta your health, fer chrissakes.

All good 'gards and amities,
Fitz

1. Lawrence visited the chief Etruscan sites in 1927; his account of the trip was published in 1932 as *Etruscan Places*, two years after his death.
2. George Elliott Clarke (b. 1960): professor of English at the University of Toronto, critic and poet (*Whylah Falls*, 1990). He has also written the libretto for James Rolfe's opera *Beatrice Chancey*.
3. Fitzgerald might be referring to "Listening to Myself" (*To Paris Never Again*).

To Sam Solecki (Toronto), from Sidney, BC, January 18, 1998

Dear Sam,

[...] Eurithe and I were both pretty dragged out from the 24 hours it took to reach Sidney, and of course we lost a night's sleep. It was a week before either of us began to feel somewhat normal.

I intend to write a piece on this trip, but first some work on the Laurence "lecture," which begins to terrify me a bit. Also, seeing all the sculptures atop their sarcophagi (or sarcophaguses?), it occurred to me that the sculptors were slaves or close to slaves, although they probably got some sort of remuneration for their work.[1] But the temptation to either flatter their masters or the opposite must sometimes have been in their minds. Altho it's probably that a few of the sculptors were

Greek emigrants, and perhaps not slaves. I think of Browning's "My Last Duchess," visitors being shown a painting of this guy's dead wife, and wonder if something similar could be done with the Etruscan sculptures. I can easily imagine that scene turned backwards, and the Etruscan widow commissioning sculpture of her dead husband. But a poem on that subject would immediately be seen as a derivation from Browning.

Anyway, the thought produced a few lines in imitation of Browning just now. Imagine an Etruscan widow taking her husband's girl friend to see the image a Greek sculptor did on his sarcophagus? "Murder in the Tombs." It'll probably come to nothing tho.

I expect you've got the Italian lit mag with your piece in it by now, and my letter expressing admiration of the piece. Because I thought you truly fathomed what's behind—or in front—of a lot of my stuff.[2]

We were treated very well by the Embassy, and especially by Laura Forconi of the Siena–Toronto Centre. We were guests at the Forconi place a couple of times. I sent about a dozen of my books, wondering if they'll get there okay, since we lost the Italian postal code for the Forconi residence (I found it later, but too late for the parcel).

Which seems to be all,

Best,

Al

1. AP saw Etruscan sarcophagi in Rome at the Museo Nationale di Villa Gulia and in Volterra's Museo Guarnacci.
2. "History and Nation in the Poetry of Al Purdy," *Rivista di Studi Canadesi / Canadian Studies Review*, No. 10 (1997).

To Judith Fitzgerald (Sundridge, Ont.), from Sidney, BC, January 26, 1998

Dear Judith,

I enclose my Etruscan poem with slight trepidation. I'm not sure how the jocular tone of the second verse would go.

I doubt if it's your only appearance in *Maclean's*. Congratulations. I've a fax but no computer.

And thanks much for the good word on some of the poems. It's a come-down after *Rooms For Rent*—, and I guess I'm not writing as well, also a little differently.

Sure, time is a human construct, and also a way of getting a handle on something we can't figure out, don't even know what it is. Time and space and human beings are the most interesting things—but everything is, for that matter, if IF you can get inside them.

I'm not sure what Adele W. went through at Windsor?

Did I mention that Bill P. modeled his lead character on me?[1] But I didn't know it, didn't recognize my supposed self, not until I read an interview, I guess in a Toronto paper, in which he said so. He never told me. I threatened him with a suit for libel, and of course he rightly disbelieved me. Eurithe, Vina and I visited his grave when we were at Granville Ferry and Annapolis. I picked up a stone there, and then forgot to take it; but no danger I'll forget Bill.

Yeah, when I was say twelve or so, I used to listen to the Leafs on radio, and yell when they scored. Before your time tho. I picked up when Jackson, Primeau, Conacher were the Leafs' big line.

Interesting that [George Elliott] Clarke loves Layton, since the latter is a very mixed bag. Sam Solecki does too. I'm fond of Irving's best, but his imitations of himself left me cold. But one should read his best.

Clambering around those tombs at Cerveteri made me very nervous. I'm probably quite brittle in bones by now. But if we didn't go to Italy on this occasion we'd never have gone. I said yes-no half a dozen times before—At Volterra we took a wrong turning on bad directions, and went down a steep hill about half a mile long. Before we could get to the top over those cobblestones again Eurithe and I were holding onto each other for support and encouragement.

Yours,

Al

1. AP also claimed that he couldn't find the character based on himself in Ondaatje's *In the Skin of a Lion* (1987).

From Sam Solecki (Toronto), to Sidney, BC, February 1, 1998

Dear Al,

Thanks for the copy of *Rivista di Studi Canadesi*. I'm glad that you liked the piece on poetry and history, though your comment that it is better and more to the matter than my book is curious since the article is really just several sections of the book added on to one of the main chapters. Speaking of books, I'm just reading a new manuscript by a McGill professor, Brian Trehearne, about the Montreal poets of the forties. He argues that *Preview* and *First Statement* weren't really that different, and that all the poets of the '40s—especially Klein, Page, Layton and Dudek—were reacting to some degree to Imagism or a poetry rooted in the image and symbol. He overstates the case, but the individual chapters show a lot of homework in the mags of the period; even the poems of Anderson and Sutherland are discussed at some length.

One thing I didn't realize is that Layton's "The Swimmer" was written in the early '40s and was followed by 7 or 8 years of weaker poems, until the great breakout of the 1951–54 period. It's difficult to accept that "The Swimmer" came out half a century ago, or that your first major period is already three decades ago. I could go on in this vein: Atwood is 58; Ondaatje is 54, and I'm not feeling so young either, etc. etc. Overall, the book's argument doesn't convince, and the closing chapter on Dudek, whom he considers seriously underrated, leaves me doubting his critical faculties. The test with Louis is always in the quotations which no matter how you slice them sound like very flat prose without the occasional spark or lyric or irony or perspective that Pound is capable of at his best. Page, Klein and Irving, on the other hand, are capable of music and of images and metaphors that linger in the mind. Still, LD has a historic importance, though that by itself will never make him happy.

I'm sending you a couple more Les Murray poems, one about Australian bat-foxes, and the other about an abandoned mill resurrected in poetry. I thought the second would bring back some local memories. Frye writes somewhere of the ruins of recently settled societies, of how many more there are than one would think, primarily because we're so willing to leave something that has failed and move on, whether a burned down or abandoned house or farm or rural factory, mill etc. I studied with Frye in 1969, an MA course on poetics and literary symbolism, and when I read him or think about him or see his name, I can still hear the voice and see the face, the twinkle in his eye. Doesn't seem as if he is dead, for a moment anyway. Whether one agreed or disagreed with him, you always knew that you were in the presence of the real thing, a mind worth disagreeing with, and disagreement would make you sharper because he wouldn't let you get away with something vague or trendy. Like F.R. Scott in your elegy, "Frye knew."

By the way, did you notice in the museum in Volterra how many of the sarcophagus covers seemed mass produced?

Take care of yourself,

Sam

To Sam Solecki (Toronto), from Sidney, BC, February 7, 1998

Dear Sam,

Thanks for the Murray poems and review.[1] [. . .]

Murray is something else. It's irrelevant to his merit to mention I met him once, sat with Tom Marshall at Queen's, listened to him read, talked to him briefly, agreed with him on how you keep yourself open for poems ("Stay stupid!"). Physically he was quite fat, and read much too fast (one of my own faults which I recognize in others), and the Aussie accent sometimes made it difficult. But that's as mentioned, irrelevant.

As a poet he's very striking; his use of image and metaphor etc. is, at times, very striking. At other times it is overwhelming, and added to his almost invariable use of rhyme and meter detracts from whatever it is he's talking about. But sometimes he will suddenly revert to ordinary language, as in the last line of "Coolongolook Mill," "But I have kept it." Very effective. Half the words—but that's exaggeration—in the poem I don't know, "pintle"—no, it's more the way he uses words that seems a bit mystifying. For instance, is "Wittgenstein" the philosopher, and what the fuck has he to do with Siberian railroads? But "The Flying-fox Dreaming" reverses my above description and does use simple language, and I love "It goes on being appropriate." And then "Neverwhere." Some of it beautiful stuff, others puzzling, and so difficult to disagree with his methods when he succeeds and flummoxes you.

But he always gives you something. There's never a poem that hasn't got something intriguing about it, something lovely or interesting or everything.

I've been working on the Laurence lecture; have a first draft done, decided I hate the name, "lecture"—shit, but then what do you call it? I also have a first draft of the Etruscan article I've been doing, something confined to our Etruscan travels etc., not Siena.[2]

Laura Forconi, incidentally, wants to translate some of my stuff. I got permission for her to publish it from Harbour. I read briefly at the University of Siena in a nearby city, and they gave me a medal. I've no idea what for, unless to flatter visiting readers. It doesn't say what for on the medal.

> best to you,
> Al

---

1. Les Murray (b. 1938): Australian poet (*New Collected Poems*, 2003). AP is refer-

ring to "Coolongolook Timber Mill" (*Conscious and Verbal*, 1999) and "Fruit Bat Colony by Day" (*Poems the Size of Photographs*, 2002).

2. "Purdy Among the Etruscans," *Canadian Forum* (June 1998).

To Jack McClelland (Toronto), from Sidney, BC, March 22, 1998

Dear Jack,

Your *Letters* are delightful.[1] And what a human guy inside them, drinking fucking talking, doing everything. And your jousting with Birney is hilarious. This is the Jack McC. I saw much too rarely. Altho once I recall sitting in a pub drinking—I guess beer for me—when you told me a story that I've never forgotten, of a competition with another guy that went on all night, and that you won just before the morning deadline. That ought to be enough to make you remember or to guess from these hints what the competition was about. One guess.

I hope you are now enjoying life and that your illness has left few traces.

All best wishes,

Al

1. *Imagining Canadian Literature: The Letters of Jack McClelland* (1998).

To Steven Heighton (Kingston), from Ameliasburgh, June 25 or 26, 1998

Dear Steve,

We leave for V.I. July 3, return July 27.

Whaddaya mean thanks for "letting us visit"—hells bells, we love to have you.

Yeah, I'm 80 Dec. 30. Helluva thing, eh? Never expected to make it, and still ain't sure.

By the way, I hope to have some *Can. Forums* here by the time I see you again. The current issue has my Etruscan piece, and a cover with a cartoon of me that makes me look several hundred years. Always thought cartoonists exaggerated present aspects of what you look like. This one gives me a long nose, and I am not flattered a damn bit. Also, when I reread the piece, I overlooked a coupla places where I had two words in too close conjunction. Shit, in other words . . .

Thanks for the words on poems . . . I'm kinda sick of them now, and think they shoulda been better, and my alibi is my age, which is a lousy alibi . . . It takes a more flexible voice than mine to read "Say the Names" well; and I'm always telling myself to slow down Steve when I mean Purdy. I don't have the dulcet voice to say *Tulameen* the way it should be said . . .

Tis the season when women take off many of their clothes in public— that got anything to do with you likin the heat?

Any more word on the novel [*The Shadow Boxer*], and do you still feel good about it, or just good because you finished it? I think I felt the latter when I finished mine. There was one weekend when it was on the best-seller list; but that was a mistake, and corrected next week. I'd rather write poems anyway, but not writing much. [. . .]

And I did the Laurence lecture. I connected the parts of it up by remembering when I was reading the Bible for the sexual passages, and remember St. Paul having a revelation on the road to Damascus. In Vancouver in the early 1950s, realizing I really wasn't very good and starting to change. I called it a luminous moment, like St. Paul on the road to Damascus, and called it by that title. For sexual passages earlier in this para., read "dirty passages," altho I wouldn't've called em that at the time.

Eurithe and I hope to see you again on our return. Make it Aug. so you can swim the lake again.

best
Al
and to Mary

To Steven Heighton (Kingston, Ont.), from Ameliasburgh, August 28, 1998

Dear Steve,
The summer ain't right: no Steve and Mary. We miss you.

I hope this secluded spot where your brains work ten times better'n here has produced that result and you're giving birth to a masterpiece. (I enclose a poem from the *Oxford Book of Comic Verse* which illustrates what happens to masterpieces.) In other words, I hope you're both enjoying yourself, plus youngster.

We're off to the Thirty Thousand Islands and Georgian Bay shortly, to write another piece for Imp. Oil.

Incidentally, I think Lynn C. is annoyed with me. She asked me to write an Intro for her Selected Poems, and I said okay. Then receive a fax from Anansi, asking me for a blurb. A blurb is short, as you know. So I write one line, and say this book will be the best book of poems this year. But I have not heard from Lynn. Maybe she's bought a gun? But there are thirty thousand islands in Georgian Bay where I can hide coweringly. "Best book" will not do, I hear borne on the wind from Paul Bernardo's biographer.[1]

Come see us if you haven't taken out US citizenship.

best
Al & Eurithe

1. AP is referring to Crosbie's controversial treatment of the Bernardo–Homolka murders in her mixed-genre novel, *Paul's Case* (1997).

From Fraser Sutherland (Toronto), to Sidney, BC, January 5, 1999

Dear Al,

[. . .] Read your and Beardsley's Lawrence book[1] with interest, though on occasion I thought you both missed the point, and generally the discussion struck me as one that might be conducted by a pair of highly intelligent and jargon-free graduate students in English—if such may be imagined. The book's main benefit for me was to see much more clearly how Lawrence was a liberating force in your own work, and how in your own way you've been searching for "gods" in the world around you.

I'll look into *Imperial Oil Review*.

Enclosed the Heaney review[2] which attempts to resolve why someone this good isn't so great. Lawrence is a different matter; the question pertaining to him is: Why is someone this great not so good? Which may be a variant of the title for Richard Aldington's biography of Lawrence: *Portrait of a Genius but . . .*

Hairy as ever, below the nose anyway,

Fraser

1. In *No One Else Is Lawrence!* AP and Doug Beardsley combined a dozen of Lawrence's best poems with a dialogue about Lawrence.
2. Sutherland had reviewed Heaney's *Opened Ground: Poems 1966–1996* and Helen Vendler's *Seamus Heaney* in the *Globe and Mail*, November 28, 1998.

To Fraser Sutherland (Toronto), from Sidney, BC, January 13, 1999

Dear Fraser,
Enclosed another review of the DHL book, with which you will no doubt disagree.

Thank you for the hints on cancer, which I'm told is unlikely or non-existent. There is a blockage to the urine, (to go into the no doubt disgusting details), and I will likely have to undergo a minor operation (I just hope it is minor). I've been taking saw palmetto and zinc pills, since three different kinds of antibiotics didn't help. The zinc and saw palmetto are not antibio, if I need to say. There is discomfort, but I don't know if that gets worse or no (the doc says it does). So I'm in a bit of a quandary right now. What's PSA incidentally?

I'm principally interested in your Heaney review and the reason for it. As you know, I feel much the same as you about Heaney, and while willing to admit merit to the guy (ain't that big of me?), don't even see him as good as you do, despite his awards. So what's wrong with me? And you? And of course I think DHL is both great and good despite your snide remarks about my gods. But yes, Lawrence meant a great deal to me, with his poetry of the moment stuff, altho I don't agree with his opinions about permanence.

"true to the impact of external reality"—said reality would differ whoever wrote about it. Sounds like shit to me, high falutin language that doesn't stand up to examination. I don't know if it's "a permanently new awareness of the world" that good poems shock us into, since my brain focuses on the poem itself, and no doubt there is a connection between said poet and world, but I'm most concerned with what the guy or gal is saying. Not that I avoid or miss the connection, but it's the poem that's the main thing. But it's easy to disagree with both this and what Heaney said. So what boots it?

How about "Those thoughts that wander through eternity"—know who wrote that?[1] I think it's a great line. And also enclose the poem I wrote that uses it. Not my line, I hasten to add.

But back to Heaney: the greater puzzle about him to me: why does everyone else but us think him great? You say "he never allows a poem to leap into its own freedom" by which you mean, I think, that he always tailors it. But so do I and so do many others, but you may mean allow it to go in a direction he didn't anticipate when he started out. I hardly ever anticipate where I'm goin, really don't know. But I agree with you anyhow, altho that "new awareness" stuff seems exaggerated.

"She walks in beauty" is euphonious, but is it a great line? Auden's, yes. How about "The mountains look on Marathon / And Marathon looks on the sea"? Or the passage beginning "A shudder in the loins engenders there—"[2]

No, I think Heaney's Nobel Prize thing is pretentious and meaningless. I guess he has "consummate craftsmanship"—but if so shouldn't he be saying something more meaningful? That external reality bit, there is really no such thing, except as something we can agree on for purposes of referring to it or doing something else with it.

I don't think Lawrence is a very profound craftsman (he doesn't know when and where to stop, for instance)

But I do.

Best,

Al

1. "For who would lose, / Though full of pain, this intellectual being, / Those thoughts that wander through eternity, / To perish rather, swallowed up and lost / In the wide womb of uncreated night, / Devoid of sense and motion." (John Milton, *Paradise Lost*, Book II, 146).
2. "She Walks in Beauty" is by Byron as are following lines about Marathon from *Don Juan* (Canto III, stanza 86). The final line—"A shudder . . ."—is from Yeats's "Leda and the Swan," and AP had just used it in "For Ann More" (*Beyond Remembering: The Collected Poems of Al Purdy*).

John B. Lee (b. 1951): Brantford, Ontario, poet (*Variations on Herb*, 1993; *Tongues of the Children: The Upper Canada Chronicles*, 1996) who is the only two-time winner of the Milton Acorn People's Poetry Award.

To John B. Lee (Brantford, Ont.), from Sidney, BC, January 23, 1999

Dear John,

Thanks for your good letter.

Of course, use my poem, and I hope yr own in the antho (I think they'll go well together). That's a true story incidentally, the kid who claimed he was Gwen MacEwen's son. I'm told he went to see Rosemary Sullivan who took him to see Peggy Atwood. It was found out later that MacEwen was somewhere else when he said she was in hospital having him; so he was kinda discredited. Odd story tho. Me sick as hell from an-tibio reaction.

That radio program, my part in it anyway, was done last summer. I didn't know it was for a birthday, my own.

Yeah, the Lawrence book. Fraser Sutherland said it read like two high school students; the guy in *Books in Canada*[1] got it entirely right; we did that book as an appreciation of DHL, since people generally think of his novels or whatever. Doug and I got an info sheet about the de luxe ed we had done. Damn thing cost us a small fortune too. And yes, of course, we are not litcrits, and don't sound like ones. Fraser S. was a bit snide, but what the hell; he's been a friend for years and I forgive him. He's a lot more literary than me.

Sure, the real snake and the snake as myth. And Lawrence's reaction to mosquitoes seems to me odd, and yet right for him. Do you know his "Fish" in which he says, "I didn't know his god" and reading that I get an odd feeling, of a different universe of water and colonnades of seaweed and coral castles . . .

I suppose he must know only the female mosquito draws blood; I think we all grew up knowing that. But when you refer to any beast or bug it's natural to use the male gender. It is for me anyway. And for Lawrence, something that bit him was likely to be male. And I suppose one of things Doug and I like about Lawrence is the naturalness of his voice, after he found his own of course. And that was with *Birds, Beasts and Flowers*, and some of the other stuff when he didn't care the way he said things, they just came out like talking.

Incidentally, did you ever read Yeats' "Mad as the Mist and Snow"?, in which Yeats' ego gets the best of him. It's a bit similar to the Ceylon poem with the English Prince of Wales, in which Lawrence's own ego slips its moorings.[2] [. . .]

And yeah, the bat in DHL is more real than the snake. I feel the snake's repugnance, not the mosquito's . . .

No, I don't remember you at the league meeting; but I don't remem-ber many many people. I have been aware of you for years though, esp after "Kitcheraboo, We are Dying"[3] and I felt so curious about what the poem was talking about. The title remained in my head, like Richards' title, *For Those Who Hunt the Wounded Down*. Your title sounds like the end of a race; Richards' of a monstrous pity, and yet we don't exactly know what he means by it.

I can remember a bat in my bedroom when I was a child, and my mother chasing it with a broom, very long ago; "as if it were flying in the mind" as you say. Such an odd thing, our reactions to various animals, bugs etc. . . . Generally, a shrinking back from them, bugs that is; not so much from animals per se.

I'm going on too long.

All the best to you,
Al

1. Jack Illingsworth reviewed the book in *Books in Canada* (November 1998).
2. Lawrence's "Elephant" describes a Ceylonese Perahera "With a little wisp of a Prince of Wales, diffident, up in a small pagoda on the temple side." The poem referred to below is "Man and Bat." Both poems are in *Birds, Beasts and Flowers* (1923), AP's favourite Lawrence collection.
3. The poem is in Lee's *Tongues of the Children: The Upper Canada Chronicles* (1996). I owe the reference to Russell Brown.

To Sam Solecki (Toronto), from Sidney, BC, January 26, 1999

Dear Sam,

Good to hear from you.

"Cities and thrones and powers" and undoubtedly Kipling, and that's where my line came from I'm sure. Interesting thought for your students, your poor students. I thought Ford[1] was hard to read years ago. Almost as bad as Mann. Of course they did help to form Lawrence's mind. As you know, he wrote a book on Hardy, which is said to be more about himself than Hardy. I haven't read that either.

You are perceptive (as Eurithe says and I agree) about Lawrence naming the turtle by means of images and metaphors. I'll have to read that one again. I agree whole-heartedly about that and "Poetry of the Present," that last having a big influence on me. I still think of it now and then. Remember also his dislike of permanence, stone buildings etc. I disagree with that, but still agree with his poetry of the present theme, which of course is impossible. Still, you can have the sense of transience in the present. We definitely should've talked about it.

I have a copy of the MO book [*Handwriting*], but haven't spent much time on it. I shall on your say-so. The turtle poem we included had such lovely rhetoric tho . . . Two turtle poems would have seemed too much. Did I say we're doing John Donne, and have rendered two poems, Elegy 19 and Elegy 5 into modern English.[2] They are not exact translation, but imitations, tho even less imitations than Lowell's with Akhmatova. I think they're interesting tho. Doug has mentioned he'd rather I didn't do any more writing at them when he wasn't there. He liked some of my additions, but thought he was being left out when credit might possibly be given later. I re-wrote much of the poem, esp. the last three lines. I can certainly understand how he feels. [...]

Irving in Etruria—too much. Yeah, I know he loved Lawrence, but Irving in a tomb seems overmuch.

I want to get this off to you before you leave, or rather that you receive it before then. Cordoba or Madrid? You have a mark below Madrid can't make out. So enjoy. If romance you're young enough—just barely.

Al

1. Ford Madox Ford (1873–1939): influential critic, editor (*English Review, Transatlantic Review*) and novelist (*The Good Soldier*, 1915; *Parade's End*, 1924–28). Ford had an almost infallible nose for genius, and is one of the godfathers of English High Modernism. Thomas Mann (1875–1955): the most important German writer of the twentieth century (*The Magic Mountain*, 1924; *Doctor Faustus*, 1947). Lawrence wrote "Study of Thomas Hardy" (1914), an unfinished study of Hardy's fiction that was not published in his lifetime. Thomas Hardy (1840–1928): novelist (*Jude the Obscure*, 1896) and poet (*Wessex Poems*, 1898).
2. *The Man Who Outlived Himself*, AP and Doug Beardsley's book on Donne, was published in 2000.

From Fraser Sutherland (Toronto), to Sidney, BC, February 2, 1999

Dear Al,

[...] You're missing the point in commenting on Heaney's allusion to poetry's being "true to the impact of external reality." He is implicitly distinguishing his stuff, which attempts to construct a bridge between signifiers (words) and the signified (the ostensible object, subject, or topic) from the kind of poetry that is seemingly all signifiers and no signified e.g. John Ashbery's. I don't think it's possible to write intelligibly without having referents, but that's another question.

By "permanently new awareness" I just mean that a phrase, line, or poem can permanently alter one's perceptions, however slightly. Or just linger like a perpetual question, enigma, or paradox. A line from Pasternak, I think in *Dr. Zhivago*, has haunted me ever since I first read it many years ago: "To live a life is not to cross a field."[1]

Heaney's fame is a little puzzling, but not terribly so. He has a grave, oracular tone that, combined with earthiness or earthboundedness, powerfully appeals to many people. But there are cultural and political reasons, too. (For an enlightening look at how literary fame gets shaped you might request from the library a book published some years ago called *The Making and Claiming of "St. George" Orwell*, I forget the author's name:[2] an academic and I think published by the University of Virginia Press. The book shows how successive generations took Orwell to be their representative, how he could become a hero to both the left and the right.) In Heaney's case he had talent to begin with, but he also made powerful friends in the places where reputations get built. And, equally important, he gained status as a witness. A talented poet gets a head start if he's writing in a war zone.

I don't really disagree with the *BiC* review of the Lawrence book. It's just that it was a little bland and middle-of-the-road (if anything, you were more professorial than Beardsley, who actually *is* a professor) and I would have preferred something more outrageous and idiosyncratic like the poem you enclosed and which I temporarily misplaced (shades of you with *Peace and War!*). The poem has a quality of rowdiness I like a lot. [...]

Tell Eurithe to keep you under control.

Yours,

Fraser

1. The last line of Boris Pasternak's "Zhivago" poem, "Hamlet."
2. John Rodden, *The Politics of Literary Reputation: The Making and Claiming of "St. George" Orwell* (1989).

To Sam Solecki (Toronto), from Sidney, BC, April 19, 1999

Dear Sam,

Enclosed the marked Contents page for Collected and three other books. Also, five Beardsley–Purdy Donne poems, plus my own unpublished stuff, of which there isn't much.

Care should be taken that poems from the Collected haven't been revised for *Rooms for Rent*—; If that turns out to be the case, poems from the latter book should be used. Also, I'd have to know the limits Howie wants to impose (obviously) before we can cut the manuscript.

Also, the Donne poems can't be used until the Beardsley/Purdy book is published.

My lung trouble is a carcinoma atop the left lung. Haven't got the results of Saturday's (today is Tuesday) CT Scan. I've had several medical procedures, including prostate surgery and a tube down my throat while

I was out. Each time things unusual happened (like the surgery, like the tube down my throat) my heart went into atrial fibrillation. In the event of surgery to remove the carcinoma, I think a stroke would be very probable. So anything we have to do shouldn't be delayed.

Best,

Al

From Susan Musgrave (Sidney, BC), to Sidney, BC, May 14, 1999

Dear Al,
Here's one of my favourite quotes from Bukowski (and I'm sure you know it): "Suicide fails, the older we get. There's less and less to kill."
  These words mean more to me every day . . .
  Continuing to spread joy, always in excessive moderation,

love,

Susan

To Margaret Atwood (Toronto), from Sidney, BC, June 1999

Dear Peggy,
I go into hospital June 21, surgery next day. I hope & expect to come out of it, but you never know. Unknown country.
  I've had a lot of respect for you over a long period of time. That line of yours many years ago was part of it. Do you remember? "That isn't true, John. You know that isn't true."[1] That one line made a large part of your character in my mind, and I think had much influence on me.
  So if I don't come out of this surgery session as "expected," your own eventual arrival will be attended with drums & flutes, welcoming signs.

Love,

Al

1. Atwood said this in response to a comment John Newlove made in front of a group of people.

From Michael Ondaatje (Toronto), to Sidney, BC, June 28, 1999

Dear Al,
I heard from Dennis this morning that he went out west to see you and he told me about the possibility of your having cancer.
  I've been roaming around the house ever since, in shock. I can't

believe the war horse that you are could be prone to mortality. I take it there will be an operation in early July. And I hope all goes well and that you will emerge from it your same self.

We never get to tell our favourite poets that they are our favourite poets. So I will now. You are the best and most important poet Canada has given the world. *And* the most enjoyable. And the least complaisant. You brought your voice alongside poetry and you changed it.

And as a person you were genuinely generous to all of us who were starting up.

Thank you Al and good wishes and love.

Michael

To Dennis Lee (Toronto), from Sidney, BC, July 5, 1999

Dear Dennis,
I go into hospital tomorrow, and I'm not really very optimistic about that.

But I wanted to say: how fortunate to have known you, and for so many years. I'll remember you for as long as I have memory,

and with love, and with admiration,
Al

To Ellen Seligman (Toronto), from Ameliasburgh, August 3, 1999

Dear Ellen,
Thanks much—for being there, being you & all your help. Do you by chance have a snapshot of yourself you could fax?

I felt much the same as you in Paris. Ran around a corner into two Hollywood movie stars whom I recognized & had just been married; they looked that new-married look. Both dead now—Mel Ferrer & Audrey Hepburn.[1] The three of us nearly ran into each other. I picked up fleas from the place we stayed at, also water was bad, my stomach turned over. I enjoyed the place much. Yes, the streets named after writers & artists. But the *feeling* was there and in Rome.

Eurithe was with me there and Michael O. expressed sympathy and said "you placed your work beside poetry and you changed it." What an odd felicitous way of saying it! I had no idea he felt that way.

Love,
Al

1. AP describes this in *To Paris Never Again*.

To Fraser Sutherland (Toronto), from Sidney, BC, September 17, 1999

Dear Fraser,
The fax & phone are the same, identical, twins, no difference. Two days
of treatment, I feel the same, lousy. I hear you say "What else is new?"
Actually the Kingston doc has given me a pretty pessimistic diagnosis, but
my own is worse. The voice is scarcely decipherable unless you're close
by. The poetic voice is silent, except for finishing off the long millennium
poem ["Her Gates Both East and West"] I got paid for. I *had* to do that
one and Sam S. thinks it comes off well. (I'd expect you to disagree.) Doc
thinks voice loss because of cancer. George's Angela[1] has been ill with cancer & related stuff for years. Tough to say, but she was bound to go. Poor
George! Jim[2] seems doing ok. But these things are invisible. I'm luxuriat-
ing in the thought of four books—one about, the rest by,[3] a feeling I spent
my life doing this, and was it worth it? To me, it is and was. I wouldn't
have it any other way. I hope you feel the same about your own life.
Love,
Al

1. George and Angela Bowering
2. AP's son Jim Purdy had suffered a heart attack.
3. AP is probably referring to *The Last Canadian Poet: An Essay on Al Purdy*,
No One Else is Lawrence!, *The Man Who Outlived Himself* and the forthcoming
Beyond Remembering: The Collected Poems of Al Purdy.

To Sam Solecki (Toronto), from Sidney, BC, March 8, 2000

Dear Sam,
Many thanks for all the interesting lit stuff you've sent my way. Especially
appreciate the *Gilgamesh* [article],[1] as will Doug Beardsley. He's really
hooked on that, the way it permeates middle-eastern myths & lit.

I've had some bad days, but got rid of them by dispensing with unnec-
essary medication that was at war inside me. We cut back to basics.

The Purdy poem[2] in *Imp. Oil Rev.* advance copy out. I hope to get one
any day now. *Do they send you copies?* Let me know, so I can send or not
send. I've worked at that poem in 1999, but that's all.

Any more reviews of *The Last Can. Doggerel Writer*?

I am told by doctor I can go along in present condition until tumour
hits a vital organ like heart or spreads. Cheerful bastards, ain't they?

I seem to get quite a few visits from people, including Beardsley who wants me to work on *Gilgamesh* with him. He doesn't have the right sort of imagination to do it alone. But, really, I can't help him. And it's not like Lawrence or Donne. And I think I'm about done anyway, unless visited by lightning.

Love,
Al

1. Jonathan Burgess's "Gilgamesh and Odysseus in the Otherworld," *Classical Views/Echos du Monde Classique*, 18:2, (1999).
2. AP is referring to "Her Gates Both East and West," published in the spring issue of the *Imperial Oil Review*, and subsequently the last poem in *Beyond Remembering: The Collected Poems of Al Purdy*.

To Sam Solecki (Toronto), from Sidney, BC, March 21, 2000

Dear Sam,

Good letter . . . Rilke remains an enigma to me. He seems inhuman in some ways. It's as if he liked women for the poems they could give him. Yet he was a great poet. Curious—I disagree with a lot of the basic attitudes of the poets. Rilke, Auden, Yeats. I wouldn't, probably, have liked Lawrence personally nor he me. But I don't want to *like* poets. I want to steal from them, but find that difficult. I can't write at all now because of the disease. Incidentally, I had "Say the Names" in mind for many years, every time I passed the Tulameen. But I didn't have the key phrase, *Say the Names*. I *knew* I had it when that entered my mind.

Eurithe is surprising and unsurprising the way she looks after me, thinks of things to help my discomfort. She knows the inevitable is death, but doesn't like talking about it. I was somewhat more raucous and physical in past years and that didn't appeal to her. But I could feel tenderness as well at the same time. I hope the ashes go together, at A-burg cemetery, I suppose. Is there communication between ashes? Of course not. But I feel that way. A little electric wire running between the chalices.

Thought I was both lucky and unlucky in old age. Did you notice "Say the Names" was cut about ten lines in *Globe*? I thought it better. I suppose I was lucky in such slow development. I was never quick finishing poems, kept going back to them.

Jeffers was always rather smug. I liked him but with reservations. But that's true of everyone I like. You can't be perfect all the time. But, yes, the peremptory "scatter the ashes" is right. Of course, like Rilke, we all stare at the darkness. But any pro-death attitude is wrong. We don't have any solid evidence. Of course I believe there's nothing; and that suits my turn of mind. But it can't have any solid basis. Also, I don't want anyone who knows all and can order me around like a fuckin doctor of souls. Yeah, sympathy, tenderness. They don't got it, I don't want that from them. I do get it from some women which makes me think they're better than men in some ways. I don't like DHL's "Ship of Death" stuff. Strikes me as cliché anyway. I want death to be sudden & silent, and I would like to know some of the scenery along the way.

Yours,
Al

To Sam Solecki (Toronto), from Sidney, BC, April 13, 2000

Dear Sam,

Good to hear—I miss your letters. I have Michael's book [*Anil's Ghost*], from Ellen, everyone says good.

Death, occasionally, too boring, to be often. But it's inevitable in next few weeks; staying alive is getting painful.

I never had anyone close to me die (except my mother) so it hasn't been bad. Eurithe & friends I would miss if I have time.

I've always (generally) thought I was finished at the end of a book. This time, the illness is pretty certain. But can you extract good stuff from my letters? Perhaps from other stuff as well?

But I dunno.

One of my life's pleasures is / has been knowing you pretty well the last few years. Not inevitably, but fairly often. Relying on your judgment.

Been having some bad times. Better stop.

Al

From Fraser Sutherland (Toronto), to Sidney, BC, April 23, 2000

Dear Eurithe,

Yesterday my sister-in-law Rosemary in Victoria told me that Al had died. I'd written him a letter a week ago, enclosing some odds and ends, but for some reason hadn't mailed it; it seems right that you should have it anyway. It's going to be very odd not to be writing and sending him things, and odder still not to be hearing back from him, but of course my loss is nothing compared to yours. Many times these past few months I've felt like phoning you. The reason I didn't, I realize, arose from the cowardly fear of getting bad news. Now the worst has happened.

Like a lot of other people, I'm numbed with grief and for years to come will probably be composing in my mind the things I want to say to you. Al could not have been the poet and the man he was without you. Besides that, I want to say at once that I know your wisdom, strength, and resilience will carry you through. Al would probably mock my grandiloquence, but it was one of his great strengths as a poet to mock the things he knew were true: that statement sounds like a paradox, but no one knows better than you that poets are complicated.

Some people are takers; some people are givers. You and Al were always givers. It's why you have good friends. Over and over you've given us hospitality, affection, practical assistance. Across many years you've given so much to others, me included, that you should let us give you some small return on the debt we all owe you. Which is just my awkward way of saying that I want very much to help in any way I can.

Alison sends her love, and joins me in blessing you for all the gifts— most of all, the gift of having made life better, richer, more joyful—that you and Al have given us,

Sincerely,
Fraser

INDEX

Page numbers appearing in **bold** indicate that the page is part of a letter to or from the subject of the entry.

Spenser, Edmund, 334–35
Steele, James, 183
Stein, Gertrude, 73–74
Steinbeck, John, 479
Stevens, Peter, 257
Strand, Mark, 469–71, 493
success/popularity, 36, 209, 278, 314–15, 382–383, 396
suicide, 13, 41, 315–16, 512, 543
Suknaski, Andy, 255, 318
Sullivan, Rosemary, 491–92, 494, 538
Sutherland, Fraser, 224, **330–31**, **338–39**, 382, **383–85**, 388, **392–93**, 396, 400, **454–56**, **469–71**, **503–04**, **507–08**, **517–20**, **536–38**, 539, **541–42**, 545, **547–48**
Sutherland, John, 50, 52
Sutherland, Ron, 93, 96, 305
Symonds, Norm, 287
Symons, Scott, 151, 153
Synge, J.M., 120–21

Tallman, Warren, 170–71, **301–02**, 504
taxes, 473
Templeton, Charles, 428–29
Theroux, Paul, 337
Thibaudeau, Colleen, 303, 305, 307, 311, 340, 354, 409
Thomas, Dylan, 29, 31–32, 34, 39–40, 43, 61, 344, 361, 399, 439, 513
Thomas, R.S., 343–44
Thompson, David, 200–01
Thompson, John, 511–12
Thompson, Wayne, 293
Thurber, James, 234–35
Tish, 81, 84
Toronto, 124, 441
Town, Harold, 157, 192–199, 203, 258, 428, 524–25
Toye, William, 354
Toynbee, Arnold, 166
Trahearne, Brian, 531–32
translations of AP, 533
travel, 8, 285
    Baffin Island/Arctic Circle, 15, 111
    British Columbia, 411, 522

travel *(continued)*
    California, 442
    Central America, 221
    Florida, 215, 372
    Galapagos Islands, 320–21
    Gulf of St. Lawrence, 239–40
    Japan, 179–80
    Mexico, 190–93, 283, 294, 309
    Netherlands, 424, 427
    Newfoundland, 15
    South Africa, 221
    Soviet Union, 271–72
    Spain, 371–73, 377–80
    Turkey, 419
Trenton, 11, 153, 168
Trotsky, Leon, 19, 509
Trower, Peter, 255, 408
Trudeau, Pierre, 14, 141, 146, **206–07**, 208, **221–22**, 235, 260, **277**, 321–22, **436–37**, 472
Turner, John Napier, 424–25, 437
Turner, W.J., 92–93, 513
Tutuola, Amos, 128–29
Twigg, Alan, 306, 308

Ustinov, Peter, 53–54

Vallejo, Cesar, 318–19
Van Toorn, Peter, 259–60
Vancouver, 411
Verne, Jules, 144–45
von Braun, Wernher, 100
Vosburgh, Abel, 65
Voznesensky, Andrei, 235, 271–73, 275, 403–04, 406–07, 468

Waddington, Miriam, 90, 160, **222–23**, 269
Wah, Fred, 370, 423, 451
Walcott, Derek, 465–66, 496
Wall, Ann and Byron, 175
Wallace, Bronwen, 476–77
Wallace, Joe, 361–62
Waller, Bob, 230–31
Ward, J.P., 344
Watson, Wilfred, 267, 269, 493